# The Complete Book of Florence Ceramics

## A Labor of Love

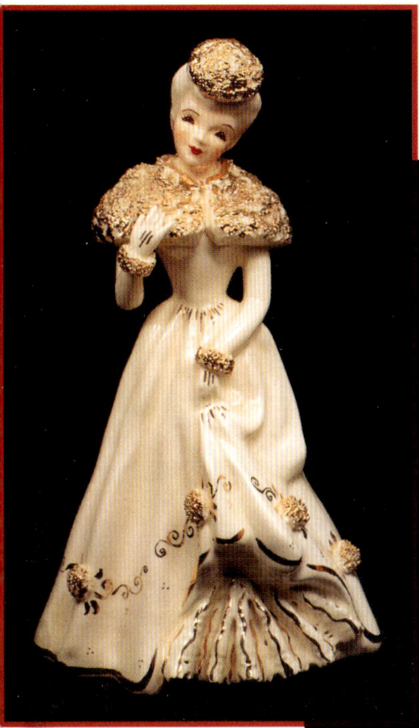

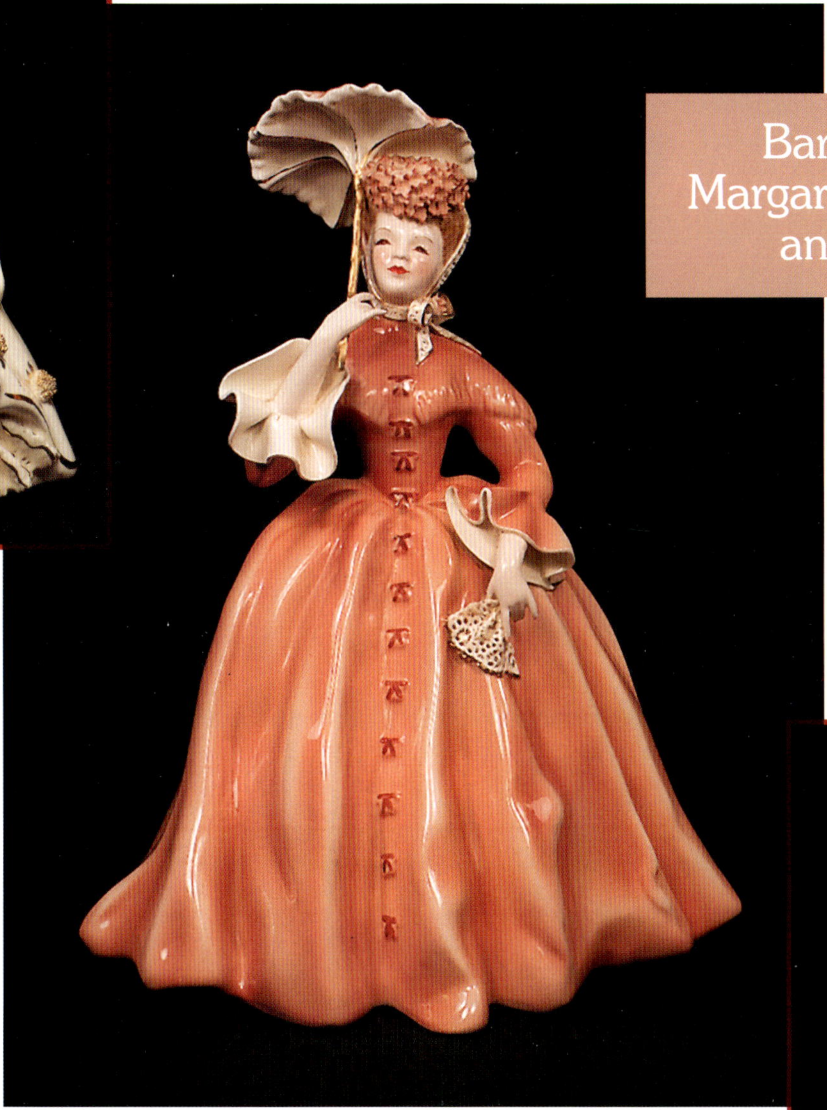

Barbara S. Kline,
Margaret C. Wehrspaun,
and Jerry Kline

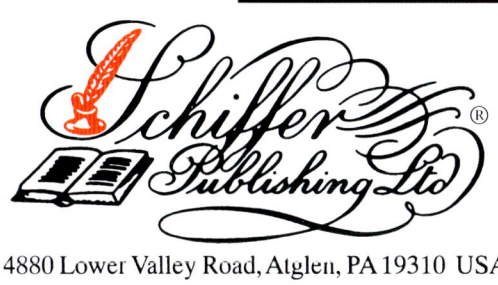

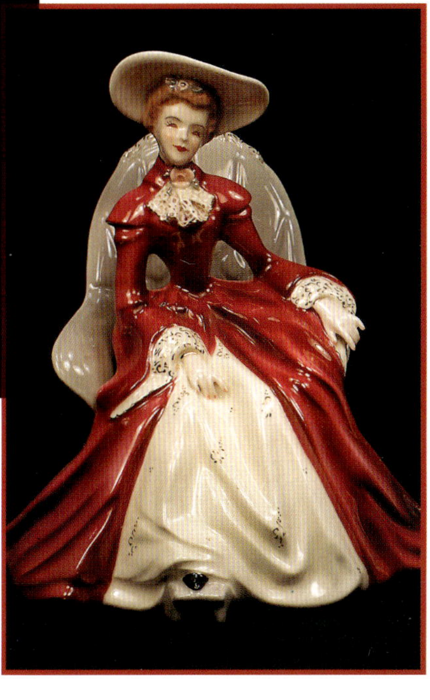

4880 Lower Valley Road, Atglen, PA 19310 USA

# *Dedication*

Dedicated to Mary, Ruth and Vivian

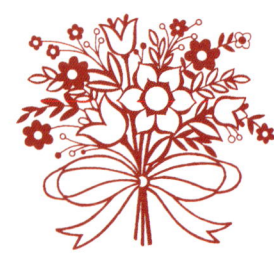

Copyright © 2002 by Barbara S. Kline,
Margaret C. Wehrspaun, and Jerry Kline
Library of Congress Control Number: 2001098059

All rights reserved. No part of this work may be reproduced or used in any form or by any means—graphic, electronic, or mechanical, including photocopying or information storage and retrieval systems—without written permission from the copyright holder.

"Schiffer," "Schiffer Publishing Ltd. & Design," and the "Design of pen and ink well" are registered trademarks of Schiffer Publishing Ltd.

Designed by "Sue"
Type set in Shelley Allegro BT/Souvenir Lt BT

ISBN: 0-7643-1528-5
Printed in China
1 2 3 4

Published by Schiffer Publishing Ltd.
4880 Lower Valley Road
Atglen, PA 19310
Phone: (610) 593-1777; Fax: (610) 593-2002
E-mail: Schifferbk@aol.com
Please visit our web site catalog at
**www.schifferbooks.com**
We are always looking for people to write books on new and related subjects. If you have an idea for a book, please contact us at the above address.

This book may be purchased from the publisher.
Include $3.95 for shipping.
Please try your bookstore first.
You may write for a free catalog.

In Europe, Schiffer books are distributed by
Bushwood Books
6 Marksbury Avenue
Kew Gardens
Surrey TW9 4JF England
Phone: 44 (0) 20 8392 8585
Fax: 44 (0) 20 8392 9876
E-mail: Bushwd@aol.com
Free postage in the UK. Europe: air mail at cost.

# Contents

Foreword ................................................................ 4

Acknowledgments ................................................. 5

Chapter I: A Labor of Love ..................................... 6

Chapter II: Plant and Process – The Making of a Figurine ........... 10

Chapter III: Showcasing Florence A to Z .............. 16

Chapter IV: Florence Fashion Parade ................... 96

Chapter V: Pairs and Groups ............................... 118

Chapter VI: Historical, Literary, and Religious ........ 130

Chapter VII: Birds and Animals ............................ 137

Chapter VIII: Artware ........................................... 143

Chapter IX: Florence Particulars ......................... 156

Appendix: Collecting, Cleaning and Care of Figurines ............ 173

Bibliography ......................................................... 174

Index .................................................................... 175

# Foreword

## Grandmother and I

It's such a privilege to be able to put down into words my feelings and thoughts about my grandmother, Florence Mae Ward. Grandmother was everything to me: a mentor, a mother, my guardian angel, my inspiration and the biggest influence in my life. As a woman, she was even more beautiful on the inside than the art she created. She was an incredibly kind and generous woman, who filled the room with joy wherever she went. Life was a wondrous adventure to her. Although she suffered tragedies, she always managed to turn them around, and to grow from them. This is how she began her artistic journey. After she had lost her second son when he was fourteen, she was so filled with sorrow that she needed to channel her grief into something constructive, which later became Florence Ceramics. As well as a ceramicist, she was a wonderful painter and seamstress, and brought beauty to everything she touched.

My Grandmother was the guiding light of my life. She suggested without insisting, praised without criticizing, and intuitively knew which path to take along the road of life. From a very young age I was exposed to art by her. She had a studio in her home, where she created most of her figurines. I remember spending hours watching, and trying to imitate what my Grandmother was creating. My attempts were quite crude, to say the least, but she took them into the plant, had them fired and painted, brought them back to me, and made me feel so special for having done something so wonderful. We went to many art galleries. I remember going to the Huntington Library and studying *Pinkie* and *Blue Boy*. Her figurines were then modeled after the original piece of art. She was always sketching ideas, and I would work right along side of her. It all was such fun, and such a new and exciting experience, every single time. When I had graduated from high school, my grandmother took me to Europe for the summer, before I started my first year of college. We saw every museum we could possibly see, as well as all the other sightseeing we could do. I was seventeen at the time and my grandmother in her sixties, and she had much more energy than I! It was an experience of a lifetime! When we returned, I started college, and became an art major, graduating with a Fine Arts degree.

Until the end of her life, Florence was always creating something of beauty. She was also a wonderful storyteller, and never skipped a detail, no matter how many times it had been told over the years. The whole family loved to hear her stories, and her many adventures; it was great entertainment for us all. My grandmother has been gone for several years now, and I continue to miss her daily. I do know that she is watching over us all, with pride and amusement. I definitely have tried to emulate her, as she was a treasure beyond measure. I have been an interior designer for over thirty years, and continue to take great joy in painting, ceramics, and artistic projects, all due to the guidance and influence of my grandmother.

Thank you Grandma, for all you passed along to me, and all the others whose lives you touched so profoundly! I love you dearly!

—Your granddaughter, *Pamela Diane Ward Perdue*

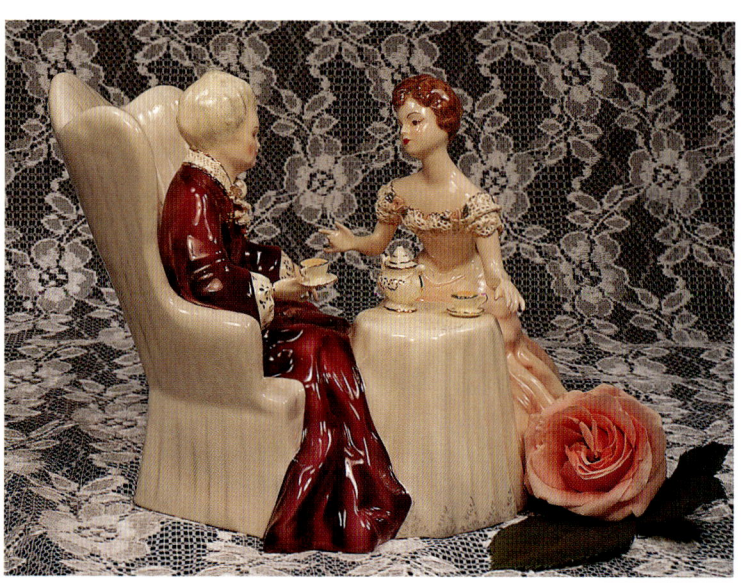

**Grandmother and I**

# Acknowledgments

The beautiful roses and daylilies photographed in the book are courtesy of the Sweet Pea garden. The wild flowers are an annual gift of the Great Smokey Mountain area of East Tennessee.

We extend special thanks to our friend and editor Donna Baker for her guidance, wisdom, and patience during the writing of this book.

We wish to express our gratitude to the following people who contributed information contained in this book:

Clifford Ward, son of Florence and Clifford Ward Sr., who gave his time, pictures, and catalogs, and who allowed us to photograph his mother's paintings.

Pamela Ward Perdue, granddaughter of Florence and Clifford Ward Sr., for recalling the wonderful moments spent with her grandmother, and for writing the foreword to this book.

David Ward, grandson of Florence and Clifford Ward Sr., for sharing memories of his grandparents, and remembrances of the Pasadena plant.

We also want to thank the following employees and artists of the Florence Ceramics company:

Pearl Sylvester for her time in describing such diverse subjects as details of the gold room and china painting; also for compiling the names of artists who signed their initials on the bases of figurines.

Margaret and Earl LaLone for the information they gave us regarding the technical aspects of the manufacturing process, with special thanks to Earl for drawing the plant layout; also for allowing us to photograph figurines from their collection. (Earl and Margaret met at Florence Ceramics in 1949, married in 1950, and were with the company until it was sold in 1964.)

Ann MacKellar for her time and for details regarding the cottage industry in the garage; also for providing valuable information concerning the art of making figurines.

Violet Kozar for her interview describing how Florence Ward and her family made employees feel "special"; also for her remembrances of the gold room where she worked as an artist.

Madeleine Lorimer for the use of old, original Florence catalogs; additional thanks go to Madeleine for her recollections of the great years at Florence.

Doris Soderquist for spending time with us and for telling her story of wonderful experiences working at Florence Ceramics.

Jim Lilleywhite, who was plant manager during his years at Florence, for his recall about various factory procedures.

A sincere "thank you" to the following collectors who shared their wonderful photographs for use in this book. Without their contributions of pictures showing rare and hard to find pieces of Florence Ceramics, this book would be incomplete: Carla and Larry Budd, Judy and Don Croy, Penney and David Miller, Nusa and Frank Pirre, Doris and Don Robertson, and Doris and Ralph Sweezey.

We extend thanks to Faith Winkler and Jim Crawford, who allowed us to borrow from their expertise.

Finally, we would like to thank Dixie, Emma, Sadie, Stella, Rainie, Brina, Hector and Hilde (the twins) for behaving long enough to allow us to complete this book.

# Chapter I
## *A Labor of Love*

*In the early days I didn't realize how talented Mother was!*
—Clifford Ward (Pasadena, California, 2001)

In 1964, production ceased for the Florence Ceramics Company, but there is so much more to the story than that. The fact that this company existed at all for any of its twenty-four years is simply fate. That a young matron with no business experience nor formal training in art or ceramics would become a respected businesswoman in the industry is equally noteworthy.

Florence Ward was a native of Lewiston, Idaho. In 1939, as a housewife and mother of two sons, she was living in Pasadena, California with husband, Clifford Ward. She enjoyed drawing and painting. Clifford was a building contractor, and Clifford Ward Jr. would soon be entering Flight School. Young Jack Ward, aged fourteen, showed promise as a budding artist. Tragically, in July of that year Jack Ward was stricken with an infectious blood disease and died within three days of the onset of his illness. The Ward family was devastated.

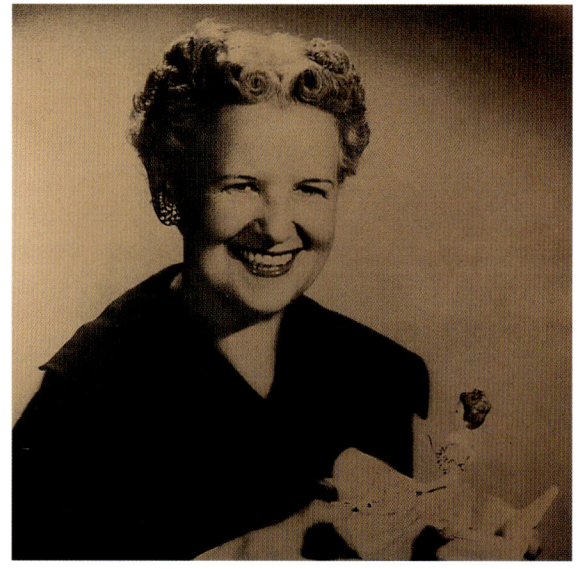

Florence Ward

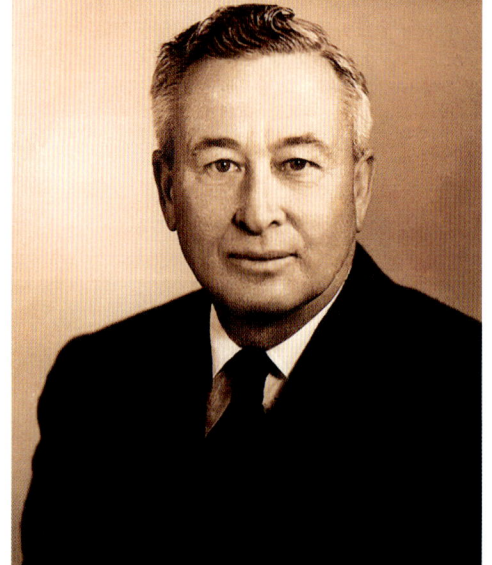

Clifford Ward Sr.

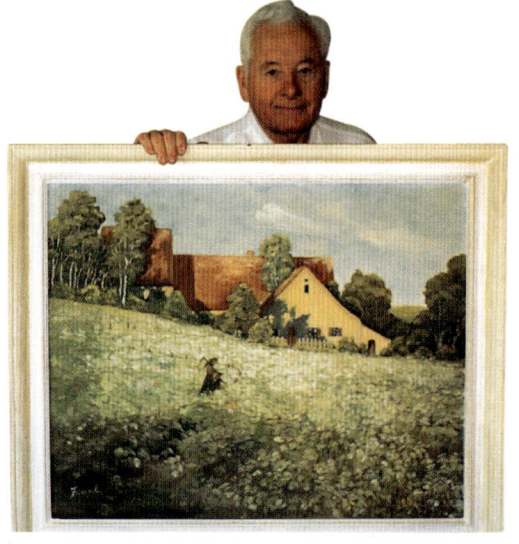

This oil painting by Florence Ward is treasured by Clifford Ward Jr.

Florence, at the urging of friends and family and in an attempt to assuage her grief, began taking art classes at the Franklin School, located at Walnut and Los Robles Streets in Pasadena. Her instructor was so taken with her work that he suggested making molds of her sketches. Florence immersed herself in this new endeavor, and for her the healing process began. She took her clay models to a studio elsewhere to be fired. The manager asked her to assist him at the studio, and it is there that she learned how to glaze, set cones, and monitor the temperatures. In addition, she learned about casting. With her aptitude for learning and her talent for modeling, she was sought out by others in the ceramics community. However, her renewed energy along with her overwhelming sense of peace as she worked the clay caused her to decline their offers.

Her first modeled pieces were of children.

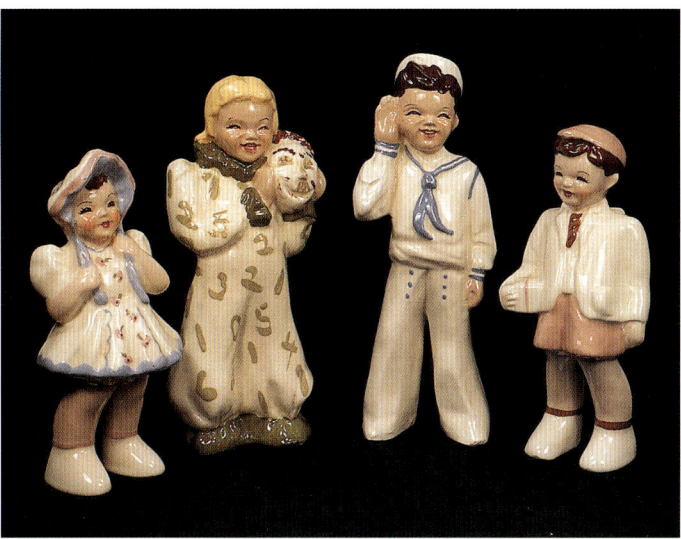

Early pieces: **Susie**, **Halloween Child**, **Sailor Boy**, **Peter**

At the beginning of World War II, the senior Clifford Ward accepted a government contract and began a project in Utah. Clifford Jr. had already joined the Marines as an aviator. Alone, Florence worked on her clay models, and concentrated on learning everything she could about her new fascination with ceramics.

In 1942, she started her own ceramics business in the family garage. She was forty-four years old then. In those years it was not at all common for a woman to have her own company.

Early garage pieces, flower holders **Loraine** and **Jo Ann**.

While on holiday from his project in Utah, Clifford Ward was so impressed with his wife's accomplishments that he offered to help her in any way he could. There were six employees working for Florence at that time, so Clifford added on to the garage both front and back. In 1946, Florence had increased the number of employees to twenty. Clifford built a small factory on Villa Street in Pasadena.

By the time Clifford's government contract expired, Florence had convinced him to join the company and take over its financial and daily management. After the war, young Clifford also joined the company.

"I thought I would try it for a few months," Clifford Junior told us, "but I found that as an engineer I was really interested in the kinds of clay used, the operation and firing of the kilns, and all the technical work involved. I wound up staying there until the end."

By 1946, the Florence Ceramics Company was displaying its wares at Los Angeles gift shows and selling directly to retailers in San Francisco, Seattle, Dallas, Chicago, Detroit, New York, and Atlanta. Additionally, their wares were sent to Hawaii, Canada, South America, and Europe.

In 1949, the company was incorporated; at the same time it expanded and moved into a modern 10,000 square foot facility located on South San Gabriel Boulevard in Pasadena. It was equipped with a continuous tunnel kiln (see Chapter II). The company's workforce was now one hundred strong and they enjoyed a workplace that was years ahead of its time. In fact, the self-imposed guidelines for the comfort and safety of the employees may have been beyond even the most stringent laws as determined by government standards today.

The company grew in volume of production and in reputation and produced some of the finest semi-porcelains ever made in the United States. Representatives

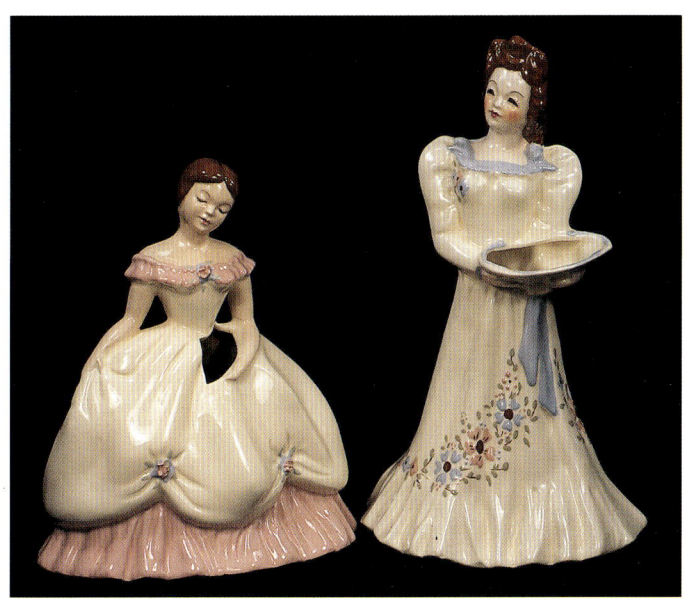

# 8  A Labor of Love

from well-known manufactories in England and elsewhere journeyed to California to speak with Florence Ward regarding the making of her figurines and other artware pieces. It is believed that Florence Ceramics was the first ever to use china spray paint finishes. Previously, finishes were brushed on by hand. Florence Ceramics was also the first to hold actual patents on production molds for porcelain figurines.

The three figurines shown here are a sampling of some of Florence Ward's finest work.

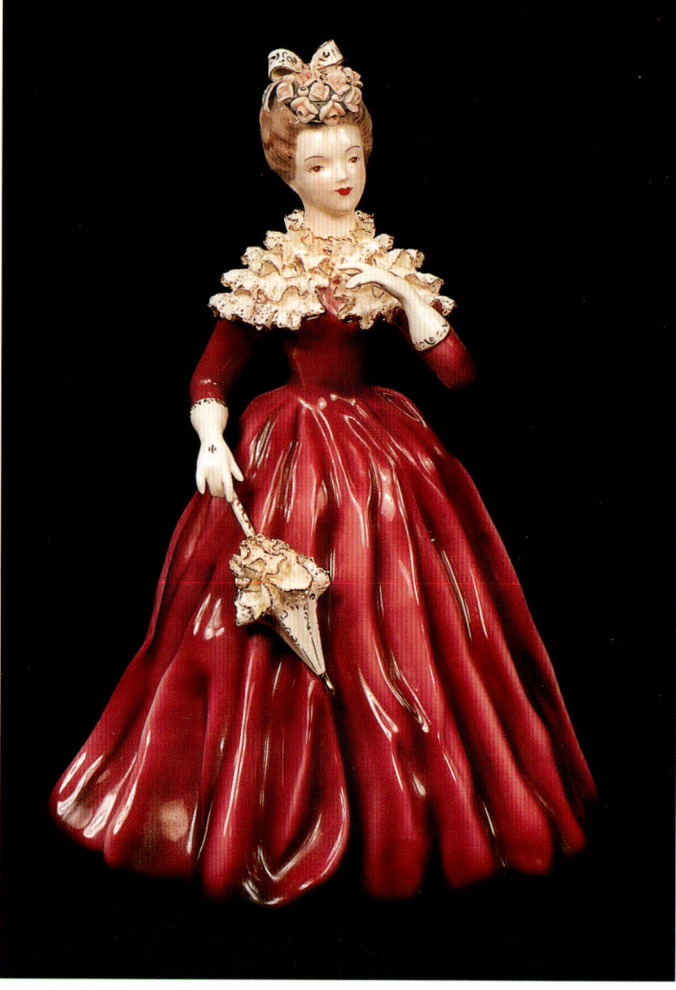

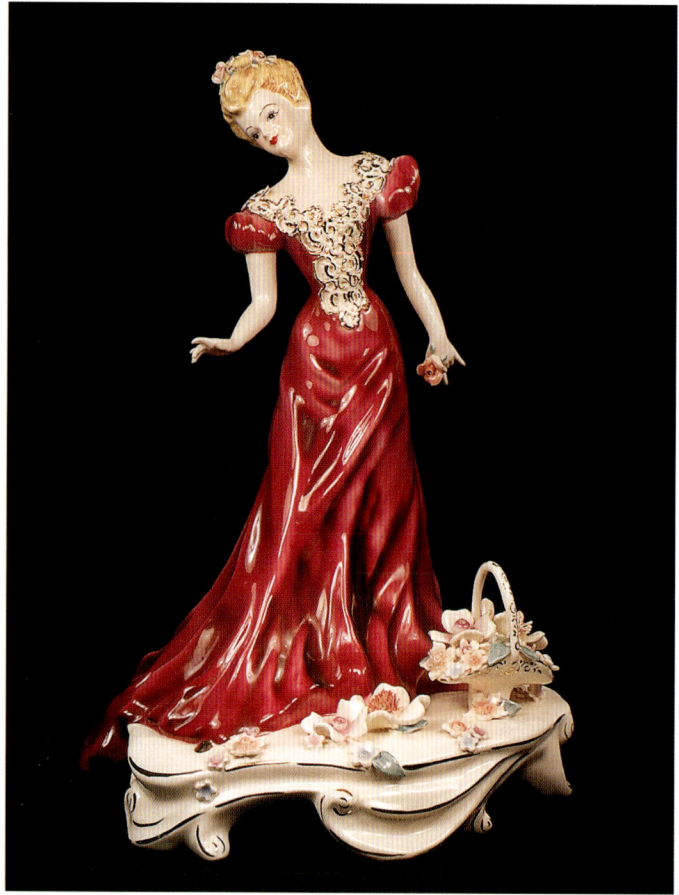

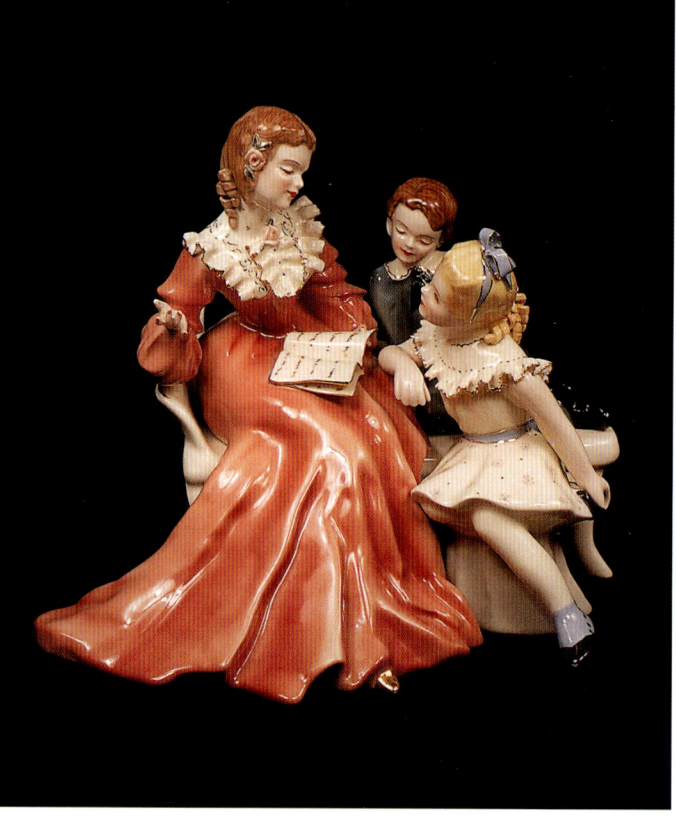

These three figurines, **Fair Lady, Margaret**, and **Story Hour**, represent some of Florence Ward's finest work.

Like other manufacturers of fine porcelains, Florence Ceramics was plagued by companies of lesser reputation who would make copies and reproductions of their wares. One such company, with production facilities in Japan, flooded the market with inferior, ill-made copies, and Florence Ceramics Company was obliged to initiate a lawsuit in order to stop the influx of those pieces. The barrage of cheap imports could not be stopped totally however, and Florence found it increasingly difficult to compete in the marketplace.

Further, at this point one could say that it is unlikely in this day and time that any company would be able to produce figurines with the same standard of excellence and quality as were produced by Florence Ceramics. Because of the labor-intensive artistic work involved, it simply would not be cost efficient in today's world.

In 1964, following the death of the elder Clifford Ward, Clifford Junior and Florence Ward sold the company to Scripto. Scripto did not continue with the production of figurines and art ware known as Florence Ceramics, but produced a different type of ceramic ware entirely.

In our conversations with former artists and employees, we heard again and again of the kindness and generosity of the Wards. They told us of the Christmas parties, and the parties at the beach house. They talked about Mrs. Ward coming to work one morning and insisting all the ladies grab their hats and purses because "Bullocks has a sale on nylon stockings, and if we wait until after work, there won't be any left!"

We heard about Florence's personal inspection of every figurine that left the plant. Her attention to detail and her insistence on quality were renowned, but her fair and unbiased treatment of every individual employee was equally renowned. For both the Wards and the artists and other employees of Florence Ceramics Company, it was truly "a labor of love."

In the pages that follow, we will show you the many facets of Florence Ward. Her artistry will be made apparent, as will her knowledge of history and her attention to detail. You will meet Florence Ward the artist, and Florence Ward the person.

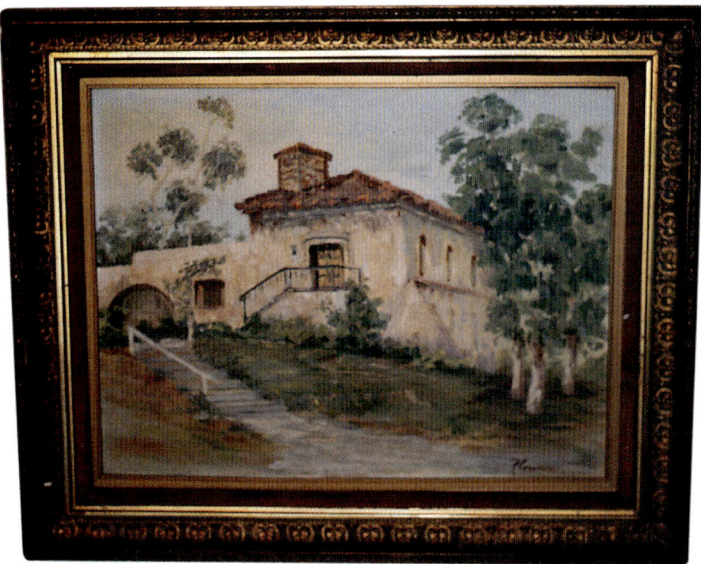

***Landscape Villa*** by Florence Ward, oil on canvas.

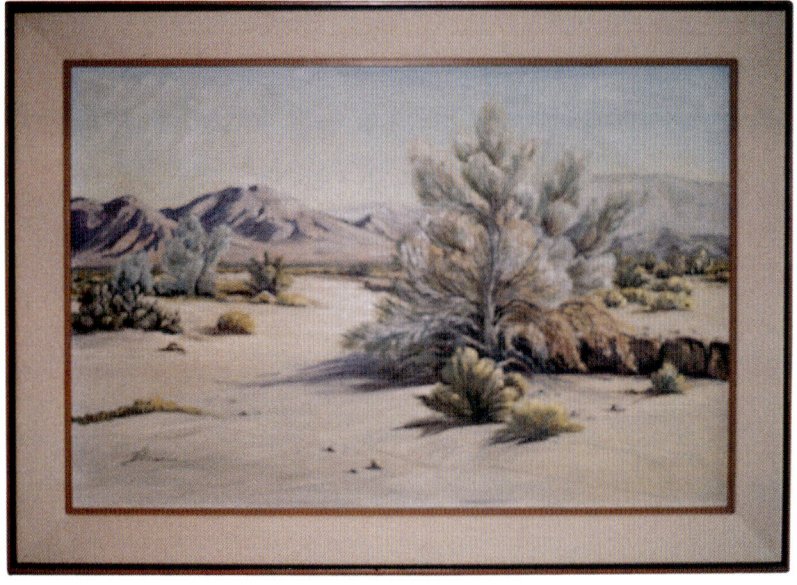

***Desert Scene*** by Florence Ward, oil on canvas.

Chapter II

# Plant and Process — The Making of a Figurine

> *It was our objective to build a ceramics facility that was better than anything known at the time. We wanted the best that anyone had ever seen.*
> —Attributed to Clifford Ward Sr., by Jim Lilleywhite, former Plant Manager (San Clemente, California, 2001)

As seen in Chapter I, Florence Ceramics Company started with very humble beginnings, then moved to a small plant on Villa Street in Pasadena.

Eventually, they built a state-of-the art ceramics plant at 74 South San Gabriel Boulevard in Pasadena.

They moved into the new 10,000 square foot plant in 1949, adding 3,600 additional square feet for storage and shipping in 1951. The company continued in that location until 1964 when the operation was sold to Scripto.

In this chapter a plant layout, details about a patent for making figurines, and other technical manufacturing information will be discussed.

We begin with two photos, one taken from an early catalog showing the new plant, and another showing the front of the building where the showroom was housed.

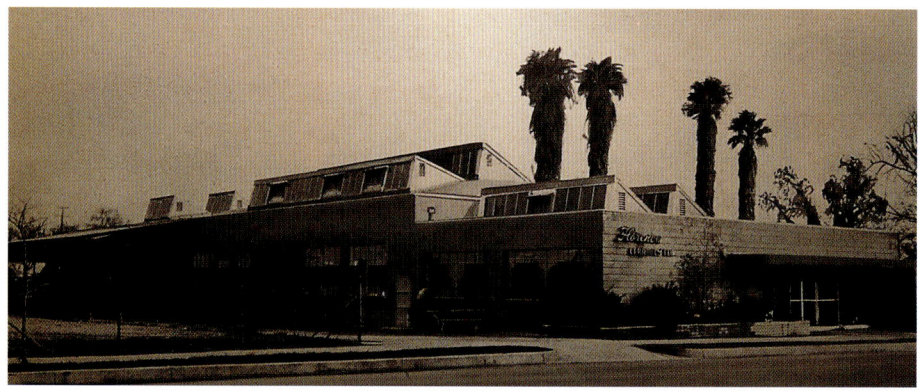

The Florence Ceramics plant on South San Gabriel in Pasadena as it looked in 1949.

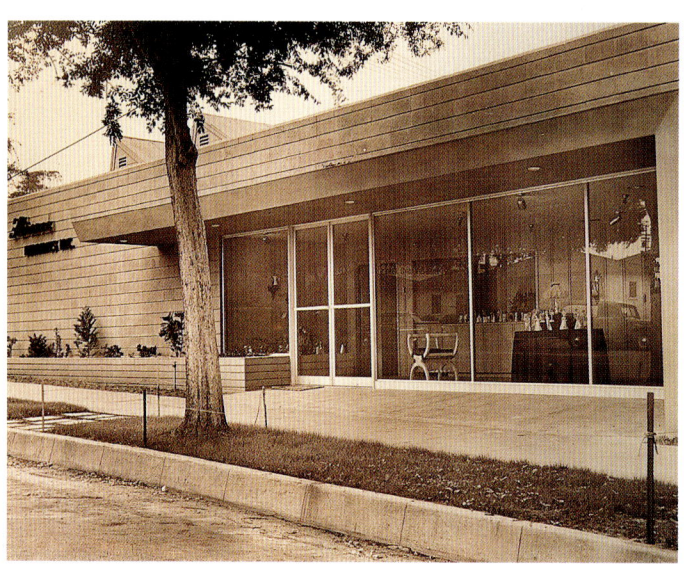

It is interesting that one can clearly see the display of several figurines in the window of the showroom. Plant tours were conducted each Wednesday, and afterwards visitors were permitted to purchase figures on display. Most reports of sales in the showroom indicate that only "seconds" were sold, but it would be very difficult to determine "seconds" due to Florence's rigid standard of quality.

Showroom at front of building.

**10**

## Plant and Process 11

In 1949, Florence applied for a patent, listing it as "mold for making figurines." Florence Ceramics Company received the patent in 1952, but by then they had already been using their patented process for several years. The drawings shown below, taken from the patent, are helpful when discussing the manufacturing process.

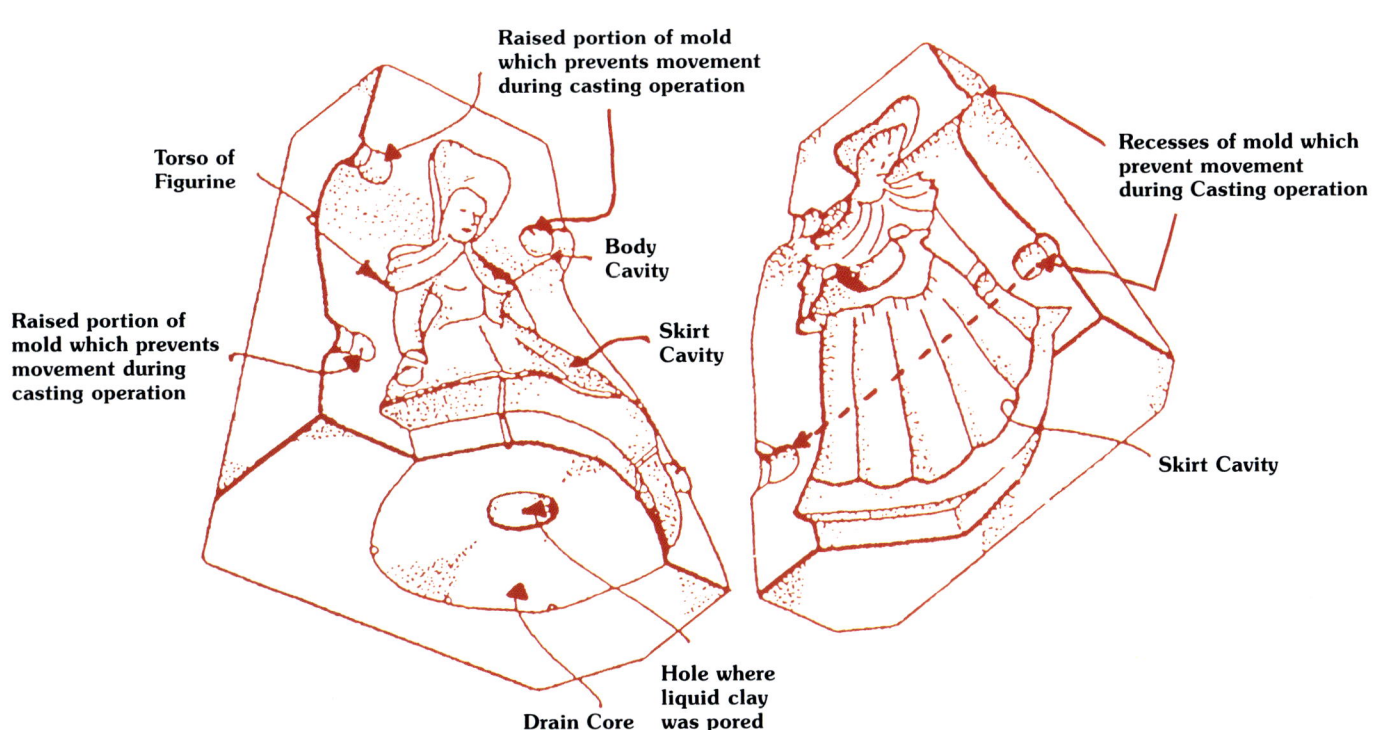

FIGURE 1. MOLD for MAKING FIGURINES

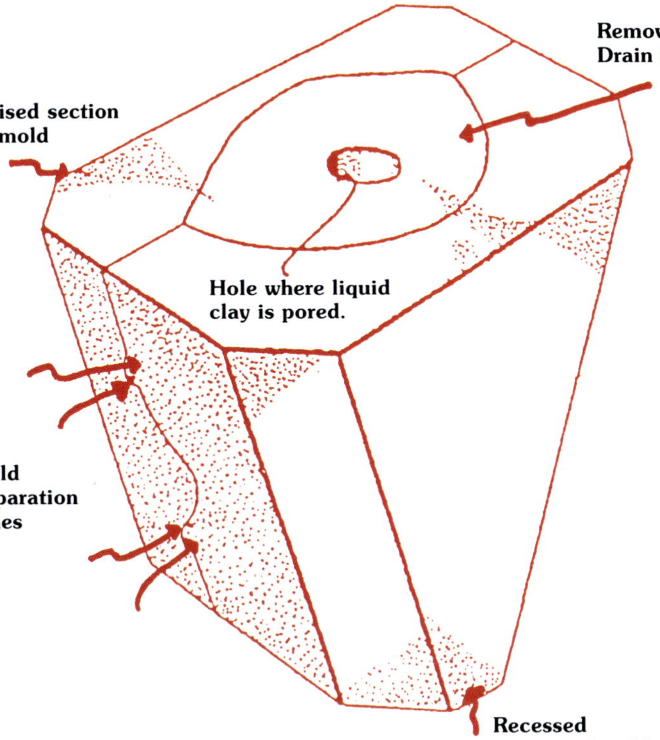

FIGURE 2. VERTICAL SECTION OF MOLD

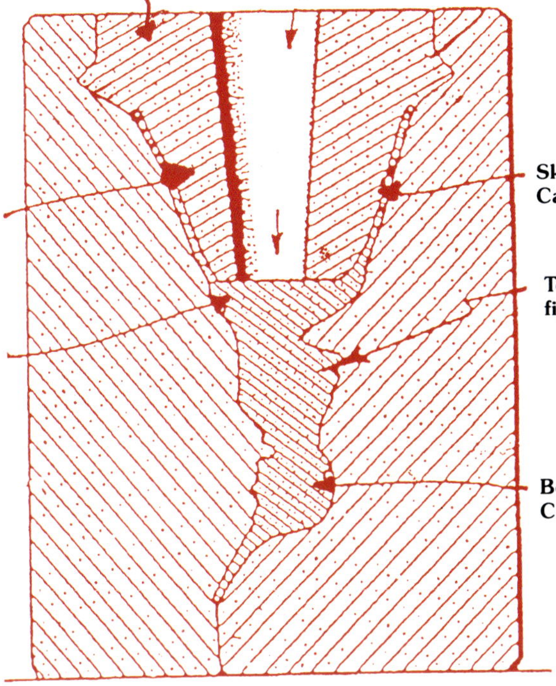

FIGURE 3. VIEW OF MOLD ON ITS SIDE WITH THE UPPER SECTION REMOVED

## 12 Plant and Process

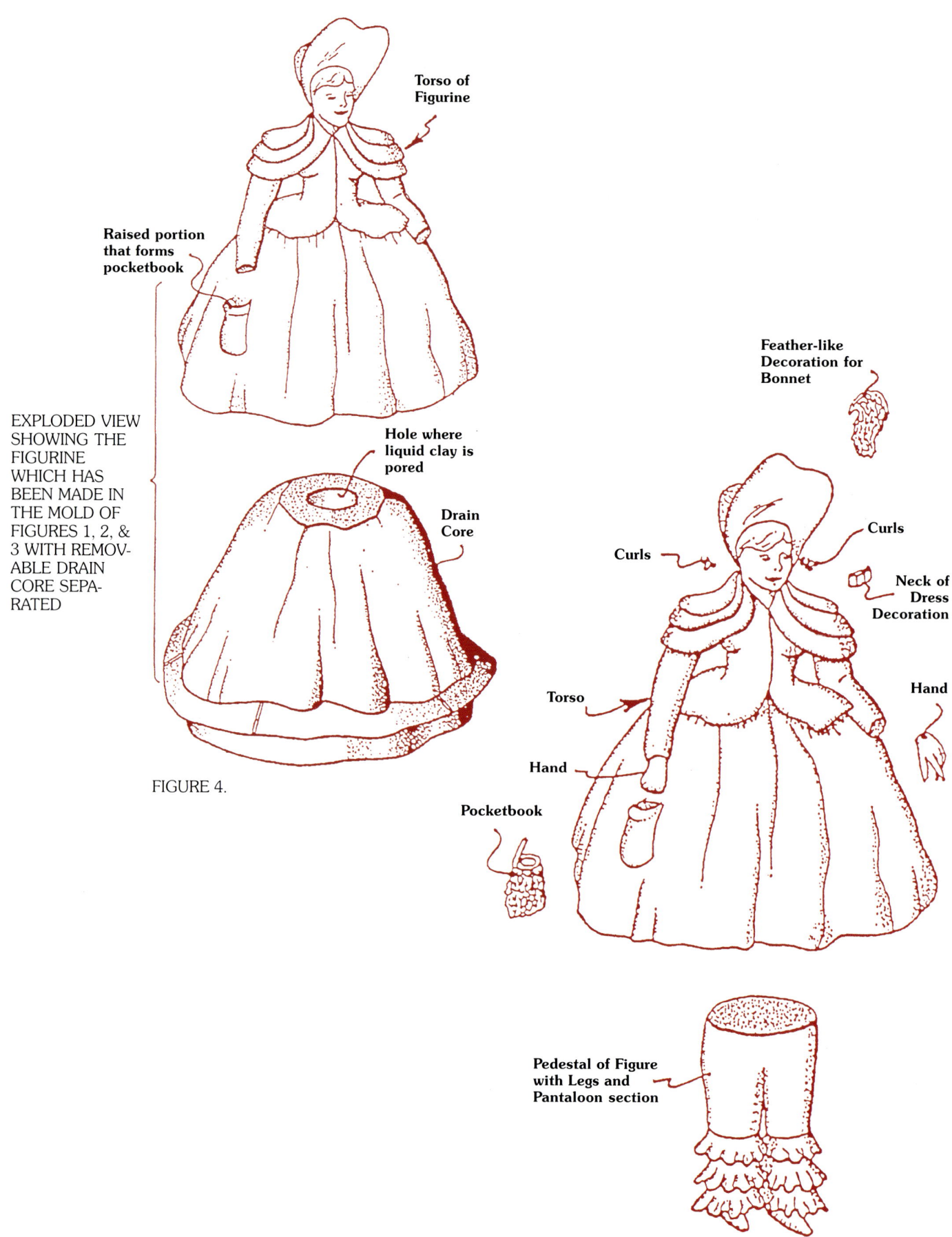

FIGURE 4.
EXPLODED VIEW SHOWING THE FIGURINE WHICH HAS BEEN MADE IN THE MOLD OF FIGURES 1, 2, & 3 WITH REMOVABLE DRAIN CORE SEPARATED

FIGURE 5.
EXPLODED VIEW SHOWING THE ADDED DECORATIONS

# Plant and Process 13

FIGURE 6.
THE FINISHED FIGURINE (CAROL)

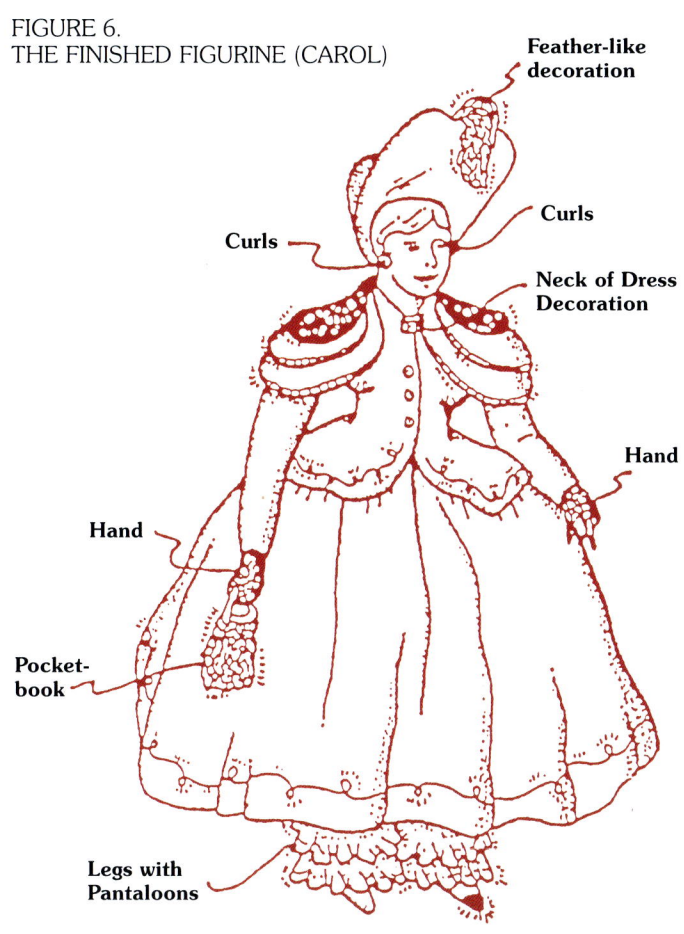

- Feather-like decoration
- Curls
- Curls
- Neck of Dress Decoration
- Hand
- Hand
- Pocketbook
- Legs with Pantaloons

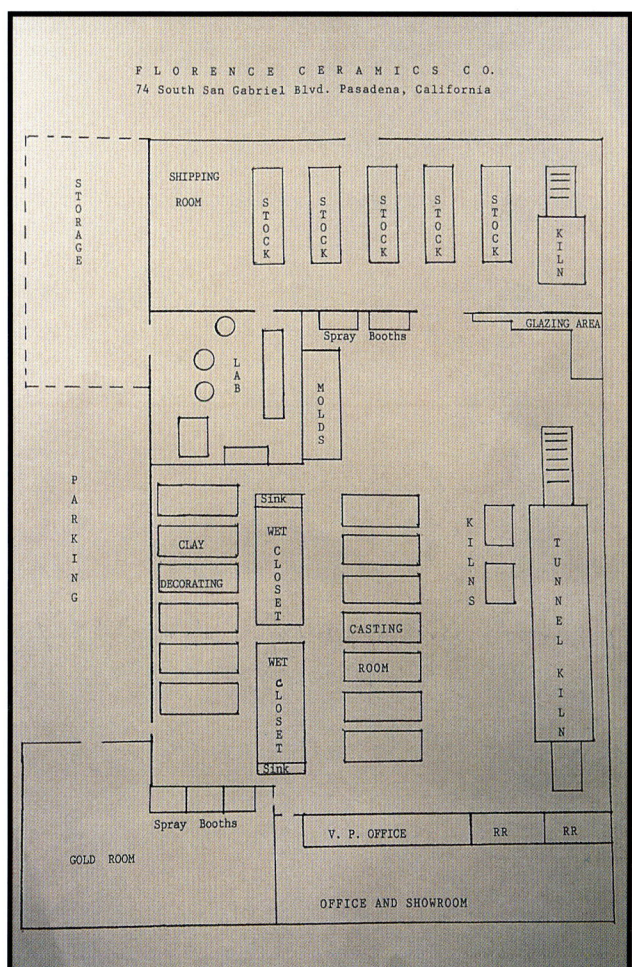

Plant layout

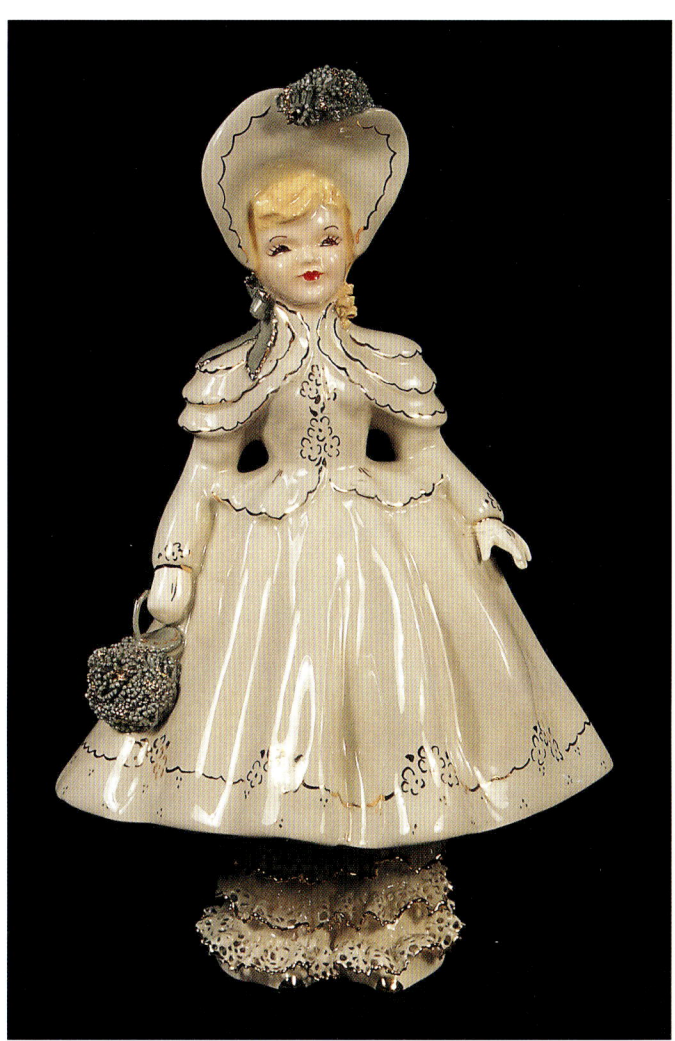

*Carol*, the finished product.

The process starts with raw materials, which were received in the back of the plant. The raw materials used and the percentage of each were: Tennessee #1 clay: 15%; OM #4 Ball clay: 15%; Kentucky clay: 15%; Kentucky Special clay: 5%; and talc: 50%. Then 40% water and silicate of soda (soda ash) were added to the mixture to form the liquid clay that was pumped to the casting room.

As shown in Figure #1 (pg. 11), the liquid clay was poured into the mold to fill the body and skirt cavity shown in Figure #2 (pg. 11). After an initial drying period, the mold was inverted end for end and all unsolidified material above the core drained out through the drain core. Moisture had been absorbed from the mold, which had a moisture absorbing nature.

The molds were made of hardened plaster of paris from a master mold that was created from the original sculpture by Florence Ward. The master molds were made by an expert mold maker in Pasadena.

Following drainage, the mold was permitted to stand in a dry atmosphere during which time added moisture was removed from the clay. The clay would then shrink away from the mold. At the end of the drying period the mold was placed on its side and the raised section lifted off, as shown in Figure #3 (pg. 11). The molded figurine could then be lifted from the recessed section by removing the drain core, followed by separating the drain core from the torso of the figurine as in Figure #4 (pg. 12). Sometimes it was necessary to aid the separation by directing compressed air between the lower edge of the skirt and the flared core portion.

The final step in the casting room was the sponging and smoothing of mold lines to eliminate any irregularities. The figures were then placed into a "wet closet" to await work the next day in the clay decorating room. The arms, hands, legs, and other small applied decorations were cast separately in very small molds.

While the figures were in the wet closets, the clay remained moist so that artists in the clay decorating room could make necessary changes or additions. The artists referred to the clay decorating room as the "crud room." It was here that arms, legs, lace, flowers, curls, and the like were added by using slip (liquid clay) and working it by hand. This allowed for a smooth joining where lines would not be visible.

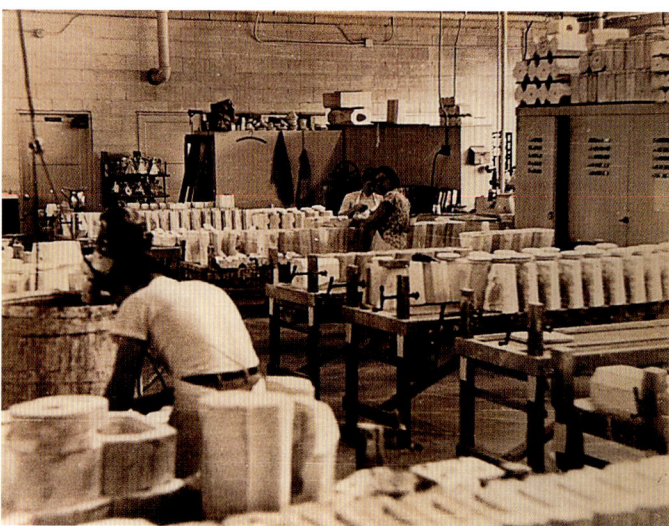

Casting room with tables full of molds.

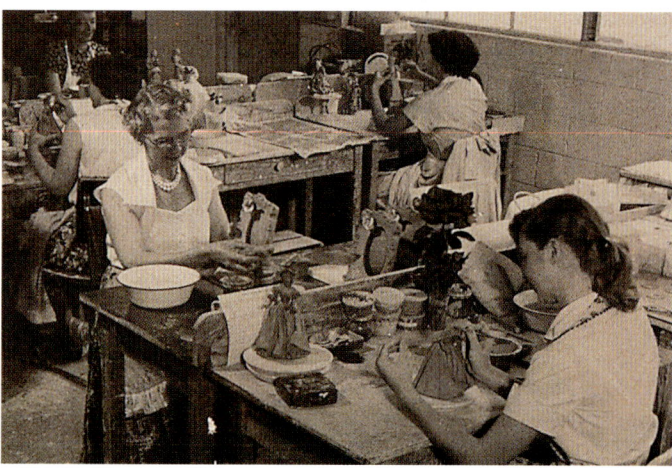

Artists working in clay decorating room (crud room).

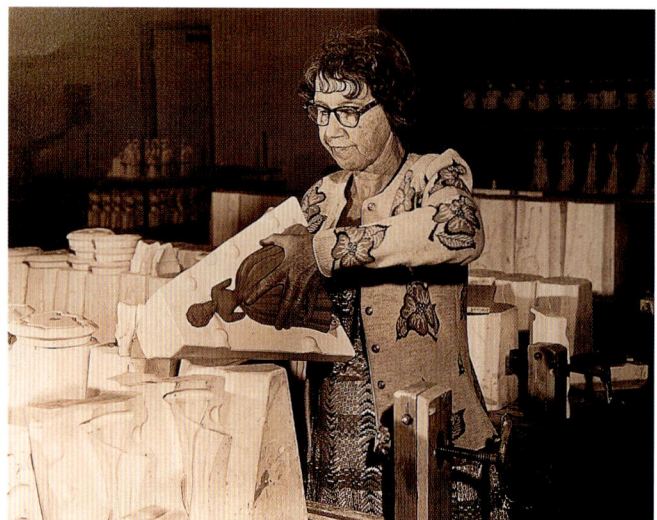

Hilda Schureman, sister of Florence Ward, removes a figure from a mold.

For the addition of lace to the figures, 100% cotton lace was used. It was dipped into liquid clay, then applied to the figurine. Once in place a string was pulled to gather the lace into folds. When fired in the tunnel kiln, the cotton lace burned away, thus creating the porcelain lace. Other applied decorations, like feathers, muffs, and fur, were made by pushing liquid clay through screens. The applied decorations shown in Figure #5 (pg. 12) comprise the creative work done by the artists working in the clay decorating room. Added details varied, depending on the particular figure.

The figurines were then sent to the tunnel kiln for the first firing (1600 degrees Fahrenheit), called the "bisque firing." The length of time for bisque firing was four and one-half hours. Following this first firing, the figures were sent to the glazing area. There they were glaze-dipped in a colored liquid solution which deposited an even coat of glaze on the figure. On plainer figures without applied decorations this was the final color; figures with decorations still to be applied were dipped in a white glaze. A second firing through the tunnel kiln, called the glaze or glass firing, was then required. Again, this firing was timed at four and one-half hours. At the end of this firing the figure had a hard, glass-like surface.

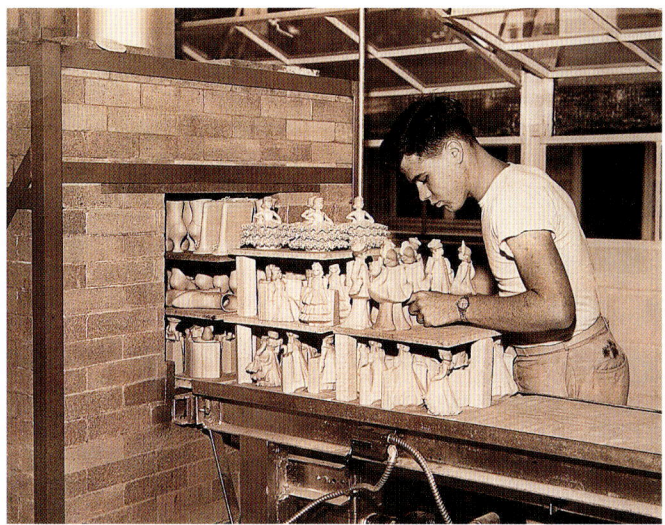

Bill Carroll loading the tunnel kiln.

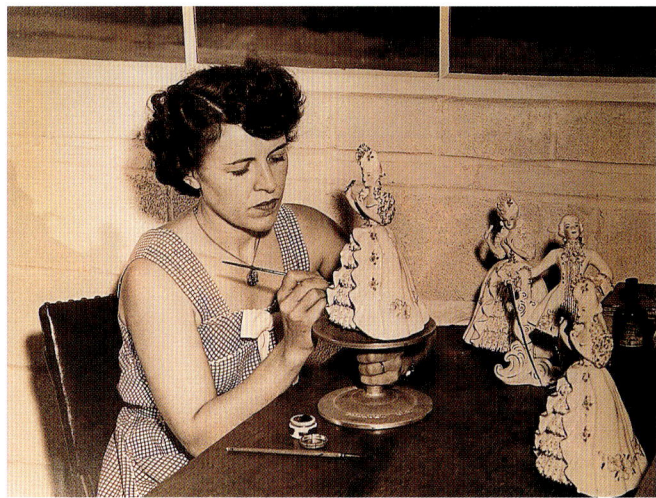

Artist LaVerne Wilkison hand painting 22-karat gold on **Marie Antoinette**.

The figures were then sent to the "gold room" for masking, where artistic detail was added. The 22-karat gold decoration was always brushed on by hand. As noted above, the fancier figures were first glazed in white. If such a figure was intended to be a color other than white, it was china spray painted at this time. Color variation in figures was due to artistic expression and any one painter applying more or less paint to a figure. This also accounts for the white sometimes bleeding through the final color, particularly at the fold of a dress. (In a glazed-dipped figure the color is universal over the entire surface.)

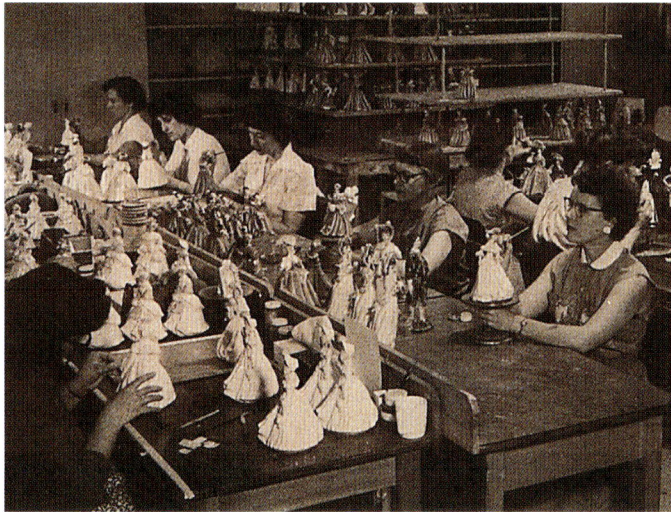

Artists working in the gold room.

With the gold and china painting completed, the figure was sent back to the tunnel kiln for the final firing. The temperature now was set at 1300 degrees for five hours. The final firing was lower in temperature and longer in duration to allow the fumes from the gold to dissipate.

Florence Ward was meticulous in her attention to detail and the most minor departure from her original model resulted in rejection of the figure. After the final quality inspection, the figurine was ready for packing and shipping.

Most of the company's business was "made to order." However, during slow periods production of the most popular figures continued. These were stored in the stock room and held for the busier fall and holiday seasons.

Many of the figures have the term "Semi-Porcelain" as part of the backstamp. This means that there is some absorption of moisture from the clay during the figure making process. The moisture absorption also causes the figure to be opaque. A full porcelain has zero absorption in the manufacturing process and is fired at a higher temperature, thus making it translucent. Too low an absorption of moisture causes crazing, which is often seen on Florence's early "garage" pieces.

Some components were not made by Florence Ceramics but were purchased from local craftsmen. These were the hardwood or brass lamp bases and the silk chiffon lamp shades.

When Scripto Company purchased Florence Ceramics in 1964, they did not obtain any rights to the copyrighted figurine line, those rights were retained by the Ward family. Scripto continued to manufacture in the same factory until 1977. They produced mugs, ashtrays, commemorative items, and other advertising specialty ware. No figurines were developed or produced by Scripto.

In 1964, when the Florence Ceramics Company closed its doors for the final time and retailers across the country no longer had a supply of these exceptional figurines, the passion for collecting Florence Ceramics was born.

Chapter III

# Showcasing Florence A to Z

*...I remember Earl LaLone...I also recall pouring clay in the casting room in the summer when I was out of school...grandmother could communicate with everyone, and had friends everywhere.*
—David Ward, grandson of Florence and Clifford Ward Sr. (Kennebunk, Maine, 2001)

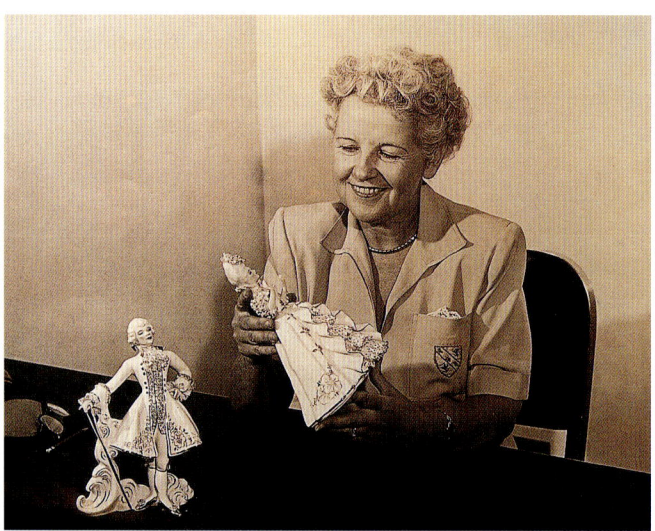

"To me my modeling was always a labor of love." Florence Ward, 1984

The figurines in this chapter are presented in alphabetic order, one by one without regard to those that are pairs. All known figures are shown, along with size and a value guide price range below each.

In the early days of Florence Ceramics, figurines were made without any identification shown on them. These figures were produced with a flat underside to the base, and with no incised name. With the introduction of the patented mold process in 1949 (discussed in Chapter II), a raised edge was now incorporated into the bottom of the mold. At this time, the name given to the figurine was incised on the underneath side of its base. There can, of course, be some exceptions relating to markings, but this represents the majority of cases.

The abbreviation (FH) shown in the caption identifies the figurine as a flowerholder.

Some figures are shown with an asterisk behind the name. This indicates names given to unknown figures by either the Florence Ceramics Collectors Society (FCCS) or by the authors. These names will provide an easy means for collectors to identify these figures in the future.

The prices reflect the average value across the continent for figures in mint condition.

In some cases, a wide price range is shown and represents a figure that is made in both plain and fancy versions. A wide price range could also relate to a figure with articulated and non-articulated fingers. Rare and hard to find pieces often have the widest margin of variance within the price range shown.

A yellow colored figure is more valuable than others; due to the cost and difficulty of producing this color, the production of yellow colored figures was limited. In general, a plain figure in yellow is worth 40-50% more than in other colors. For a fancy yellow figure, add 50-60% more. Note that for any yellow figurines shown in the pictures that follow, the higher value has already been listed.

Additionally, Florence Ceramics produced a line of figurines dressed in brocade fabric. These fabric costumes were hand crafted by seamstresses residing in or near the Pasadena community. Due to the exceptional detail and draping of the fabric on these figurines, production was time consuming and expensive. The brocade dressed figurines were produced for a relatively brief period of time in the mid 1950s, and Florence advertised and promoted these beautiful creations as "Fashions in Brocade."

Lastly, there is one other issue that we should address here. Differences in applied decorations on a figurine are due to a freedom of artistic expression, and values of various figures are affected only insofar as collectors are willing to pay more or less for a certain finished look. No one, the authors included, can state that an application of a hat is more valuable than an applied rose, or other treatment. All are beautiful, and what remains then, is for the collector to decide which one is his or her favorite.

Showcasing Florence A to Z 17

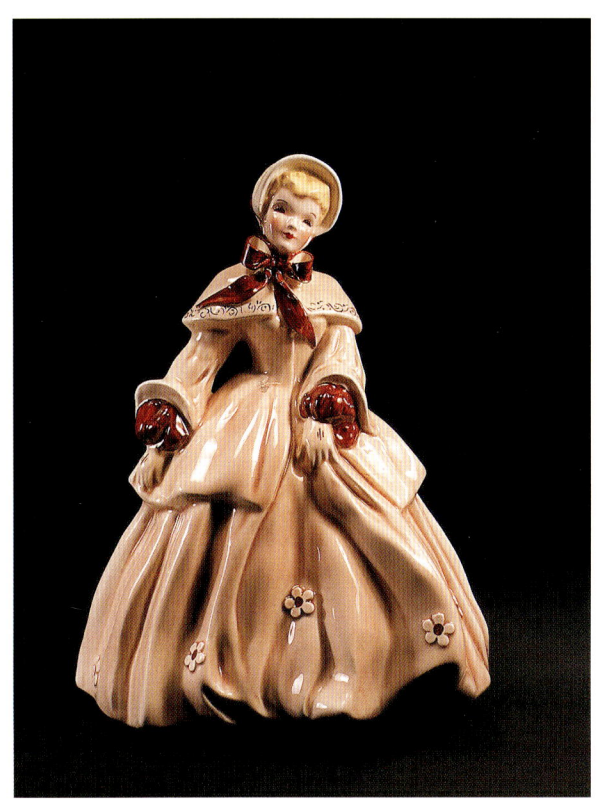

**Abigail**, 8"
$175-200

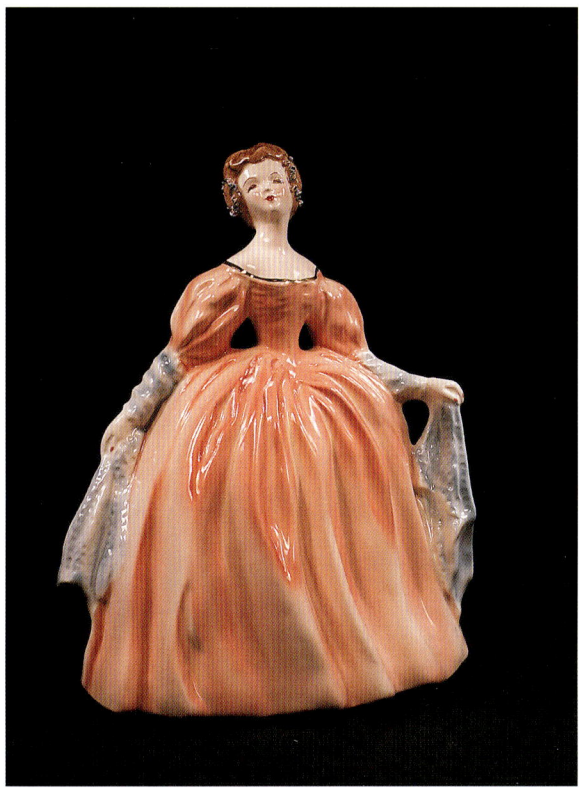

**Adeline**, 8.75"
$300-350

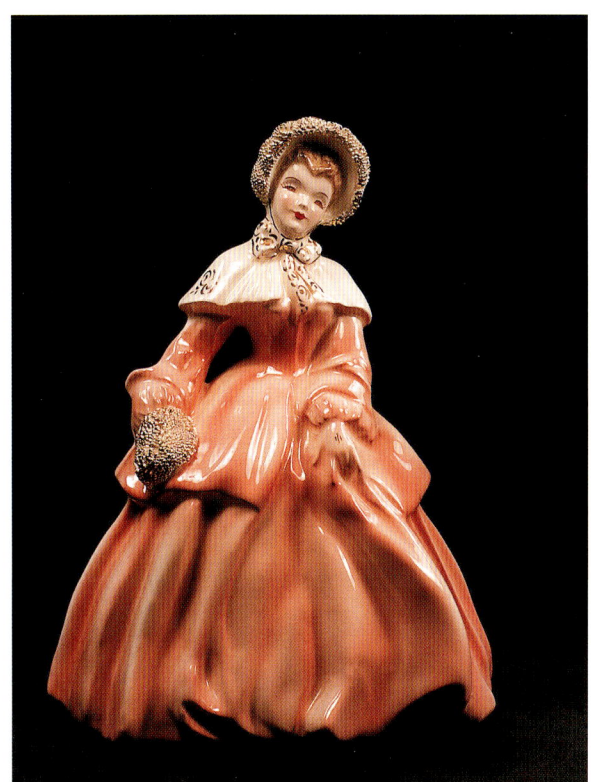

**Abigail**, 8"
$175-200

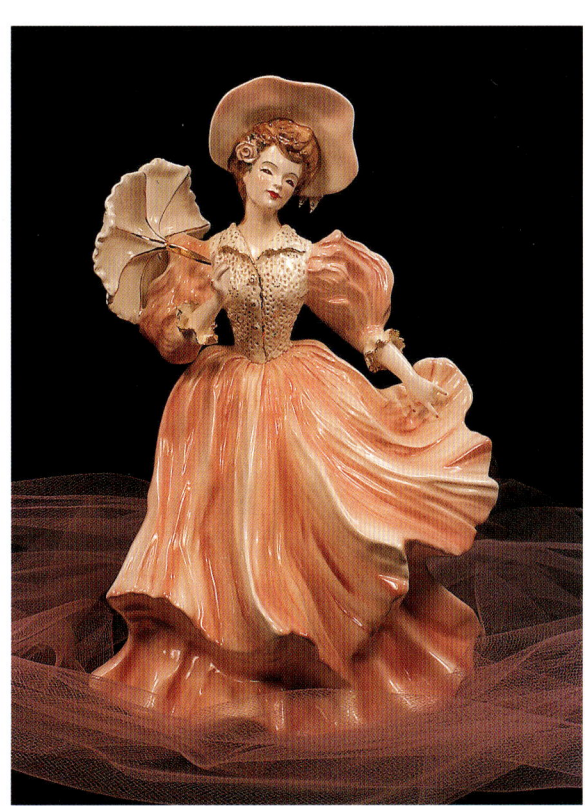

**Amber**, 9.25"
$700-750

## 18  Showcasing Florence A to Z

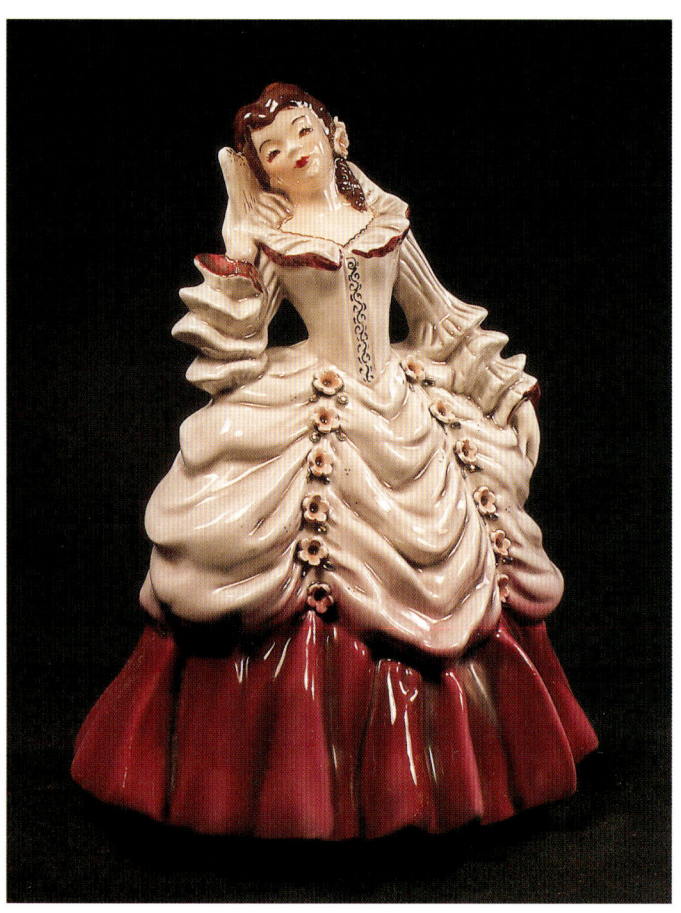

**Amelia**, 8.25"
$275-300

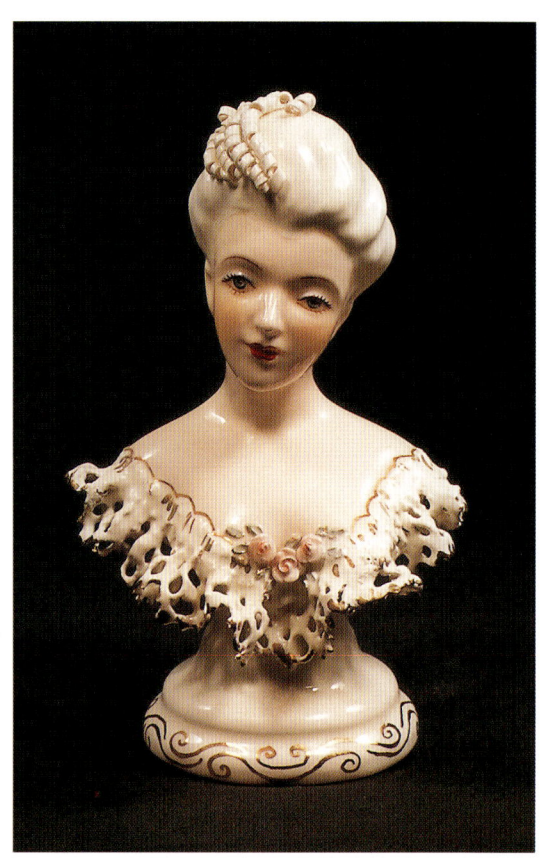

**American Lady**, 6.5"
$400-450

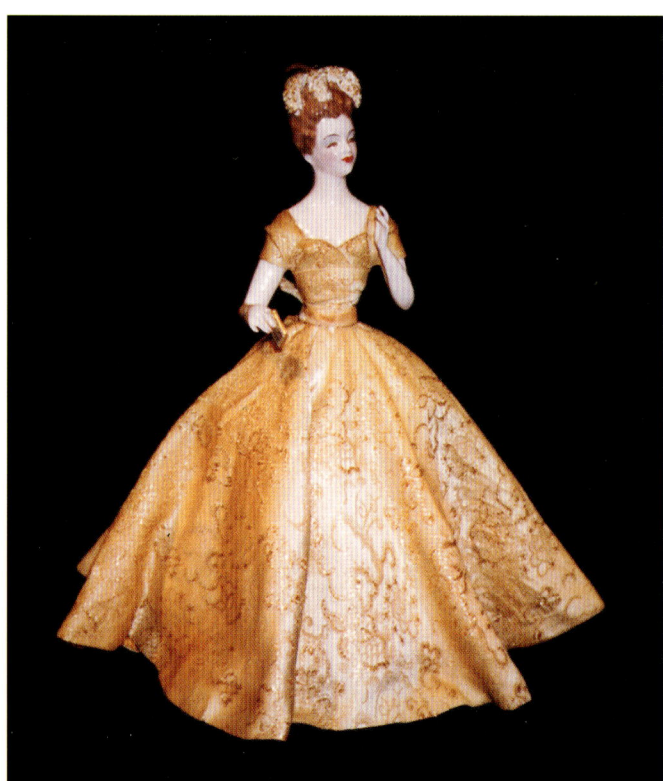

**Amelia Brocade**, 12"
$2,750-3,000

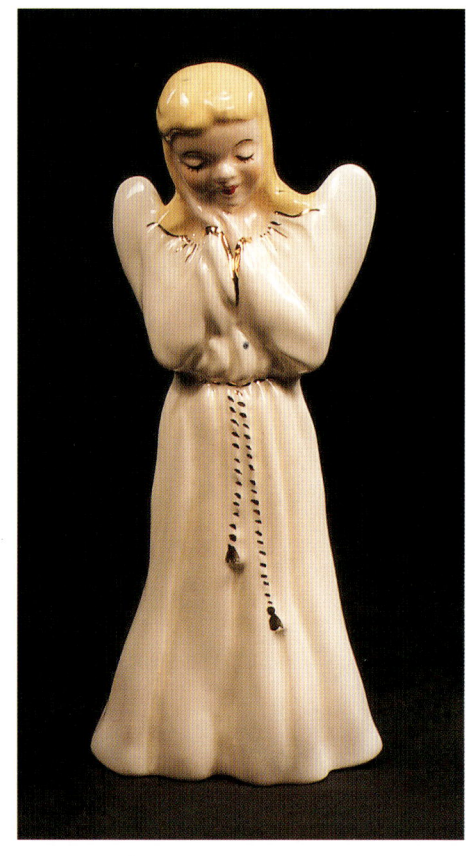

**Angel,** arms clasped, 7"
$150-175

Showcasing Florence A to Z  19

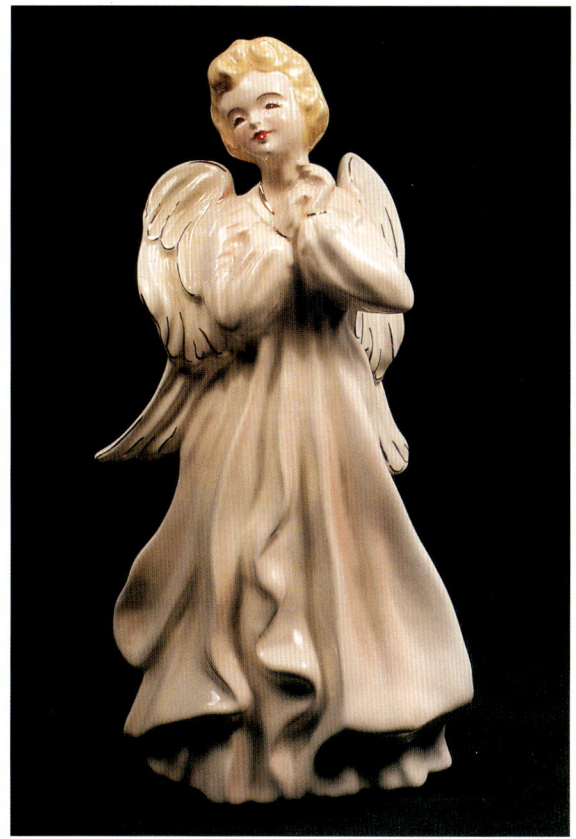

**Angel,** wings spread, 7"
$325-350

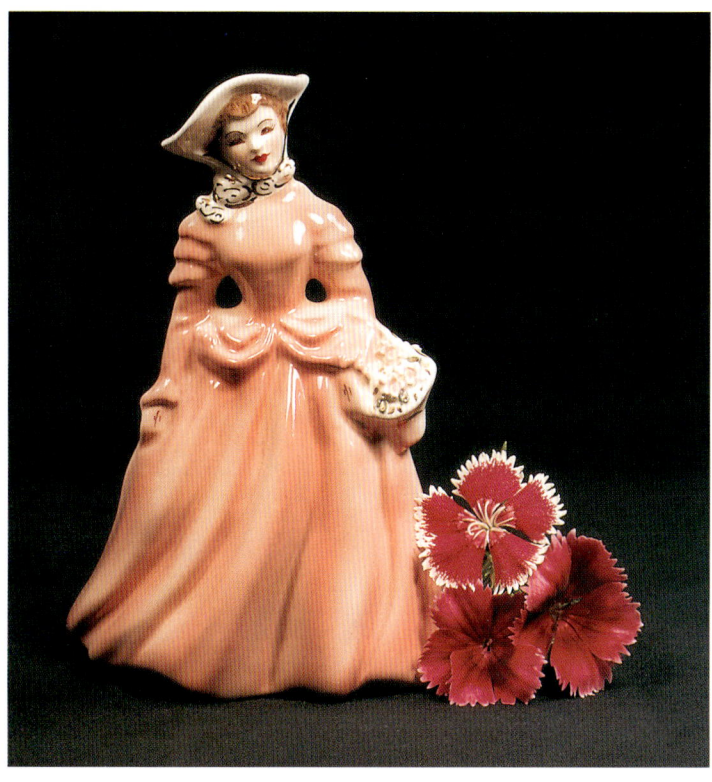

**Ann**, 6"
$70-80

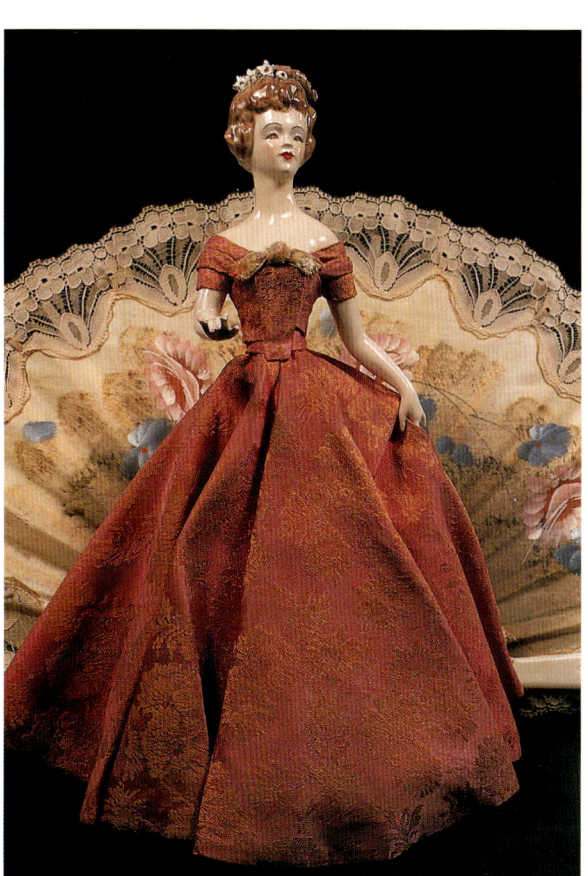

**Anita Brocade**, 10"
$2,750-3,000

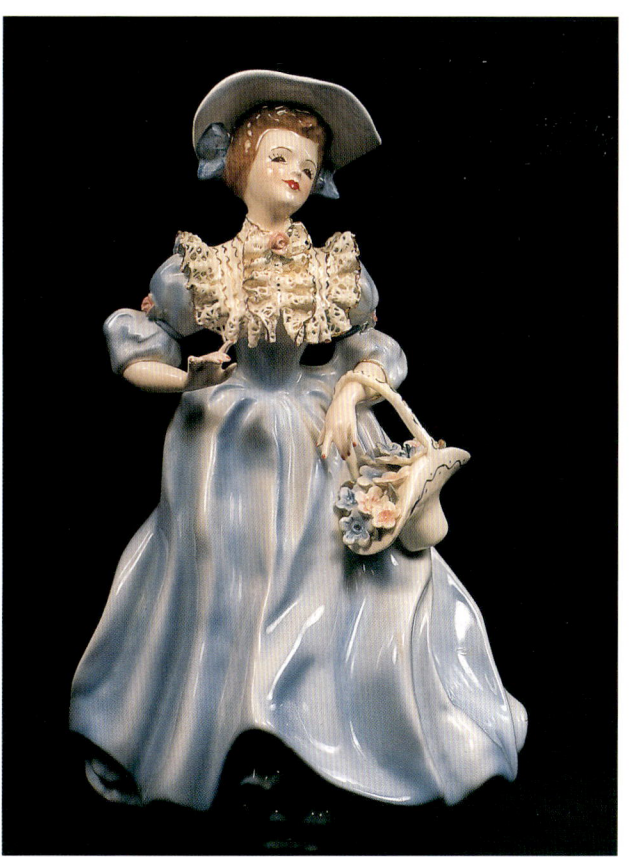

**Annabel,** with flower basket, 8.25"
$600-650

## 20  Showcasing Florence A to Z

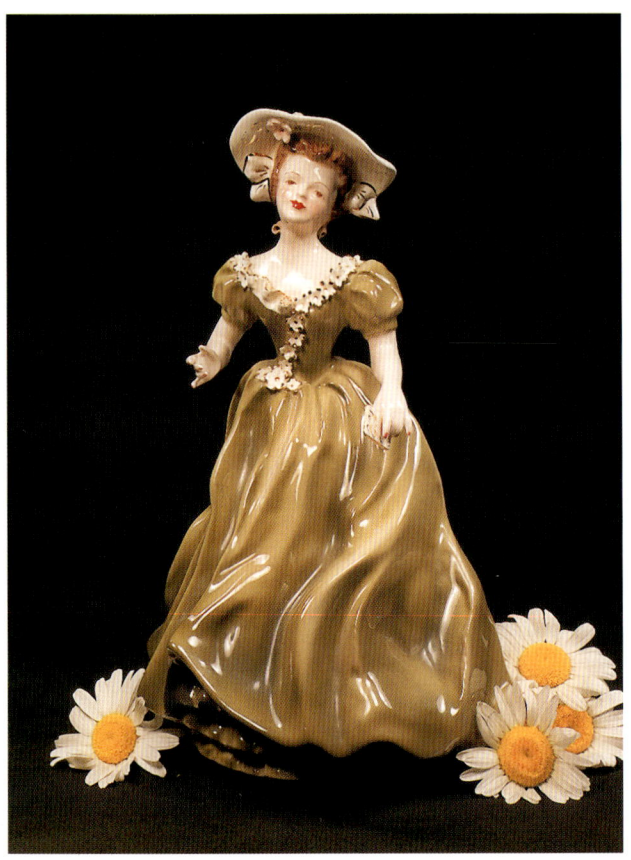

**Annabel,** with card in hand, 8.25"
$650-700

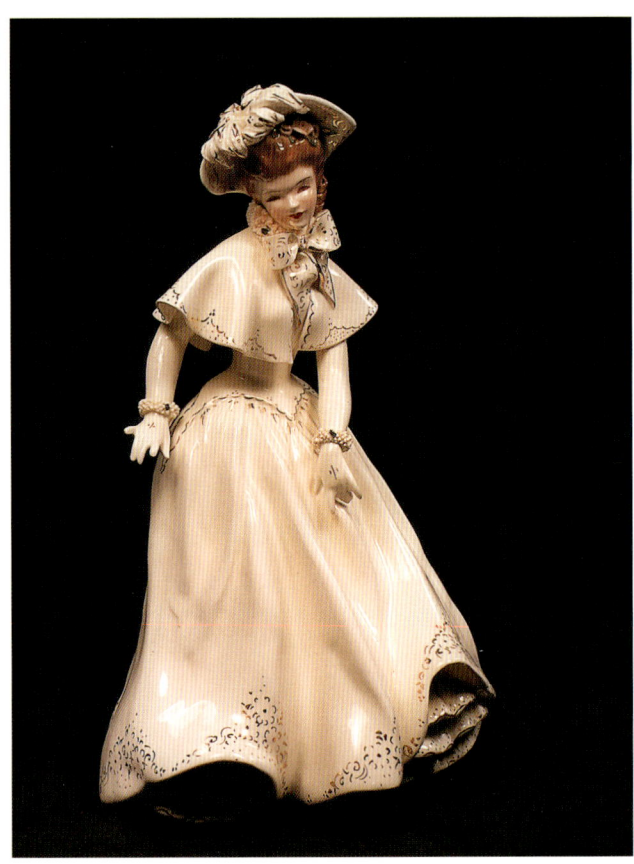

**Annette,** 8.25"
$500-550

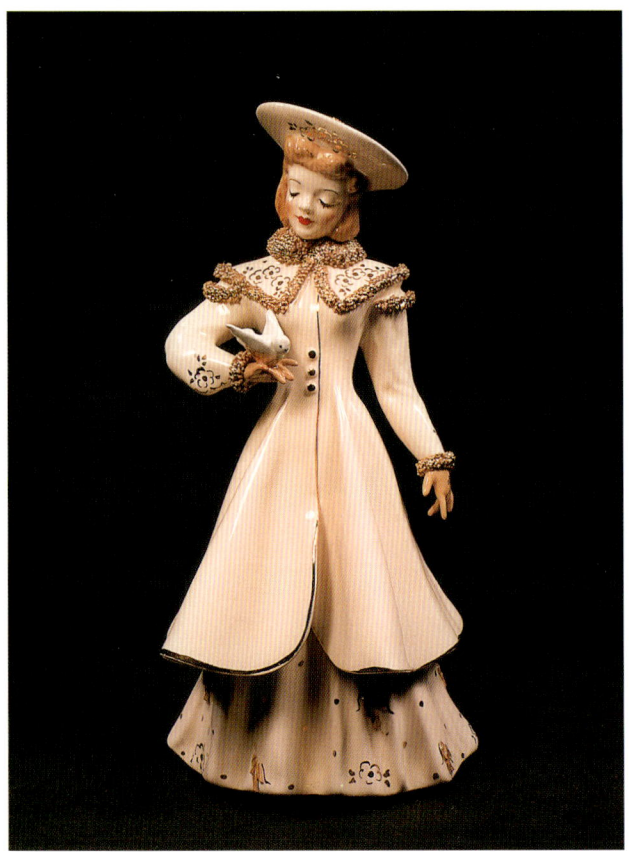

**Annabelle,** with blue bird, 8.75"
$550-600

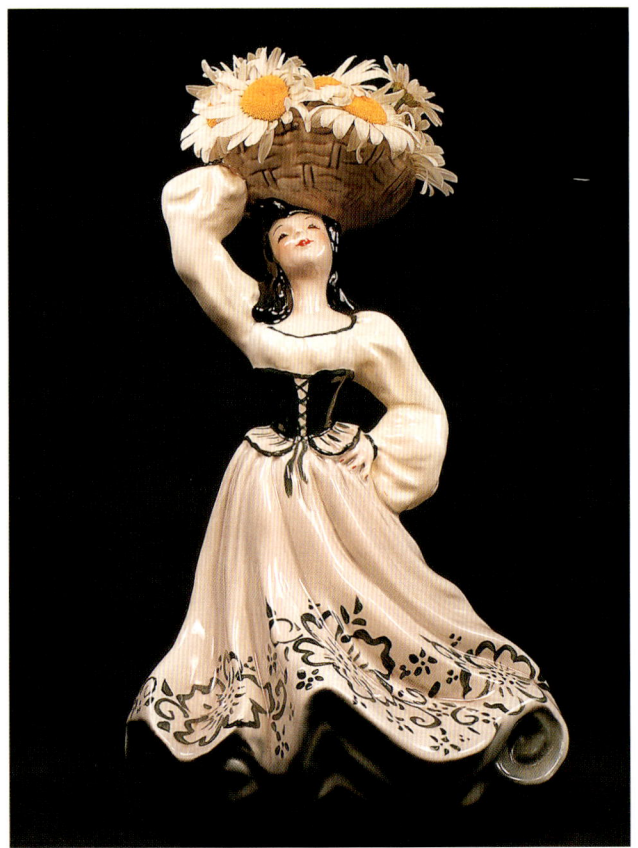

*Ava*, 10.5" (FH)
$300-350

Showcasing Florence A to Z   21

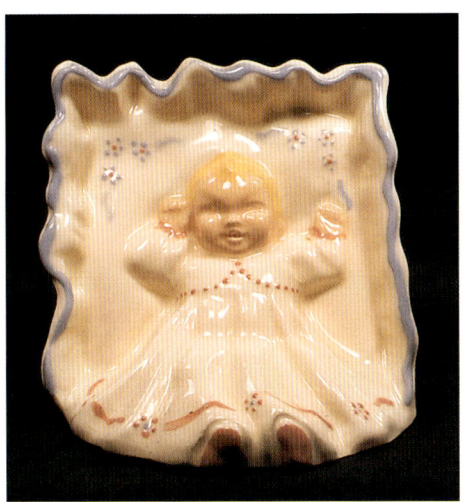

***Baby***, 4.5" (FH)
$75-100

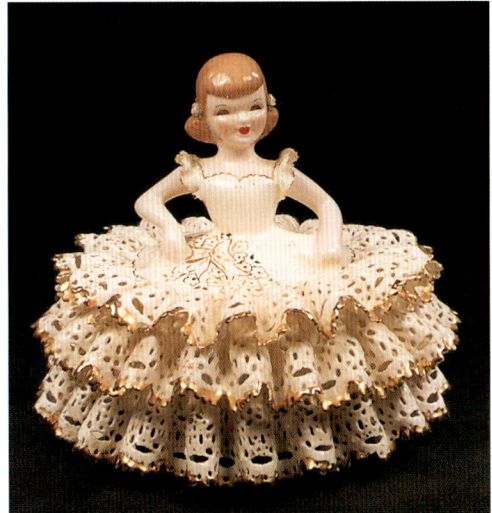

***Ballet Powder Box***,
6" x 6"
$600-650

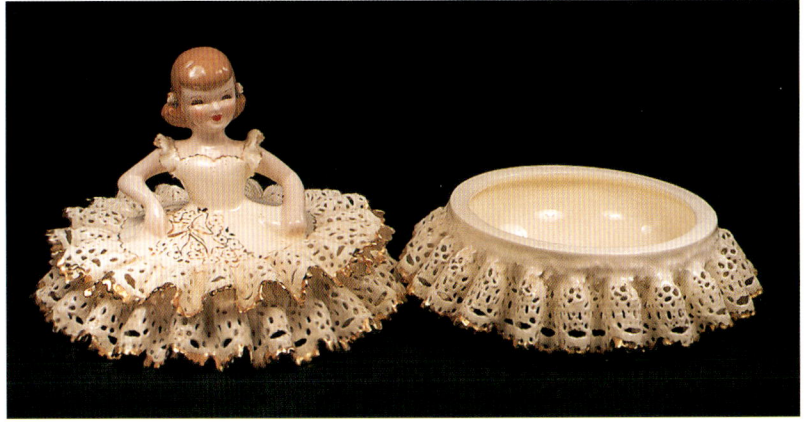

***Barbara,*** adult, 8.5"
$700-750

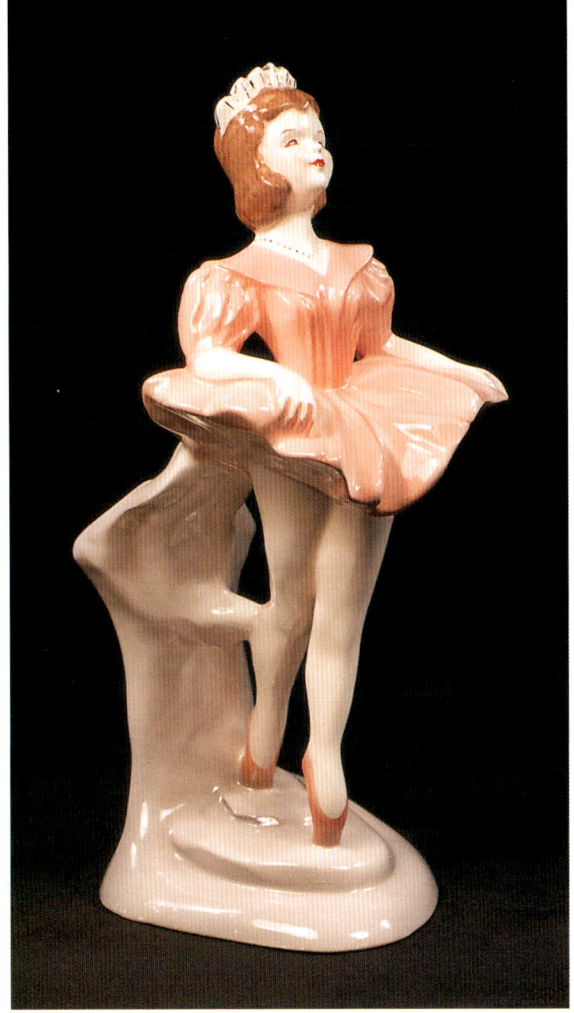

***Ballet***, 7.75"
$400-450

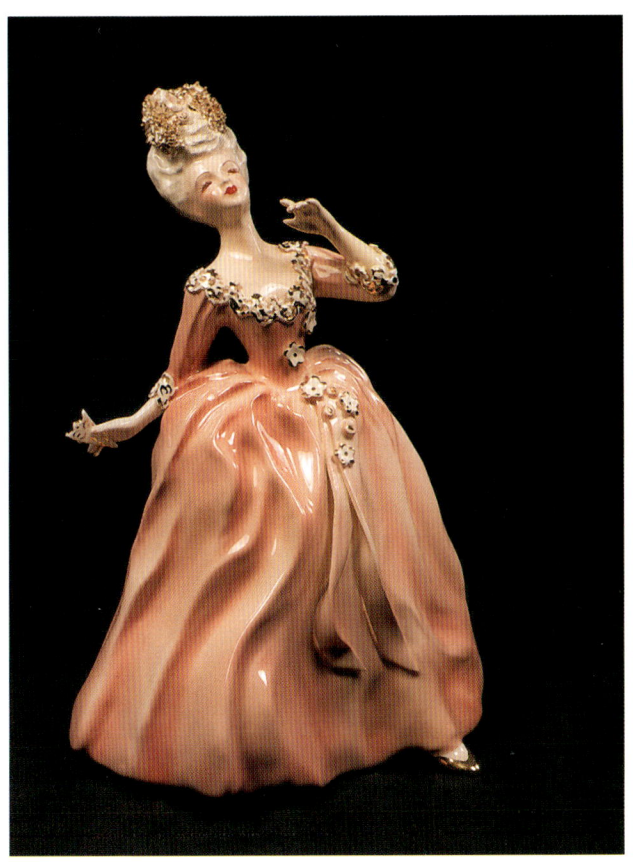

## 22   Showcasing Florence A to Z

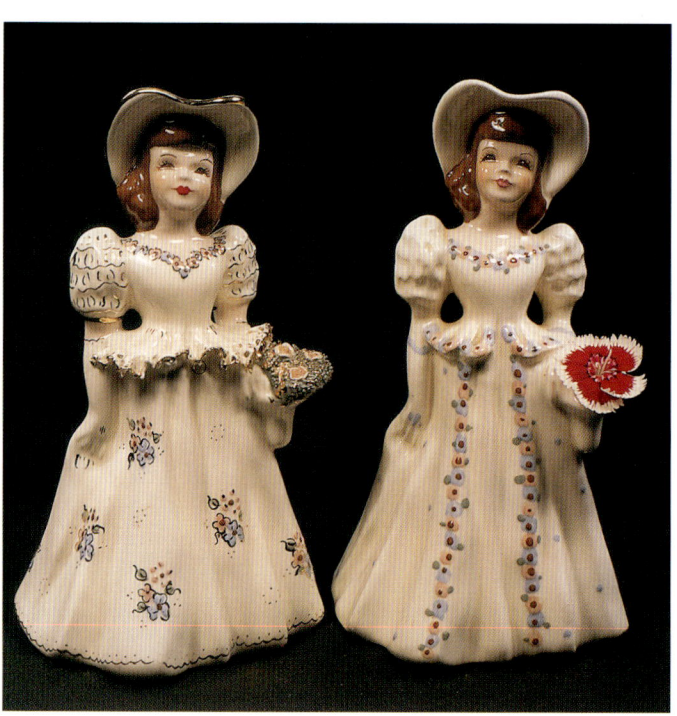

Left: **Barbara,** youth, 7"; Right: **Bee**, 7" (FH)
Left: $150-175; Right: $50-60

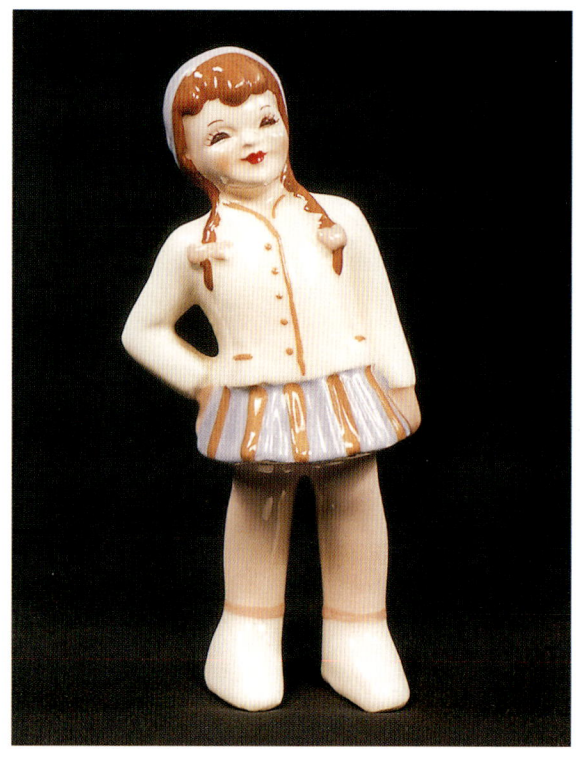

**Becky,** child, 5.5"
$175-200

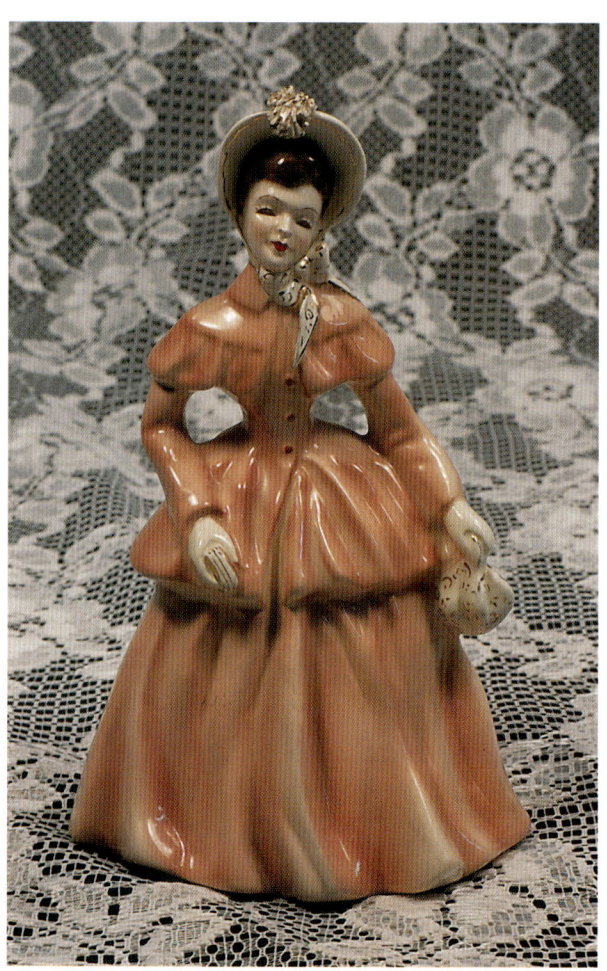

**Bea**, 6"
$150-175

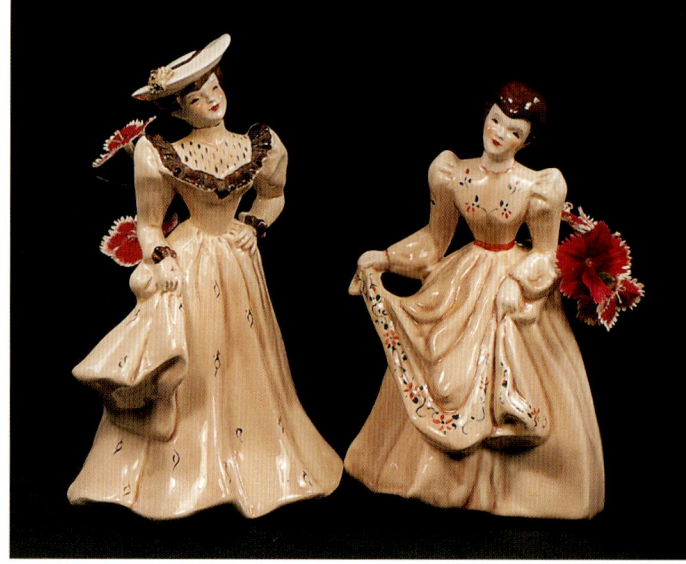

Left: **Belle**, 8" (FH); Right: **Beth**, 8" (FH)
Left: $140-150; Right: $140-150

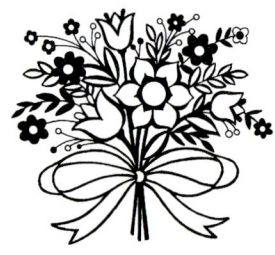

Showcasing Florence A to Z   23

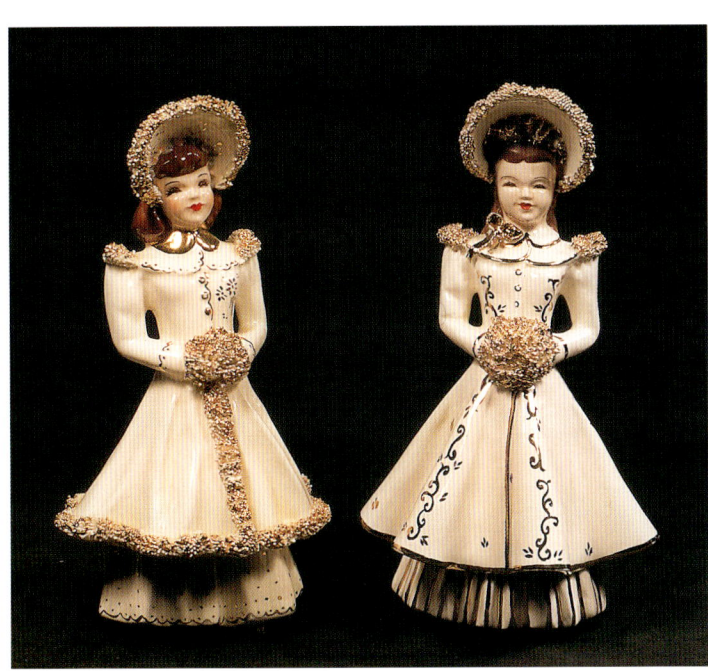

**Betsy,** youths, two different molds, 7.5"
$140-150

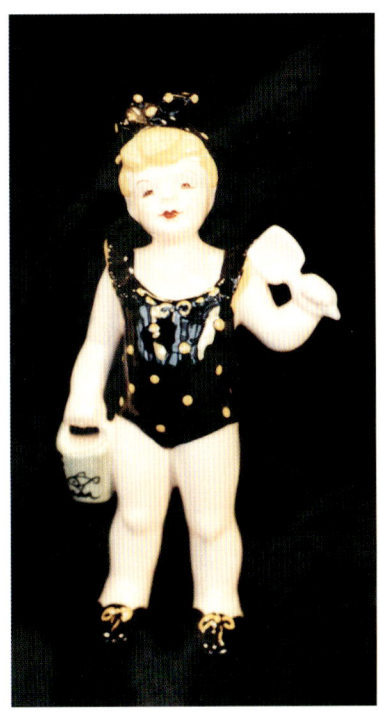

**Blondie,** youth, 7.5"
$1,250-1,500

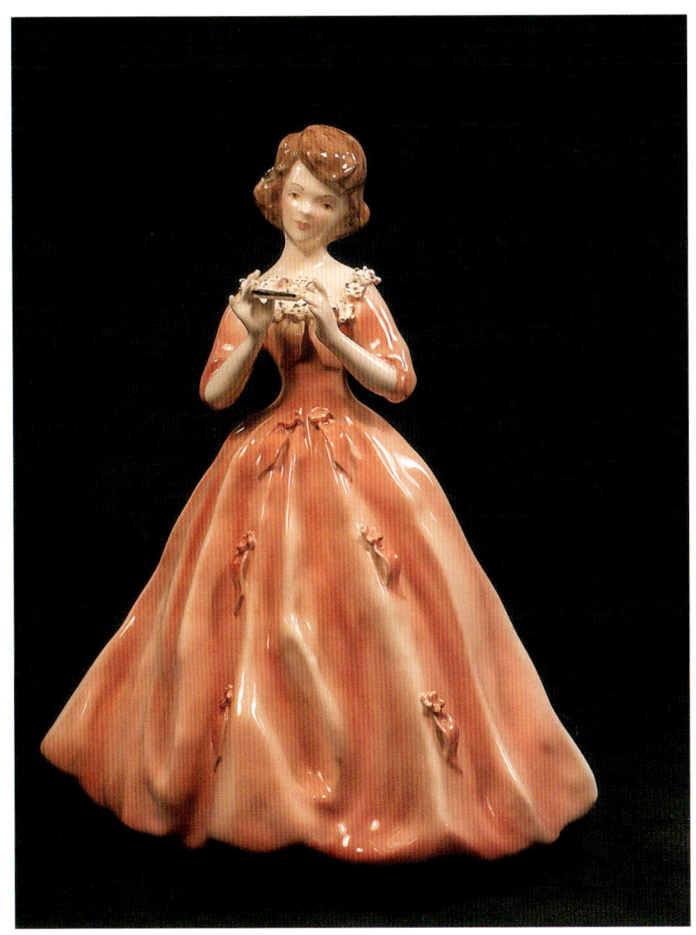

**Birthday Girl**, 9"
$2,500-2,750

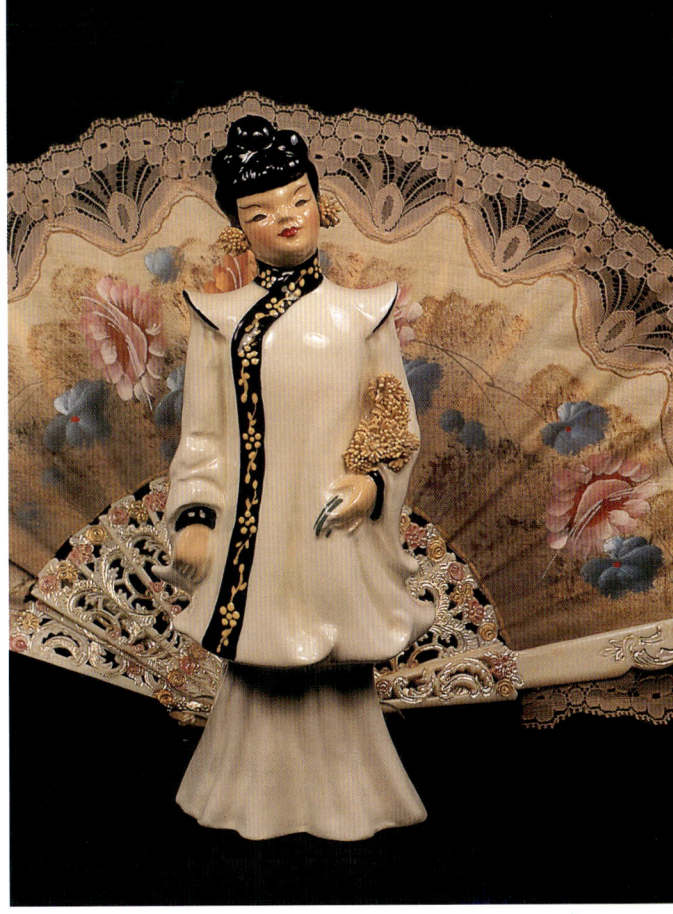

**Blossom Girl**, 8.25" (FH)
$125-140

**24** Showcasing Florence A to Z

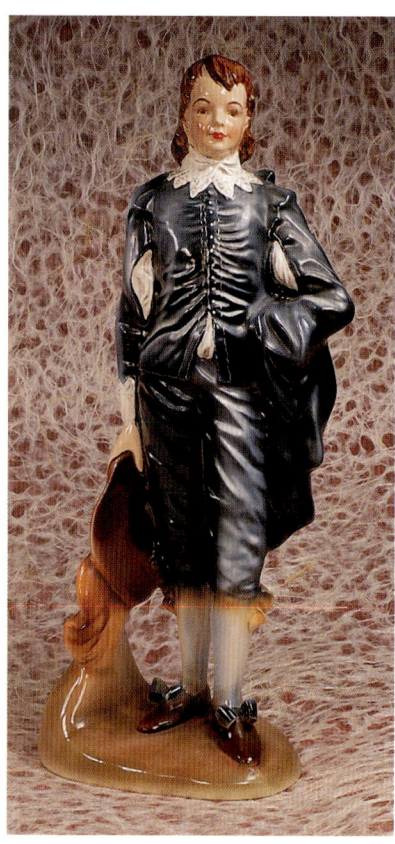

**Blue Boy**, 12"
$400-450

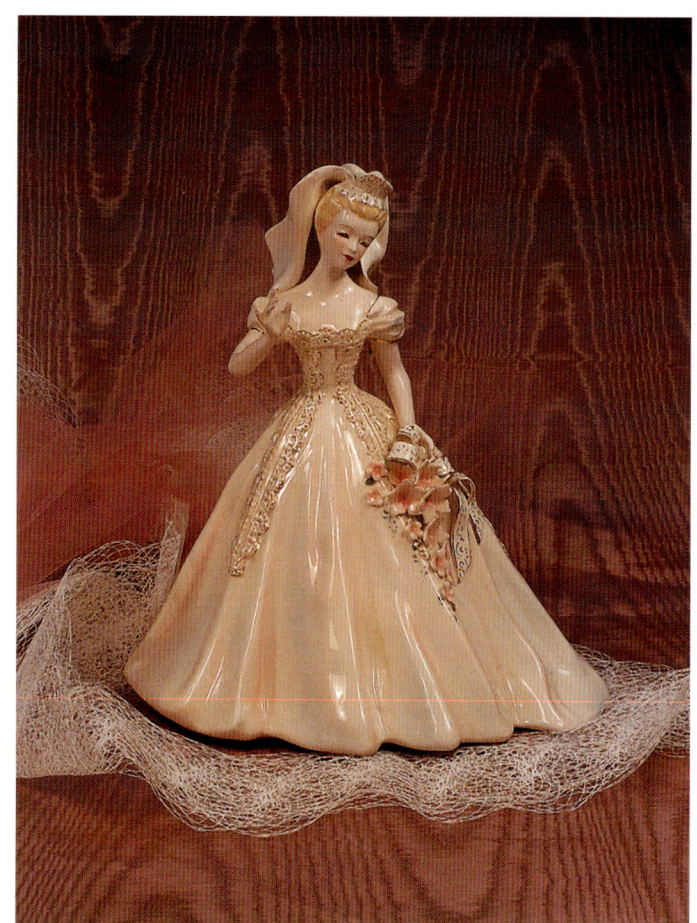

**Bride**, 8.75"
$1,800-2,000

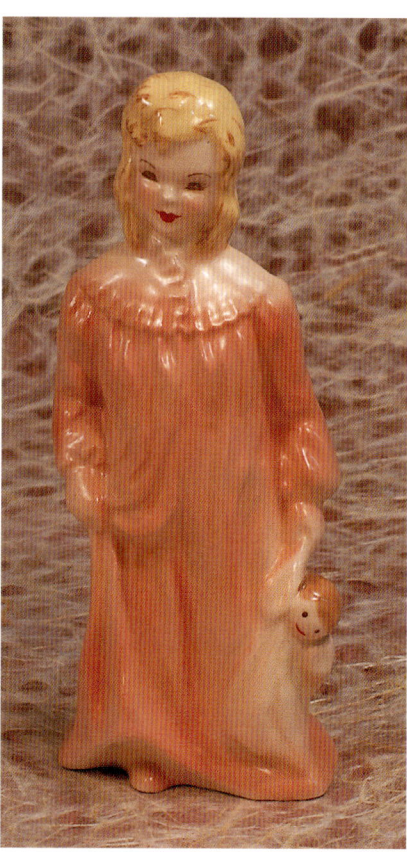

**Blynkin**, child, 5.5"
$200-225

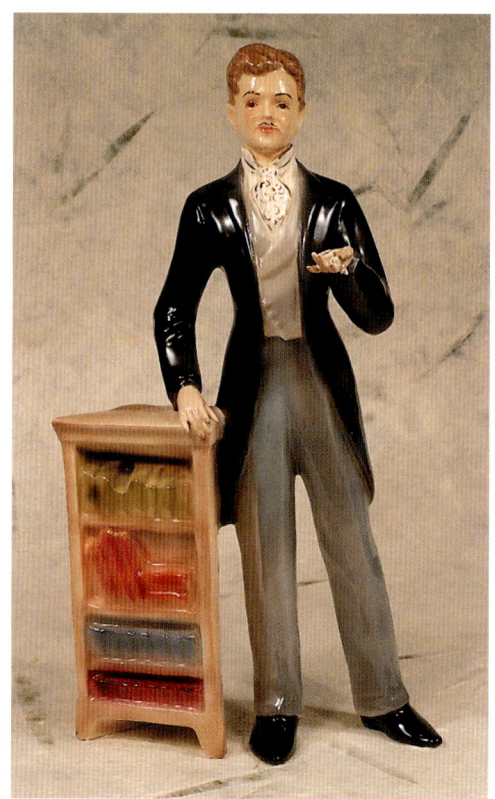

**Bryan**, 10.5"
$2,750-3,000

**Showcasing Florence A to Z 25**

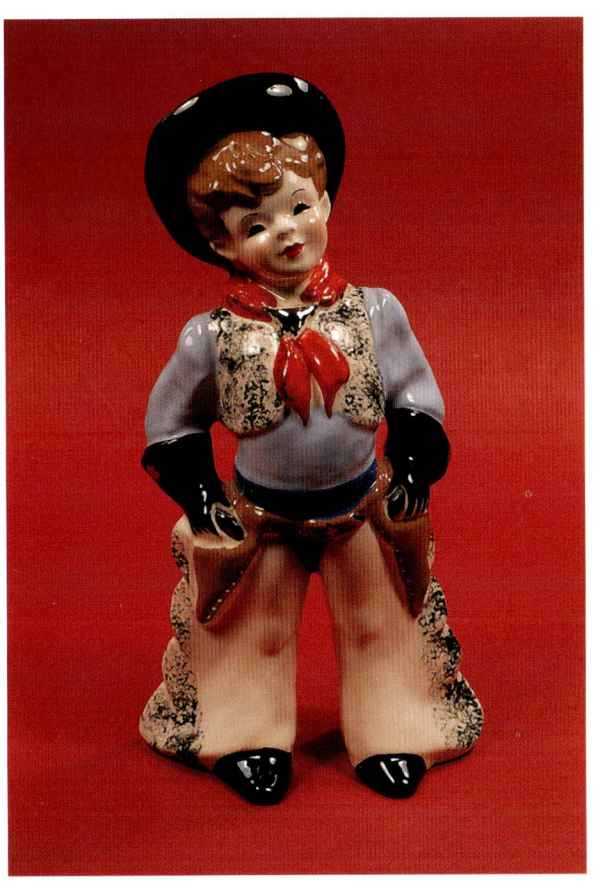

**Bud,** youth cowboy, 7.5"
$700-750

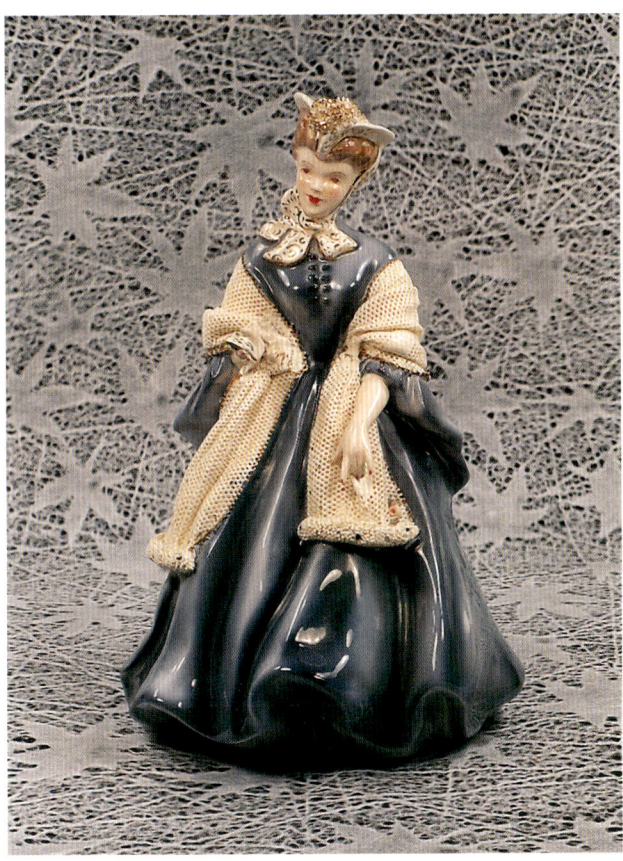

**Camille,** with card in hand, 8.5"
$350-400

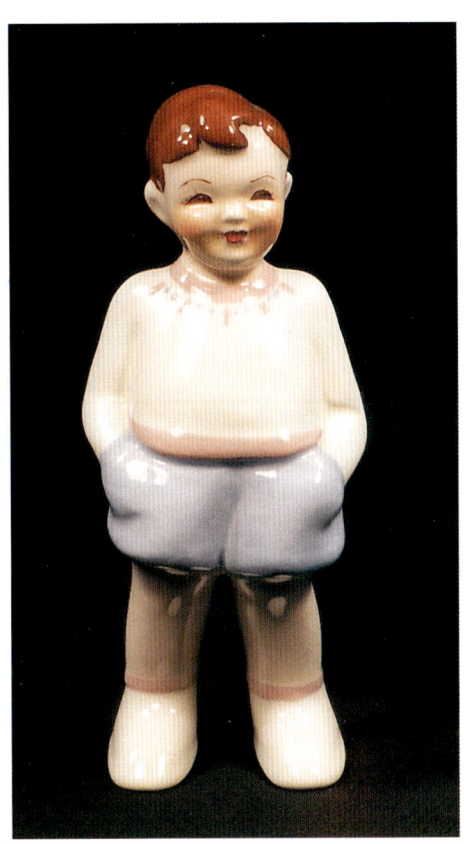

**Butch,** child, 5.5"
$175-200

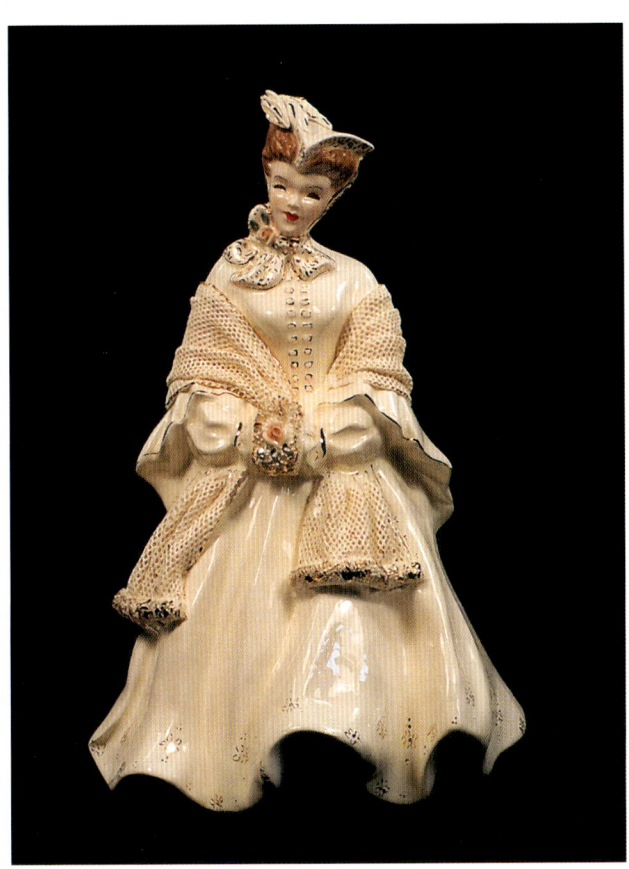

**Camille**, 8.5"
$225-250

## 26 Showcasing Florence A to Z

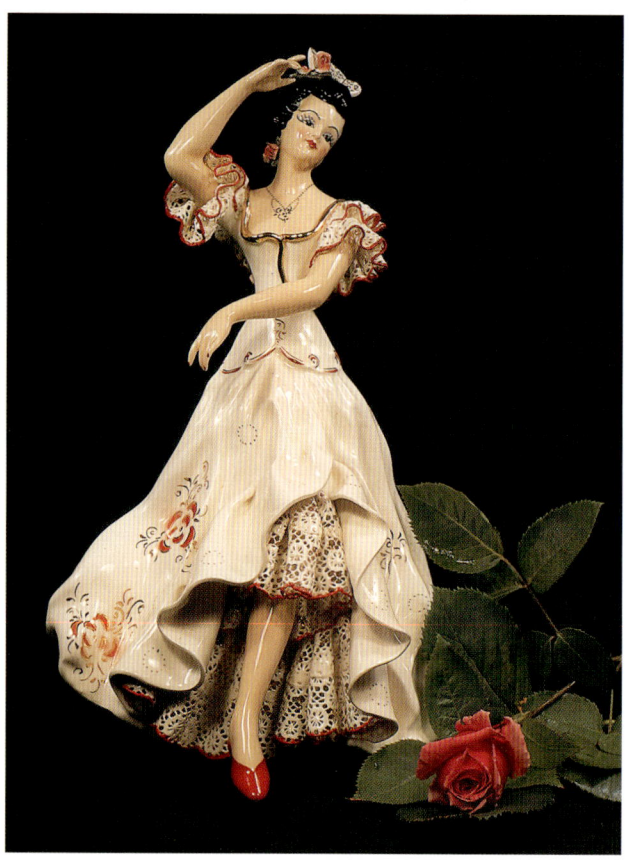

**Carmen**, 12.5"
$2,750-3,000

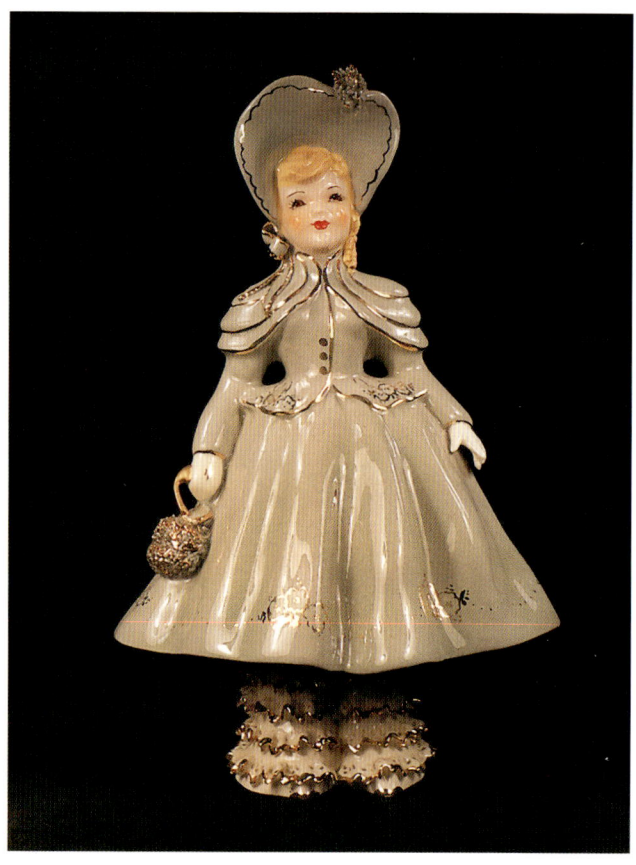

**Carol with Pantaloons**, youth, 7.5"
$400-450

**Caroline Brocade**, 15"
$3,000-3,500

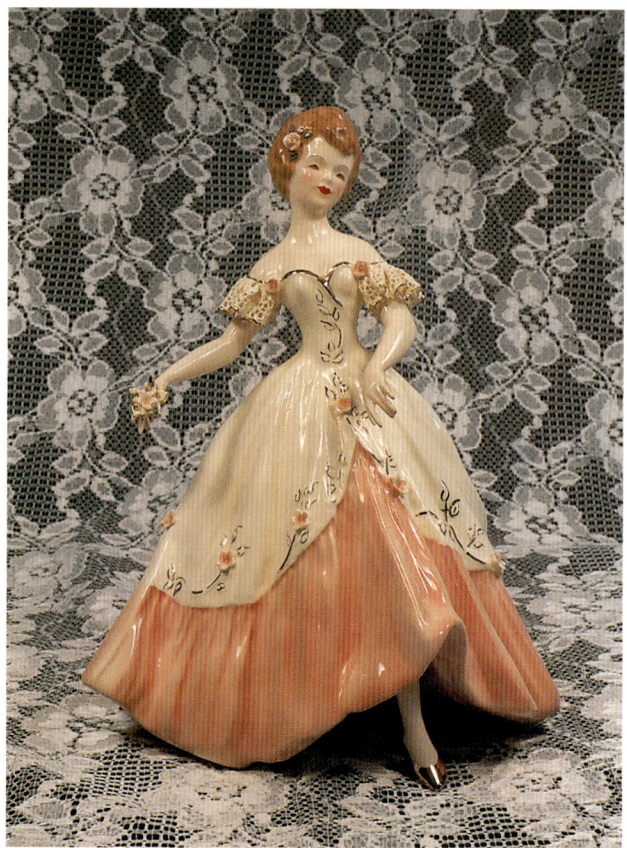

**Carol,** adult, 10"
$775-850

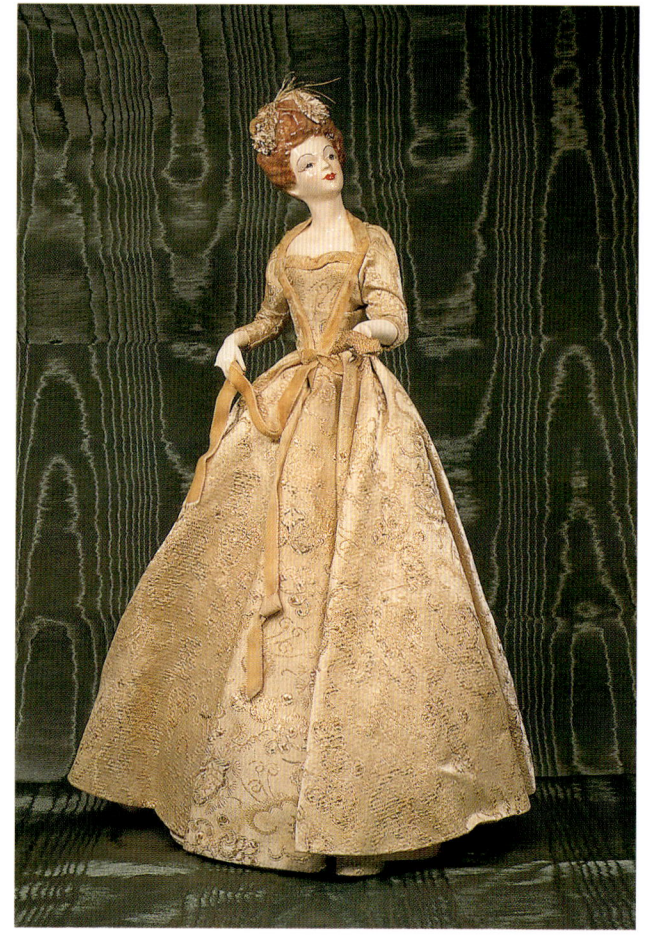

Showcasing Florence A to Z   27

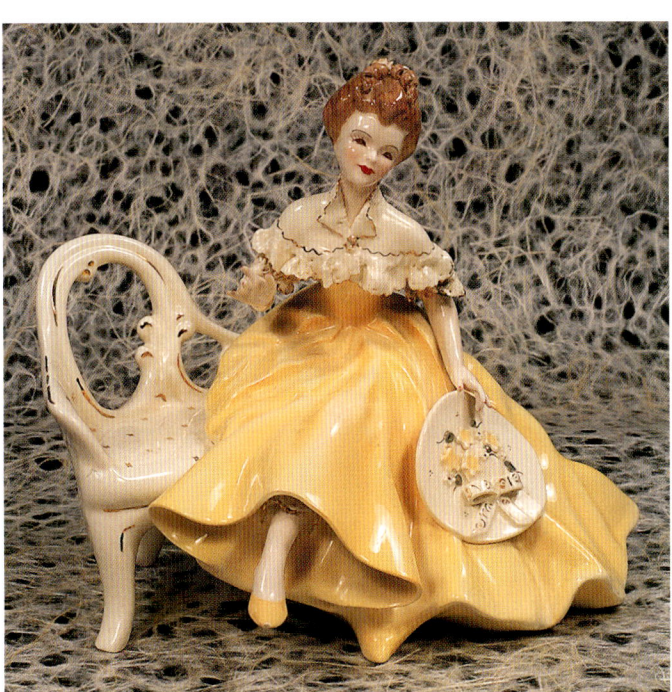

**Catherine,** yellow, with hat, 7.75" x 6.75"
$1,000-1,100

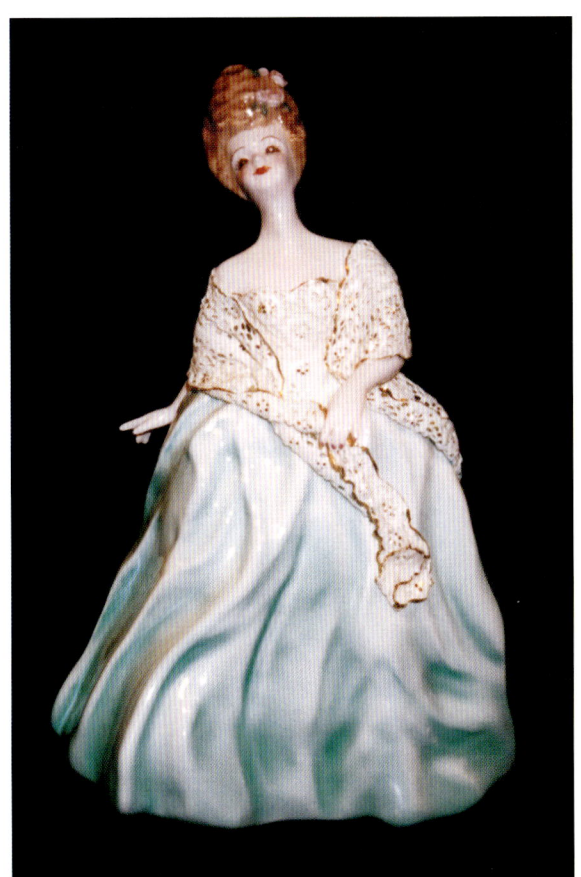

**Cecile**, 8.5"
$1,000-1,250

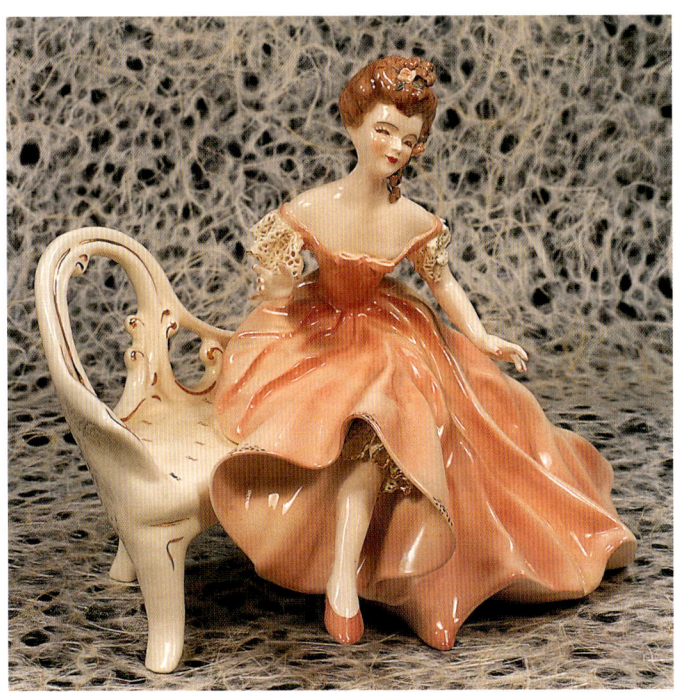

**Catherine,** without hat, 7.75" x 6.75"
$700-750

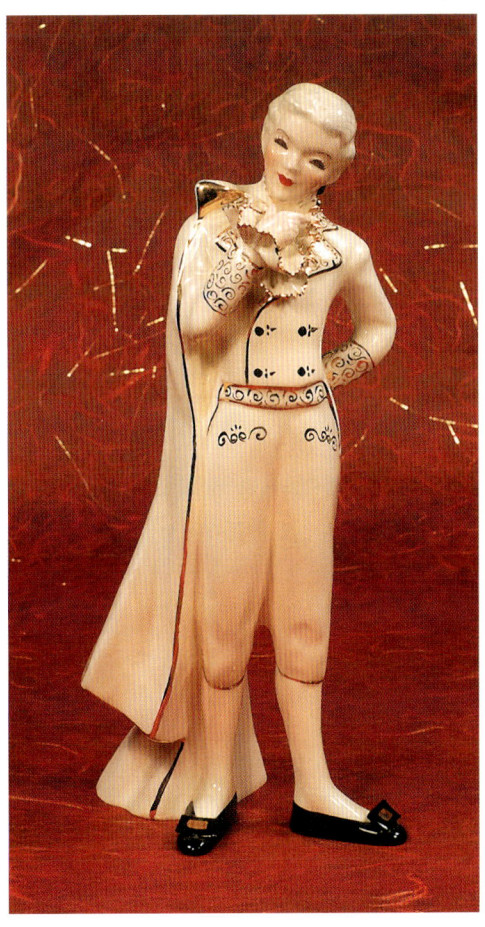

**Charles**, 8.5"
$325-375

## 28  Showcasing Florence A to Z

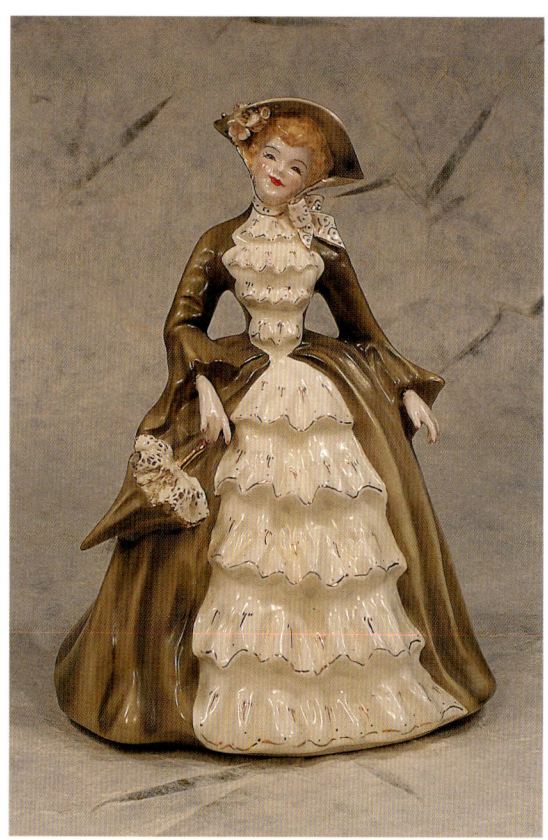

***Charmaine***, 8.5"
$275-375

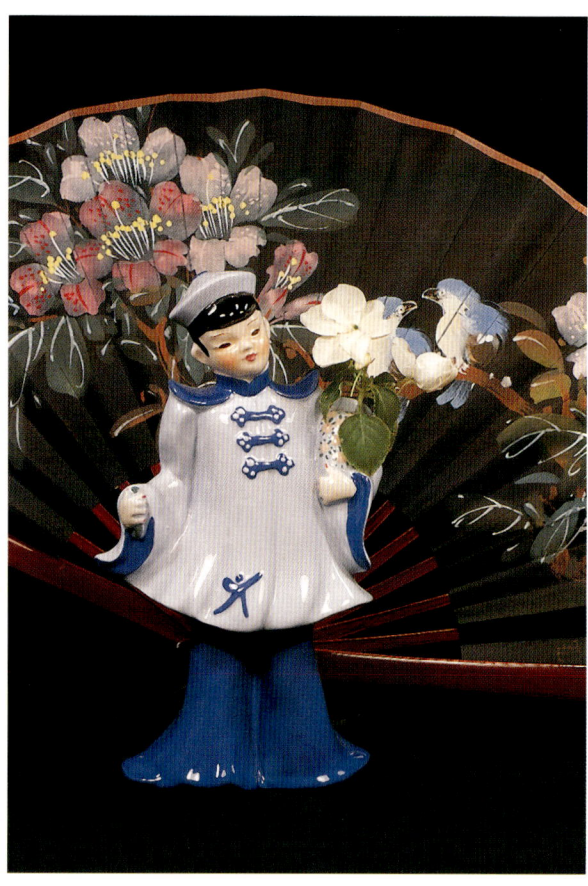

***Chinese Boy***, 7.75" (FH)
$65-80

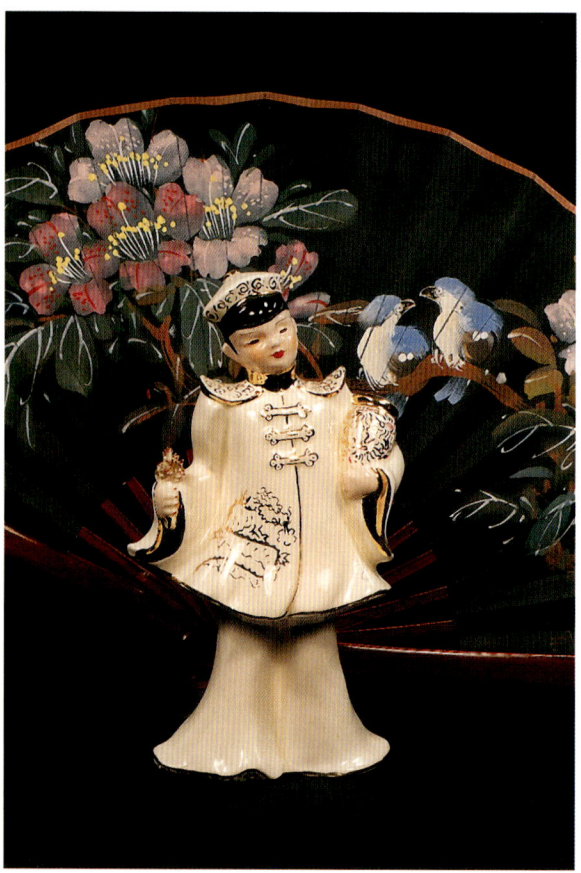

***Chinese Boy***, 7.75"
$75-90

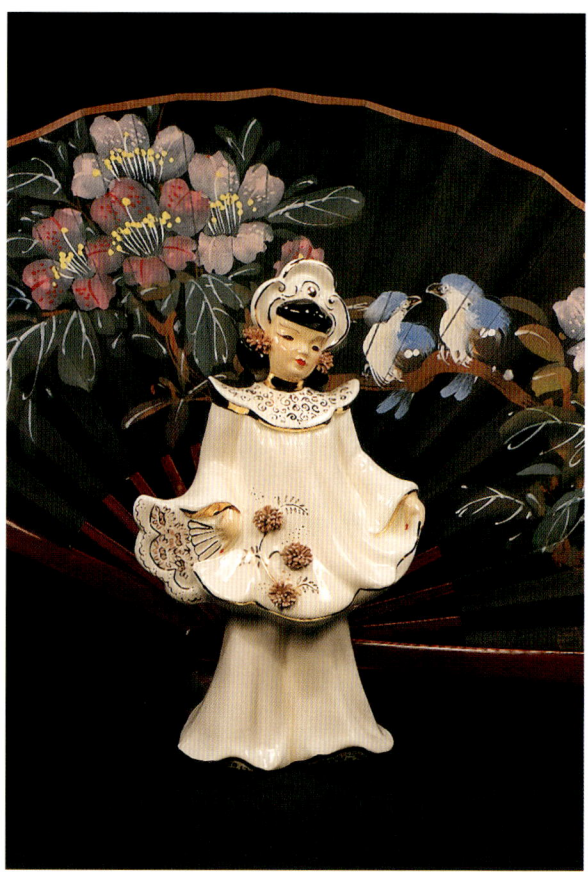

***Chinese Girl***, 7.75"
$75-90

Showcasing Florence A to Z   29

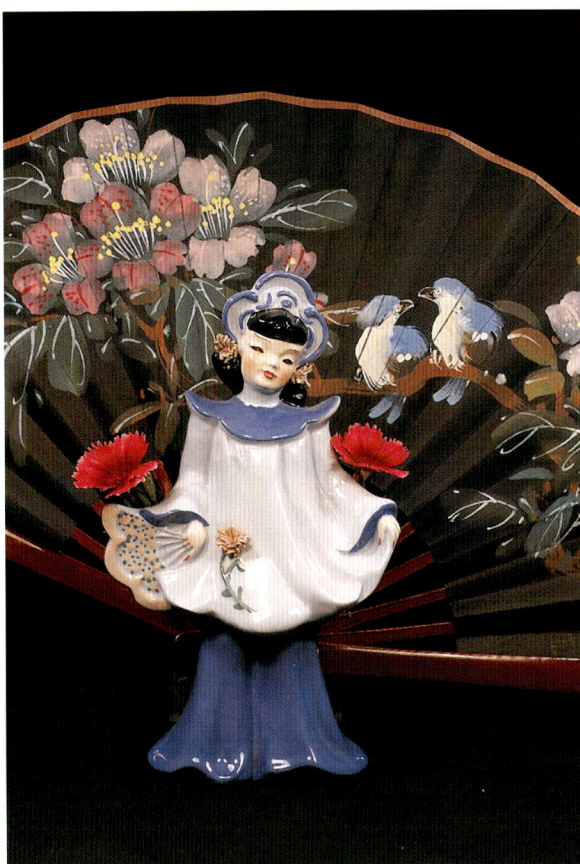

**Chinese Girl**, 7.75" (FH)
$65-80

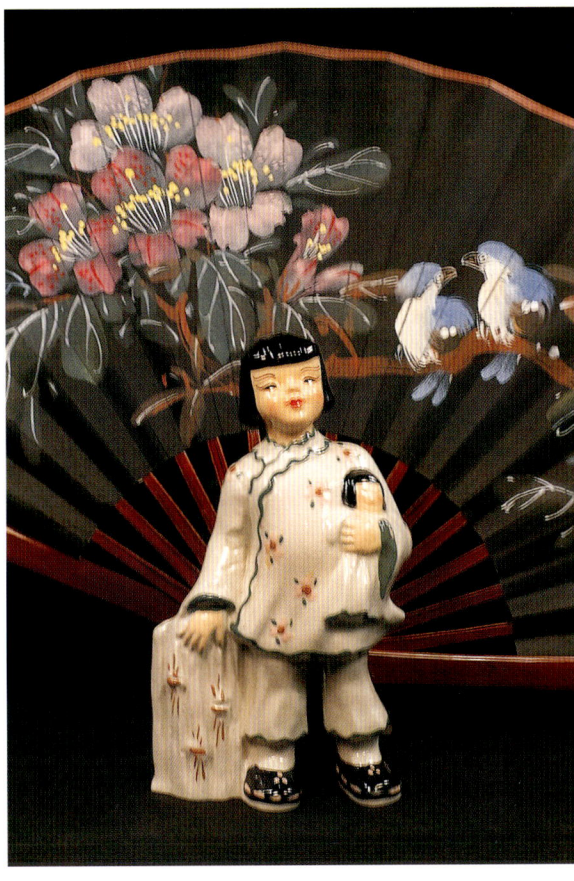

**Chinese Girl Twin**, 7.75" (FH)
$90-100

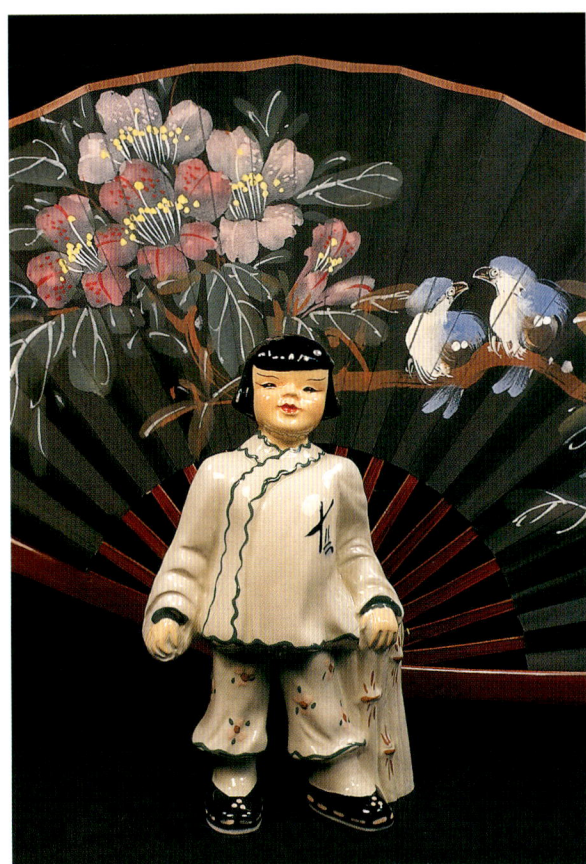

**Chinese Boy Twin**, 7.75" (FH)
$90-100

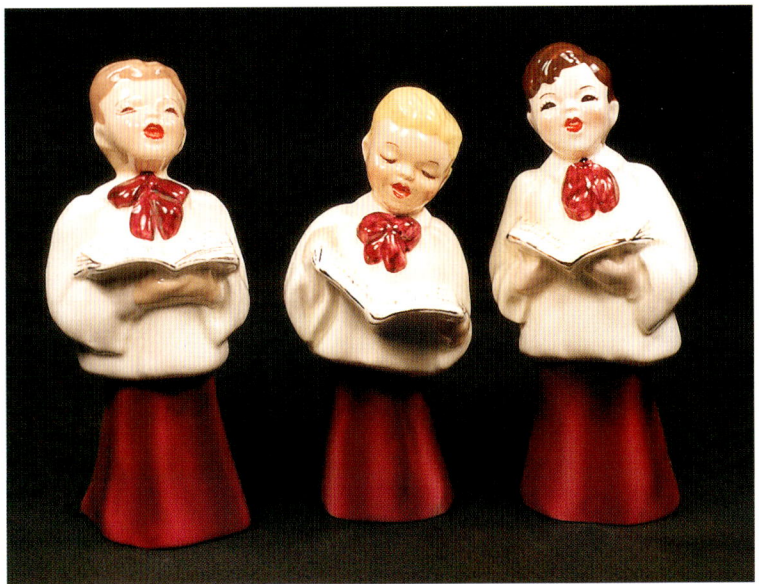

**Choir Boys**, 6"
$400-450 group

## 30 Showcasing Florence A to Z

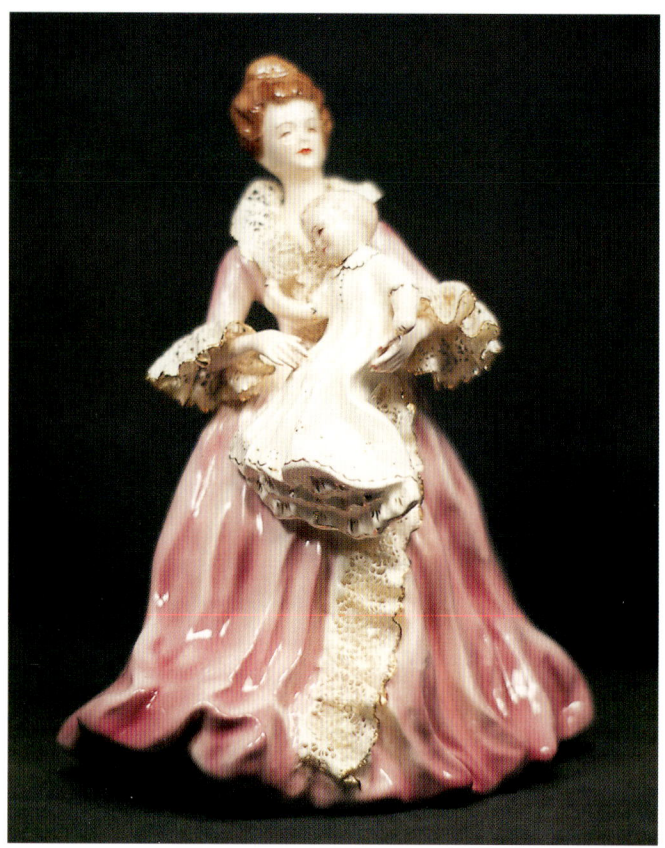

**Christening**, 9.75"
$2,250-2,500

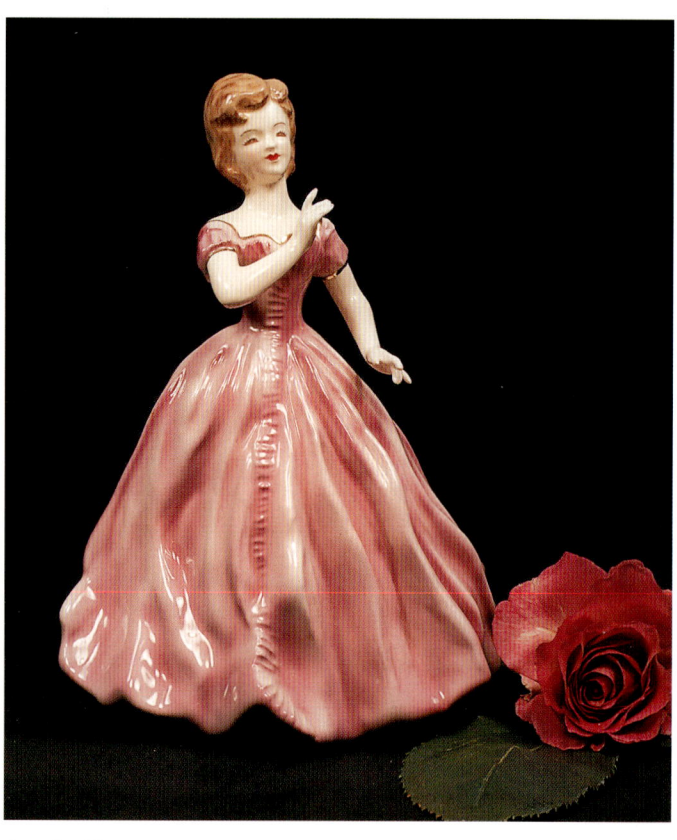

**Cindy**, 8"
$425-475

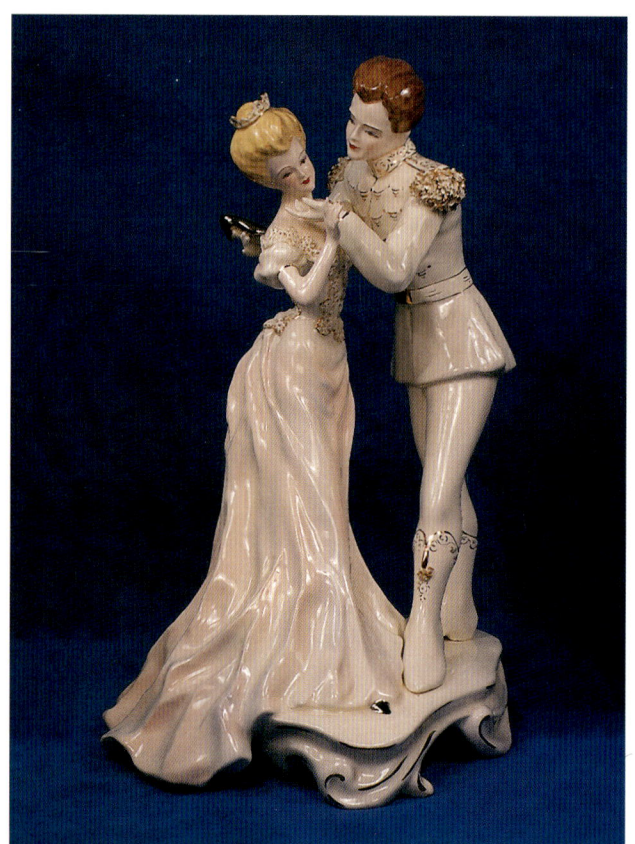

**Cinderella and Prince Charming**, 11.75"
$2,800-3,200

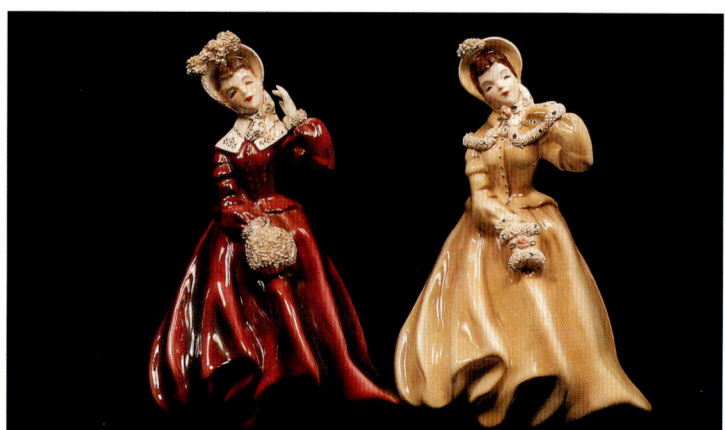

**Clarissa**, two versions, 7.75"
Left: $275-325; Right: $200-250

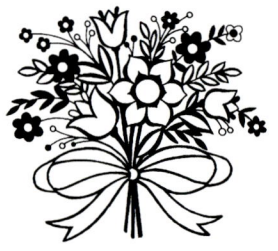

Showcasing Florence A to Z   31

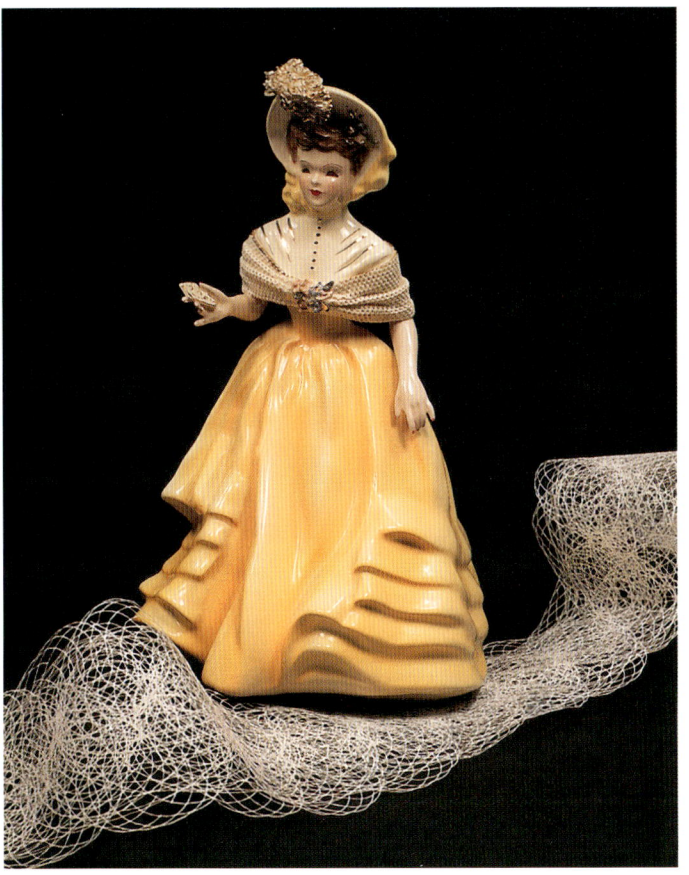

**Claudia**, in yellow, 8.25"
$800-850

**Claudia**, three versions, 8.25"
$300-475

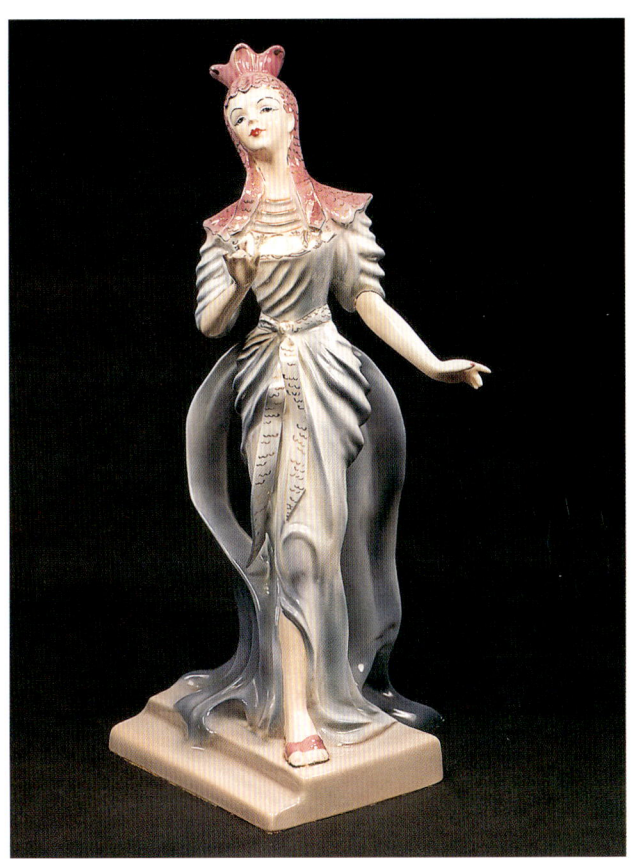

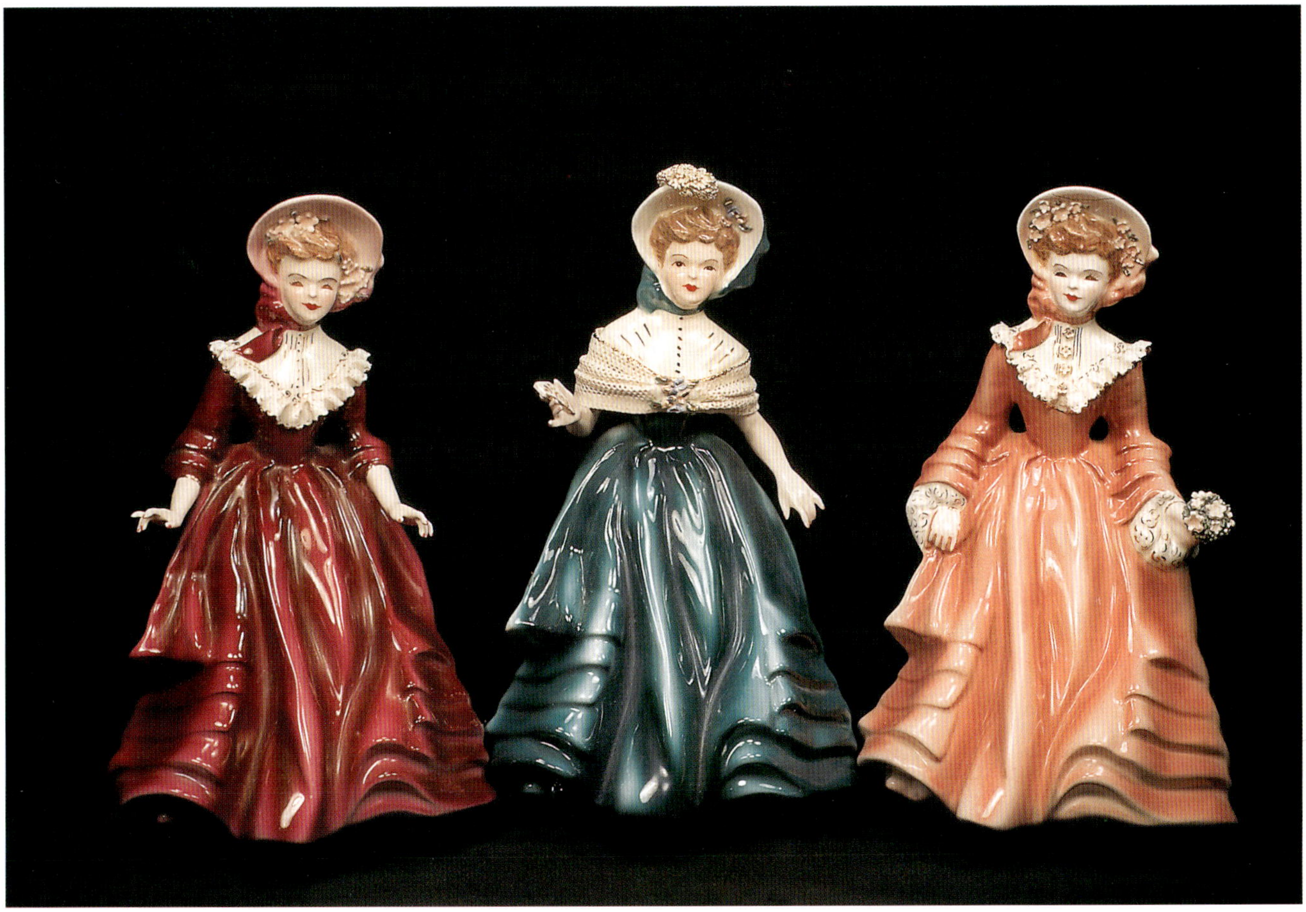

**Cleopatra**, 12"
$1,400-1,600

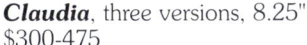

## 32    Showcasing Florence A to Z

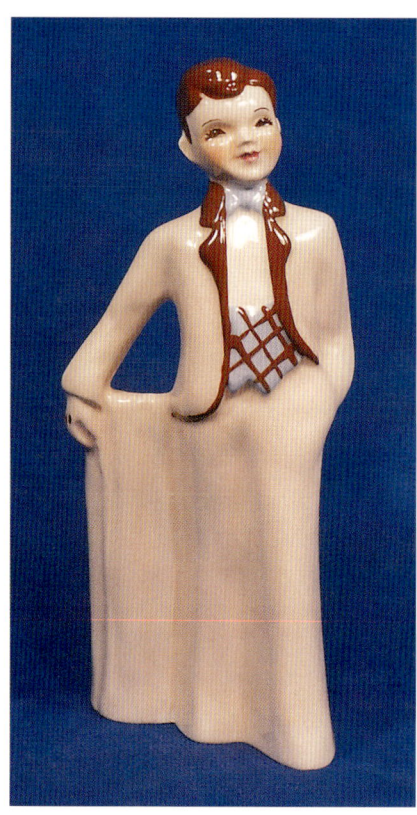

***Clifford,*** young man, 6.5" (FH), *
$65-75

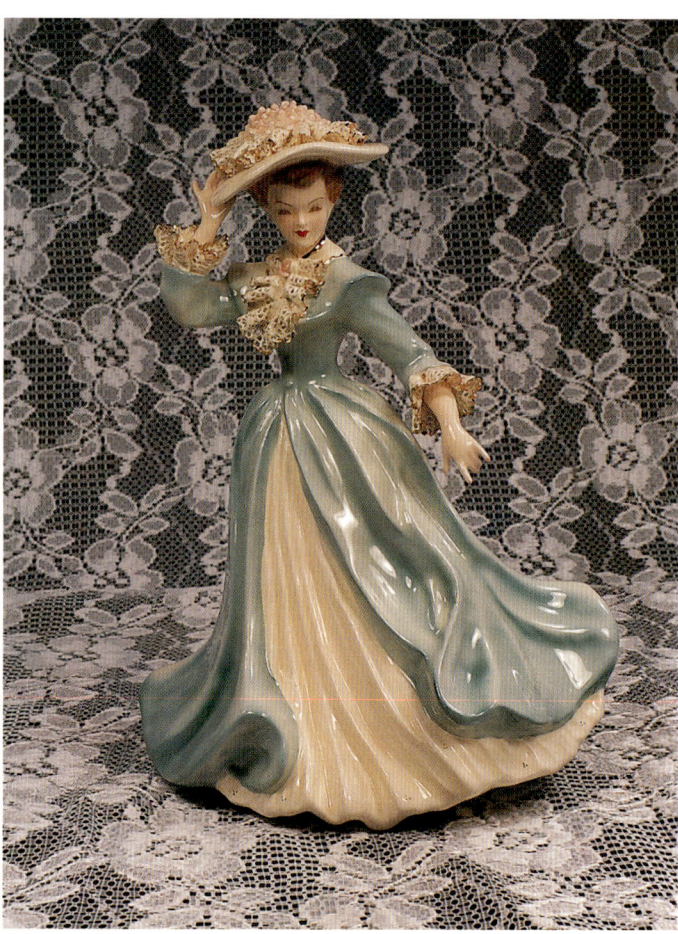

***Cynthia***, 9.25"
$700-750

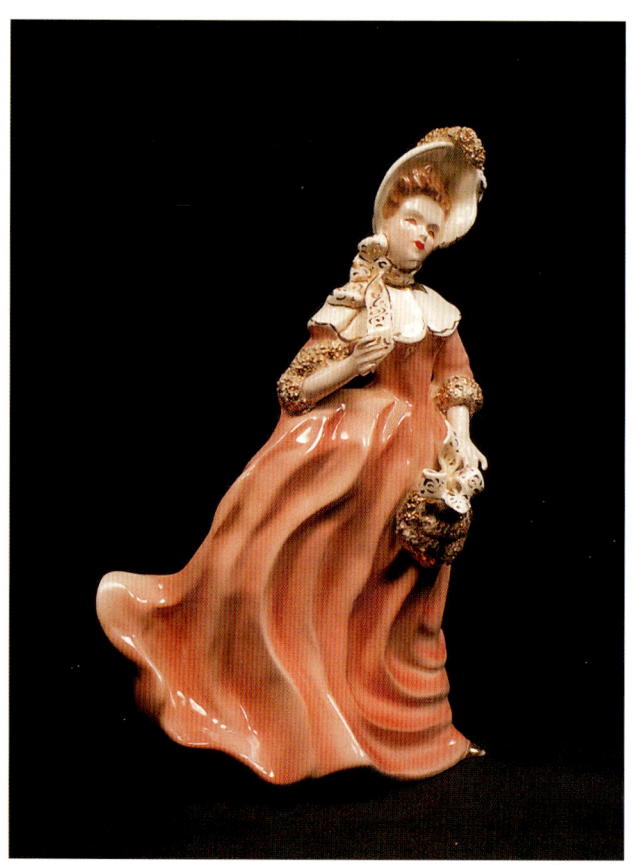

***Coleen***, 8"
$350-400

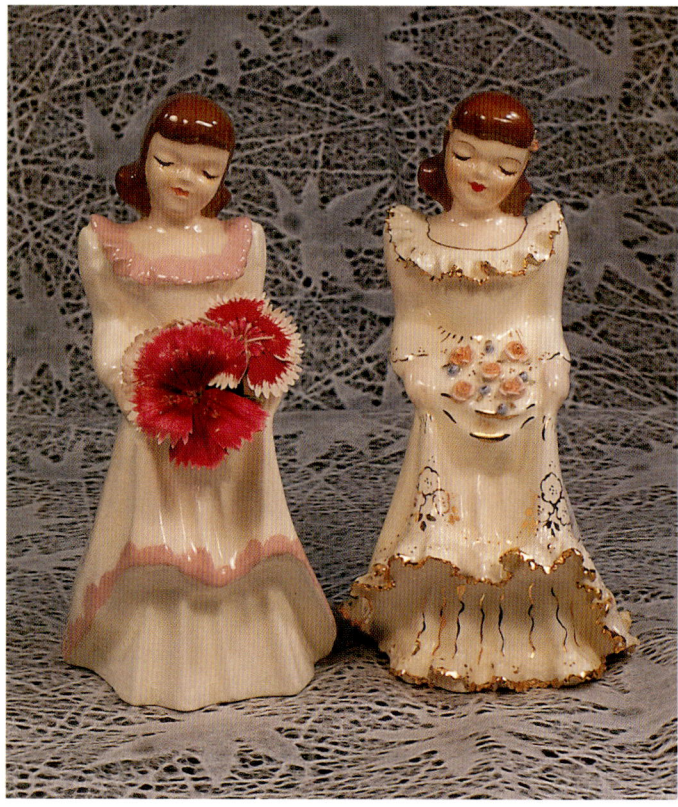

Left: ***Daisy,*** 6.25" (FH); Right: ***Daisy,*** 6.25", *
$75-100 each

Showcasing Florence A to Z  33

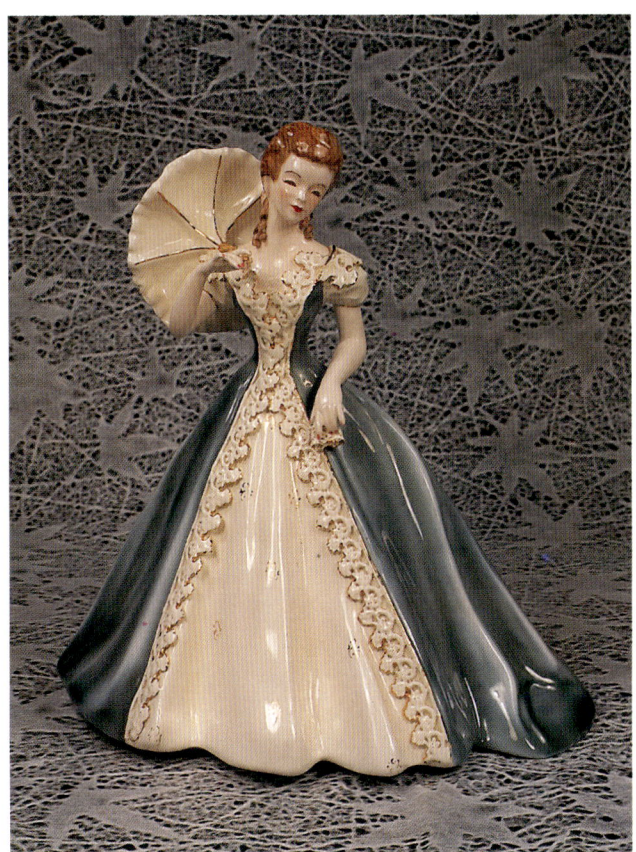

**Darleen**, 8.25"
$800-900

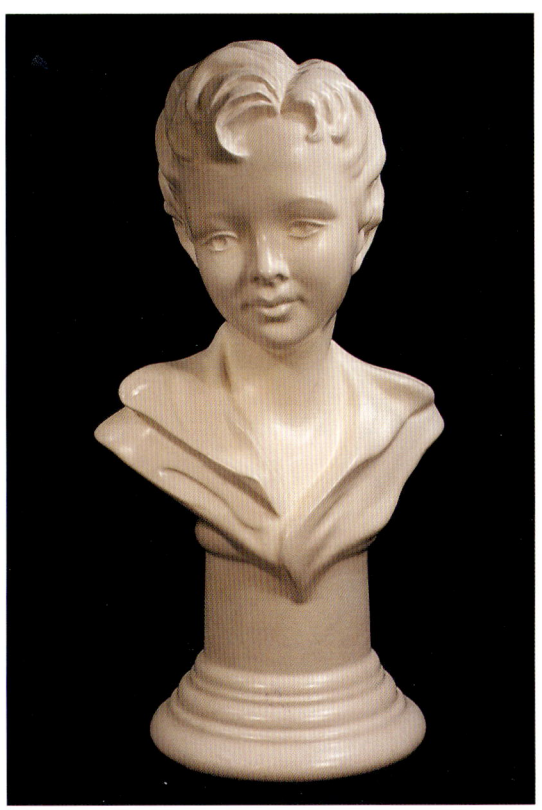

**David,** bust, 11.5"
$275-300

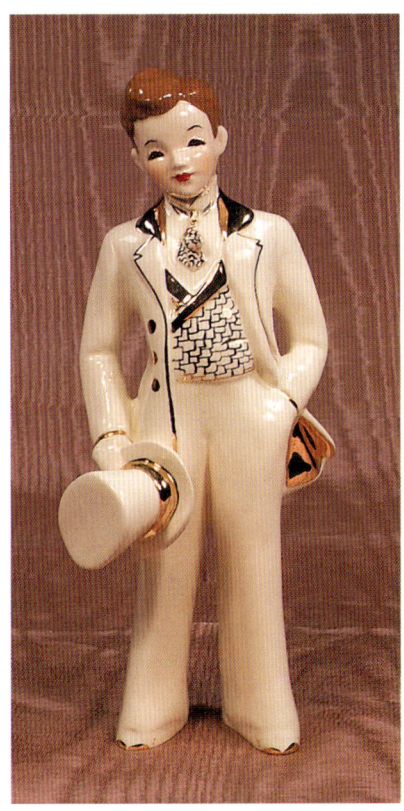

**David,** youth, 7.5"
$140-160

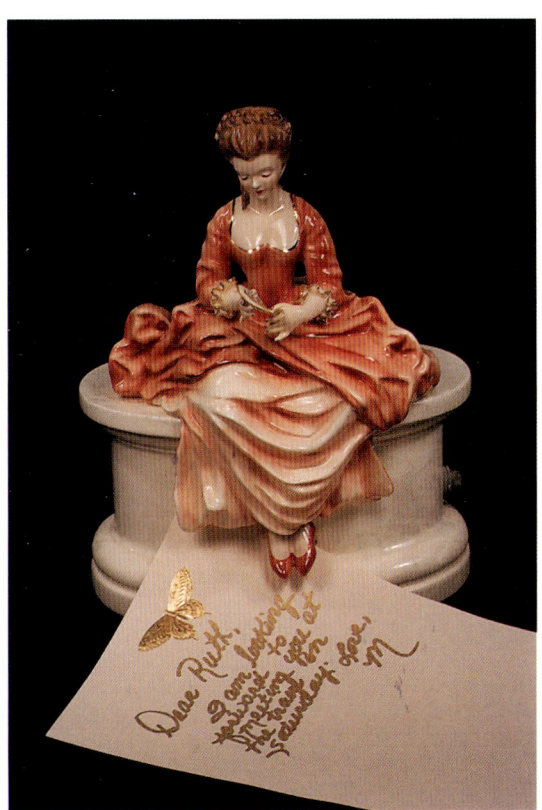

**Dear Ruth**, TV lamp, 9"
$1,200-1,400

## 34  Showcasing Florence A to Z

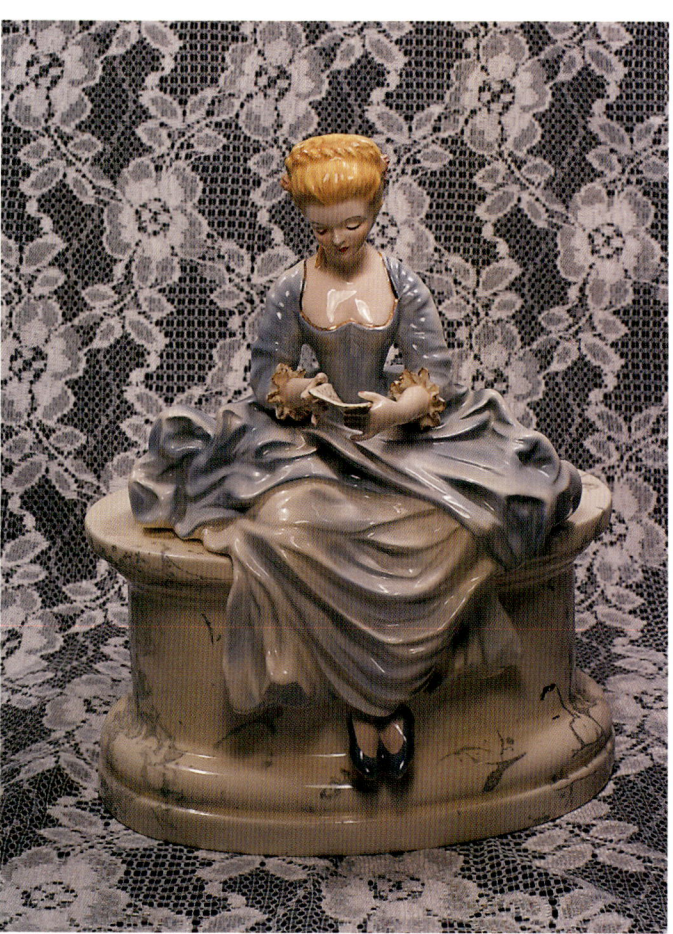

**Dear Ruth**, on oval base (not a lamp), 9"
$1,200-1,400

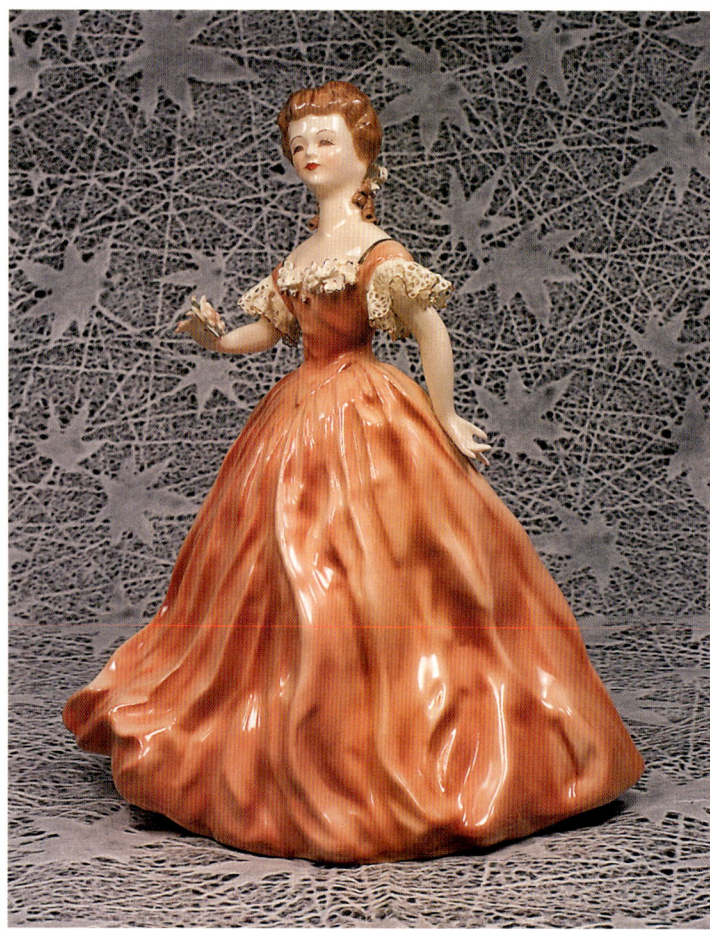

**Deborah**, 9.5"
$700-750

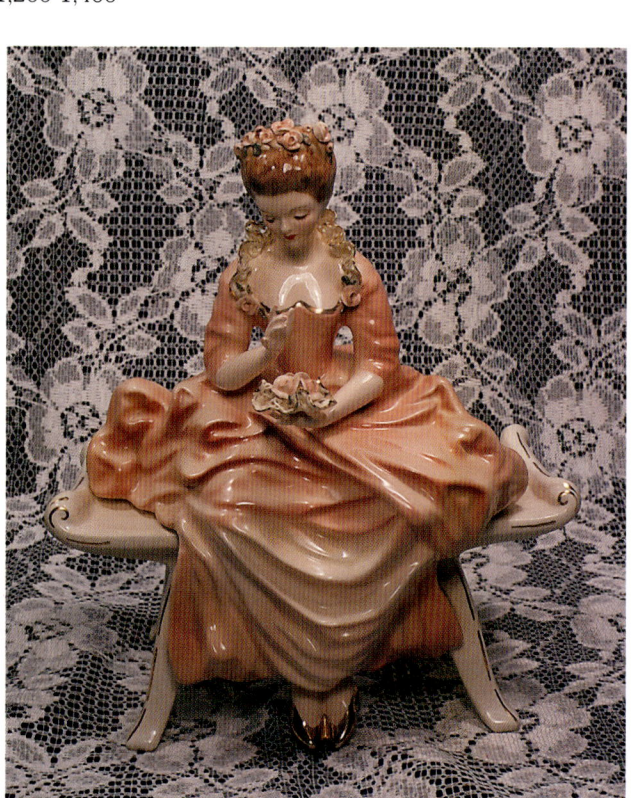

**Dear Ruth**, on bench, 9"
$1,750-2,000

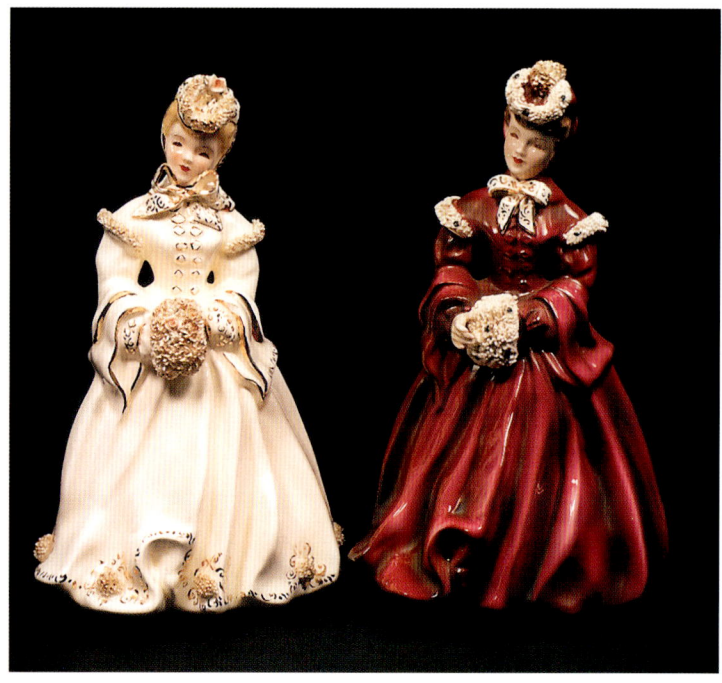

**Delia**, two styles, 7.75"
Left: $135-150; Right: $200-250

Showcasing Florence A to Z   35

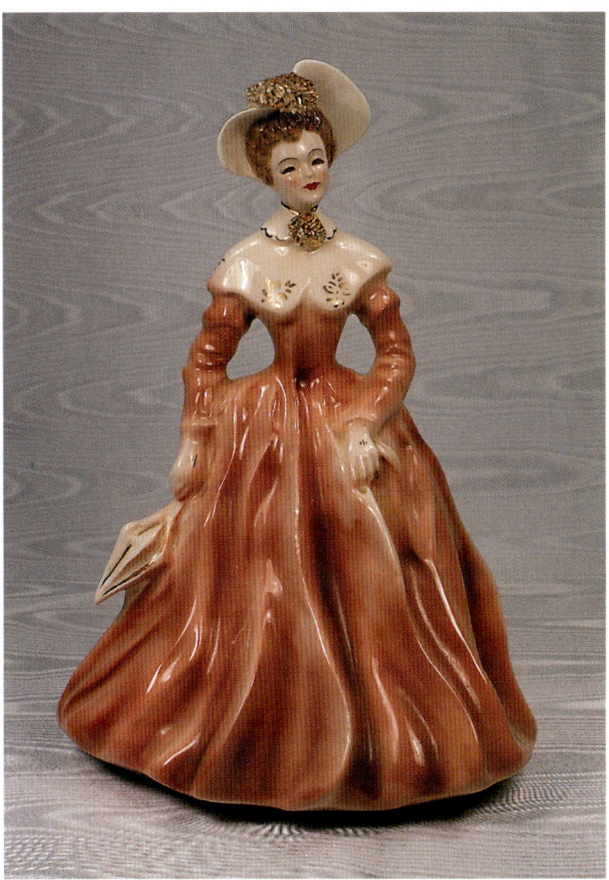

**Delores**, 8"
$225-250

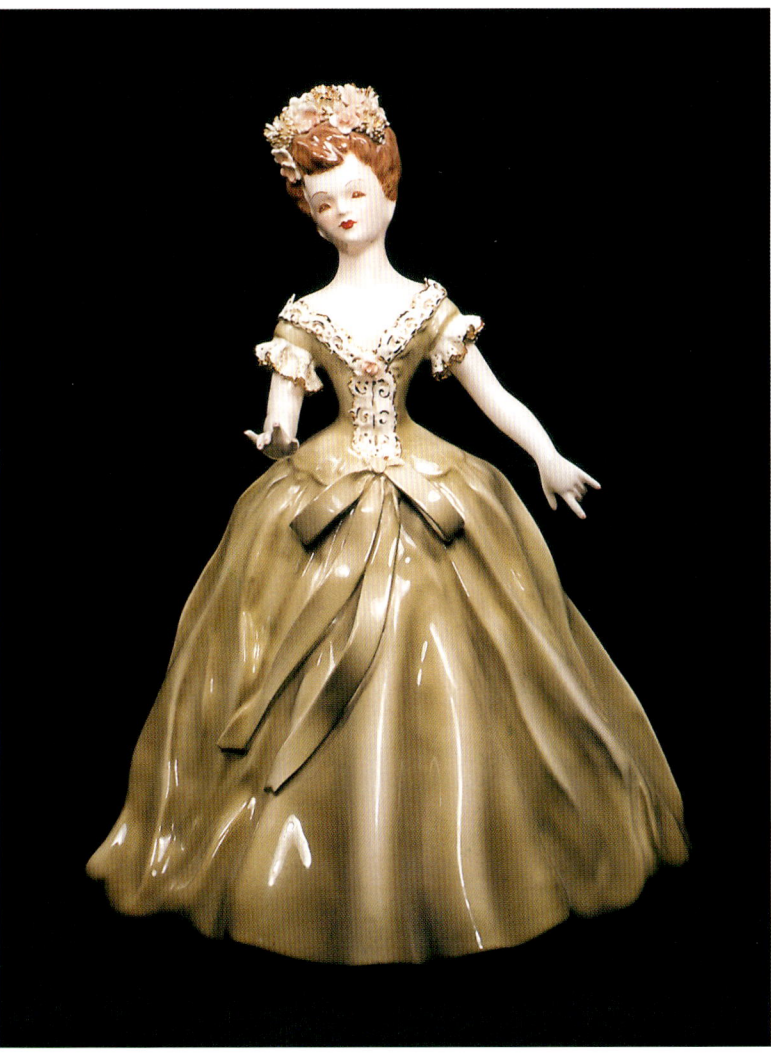

**Denise**, without fan, 10"
$950-1,000

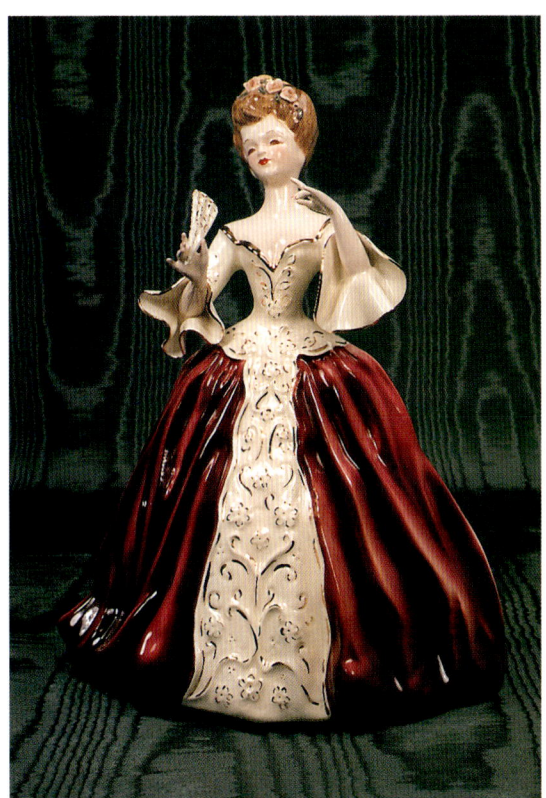

**Denise**, with fan in hand, 10"
$800-850

## 36  Showcasing Florence A to Z

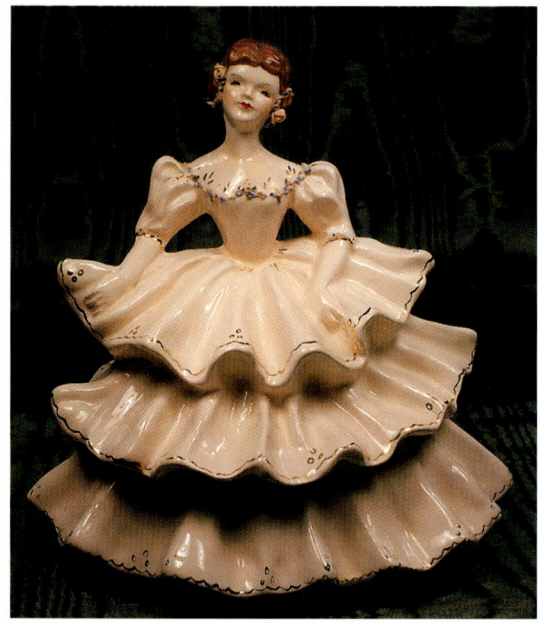

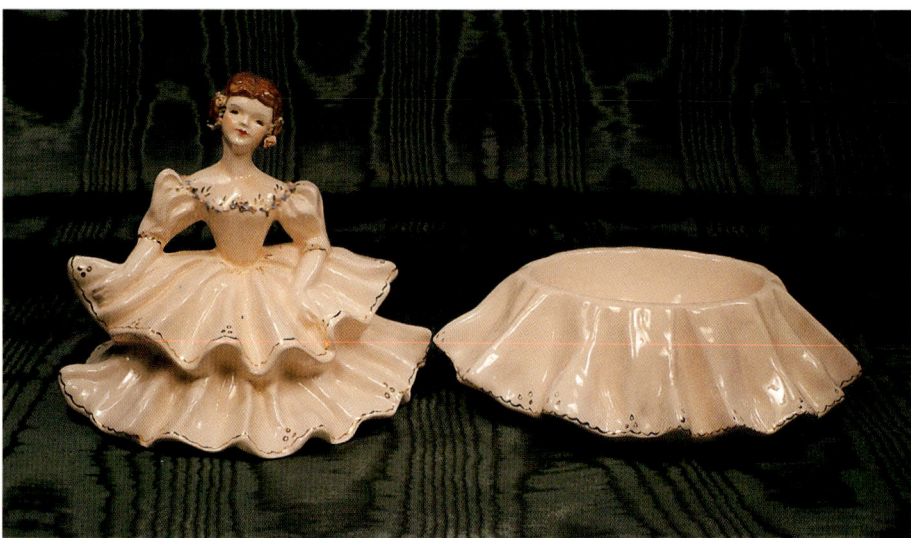

**Diana Powder Box**, 6.25"
$550-600

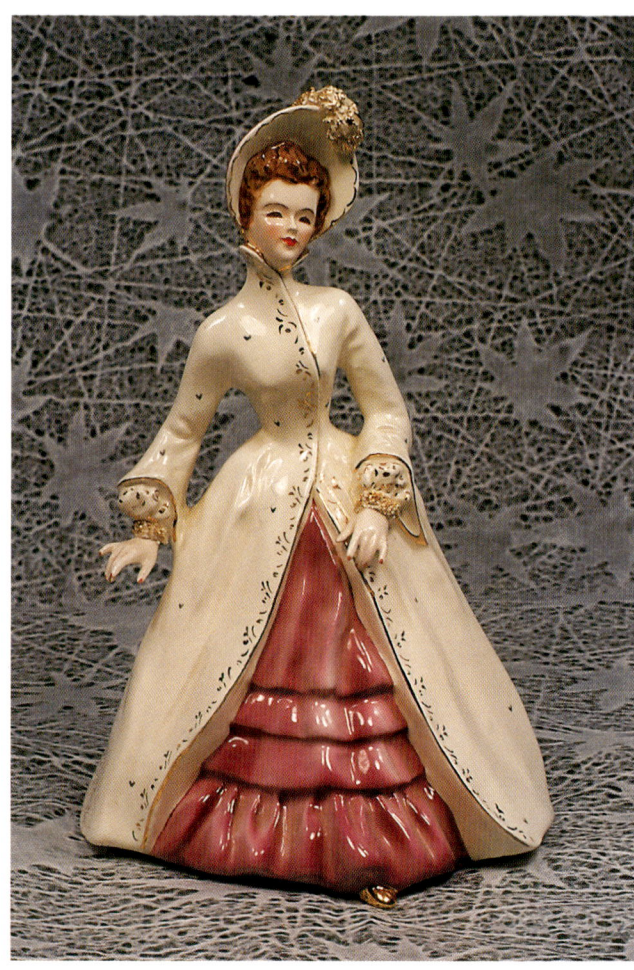

**Diane**, 7.75"
$450-500

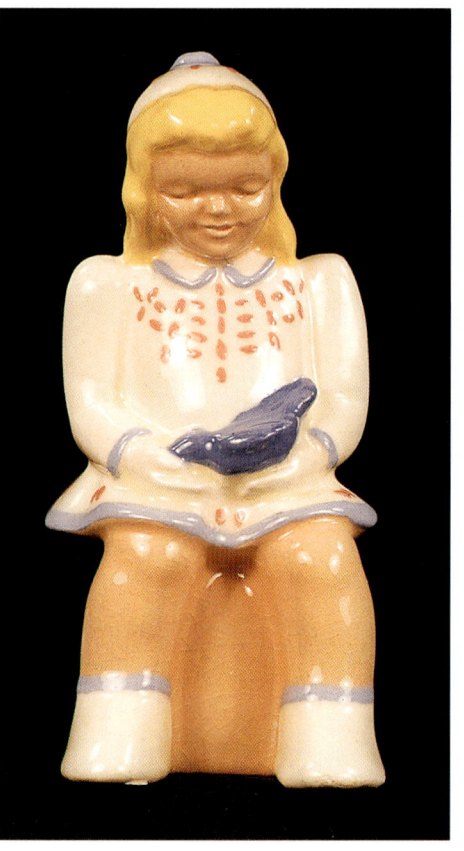

**Dixie**, girl with bluebird, 5", *
$150-175

Showcasing Florence A to Z   37

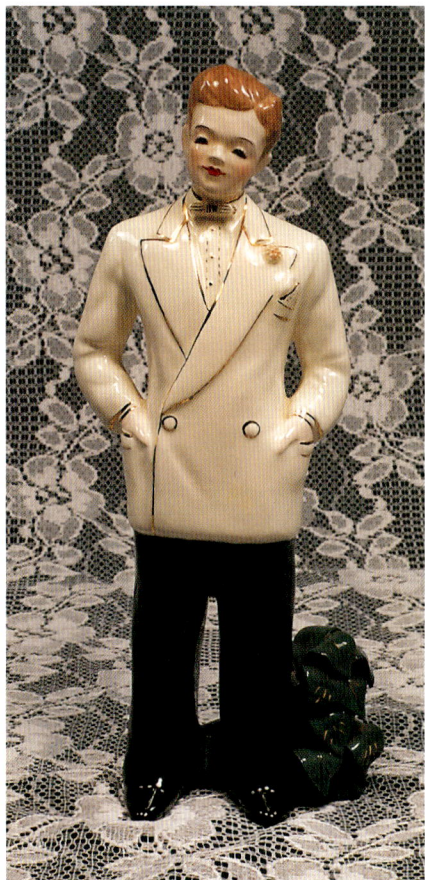

**Don**, 9.5"
$425-475

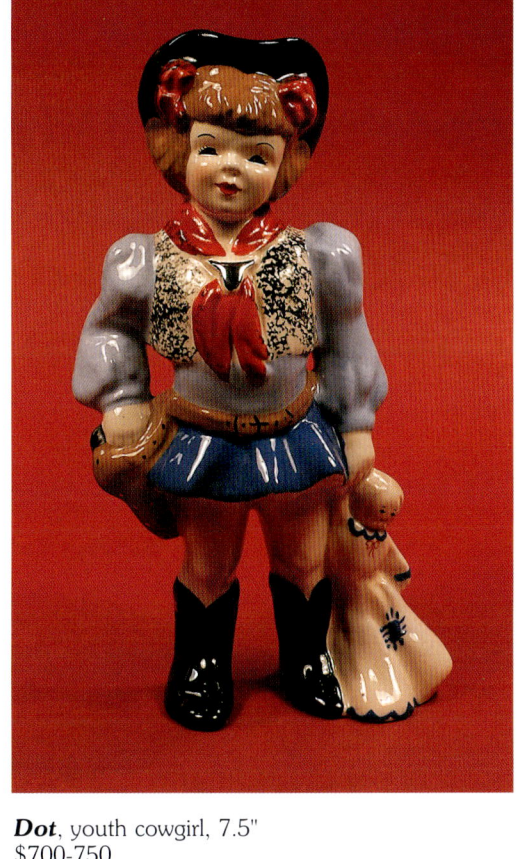

**Dot**, youth cowgirl, 7.5"
$700-750

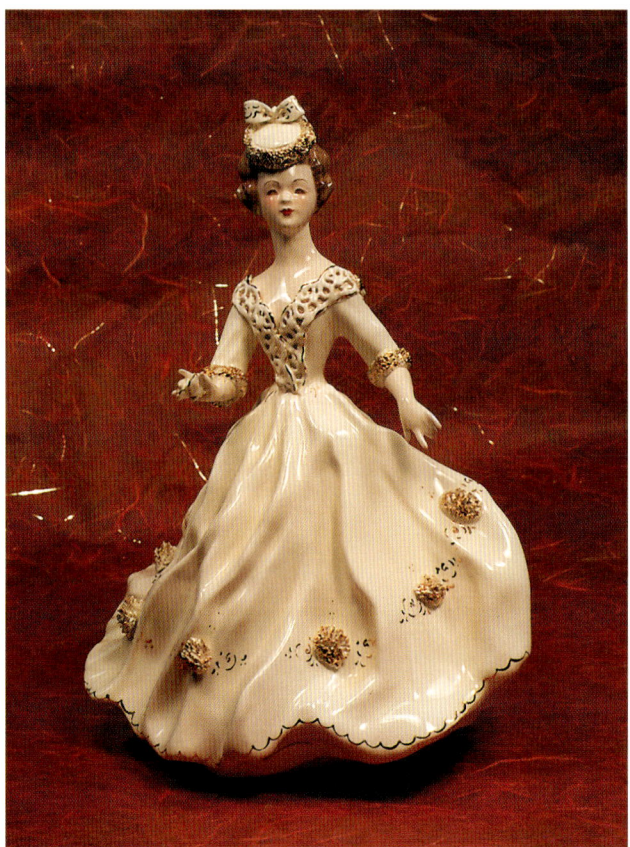

**Dora Lee**, 9.5"
$1,500-1,750

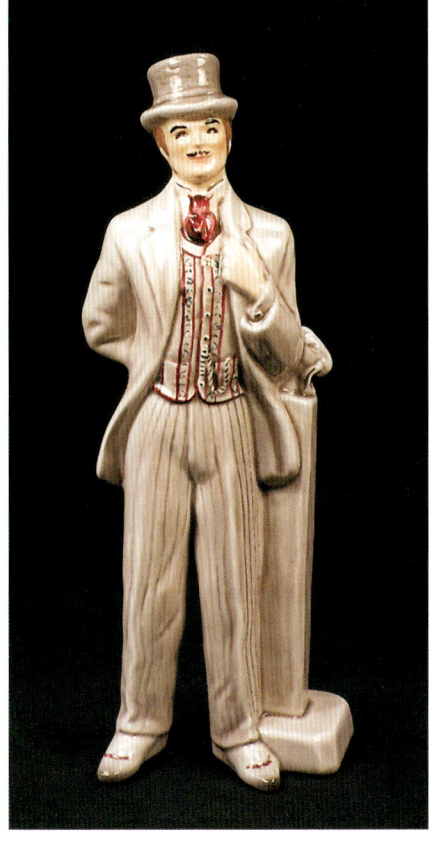

**Douglas**, 8.25"
$140-160

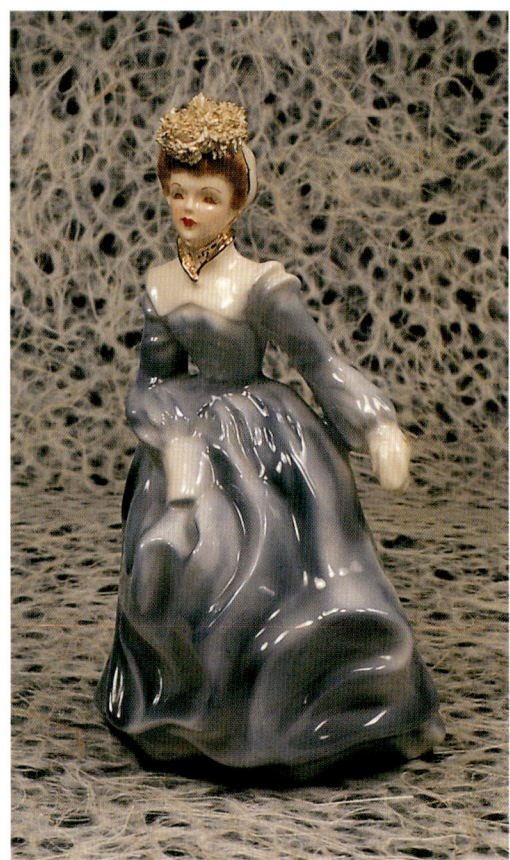
*Edith*, 7.25"
$175-200

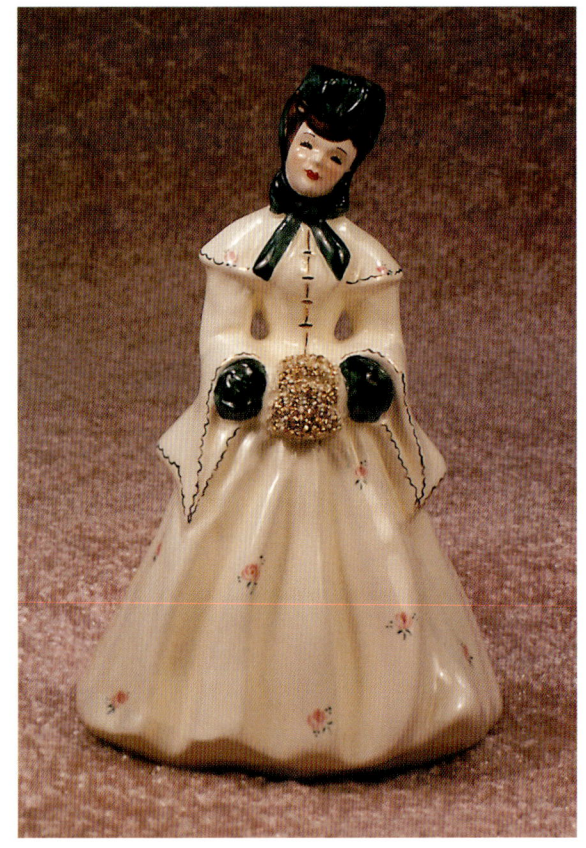
*Elaine*, 6"
$60-70

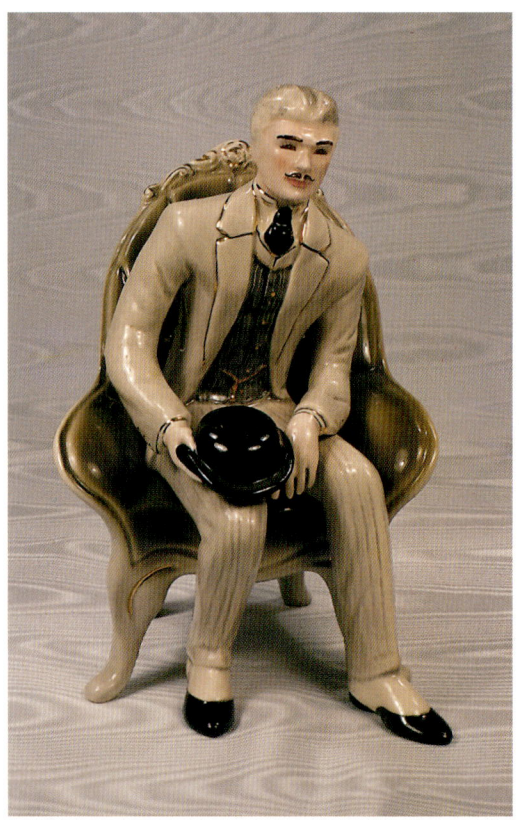
*Edward*, 7"
$450-500

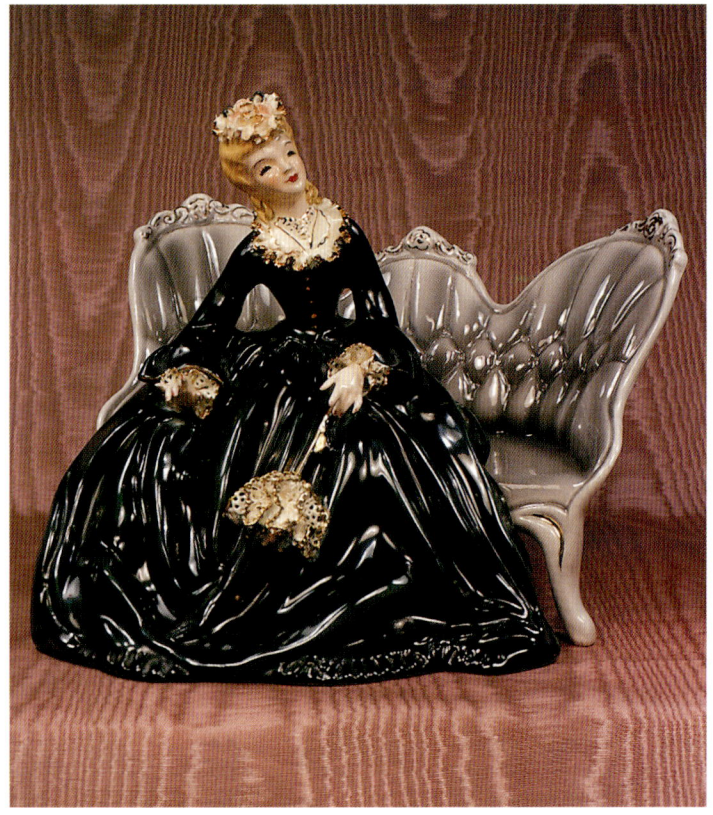
*Elizabeth*, with parasol, 8.25" x 7"
$400-450

**Showcasing Florence A to Z** 39

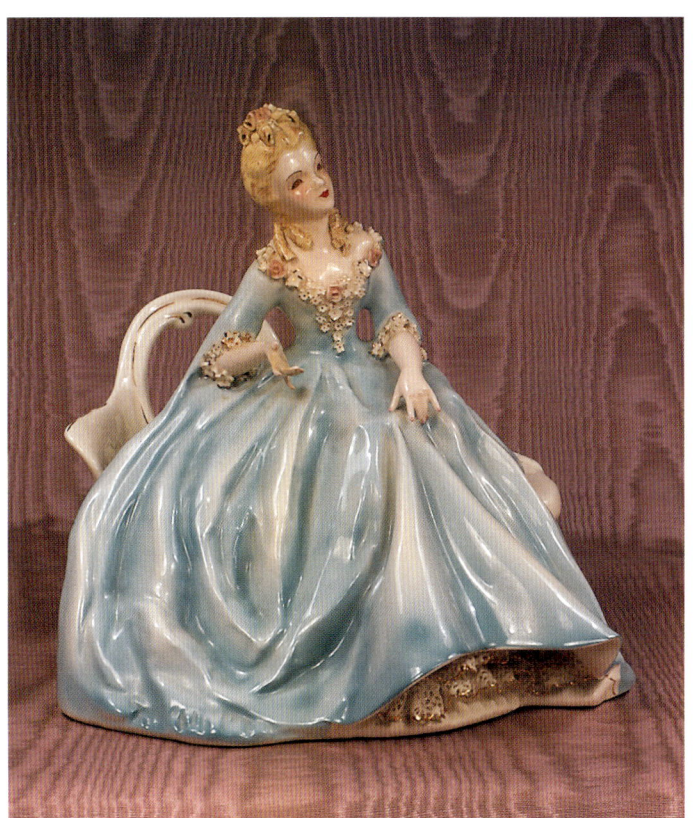

***Elizabeth***, with hands out, 8.25" x 7"
$900-950

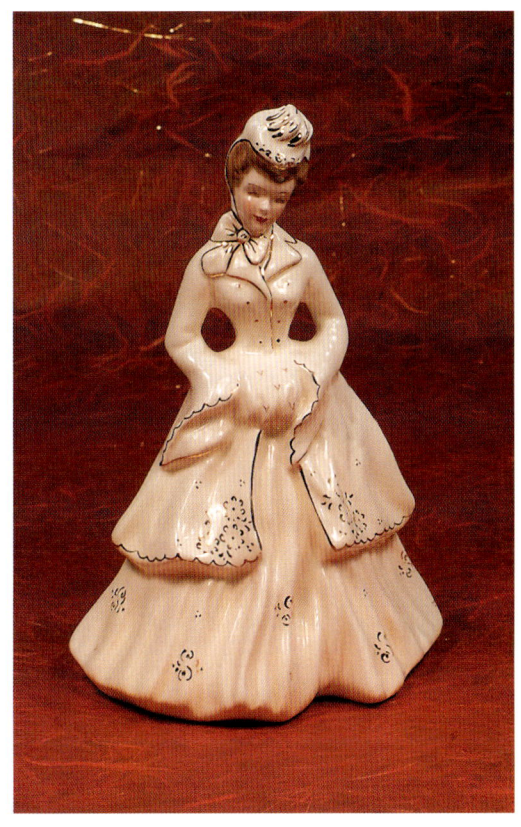

***Ellen***, 7"
$225-250

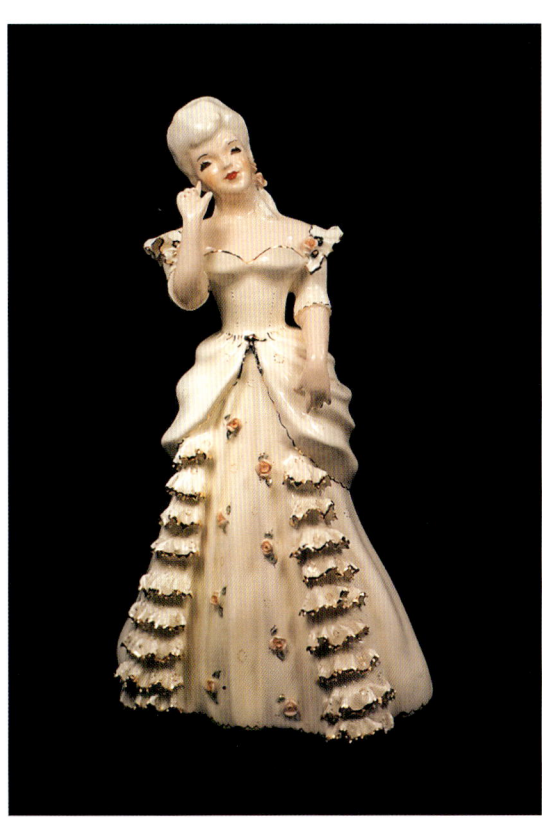

***Elizabeth***, early figure, 8.25"
$500-550

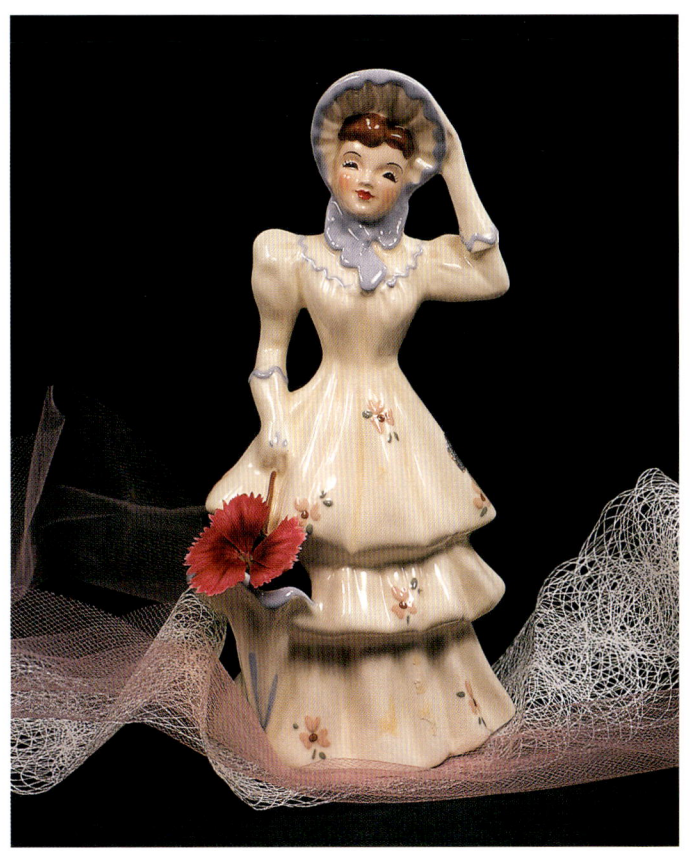

***Emily***, 8" (FH)
$100-125

**40** Showcasing Florence A to Z

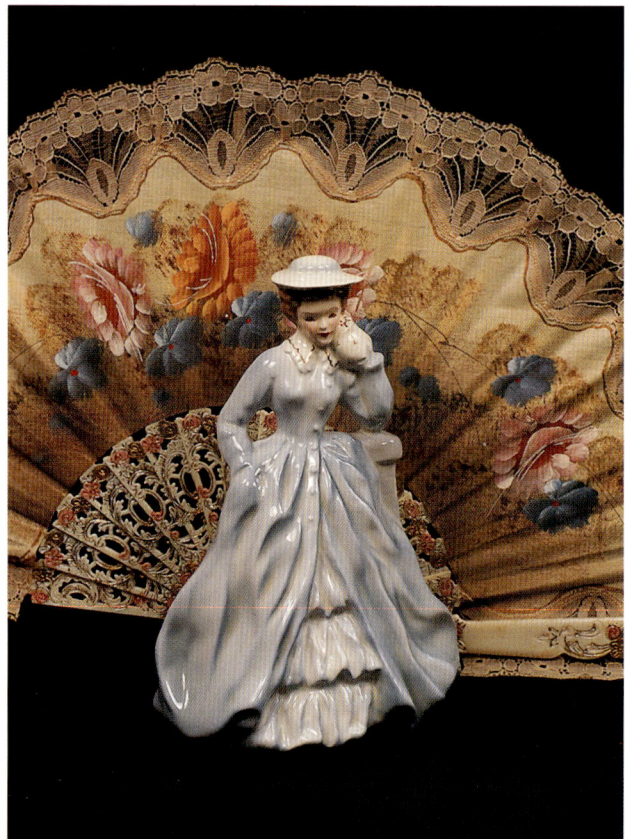

***Emma***, 7" (FH), *
$90-100

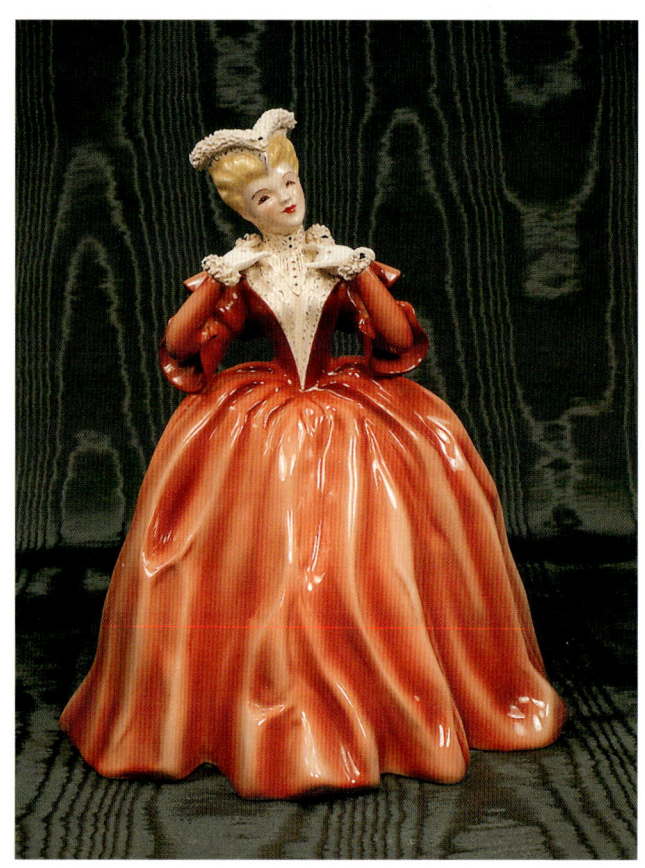

***Eugenia***, 9"
$450-500

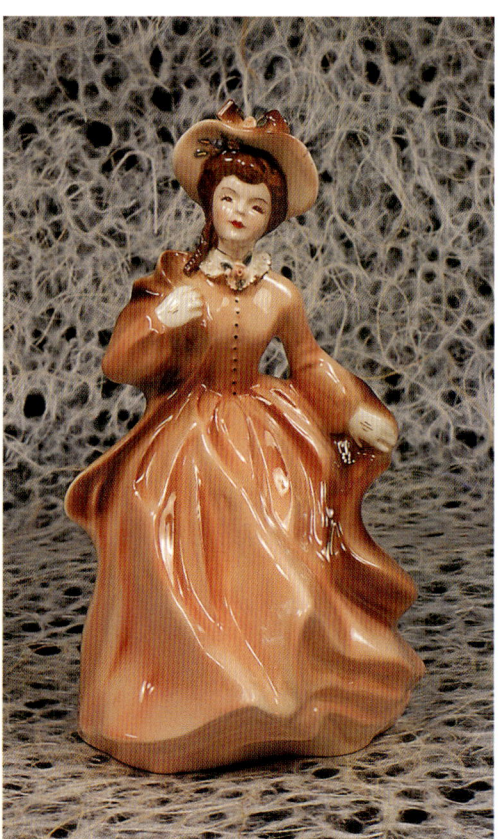

***Ethel***, 7.25"
$160-180

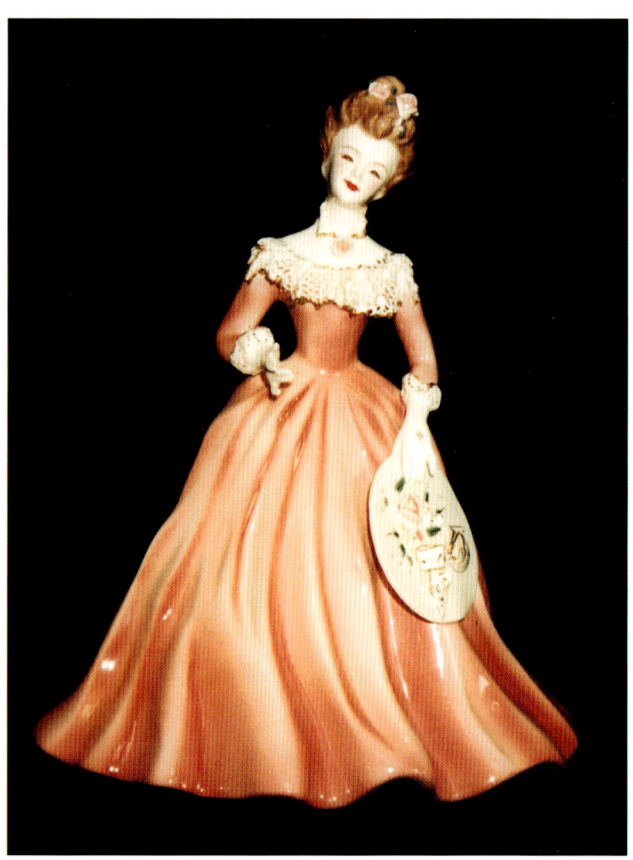

***Eve***, made from a Lavon mold, 8.5"
$600-700

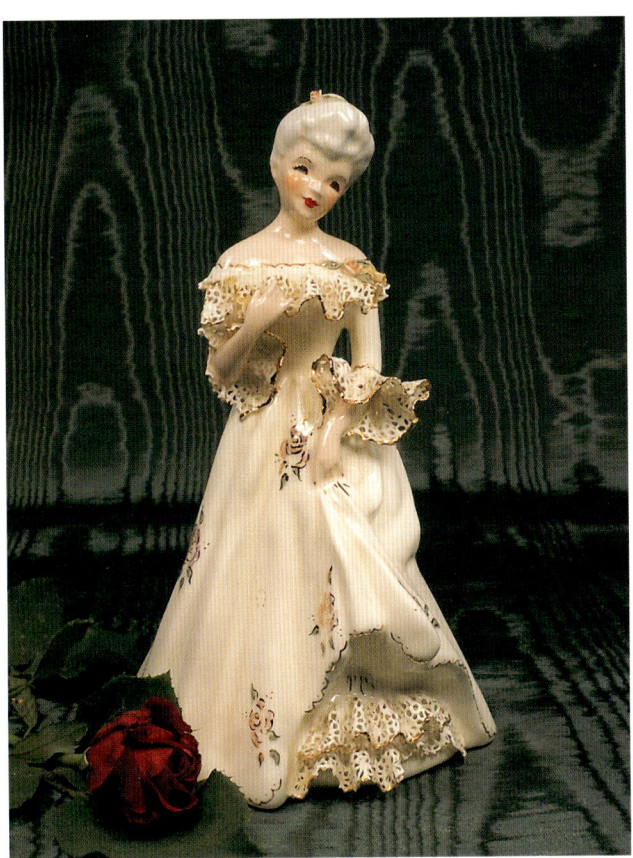

***Eve***, 8.5"
$375-425

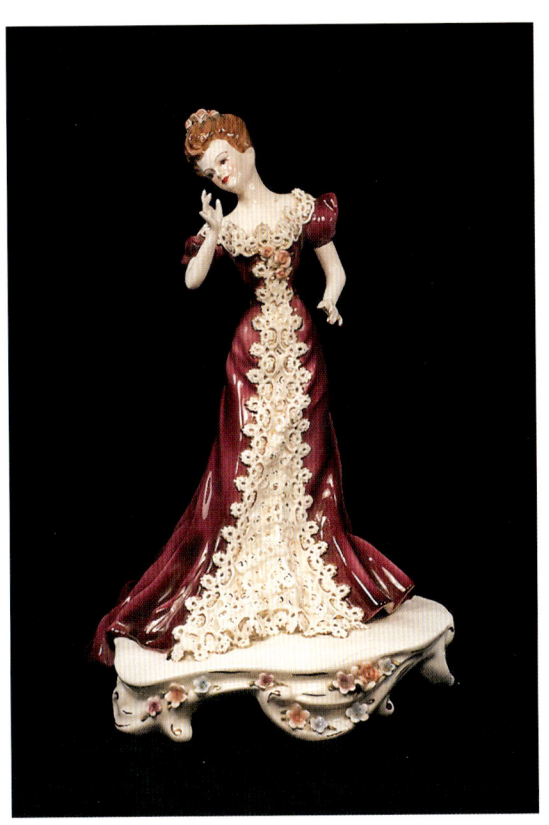

***Fair Lady*** without basket, 11.5"
$3,300-3,500

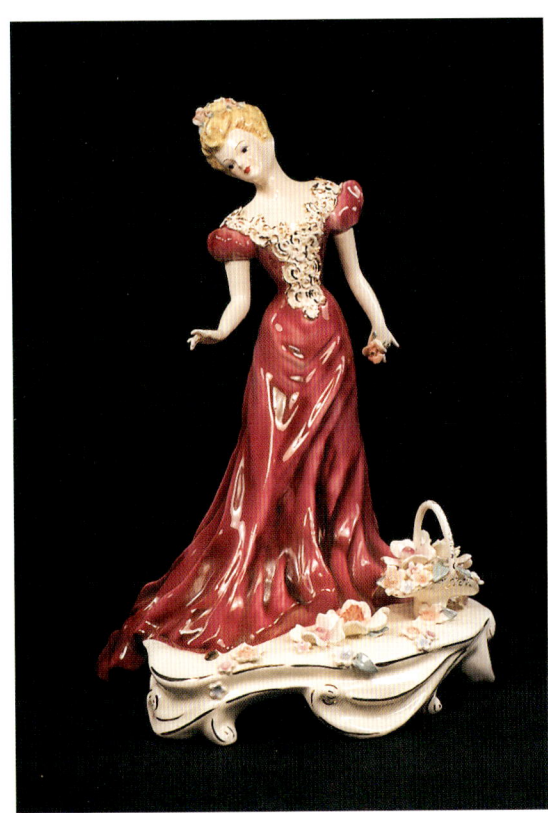

***Fair Lady***, with basket, 11.5"
$3,500-3,750

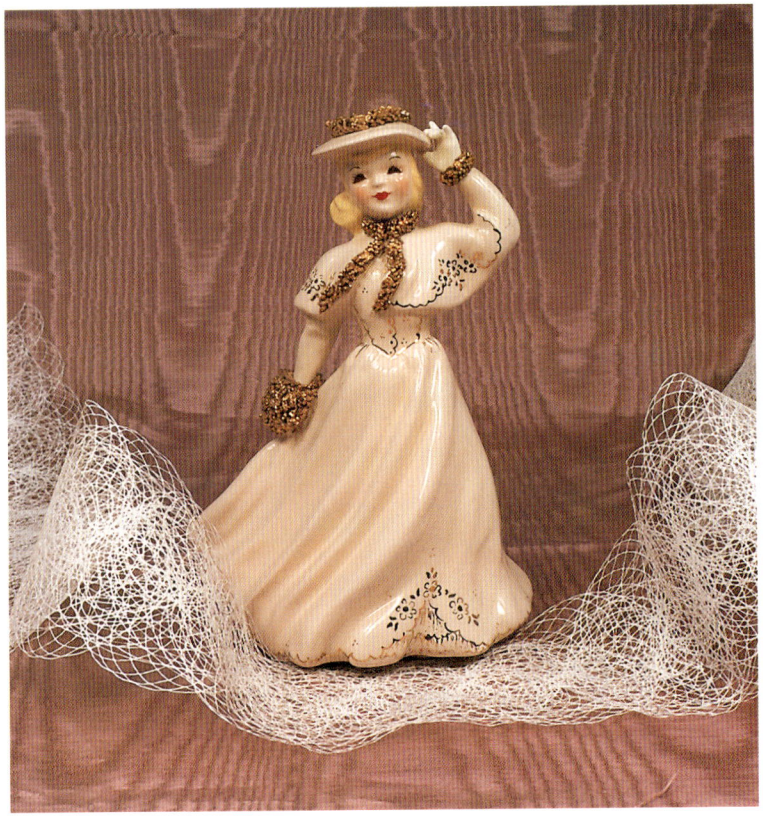

***Fall***, 6.5"
$175-200

## 42  Showcasing Florence A to Z

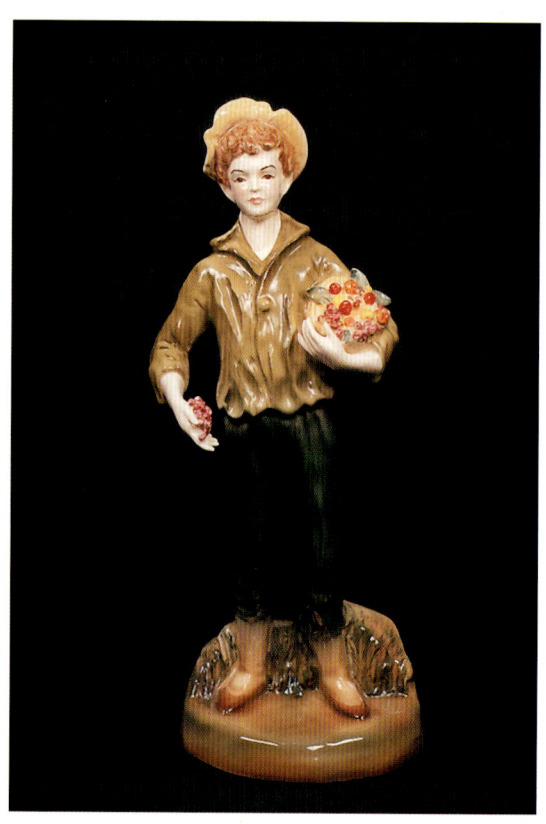

**Fall Reverie**, 12" (also called **Summer Harvest**)
$1,750-2,000

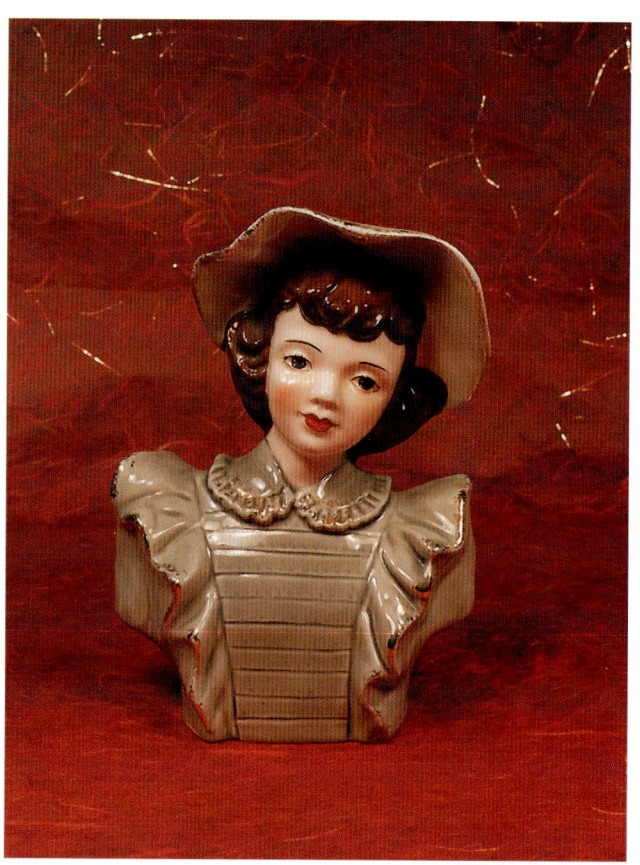

**Fern**, head vase, 7" (FH)
$150-160

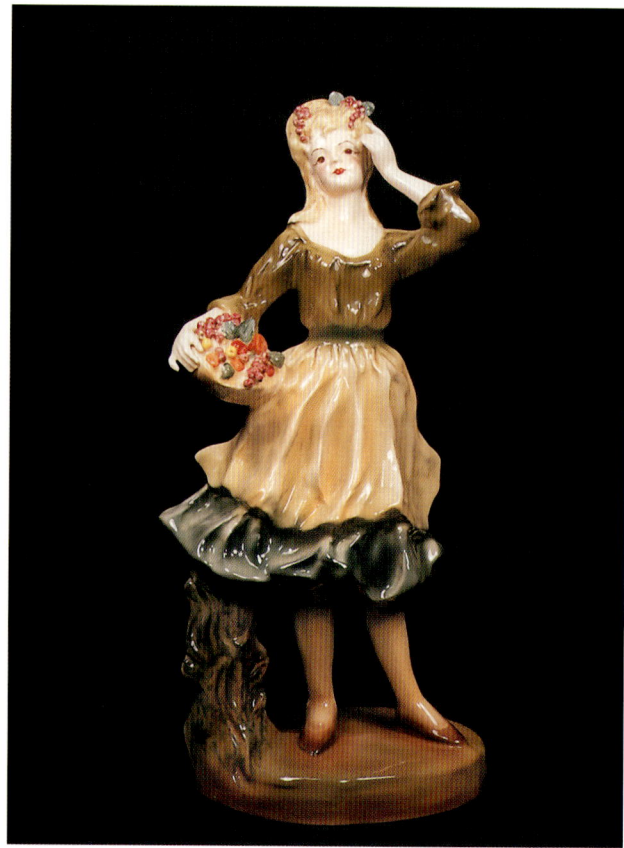

**Fall Companion**, 12" (also called **County Fair**)
$1,750-2,000

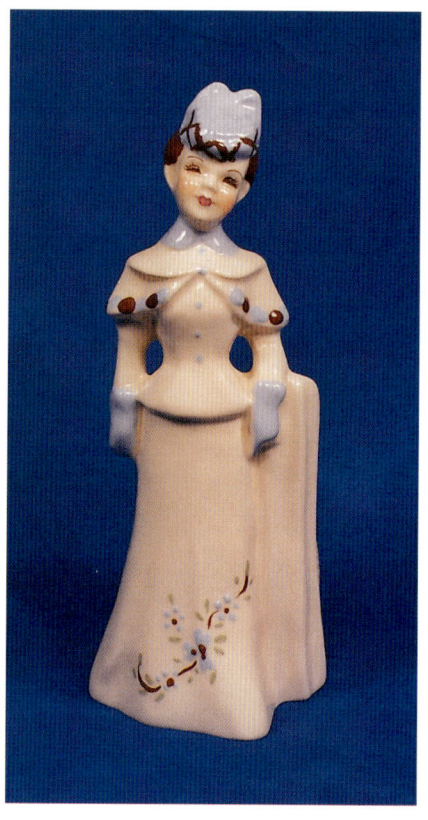

**Florence,** youth, 6.5" (FH), *
$65-75

Showcasing Florence A to Z   43

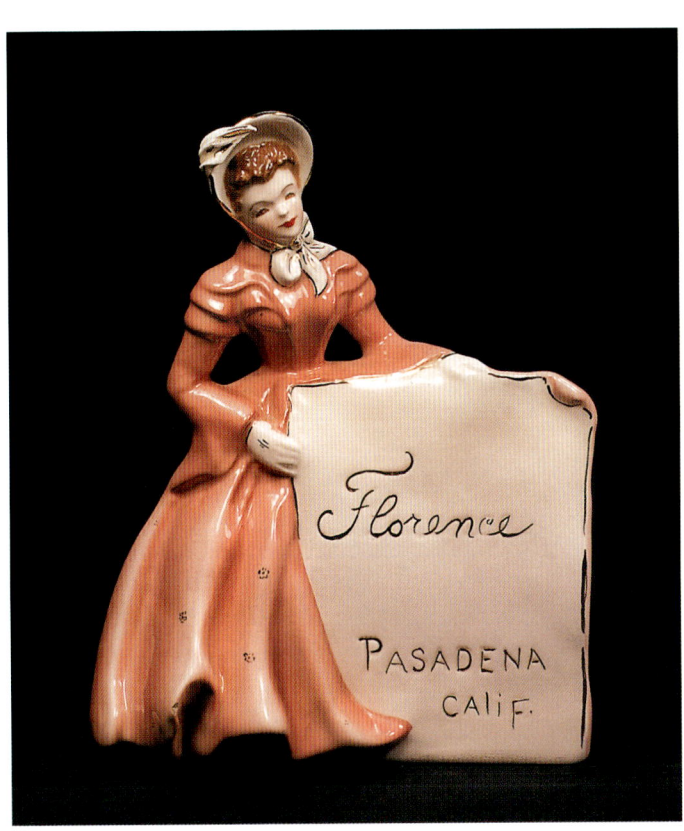

**Florence Lady Dealer Sign**, 6.5"
$650-700

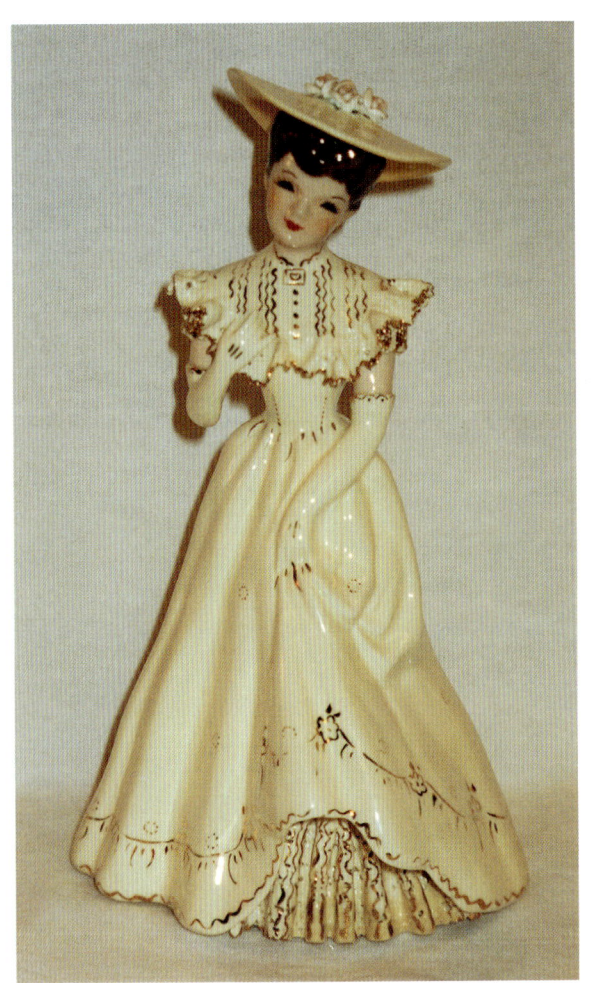

**Frances**, 8.5"
$500-550

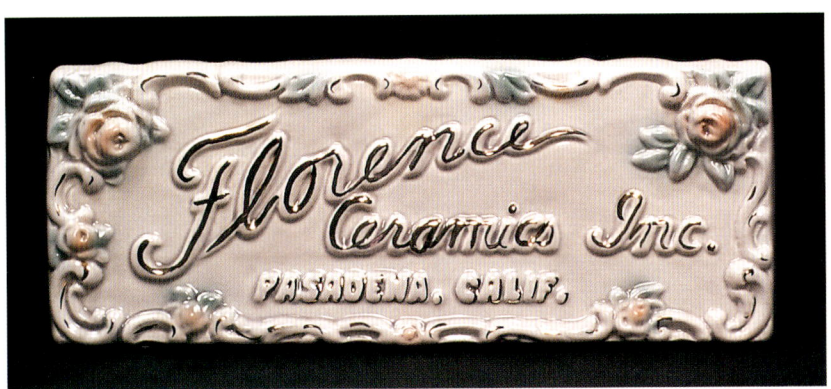

**Florence Rectangle Dealer Sign**, 9" wide
$700-750

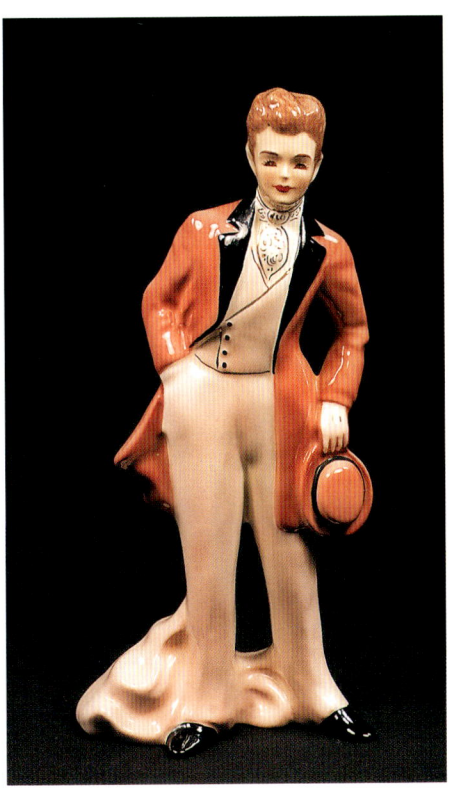

**Gary**, 8.5"
$160-175

**44 Showcasing Florence A to Z**

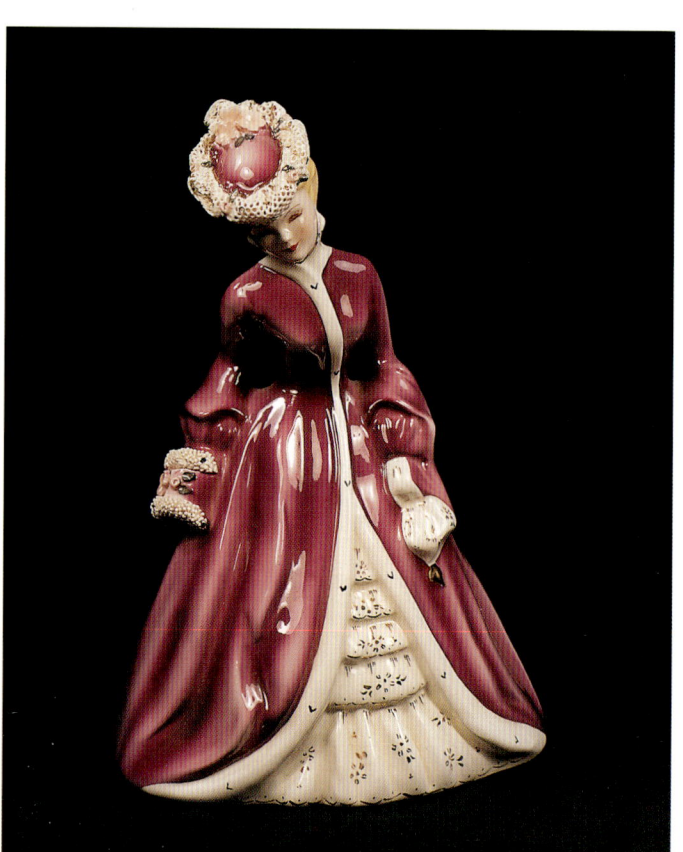

**Genevieve**, 8" (Also spelled **Jenevieve**)
$175-200

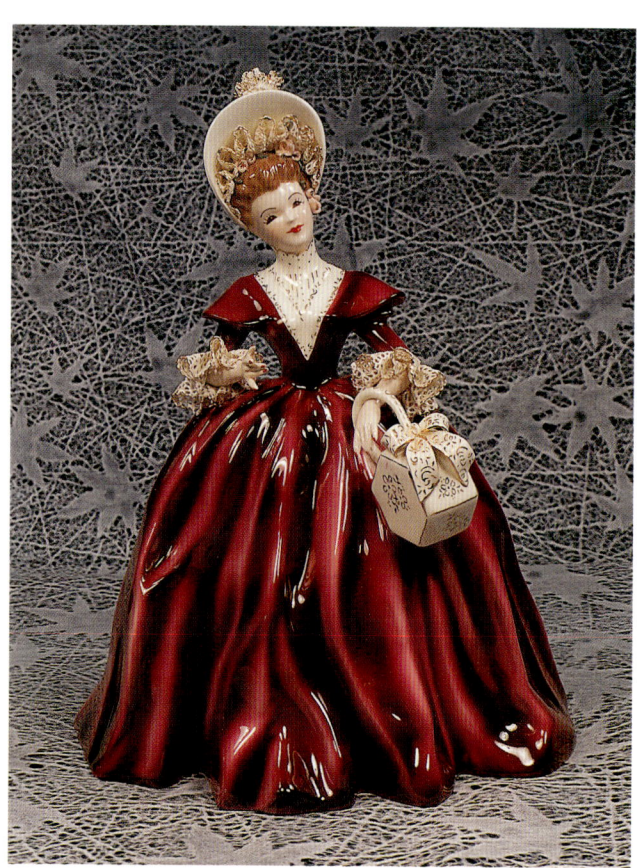

**Georgette**, 10"
$700-750

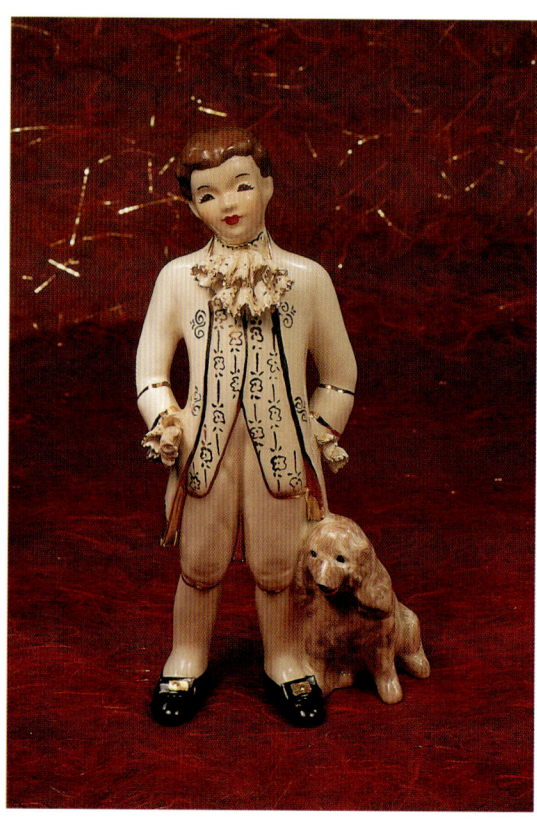

**Geoff**, boy with dog, 7.25", *
$1,250-1,400

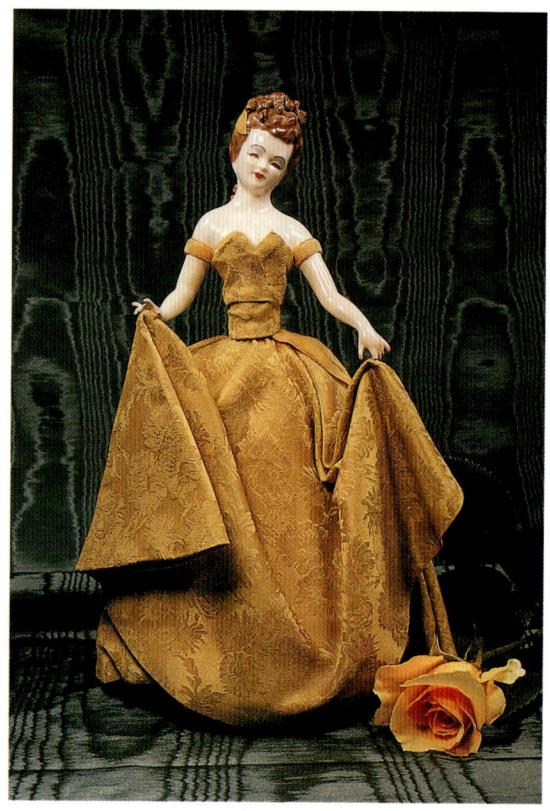

**Georgia Brocade**, 12"
$2,750-3,000

# Showcasing Florence A to Z 45

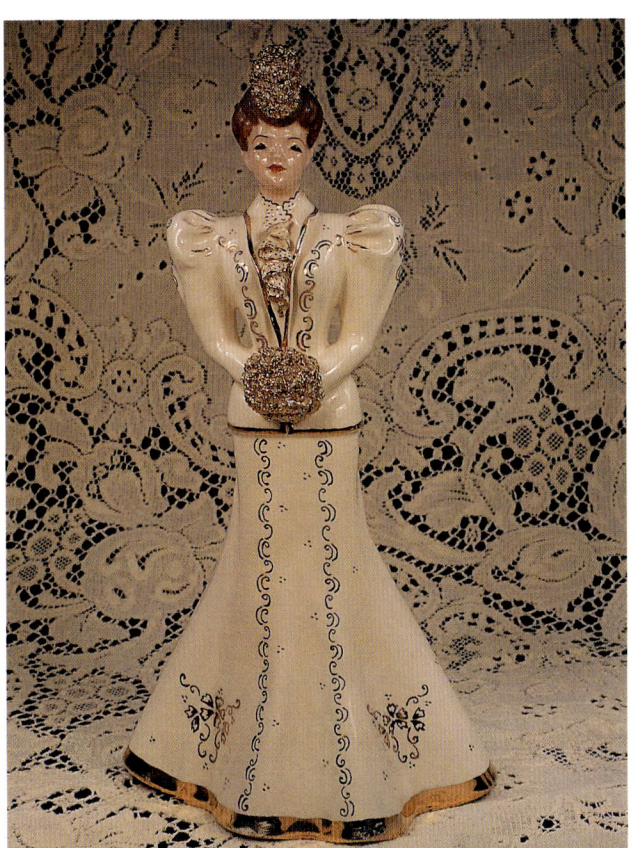

**Gibson Girl**, with muff, 10.75"
$700-800

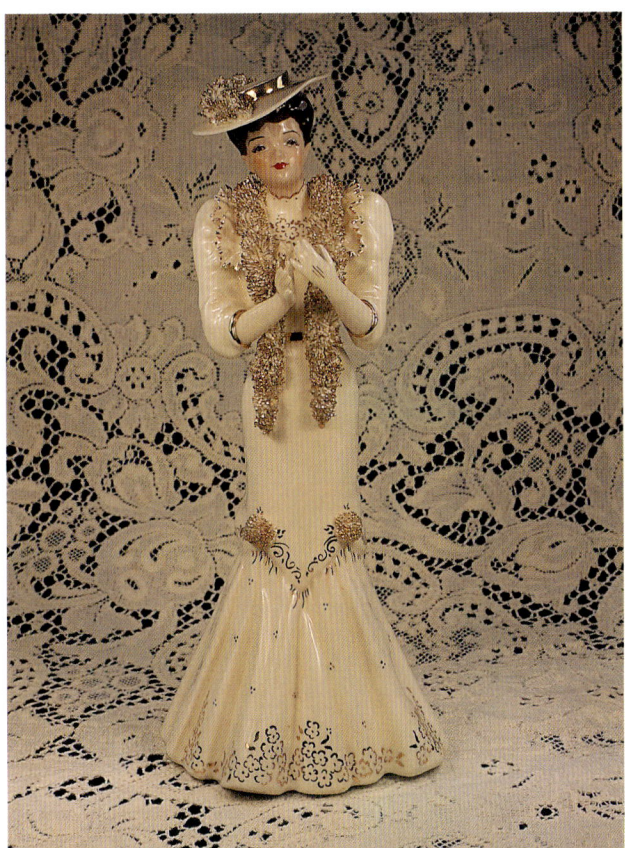

**Gibson Girl**, with boa, 10.75"
$700-800

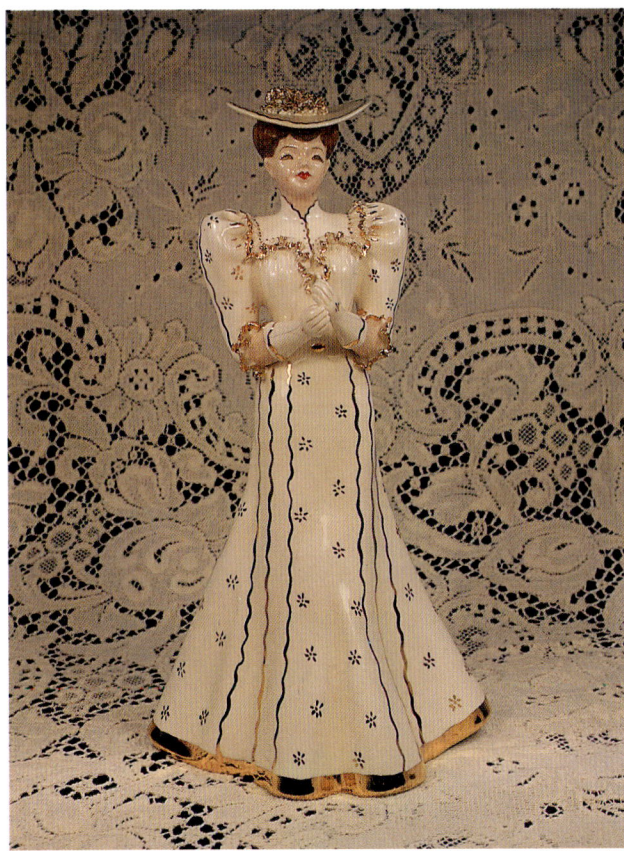

**Gibson Girl**, hands together, 10.75"
$700-800

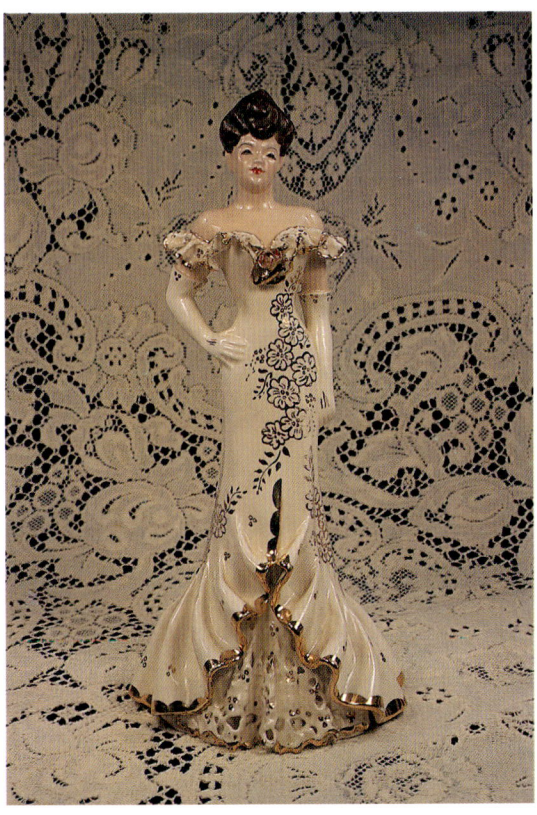

**Gibson Girl,** hand at waist, 10.75"
$700-800

## 46  Showcasing Florence A to Z

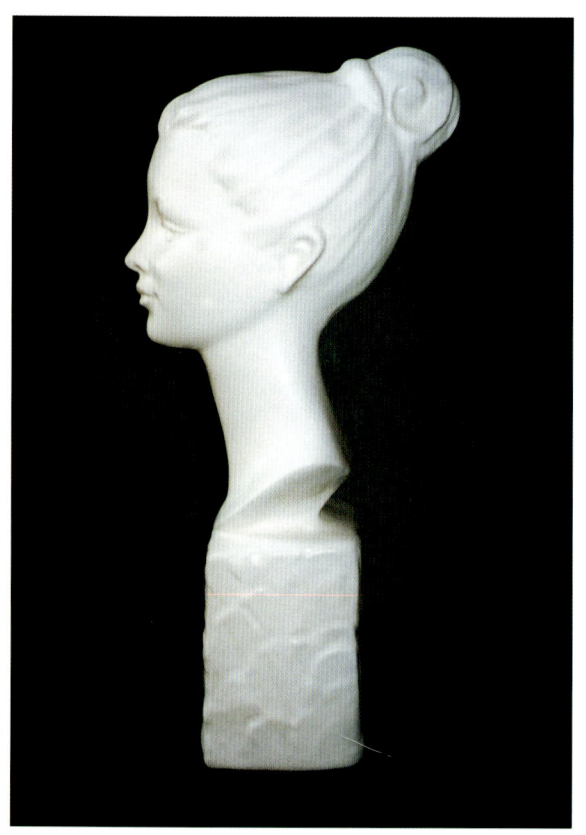

**Gigi,** bust, 11.5"
$400-450

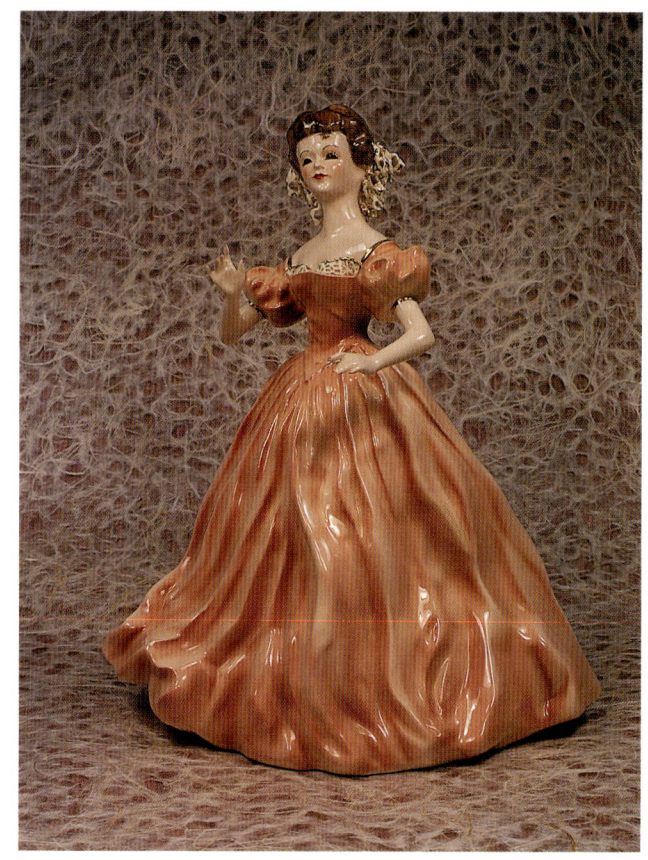

**Giselle**, 9.5"
$1,500-1,750

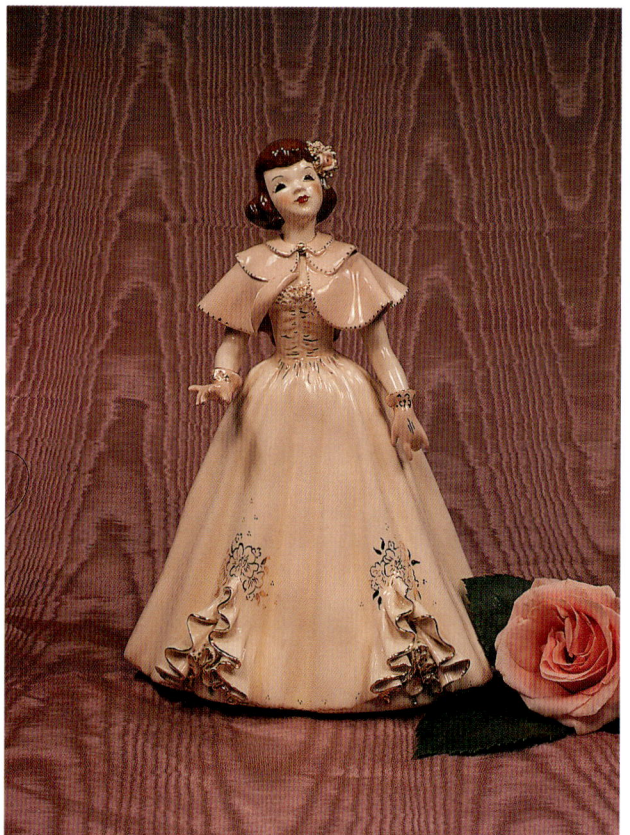

**Ginger**, 8.75"
$500-550

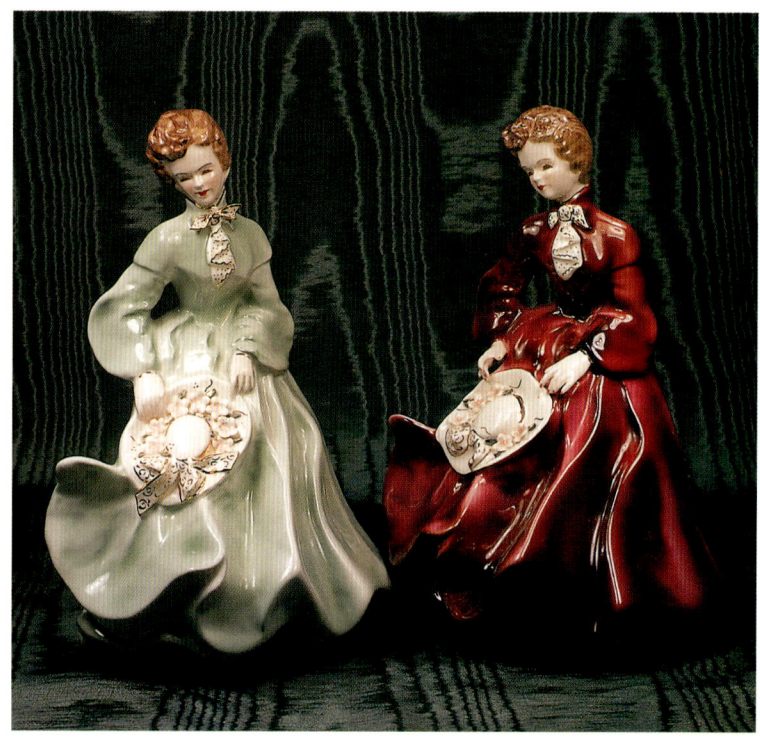

**Grace**, two styles, 7.75"
Left: $250-300; Right: $300-350

Showcasing Florence A to Z  47

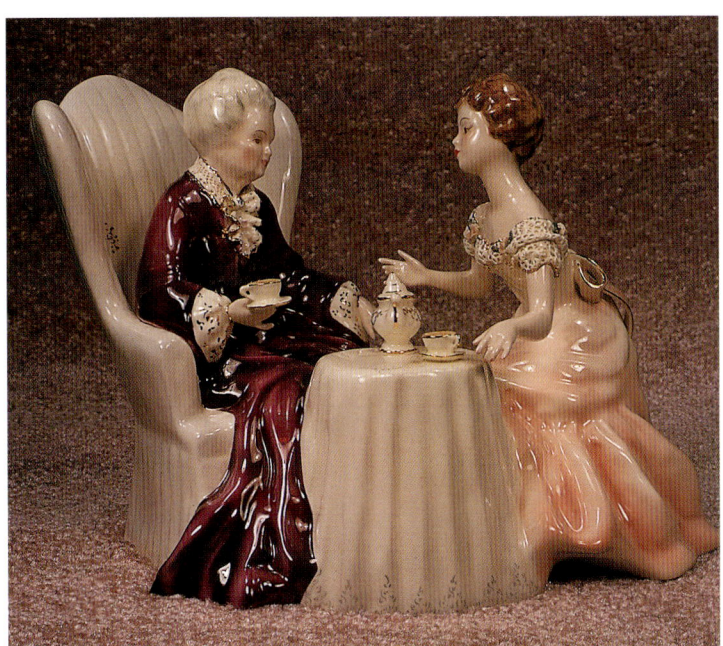

***Grandmother and I***, 9" x 7"
$2,500-2,750

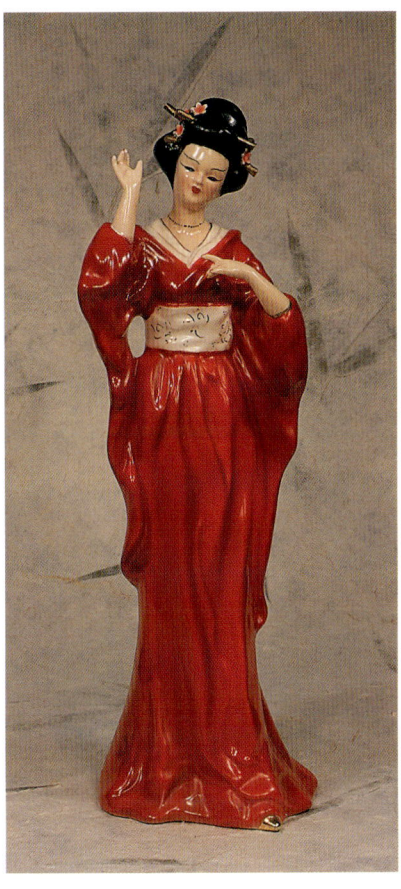

***Haru***, 10.5"
$400-450

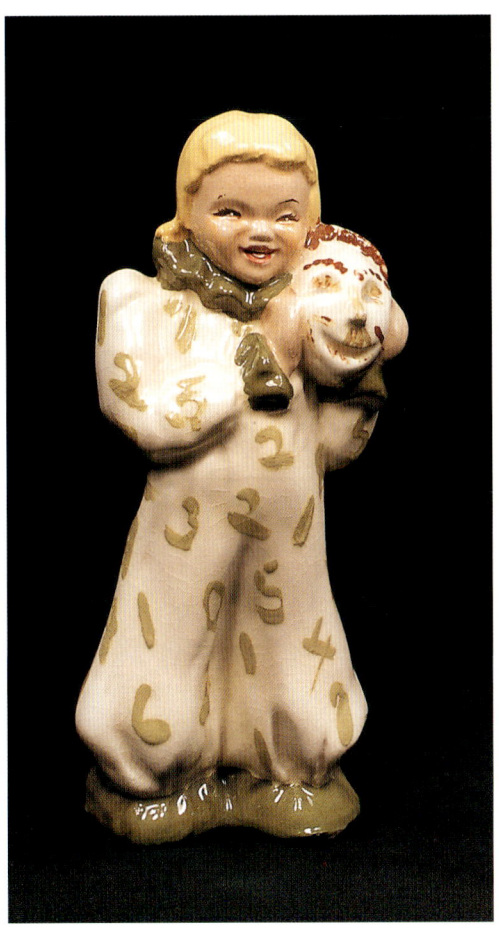

***Halloween Child***, 5.5"
$600-700

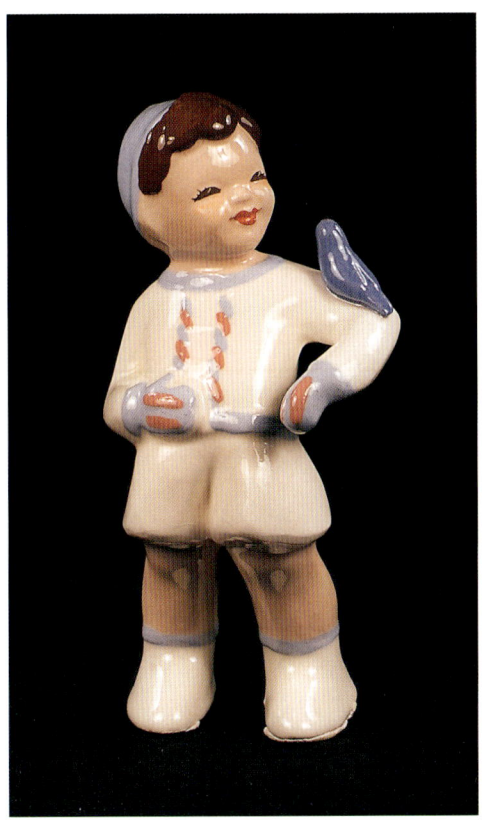

***Hector,*** with blue bird, 5.5", *
$150-175

**48** Showcasing Florence A to Z

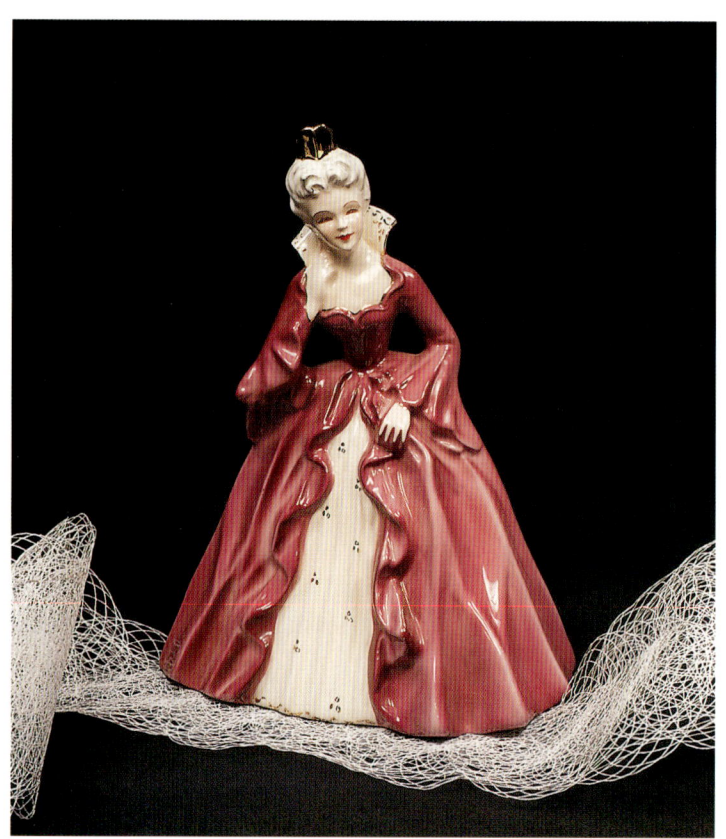

***Her Majesty***, 7.25"
$200-250

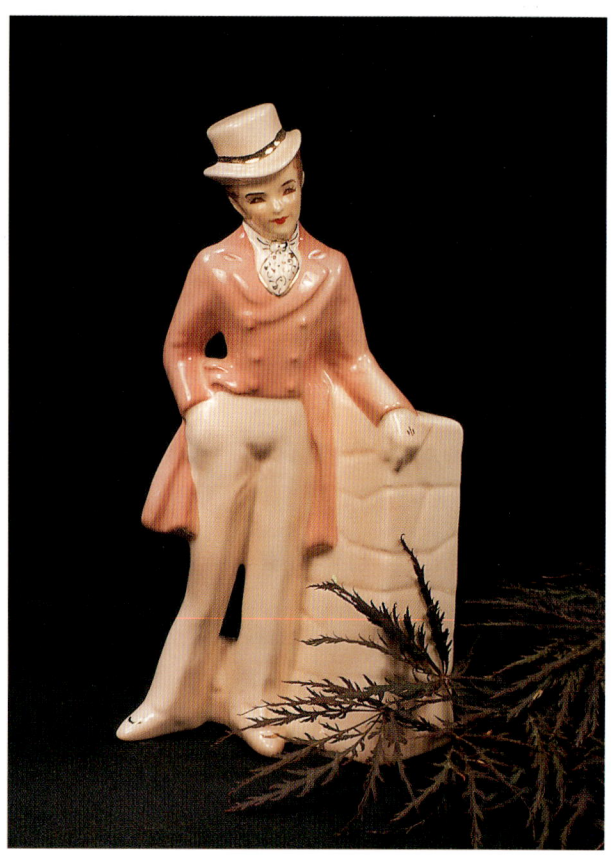

***Jay,*** 7.5"
$150-180

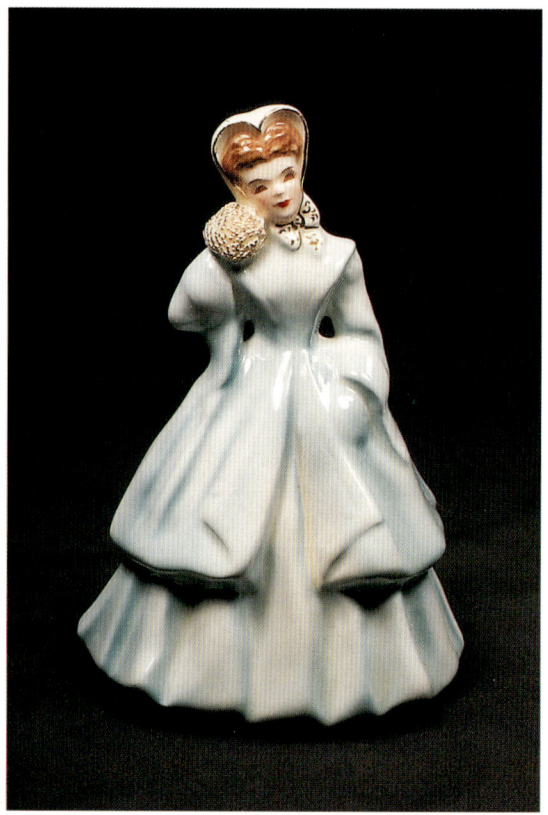

***Irene***, 6"
$60-70

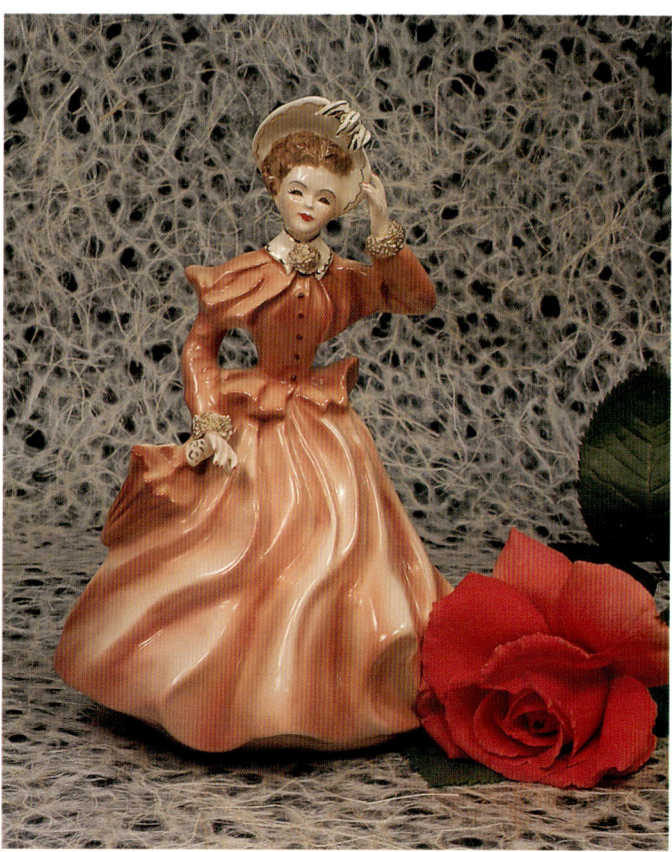

***Jeanette***, 7.75"
$250-350

Showcasing Florence A to Z  49

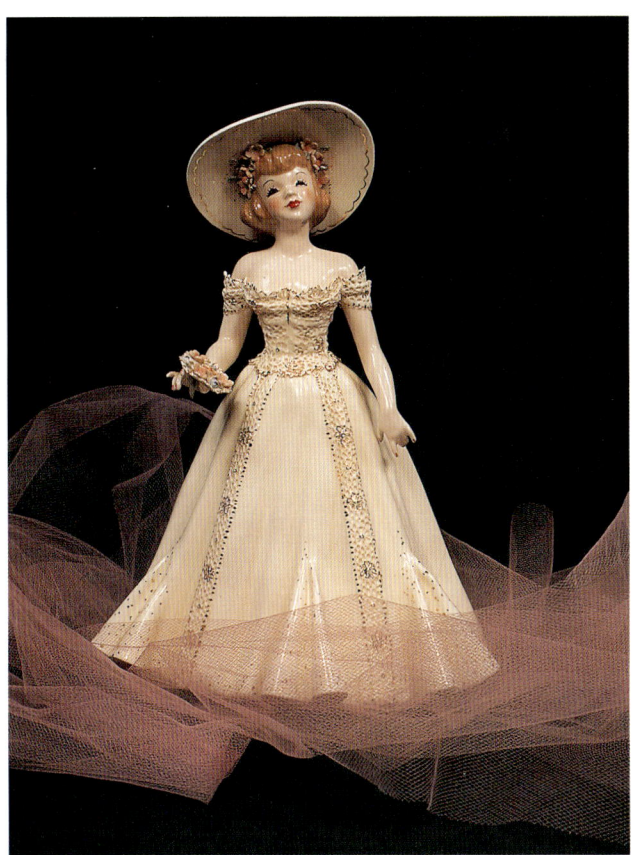

*Jeanie*, 8.75"
$600-675

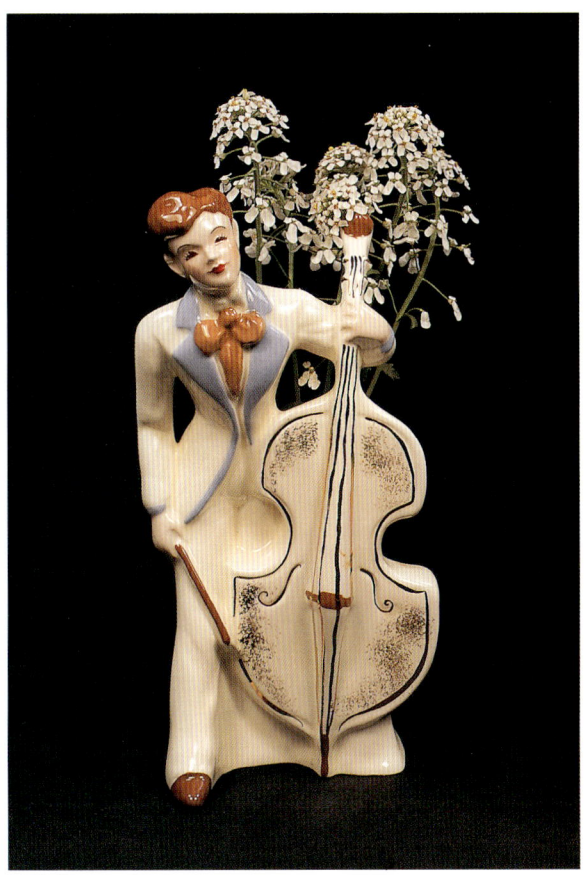

*Jerry*, 7" (FH)
$175-200

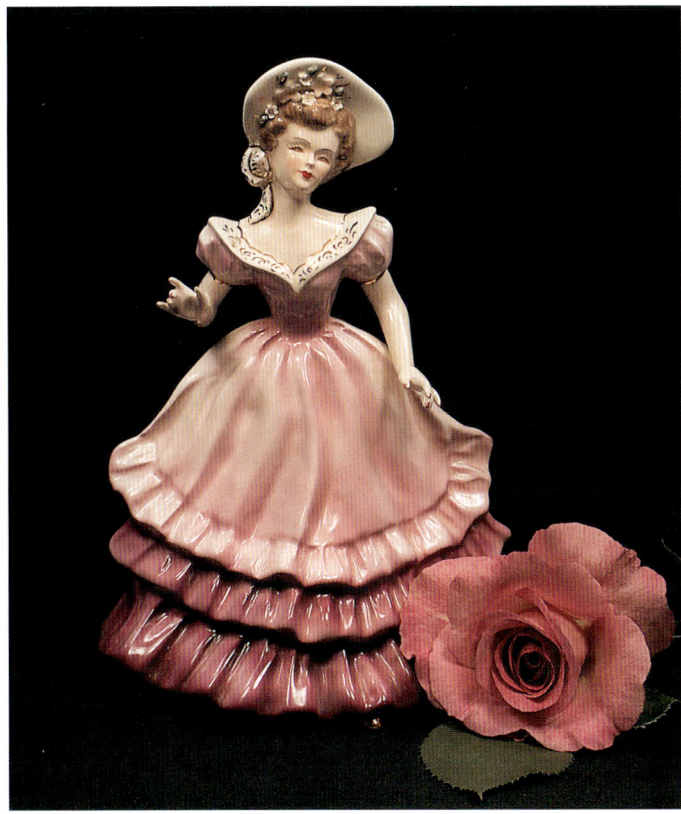

*Jennifer*, 8"
$450-500

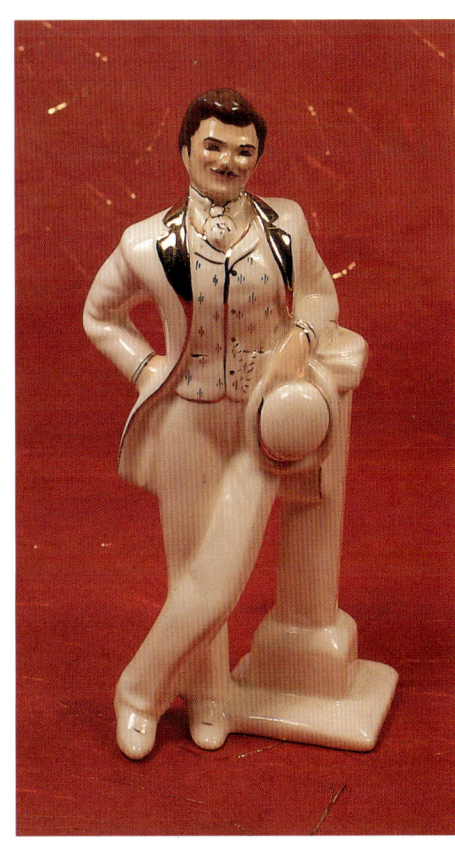

*Jim*, 6.25"
$60-70

# 50 Showcasing Florence A to Z

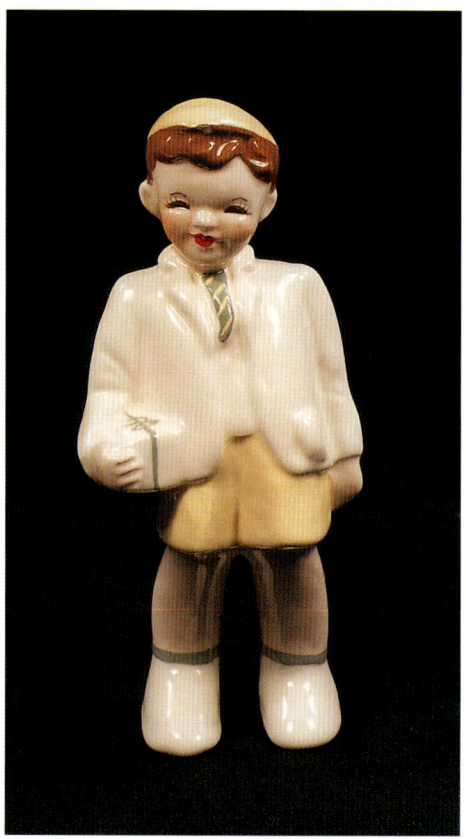

**Jim,** child, 5.5"
$250-275

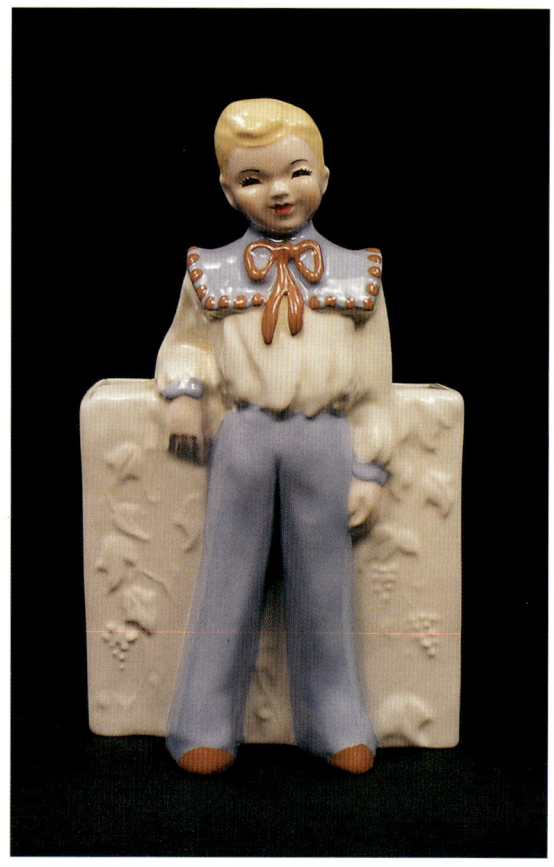

**Joe**, 6.5" (FH), *
$50-60

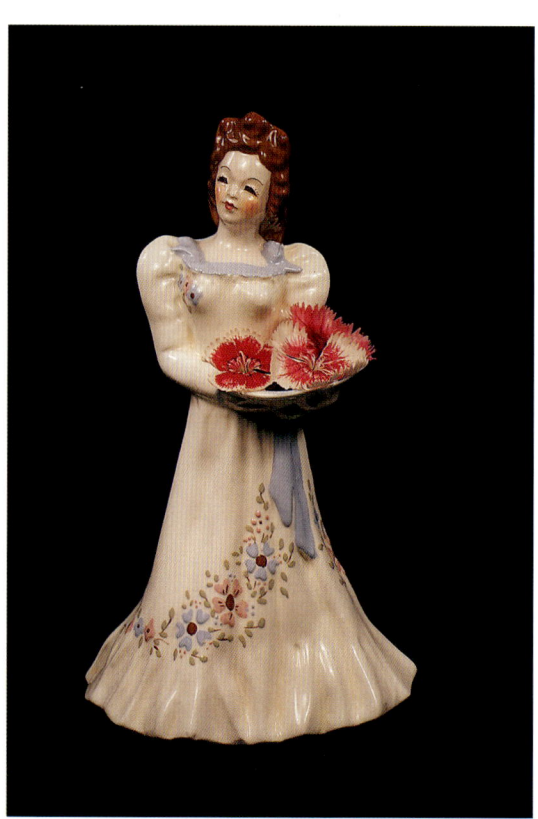

**Jo Ann**, 9.5" (FH), *
$175-200

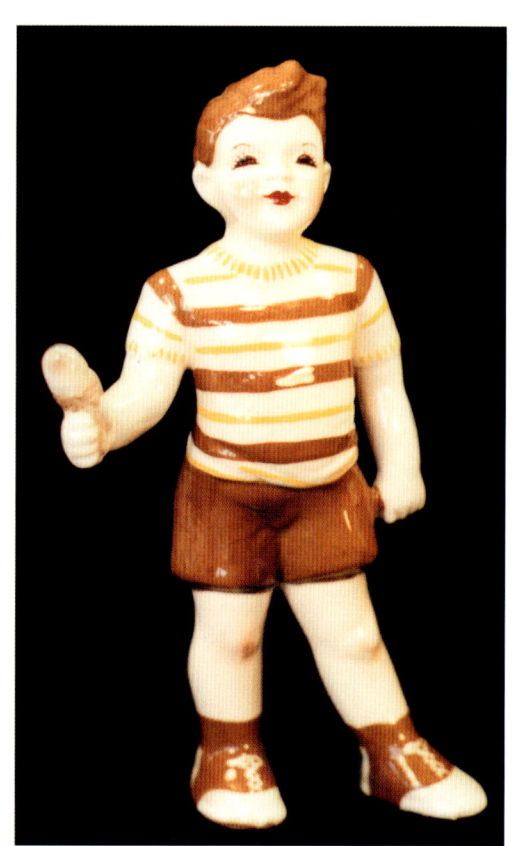

**John,** youth, 7.5"
$1,250-1,500

Showcasing Florence A to Z  51

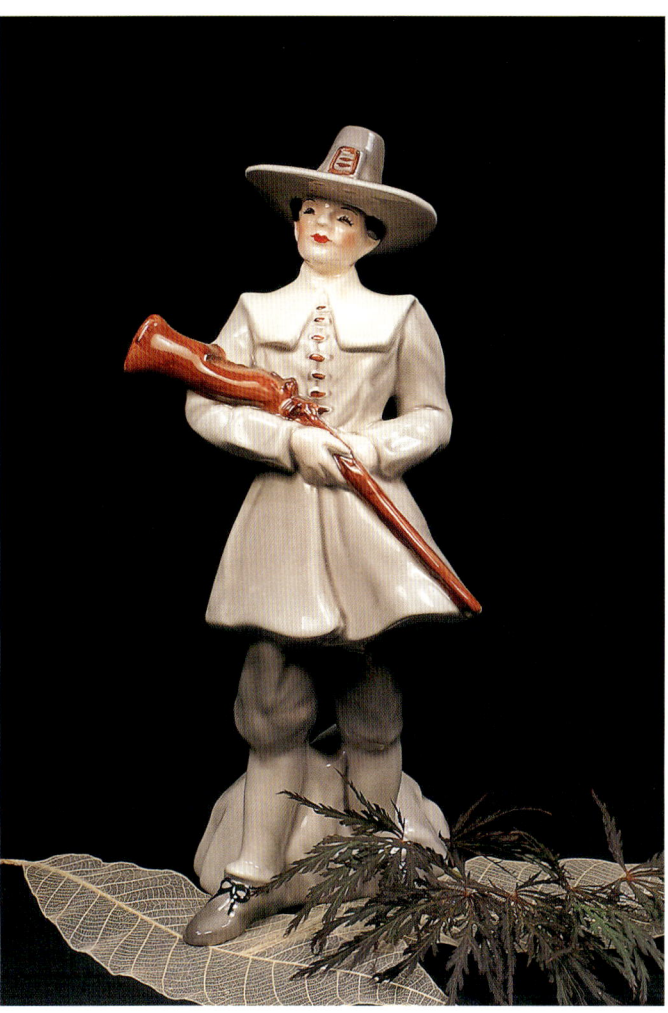

**John Alden**, 9.25"
$275-300

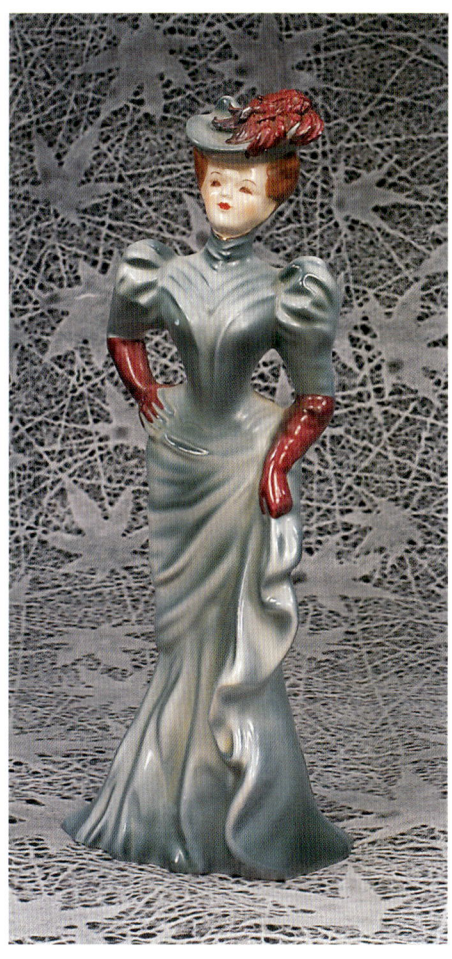

**Josephine**, 9"
$350-375

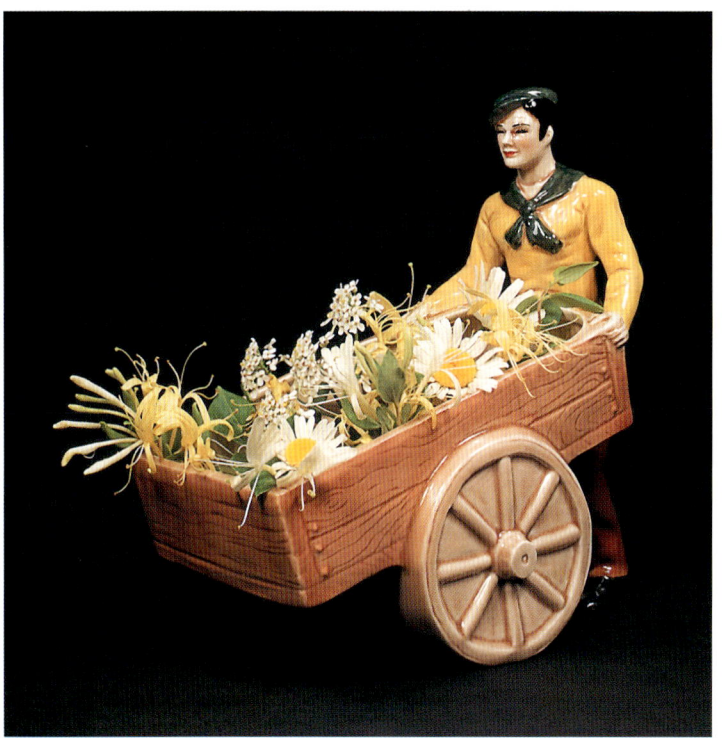

**Jose** with cart, 7.75" (FH)
$650-700

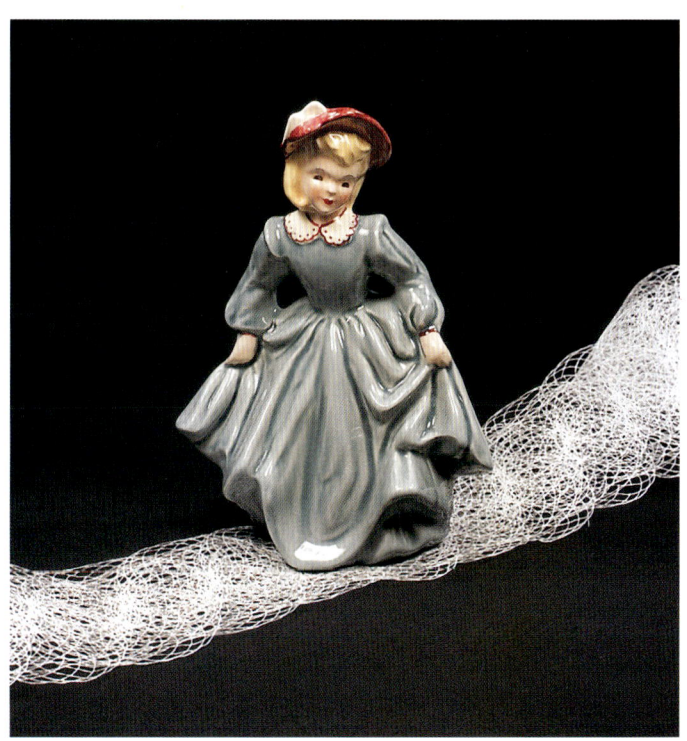

**Joy**, child, 6"
$175-200

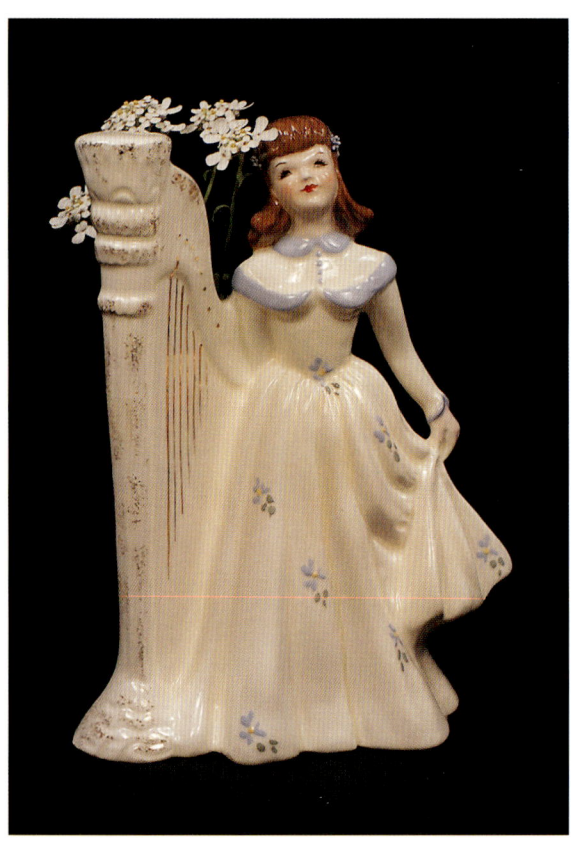

**Joy**, 7" (FH)
$175-200

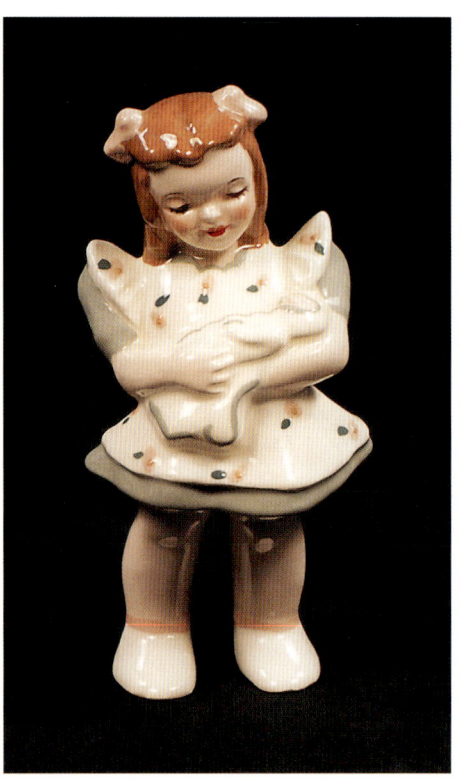

**Joyce**, child, 5.5"
$175-200

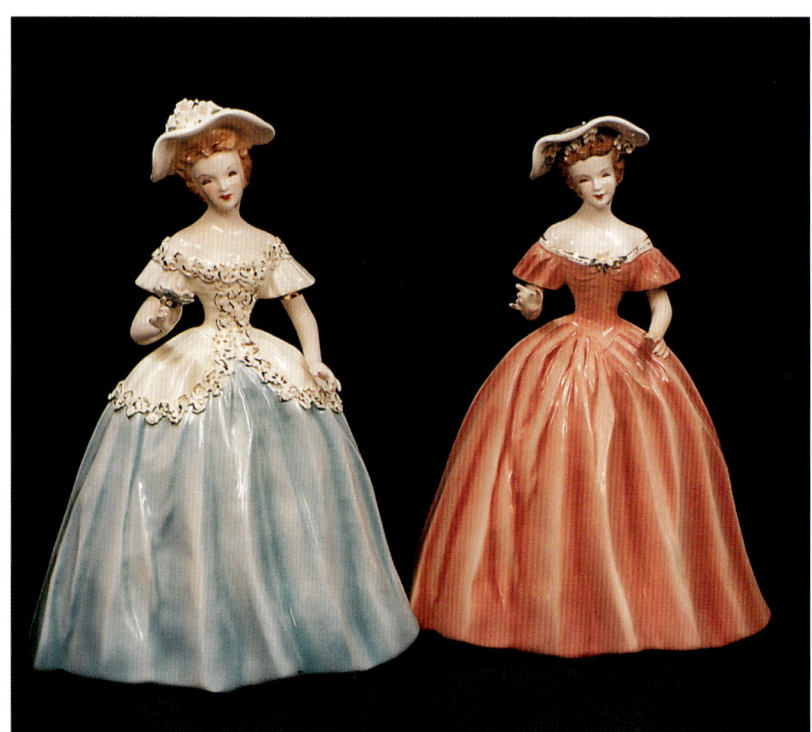

**Joyce**, adult in two styles, 9"
$550-600

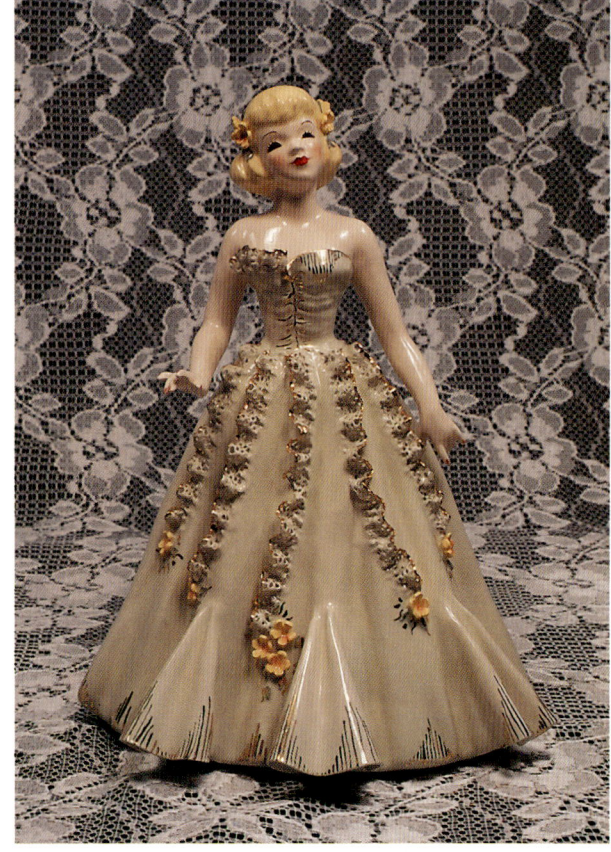

**Judy**, 9"
$450-500

Showcasing Florence A to Z 53

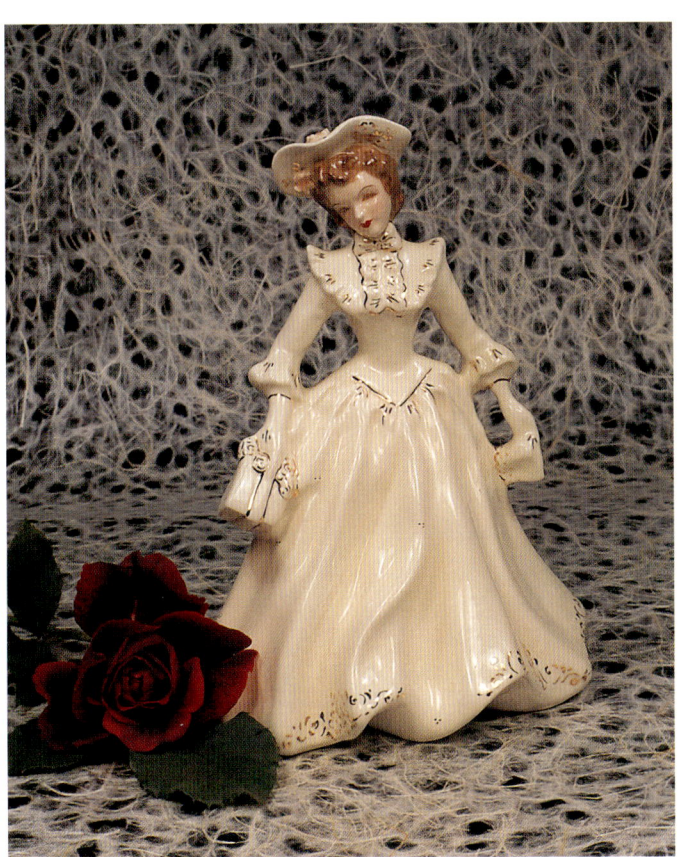

***Julie***, 7.25"
$200-250

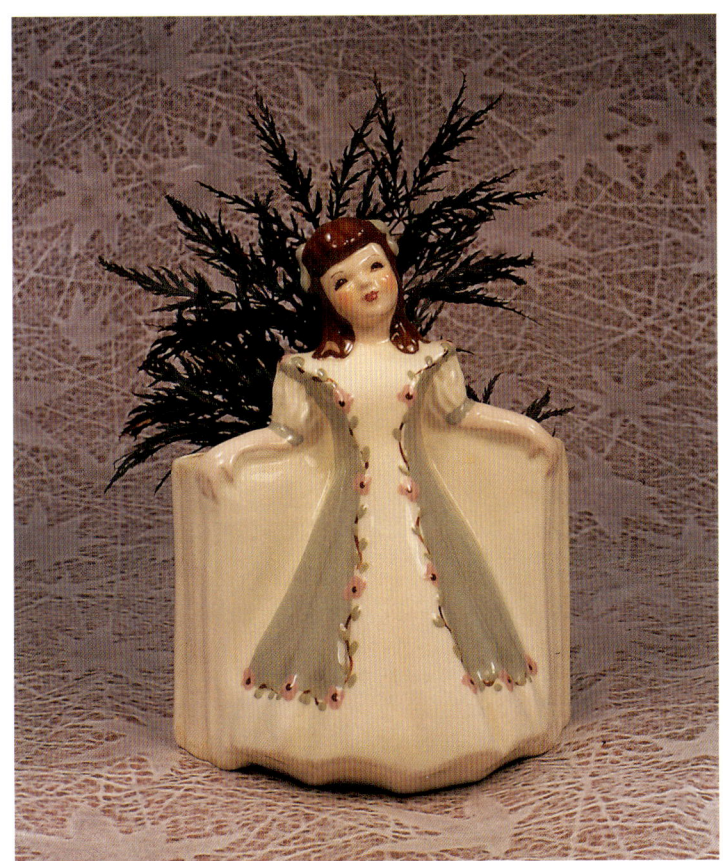

***June***, 8.5 (FH)
$50-60

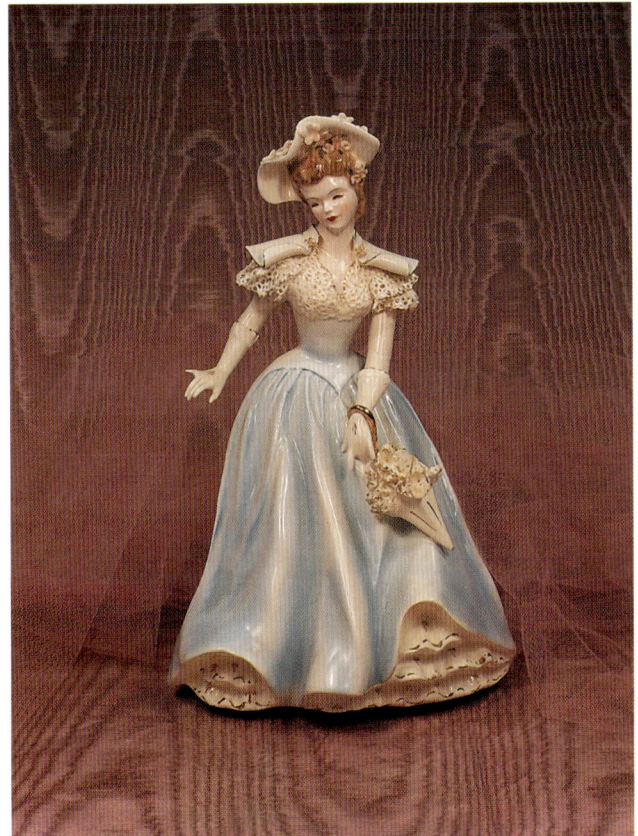

***Juliet***, 8.5"
$650-700

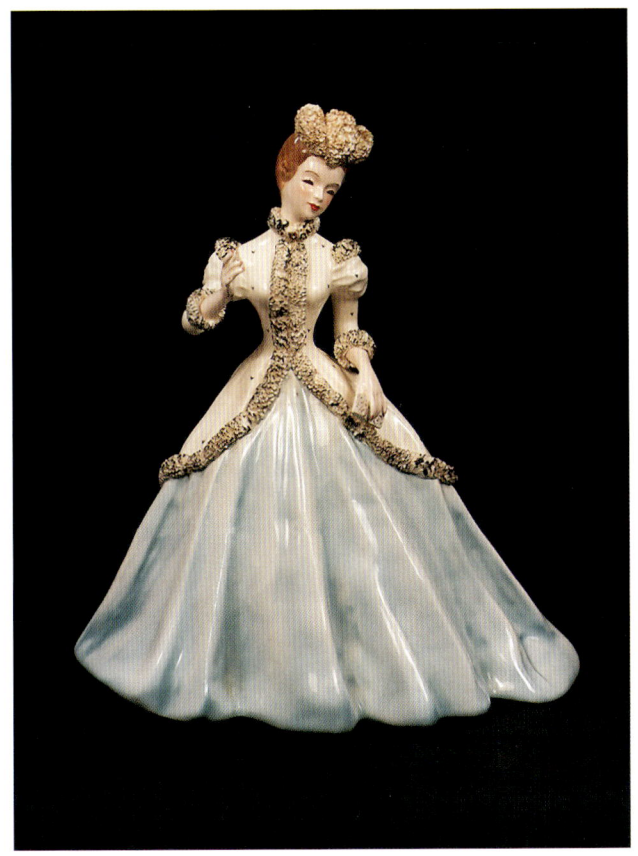

***Karen***, 8.25"
$2,000-2,250

## 54 Showcasing Florence A to Z

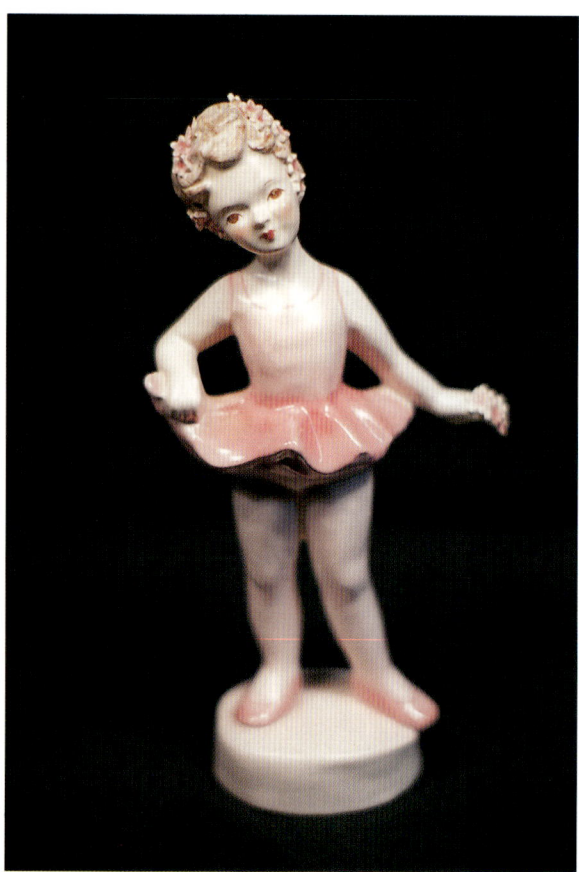

**Karie,** child, 9.5", *
$600-650

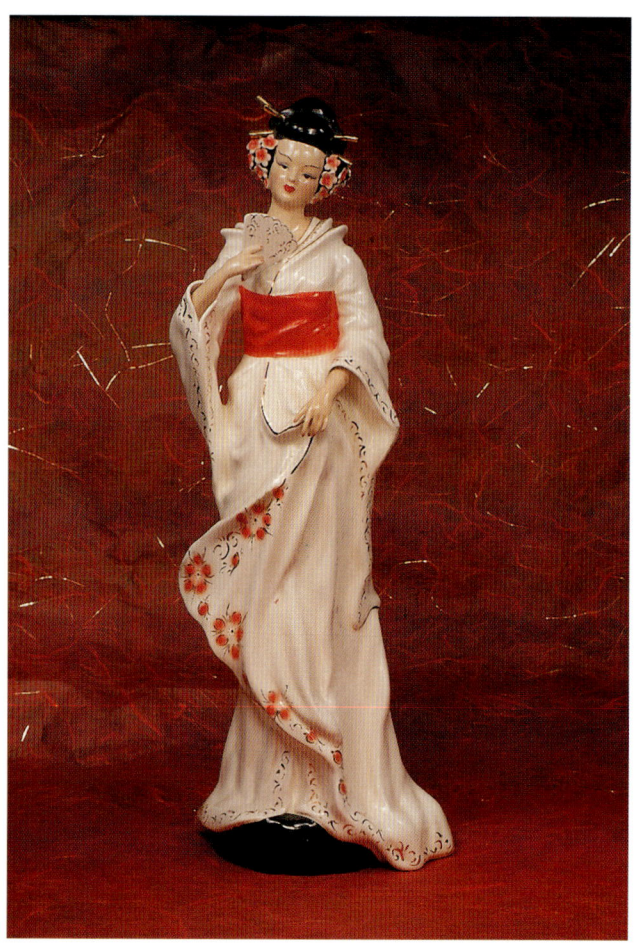

**Karlo**, 11"
$750-850

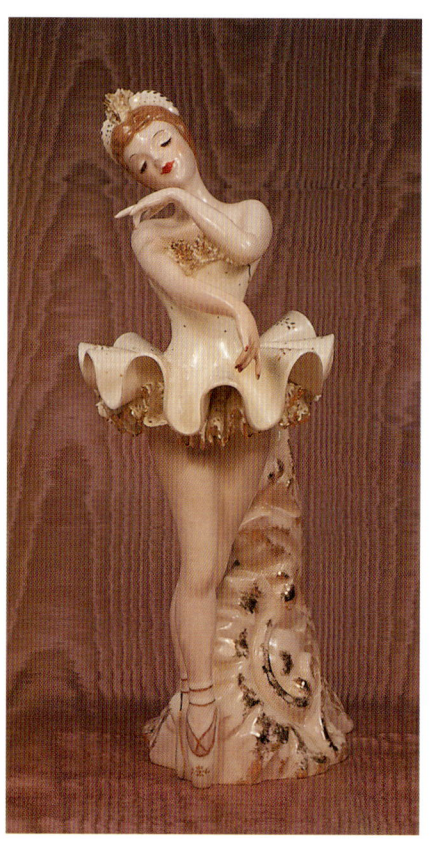

**Karla Ballerina**, 9.75"
$450-500

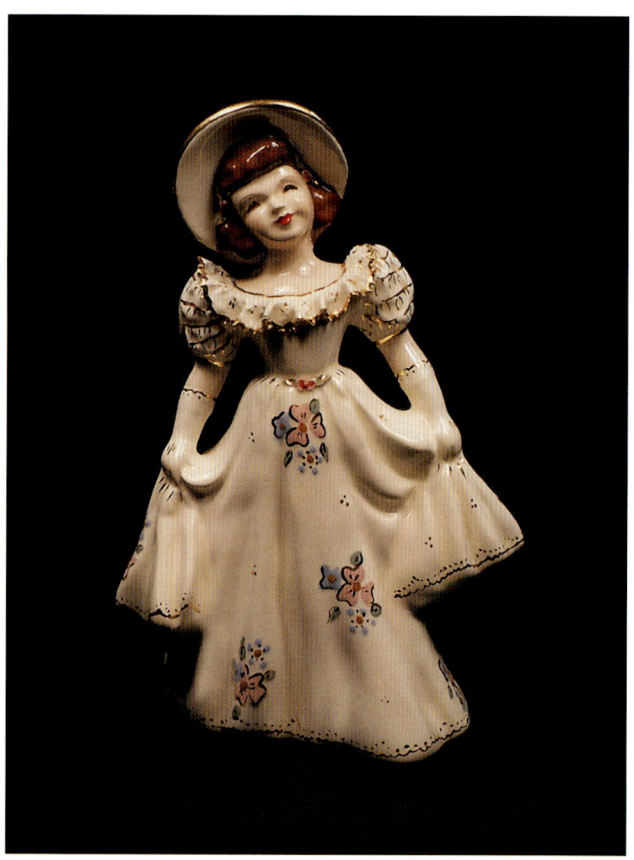

**Kathy**, 7"
$100-125

Showcasing Florence A to Z  55

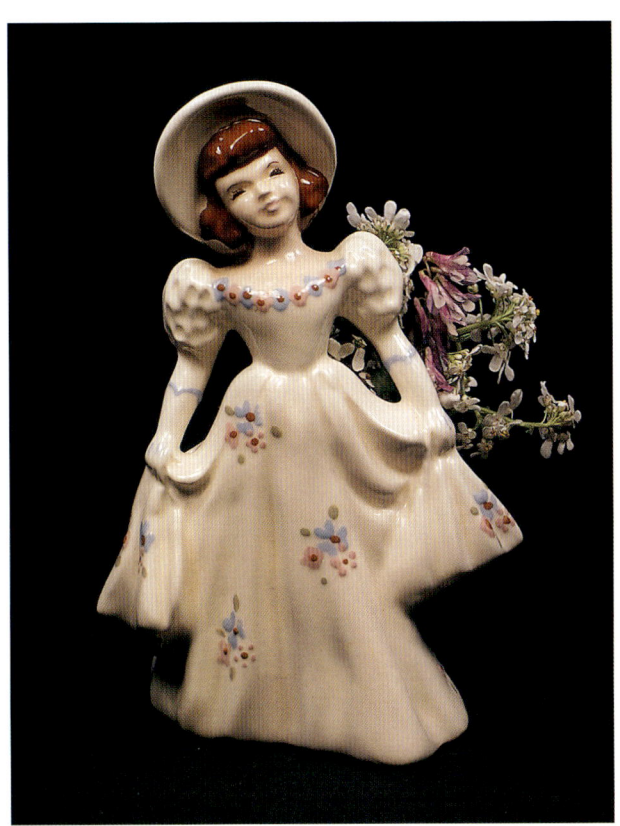

**Kay**, 7" (FH)
$60-70

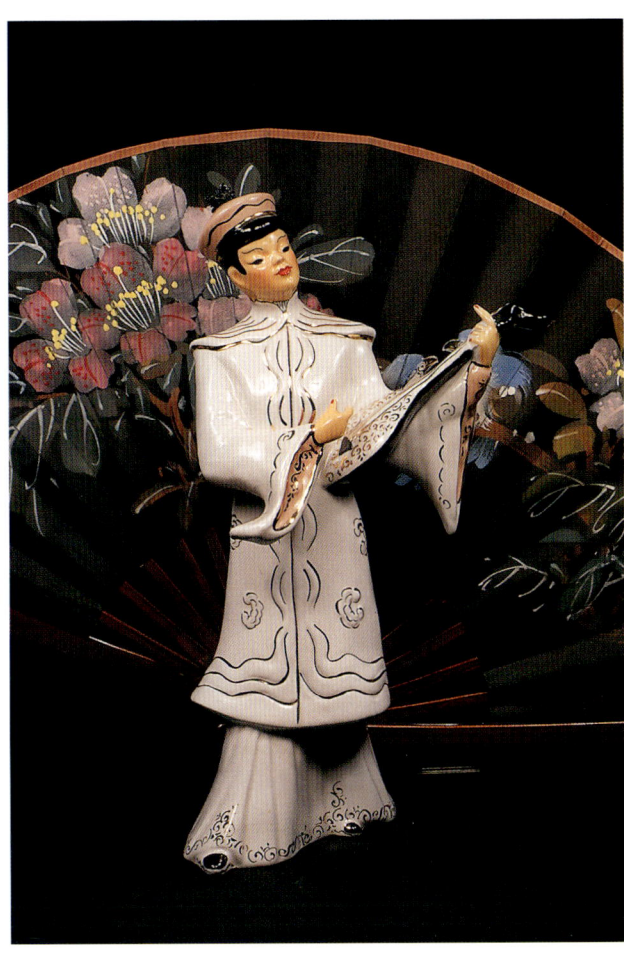

**Kiu**, 10.25"
$225-250

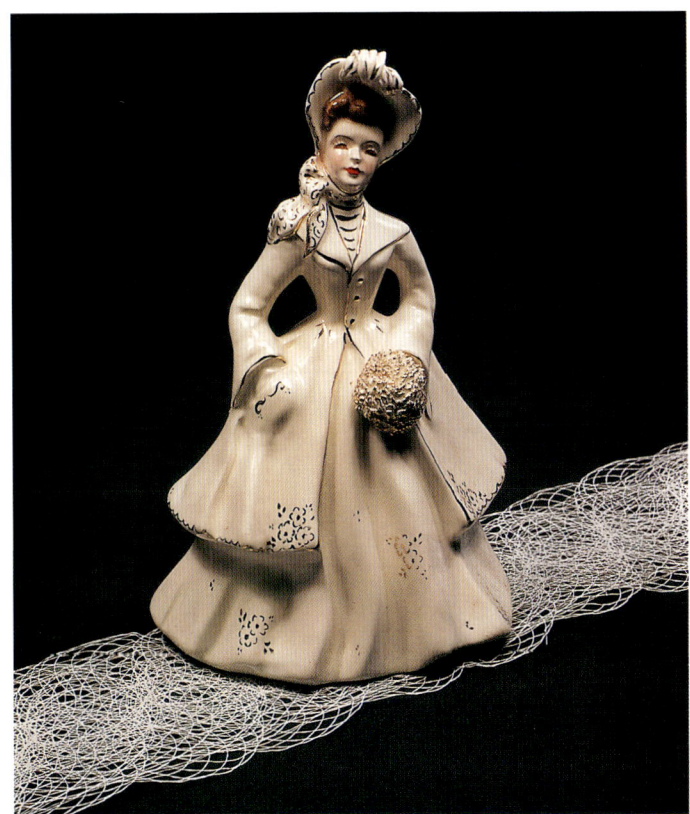

**Kay**, 6"
$125-140

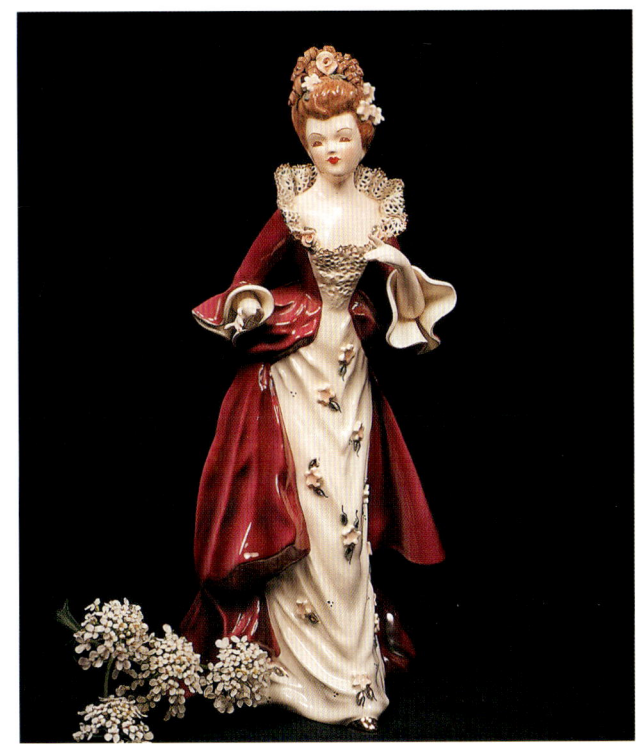

**Lady Diana**, 10"
$1,250-1,400

## 56  Showcasing Florence A to Z

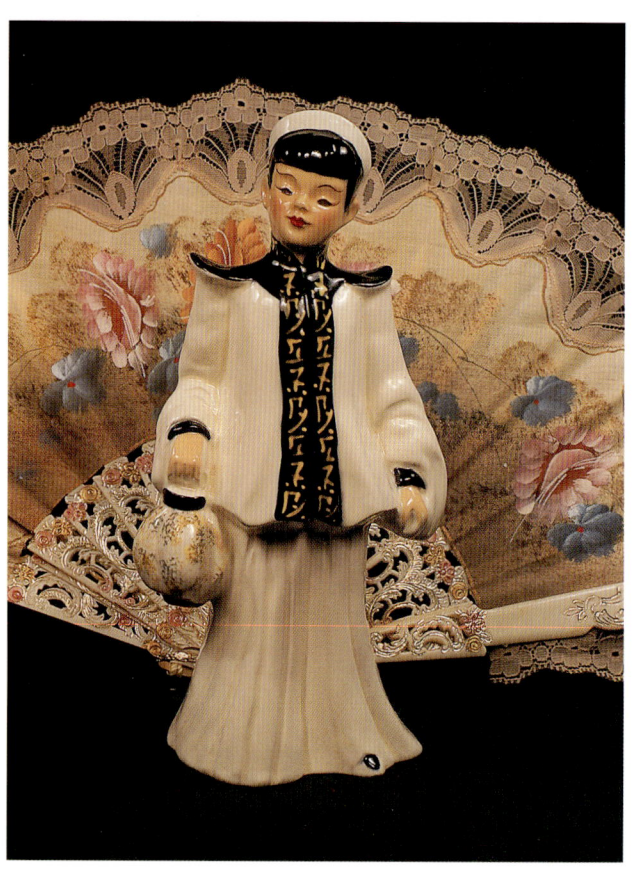

**Lantern Boy**, 8.25" (FH)
$125-140

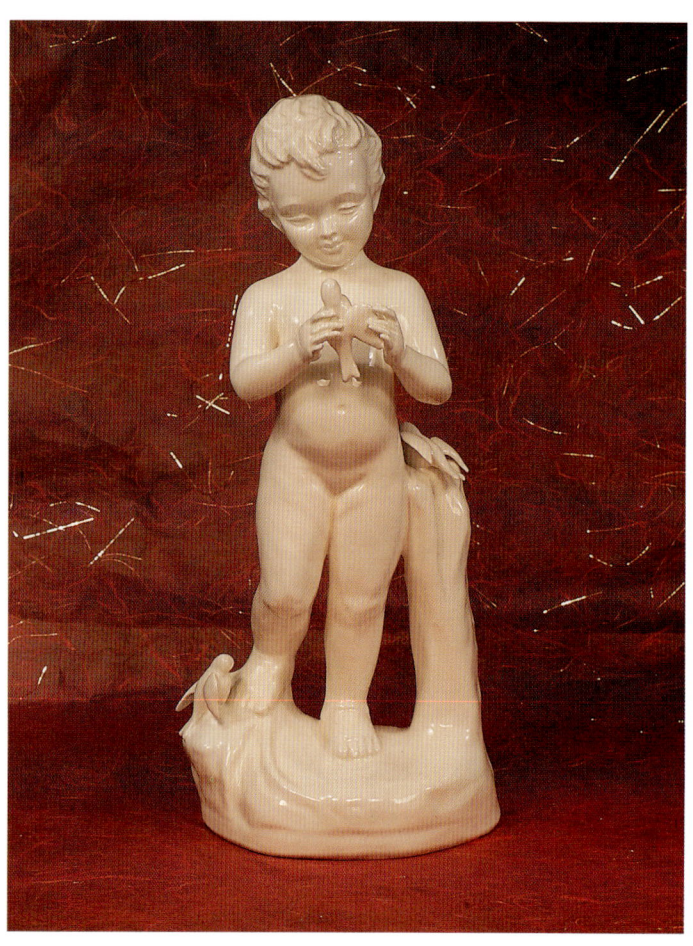

**Larry**, 12.5", *
$700-750

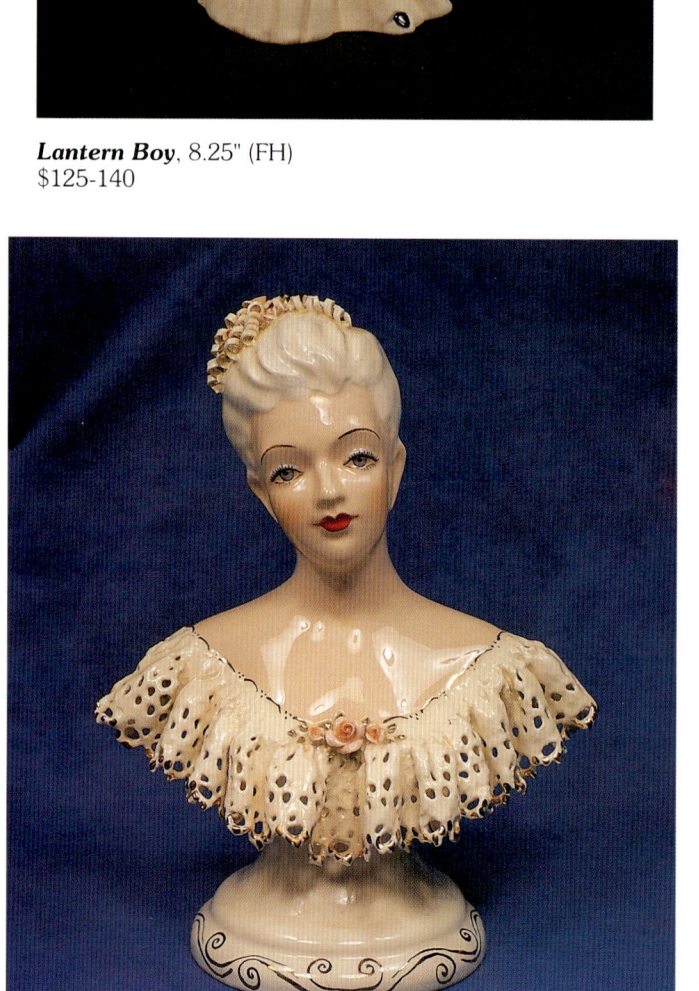

**La Petite**, 8.25"
$500-600

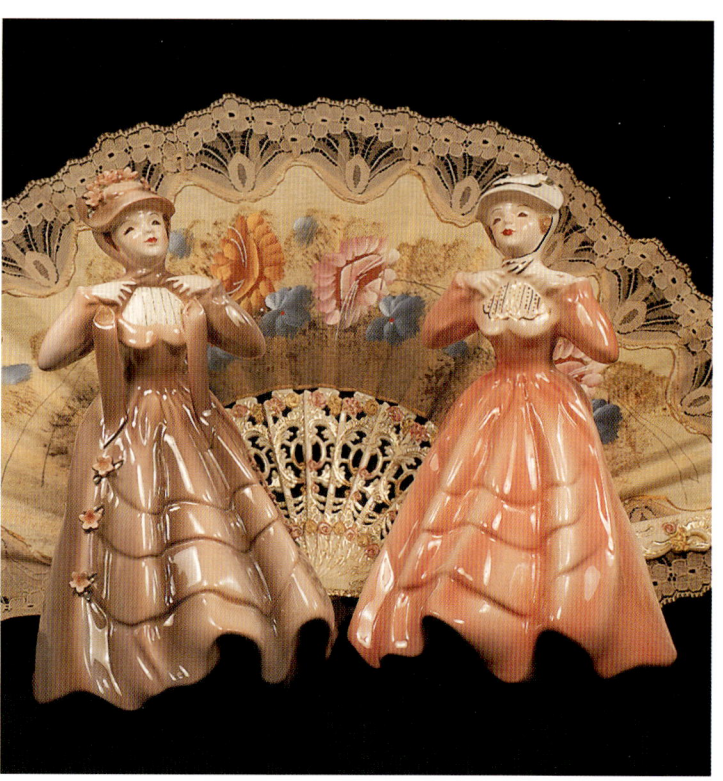

Left: **Laura** with ribbon, 7.5"; Right: **Laura** plain, 7.5"
Left: $250-275; Right: $200-225

Showcasing Florence A to Z  57

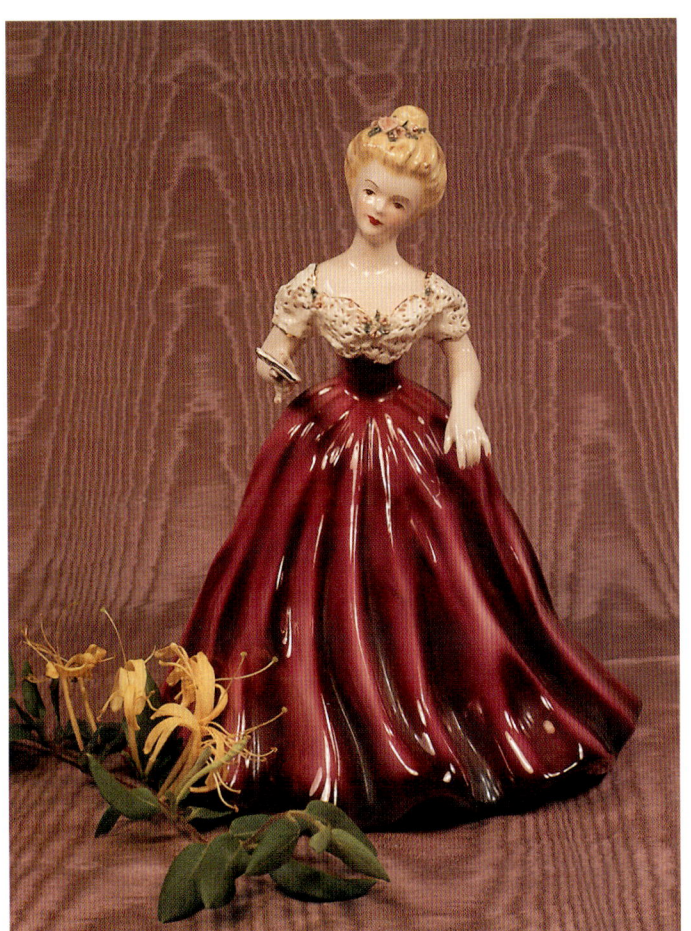

**Lavon**, 8.5"
$500-550

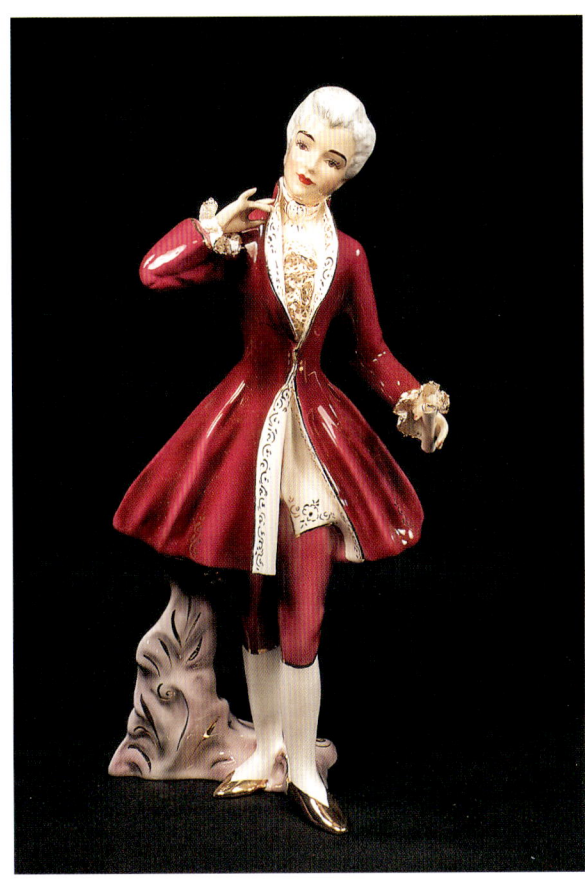

**Leading Man**, 10.25"
$475-500

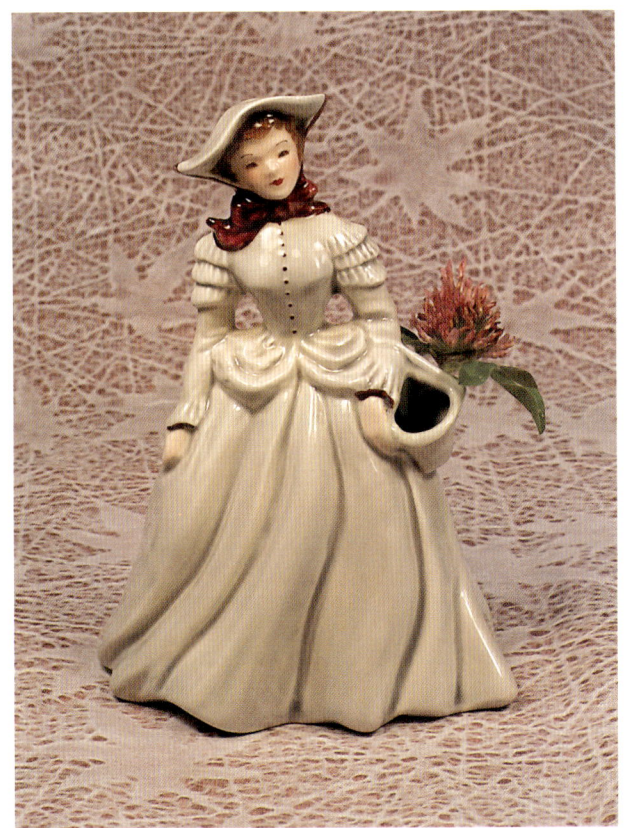

**Lea**, 6" (FH)
$80-100

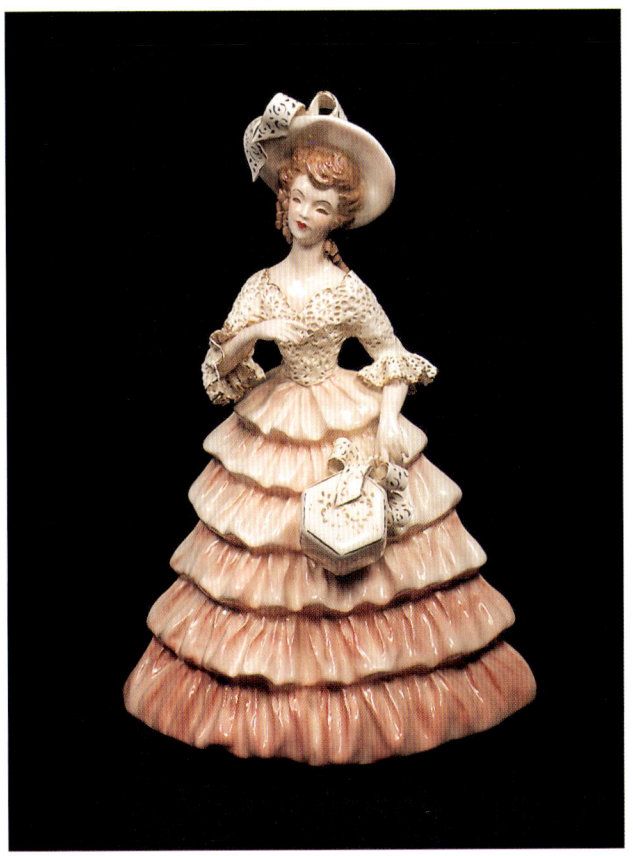

**Lee Ann**, 9.5"
$2,400-2,600

**58   Showcasing Florence A to Z**

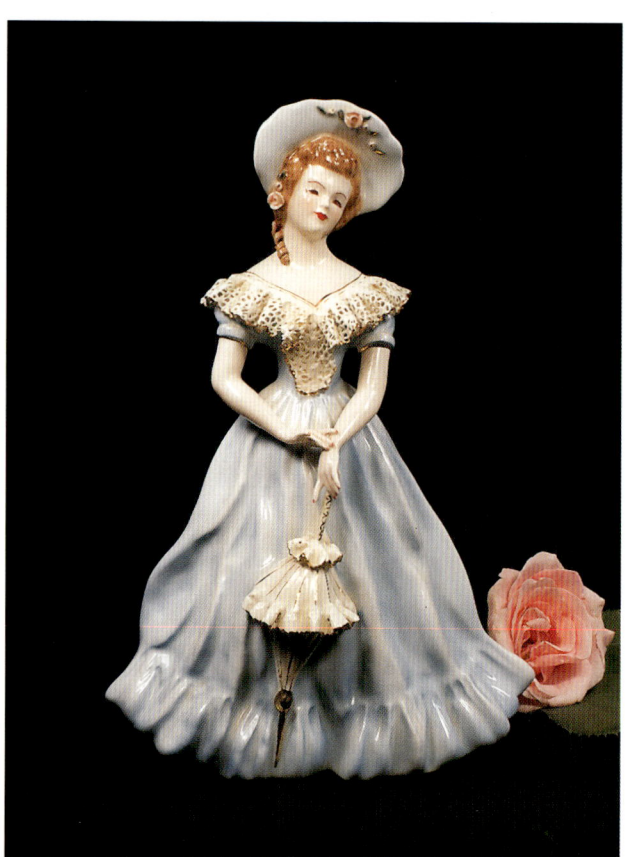

**Lila**, 9"
$1,000-1,200

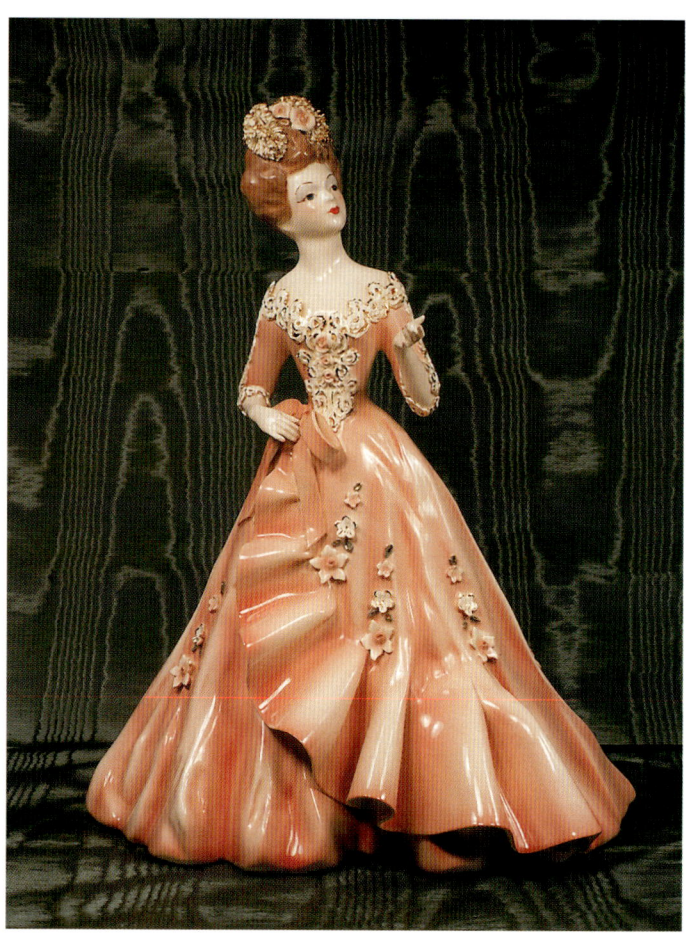

**Lillian Russell**, 13.5"
$2,700-2,900

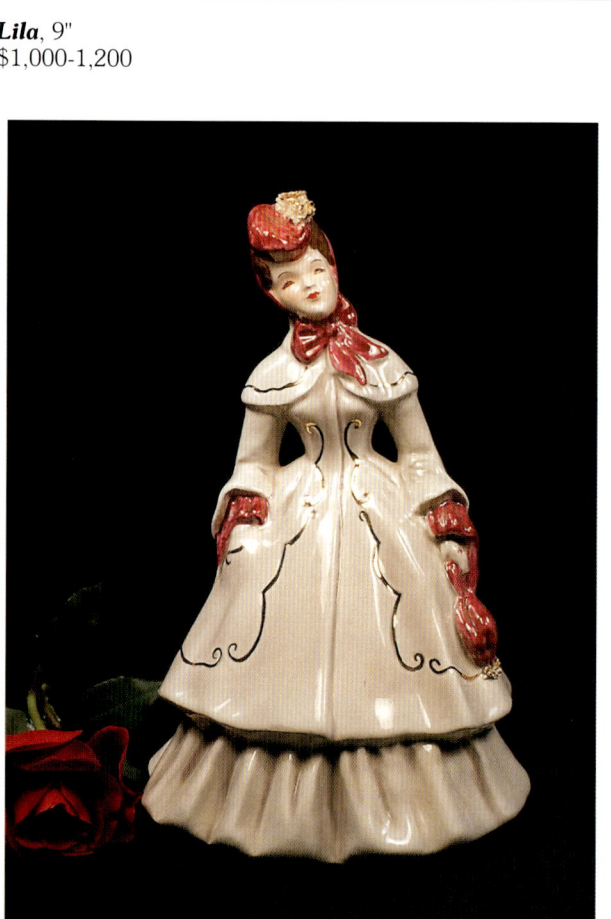

**Lillian**, 7.25"
$135-150

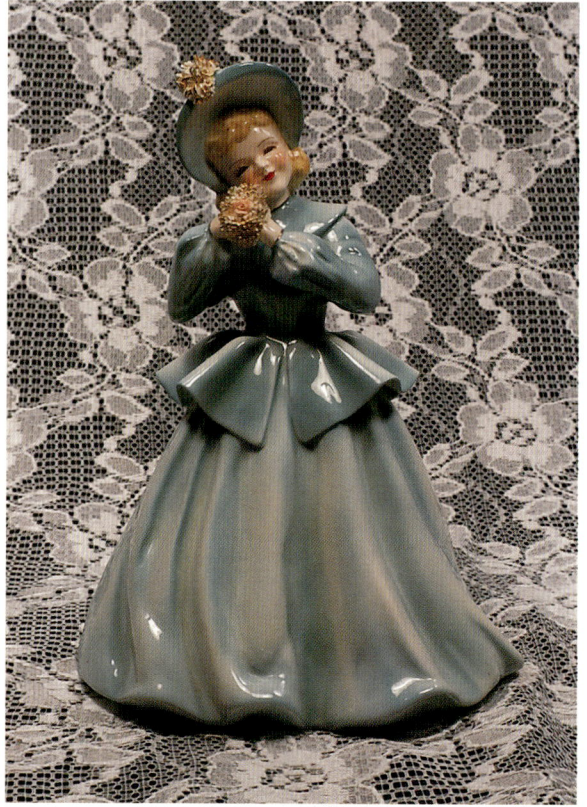

**Linda Lou**, 7.75"
$375-425

Showcasing Florence A to Z   59

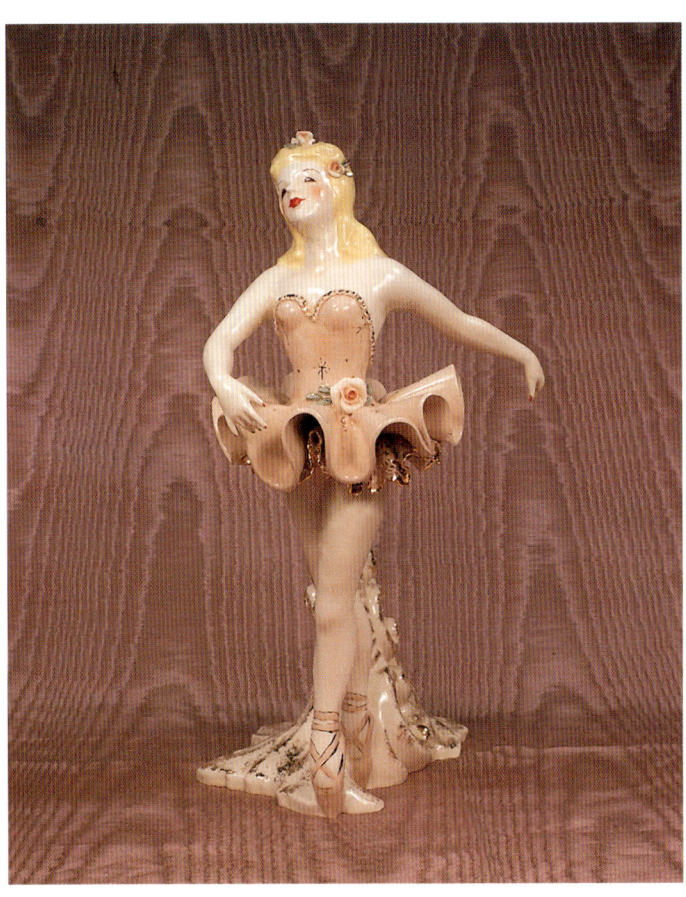

***Lisa Ballerina***, 9.75"
$450-500
***Lisa***, 7.25"
$180-200

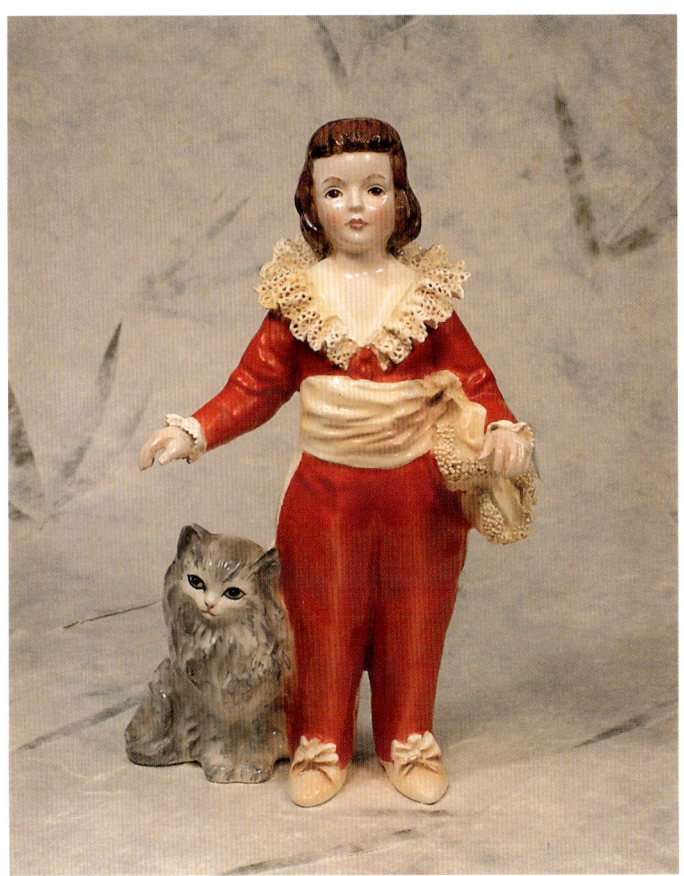

***Little Don***, 7.75"
$2,250-2,500

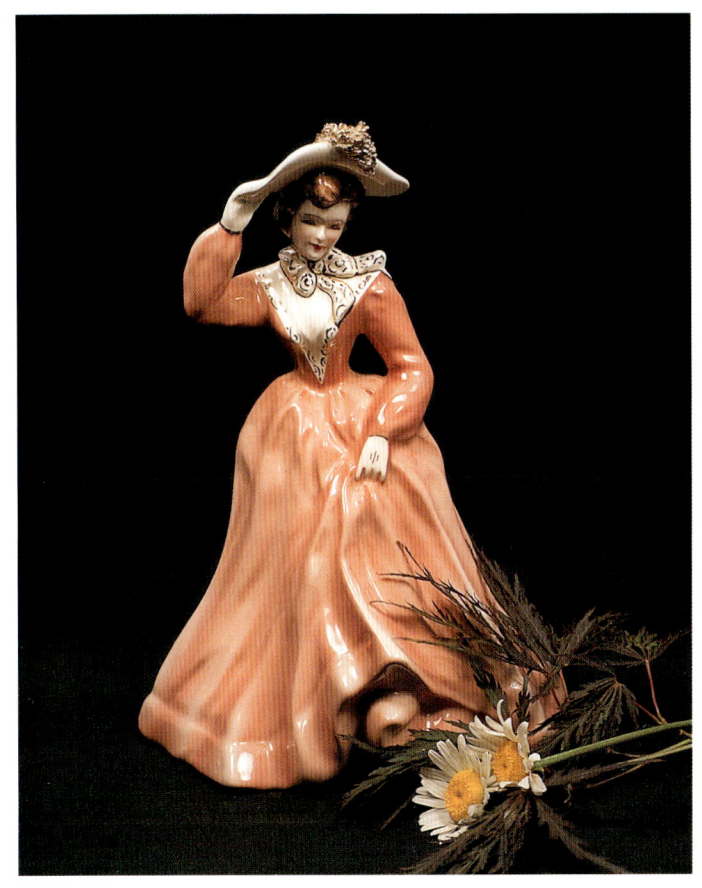

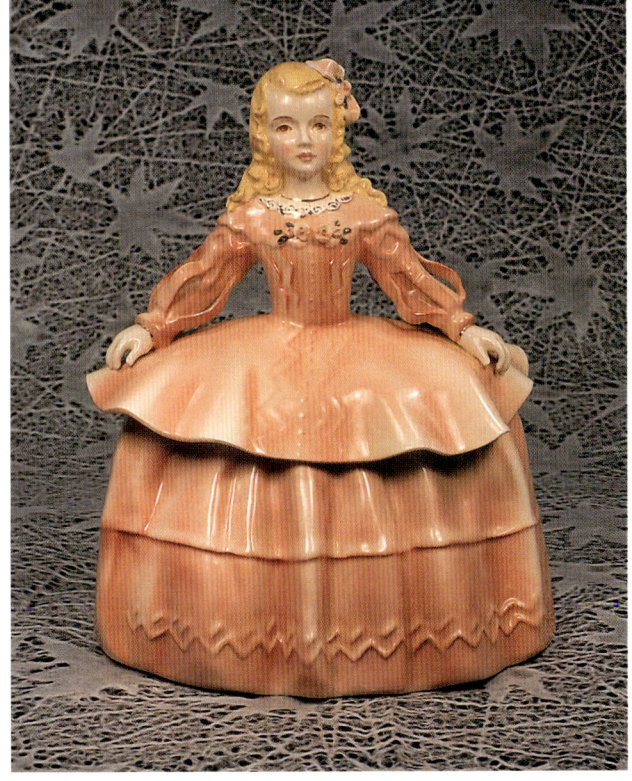

***Little Princess***, 8"
$2,250-2,500

# 60 Showcasing Florence A to Z

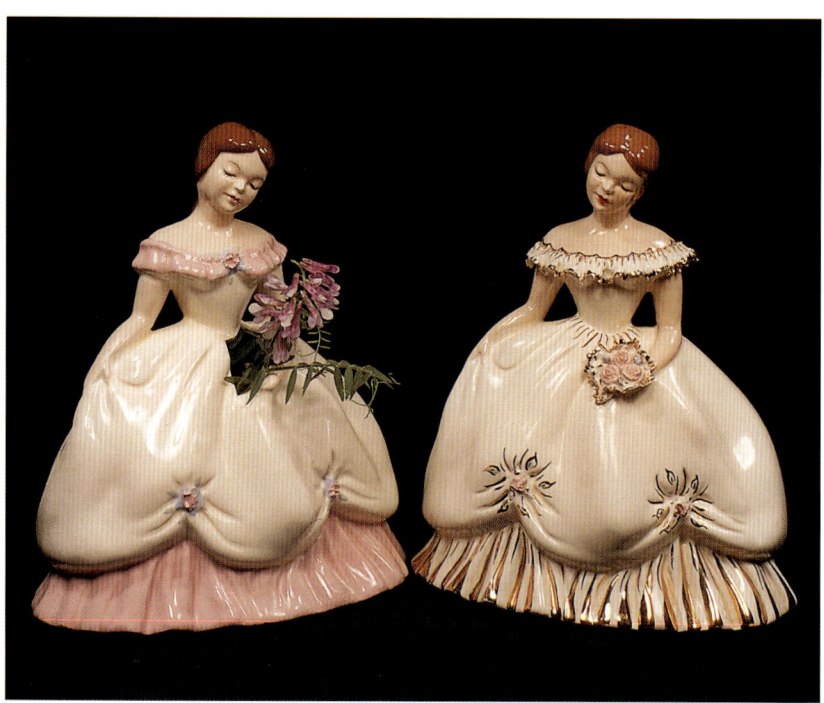

Left: **Loraine**, 7.25" (FH); Right: **Loraine**, 7.25", *
Left: $125-140; Right: $140-160

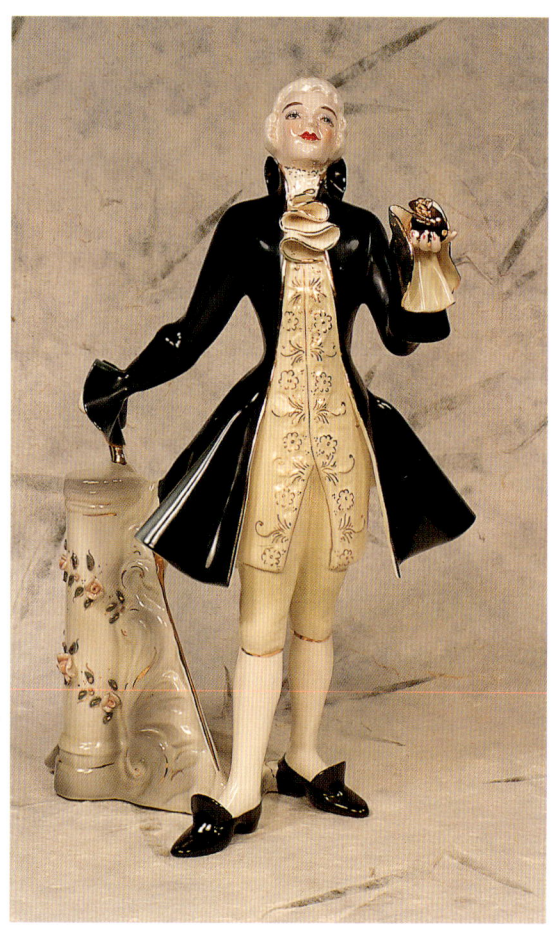

**Louis XV**, 12.5"
$375-400

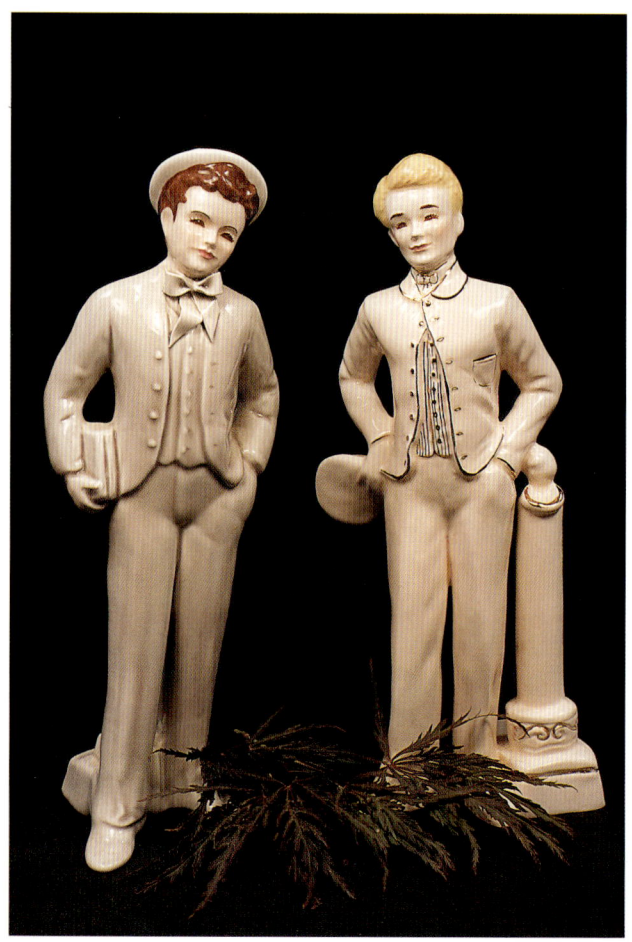

Left: **Lorry,** with book, 8"; Right: **Lorry,** with cap, 8"
Left: $1,200-1,400; Right: $1,200-1,400

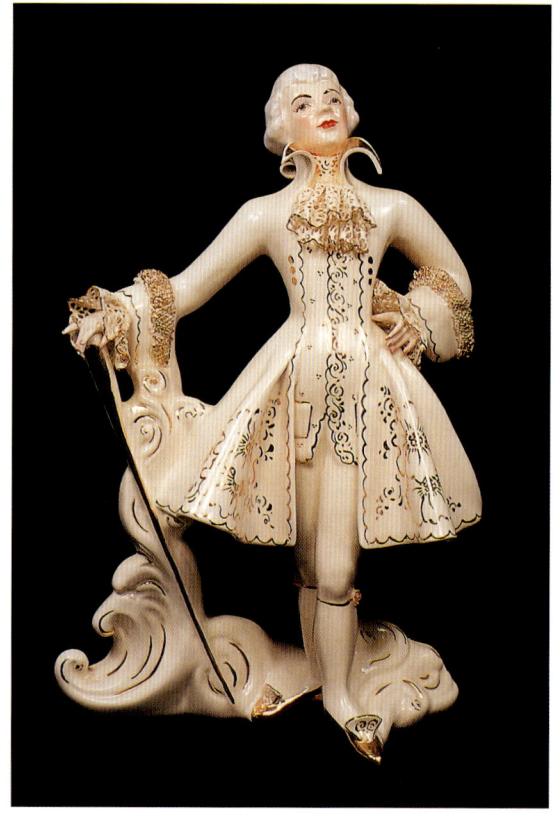

**Louis XVI**, 10"
$375-400

Showcasing Florence A to Z  61

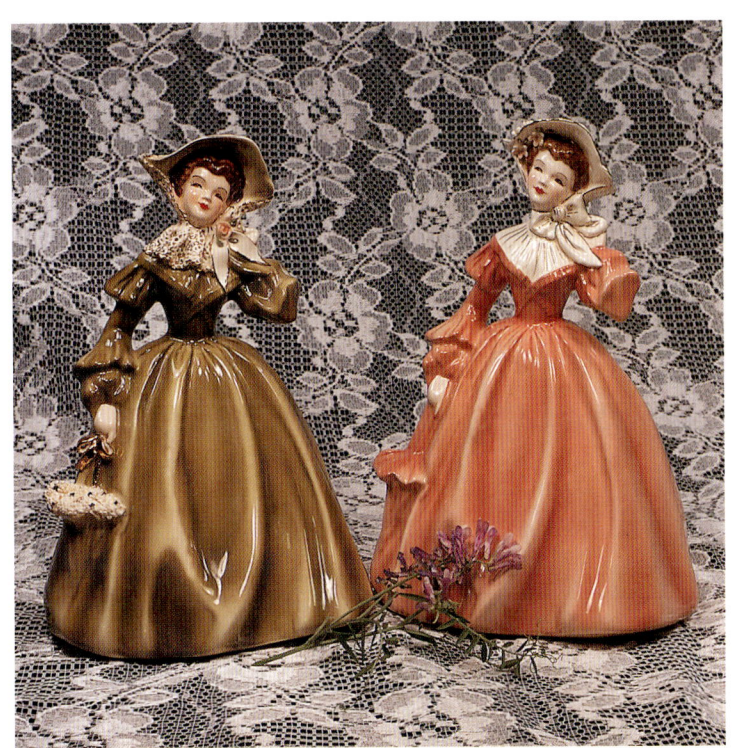

**Louise**, two styles, 7.25"
Left: $175-200; Right: $150-175

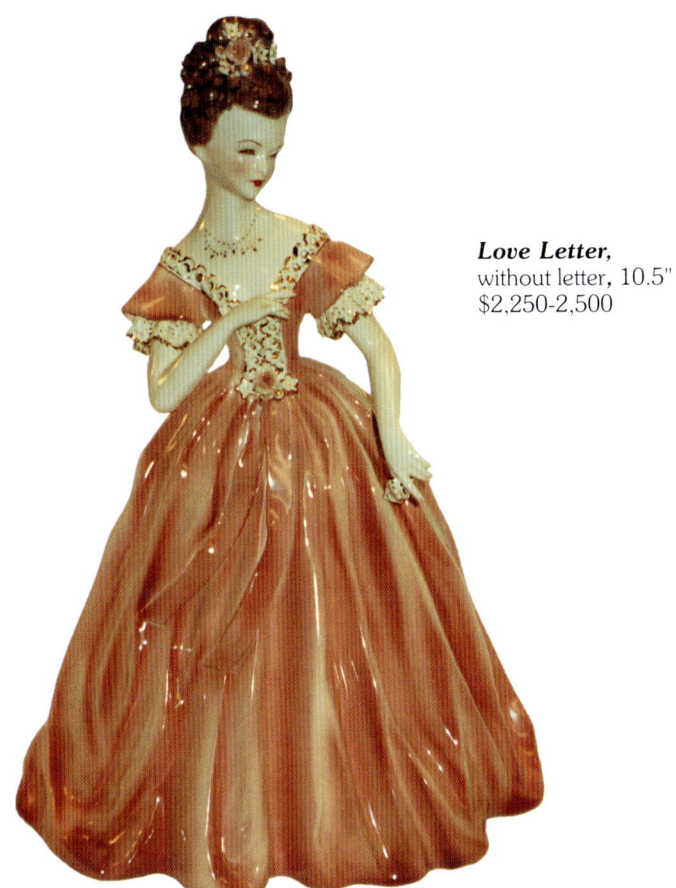

*Love Letter,*
without letter, 10.5"
$2,250-2,500

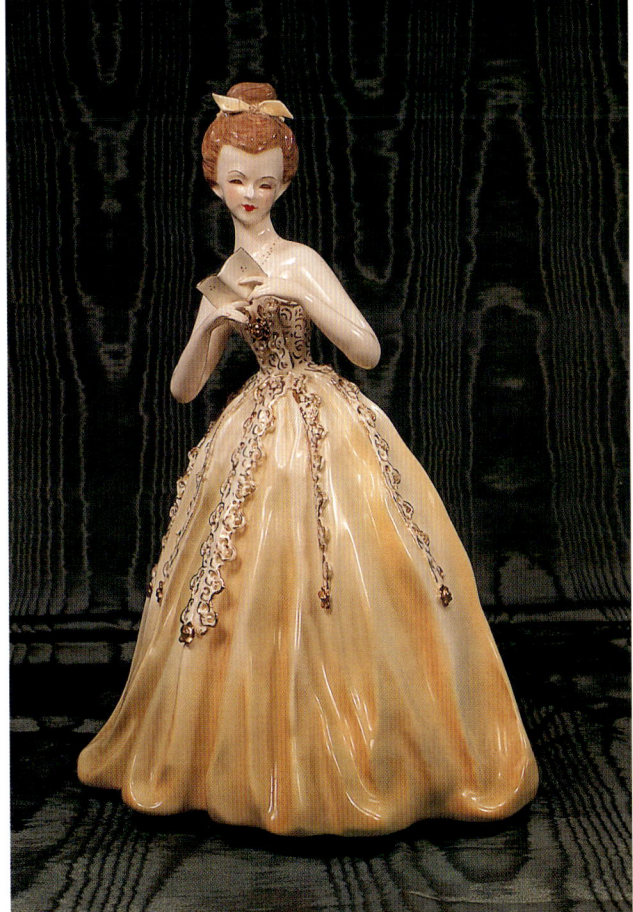

*Love Letter,* with letter, 10.5"
$2,250-2,500

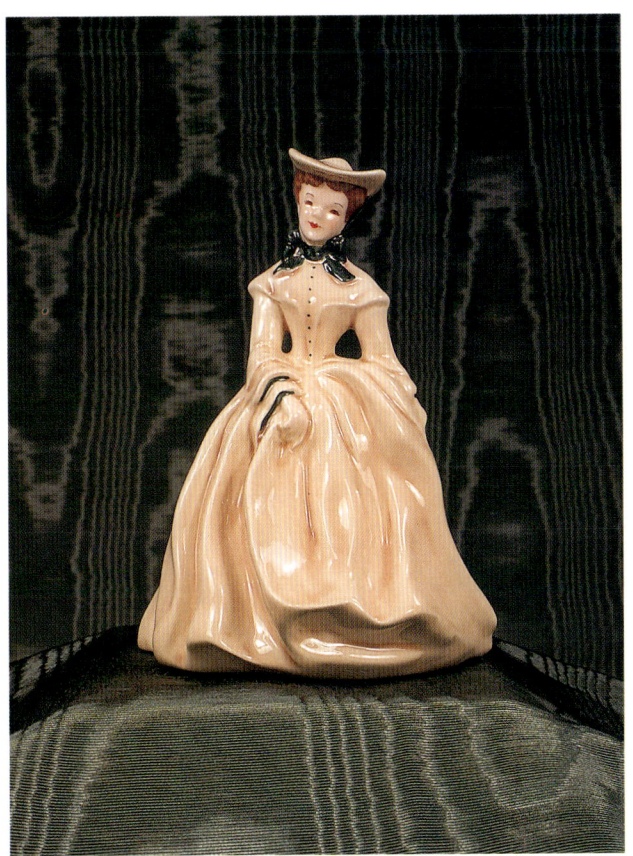

*Lyn*, 6" (FH)
$80-100

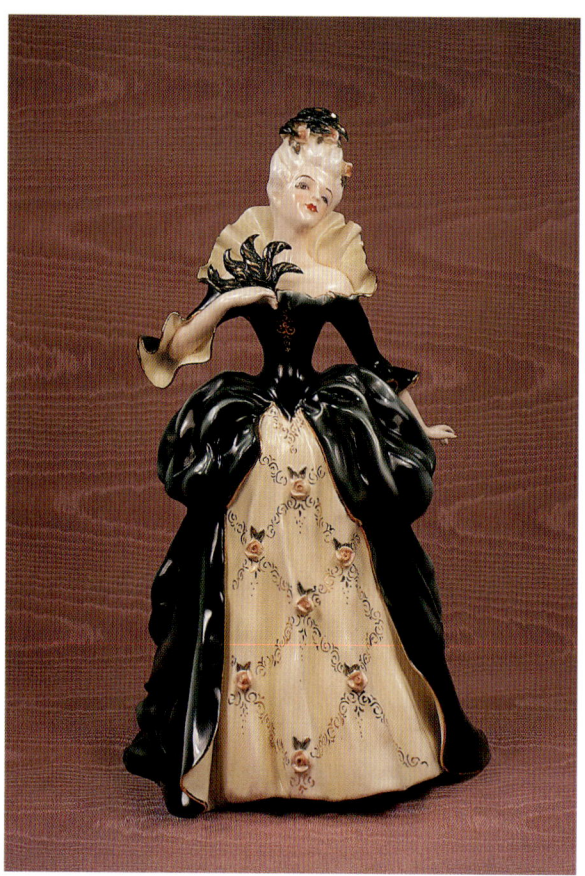

**Madame Pompadour**, 12.5"
$375-400

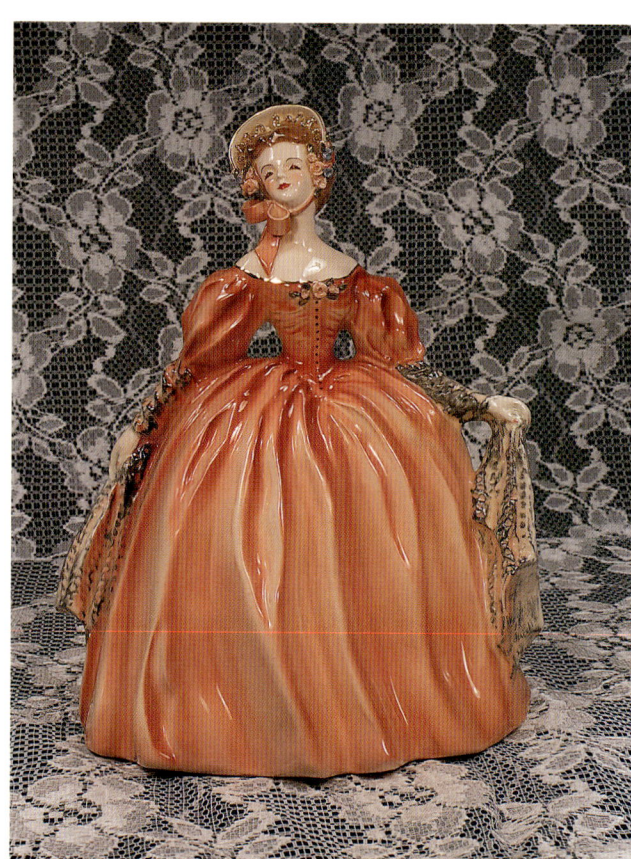

**Madeline**, 8.75"
$400-425

**Madame DuBarry**, 8.5"
$500-550

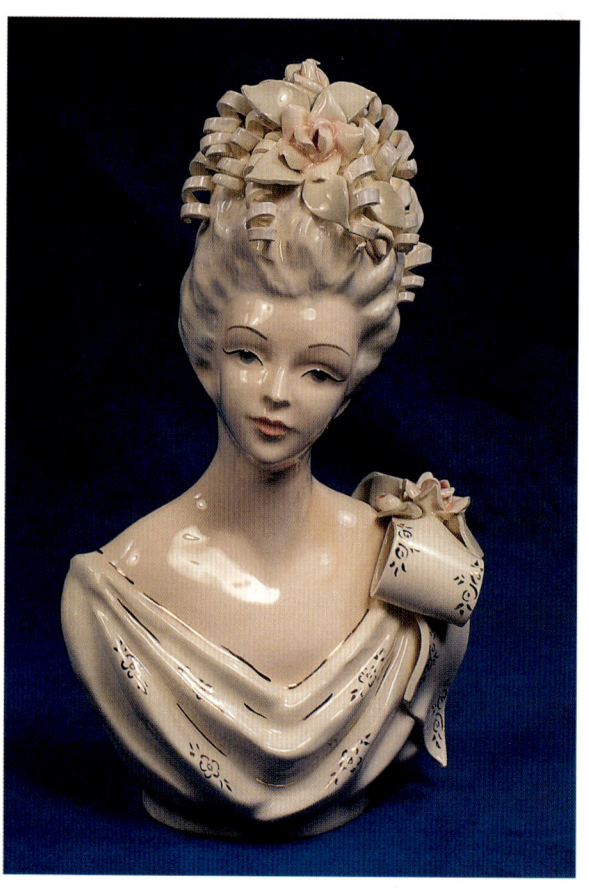

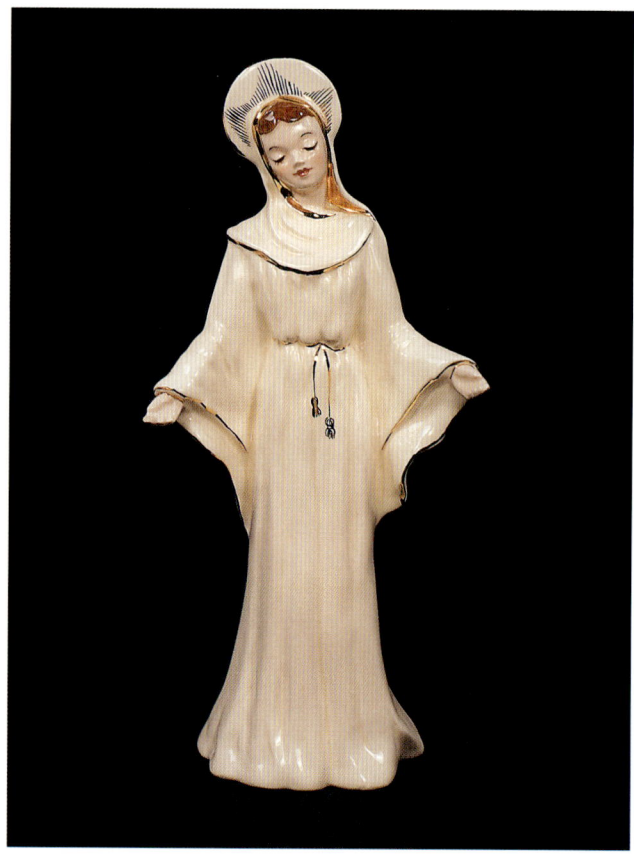

**Madonna**, with arms outstretched, 10"
$150-175

**Showcasing Florence A to Z   63**

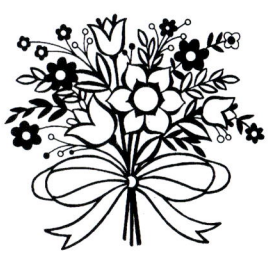

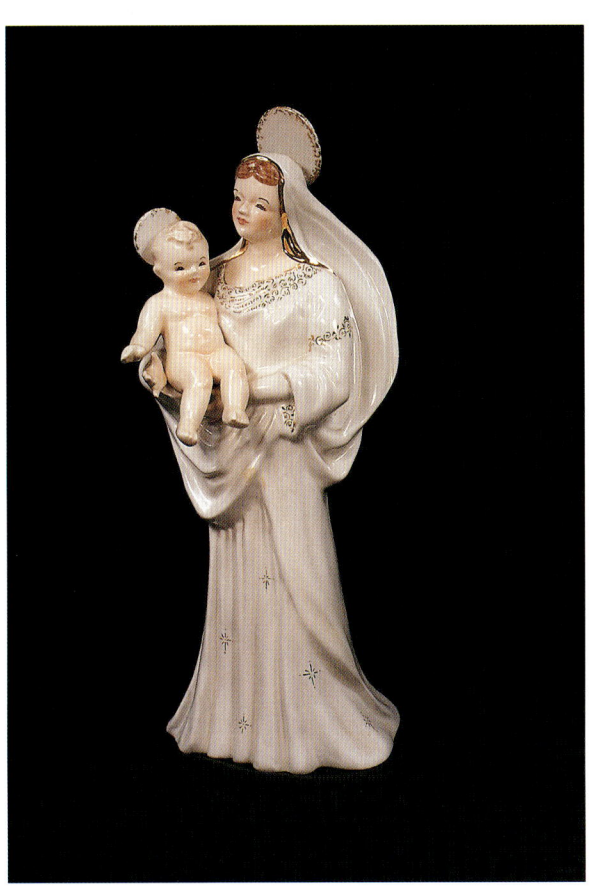

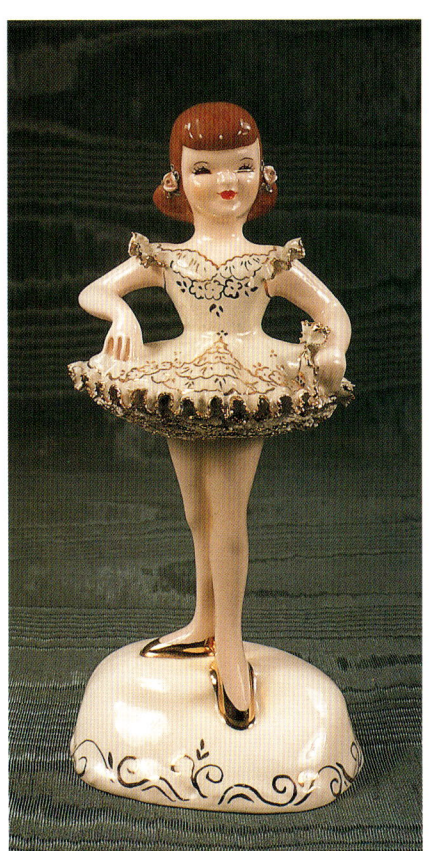

*Marcella,* child ballerina, 6.75"
$350-375

**Madonna and Child**, 10.5"
$500-550

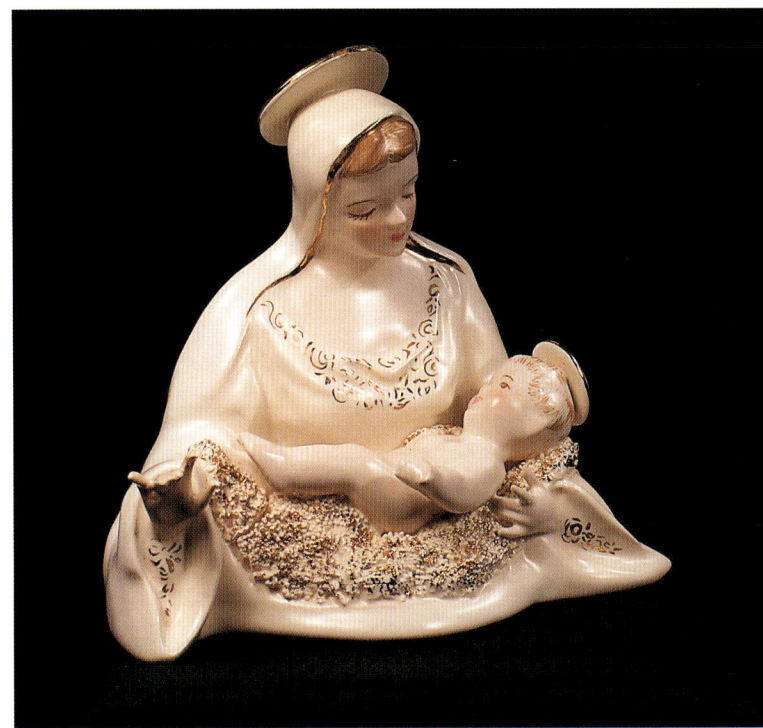

**Madonna and Child Bust**, 4.75"
$400-450

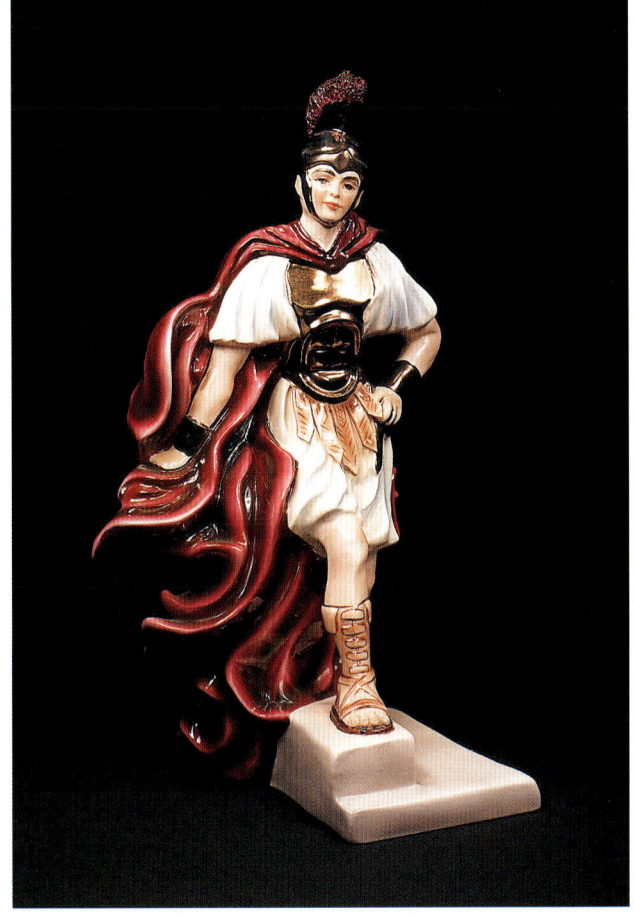

*Mark Anthony*, 12.5"
$1,400-1,600

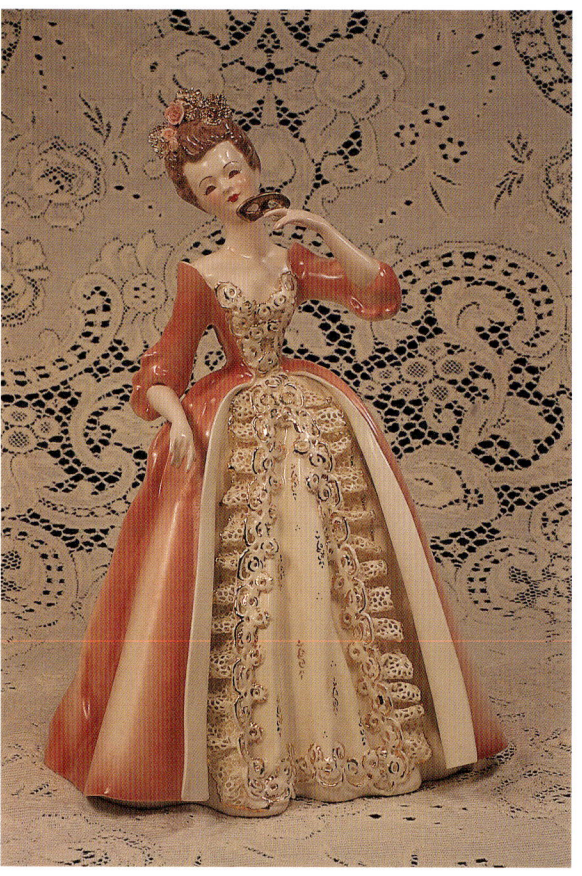

**Mardi Gras**, 10.5"
$2,500-2,700

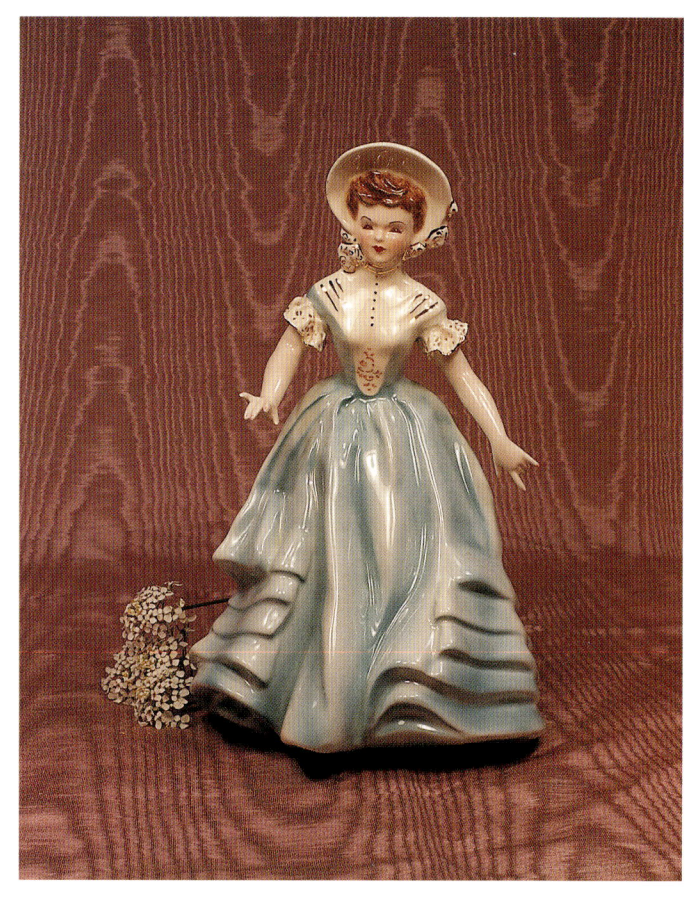

**Margo**, 8"
$650-700

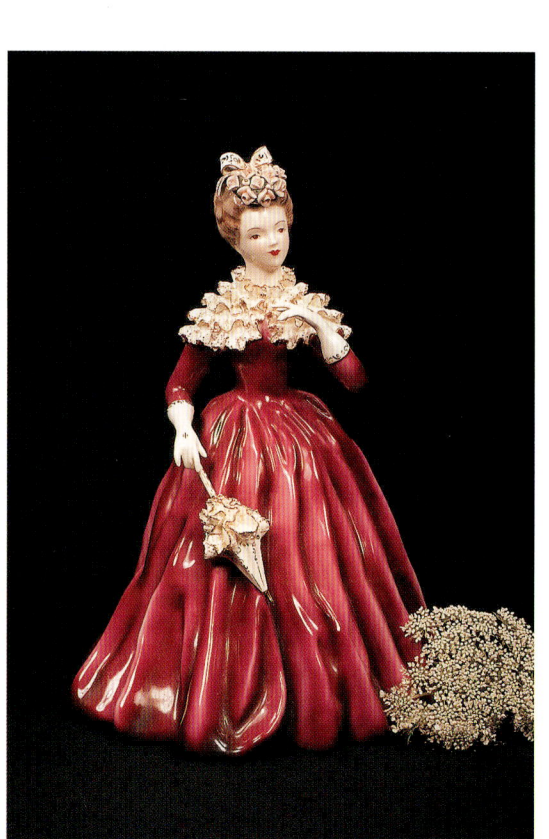

**Margaret**, 9.75"
$1,600-1,750

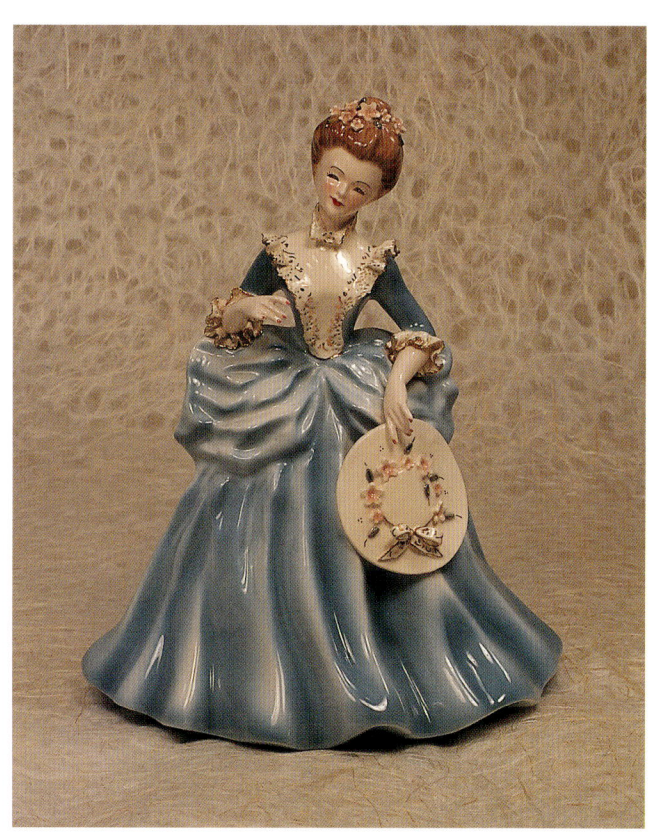

**Marianne**, 8.25"
$600-700

Showcasing Florence A to Z   65

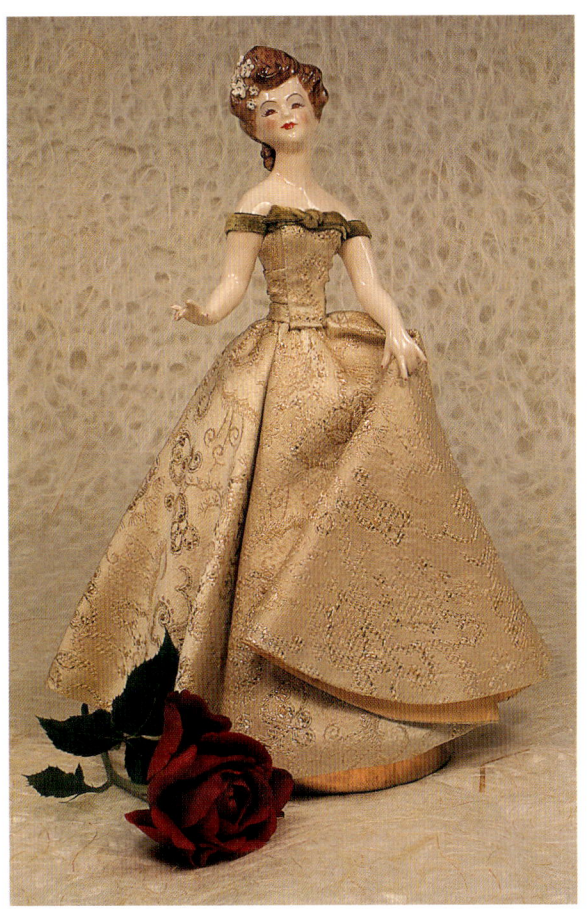

**Marleen Brocade,** 10"
$2,750-3,000

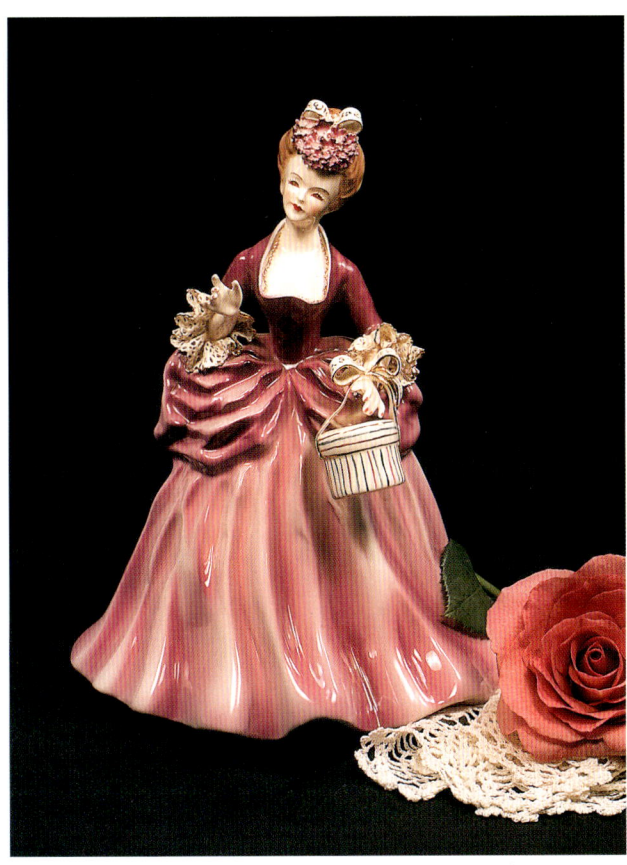

**Marilyn**, 10.5"
$500-550

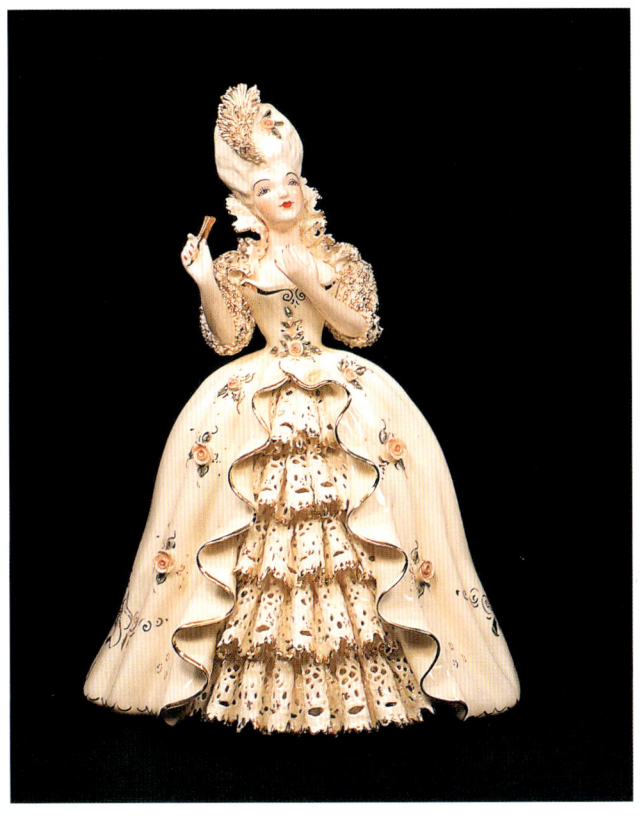

**Marie Antoinette**, 10"
$375-400

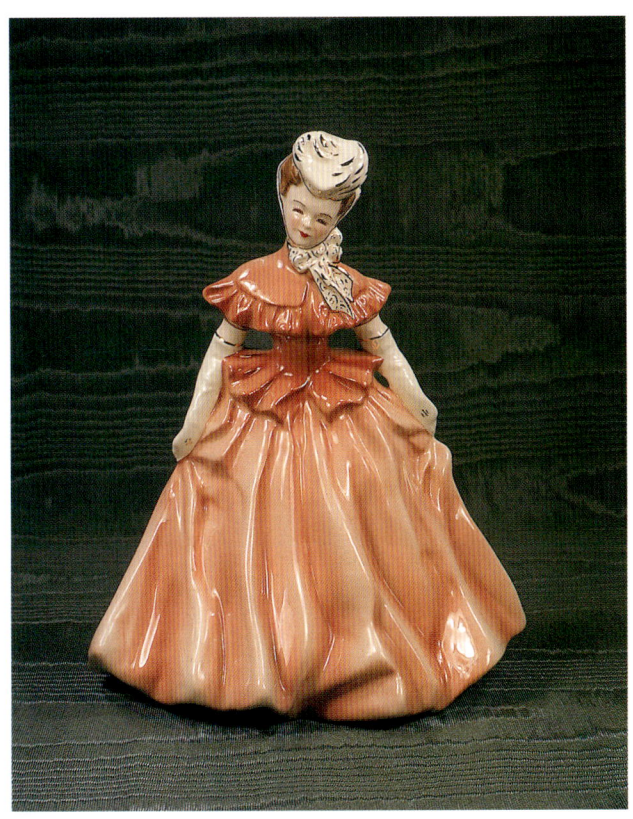

**Marsie**, 8"
$425-475

## 66 Showcasing Florence A to Z

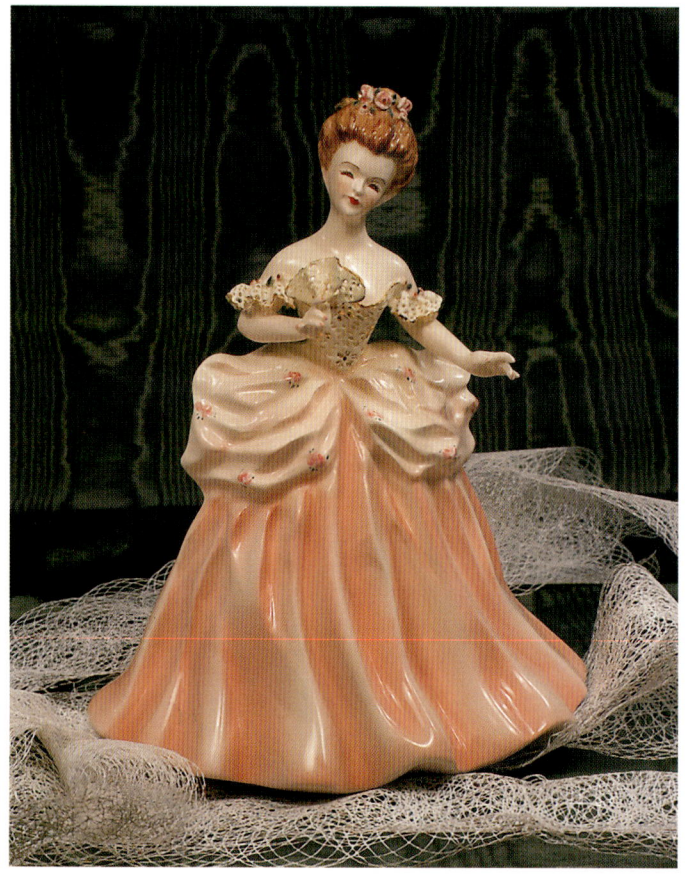

**Martha**, 8.25"
$600-650

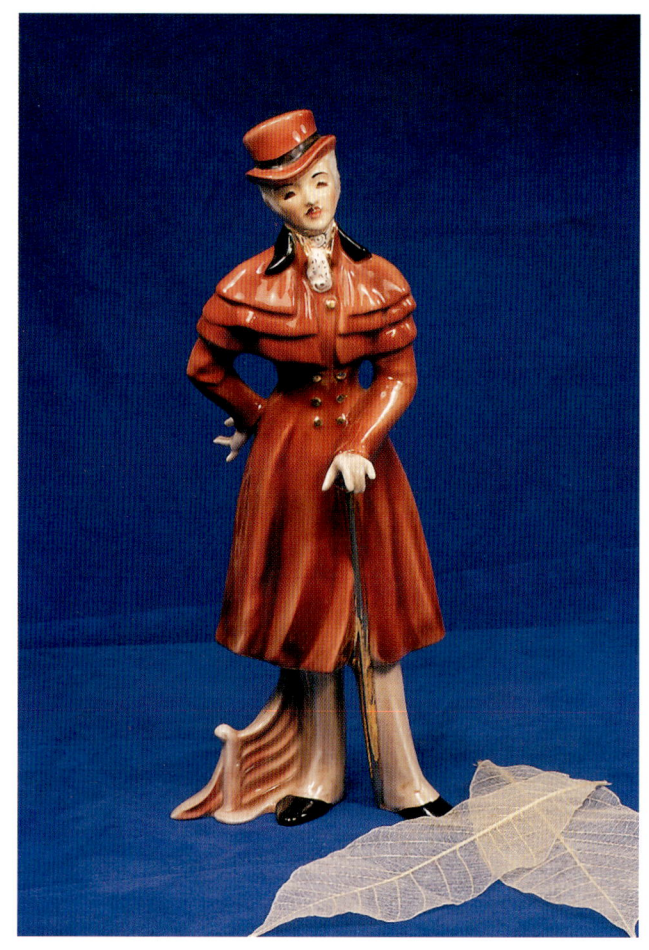

**Martin**, 10.5"
$400-450

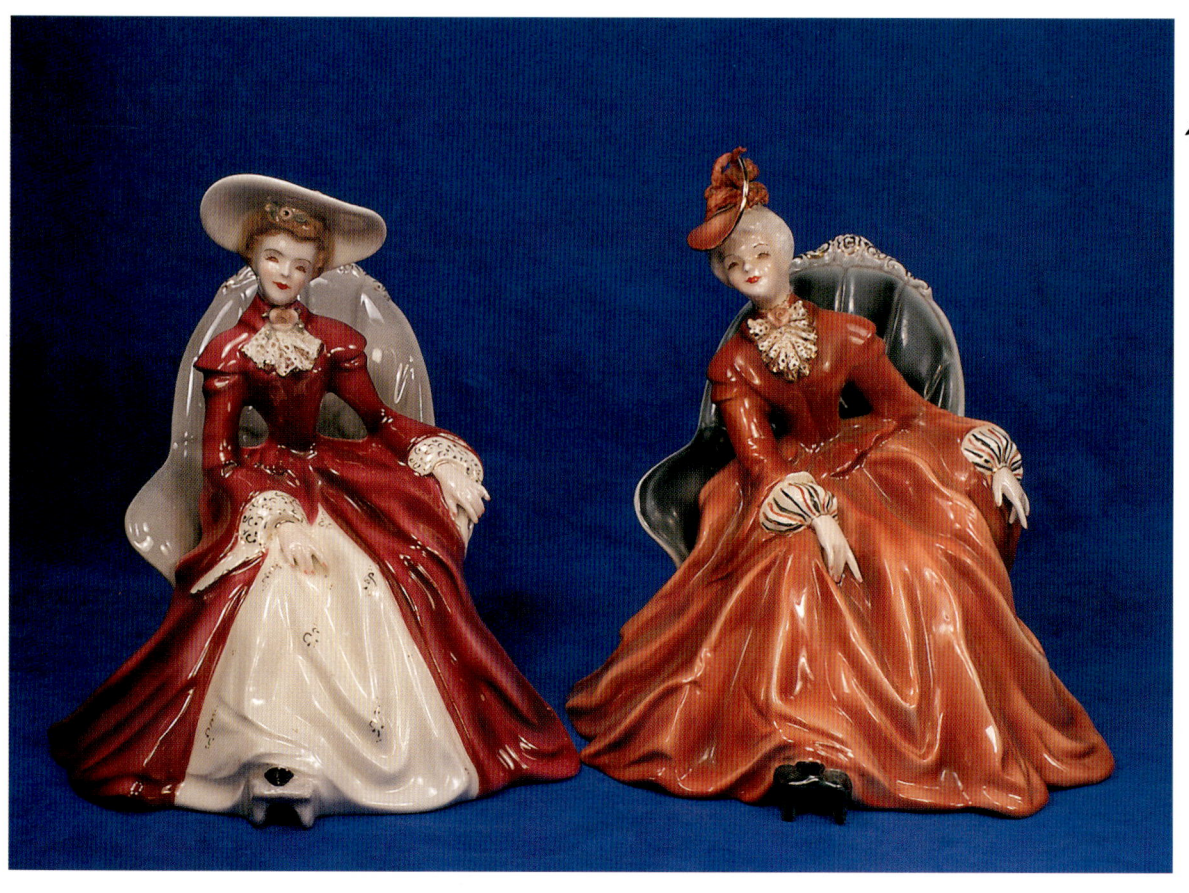

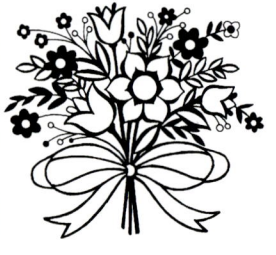

**Mary**, two styles, 7.5"
$650-700

Showcasing Florence A to Z 67

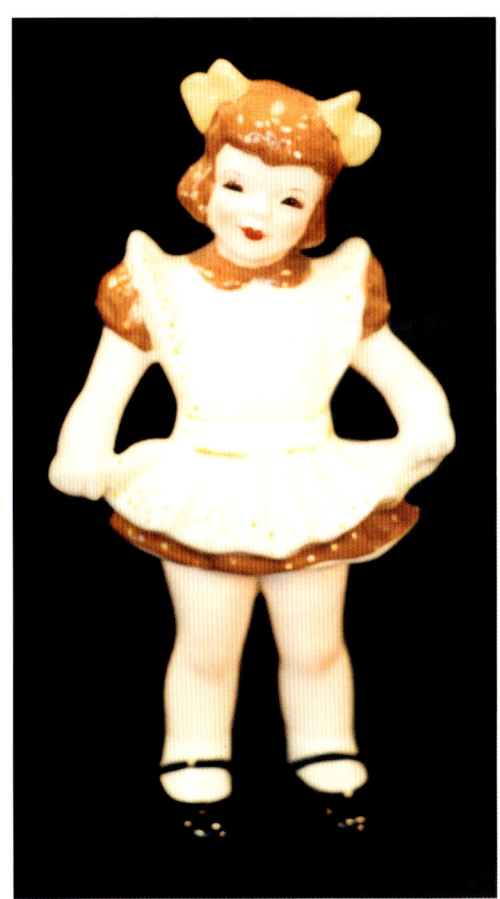

**Mary,** youth, 7.5"
$1,250-1,500

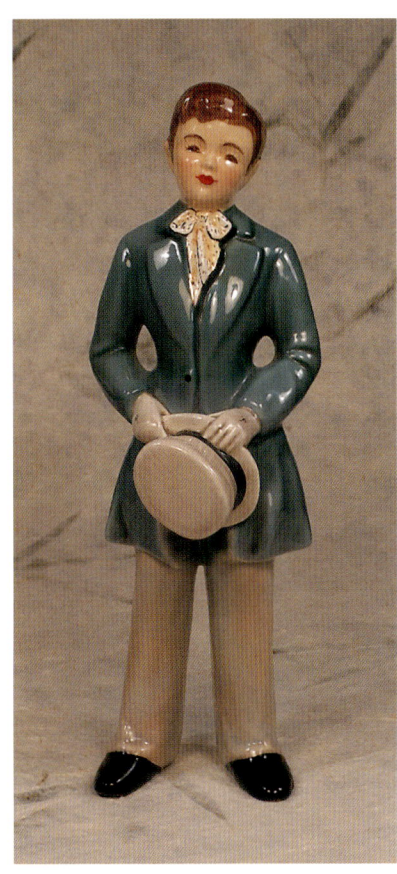

**Master David**, 8"
$500-550

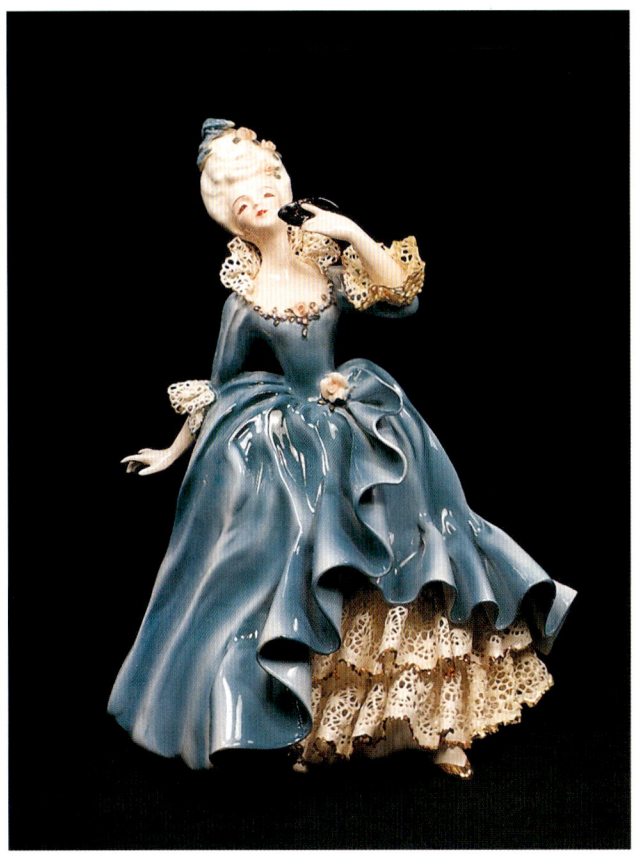

**Masquerade**, 8.25"
$800-900

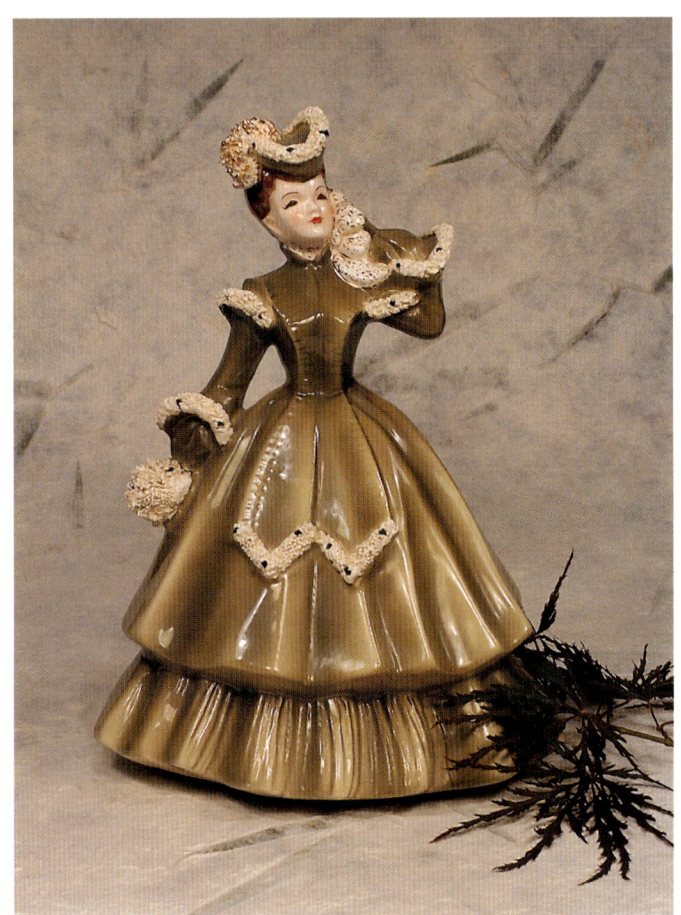

**Matilda**, 8.5"
$165-190

## 68  Showcasing Florence A to Z

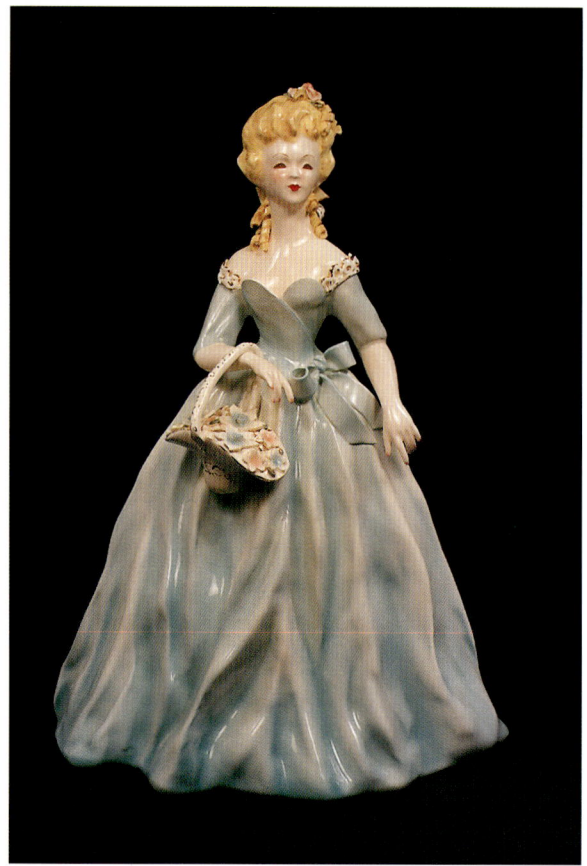

**Maybelle**, 10.5"
$2,500-2,700

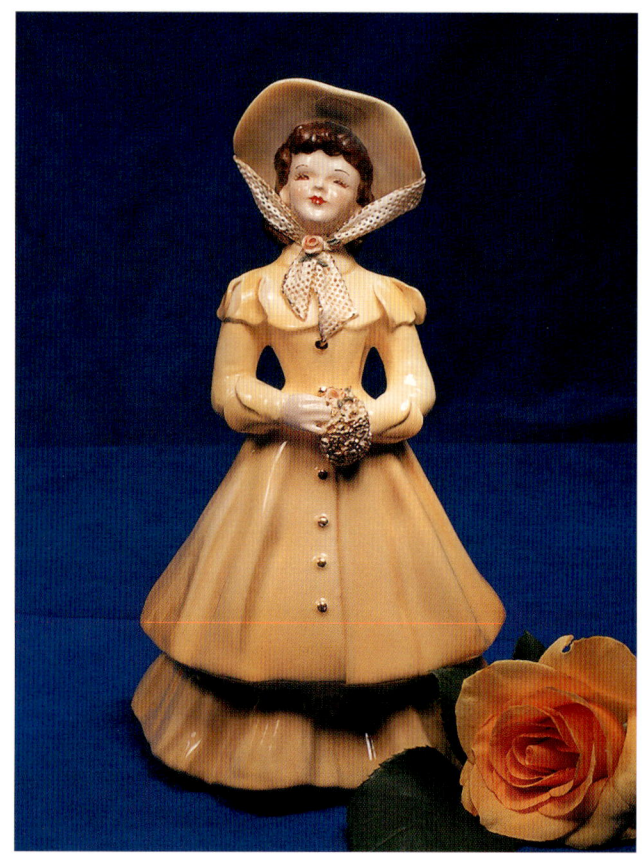

**Meg**, 7.75"
$250-300

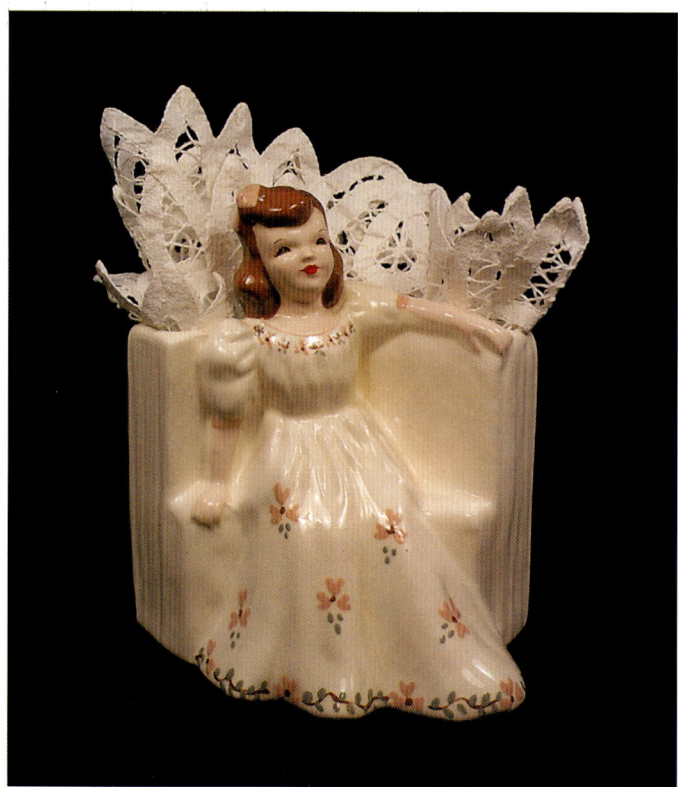

**May**, 6.5" (FH)
$50-60

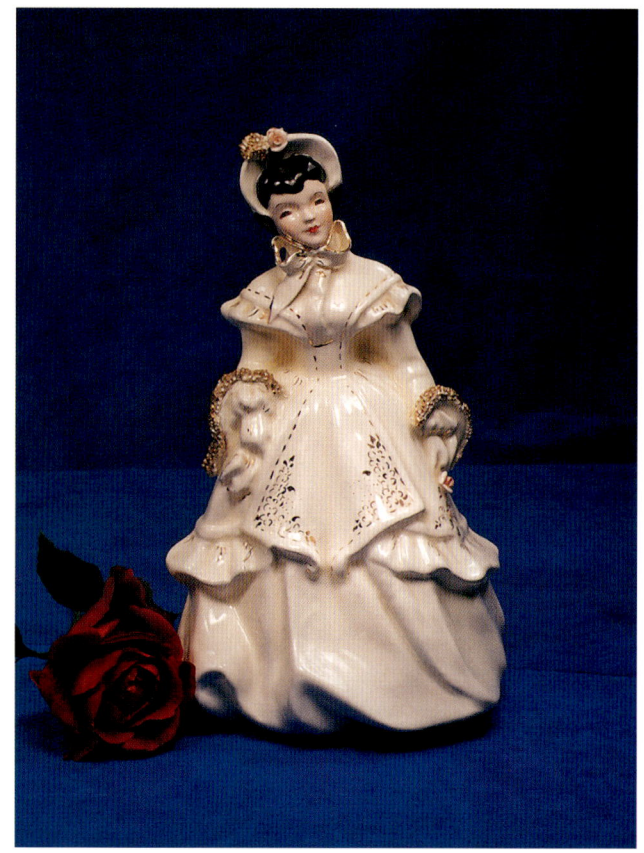

**Melanie**, 7.5"
$135-150

Showcasing Florence A to Z   69

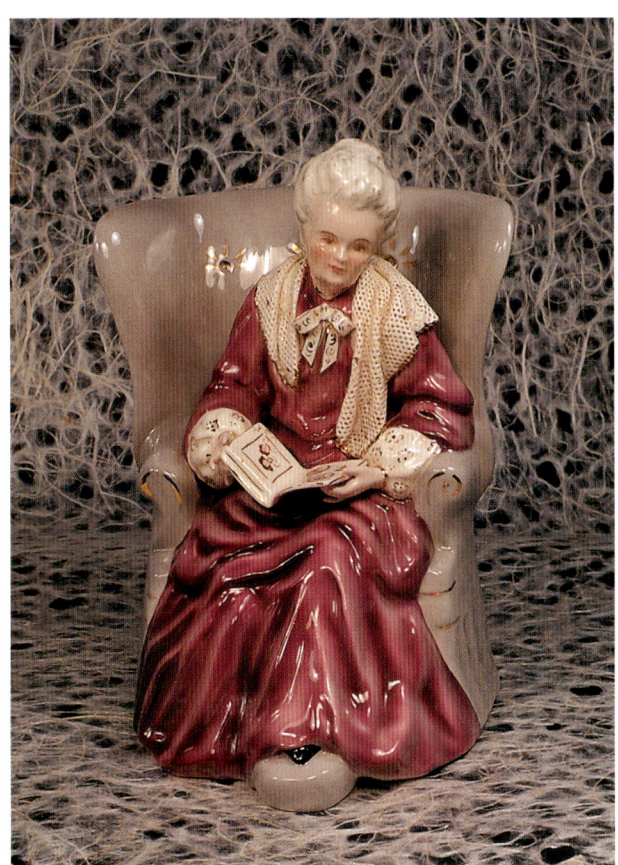

**Memories**, 7.5"
$1,250-1,400

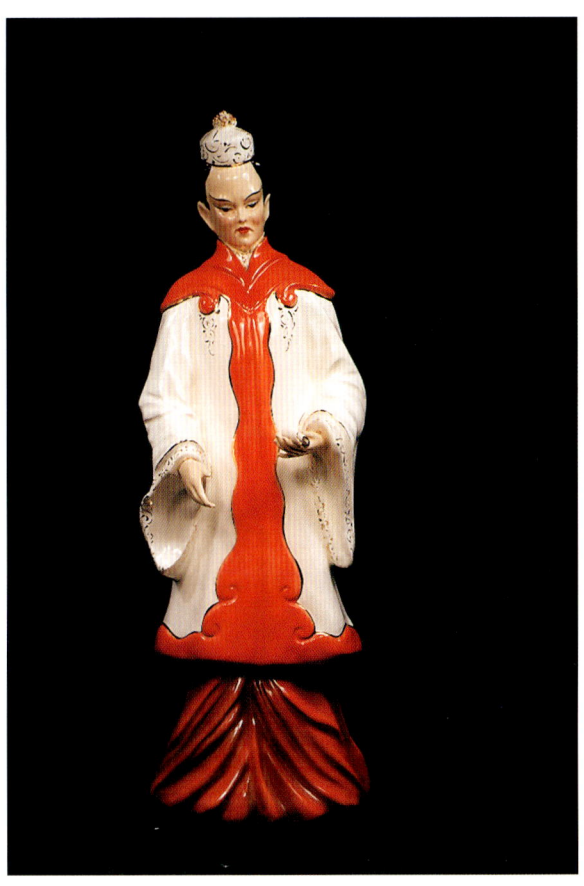

**Mikado**, 14"
$1,000-1,250

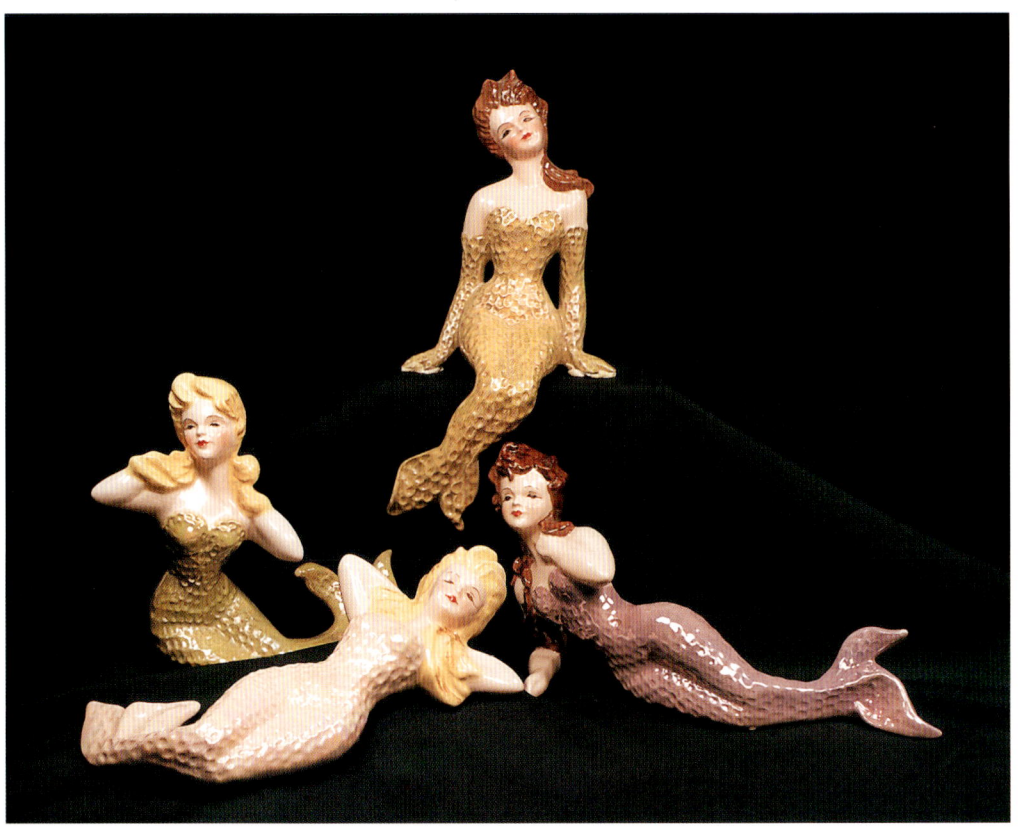

**Merrymaids: Betty** sitting, **Lil** reclining, **Jane** sitting, **Rosie** on side
Betty: $200-225; Lil: $400-450; Jane: $200-225; Rosie: $200-225

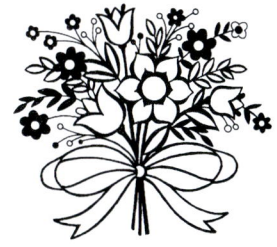

**70  Showcasing Florence A to Z**

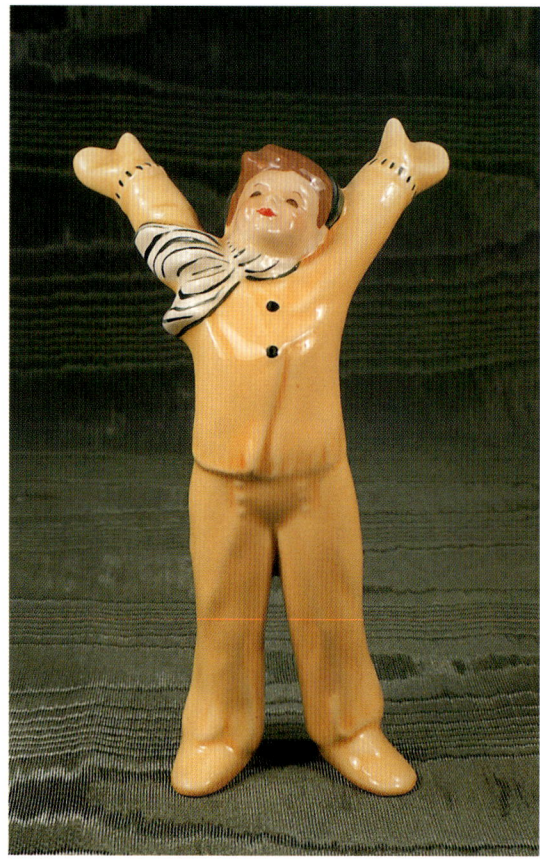

**Mike**, 6.25"
$200-225

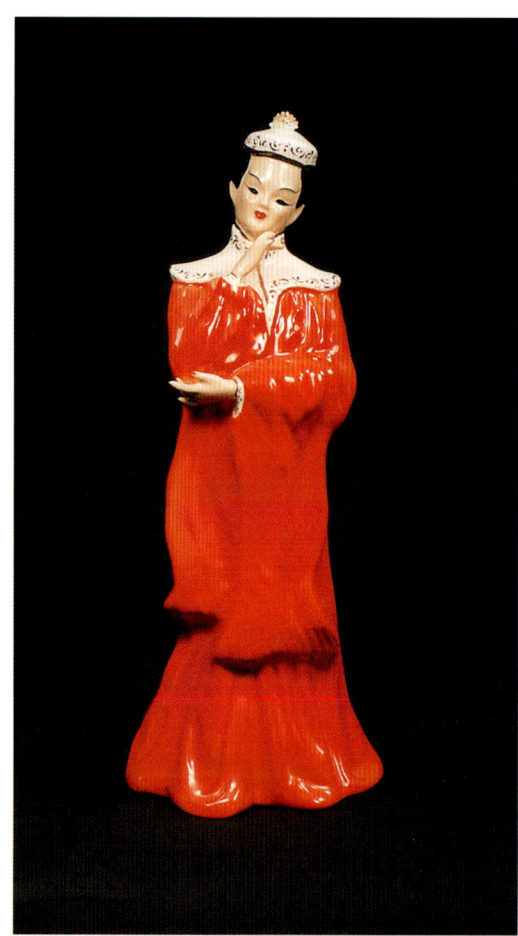

**Ming**, 9"
$325-350

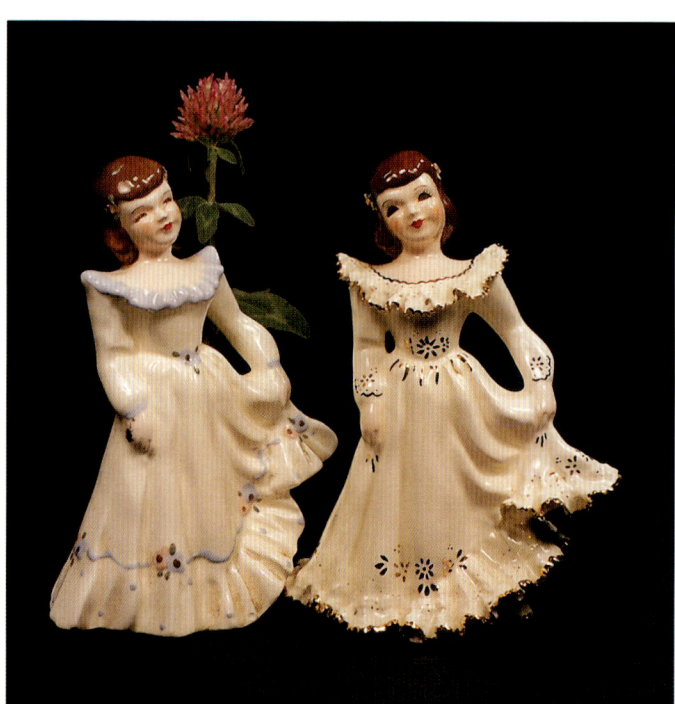

**Mimi**, 6" (FH), and **Mimi**, 6"
Left: $70-80; Right: $110-125

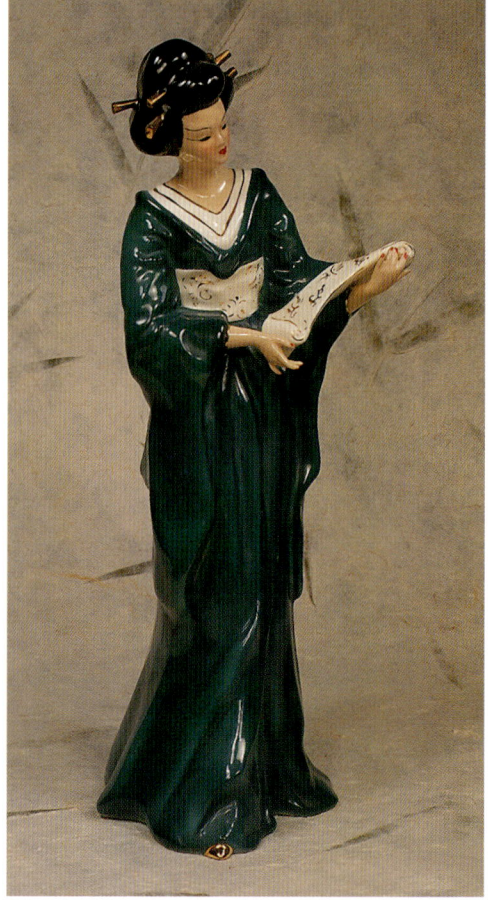

**Misha**, 11"
$350-400

Showcasing Florence A to Z   71

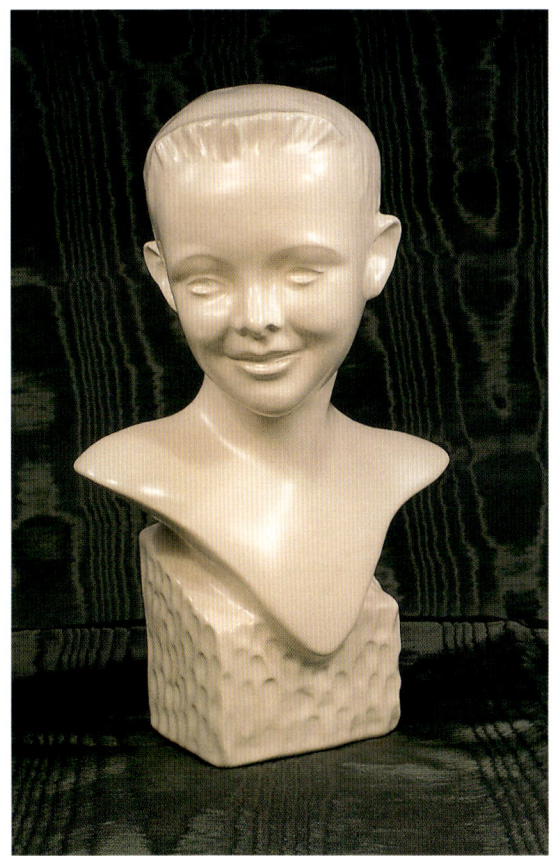

**Modern Boy**, 9.75"
$275-300

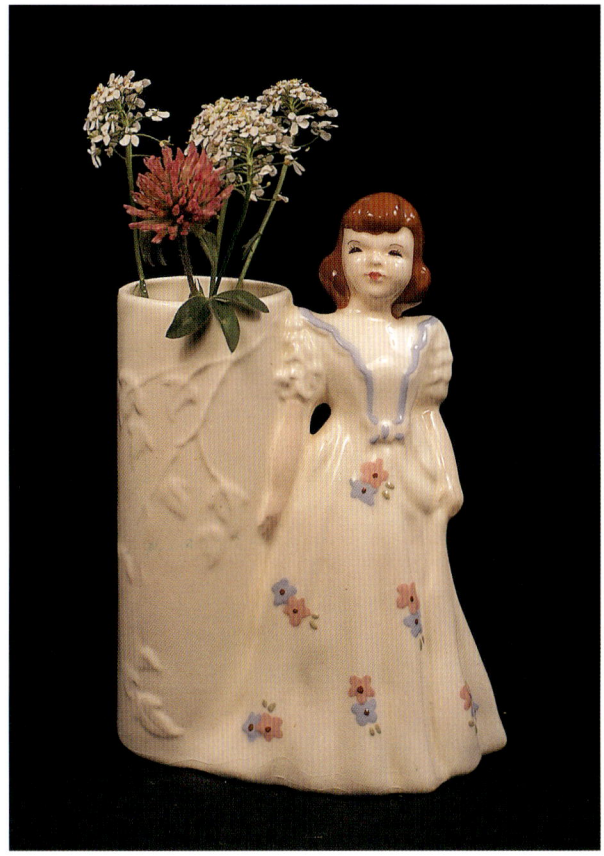

**Molly**, 6.5" (FH)
$50-60

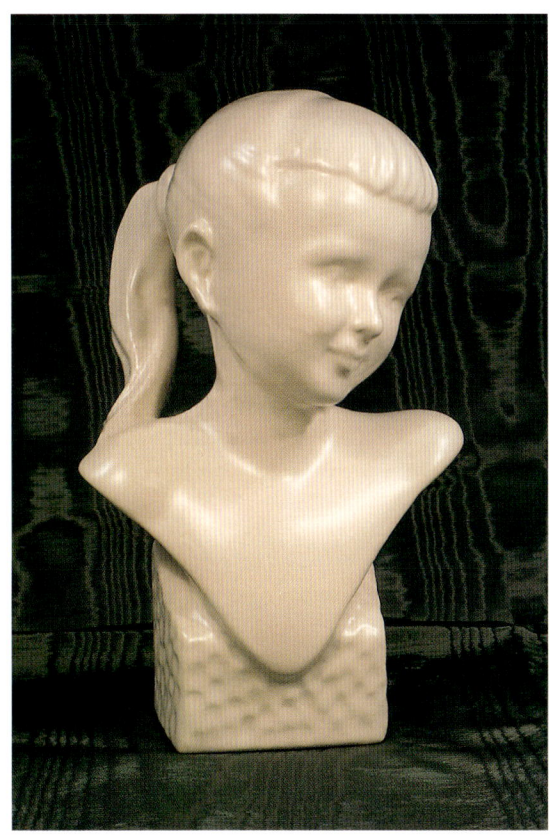

**Modern Girl**, 9.5"
$275-300

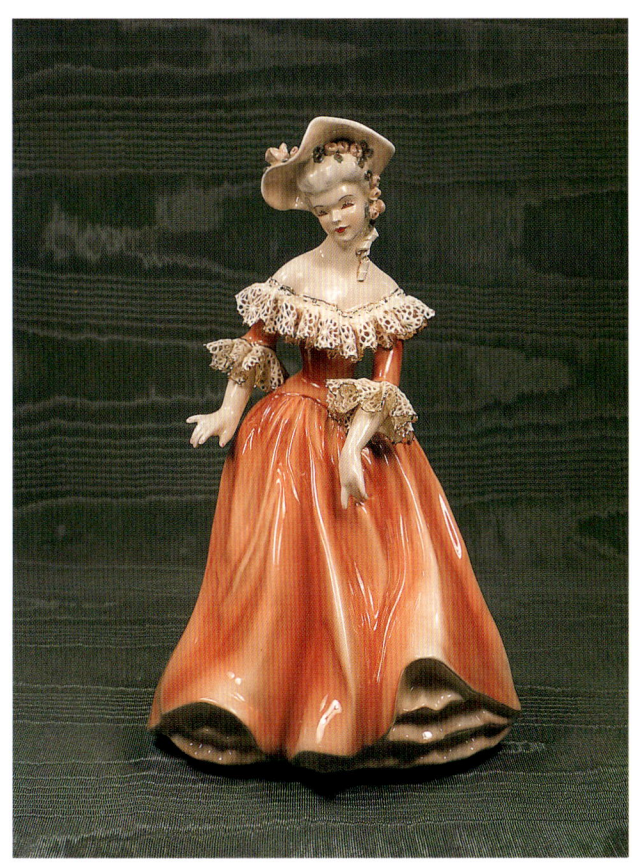

**Musette**, 8.75"
$600-650

## 72  Showcasing Florence A to Z

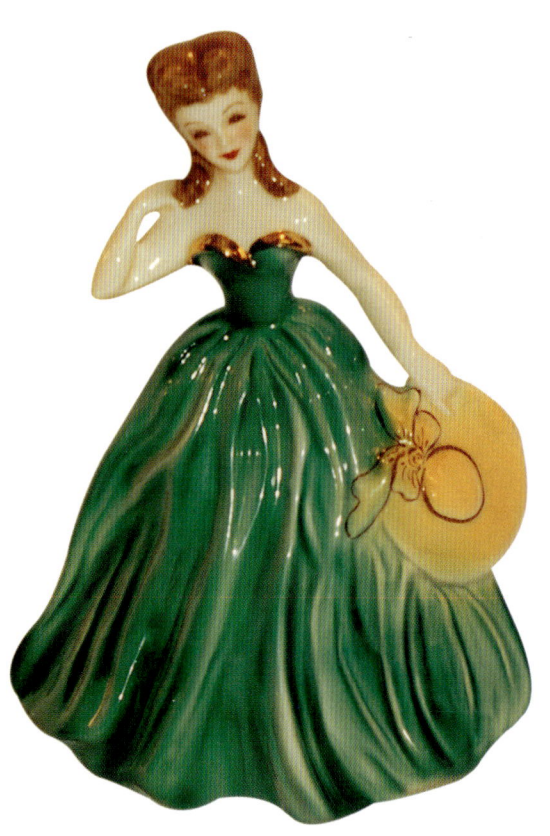

**Nancy**, 6.75"
$175-200

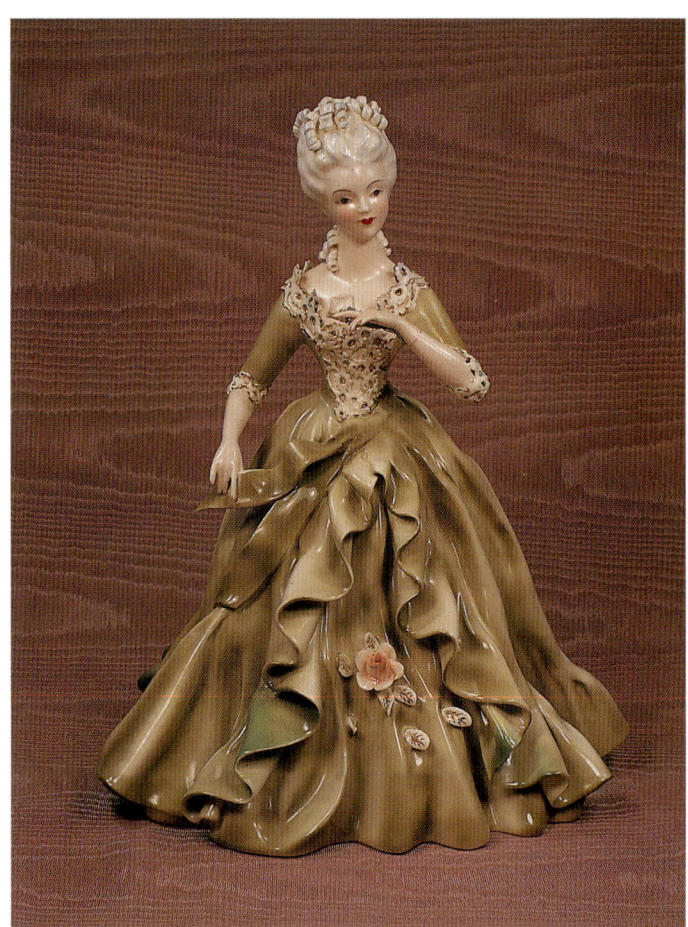

**Nell Gwynn**, 12"
$2,500-2,750

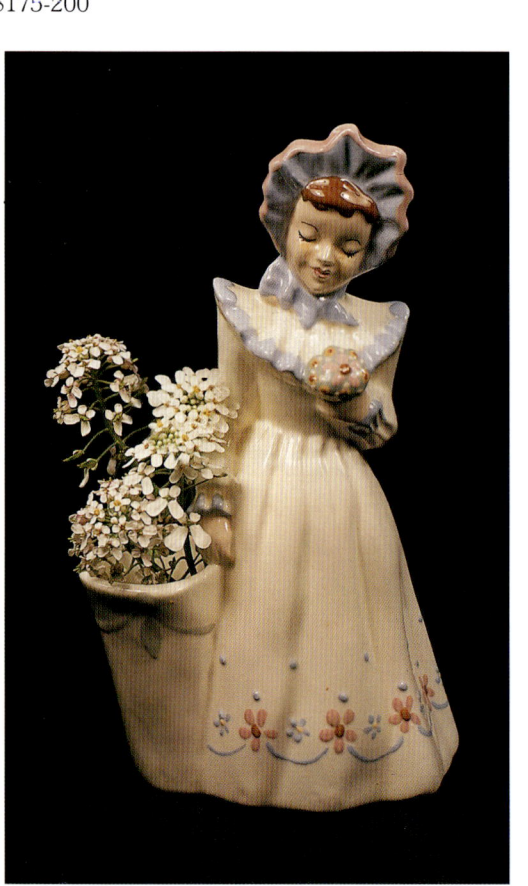

**Nan**, 7" (FH), *
$100-125

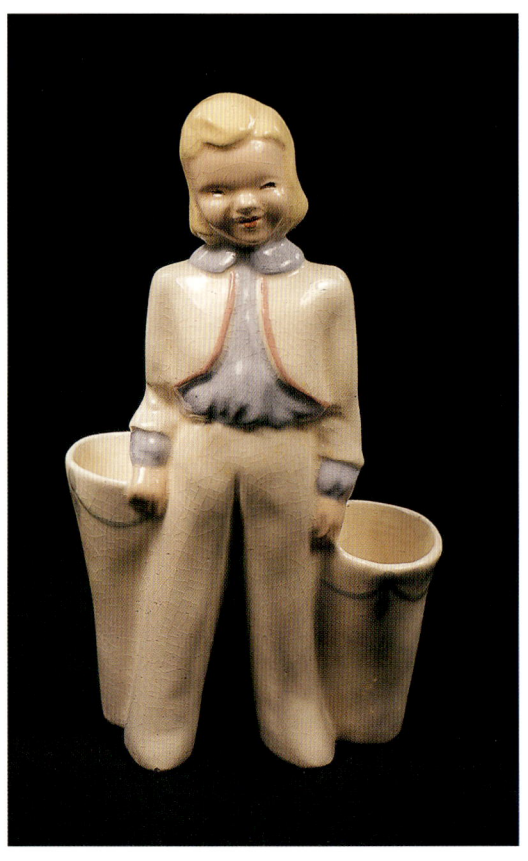

**Nick**, 7" (FH), *
$100-125

Showcasing Florence A to Z   73

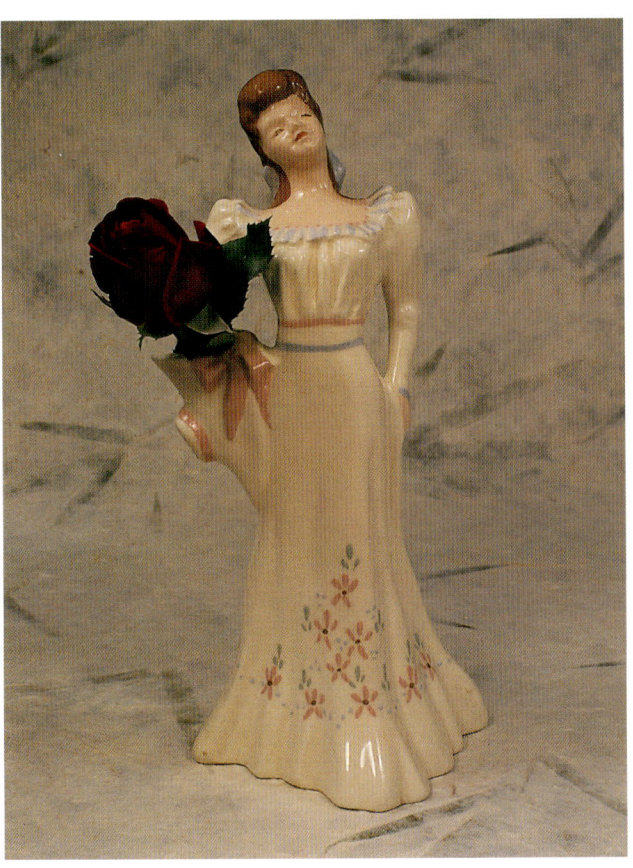

***Nina***, 8" (FH), *
$175-200

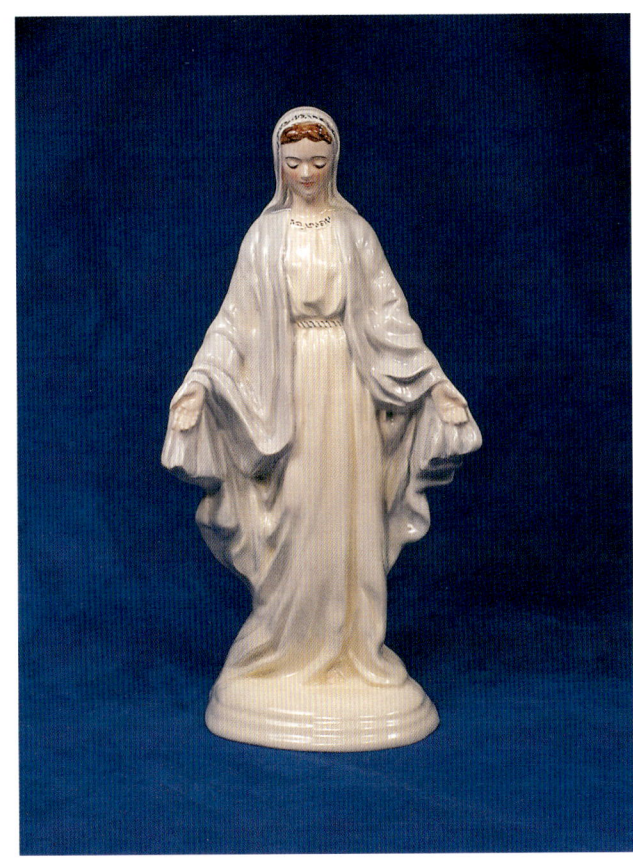

***Our Lady of Grace***, 9.75"
$250-300

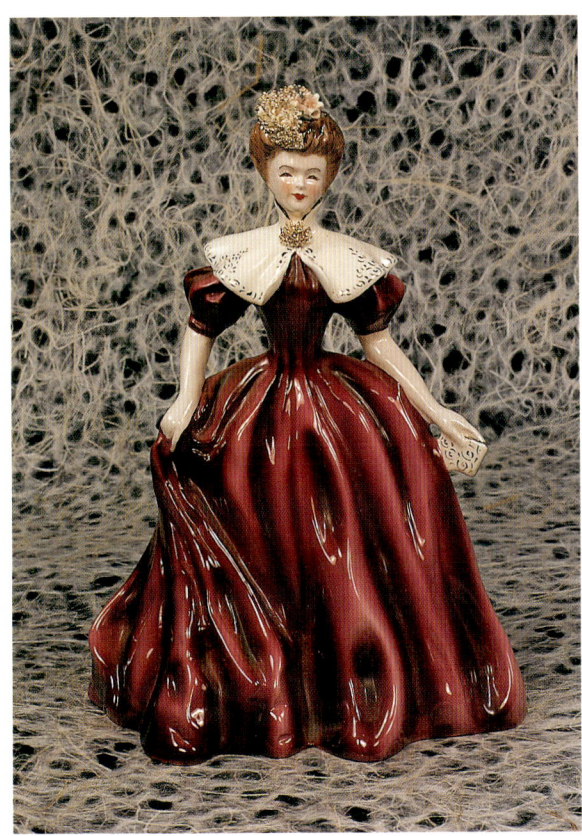

***Nita***, 8"
$500-550

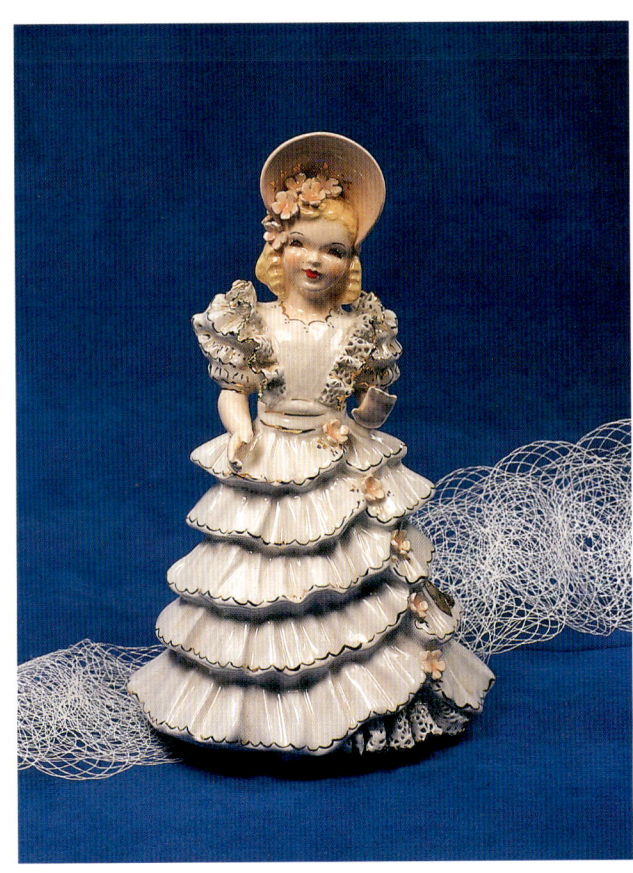

***Pamela,*** youth, 7.25"
$350-400

## 74  Showcasing Florence A to Z

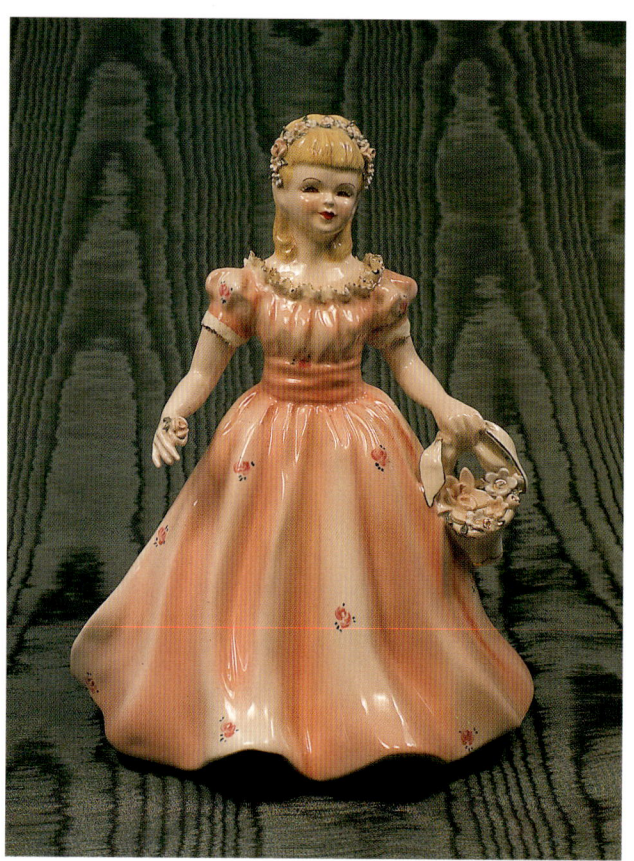

**Pamela,** with basket, 7.5"
$600-650

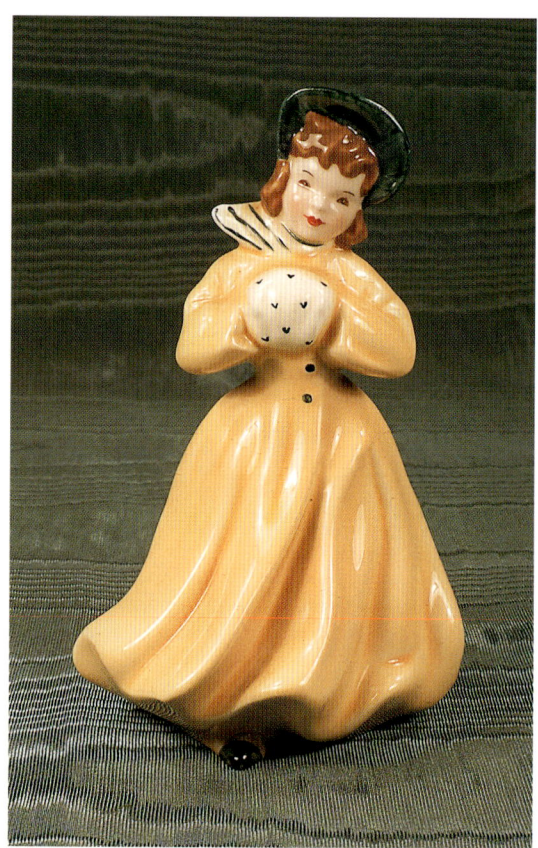

**Pat**, 6"
$170-190

**Pamela** bust, 11.5"
$275-300

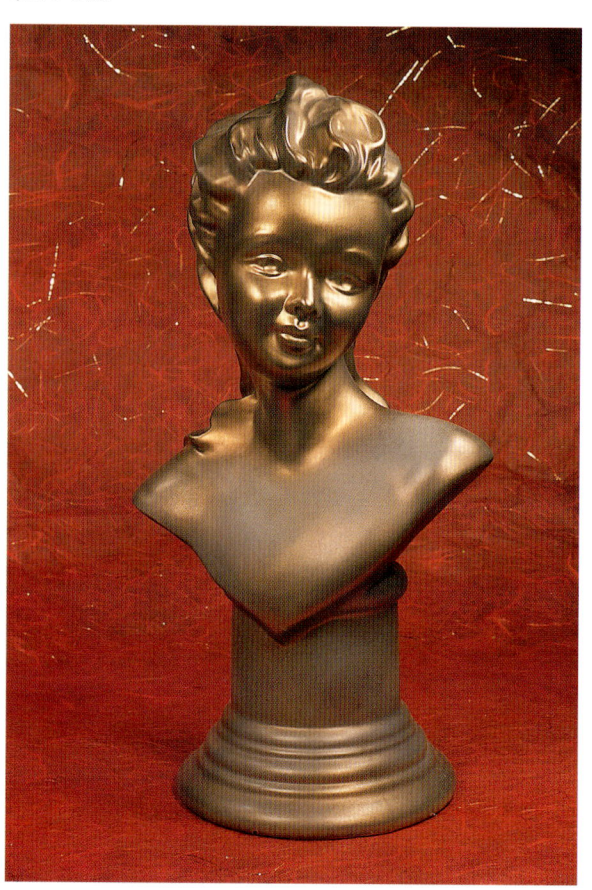

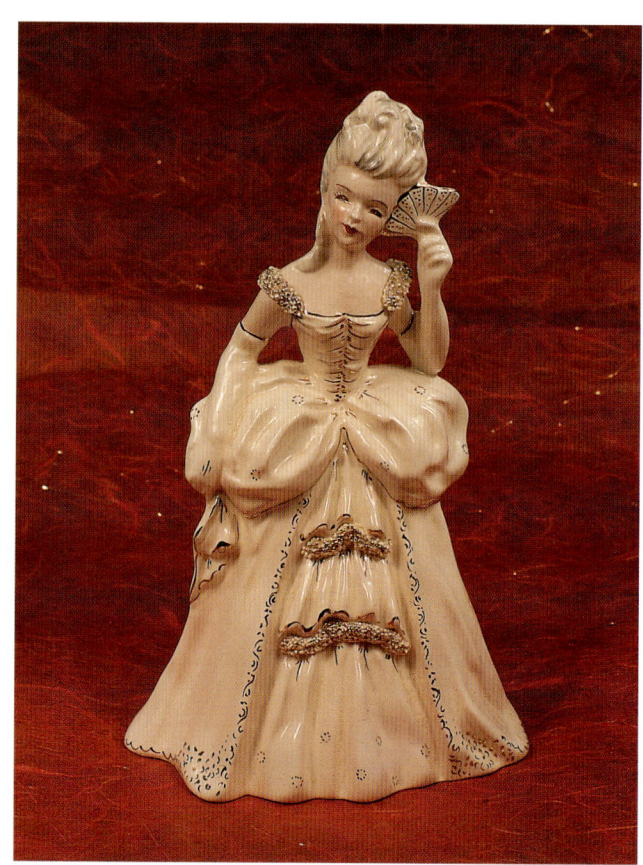

**Patrice**, 7.25"
$200-225

Showcasing Florence A to Z  75

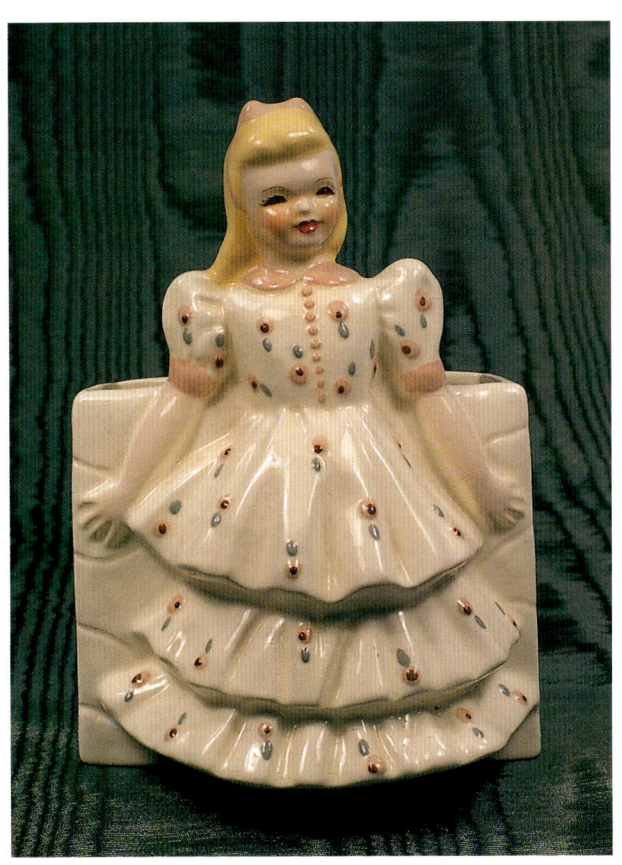

**Patsy**, 6" (FH)
$50-60

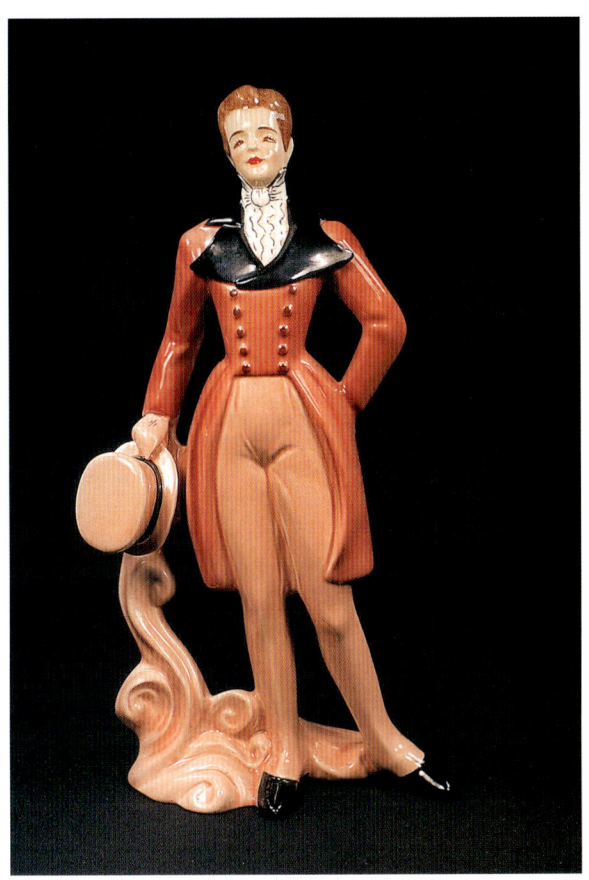

**Peter**, 9.25"
$500-550

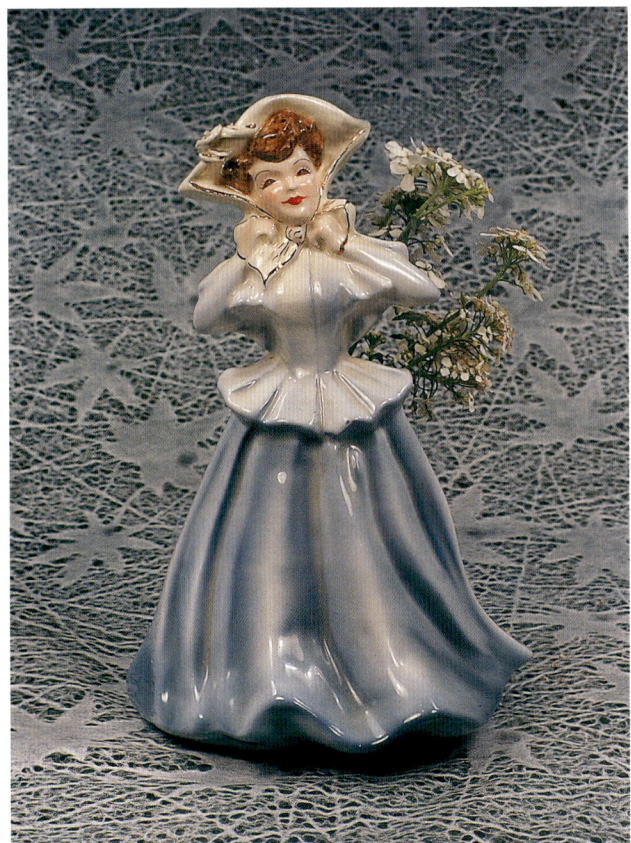

**Peg**, 7" (FH)
$140-150

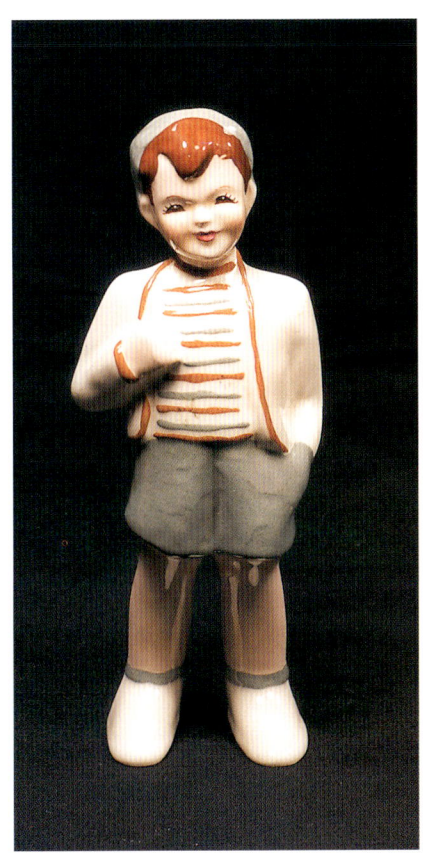

**Peter**, child, 5.5"
$175-200

## 76 Showcasing Florence A to Z

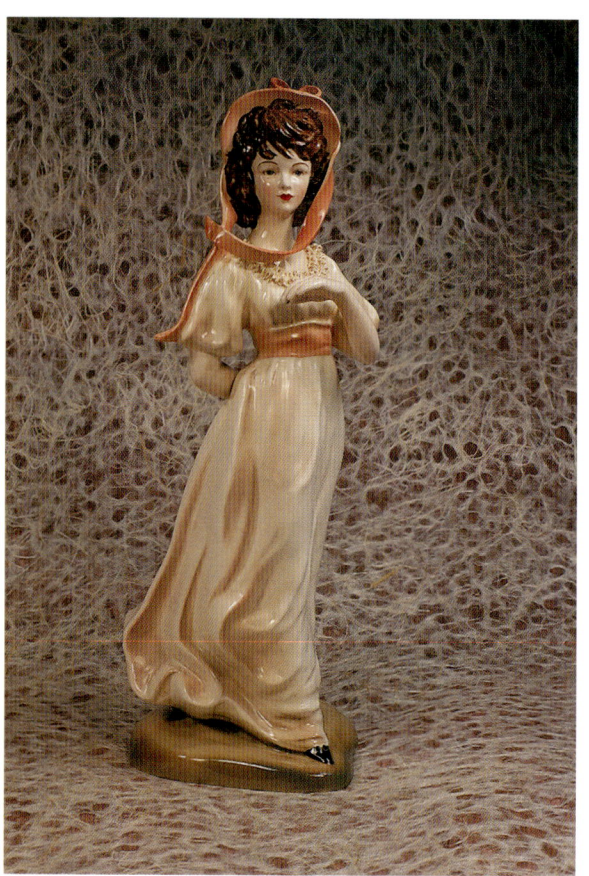

**Pinkie**, 12"
$400-450

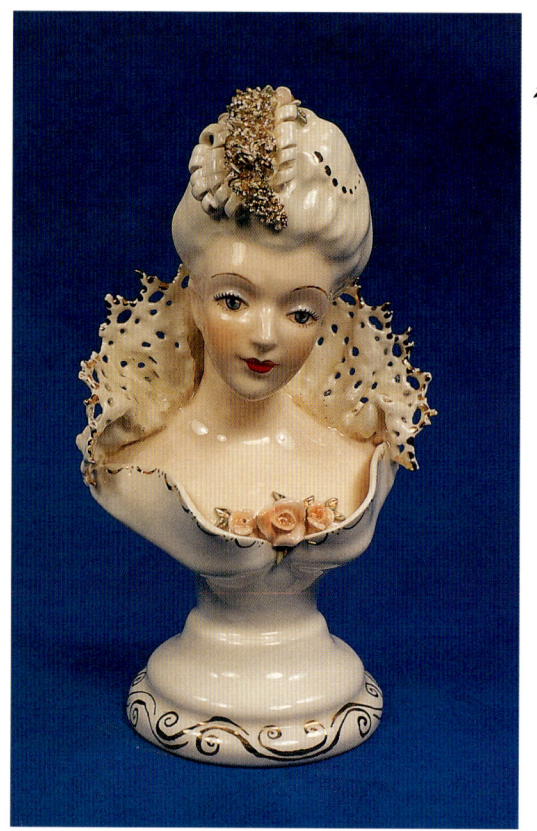

**Pompadour**, 6.5"
$400-450

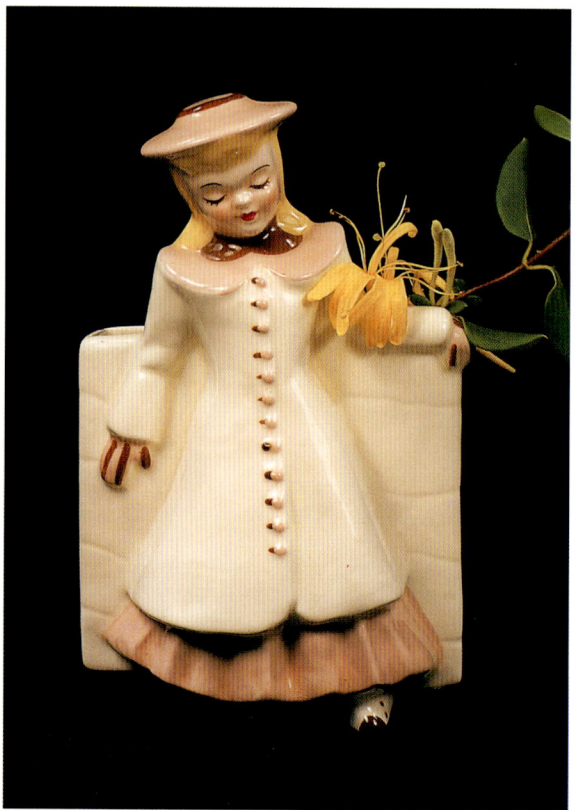

**Polly**, 6" (FH)
$50-60

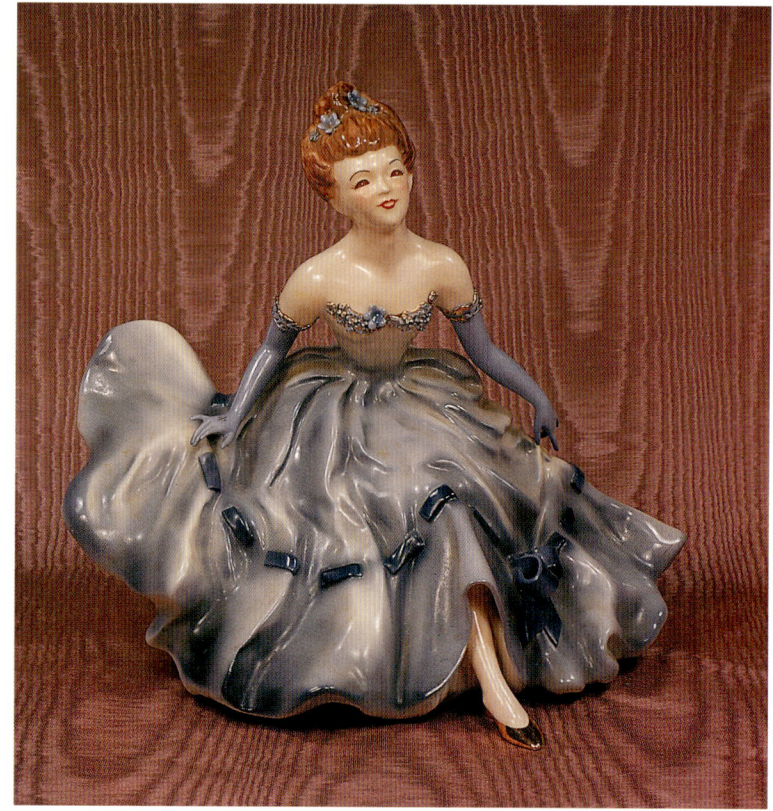

**Portrait**, 8.5"
$2,250-2,500

Showcasing Florence A to Z 77

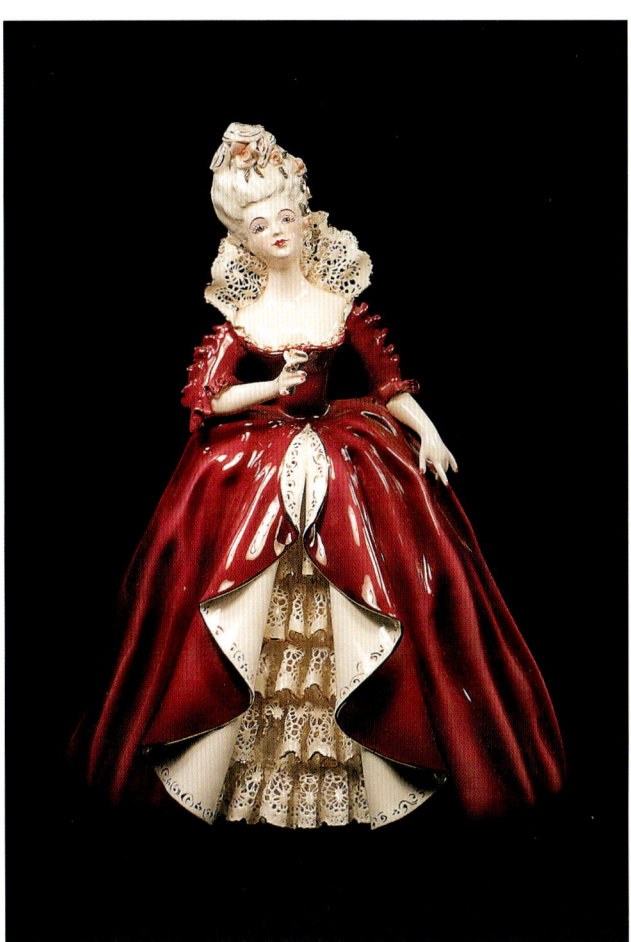

**Prima Donna**, 10"
$1,000-1,200

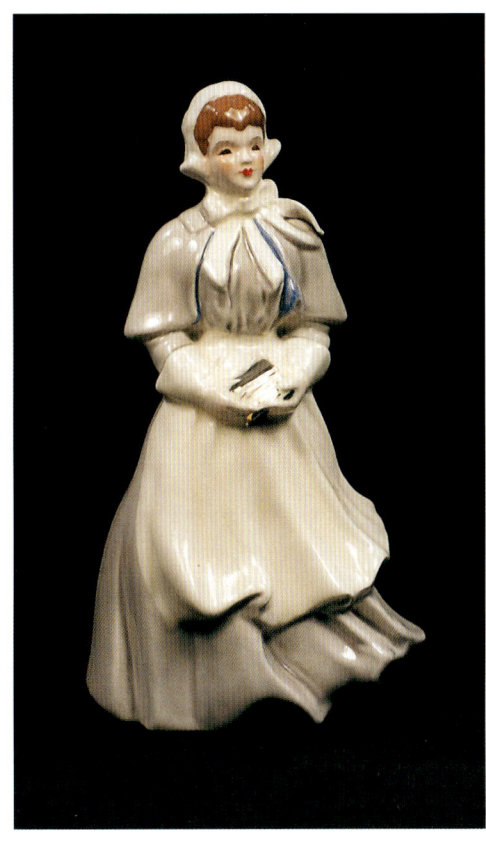

**Priscilla**, 7.75"
$275-300

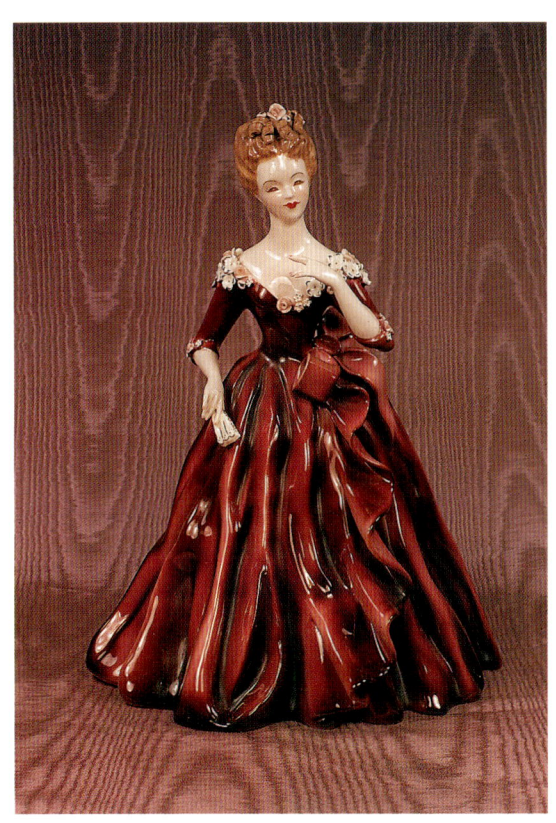

**Princess**, 10.25"
$1,150-1,250

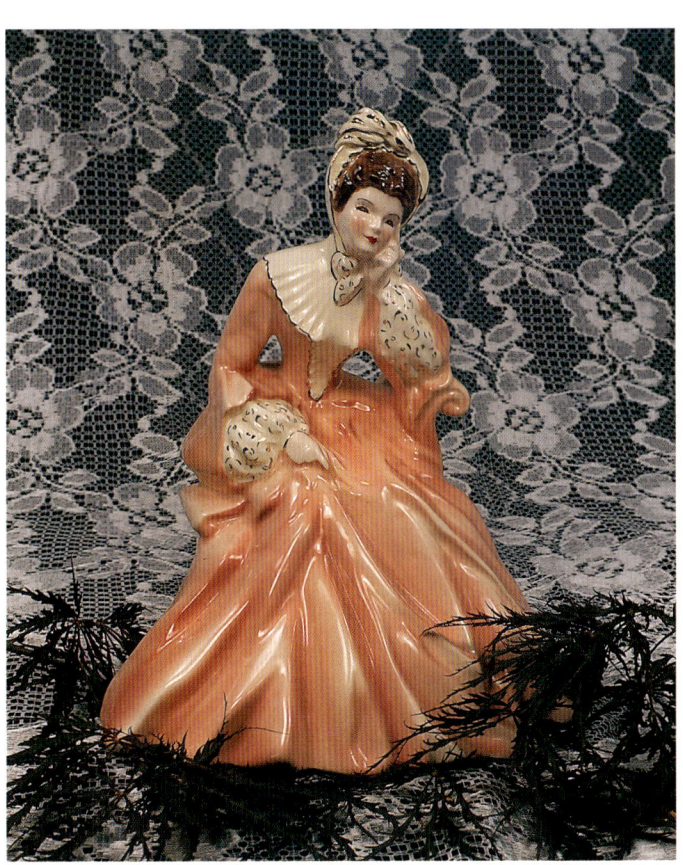

**Rebecca**, 7"
$225-250

## 78 Showcasing Florence A to Z

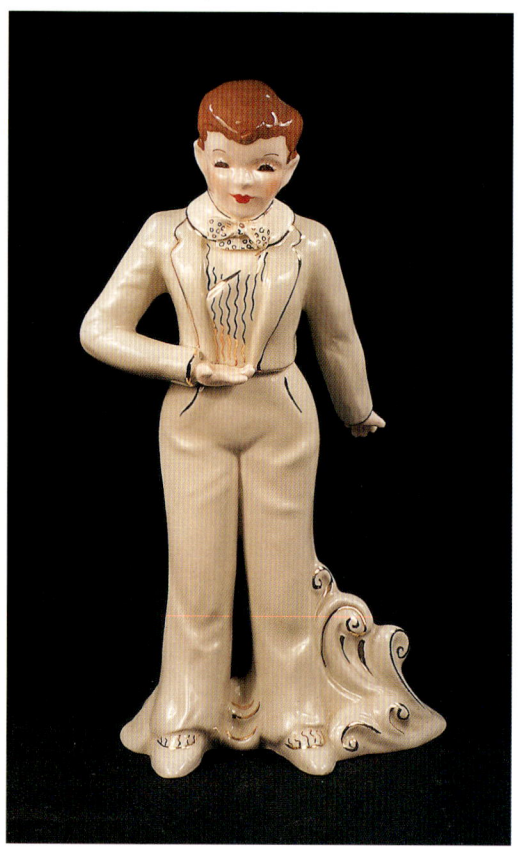

**Reggie**, 7.5"
$400-450

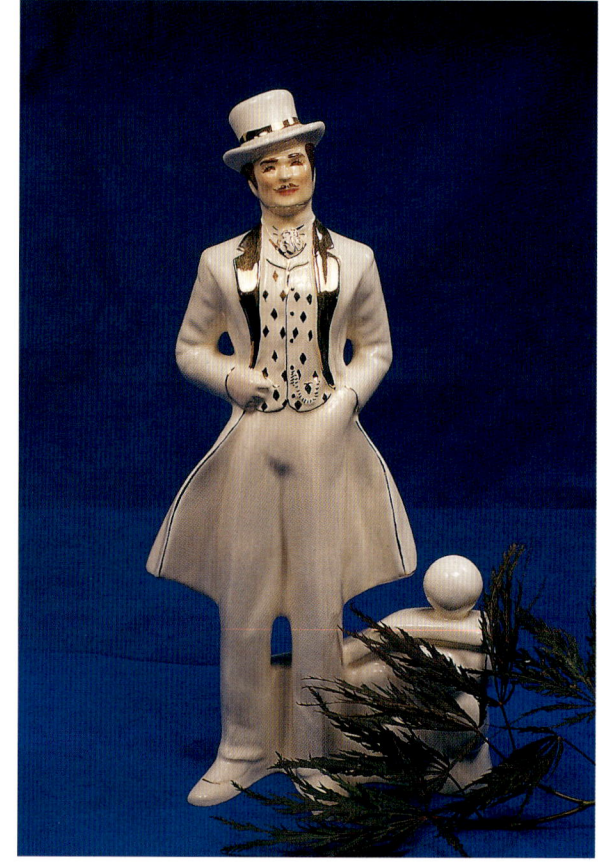

**Rhett,** by stone wall, 9"
$325-375

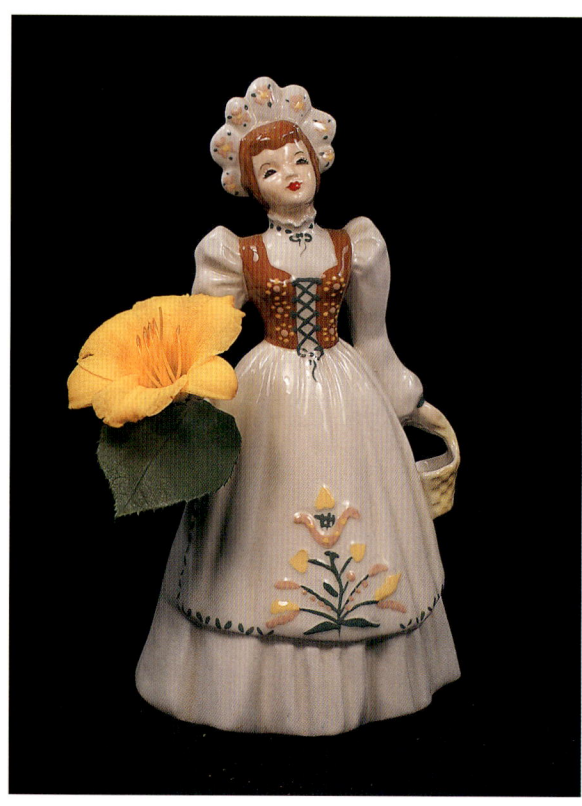

**Rene**, 9" (FH)
$180-200

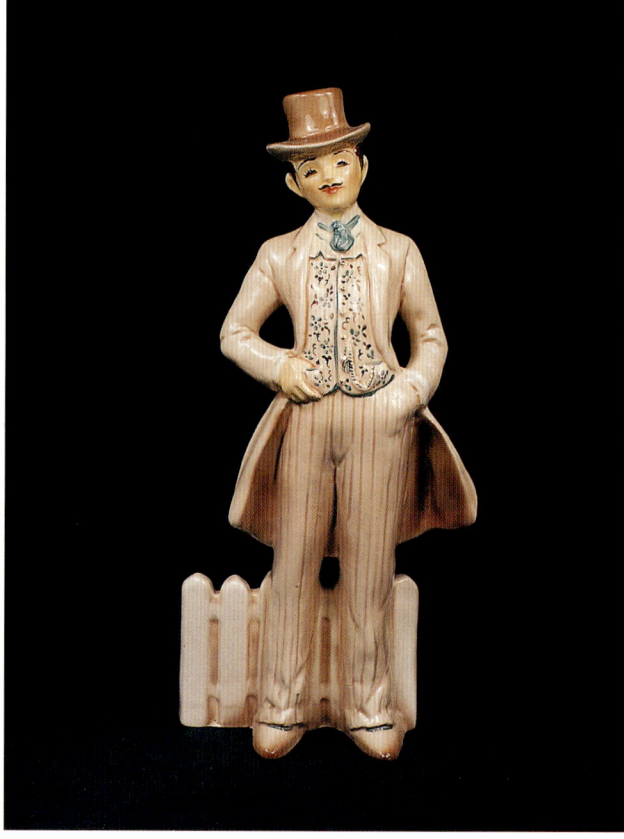

**Rhett**, by picket fence, 9"
$400-450

Showcasing Florence A to Z   79

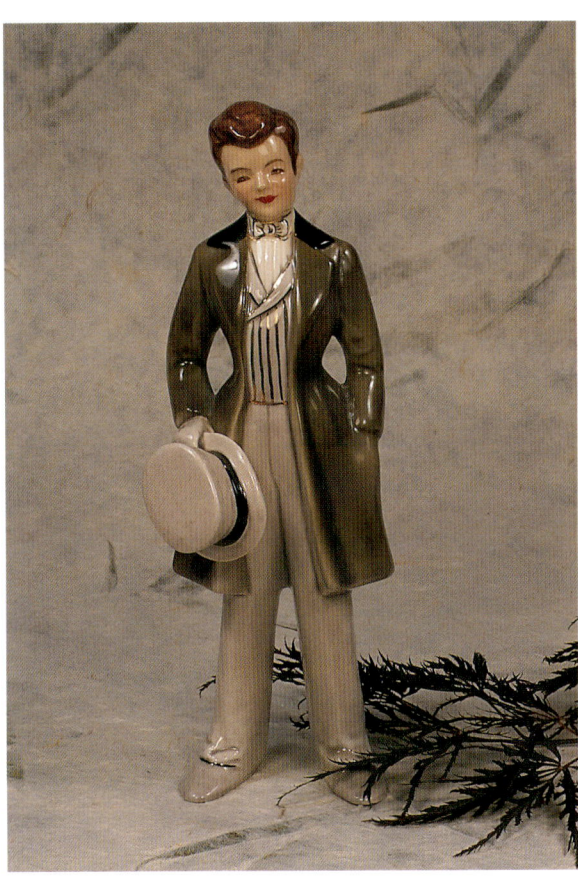

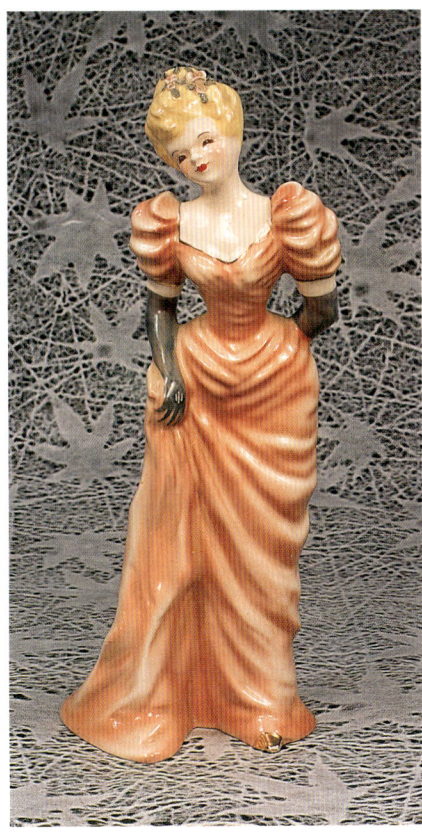

***Roberta***, 8.5"
$350-375

***Richard***, 8.5"
$500-550

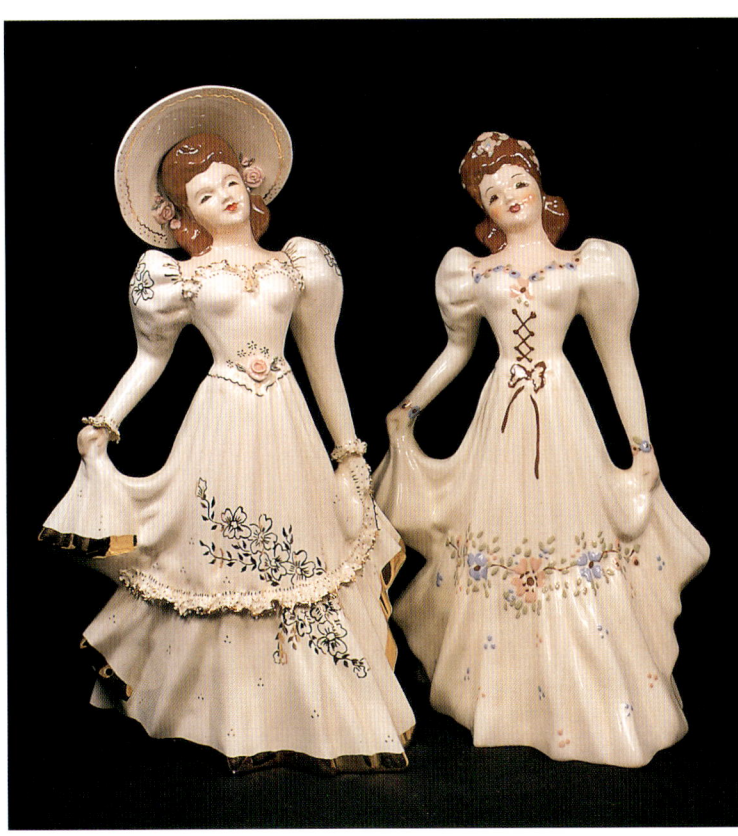

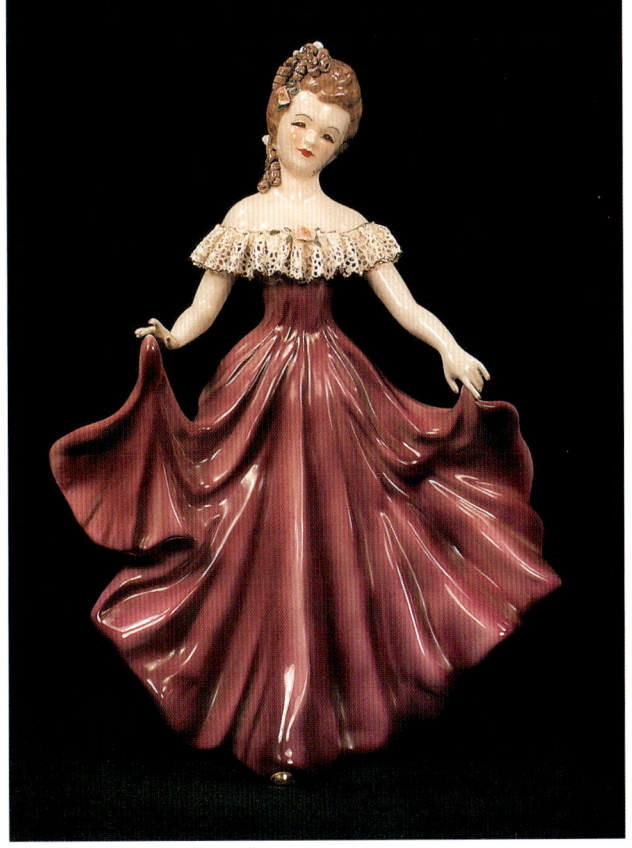

Left: ***Rita***, 9.25"; Right ***Rita***, 9.25" (FH)
Left: $250-300; Right: $200-225

***Rosalie***, 9.5"
$1,000-1,100

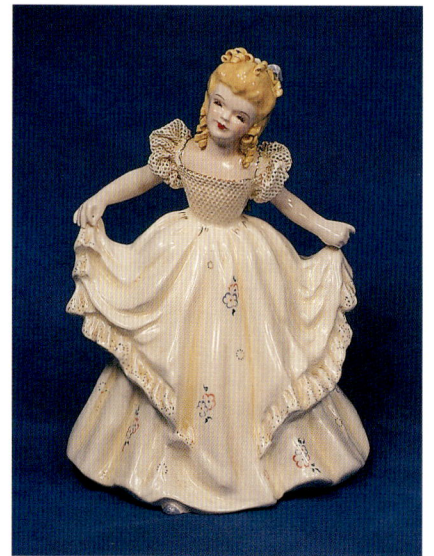

**Rose Marie,** youth, 7"
$400-450

**Rose Marie,** adult, 9.5"
$1,200-1,400

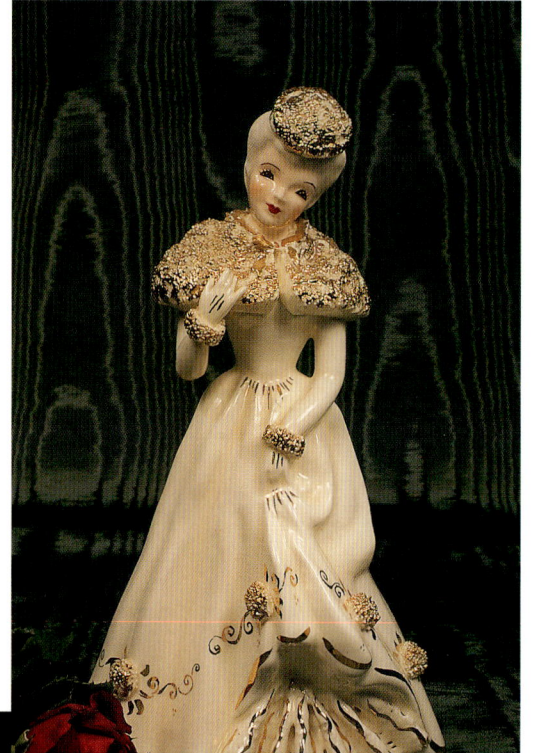

**Ruth,** with cape, 8.5"
$350-400

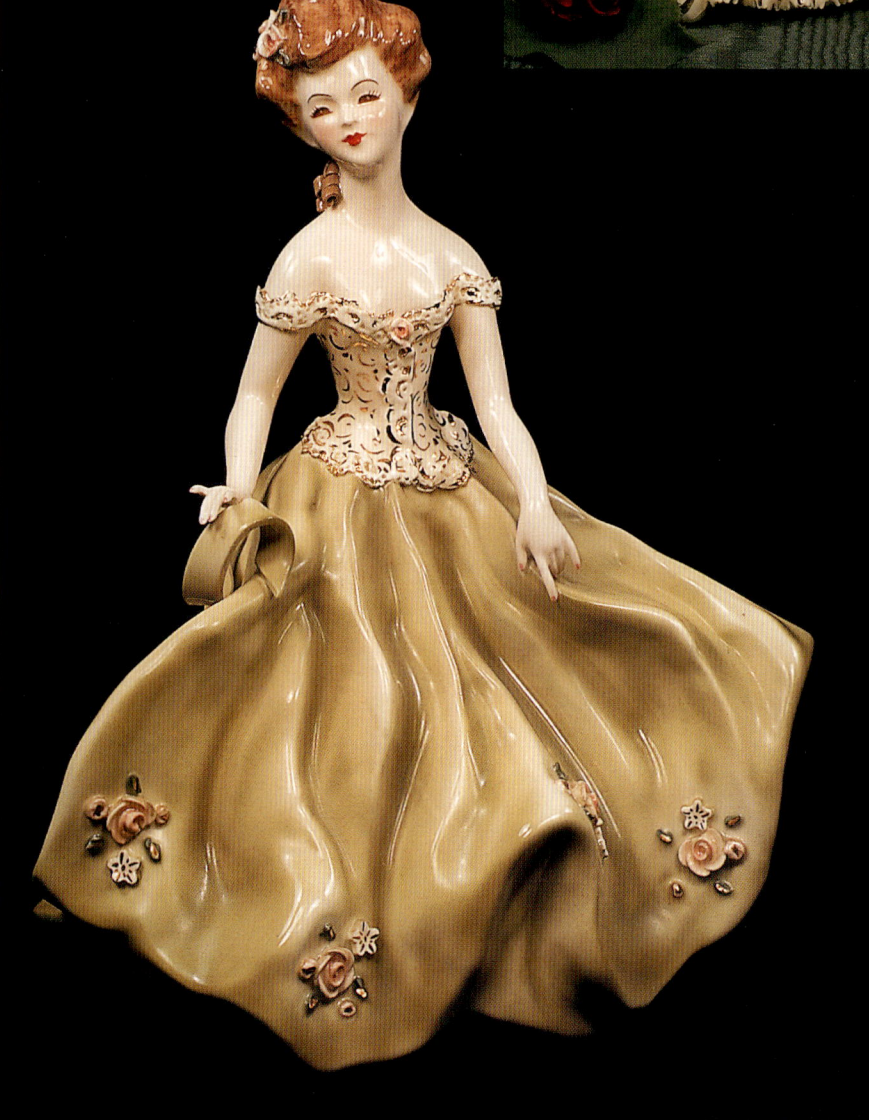

**Ruth,** with high neck dress, 8.5"
$350-400

**Showcasing Florence A to Z  81**

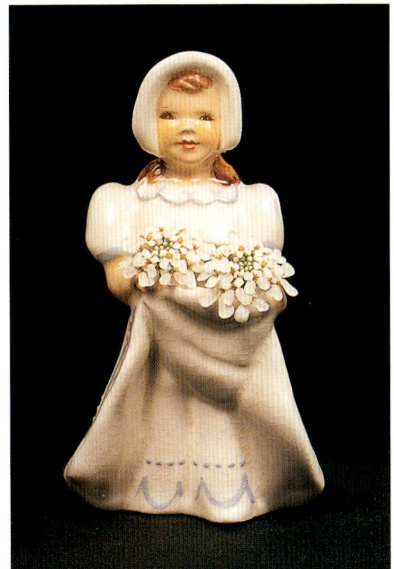

***Sabrina***, 5.25" (FH), *
$75-100

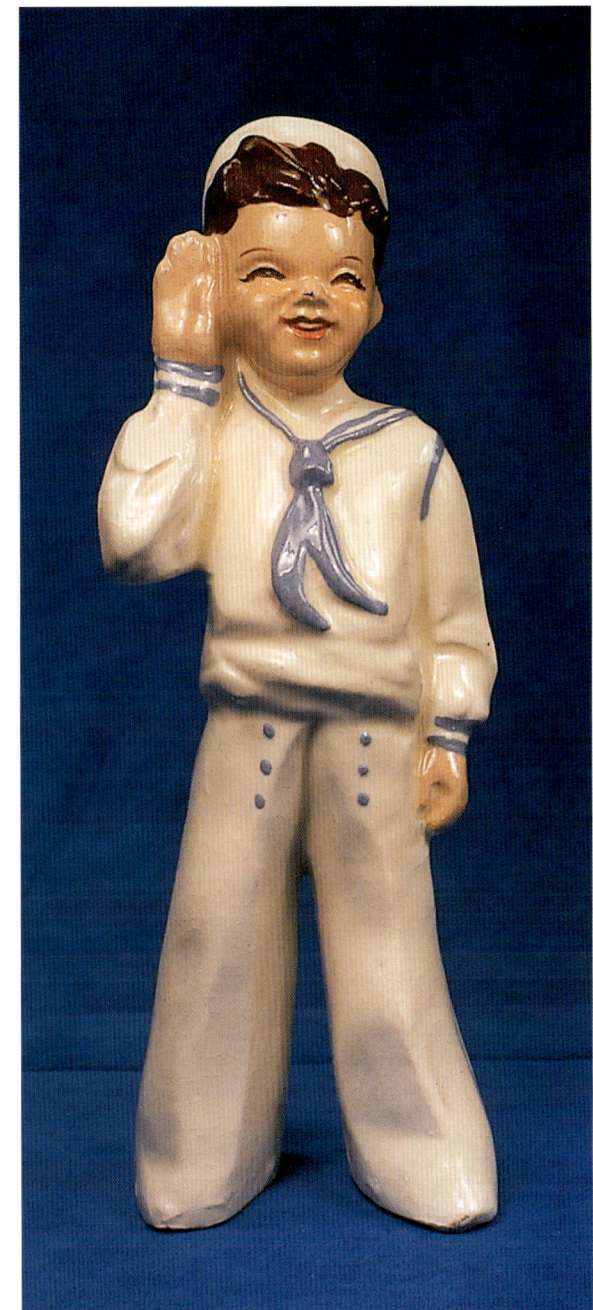

***Sailor Boy***, 6.75"
$300-350

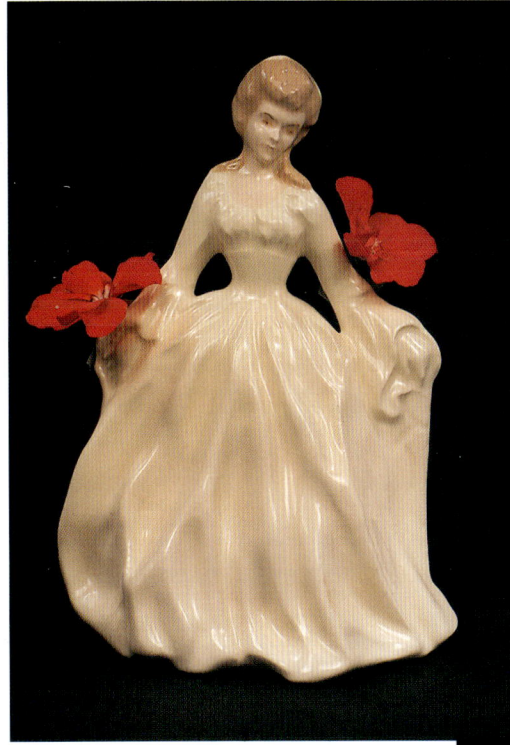

***Sadie***, 6.5" (FH), *
$90-110

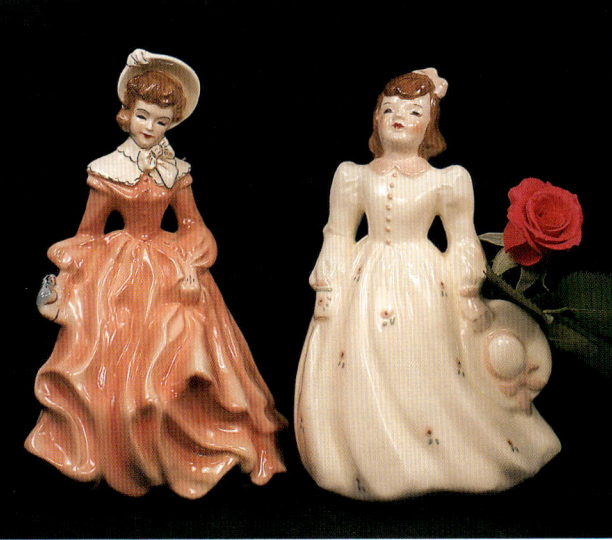

Left: ***Sally***, 6.75"; Right:
***Sally***, 6.75" (FH)
Left: $175-200; Right:
$100-115

## 82 Showcasing Florence A to Z

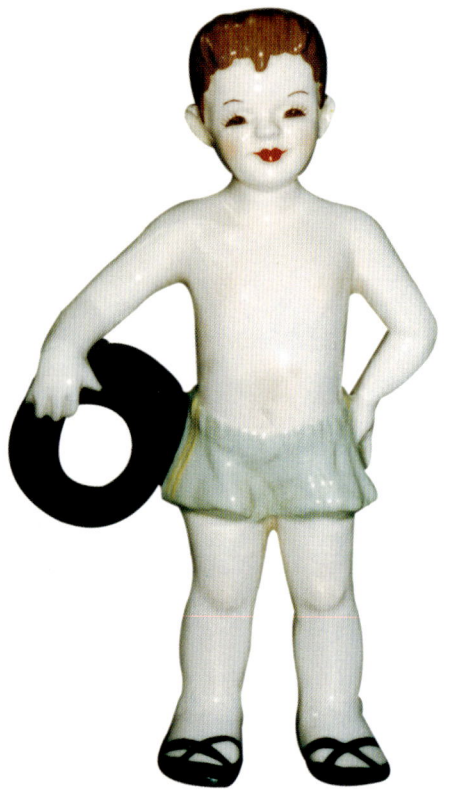

**Sandy,** youth, 7.5"
$1,250-1,500

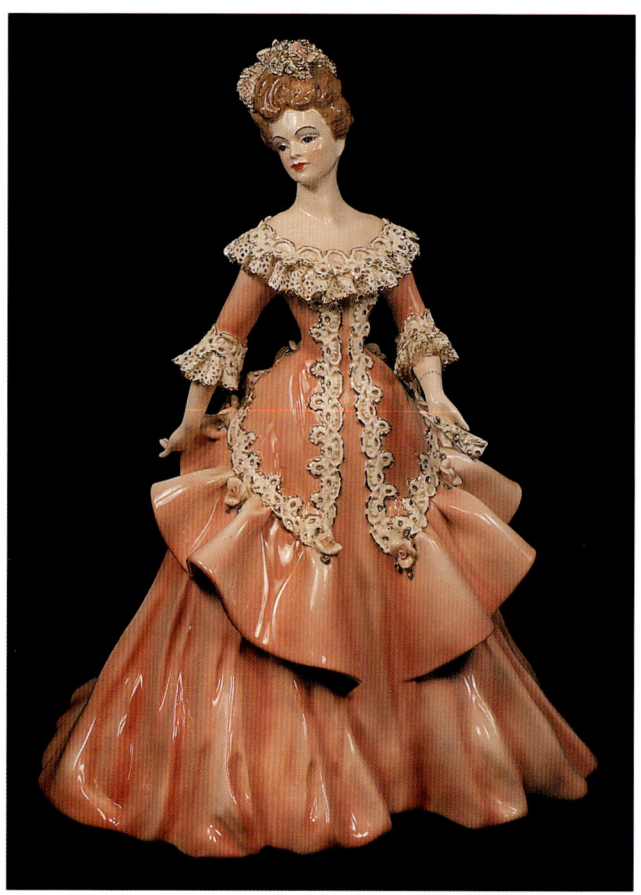

**Sarah Bernhardt**, 13.25"
$3,800-4,200

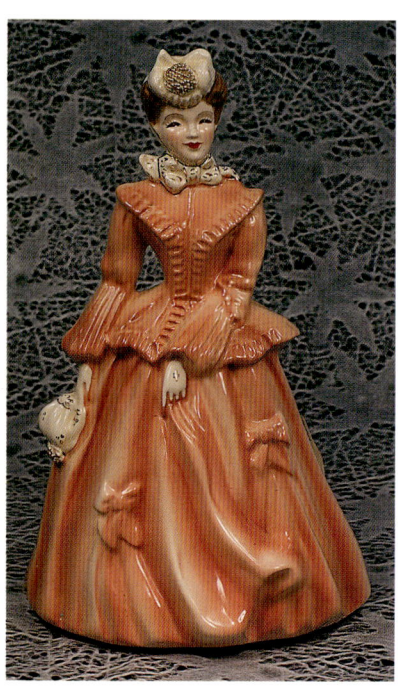

**Sarah**, 7.5"
$125-140

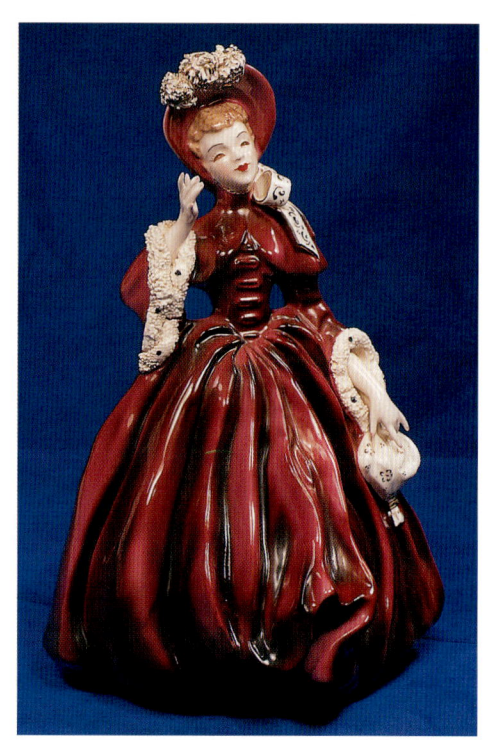

**Scarlett**, both hands articulated, 8.75"
$500-550 with both hands articulated
$400-450 with one hand articulated
$200-250 with hands in muff

Showcasing Florence A to Z  83

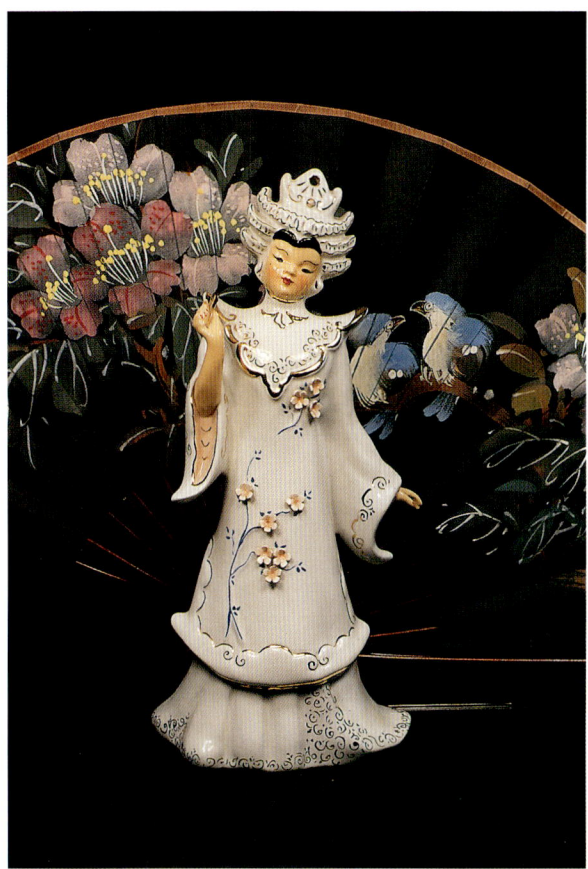

**She-Ti**, 10.25"
$225-250

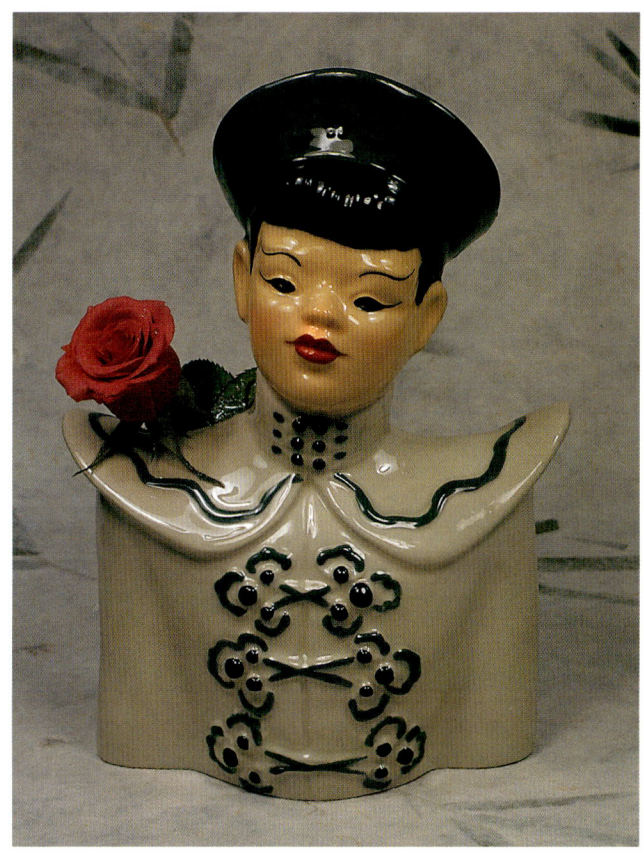

**Shen**, 7.5" (FH)
$150-175

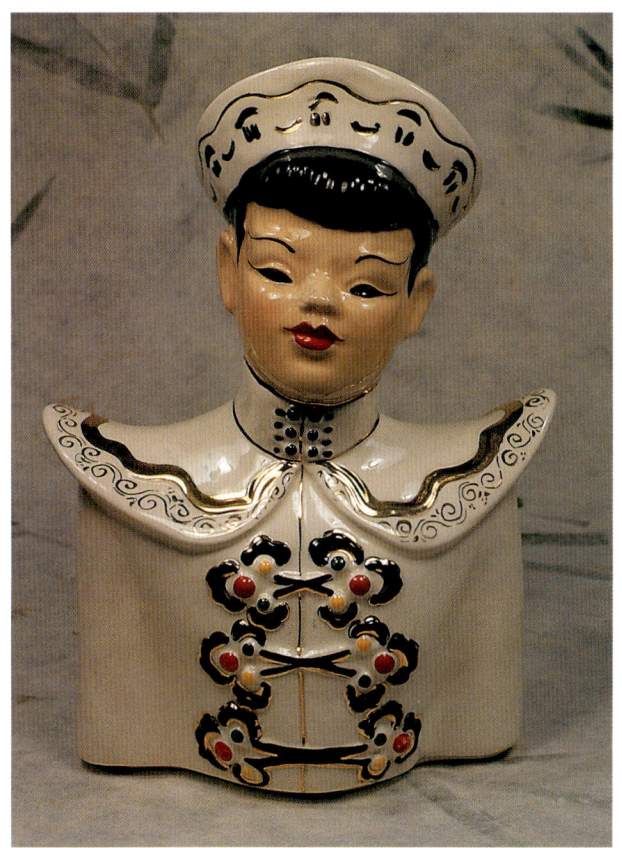

**Shen**, 7.5"
$175-200

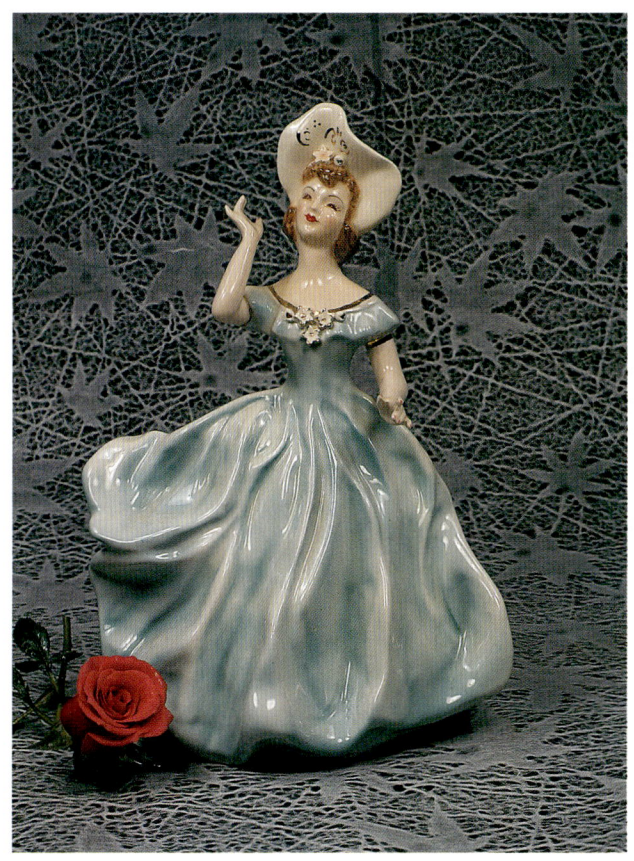

**Sherri**, 8.5"
$450-500

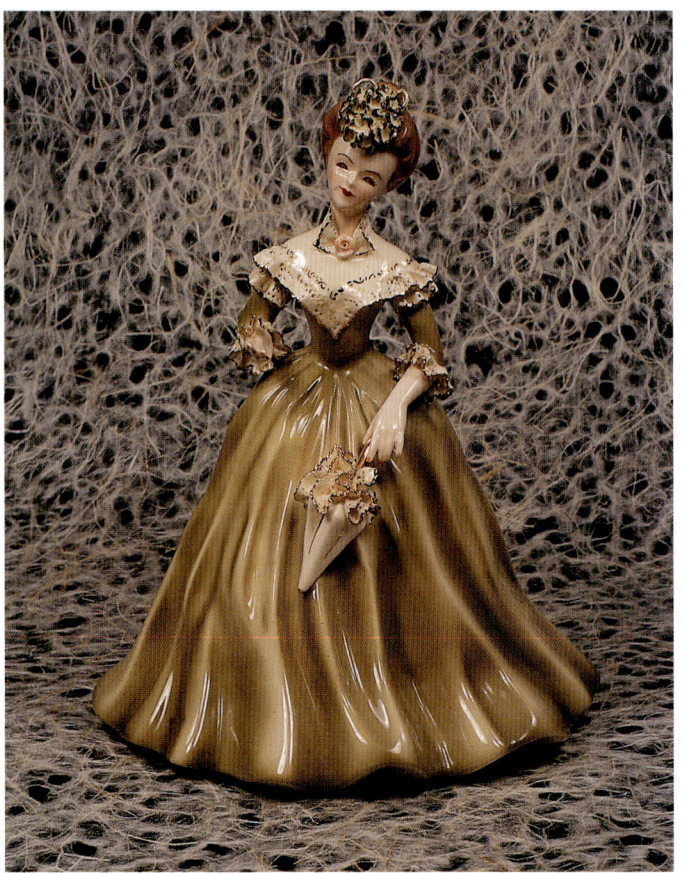

**Sherry**, 8.5"
$700-750

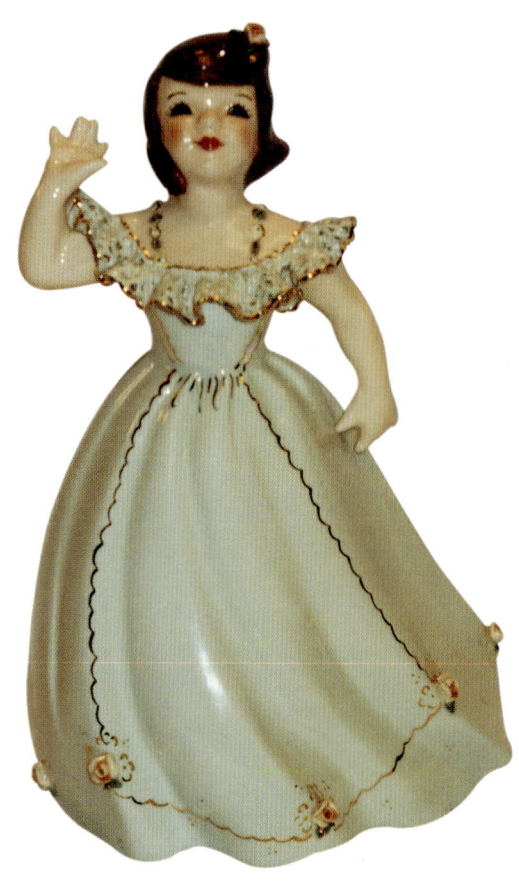

**Spring,** child, 6.25"
$400-450

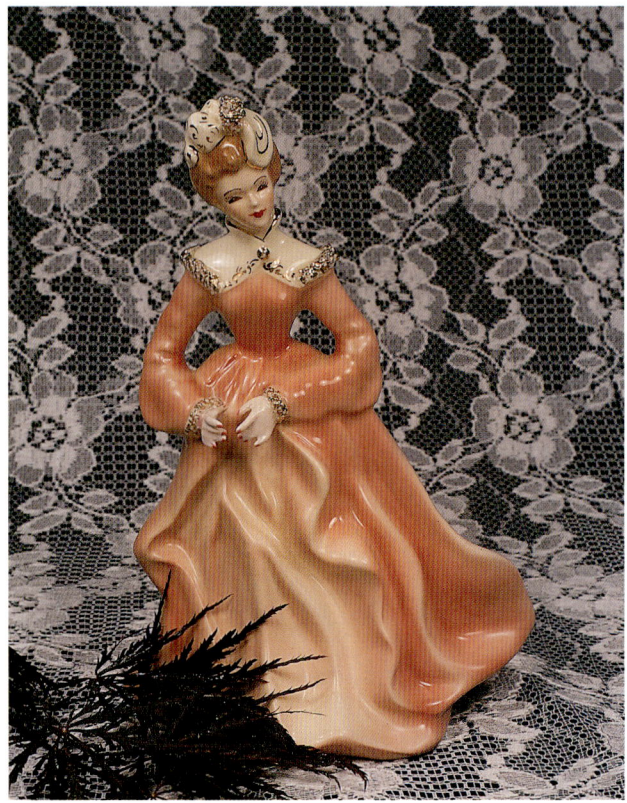

**Shirley**, 8"
$250-350

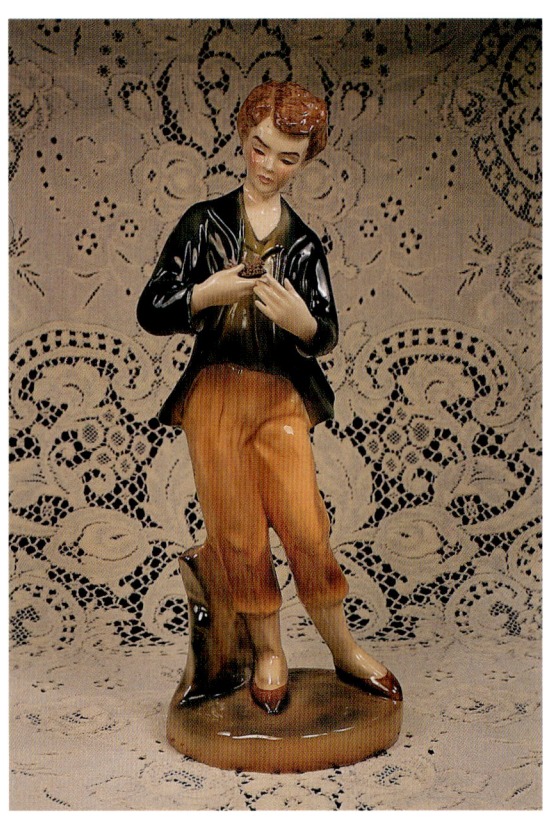

**Spring Reverie**, 11.5"
$1,250-1,500

Showcasing Florence A to Z   85

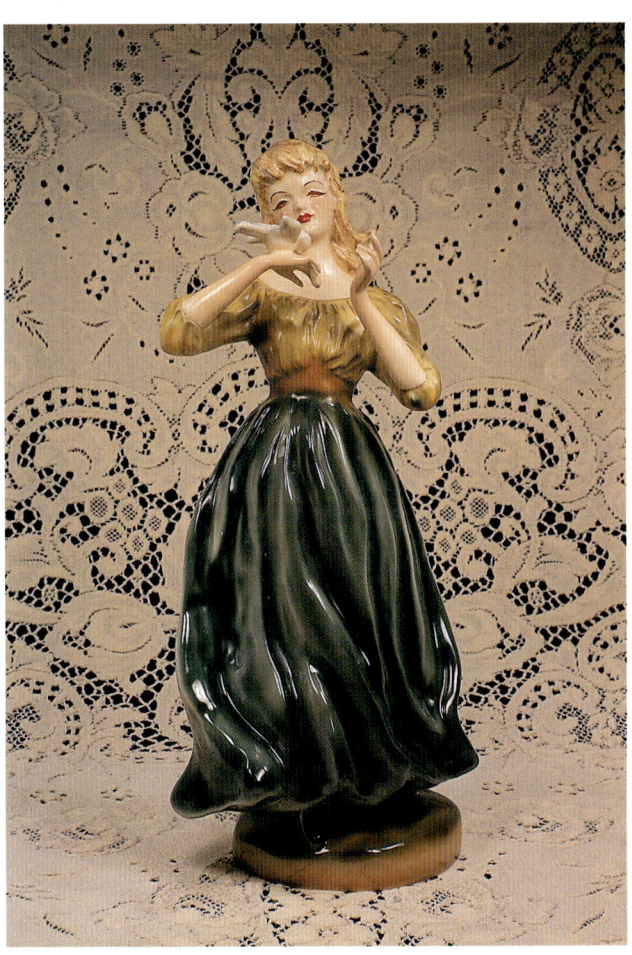

**Spring Companion**, 11.5"
$1,250-1,500

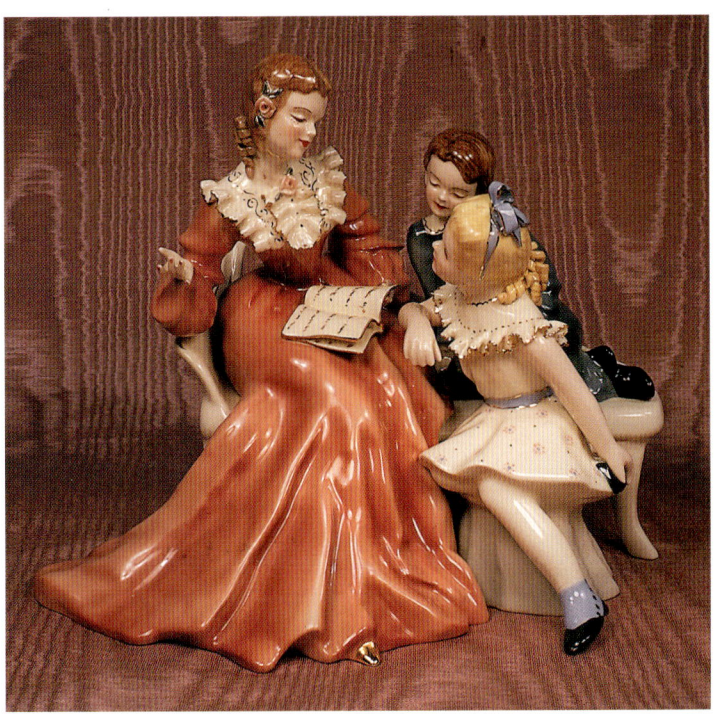

**Story Hour,** with boy and girl, 8" x 7"
$1,100-1,250

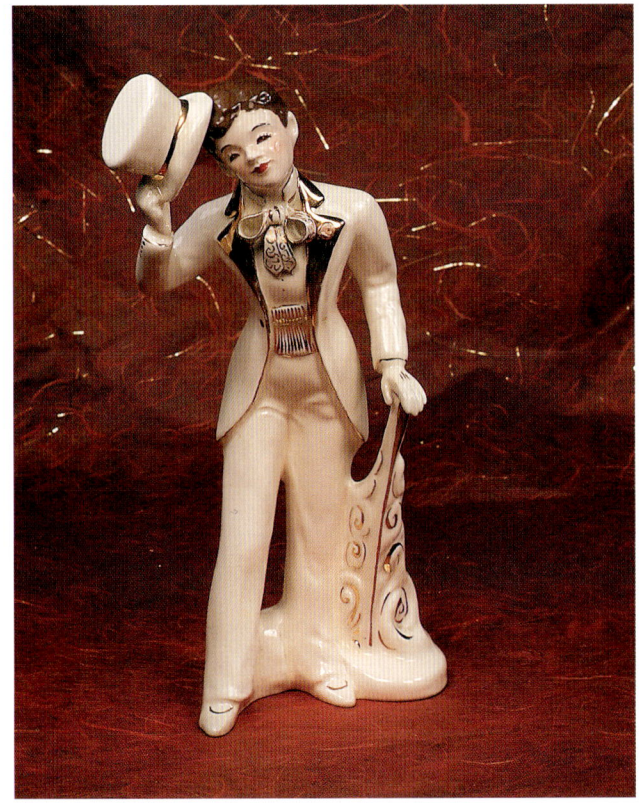

**Stephen**, 8.75"
$450-500

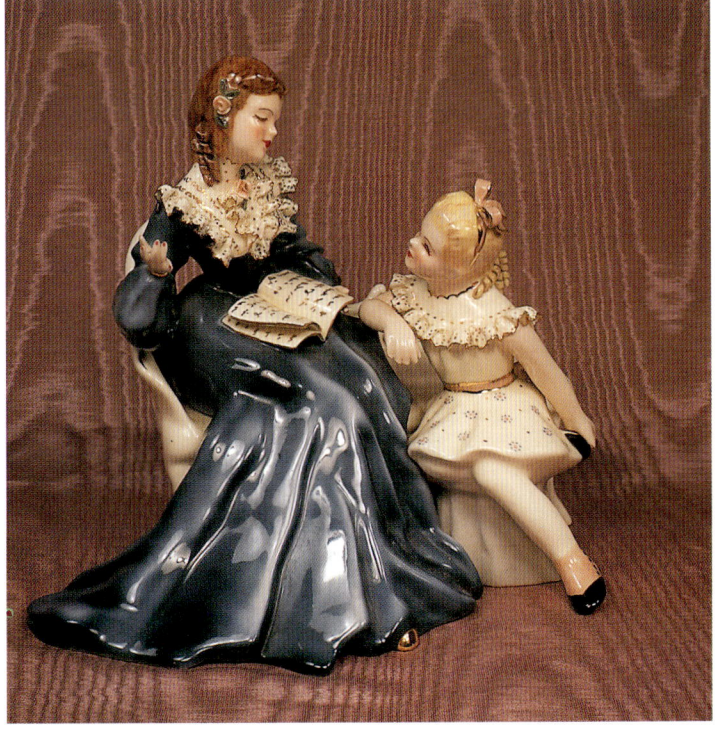

**Story Hour,** with girl, 8" x 7"
$1,000-1,100

86  Showcasing Florence A to Z

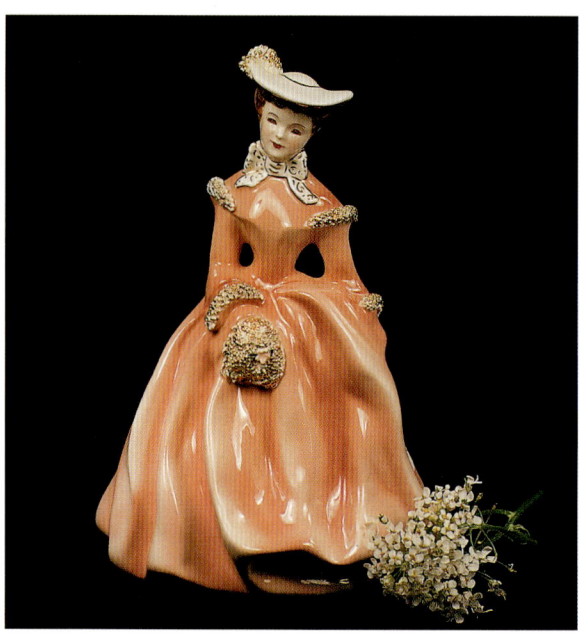

**Sue**, 6"
$60-70

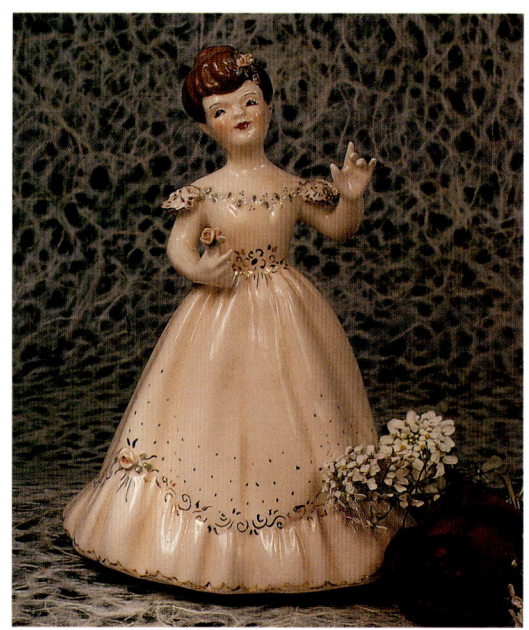

**Summer,** child, 6.25"
$400-450

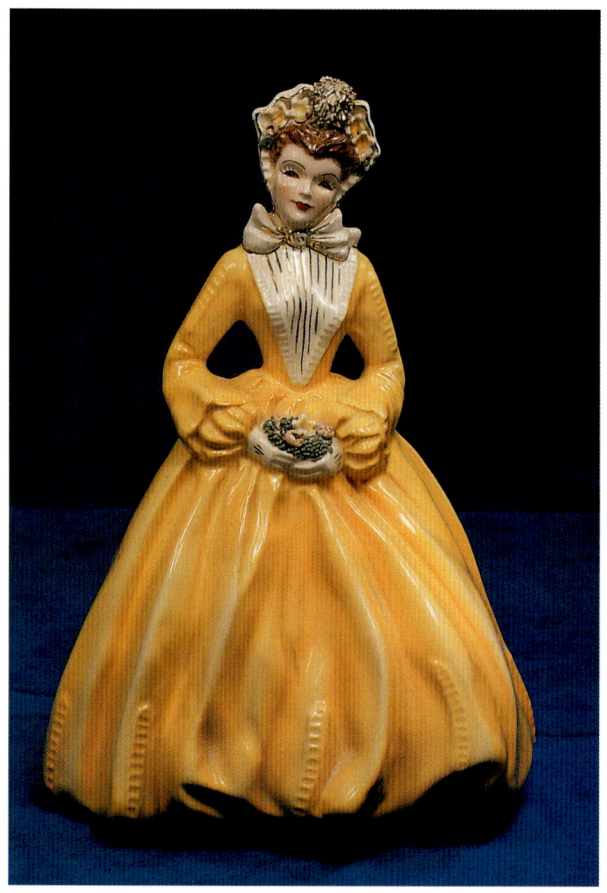

**Sue Ellen**, yellow, 8.25"
$300-350

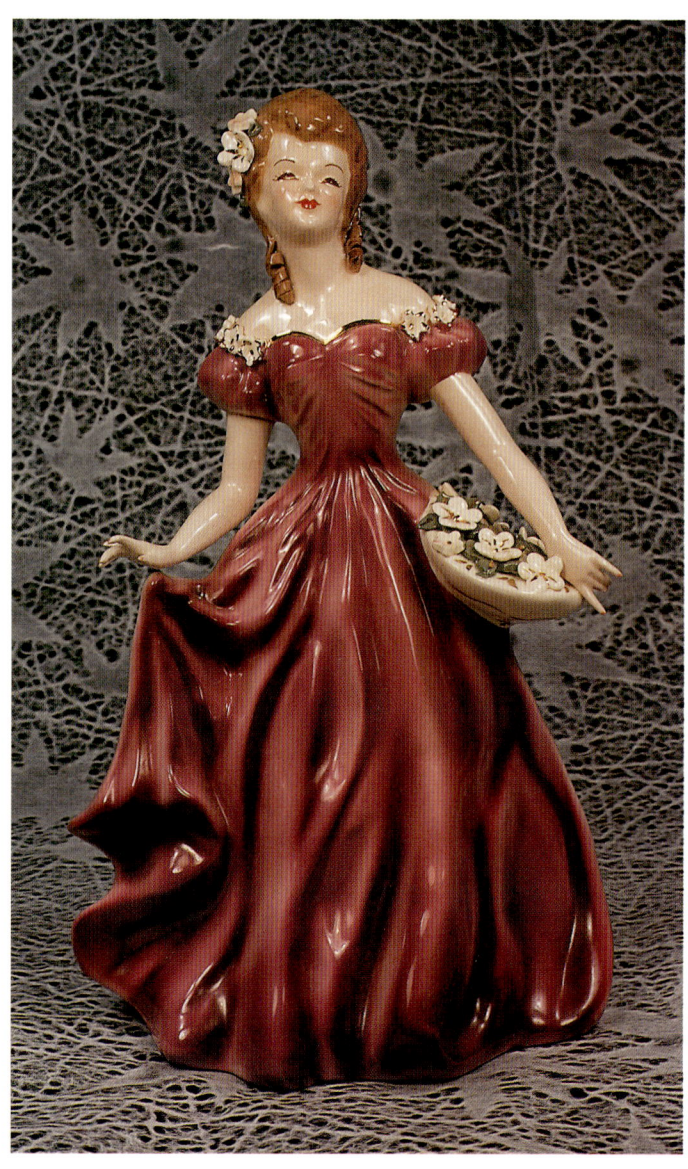

**Susann,** with basket, 9"
$475-500

Showcasing Florence A to Z   87

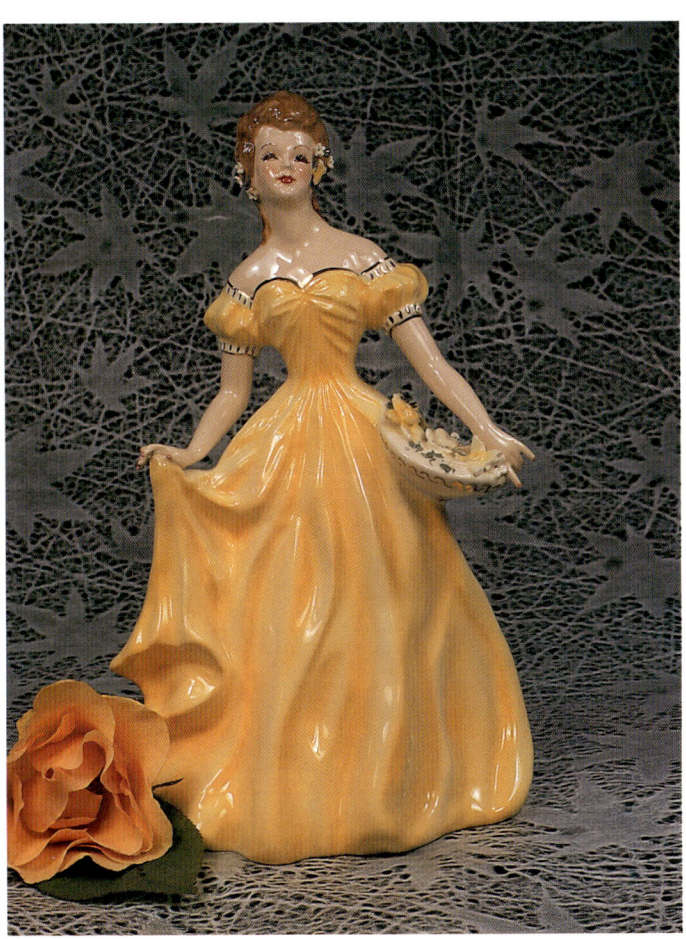

**Susann,** yellow, with basket, 9"
$750-800

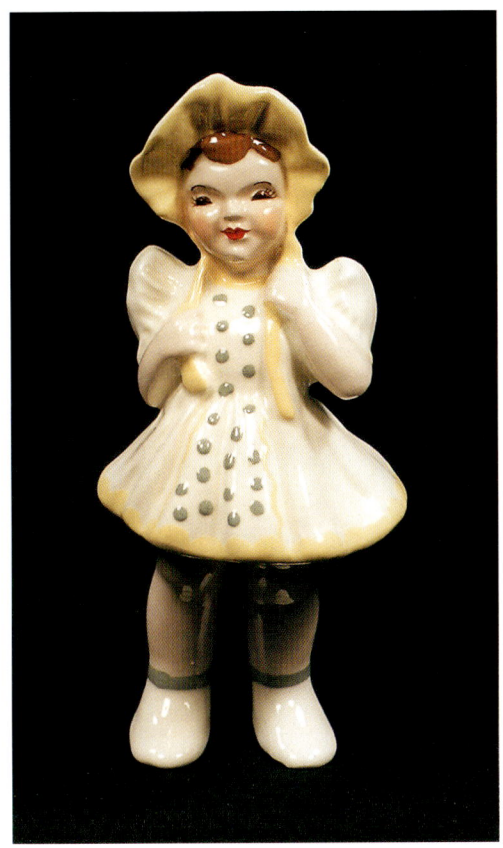

**Susie,** child, 5.5"
$250-275

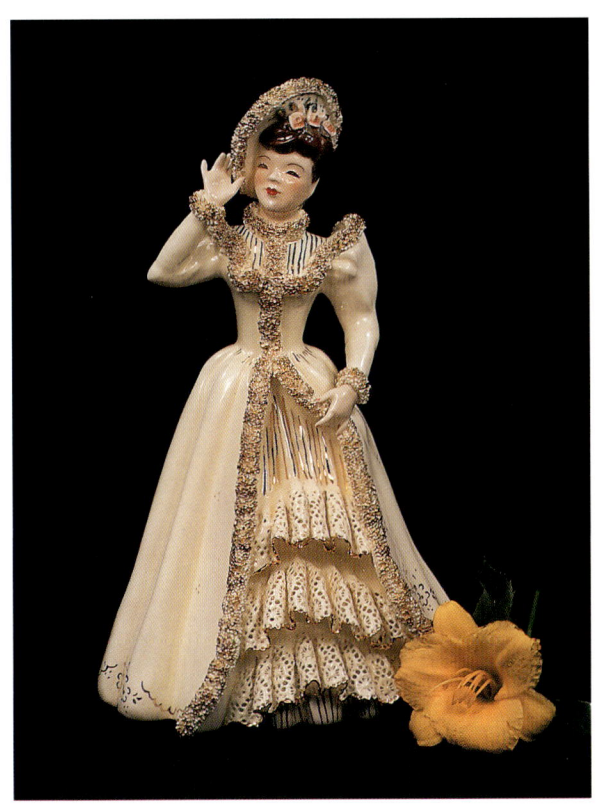

**Susanna**, 8.75"
$550-600

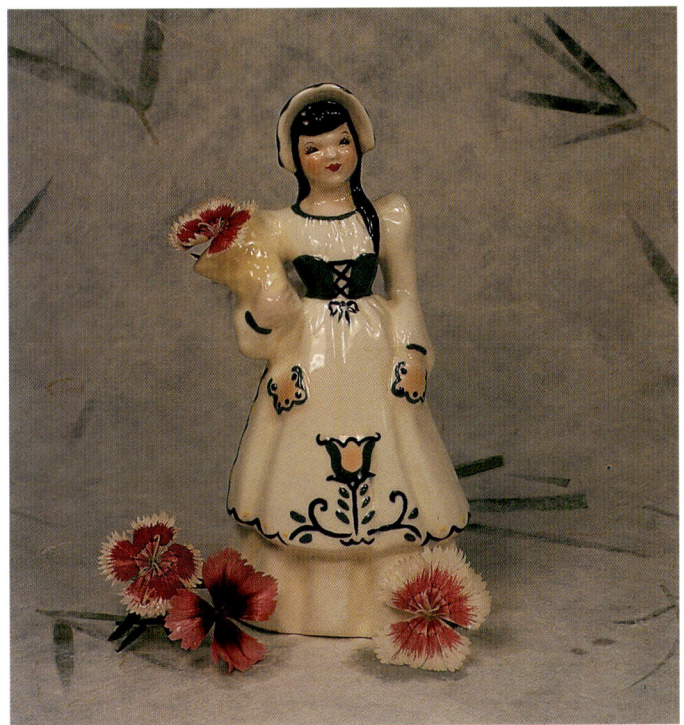

**Suzette**, 7" (FH)
$140-160

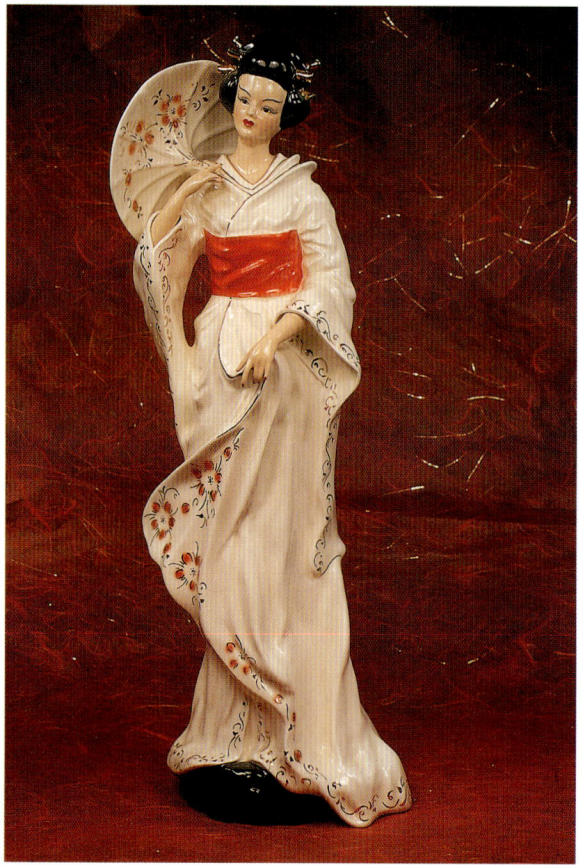

**Taka**, 11"
$750-850

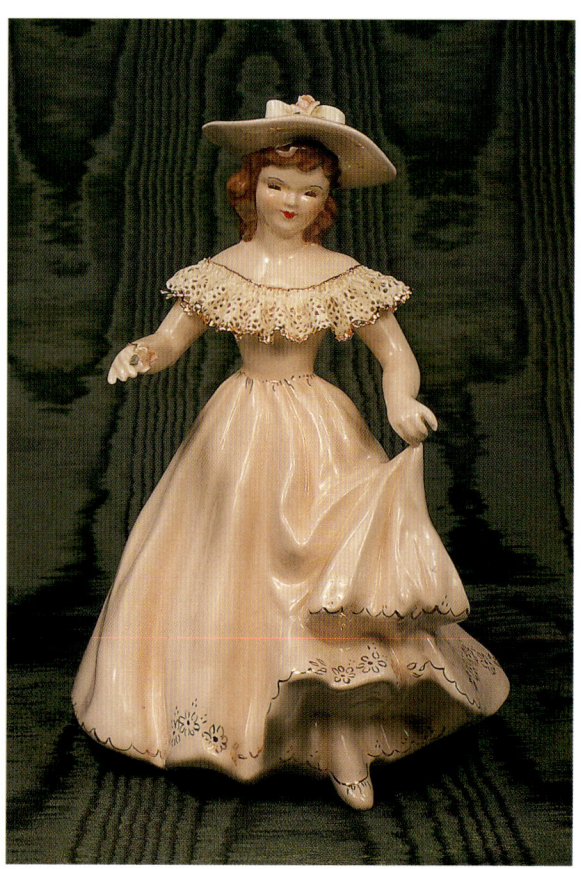

**Tess**, with lace, 7.25"
$500-550

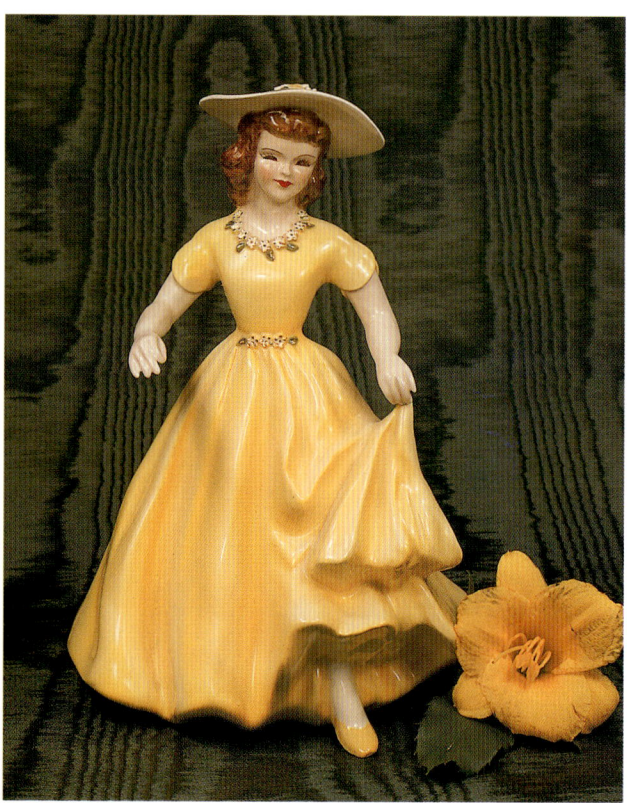

**Tess**, in yellow, 7.25"
$700-750

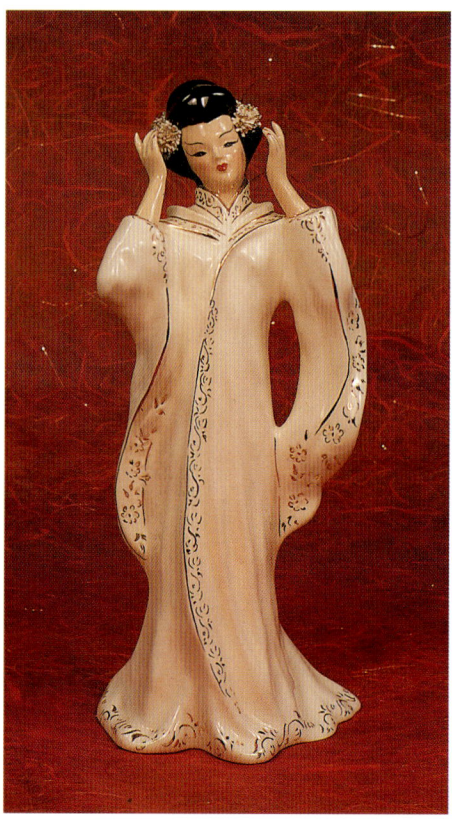

**Toy**, 9"
$325-350

Showcasing Florence A to Z   89

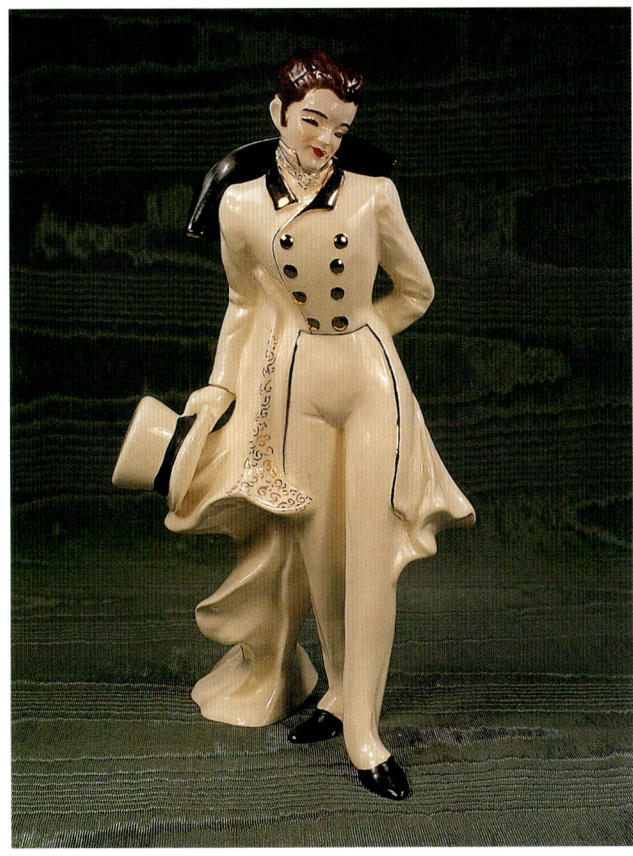

**Victor**, 9.25"
$275-325

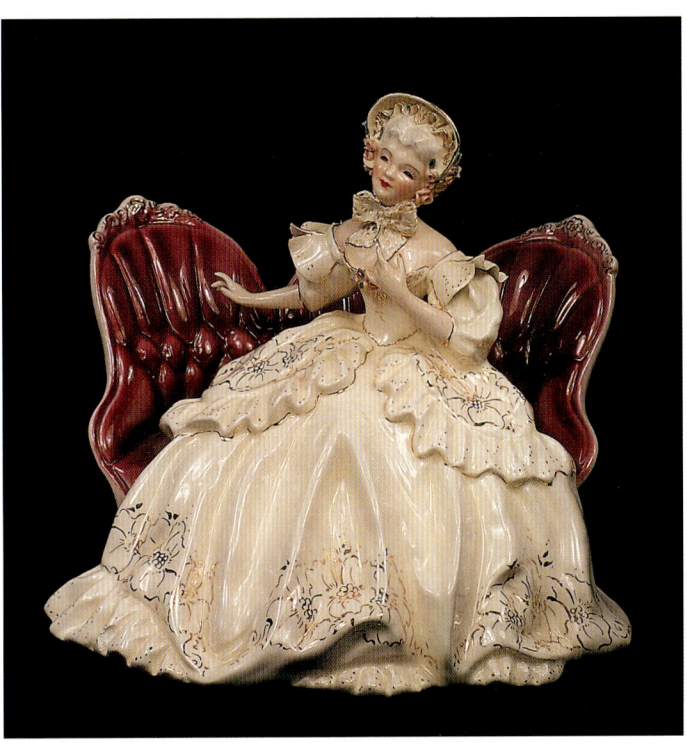

**Victoria**, with bonnet, 8.25" x 7"
$575-625

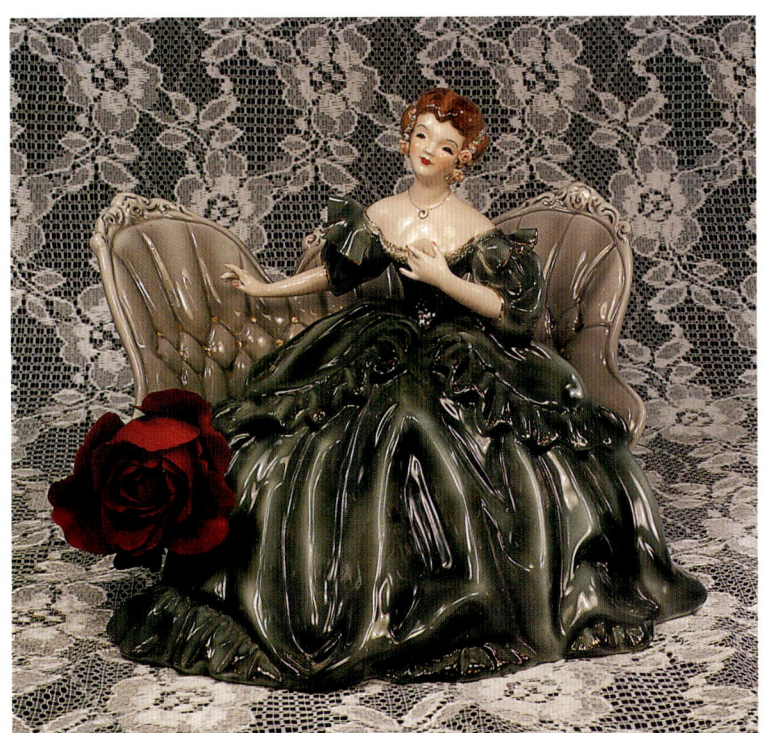

**Victoria**, 8.25" x 7"
$550-600

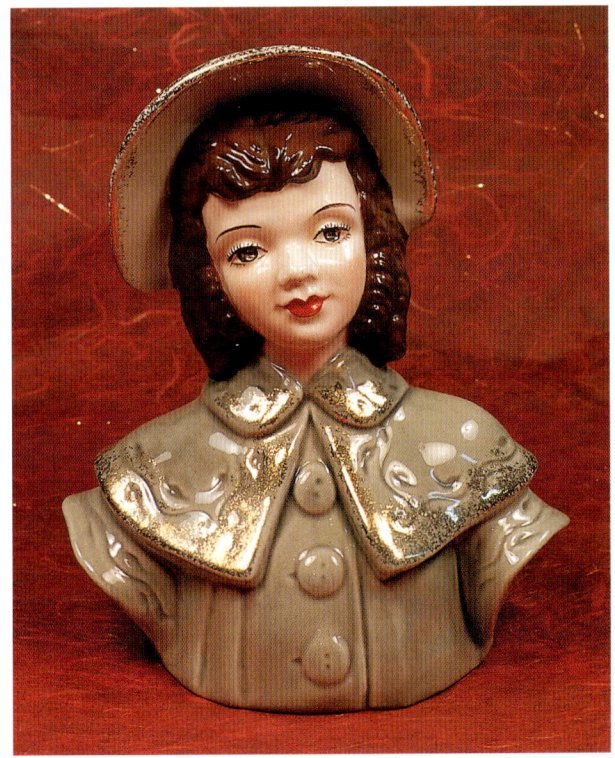

**Violet**, 7" (FH)
$150-160

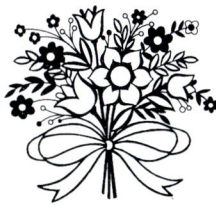

## 90 Showcasing Florence A to Z

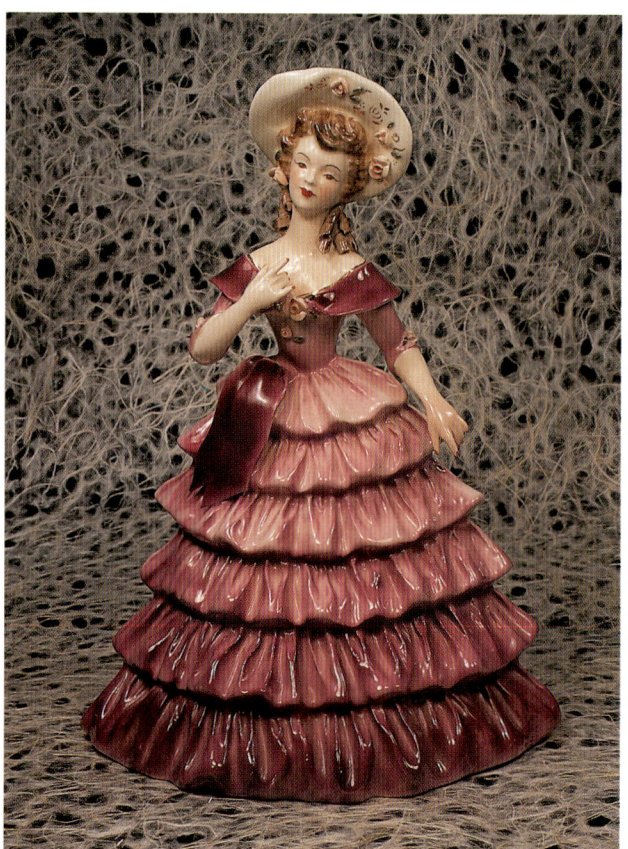

**Virginia**, 9.5"
$2,250-2,500

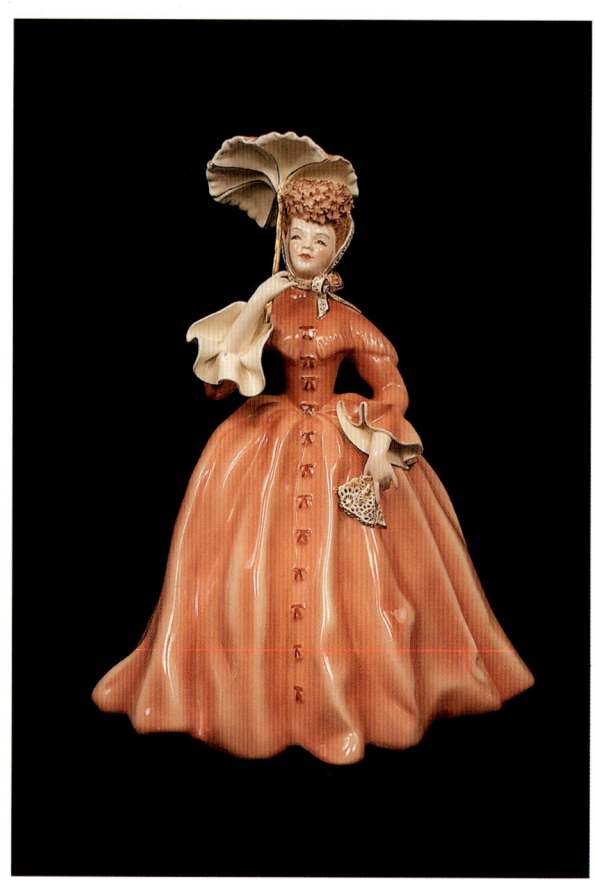

**Vivian**, 10"
$350-400

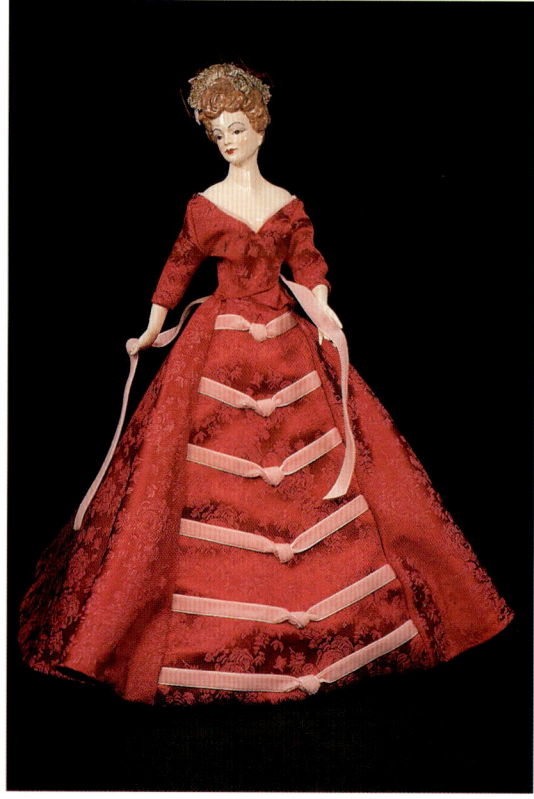

**Virginia Brocade**, 15"
$3,000-3,500

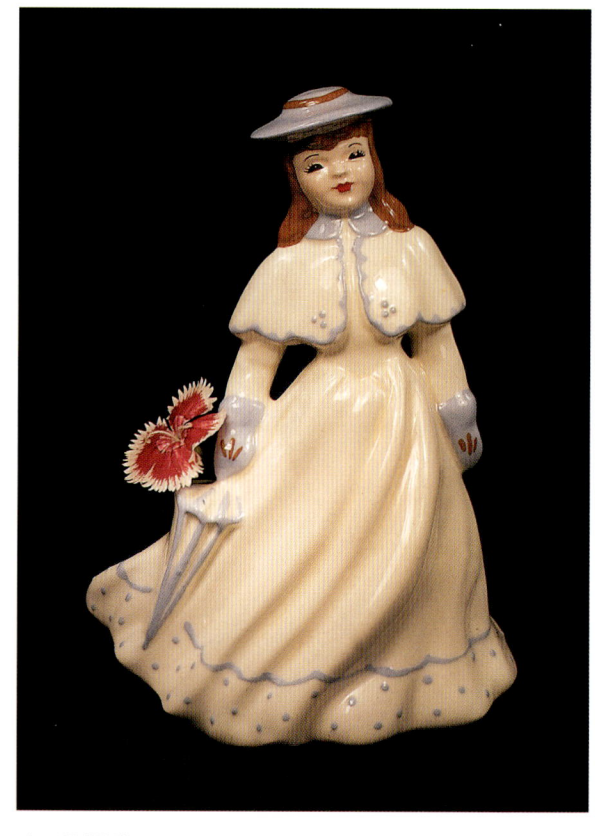

**Wendy**, 6" (FH)
$90-110

**Showcasing Florence A to Z    91**

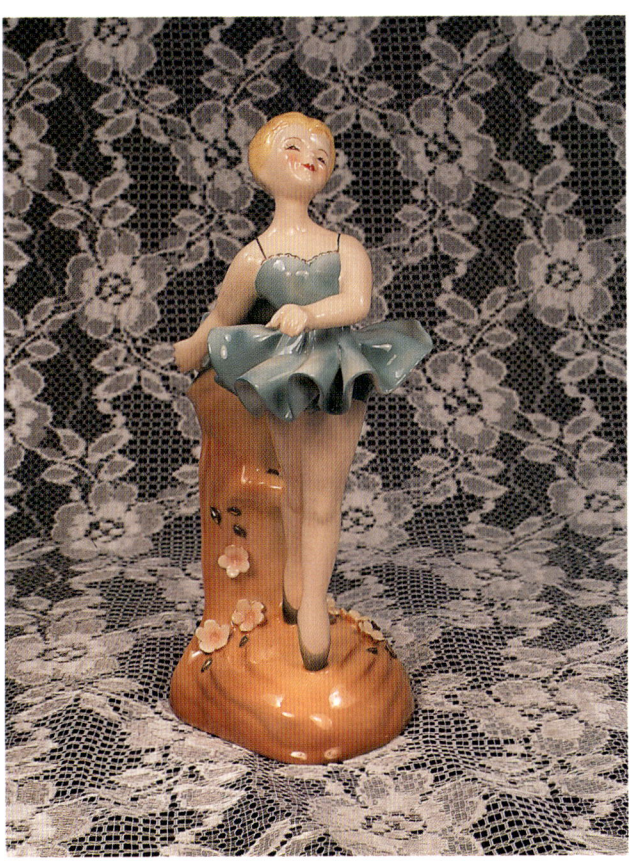

**Wood Nymph Ballerina**, 7.75"
$400-450

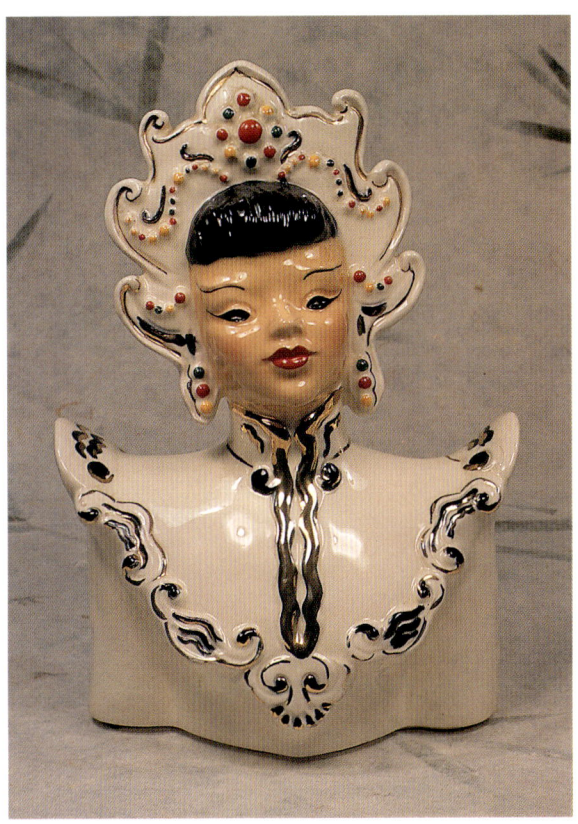

**Yulan**, 7.5"
$175-200

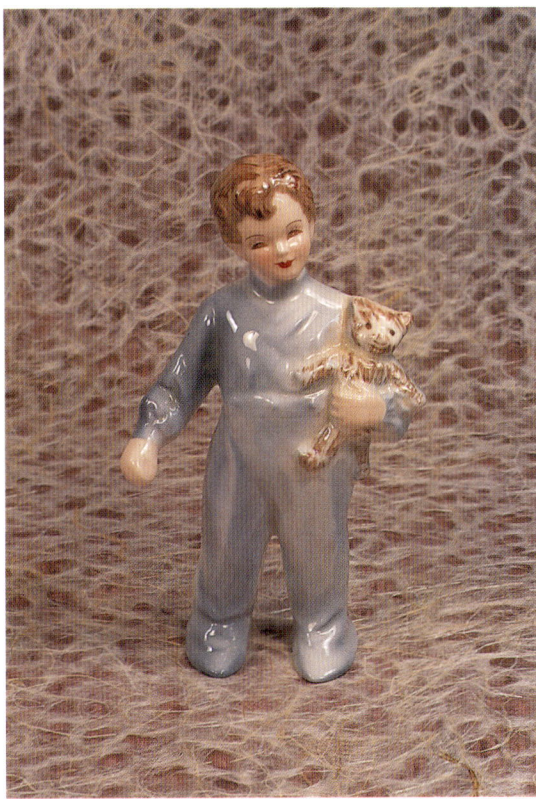

**Wynkin**, child, 5.5"
$200-225

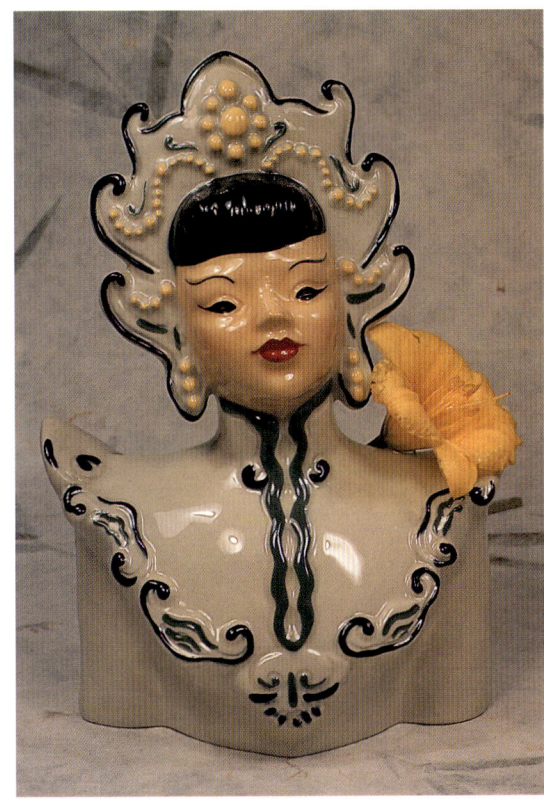

**Yulan**, 7.5" (FH)
$150-175

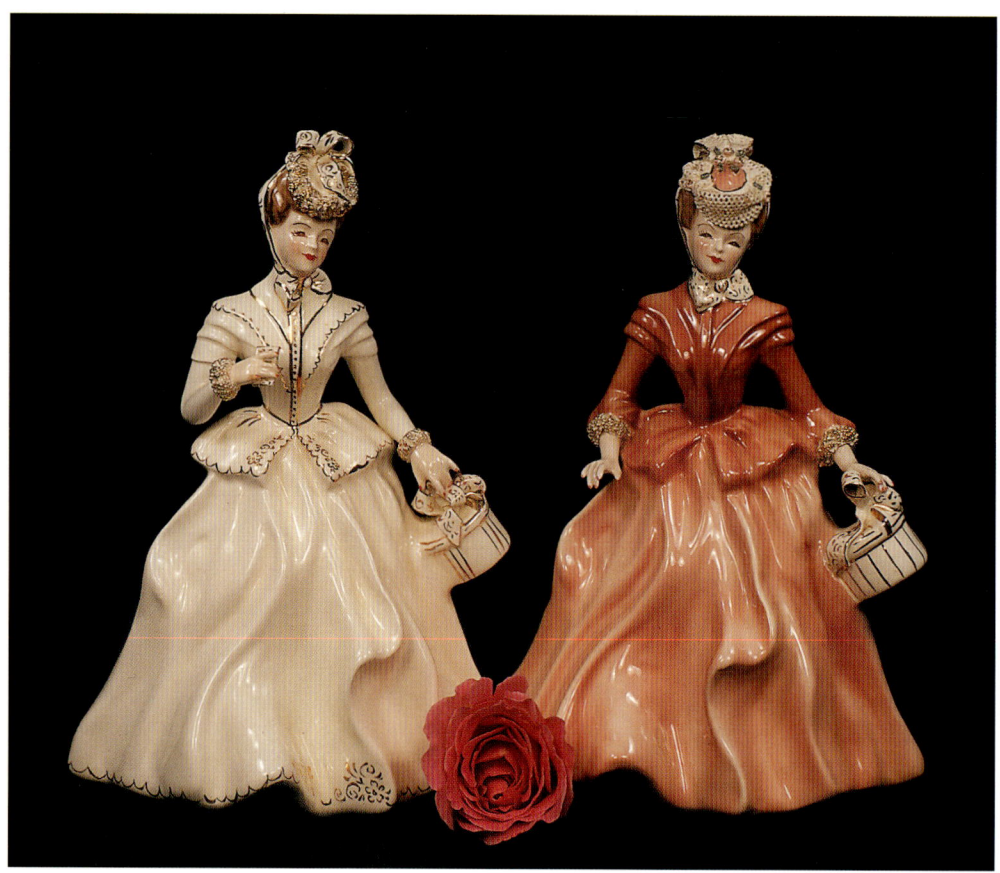

**Yvonne**, two styles, 8.75"
$425-500

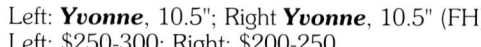

Left: **Yvonne**, 10.5"; Right **Yvonne**, 10.5" (FH)
Left: $250-300; Right: $200-250

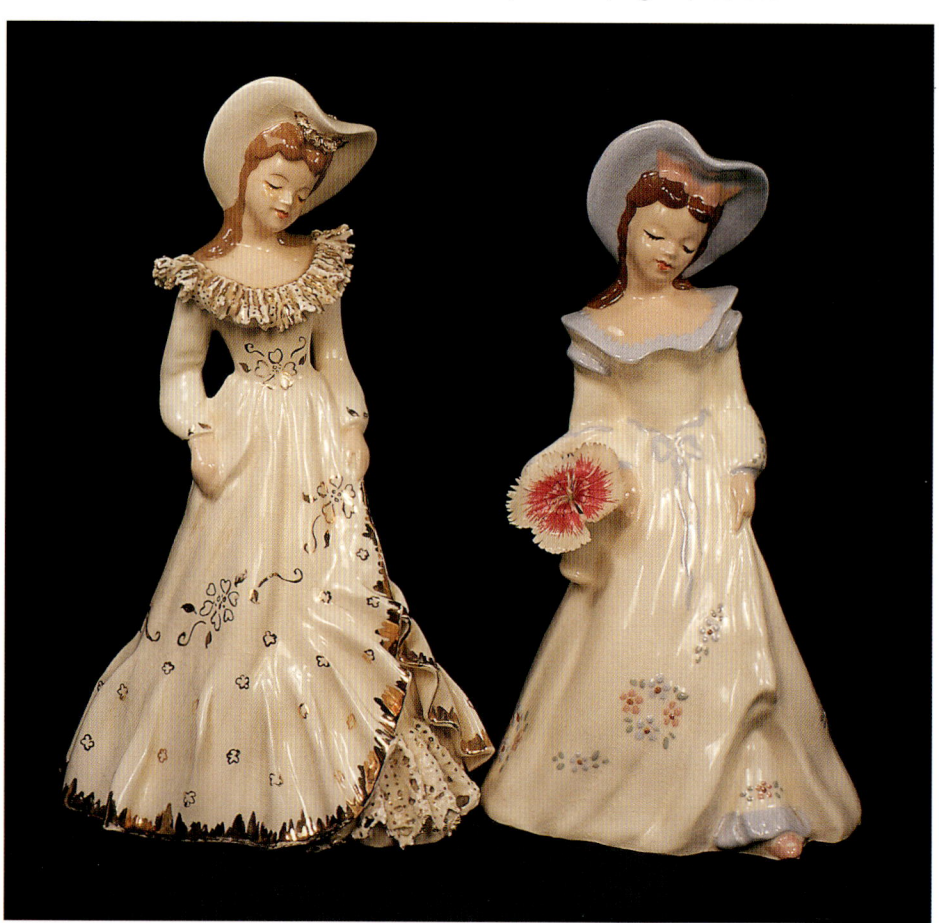

Showcasing Florence A to Z  93

*Lamps*

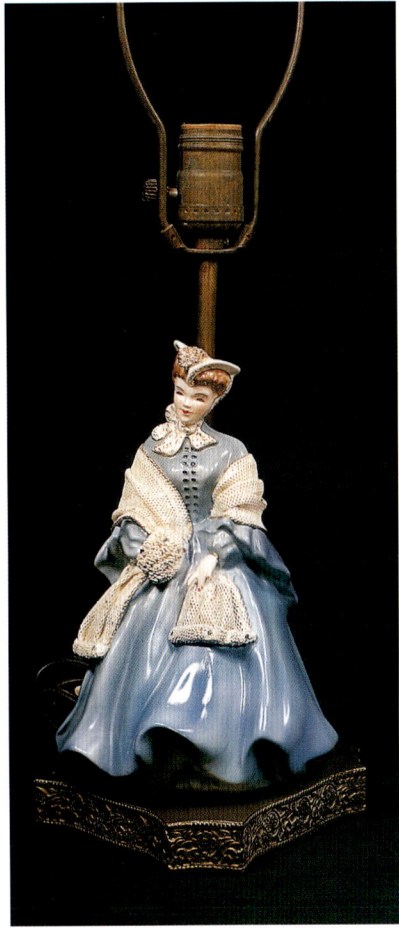

**Camille,** lamp, with hand out, figure is 8.5" and lamp is 21.5"
$500-550

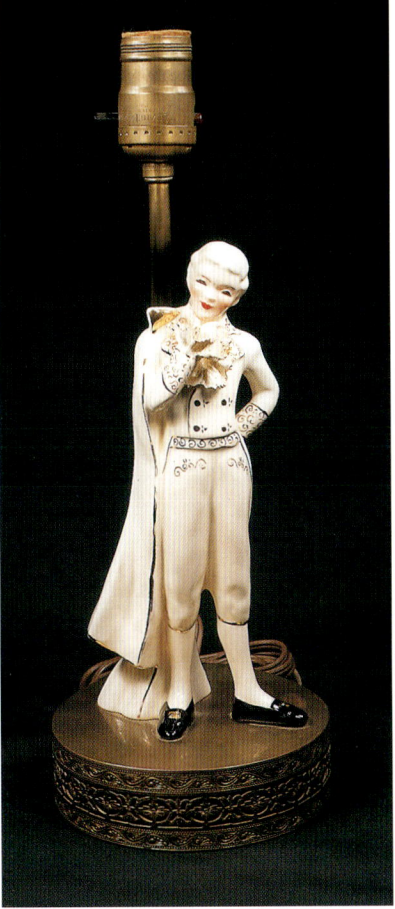

**Charles**, lamp, figure is 8.5" and lamp is 18"
$500-550

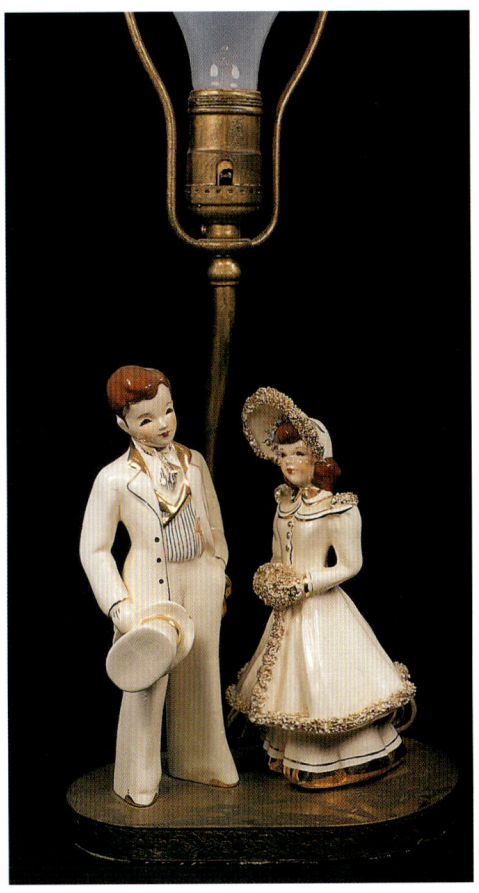

**David and Betsy,** lamp, figures are 7.5" and lamp is 21.5"
$550-600

**Delia,** lamp, figure is 7.5" and lamp is 19.5"
$400-450

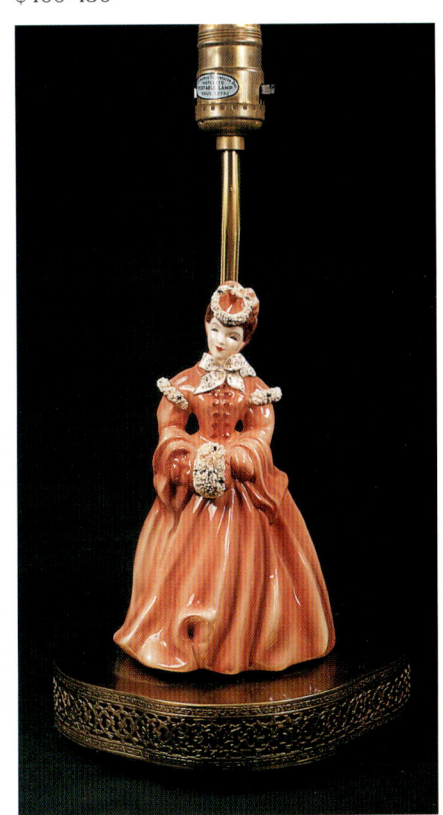

## 94  Showcasing Florence A to Z

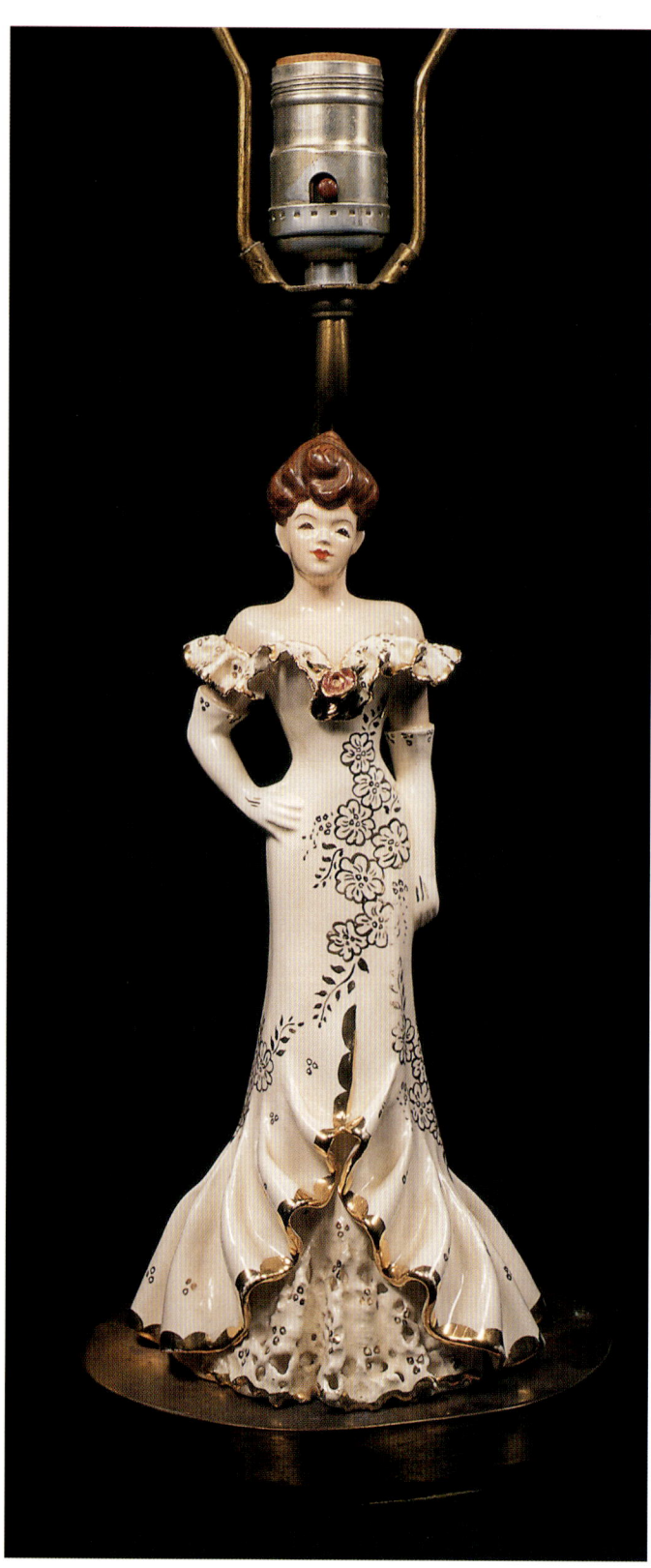

**Gibson Girl,** lamp, figure is 10.5" and lamp is 21.5"
$950-1,000

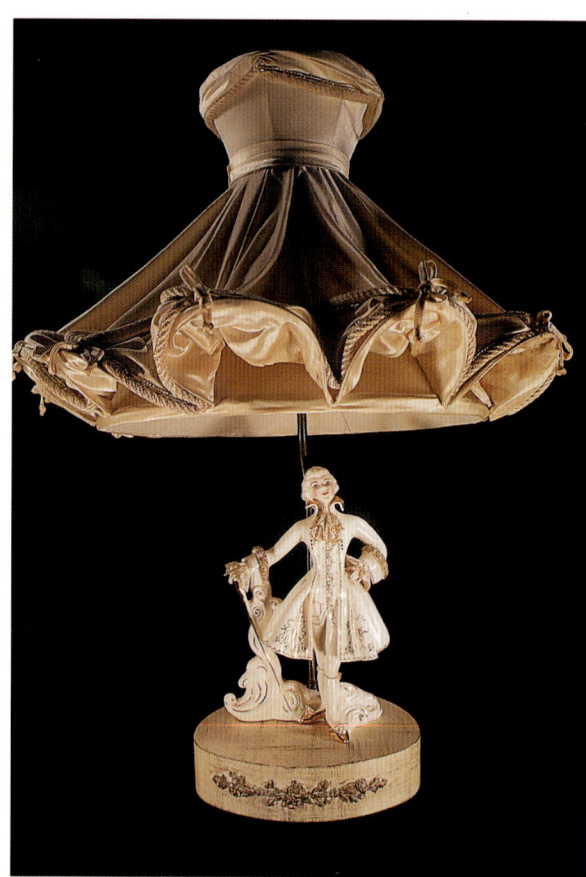

**Louis XVI,** lamp, figure is 10" and lamp is 26" with original shade
$650-700

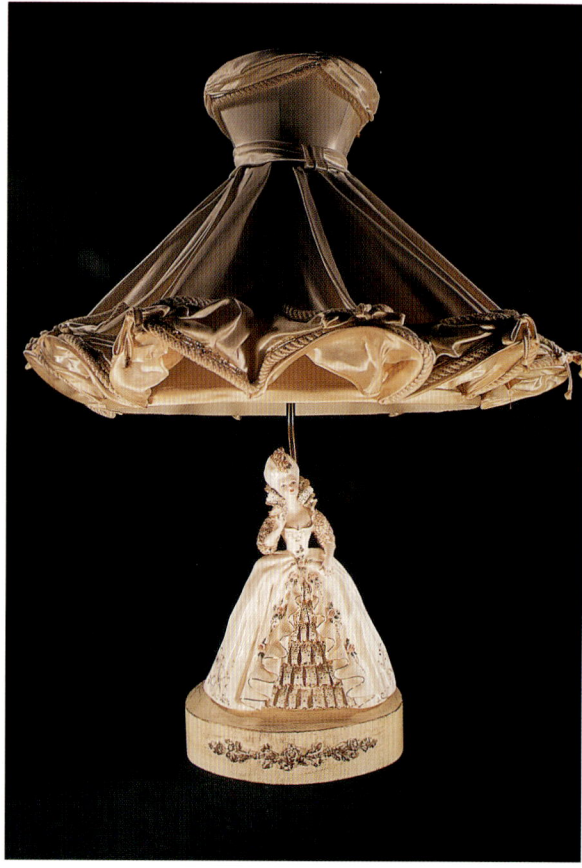

**Marie Antoinette,** lamp, figure is 10" and lamp is 26" with original shade
$650-700

Showcasing Florence A to Z  95

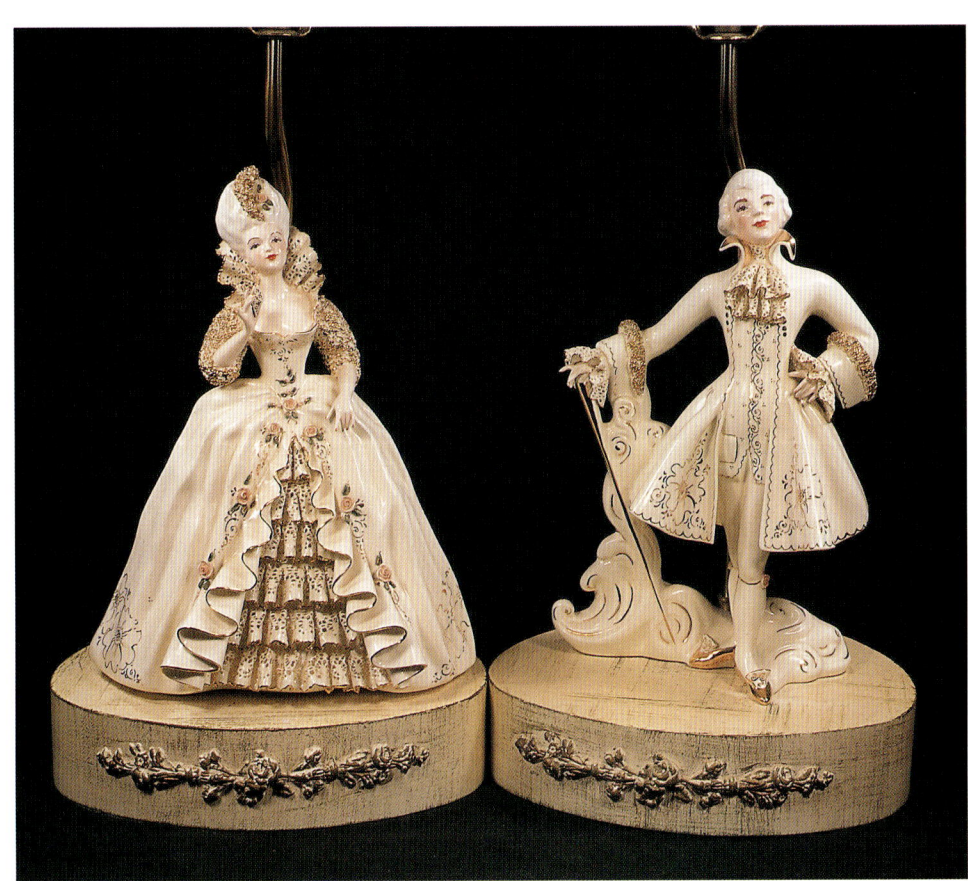

**Marie Antoinette and Louis XVI,** lamps with original shades $1,300-1,400

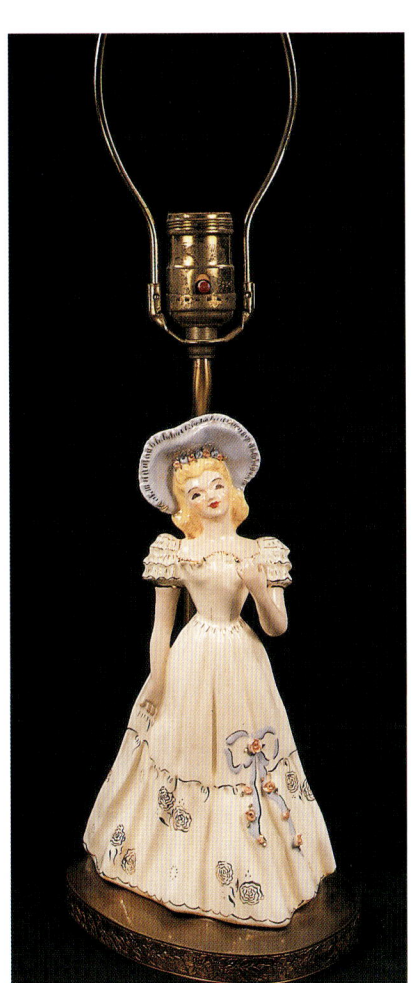

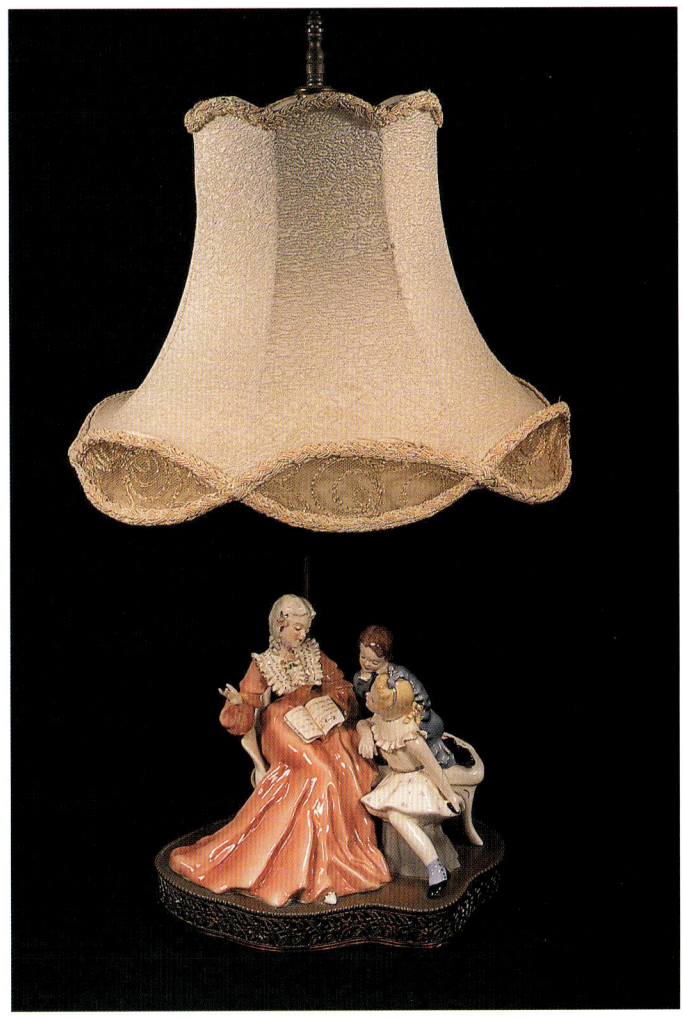

*Left:*
**Stella,** lamp, figure is 10" and lamp is 20.5", * $550-600

*Right:*
**Story Hour,** lamp, figures are 6.75" and lamp is 22" with original shade $1,500-1,750

Chapter IV

# Florence Fashion Parade

*Florence allowed us a certain amount of freedom of expression, while still keeping a close eye on what we were doing. One day she came into the 'gold room,' and holding up two of the same figurine said, 'This one has too much decoration, and this one has not enough. Will the people who did these please come up and get them?' Well, I found I had to go get both!*

—Violet McCorkle Kozar (Pasadena, California, 2001)

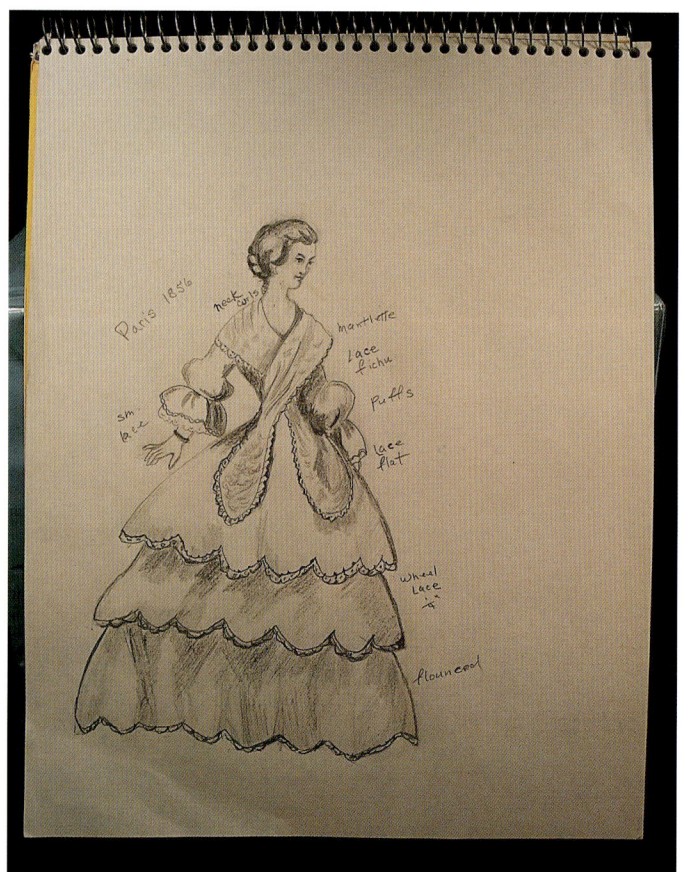

Although this is a contemporary sketch, no doubt Florence would have used a sketch pad like this when designing period costumes for her figurines.

## Why a Fashion Parade?

First of all, we wanted to examine an aspect of collecting Florence Ceramics figurines that hadn't been discussed before. We have long believed that Florence Ward's faithfulness to detail in designing her period costumes was not solely the result of her copying from *Godey Lady's Book* of 1860. We think it is unlikely that the array of gowns her figurines are wearing are all from the same year of 1860, or even from the same decade, yet this reference is the only one recorded in Florence Ceramics catalogs. Aside from the obvious *Cleopatra,* or *John Alden,* or other historical figures, where do all these designs come from? Considering the time frame of Florence Ward's life, she might have had portraits or perhaps photographs of her own mother and grandmother as examples of fashions from the nineteenth century. She may have found pictures of period costumes in old magazines and book publications as well.

We are also curious as to the use of accessories shown with her designs. Suppose Florence copied a gown of a certain period and in the picture she was sketching there was a hat or parasol. Then suppose she wanted to use that same model with different accessories. It would seem the only answer would be to research the time period of that dress and hopefully find the year the gown was made, and finally the accessories that went with it. Such detailed research requires patience and perseverance, not to mention several trips to the library.

We set out then, "to be Florence" for a brief period of time. We took a random sampling of figurines and researched the gowns, the era that gown was worn, and the accessories that went with it. It is doubtful that we used the same research methods as did Florence, because researching has changed in the last sixty years. Imagine our excitement when we found every article of clothing and every accessory to be totally coordinated to a particular year in time! Each figurine is "authentic" from gown, to purse, to hat, and so on. Even the lady's hairstyle is exactly as it would have been for that year!

We have used the proper name for the styles of fashion and accessories whenever we can, because we believe Florence Ward would have known these names.

# Florence Fashion Parade

Her research, which of necessity was so much more extensive than ours, would have given her all the information she needed to make the perfectly gowned figurine. She did just that, and because of the magnitude of her research we are able to present this Parade of Fashions. The fashions are presented in chronological order.

From the eighteenth century, young *Geoff* wears attire suitable for an afternoon visit, or perhaps a carriage ride in the park. His suit has less trimmings than one for a *grande gala*, so it is called a *habit de demi-gala*, a costume for less formal events. It is French and dates to 1779.

There are other examples that can be set forth to illustrate Florence's accuracy of design and detail. A typical morning dress of the early 1830s has gigot sleeves, which are enormously full and attached to a closed corsage (bodice). The bodice is form fitting and opens in a "V" neck with turned-back lapels. The waist is round and the skirt is very full. Hats are broad brimmed and set from the top of the head to slightly back from the crown. Parasols are popular accessories. *Amber* is an excellent example of this style.

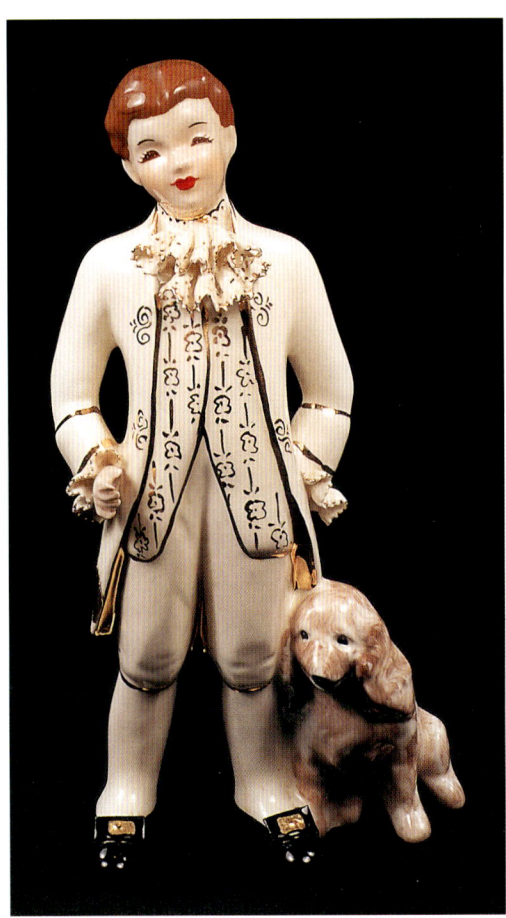

***Geoff***, French social attire, 1779.

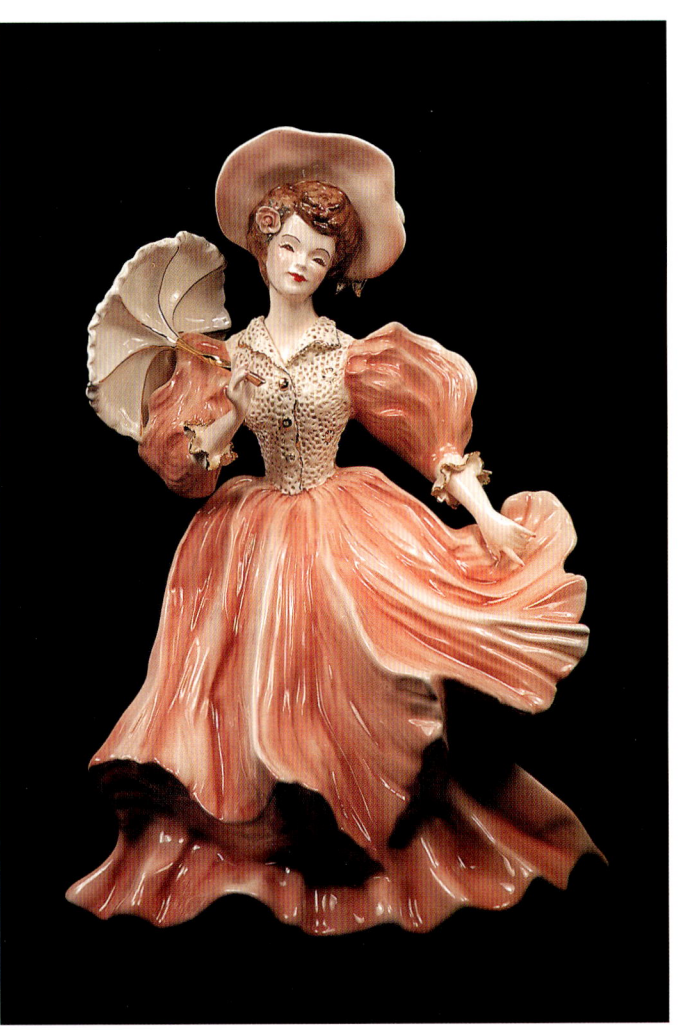

***Amber***, morning dress, 1834.

When one considers the technical expertise that was required of dressmakers to create these elaborate period costumes, it is even more astounding that Florence achieved this same technical expertise in her porcelain figurines. After all, if an actual dress once completed turned out to be unsuitable, it could be redone, albeit with time and effort. However, once the clay lady is completed with all her added flounces, laces, and accoutrements, she is set and cannot be undone. Painstaking time and research preceded each figurine so that the finished lady was gowned exactly as a representative of her particular era.

If the Florence figurine collector wonders why a certain dress might appear first as a day dress and then later as evening attire, he or she should note that this may be more than mere coincidence or the whim of the artist. We prefer to think it was done so on purpose, because of a fact we stumbled upon while doing our own research for this book. In the decade of the 1840s, a novelty was introduced regarding the bodice of the dress. It was the dress with two bodices, one for day and one for evening, either of which could be tacked on to the skirt band as needed. Another option was to simply cover the bared bodice of the ball gown with the closed and sleeved bodice for daywear. Florence shows the versatility of this particular 1840s dress modeled by *Marilyn* and *Marianne*.

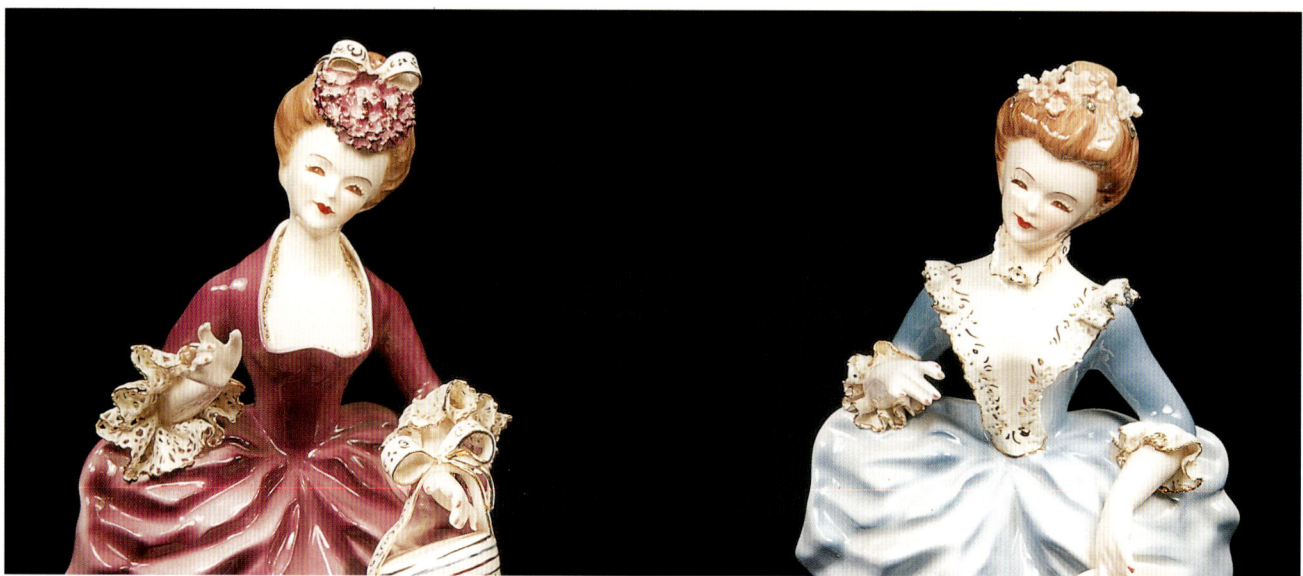

**Marilyn and Marianne**, dress with two bodices, c.1840s.

In 1780, French designers adapted the redingote from the English gentleman's riding coat of that period. The redingote became almost a permanent form of ladies' attire well into the nineteenth century, popular in France, England, and America. For day dress, the redingote is commonplace. In the 1840s, the redingote has a plain high corsage with long tight sleeves, often expanding over an under sleeve of muslin or tarlatan at the wrist. It is usually buttoned high to the neck. Two examples of the riding coat are worn by *Genevieve* and *Diane*.

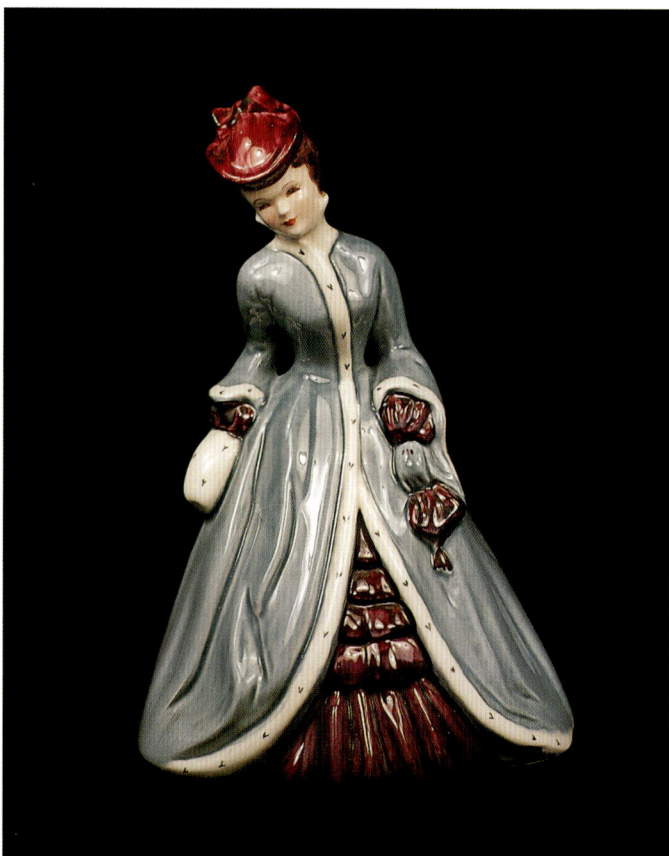

**Genevieve**, redingote trimmed in fur, c.1845-1860.

More fashion news of the 1850s refers to the caraco, which is a short jacket fitted at the waist and flared out just to hip level. It is worn over a matching skirt and generally has flounces around the hem. It probably had its origins in France around 1775-1780, and became popular again in England and America around 1855.

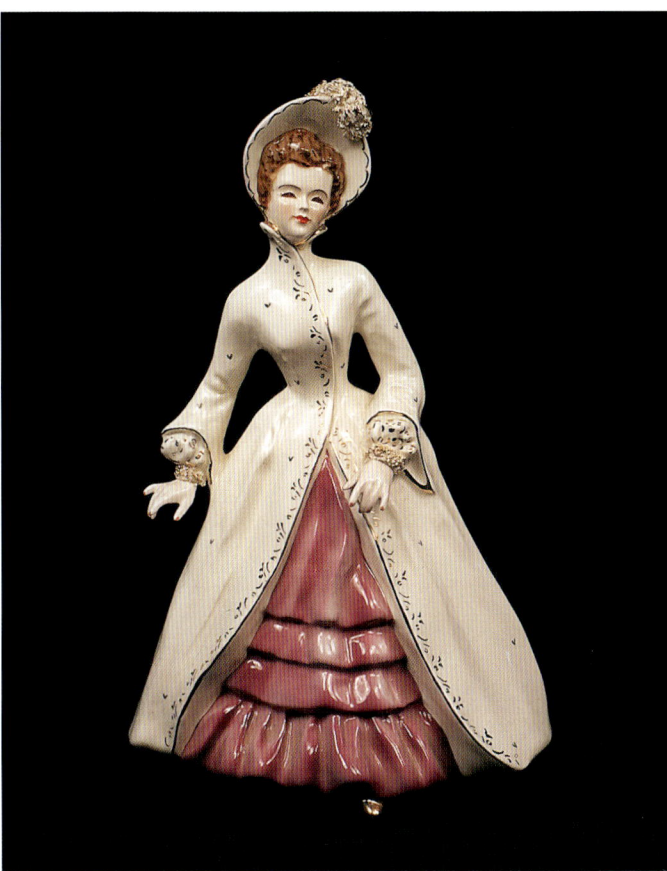

**Diane**, redingote and promenade bonnet, c.1842-1848.

The pelisse-robe or redingote of the 1850s is shorter in length than the full redingote. The corsage is high and close fitting, and the pelisse is trimmed in fur, most probably ermine. *Karen*, with her long waist and wide skirt, is gracefully elegant in this Florence model.

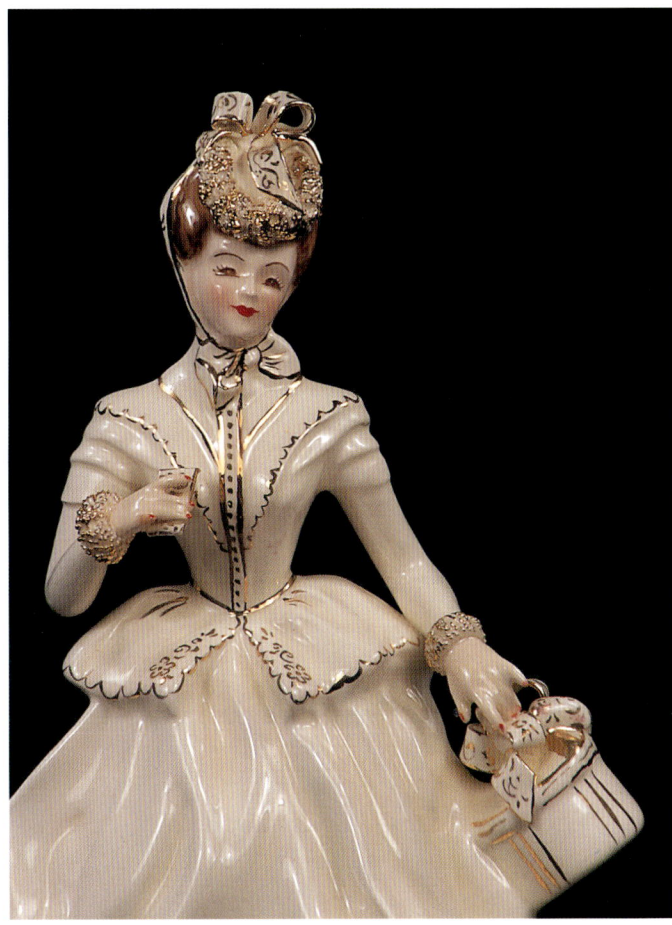

**Yvonne**, caraco jacket, c.1850s.

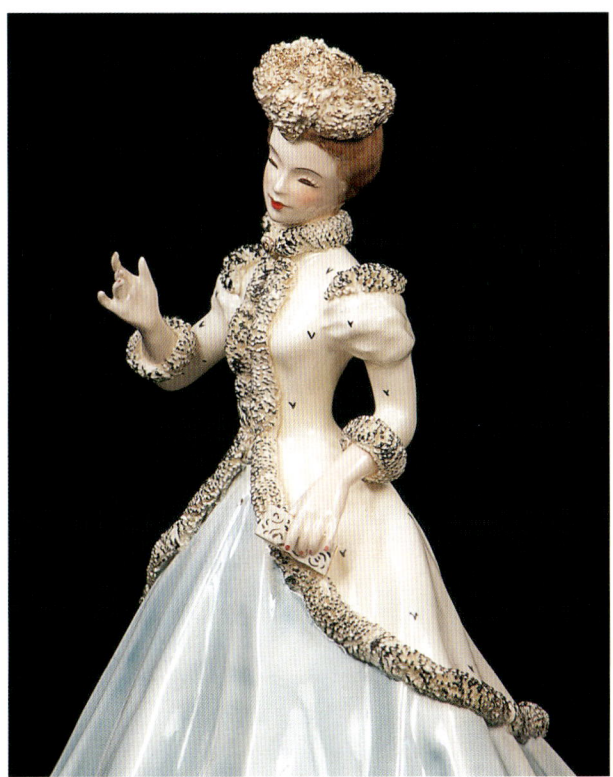

**Karen**, pelisse-robe, ermine trimmed, c.1848-1855.

## Florence Fashion Parade

Panniers circulated in and out of the latter eighteenth to mid nineteenth centuries with more grace than the actual apparel itself. A pannier was originally an eighteenth century oval hoop worn under skirts to produce the fashionable hip extensions. It eventually evolved into a crinoline pannier, which was probably not as unwieldy. In the decade of the 1850s, dresses continued to broaden, thus the very large grand pannier was used. In 1856, a pundit in England worried that it "might become necessary to widen all the public walkways." By 1857, a silk dress now needed up to eighteen yards of material! Florence faithfully recreates the enormously wide skirts of the 1850s. *Victoria* is lovely in a very grand dress.

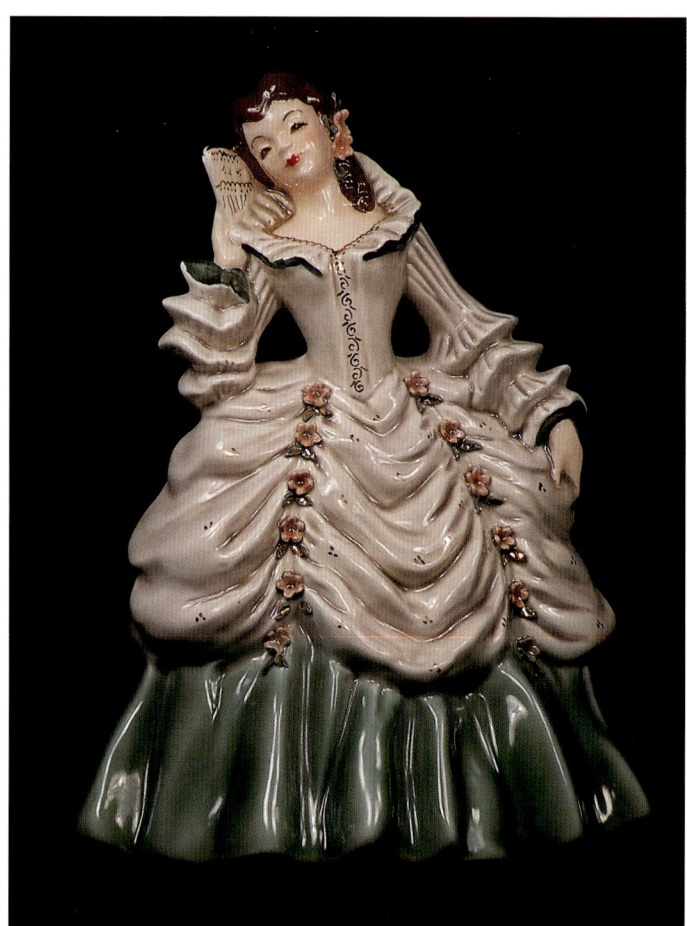

*Amelia*, panniers, c.1860-1865.

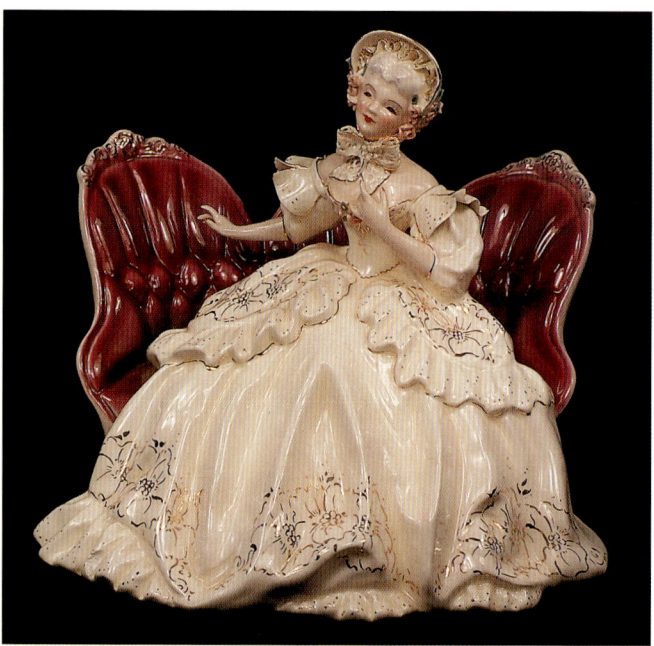

*Victoria*, grand pannier, c.1856-1859.

Florence gives us another example of the melding of French and English fashion as shown by the figure, *Amelia*. *Amelia* is wearing a pannier dress reminiscent of a French Court dress, or *Robe de Cour*, popular once again in the 1860s. The sleeves of her dress are gathered into multiple puffs.

In 1860, the gigot sleeve (see *Amber*, pg. 97) turns upside down and becomes the bishop sleeve that *Grace* is wearing. Whereas the gigots have their fullness between the bodice and slightly below the elbow, the bishop sleeve is very narrow from the bodice and over the shoulder and becomes fuller from slightly above the elbow down to the wrist. The bishop sleeve was in and out of favor throughout the nineteenth century.

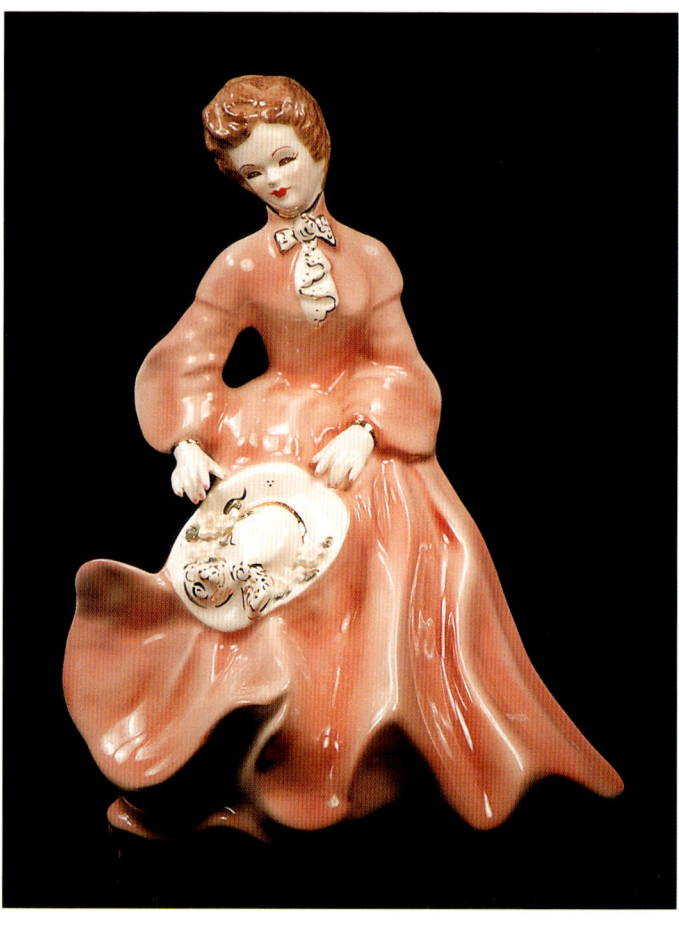

*Grace*, bishop sleeves, c.1860-1862.

Costume designers' fascination with the female derriere continued throughout the nineteenth century, with many kinds of bustles and near-bustles worn. In 1868, the pannier puff is introduced. Whereas the grand pannier is accomplished by the use of very large hoops, the pannier puff requires more material and a crinoline. Half a yard of extra fabric is added to the top of the back widths and gathered into the side seams, with the fullness extending approximately ten inches below the belt. A drawing string extends across the back widths and draws the back in to fit closely over the crinoline, allowing the full fabric to fall over the drawing string into a puff. The puff may belong to either the underskirt, as Florence has molded for *Marianne*, or it may be part of the overskirt, as demonstrated by *Patrice*. *Marianne* is holding a large brimmed Leghorn hat popular for the garden. *Patrice* is carrying a fan that is indicative of the painted sandalwood fans of the era.

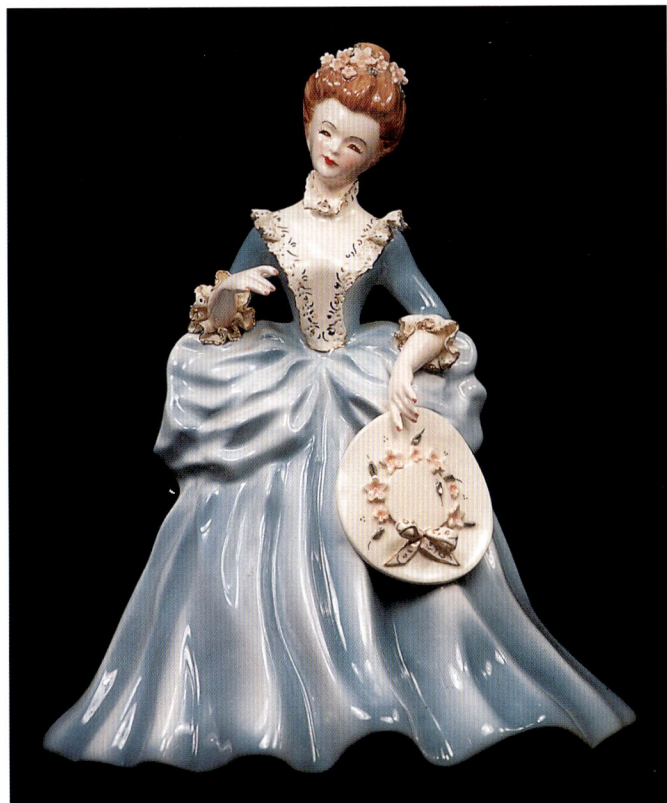

*Marianne*, pannier puff, c.1869.

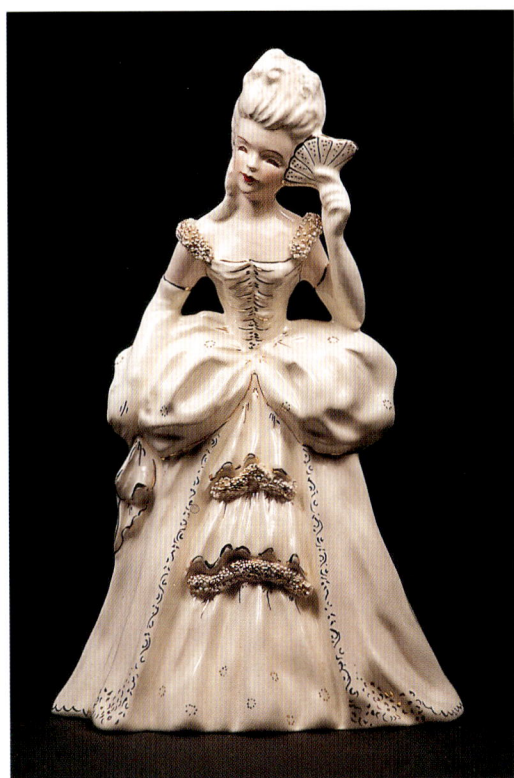

*Patrice*, pannier puff, 1868.

Many styles were repeated. One such fashion is the polonaise, a jacketed dress with skirt fronts pulled back to form coattail sections that are held up in a draped fashion by ties or drawstrings. The polonaise is worn over either a matching or a contrasting skirt. Florence demonstrates two polonaise dresses. *Elizabeth's* French dress is from the eighteenth century and *Lady Diana* (see next page) is resplendent in an English polonaise from a hundred years later.

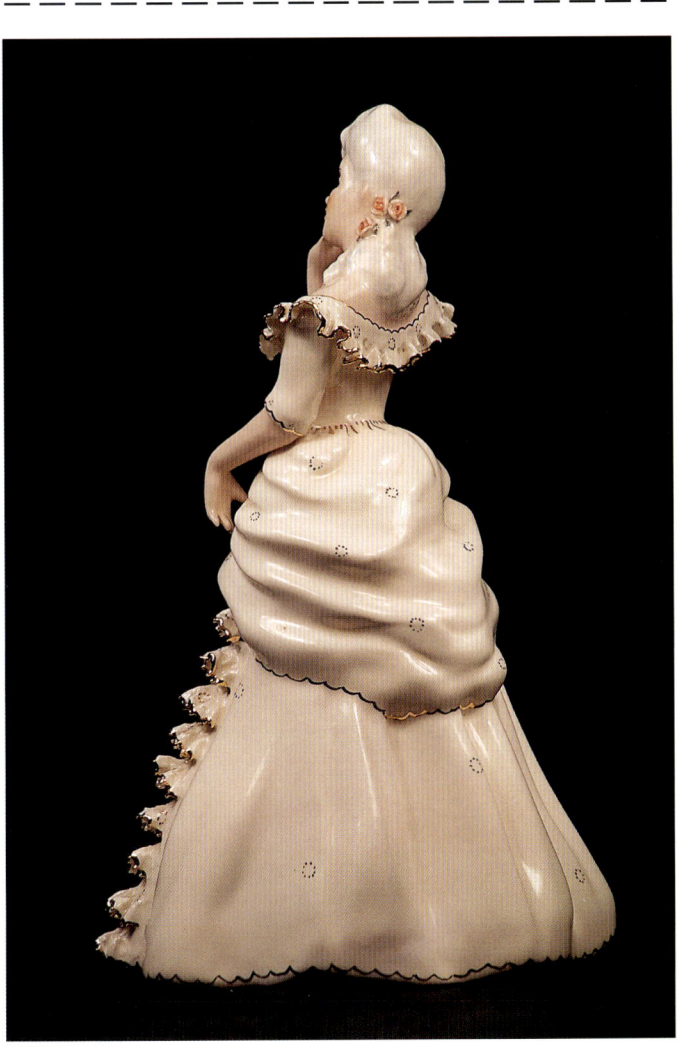

*Elizabeth*, French polonaise dress, c.1780.

## Florence Fashion Parade

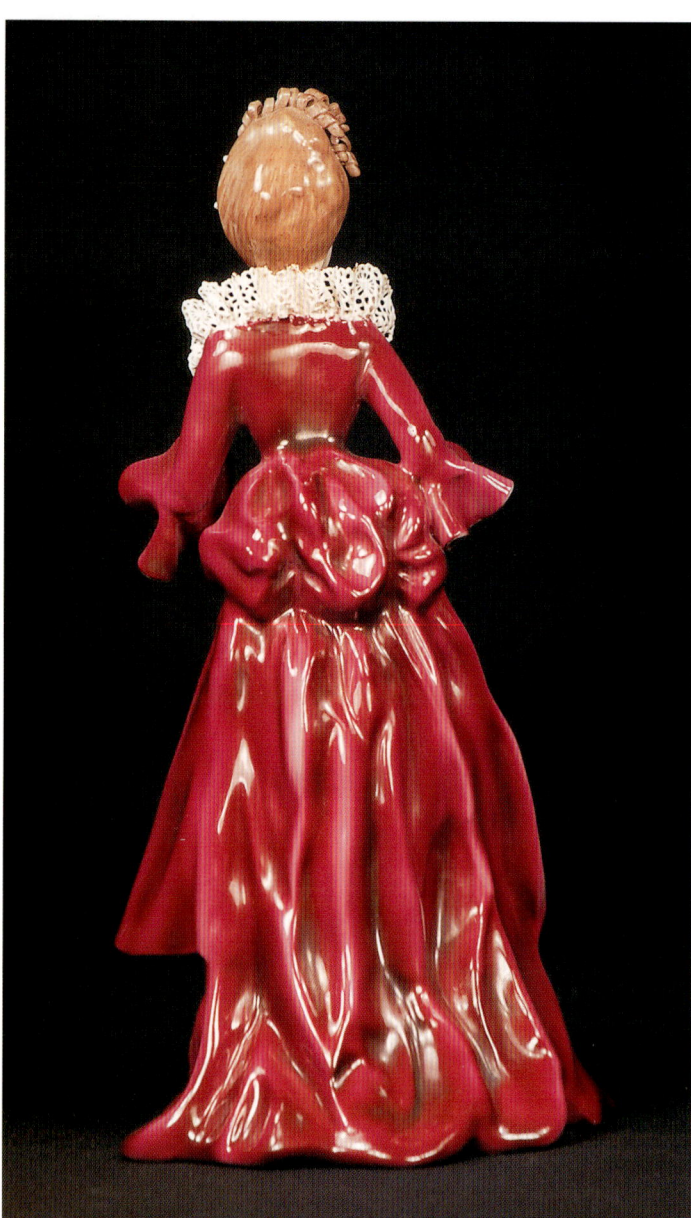

**Lady Diana,** English polonaise dress, c.1871.

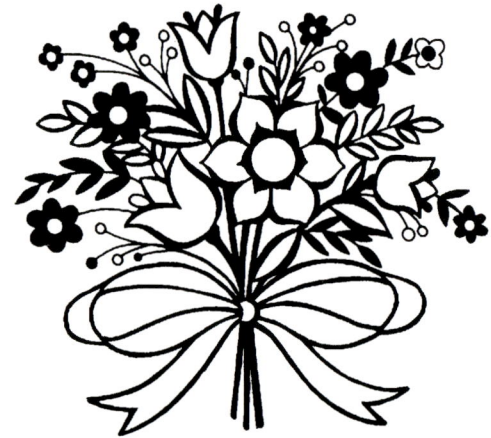

Just as individual garments appeared and disappeared, whole outfits seemingly did the same thing. Beginning in the 1880s, fashion dictated that gowns become narrower so women's clothing now begins to resemble the clothing of the 1820s. The main difference between the beginning of the century and the ending of the century is in attitude. In the 1880s, dresses are a tailored style, lacking the feminine softness of the earlier era. As accessories, gloves are worn for day and evening. They are extremely long and tucked up under the sleeve, even if the sleeve is above the elbow. Florence created two beautiful examples of the enlightened women of the 1880s in *Roberta* and *Josephine*. *Roberta's* dress is a stylish ball gown or dinner dress. Her hair is fashionably upswept in the style of the day. *Josephine* is shown in a day dress or walking dress and wears a Niniche bonnet with brim turned down in front and raised in back, adorned with a brightly colored feather.

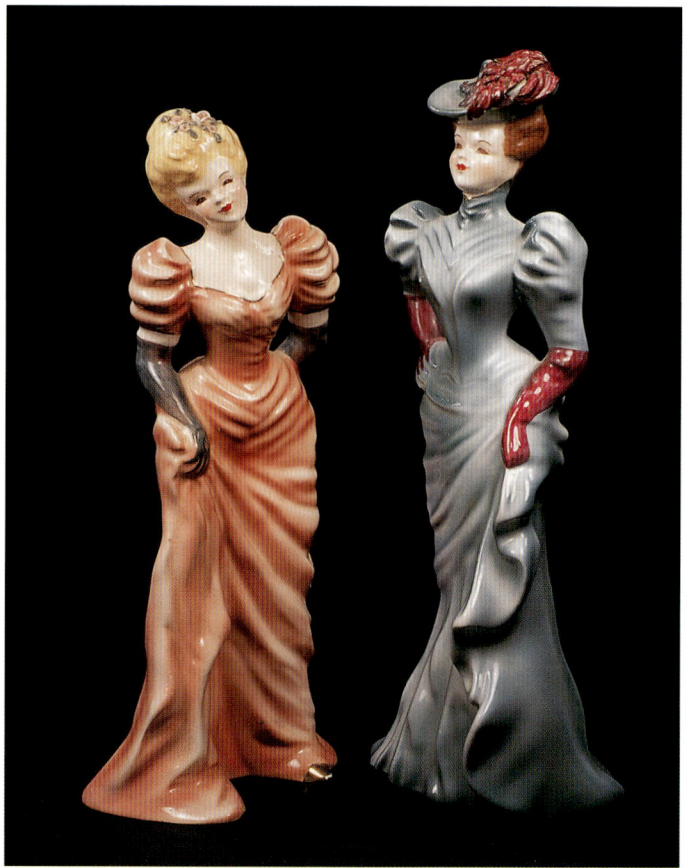

**Roberta and Josephine,** evening and daywear dress, c.1880s.

# Florence Fashion Parade

In keeping with the svelte elegance of the late nineteenth century and the new sophistication of the twentieth century, Florence created *Fair Lady*. The back of the dress, while not precisely a bustle, is more like a gathering of material to portray a perception of the bustle. Rather than being formed by a hoop device, the fullness is achieved by the wearing of petticoats. The petticoat is more than two yards wide at the hem, with gores and drawstrings at the top. Its bell shape is meant to match the shape of the dress and may be gathered at the top and again farther down the back. It may have endless rows of tucks, lace insertions, and puffings. *Fair Lady's* hairstyle is upswept into a knot at the top of the head. For evening wear, flowers encircle the topknot.

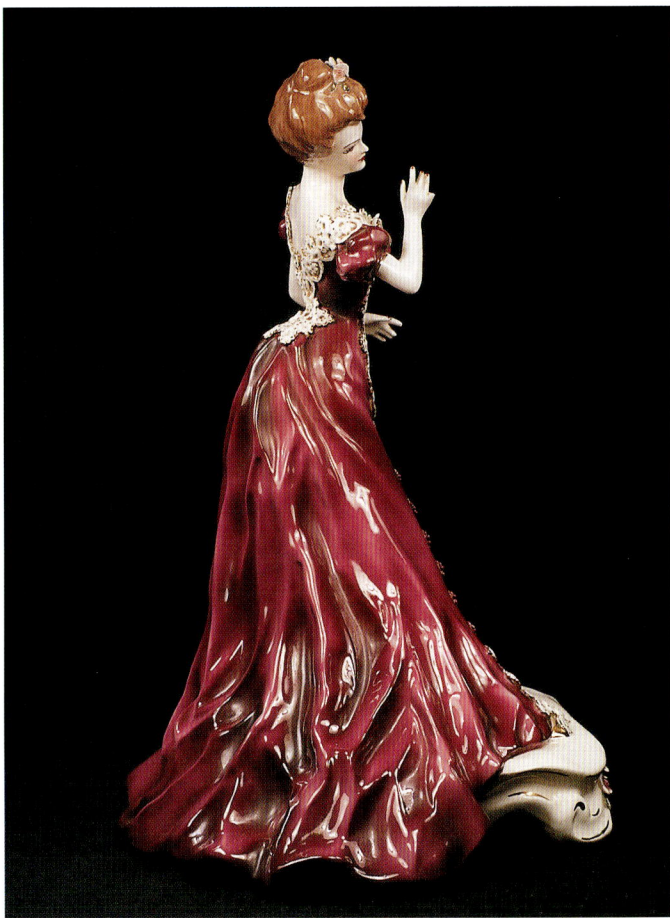

**Fair Lady**, dress gathered into bustle, 1890-1900.

## Attention to Detail

The attention to detail extends beyond clothing. Here, *Spring Reverie* holds a delicate bird's nest resplendent with two tiny eggs. The eggs are formed by using pieces of clay and the nest is created by pressing clay through a finely meshed screen. This is the same process for making ermine fur decoration. The lengths of screen meshed clay determine whether the application is to be made to look like twigs in a nest, feathers in a boa, or fur trim on a collar. The bird's nest "twigs" are three-quarters of an inch long.

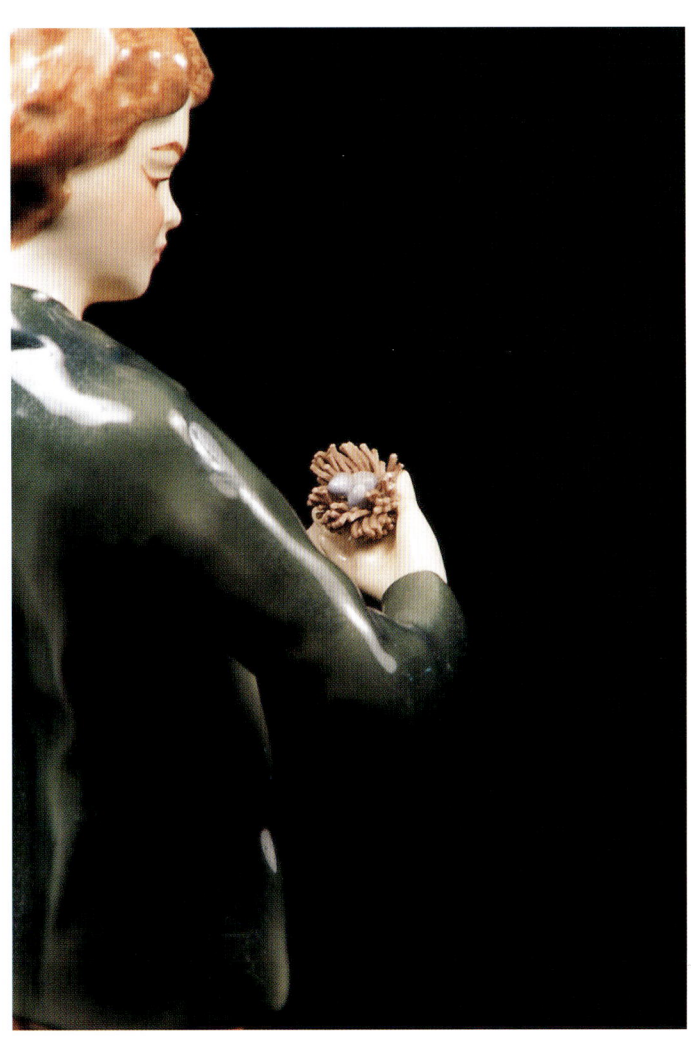

**Spring Reverie,** with nest of meshed clay.

## 104   Florence Fashion Parade

Not all the roses in Pasadena made it to the Rose Parade. Some of the most stunning ones are included in our Florence Parade of Roses. A talented artist, Margaret LaLone, demonstrates the intricate details of making a ceramic rose, petal by petal.

Florence's Parade of Roses

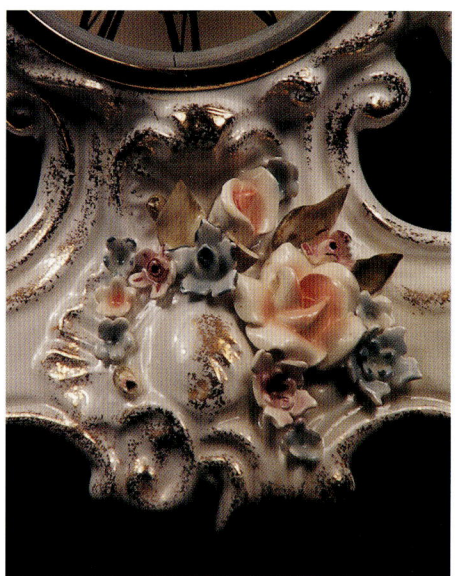

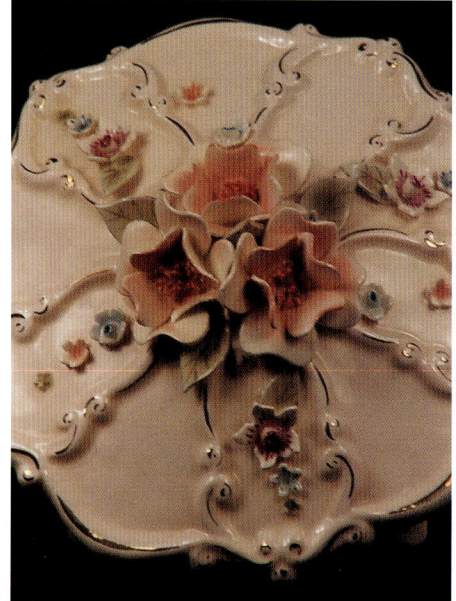

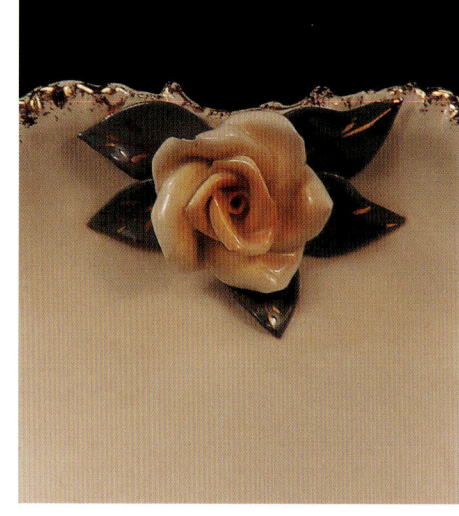

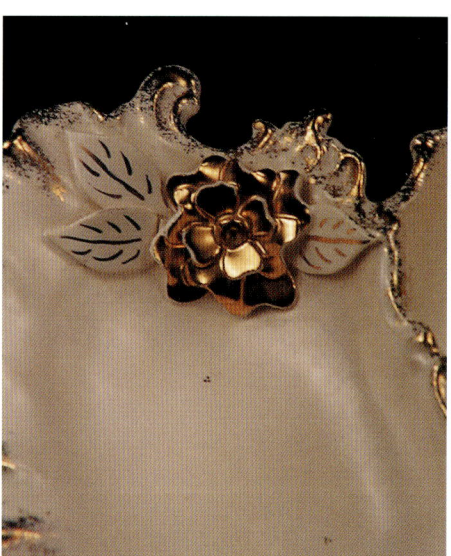

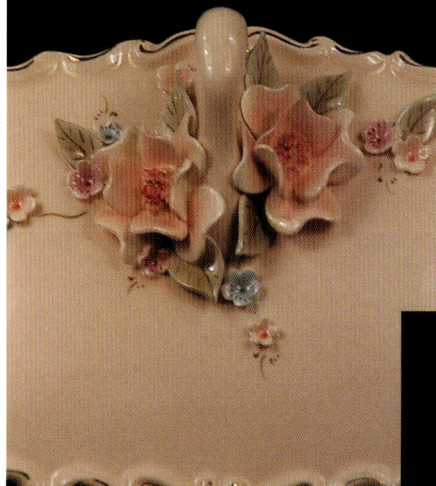

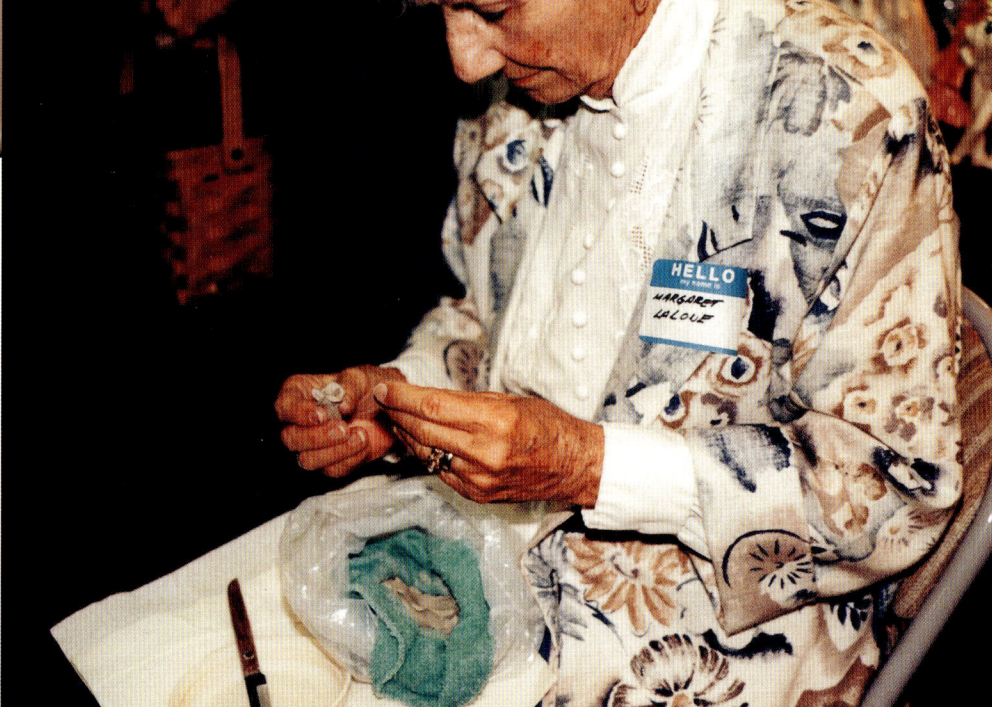

Margaret LaLone demonstrates the making of a ceramic rose at the Florence Convention 1998 in Pasadena, California.

# Florence Fashion Parade 105

After World War II, artist and designer Amy Delphino joined the Florence Ceramics Company. During the war, Delphino had been detained in a prisoner of war camp in Shanghai. Unfortunately, not much is known about this woman except that she spoke Chinese and had an extensive knowledge of the culture. She inspired Florence to model Chinese figures. Thus was born Florence's popular and extensive line of traditional Oriental figurines.

The company filed for a design patent on *Chinese Boy* and *Chinese Girl* in 1946 and the patent was approved in 1949. These seemingly are the only figures for which design patents were filed. Starting in 1949, Florence Ceramics copyrighted many of the figures under "Works of Art and Designs for Works of Art as Ceramic Statuettes." A listing of the copyrights Florence held is included in Chapter IX.

Many of the Chinese figures exhibited detailed artwork. For example, Amy Delphino designed a beautiful coat for *Kiu*, whose name means "Minister of High Estate."

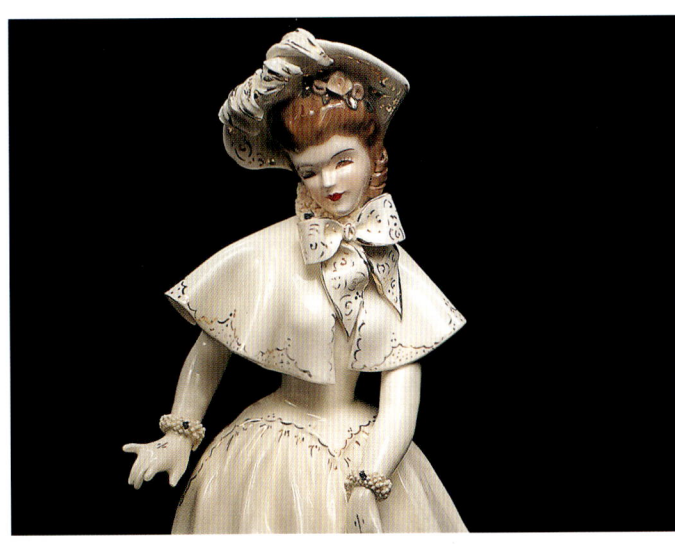

**Annette,** clay cape applied separately.

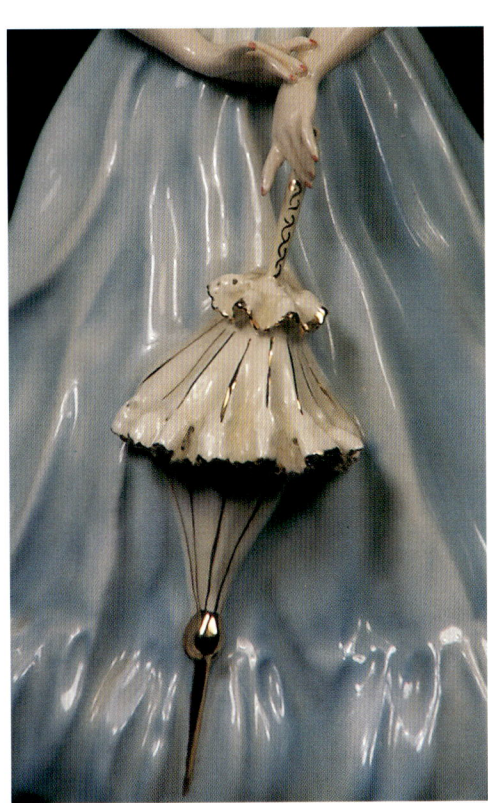

Pagoda style parasol.

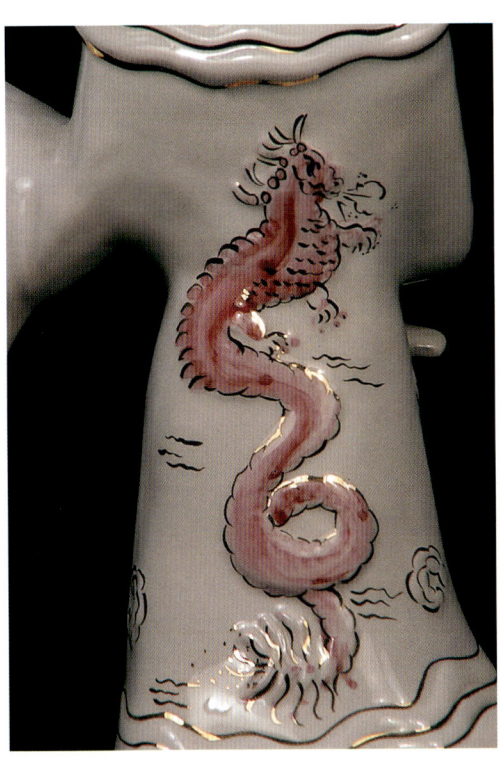

**Kiu,** with embossed and hand painted dragon.

Continuing with more attention to detail in fashions, *Annette* wears a mantlet cape, which is a separate application of clay. Her bow and the decoration on her hat are also individually applied pieces; her fingers are articulated. Other examples of accessories used by Florence (shown here and on next page) include a pagoda-style parasol; six-sided, beribboned hat box; round hatbox with ribbons and gold stripes; and nosegay. Each is a separate application done by the artists in the clay room.

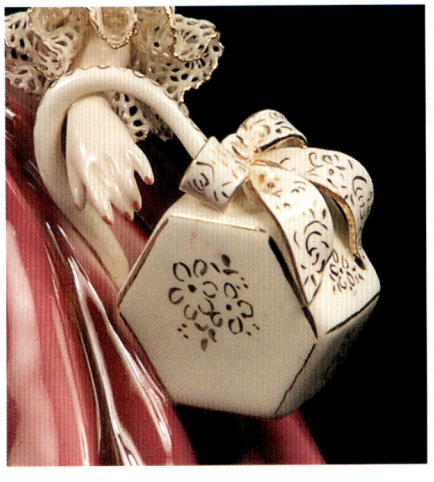

Six-sided hatbox with applied ribbons.

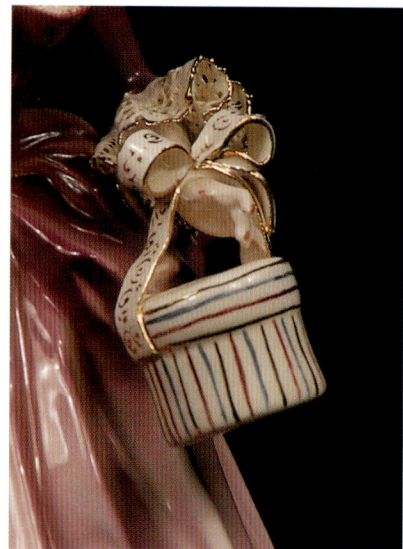

Hatbox with gold stripes.

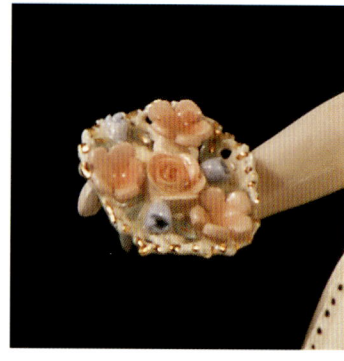

Nosegay with applied flowers.

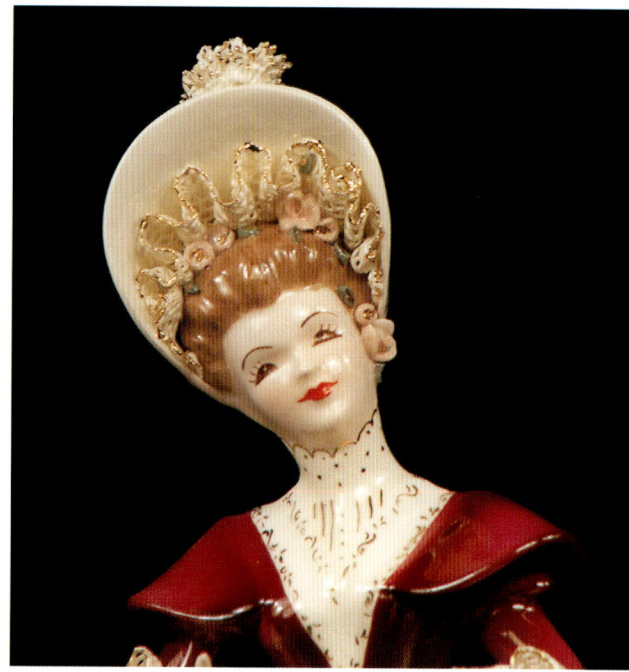

**Georgette,** elaborate, labor intensive hat.

For a change of pace, we can view the lovely little scene hand painted on the lid of a cigarette box (pg. 108). It is a work of art in miniature!

Consider the time involved in decorating *Georgette's* hat. The hat is separately applied to the figure, then gathered lace is inserted into the hat, and, lastly, tiny flowers are added as an embellishment. These additions are affixed with slip (liquid clay), then all are hand painted.

*Annabel* strolls through her garden wearing her sun hat and carrying a basket for gathering flowers. Note the rose-decorated garter on her sleeve.

*Mary* exhibits a lace bow, hand painted striped cuffs, and articulated fingers. Seated figures like Mary are also fastened to the ceramic furniture with liquid clay.

*Madame DuBarry* is an especially good example of applied curls. Cutting a narrow strip of flattened clay creates the curls. This strip is wound around a tiny rod. Again, the tendrils are affixed with slip. The curls are sized proportionately to the figurine. *Rosalie* and *Virginia* demonstrate the different proportions of the curls to the smaller sized figures.

*Vivian* (shown on pg. 108) is an outstanding example of the painstakingly detailed work that went into Florence figurines. Take a close look at *Vivian's* hat. It is made from tiny flowers that are individually pressed through a mold. Each tiny flower is picked up on the tip of the handle of the artist's brush. Then it is coated with slip and gently pressed to the hat. The petal-shaped parasol with handle is another individual application. The bell sleeves are added, being similarly formed and applied as the mantlet cape that *Annette* (pg. 105) wears.

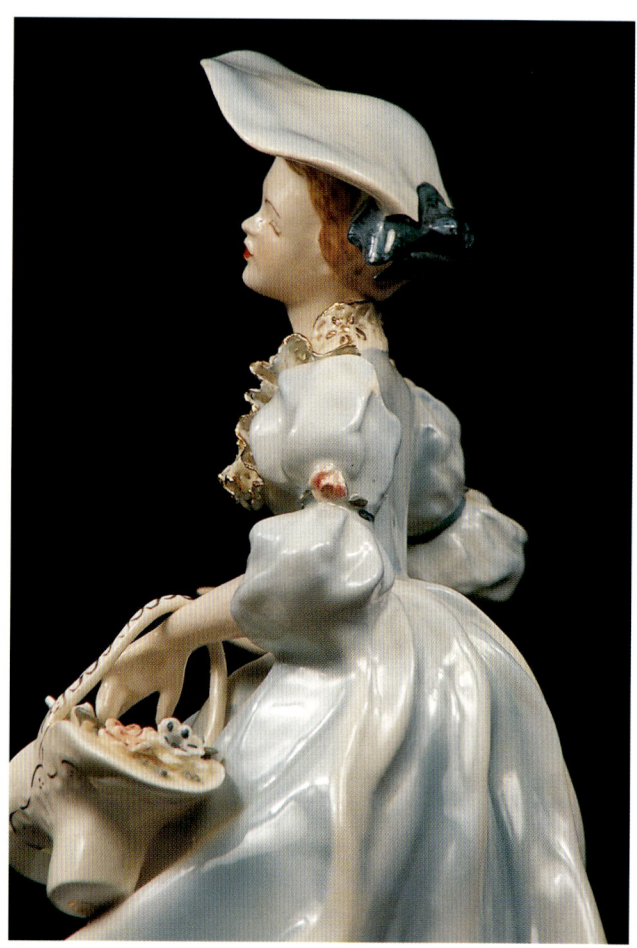

**Annabel,** decorated garter.

**Florence Fashion Parade** 107

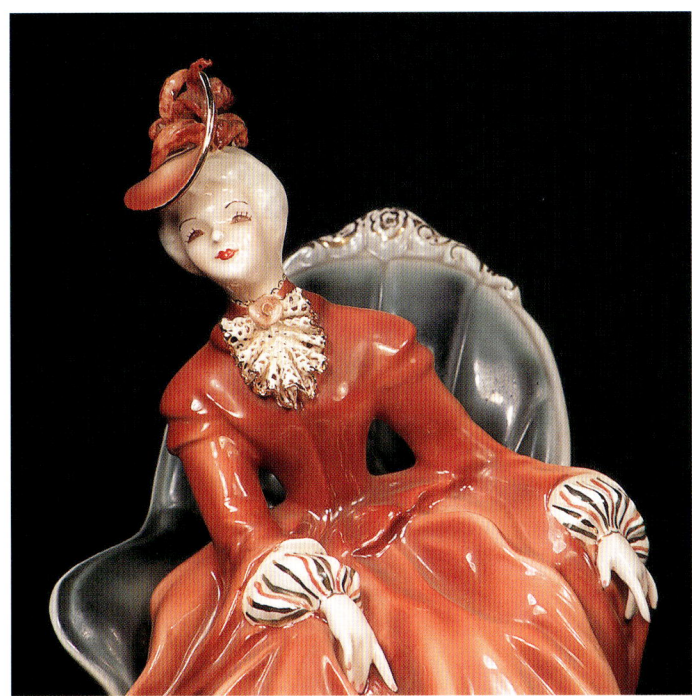

**Mary,** fancy bow and hand painted cuffs.

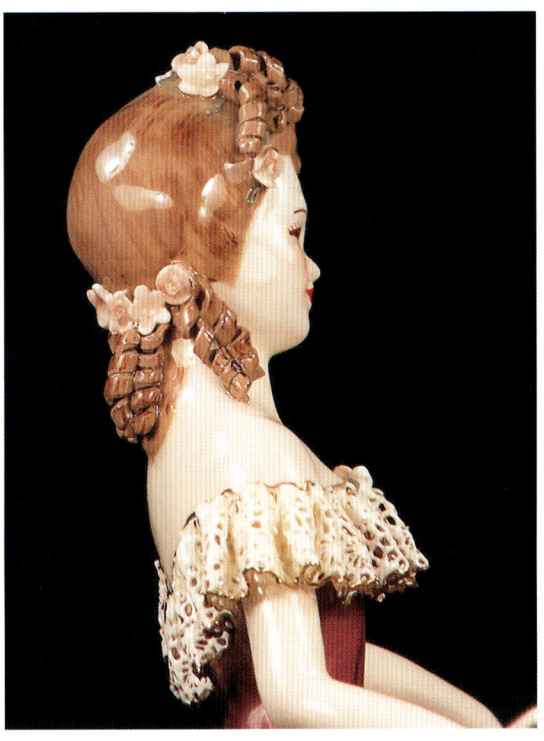

**Rosalie,** smaller curls.

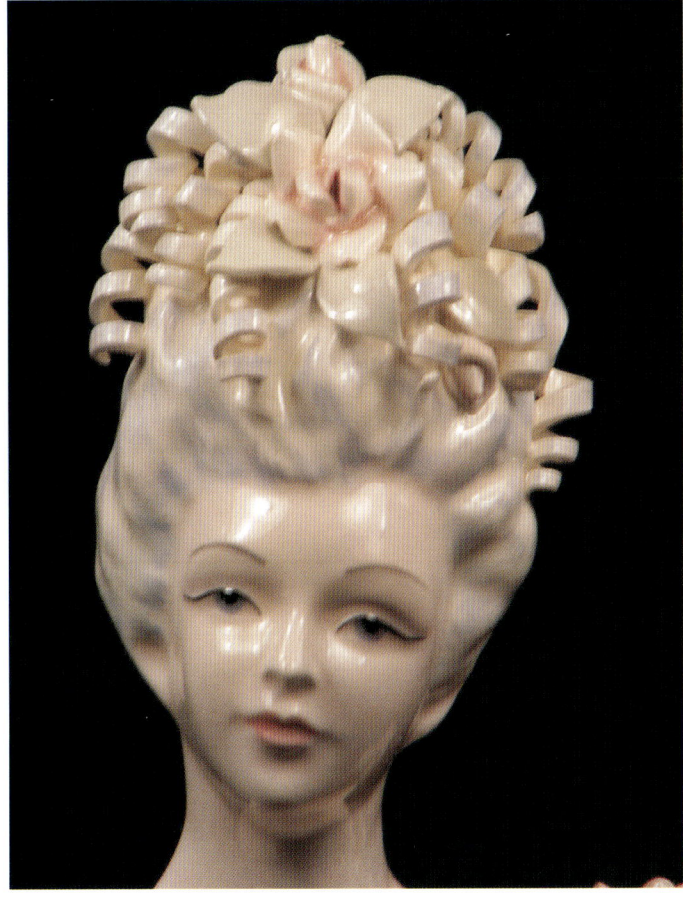

**Madame DuBarry,** large curls.

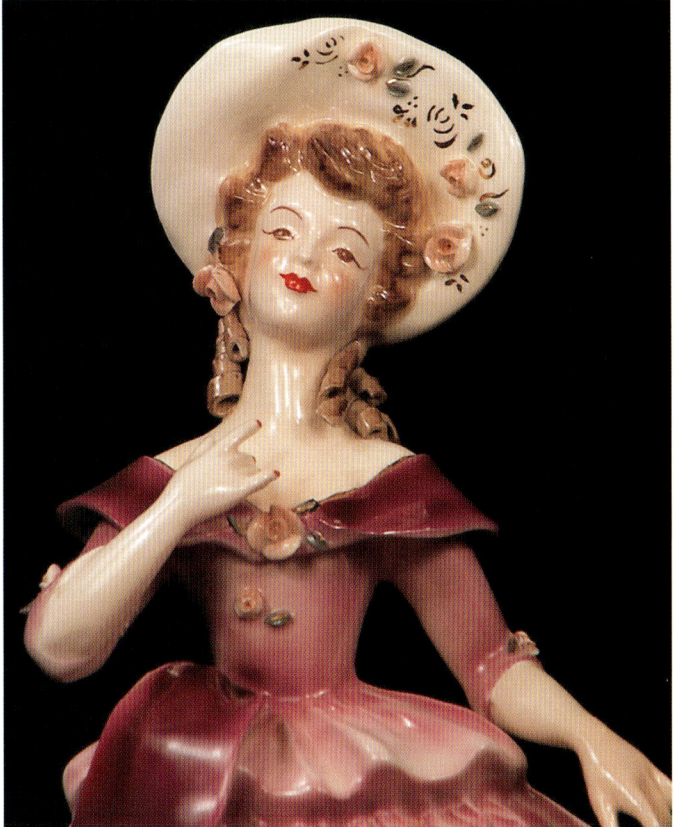

**Virginia,** proportioned curls.

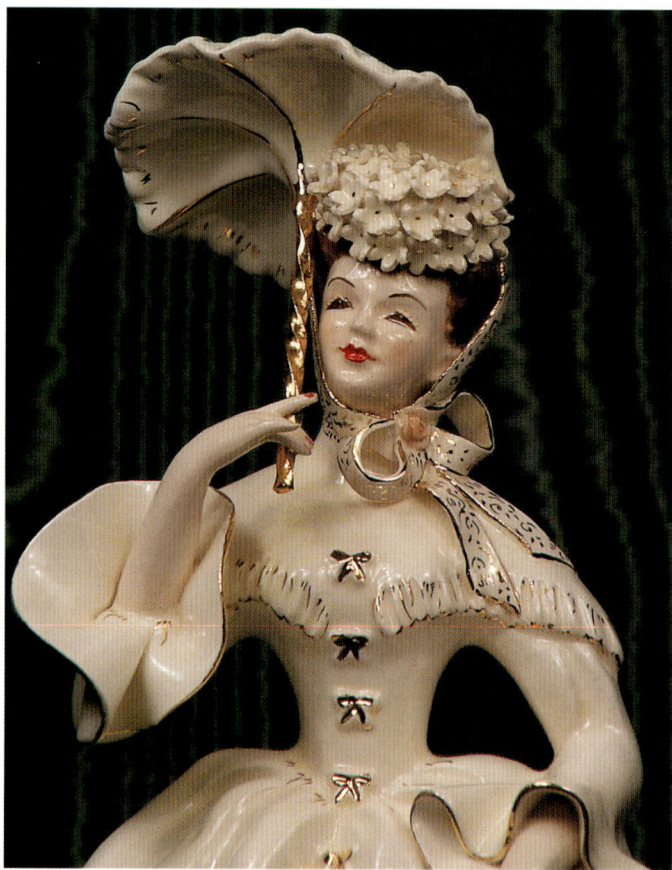

**Vivian,** look closely at her hat.

The bodice for *Rose Marie's* dress is created by dipping scalloped lace in a heavier solution of slip and then applying it to the figurine's form. The thickened slip fills the holes in the lace, giving it the appearance of tulle. A tiny, hand crafted rose is tucked into the décolletage of *Rose Marie's* gown. Matching roses adorn the folds of her hem.

Reminiscent of *Vivian's* bell sleeves and *Annette's* mantlet, the ballet tutu that *Lisa* wears is also clay that has been cut, molded, and applied separately.

The *Bride's* bouquet is a cascade of individually pressed flowers of varying sizes and a separately applied ribbon. Each flower is hand painted after it is applied to the figurine.

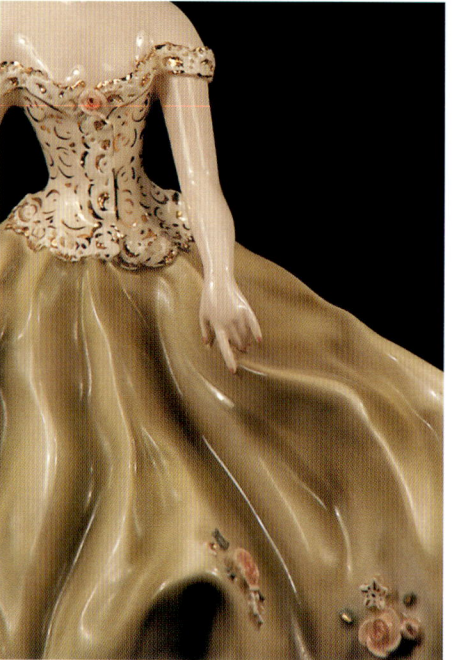

**Rose Marie,** "tulle" bodice, rose trimmed.

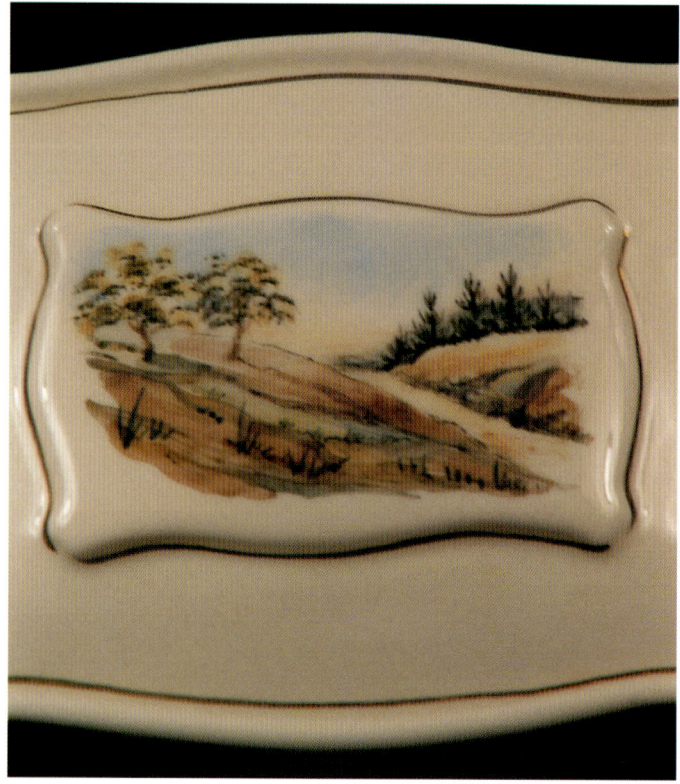

**Cigarette box,** art in miniature.

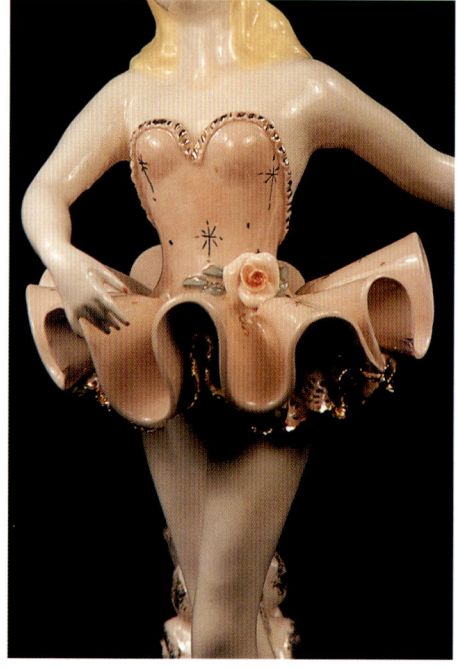

**Lisa,** molded and applied tutu.

# Florence Fashion Parade 109

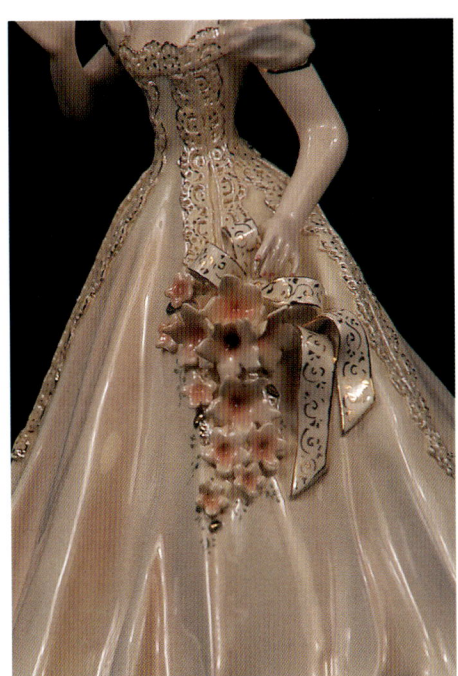

The **Bride's** bouquet.

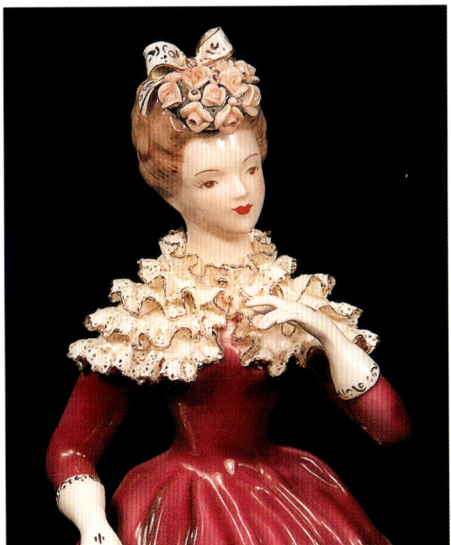

***Margaret,*** ruffles and roses.

Elegant details! Roses and tiny pressed flowers are used around the neckline and at the bottom of the elbow length sleeve of the dress worn by *Princess*. Her upswept hairdo features applied curls and roses. A beautiful bow sash is cut from a strip of flattened clay and then applied at the waist of her gown.

Tiny rows of one-eighth inch lace form *Margaret's* lace canezou. Her articulated gloved hand draws attention to her rows of ruffles. A small bow is cut from clay, formed, and added to her coiffure along with hand painted roses.

Detailed scalloped lace is used to form a charming insert to *Fair Lady's* ball gown. The scallops around the neckline are slightly raised, perhaps for the sake of modesty. A tiny rose is formed petal by petal and then placed in her outstretched hand.

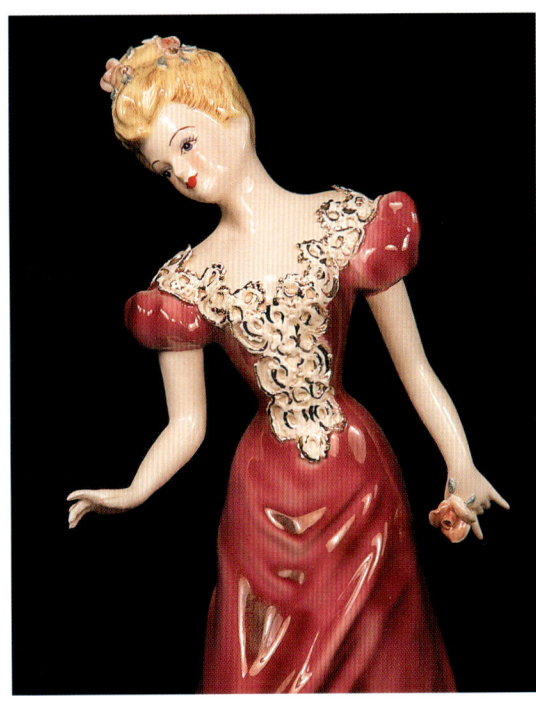

***Fair Lady,*** with rose in hand.

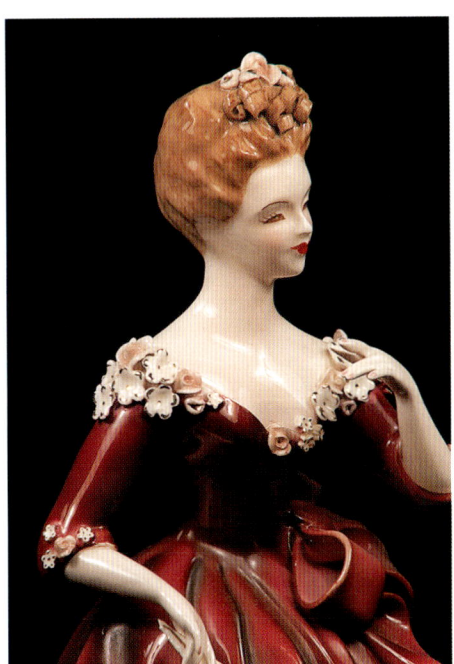

***Princess,*** elegant details.

Shown on the next page, four more figurines illustrate additional details. Elegant in brocade, *Virginia* shows off her aigrette accented coiffure. Her hat is a tiny velvet bow.

*Claudia's* lace pelerine bodice is decidedly feminine. Her broad brimmed hat is a miniature garden of tiny pressed flowers, complemented by an applied ribbon.

*Matilda* displays an excellent example of ermine decoration. Clay is pressed through a finely meshed screen to approximately one-quarter inch in length. Then small dots of black enamel are applied to make the "ermine fur" trim. The clay is gently tamped down to give the appearance of dense fur.

*Carmen* is the only figurine we have seen that has lace with red painted edges. A delicate, hand painted 22-karat gold necklace encircles her neck. *Victoria's* necklace is, however, a raised decoration made by the addition of a tiny piece of applied clay.

## 110 Florence Fashion Parade

*Caroline* is most fashionable in brocade trimmed in velvet. In her hand is a tiny evening purse made to look like gold mesh. Imagine fashioning a fabric purse that is only one-quarter inch wide and less than a half inch in length!

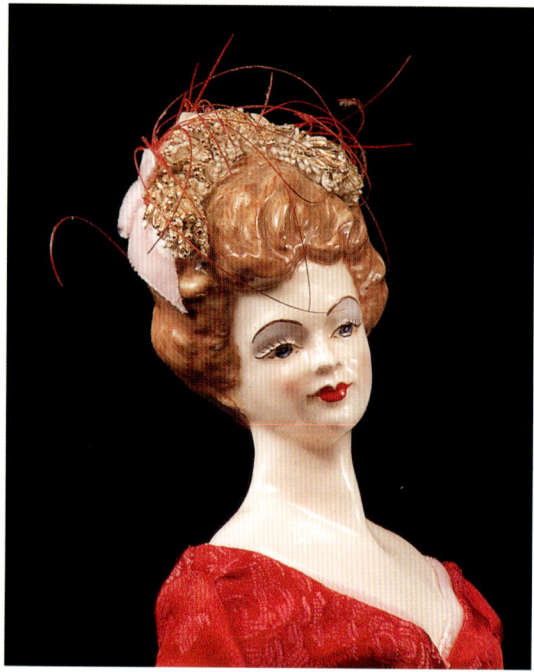

**Virginia,** velvet hat with feather.

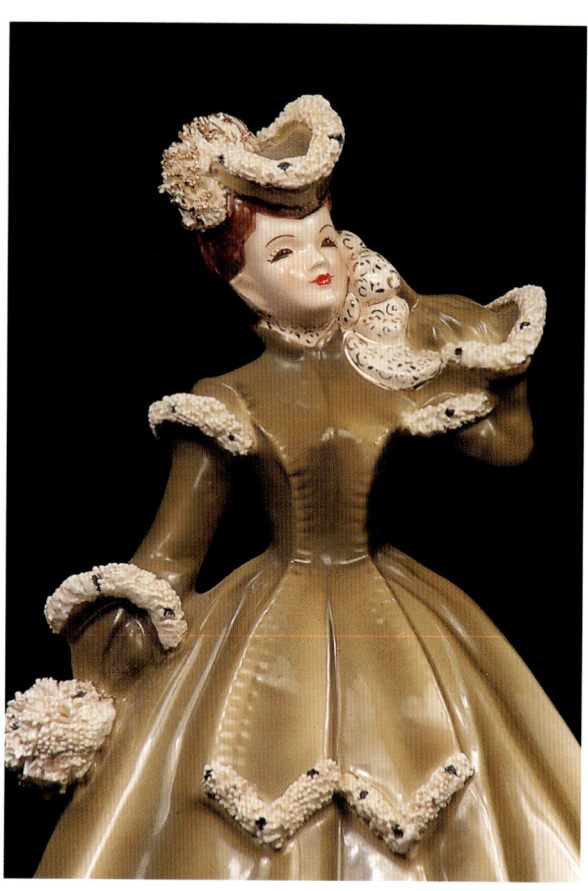

**Matilda,** ermine fur decoration.

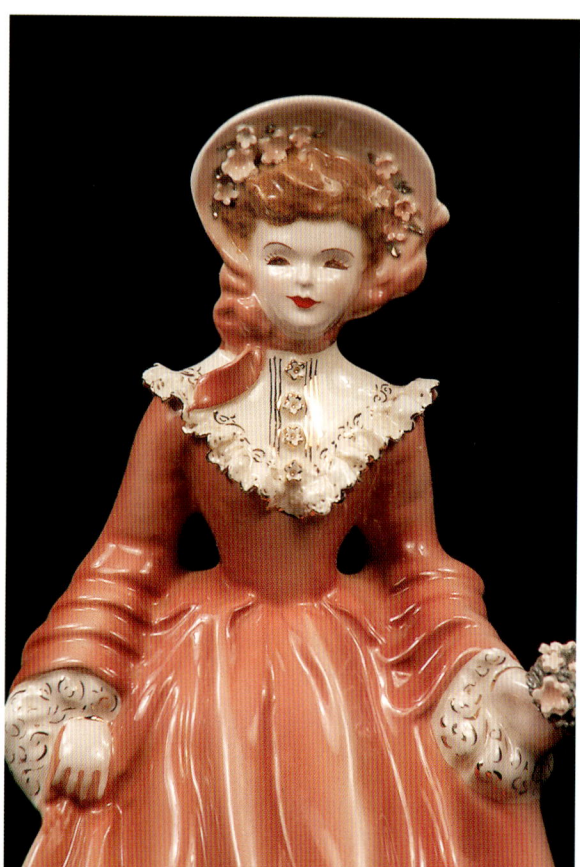

**Claudia,** hat with tiny pressed flowers and applied ribbon.

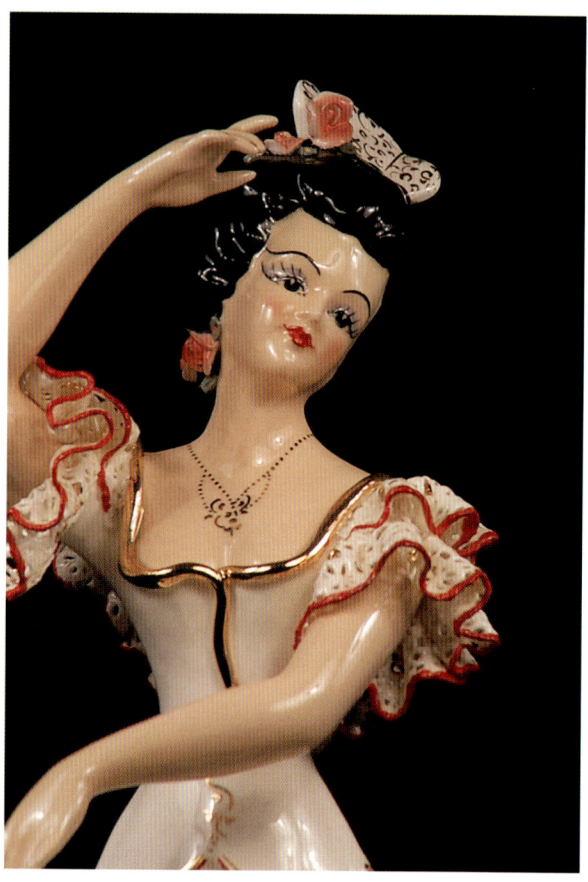

**Carmen,** red edged lace.

## Florence Fashion Parade 111

More gold decoration is shown on *Annabelle* and *Gibson Girl*. *Annabelle* is holding a tiny blue bird in her articulated hand. Her mantlet and sleeves feature hand painted gold and screened mesh designed to look like gold braid trim. *Gibson Girl's* feather boa is screen meshed clay as well, one-half inch in length. The threads of the mesh are separated slightly to give the boa a light feathery look.

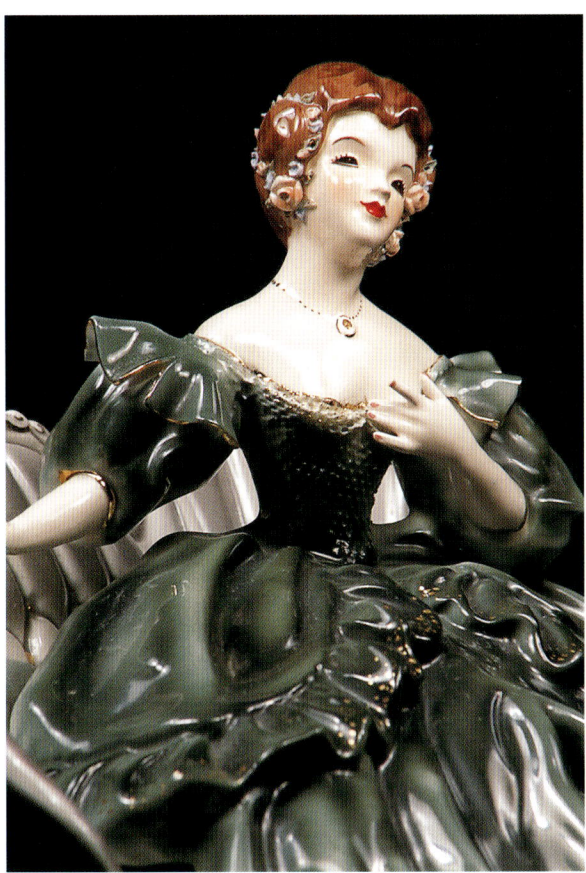

**Victoria,** applied necklace.

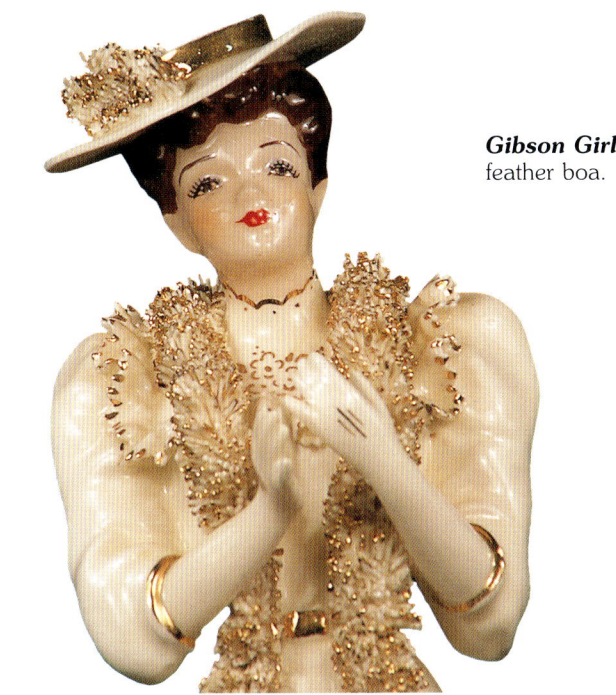

***Gibson Girl,*** feather boa.

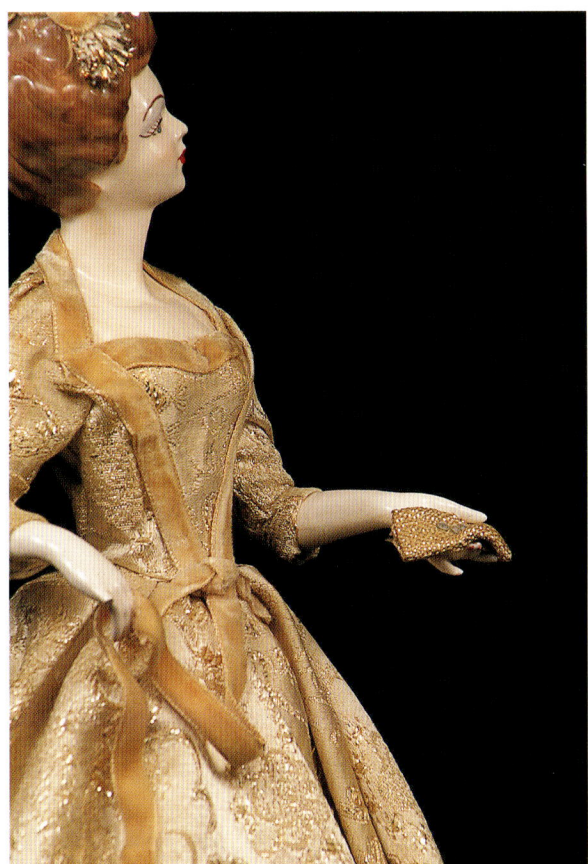

**Caroline,** tiny fabric purse.

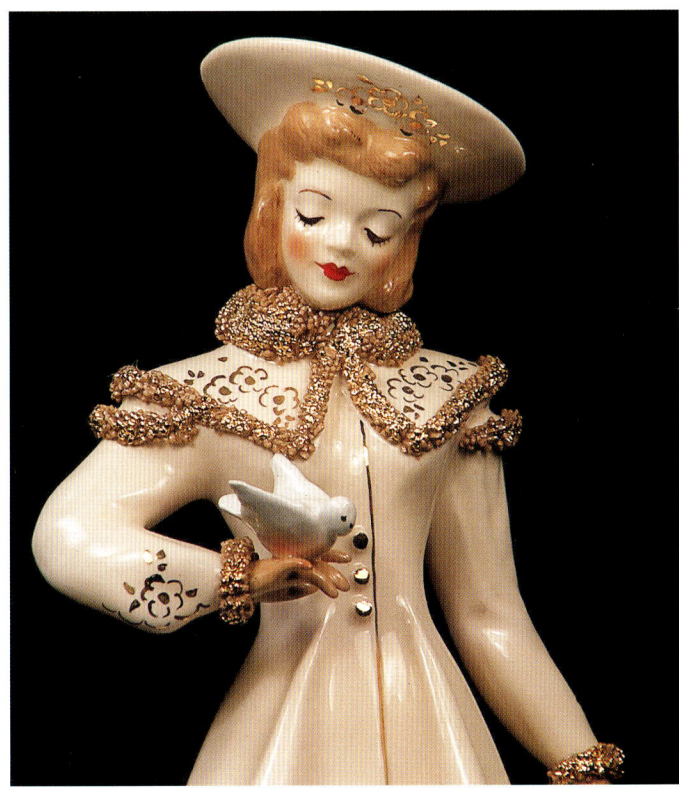

**Annabelle**, blue bird and gold ermine trim.

Looking over Grandmother's shoulder on the *Memories* figurine, we can see the hand painted photos in her album. And, if we peek over *Dear Ruth's* shoulder we can read her letter written in 22-karat gold.

*Yvonne's* stylish hat is formed from net lace. The net lace is gathered into ribbon folds, dipped in liquid clay, and applied to the crown of her head. Again, as with *Matilda*, we can glimpse an example of ermine fur on her sleeve cuffs.

Both *Lady Diana* and *Prima Donna* are high fashion examples of a portrait collar made from wheel lace that has been immersed in slip. *Lady Diana* wears the bell cuffs formed from clay and then attached at the wrist of her garment. *Prima Donna's* puffings in her Gabrielle sleeves are formed by crimping the clay into place.

The cherub used on the clocks is made in a separate mold and fired as a single entity. It is then placed carefully on the clock later in the production.

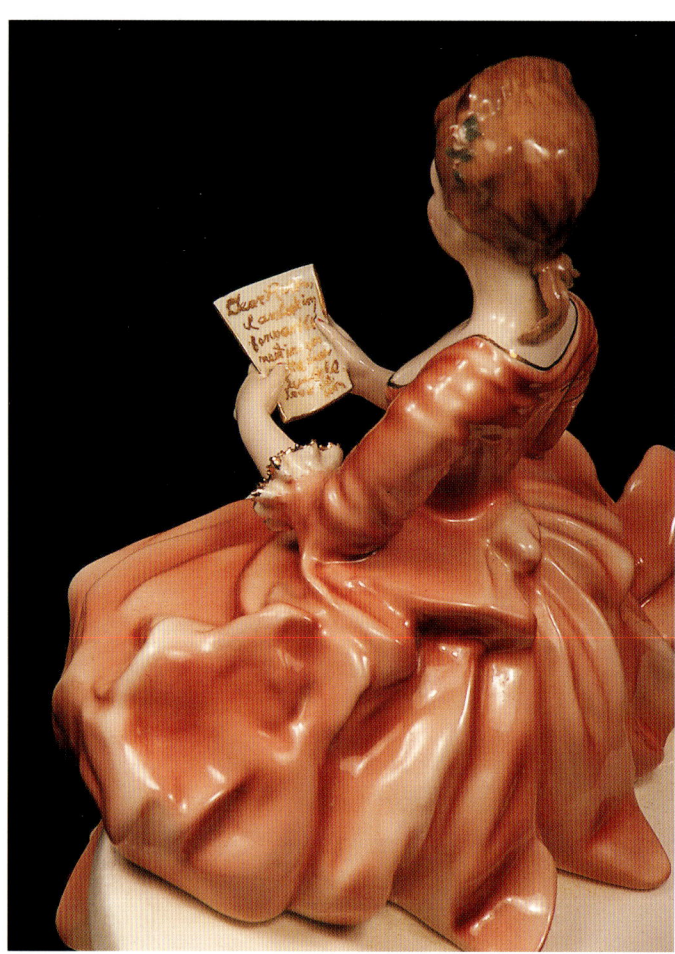

**Dear Ruth,** gold lettering in letter.

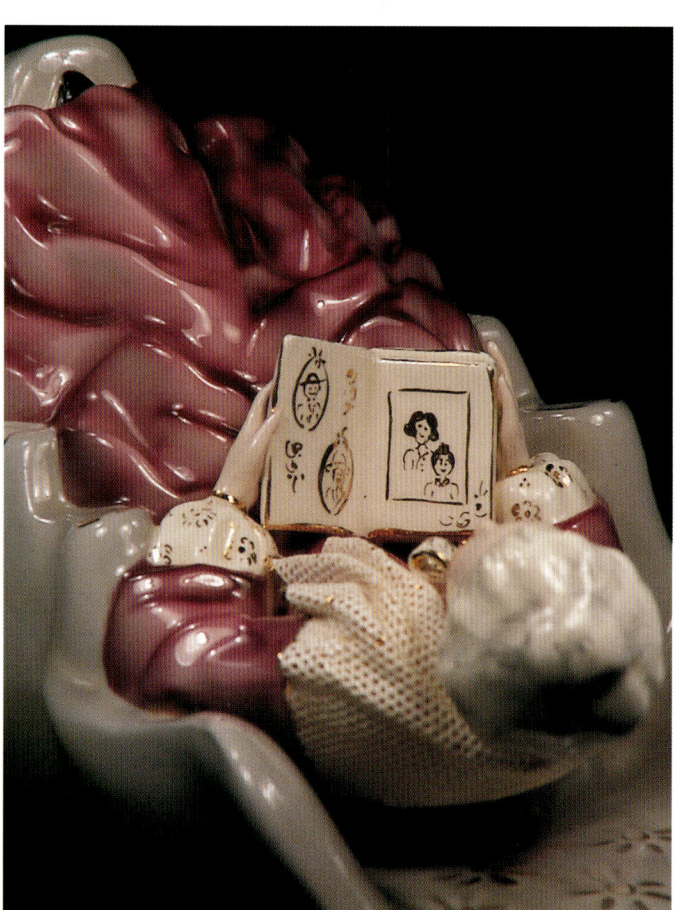

**Memories,** hand painted pictures.

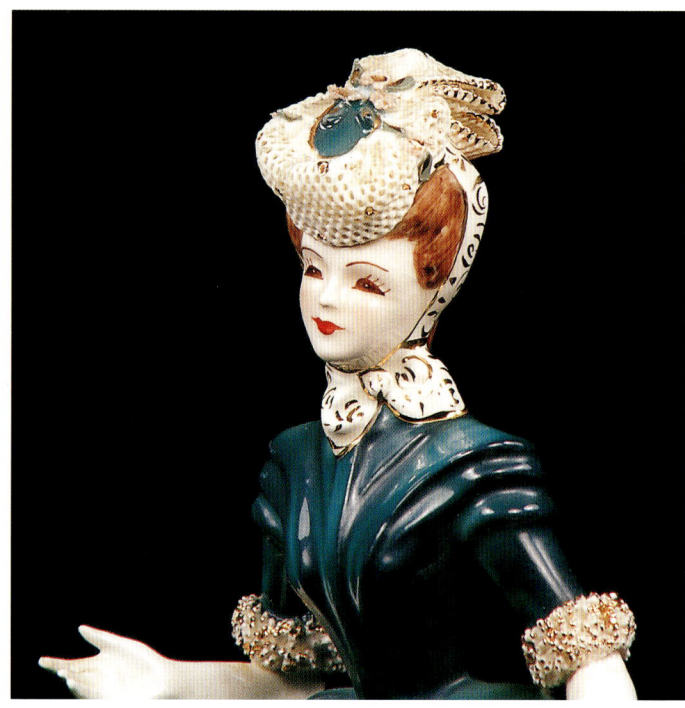

**Yvonne,** net lace hat.

**Florence Fashion Parade** 113

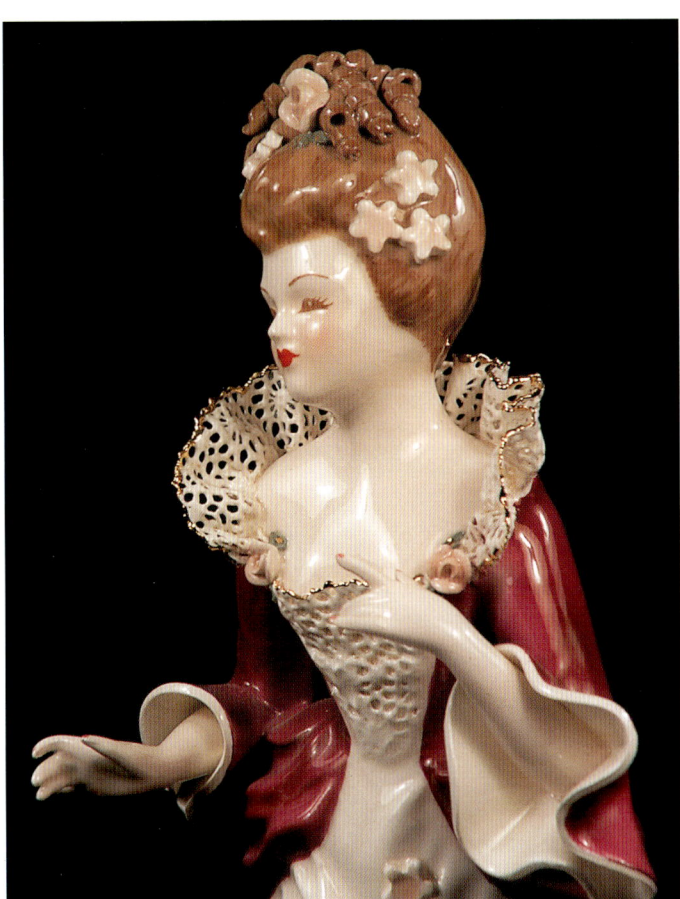

**Lady Diana,** portrait collar and bell sleeves.

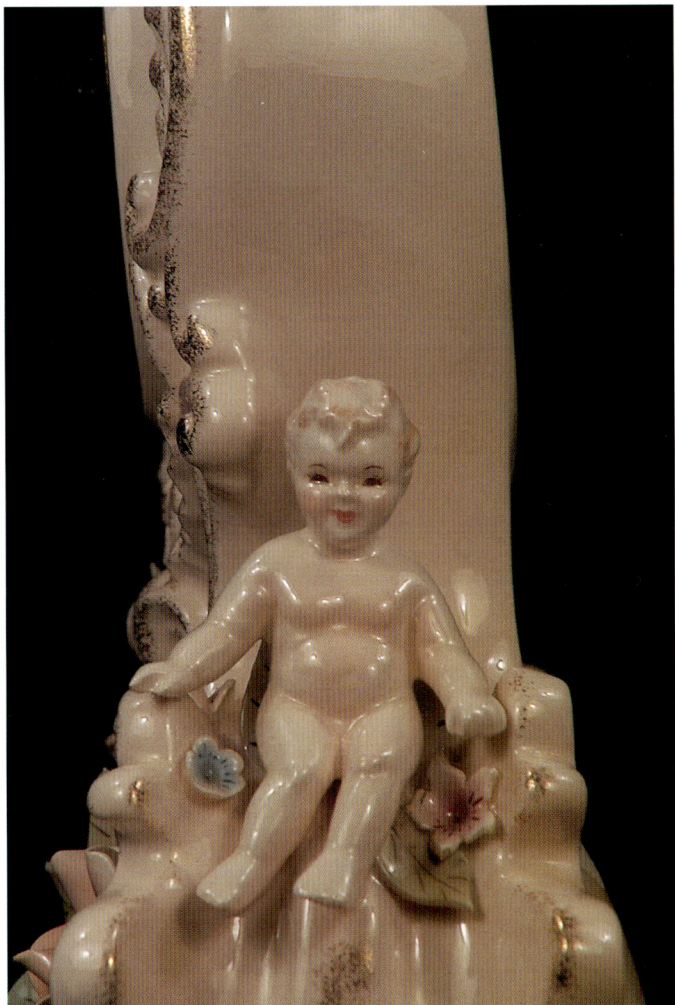

Cherub applied to side of clock

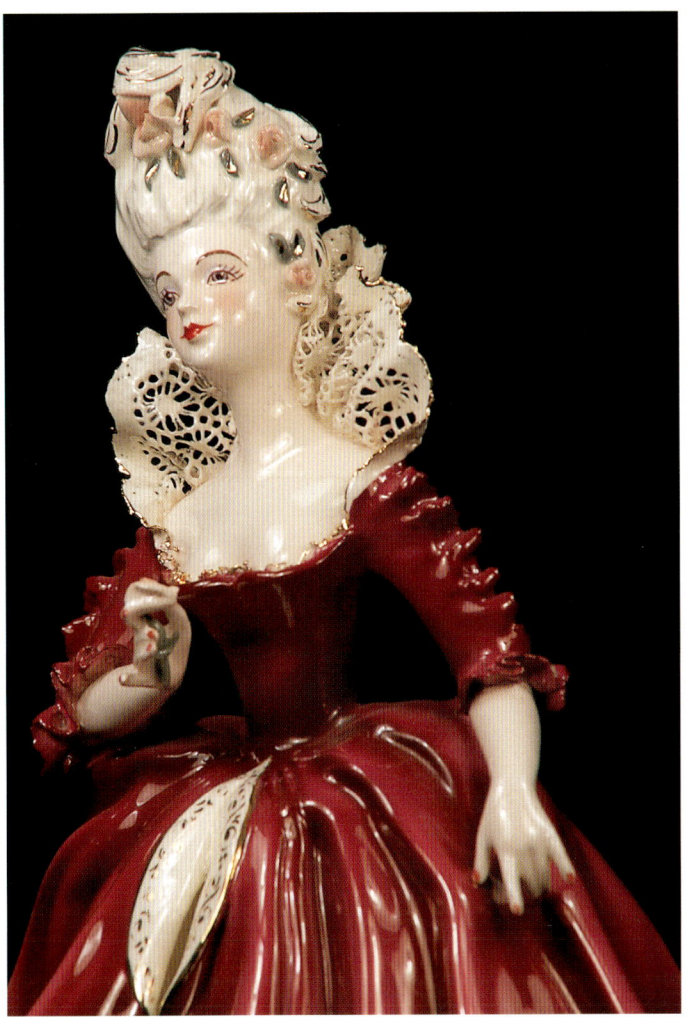

**Prima Donna,** portrait collar and Gabrielle sleeves.

**114  Florence Fashion Parade**

## *Lace*

Following are the different kinds of lace used by Florence Ceramics. They vary in size and type and are named accordingly. Clifford Ward stated that only 100% cotton lace is used in ceramic production – synthetic laces do not burn away cleanly during the firing process. We have no examples of the original cotton lace used by the company. Therefore, we have photographed the finished products and named the type and size of lace used on each figure.

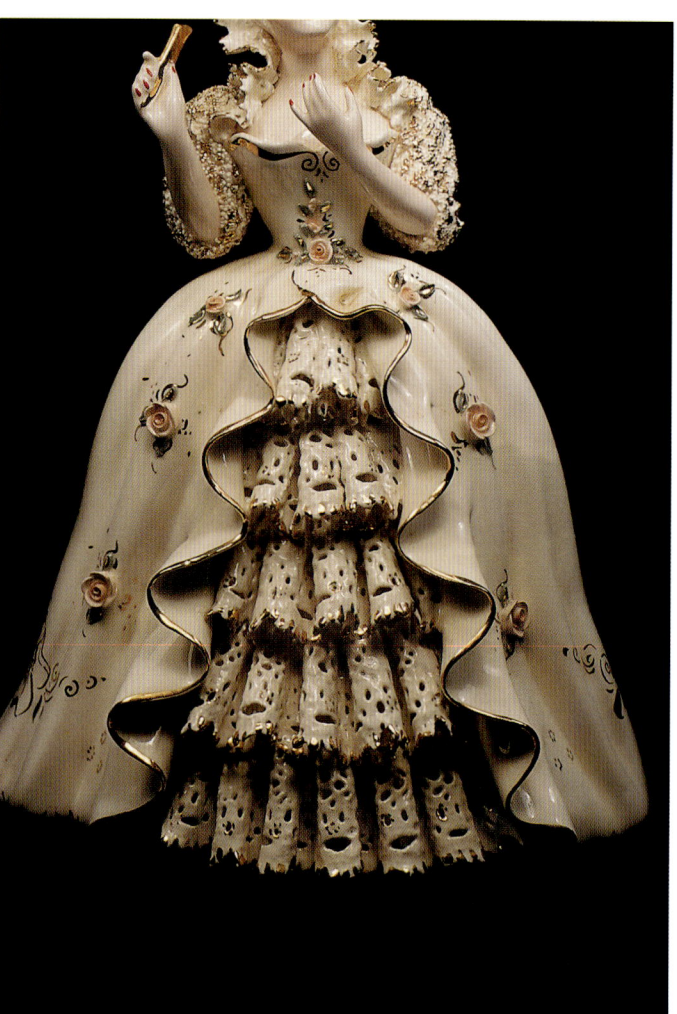

Wheel lace large, 1", as used on **Marie Antionette**.

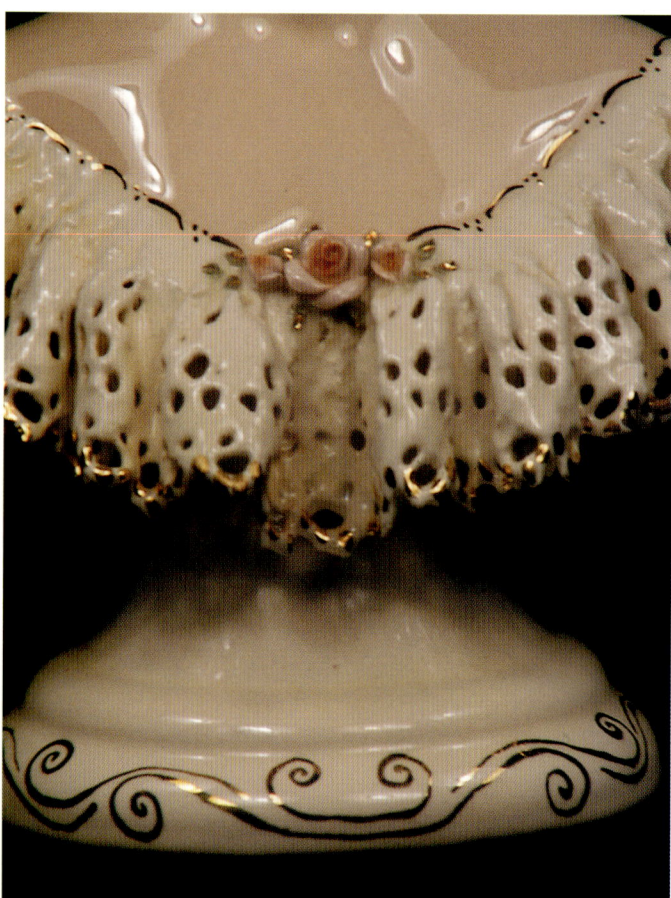

Wheel lace extra large, 1.75", as used on **American Lady**.

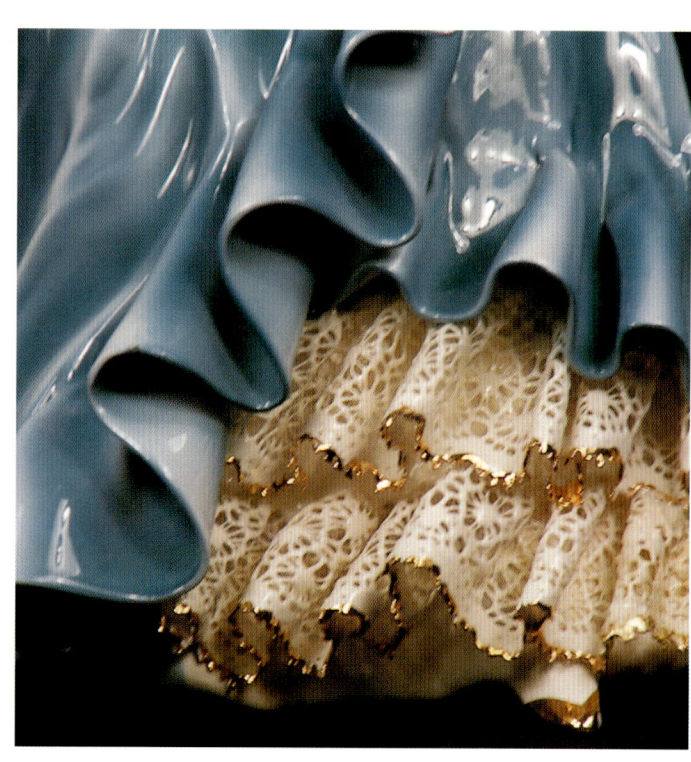

Wheel lace medium, .5", as used on **Masquerade**.

**Florence Fashion Parade 115**

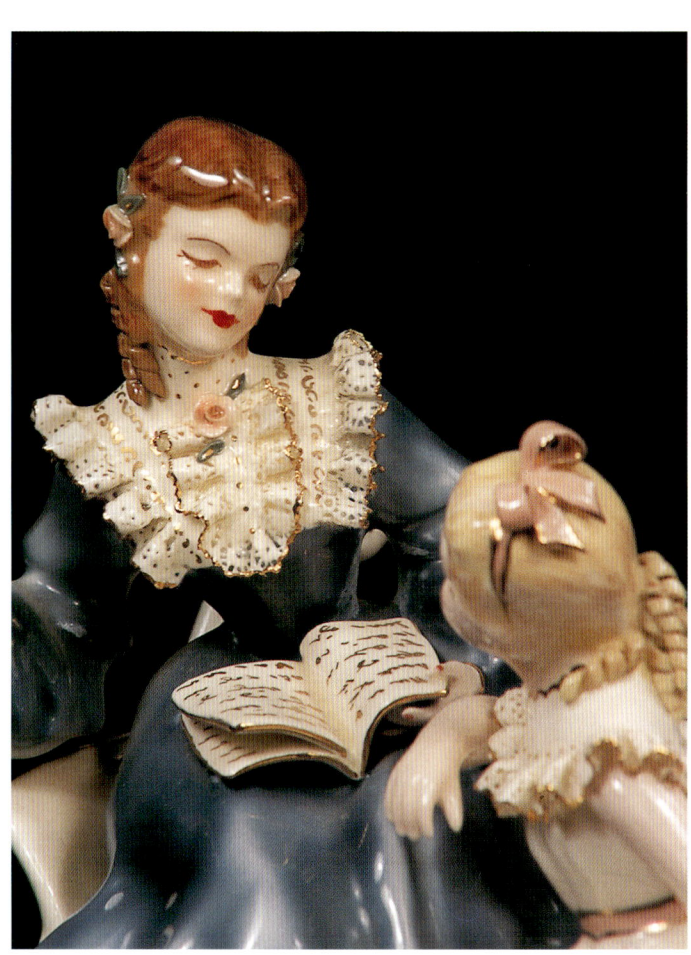

Wheel lace small, .25", as used on lady in **Story Hour**.

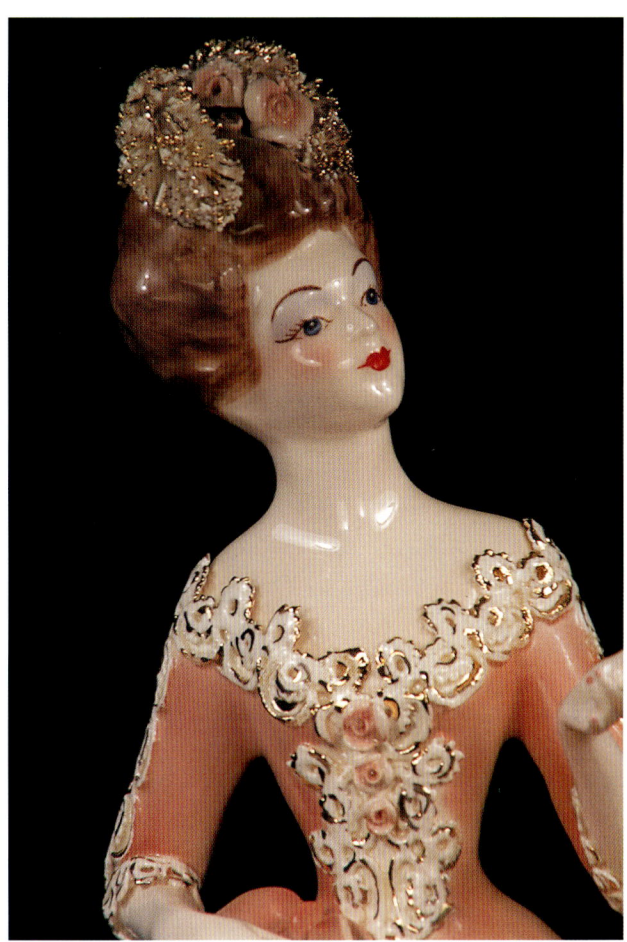

Scalloped lace medium, .5", as used on **Lillian Russell**.

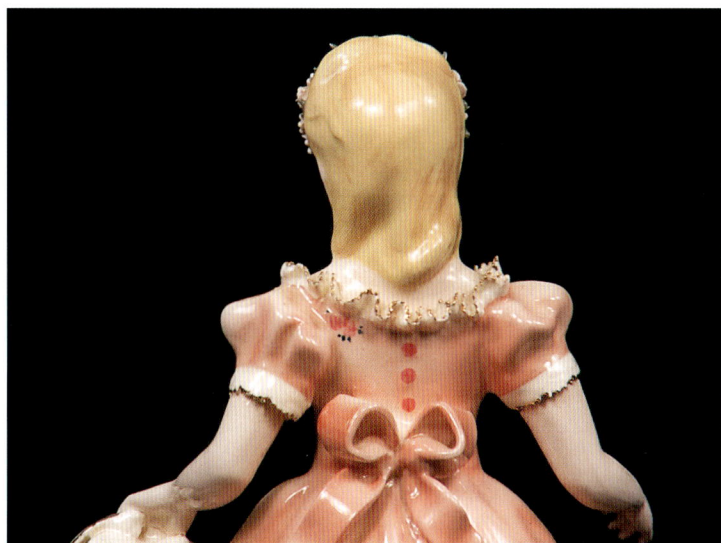

Wheel lace small, .25", as used on **Pamela with Basket**.

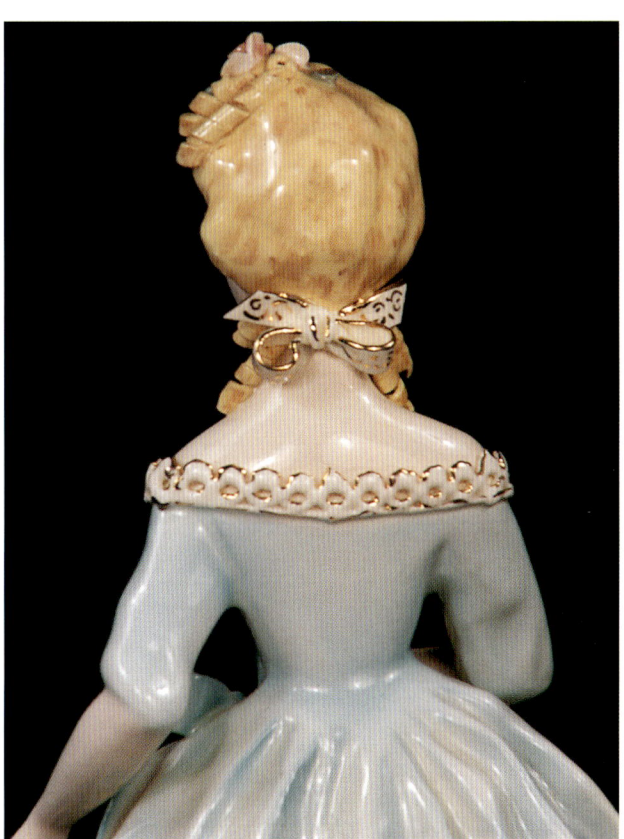

Scalloped lace small, .25", as used on **Maybelle**.

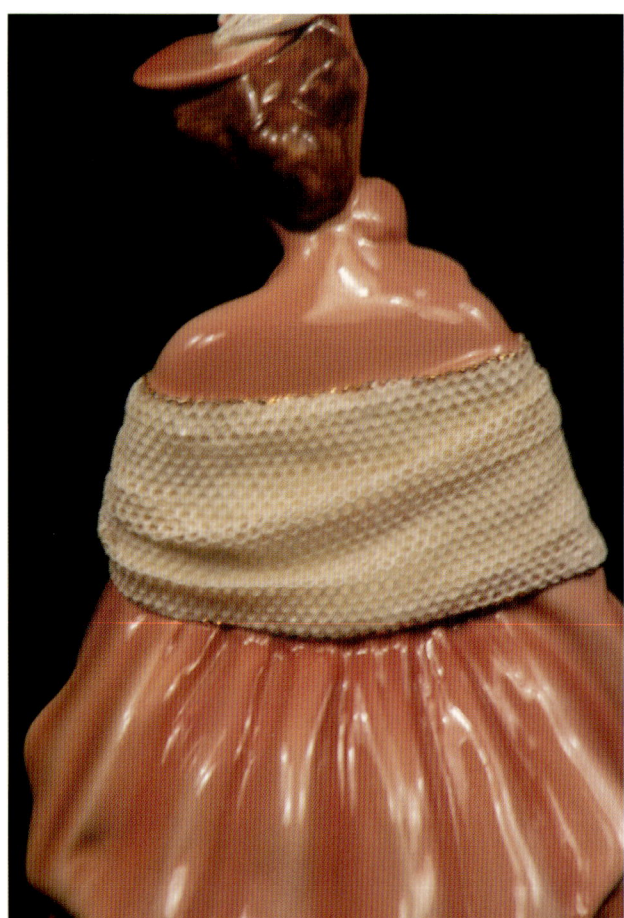

Net lace, 14 hole to the inch, as used on **Camille**.

Twig fur decoration, .25", as used on **Gibson Girl**.

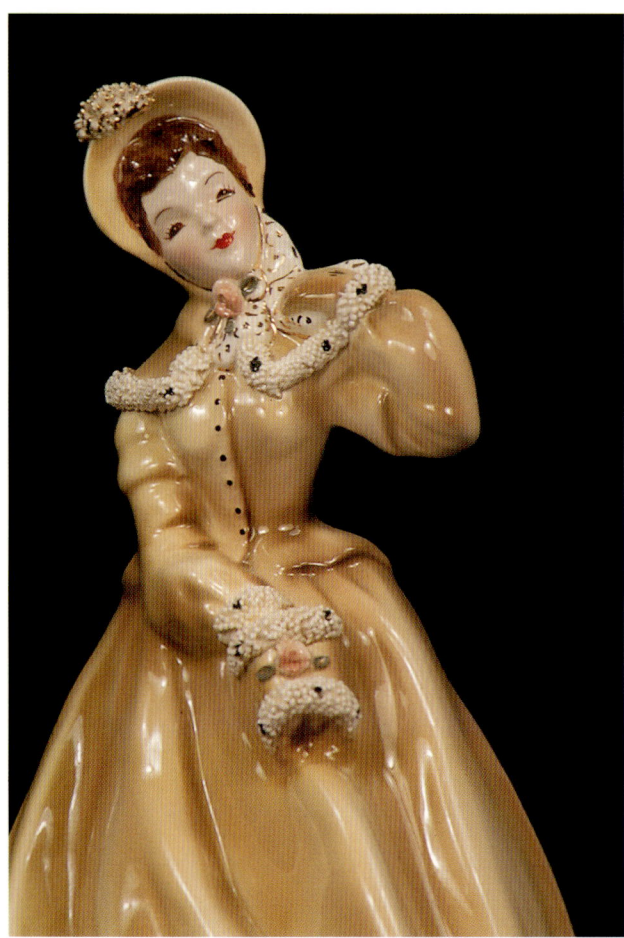

Ermine fur decoration, .125", as used on **Clarissa**.

## Florence Fashion Parade 117

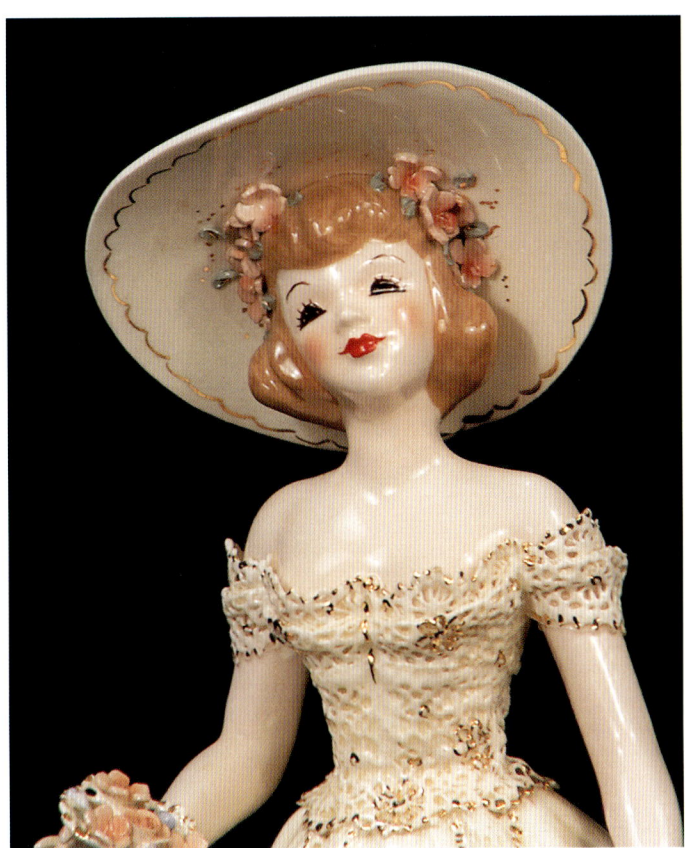

Wheel lace flat applied, .25", as used on **Jeanie**.

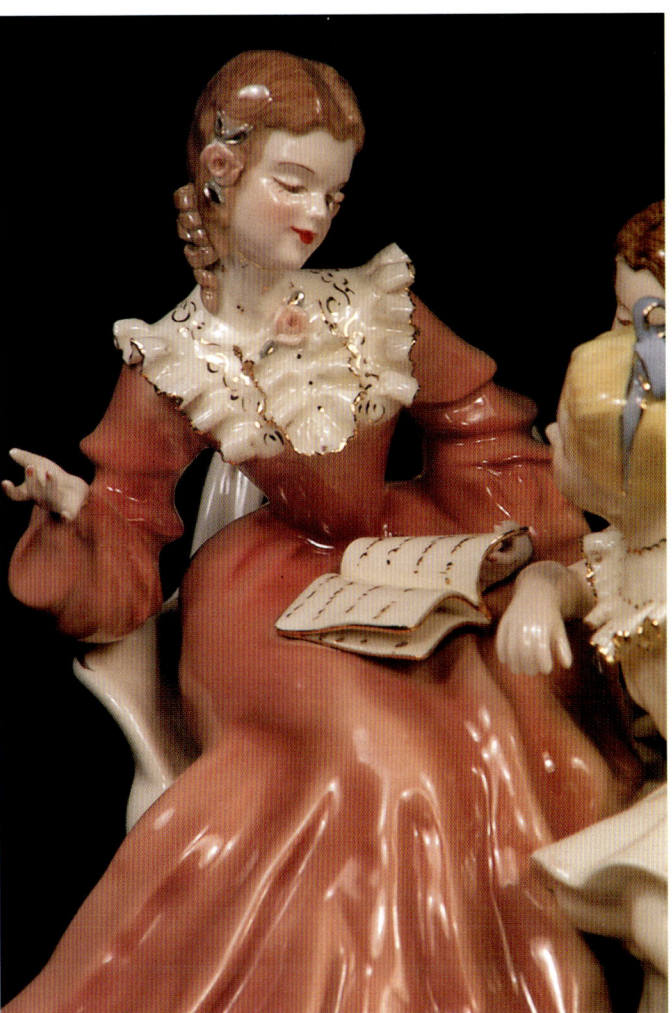

Wheel lace filled with slip, .25", as used on lady in **Story Hour**.

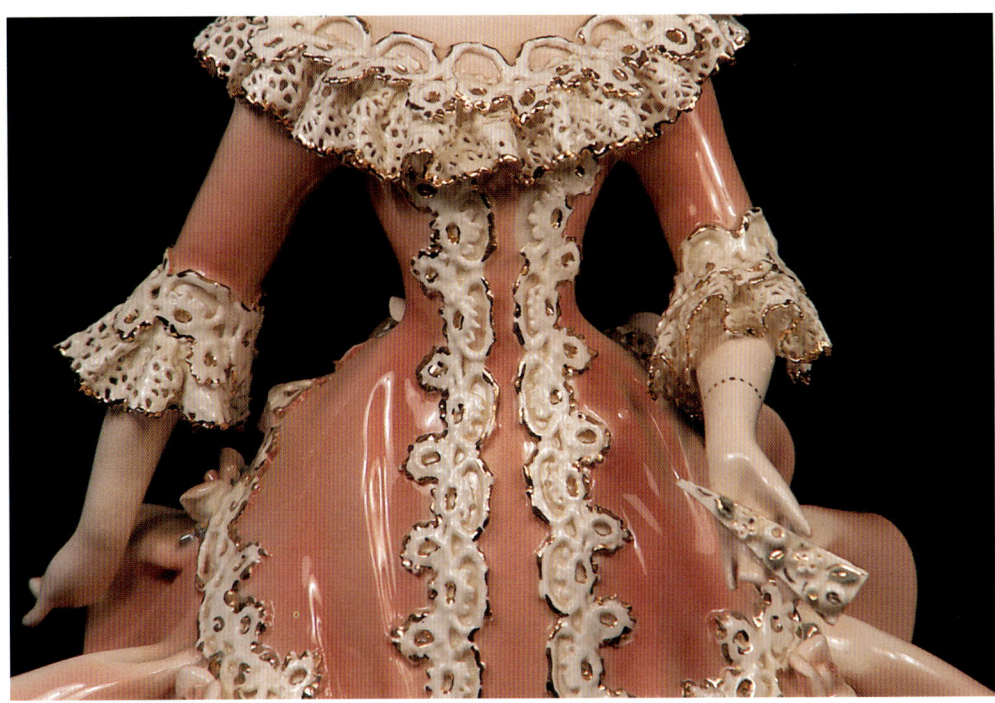

Dual applied scalloped and wheel lace, as used on **Sarah Bernhardt**.

Chapter V

# Pairs and Groups

*I remember as a child going to the Huntington Museum in Pasadena with my grandmother. She would sketch for what seemed like hours, and as she did so, I tried to be quiet. I wasn't always successful, but I knew if I behaved, there would be an ice cream cone waiting for me.*
— Pamela Ward Perdue (Irvine, California, July 2001)

This chapter displays the pairs and groups of figures that Florence Ward designed as companion pieces. Many are obvious, and some are a product of Florence's imagination. In some instances, the company's advertising brochures and catalogs paired certain figures; in those cases, we have shown them as a pair or group. From our research of Florence catalogs and order forms, we have determined that many figures were given sequential stock numbers, which might indicate that they were meant to go together.

The prices shown below the figures are for the pair or group.

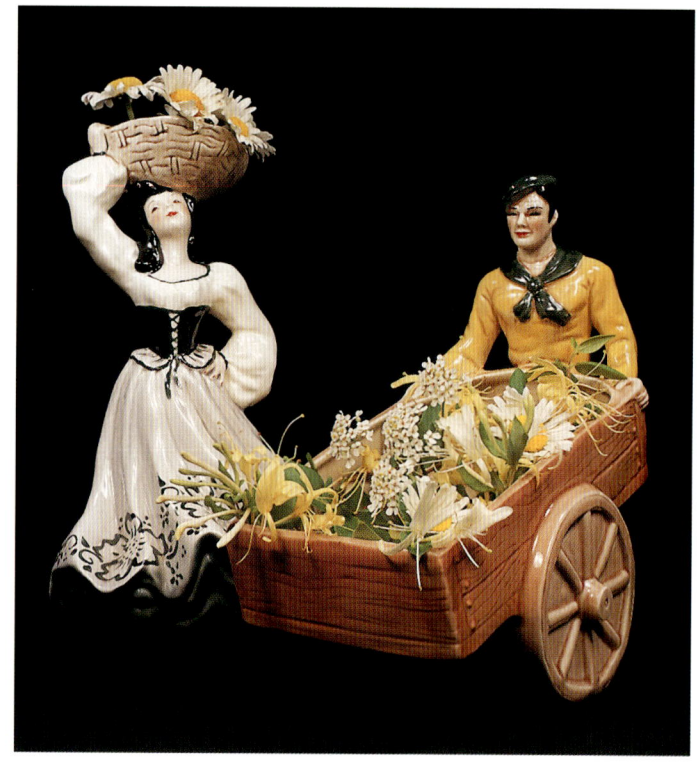

**Ava and Jose**
$900-1,050 pair

**Butch, Susie, Jim, Becky, Peter, Joyce**
$1,250-1,350 group

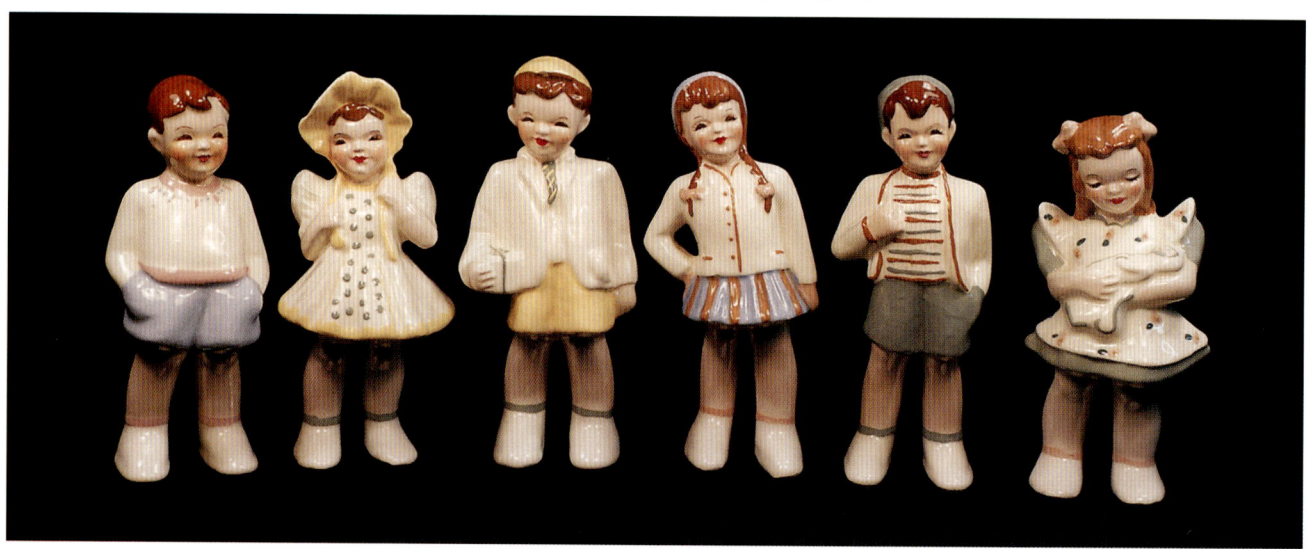

# Pairs and Groups 119

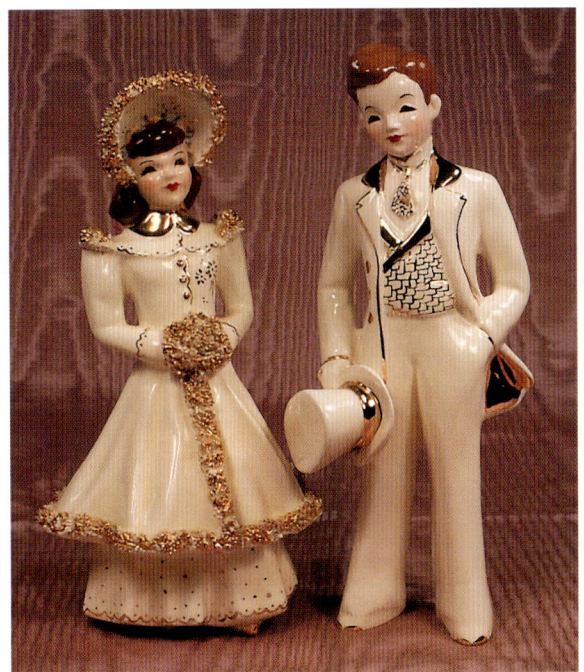

***Betsy and David***
$275-325 pair

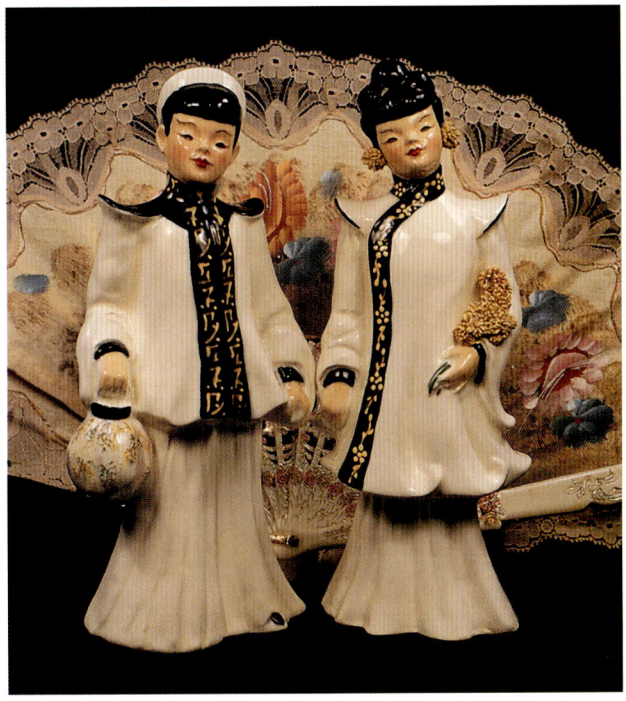

***Lantern Boy and Blossom Girl***
$250-280 pair

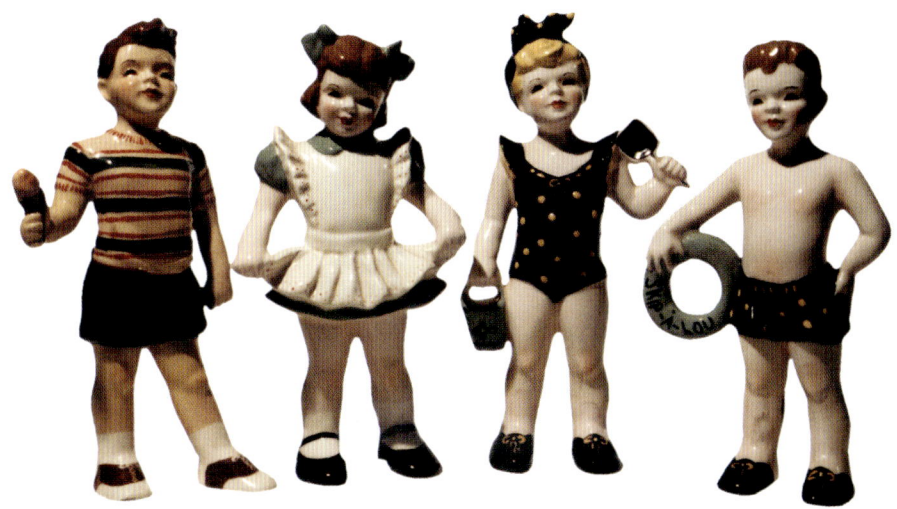

***Blondie, Sandy, Mary, John***
$5,000-6,000 group

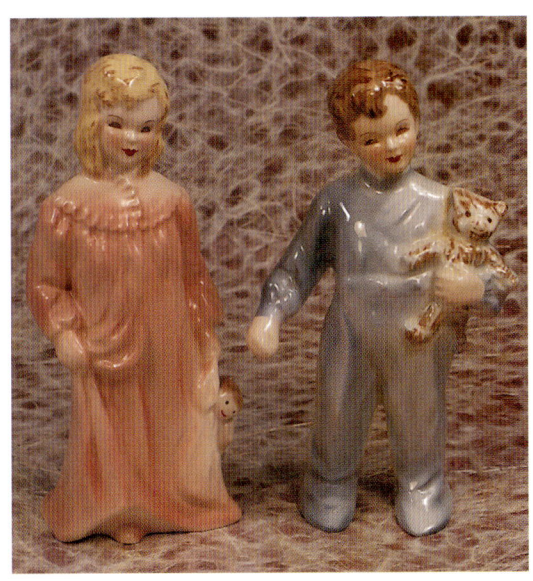

***Blynkin and Wynkin***
$400-450 pair

## 120 Pairs and Groups

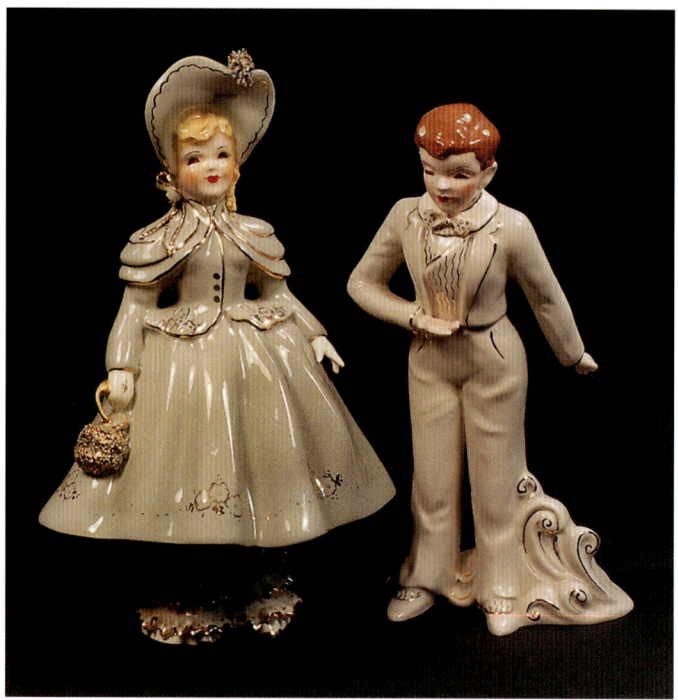

**Carol and Reggie**
$800-900 pair

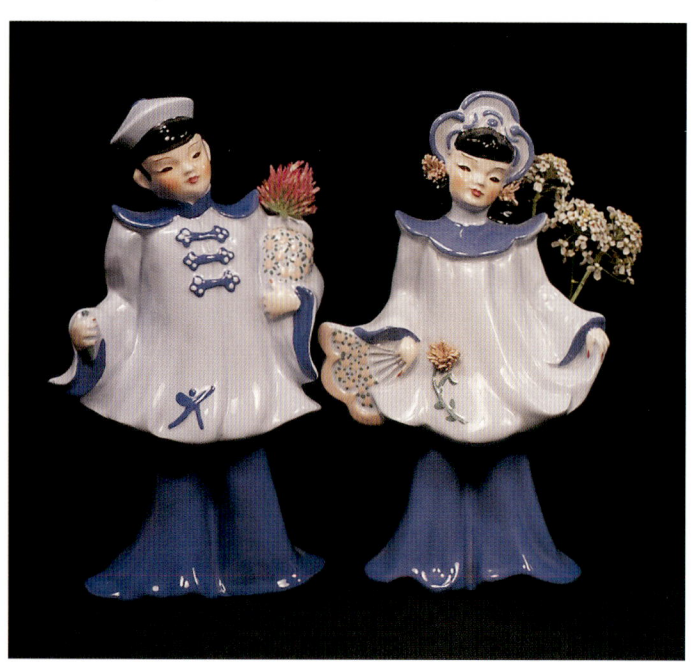

**Chinese Boy and Girl** (FH)
$130-150 pair

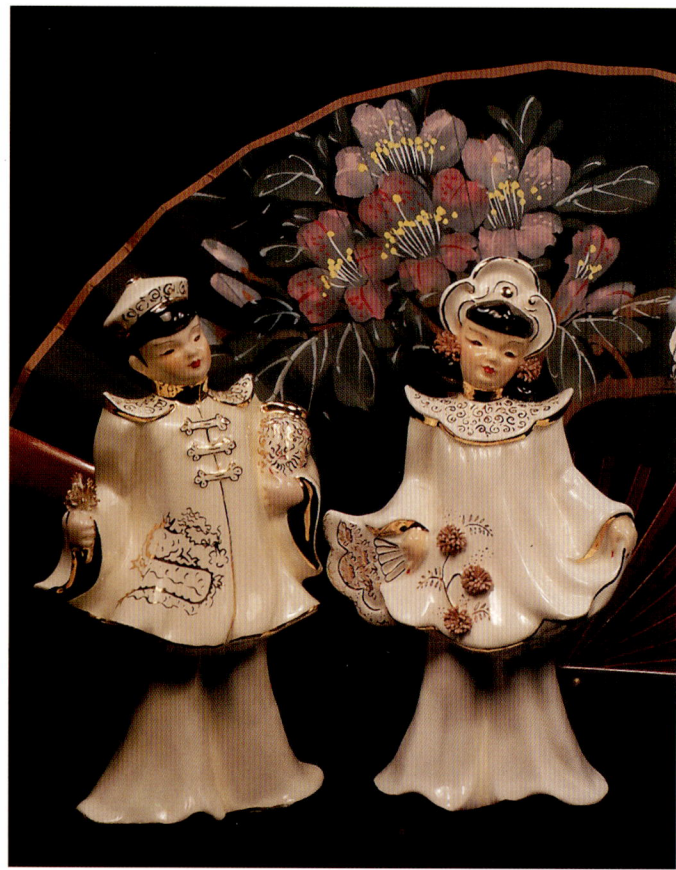

**Chinese Boy and Girl**
$150-180 pair

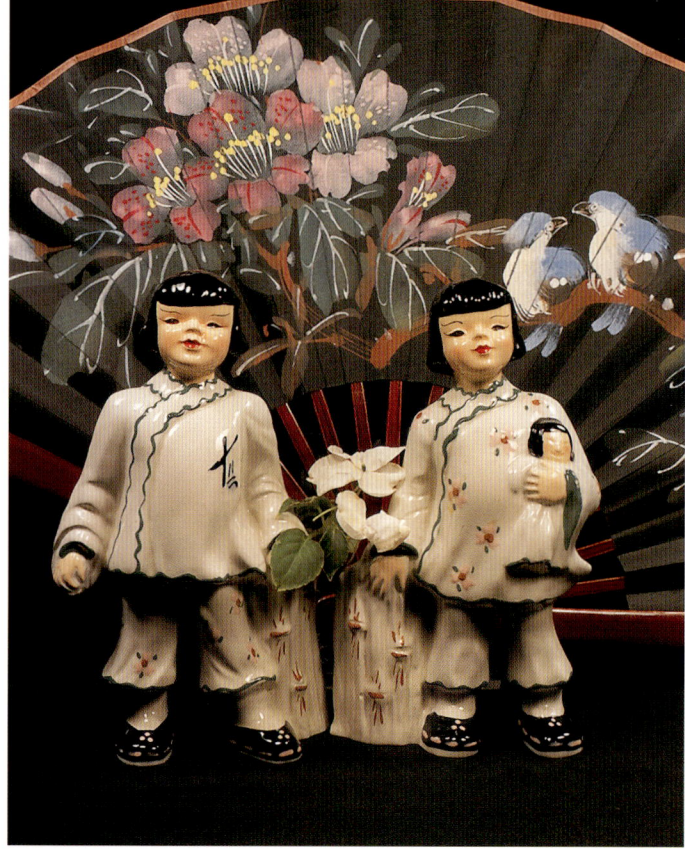

**Chinese Boy and Girl Twins** (FH)
$180-200 pair

Pairs and Groups 121

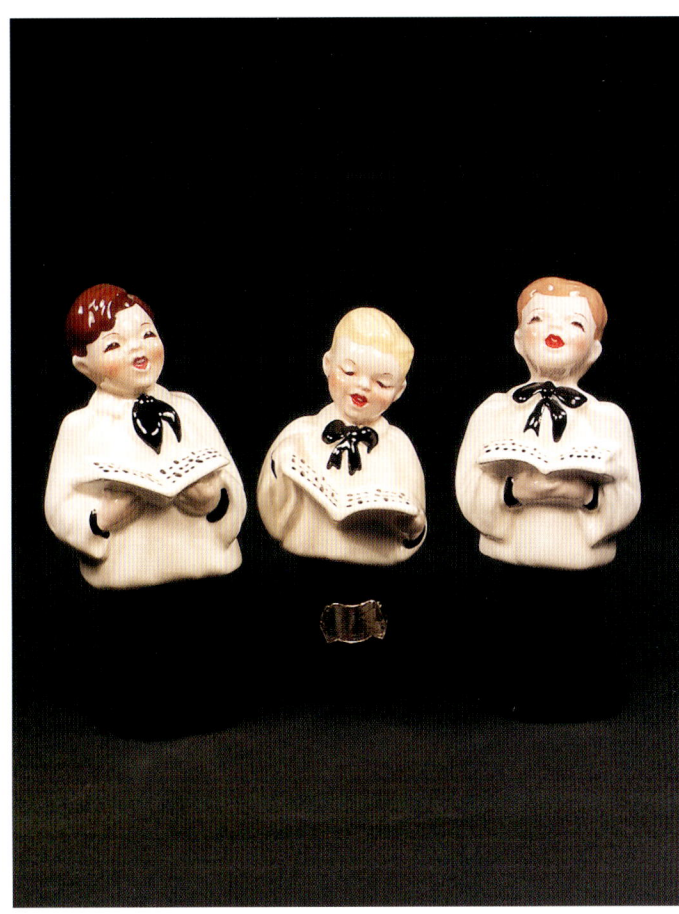

**Choir Boys**
$400-500 group

**Cinderella and Prince Charming**
$2,800-3,200

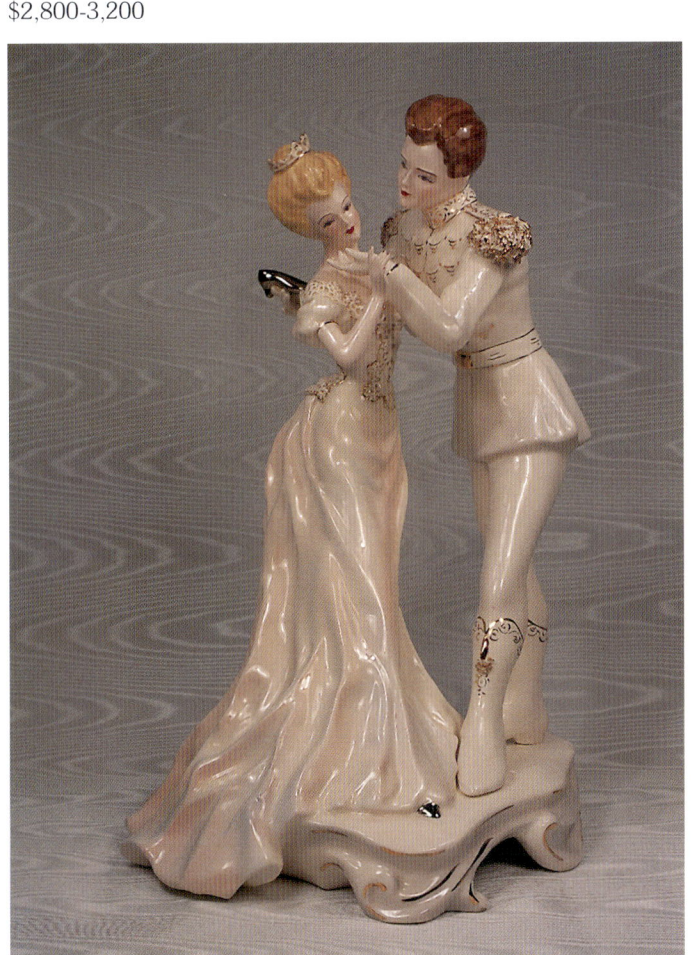

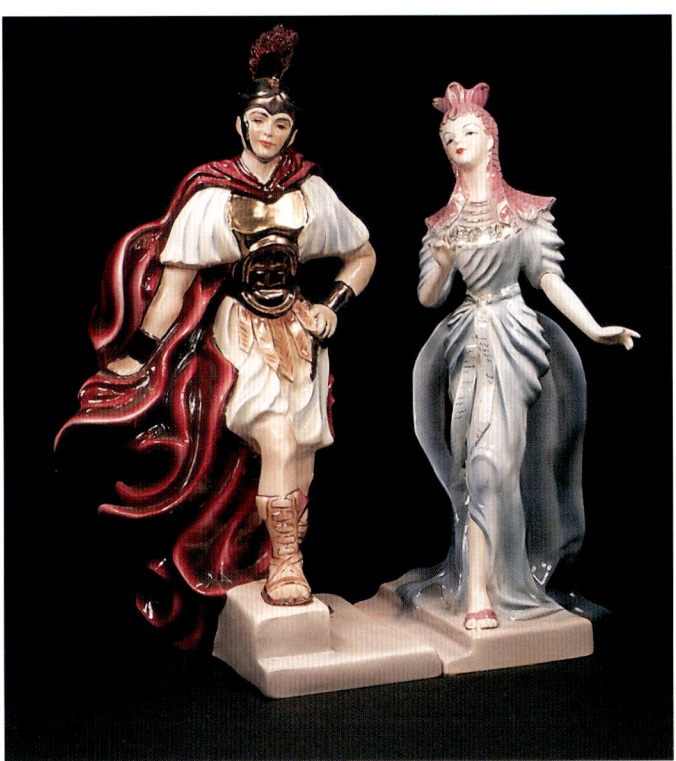

**Mark Anthony and Cleopatra**
$2,800-3,200 pair

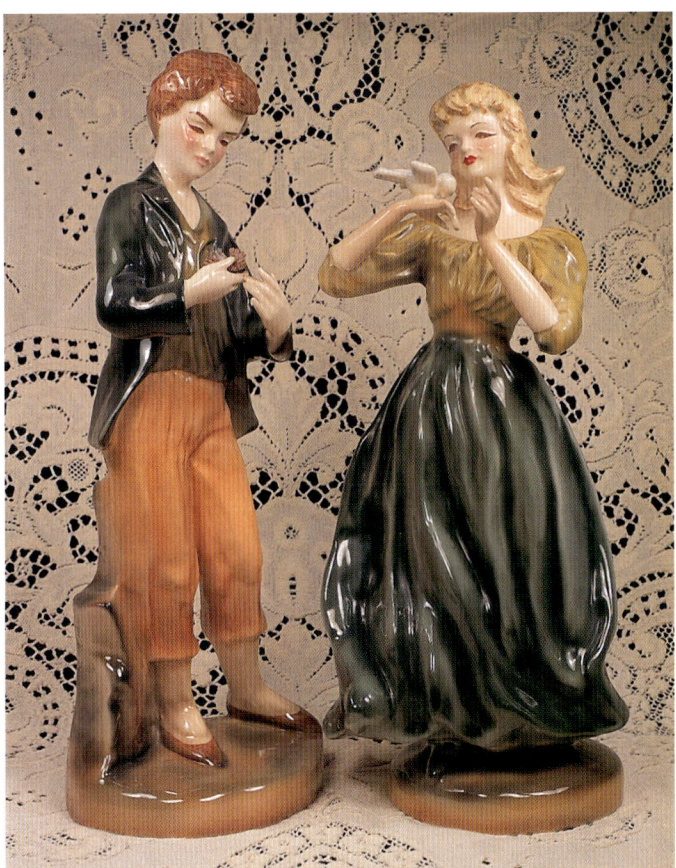

**Spring Reverie and Companion**
$2,500-3,000 pair

## 122 Pairs and Groups

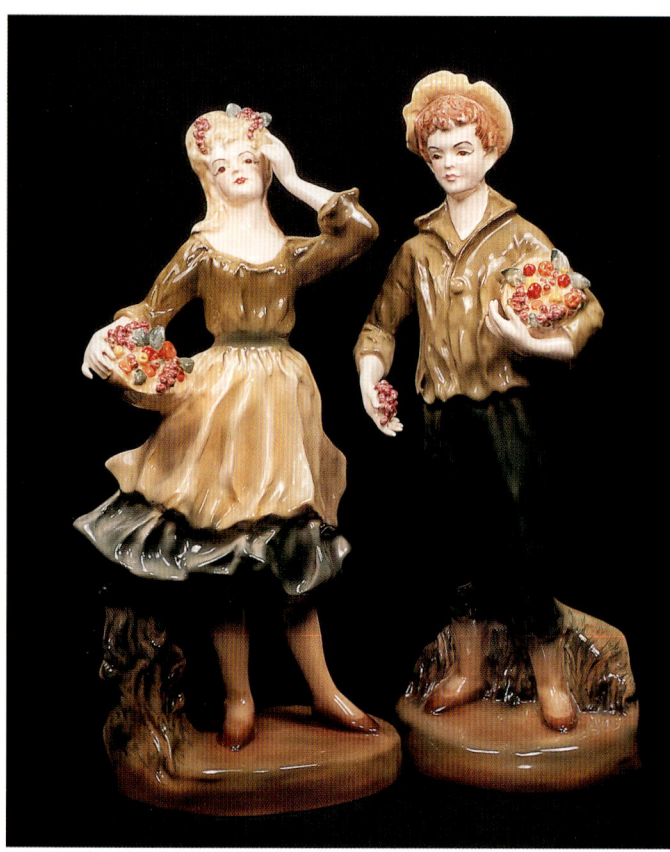

**Companion and Fall Reverie**
$2,500-3,000 pair

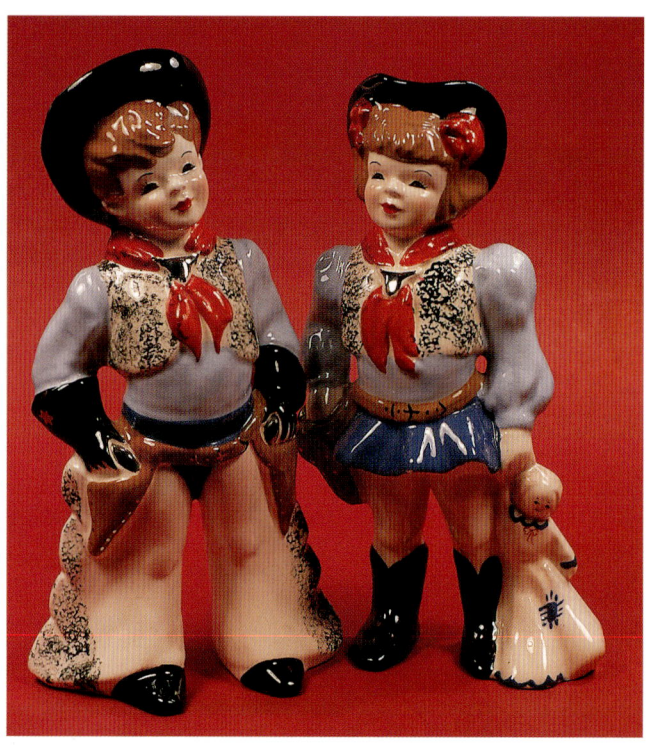

**Bud and Dot**
$1,400-1,500 pair

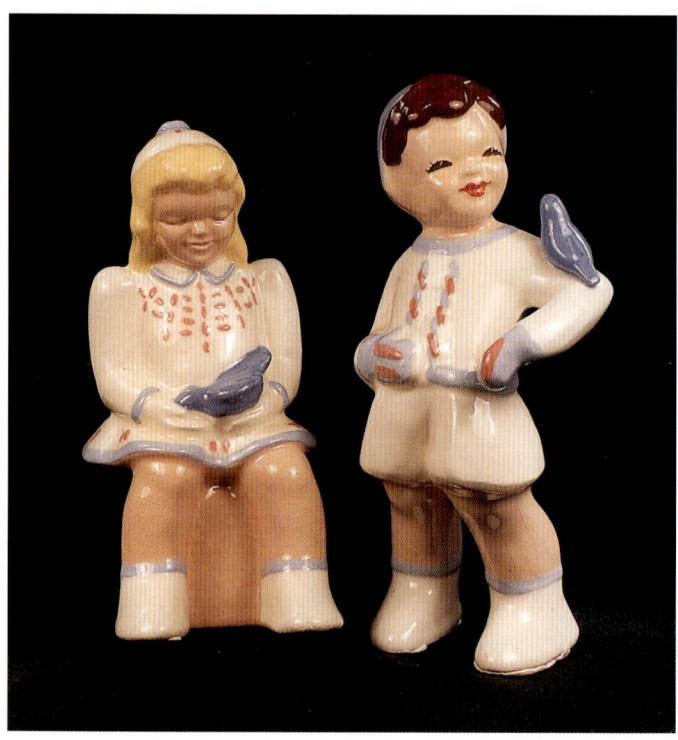

**Dixie and Hector**
$300-350 pair

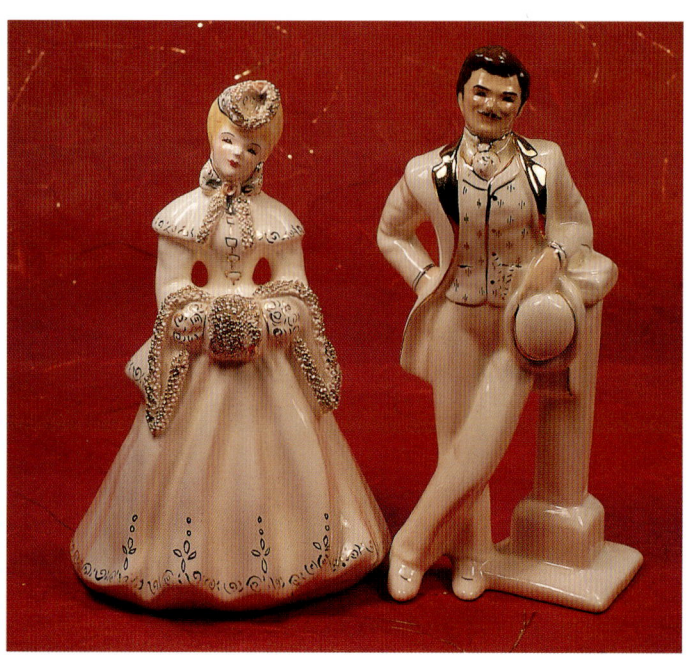

**Elaine and Jim**
$120-140 pair

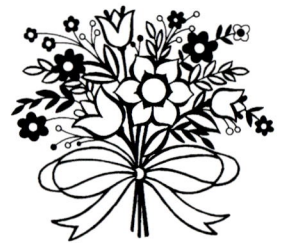

Pairs and Groups  123

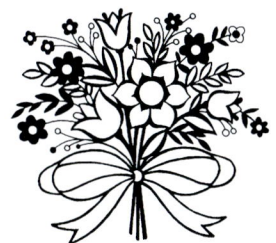

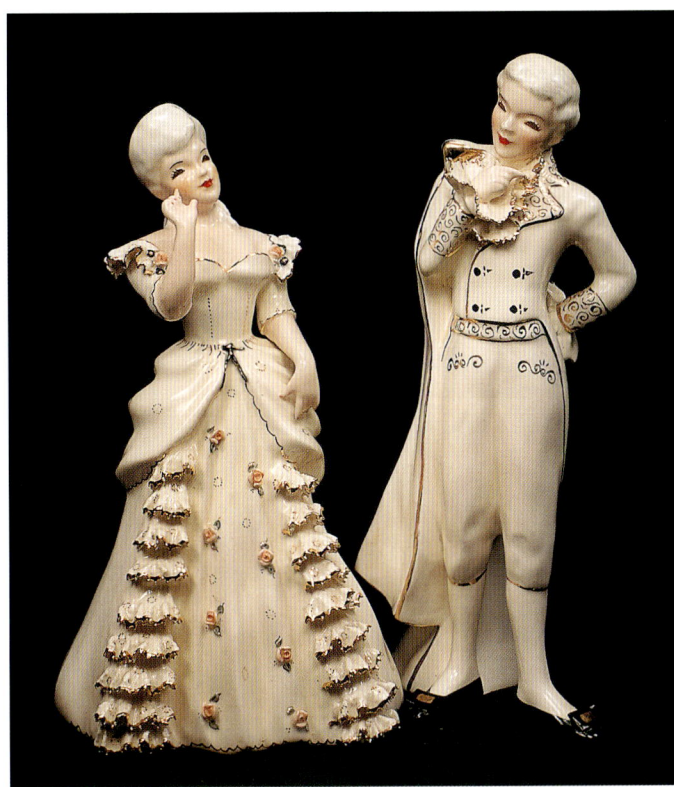

**Elizabeth and Charles**
$975-1,050 pair

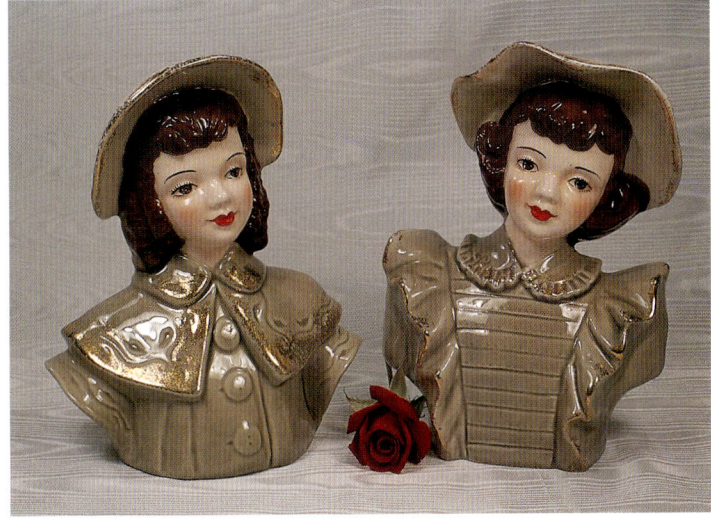

**Fern and Violet** (FH)
$300-320 pair

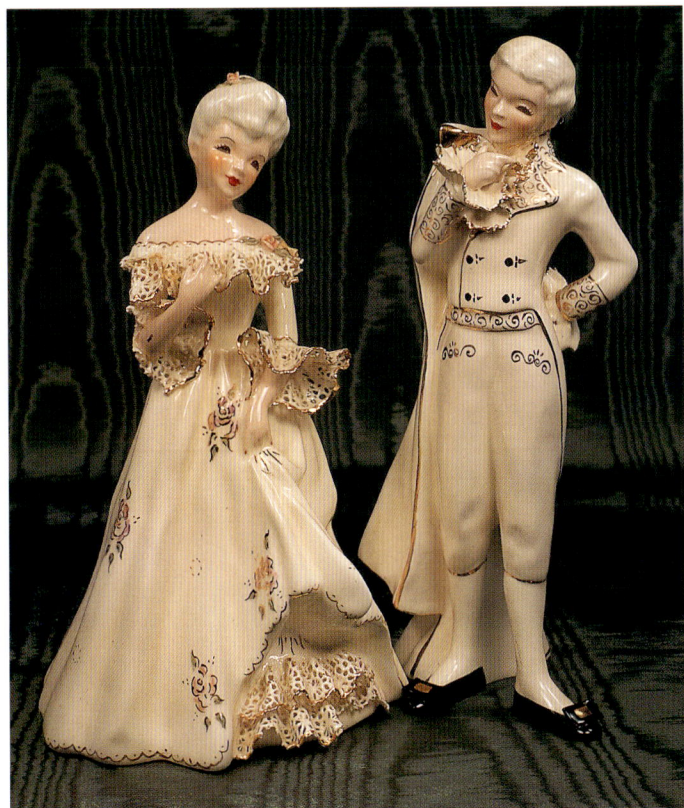

**Eve and Charles**
$700-750 pair

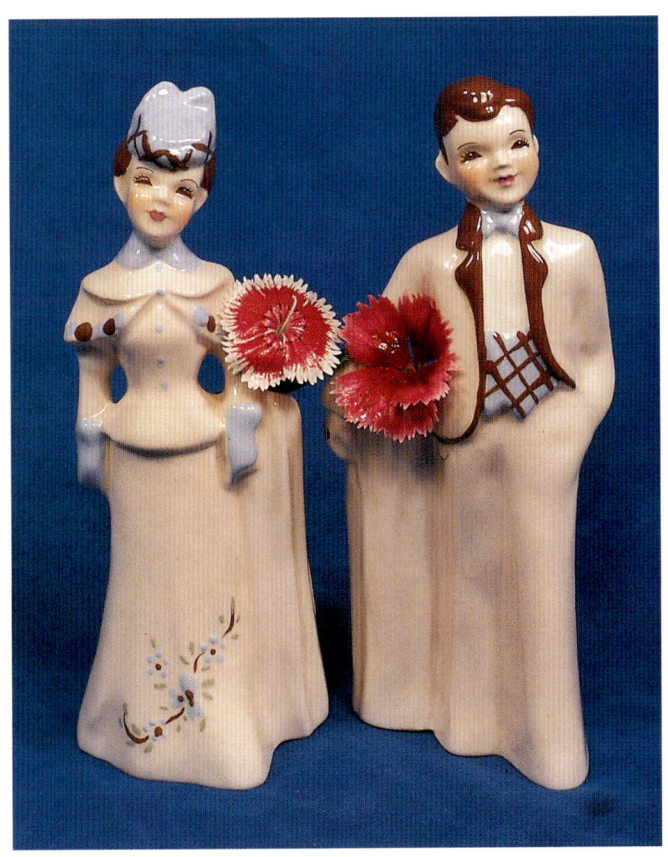

**Florence and Clifford** (FH), *
$130-150 pair

## 124  Pairs and Groups

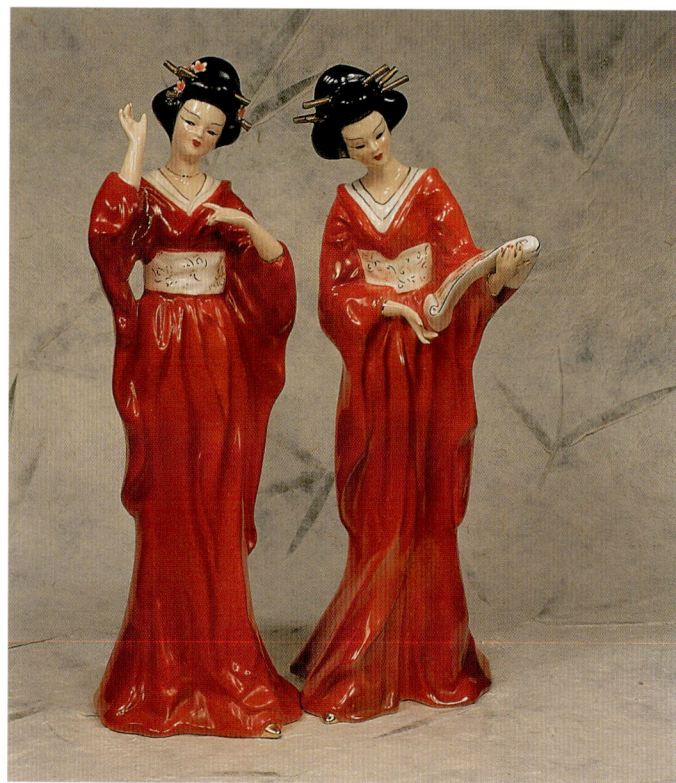

**Misha and Haru**
$700-800 pair

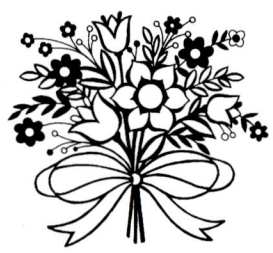

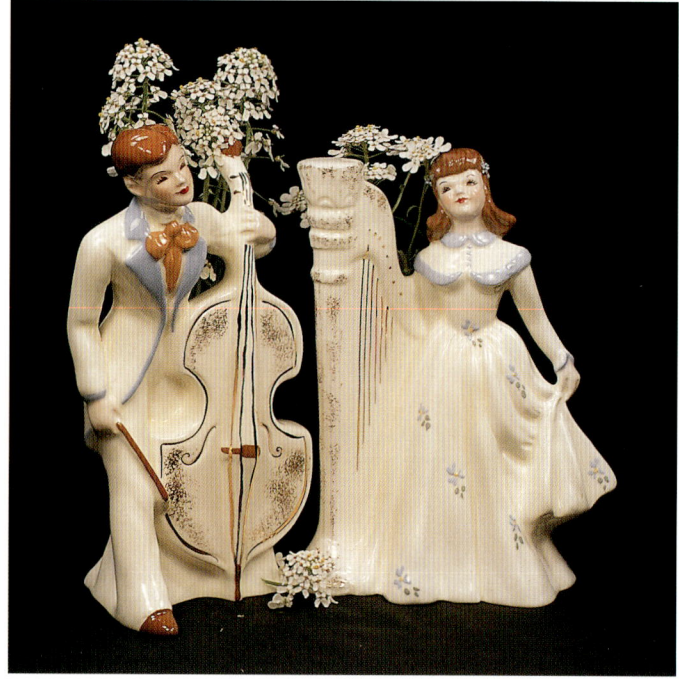

**Jerry and Joy** (FH)
$350-400 pair

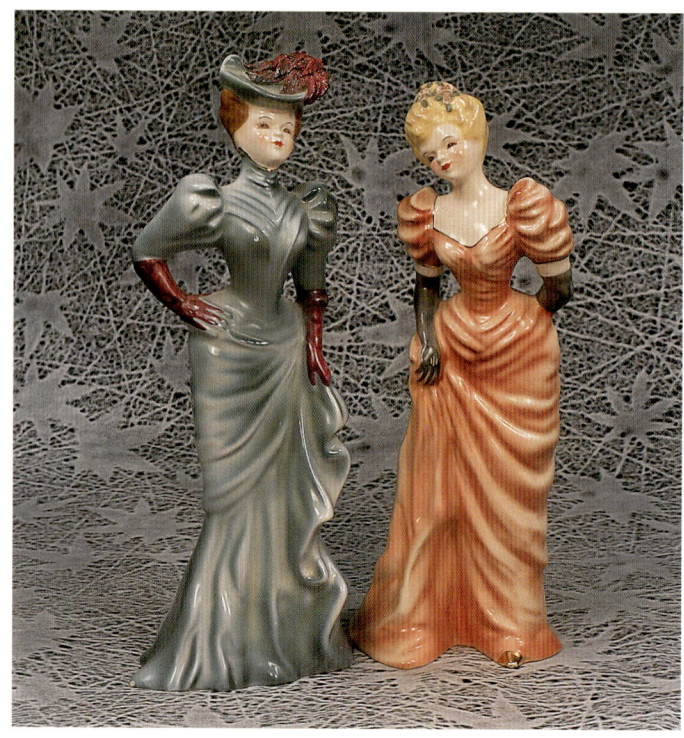

**Josephine and Roberta**
$700-750 pair

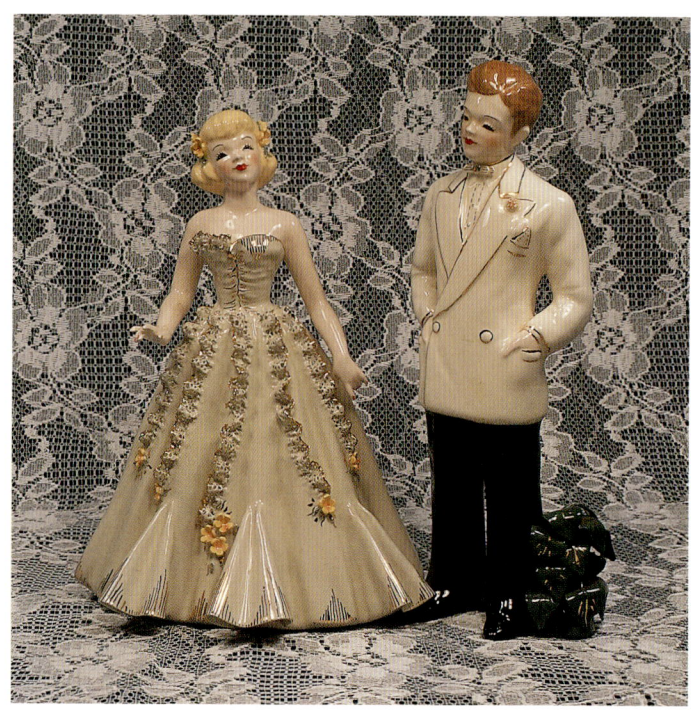

**Judy and Don**
$875-950 pair

Pairs and Groups 125

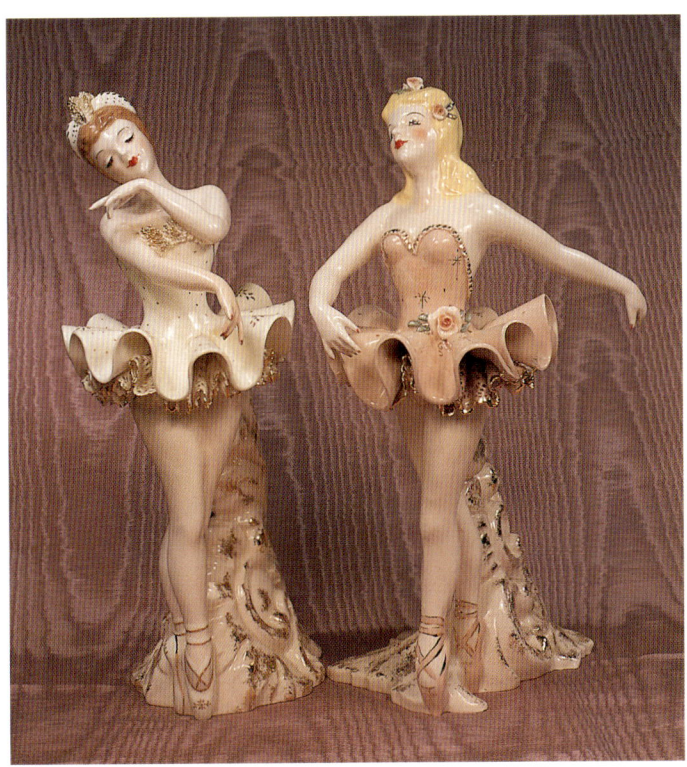

**Karla and Lisa Ballerinas**
$900-1,000 pair

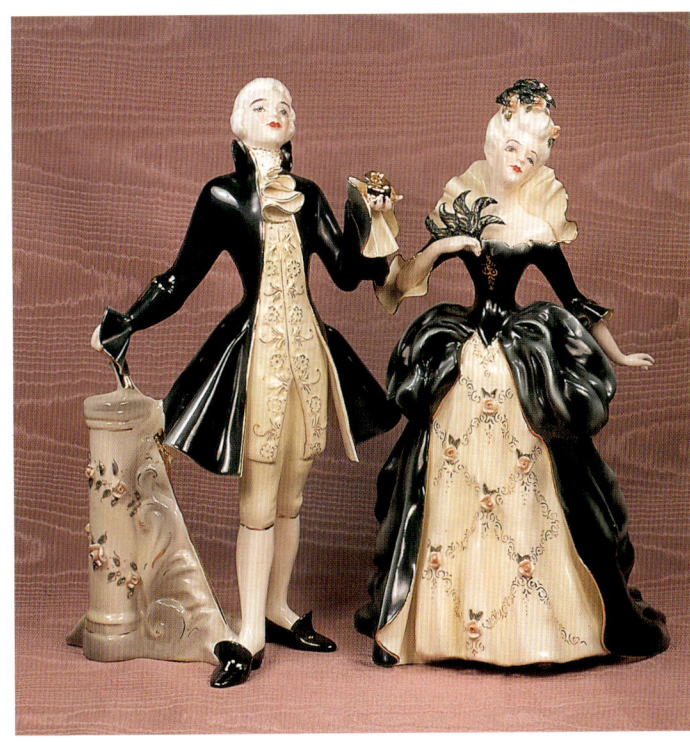

**Louis XV and Madame Pompadour**
$750-800 pair

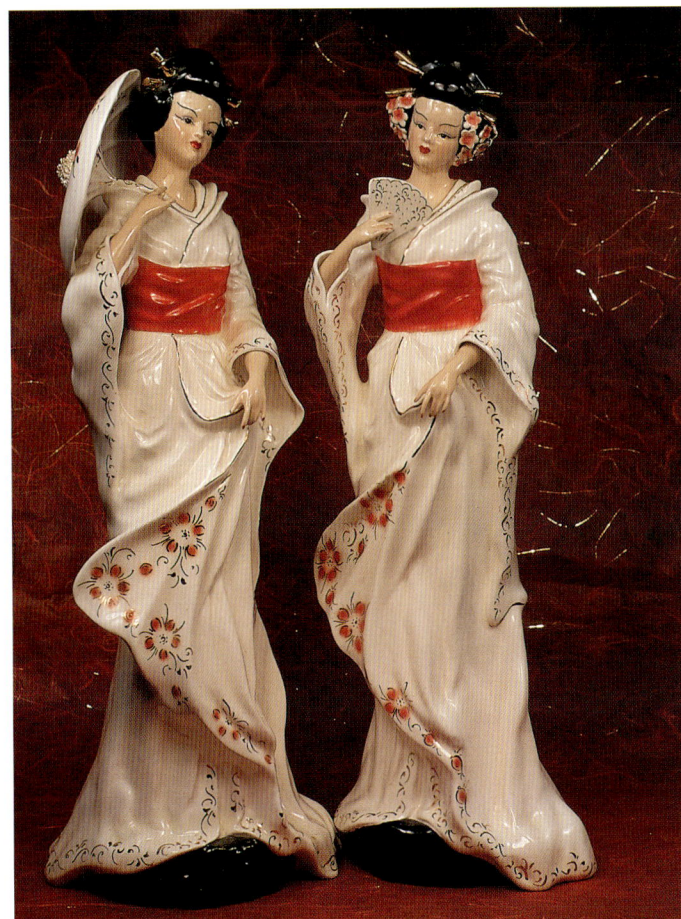

**Taka and Karlo**
$1,500-1,700 pair

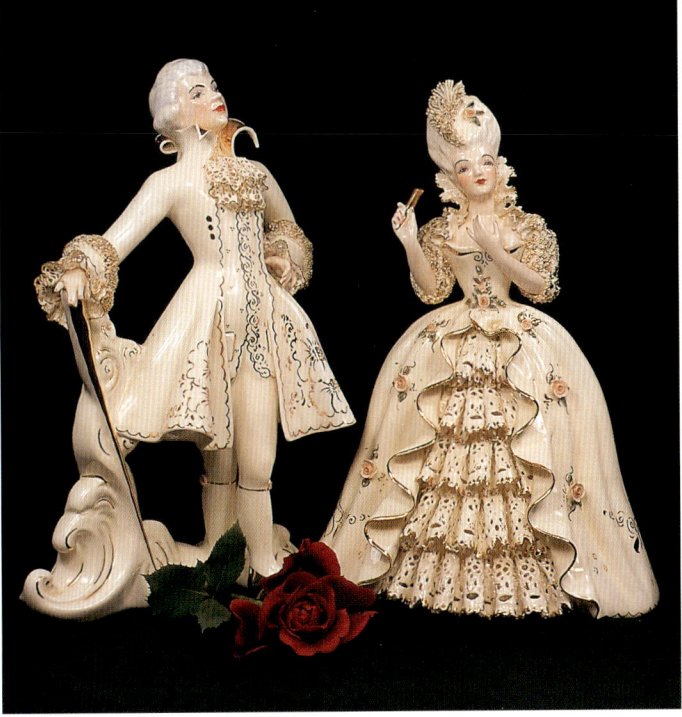

**Louis XVI and Marie Antoinette**
$750-800 pair

## 126  Pairs and Groups

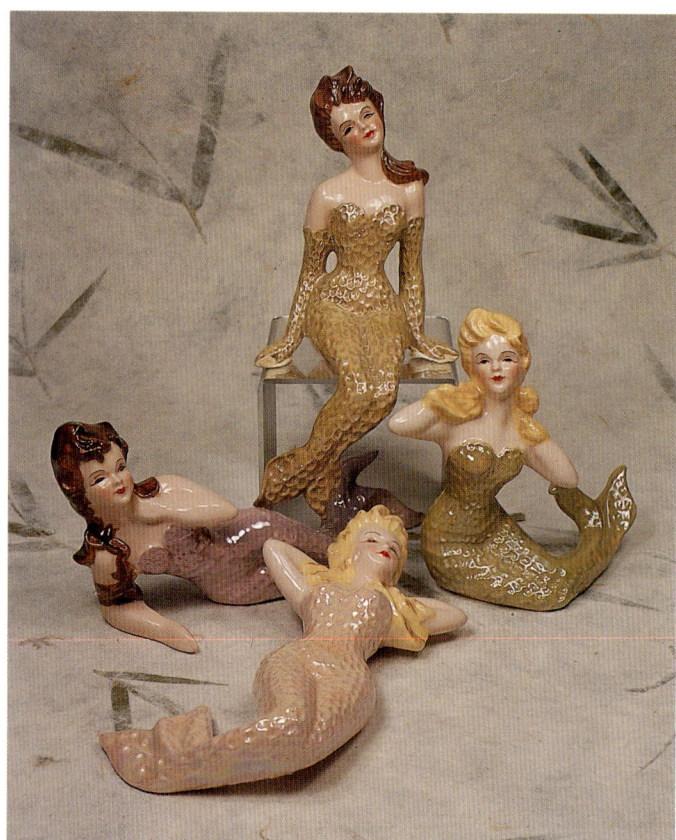

**Merrymaids: Rosie, Lil, Jane, Betty**
$1,000-1,125 group

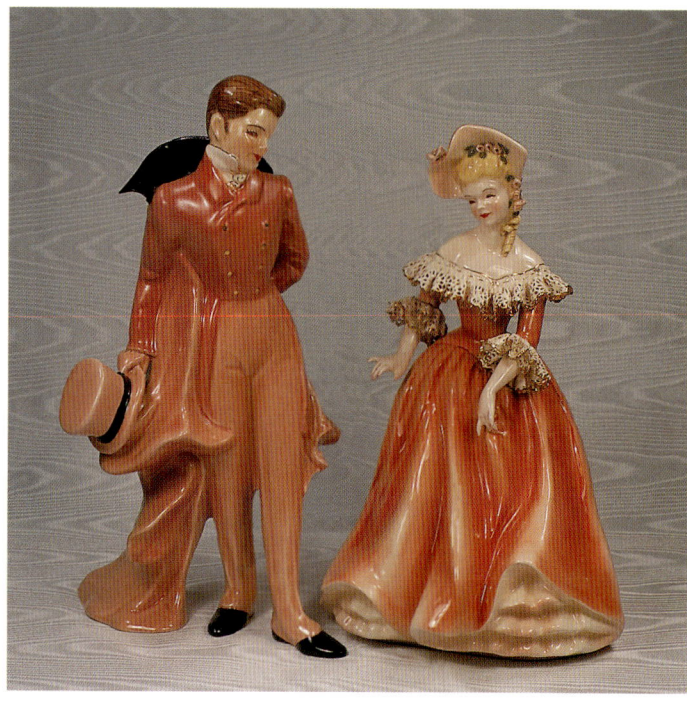

**Victor and Musette**
$875-975 pair

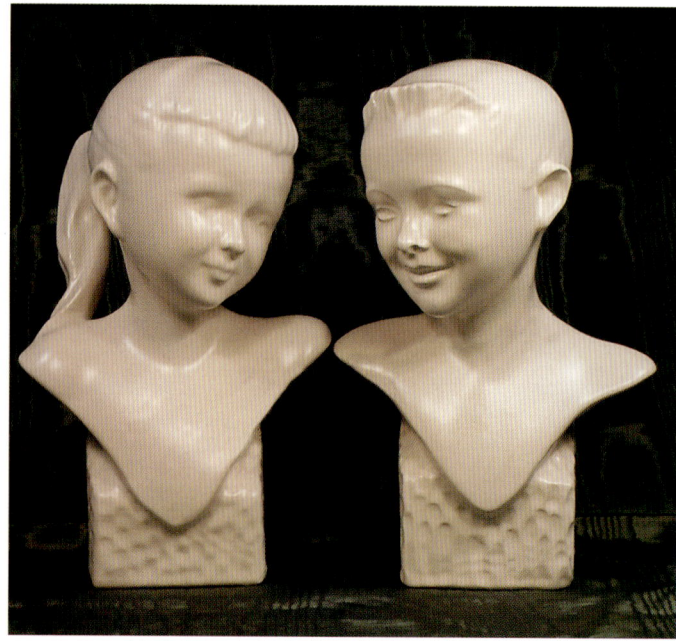

**Modern Girl and Modern Boy**
$550-600 pair

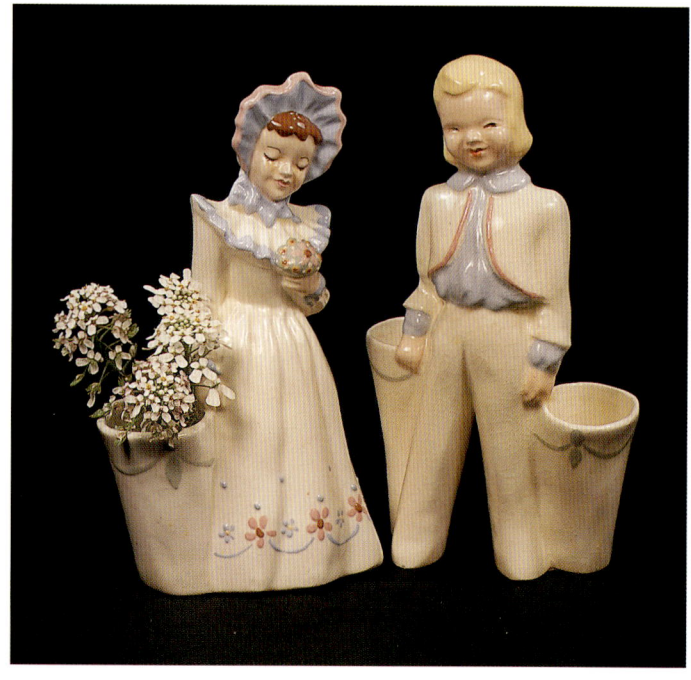

**Nan and Nick** (FH)
$200-250 pair

Pairs and Groups 127

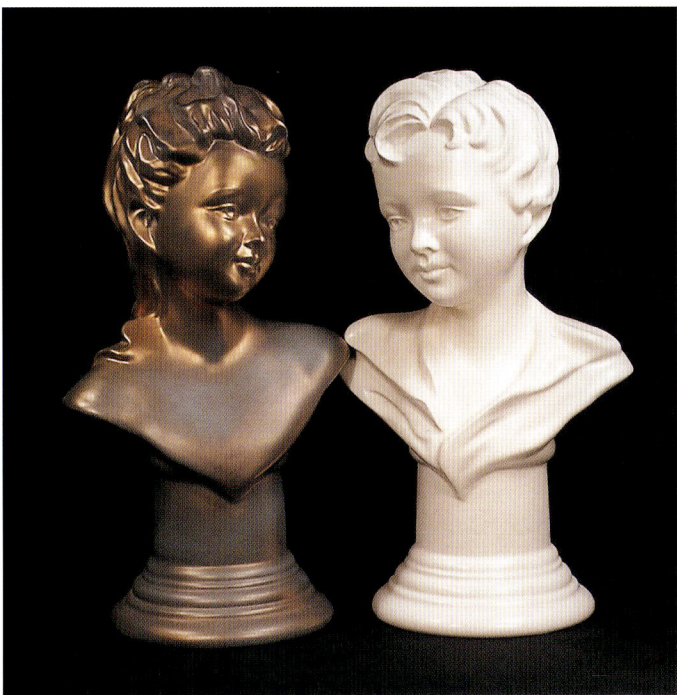

**Pamela and David**
$550-600 pair

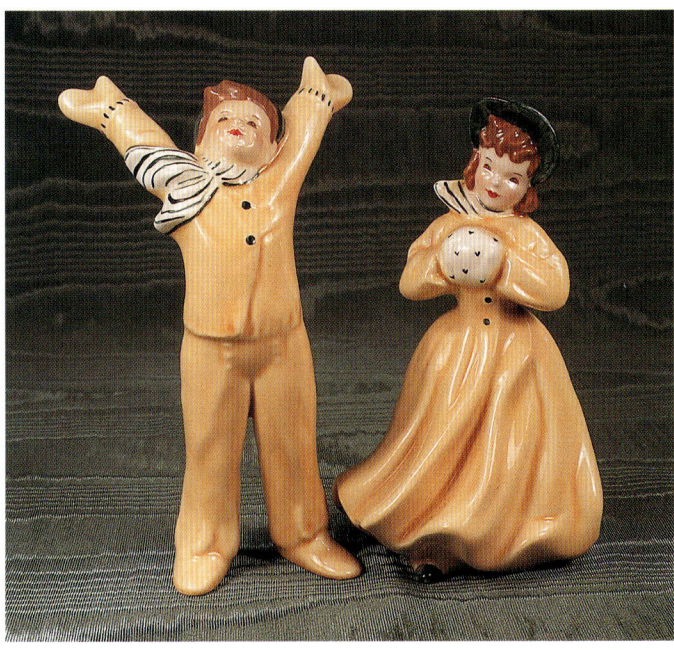

**Mike and Pat**
$400-450 pair

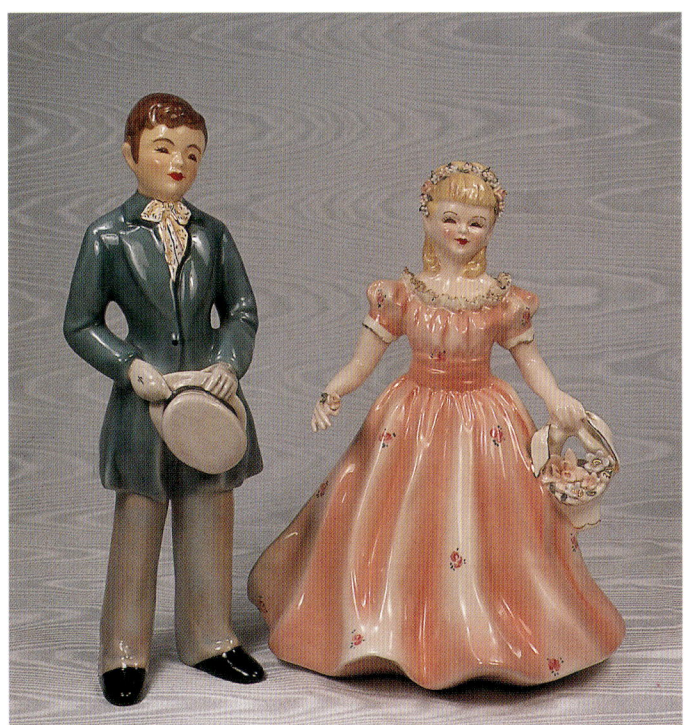

**Master David and Pamela**
$1,100-1,200 pair

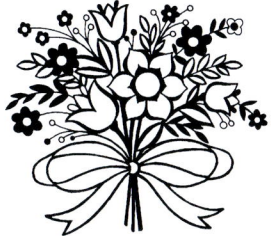

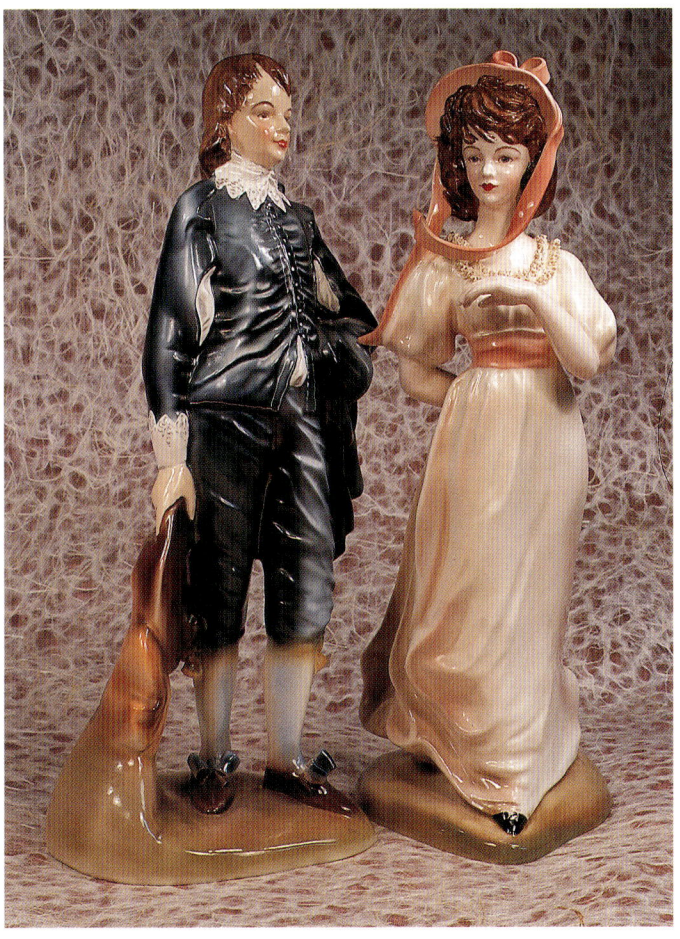

**Blue Boy and Pinkie**
$800-900 pair

## 128  Pairs and Groups

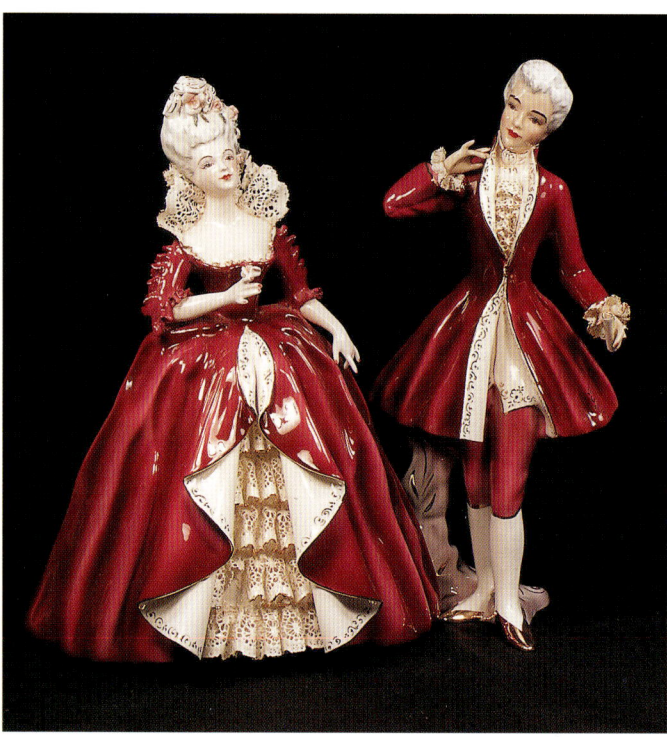

**Prima Donna and Leading Man**
$1,475-1,700 pair

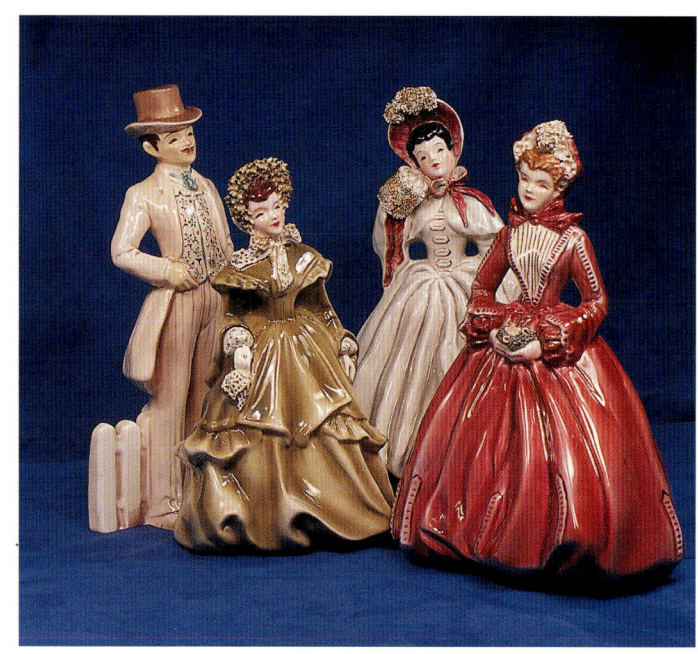

**Rhett, Melanie, Scarlett, Sue Ellen**
$800-1,100 group

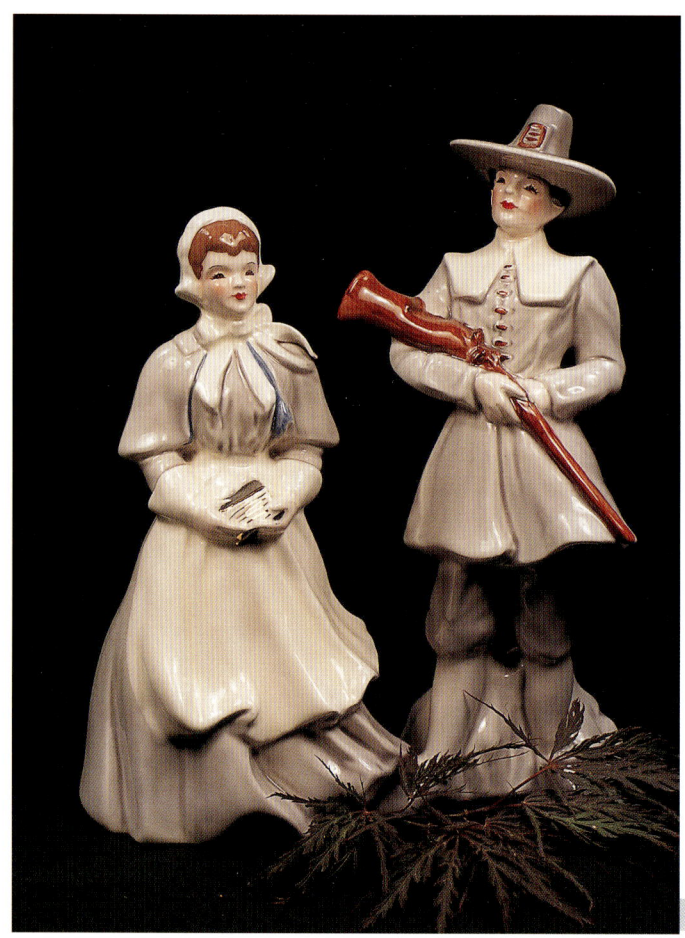

**Priscilla and John Alden**
$550-600 pair

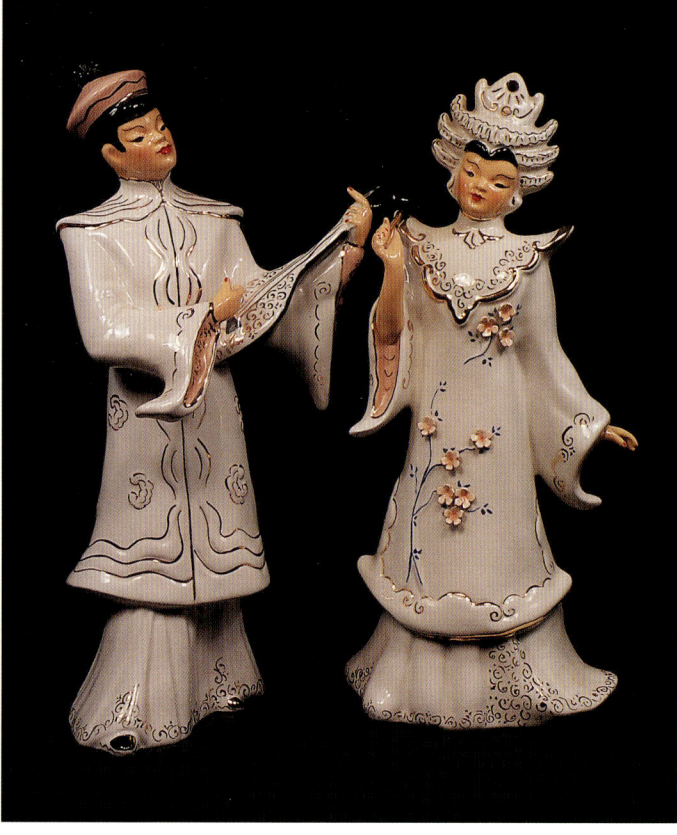

**Kiu and She-Ti**
$450-500 pair

# Pairs and Groups 129

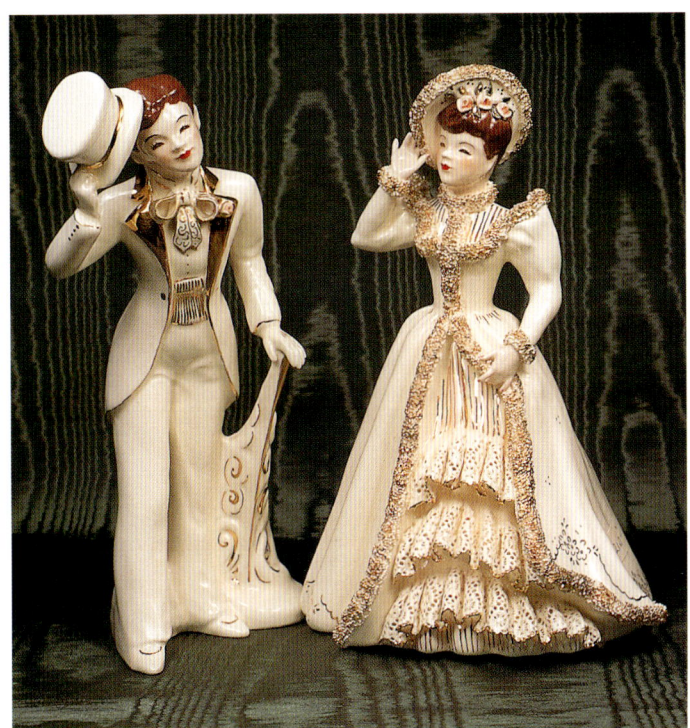

**Stephen and Susanna**
$950-1,050 pair

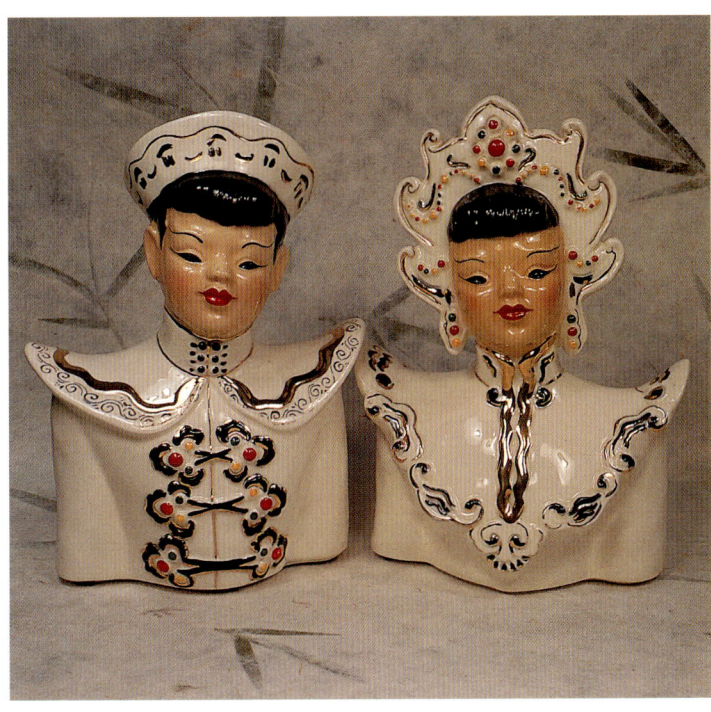

**Shen and Yulan**
$350-400 pair

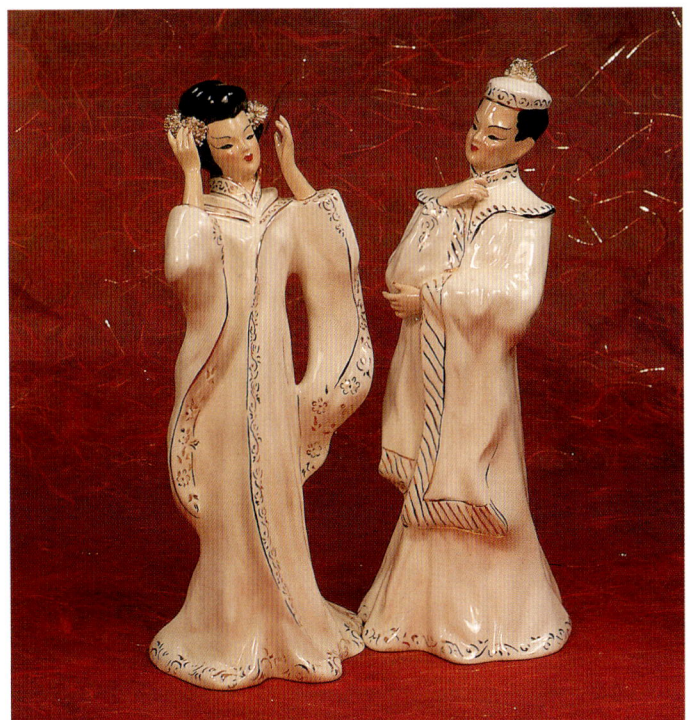

**Toy and Ming**
$650-700 pair

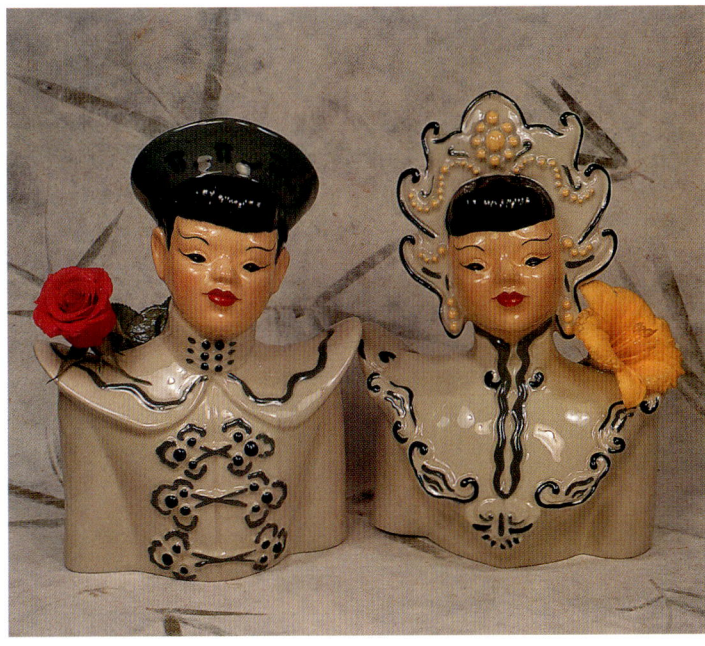

**Shen and Yulan** (FH)
$300-350 pair

Chapter VI

# Historical, Literary, and Religious

*...got her inspiration from books, plays, movies, paintings, even advertisements...Marie Antoinette came into being after Mrs. Ward attended the play "New Moon" and Diane and Charles owe their existence to a whiskey advertisement.*
—Pasadena Star-News (January 18, 1948)

**Carmen**: Florence captured the fiery beauty of this Gypsy woman as she dances her way into the arms of her Spanish officer. The original story of *Carmen* was written by Prosper Merimee in 1845. It was composed for the opera *Carmen* by George Bizet and opened in Paris in 1875, though it was considered too shocking even for that sophisticated audience. However, just as we expect the popularity of the figurine Carmen to endure, so has the opera. Today, *Carmen* is considered one of the most popular operas of all time. There is no reference to the opera *Carmen* in any Florence catalogs.

**Cinderella and Prince Charming**: The origins of this popular fairy tale are unknown, but one of the oldest known written renderings of the theme is a Chinese version from the ninth century. Charles Perrault's *Cendrillon*, written in 1697, is the most popular version. Perrault's story is the only version to mention the glass slipper. In Florence's timeless setting, the Prince holds the "glass" slipper as he gazes upon the face of the shy cinder girl.

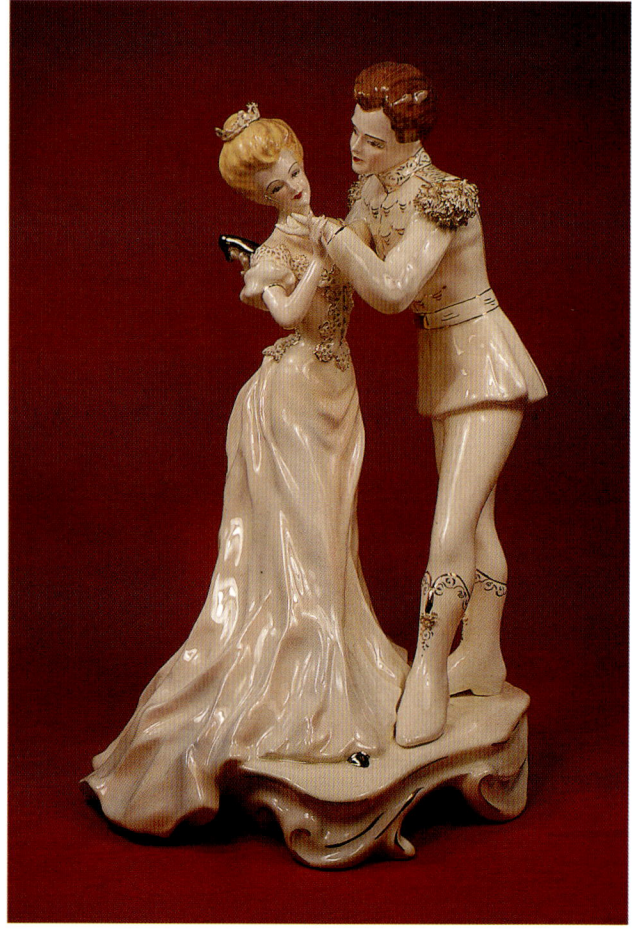

**Cinderella and Prince Charming**, popular fairy tale.

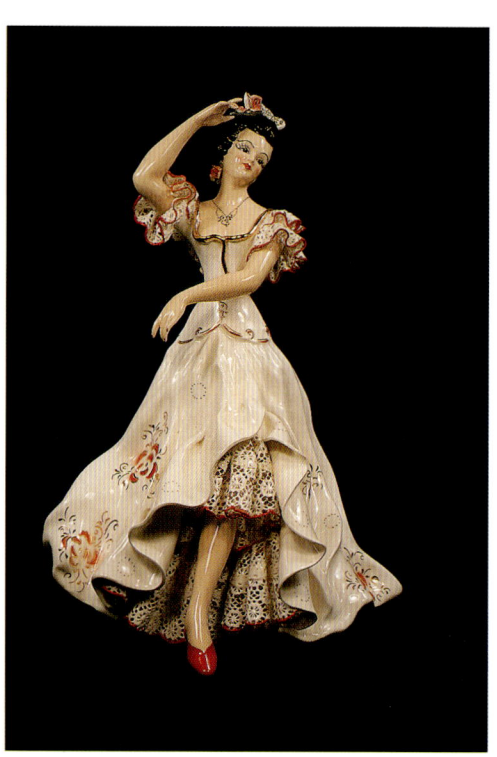

**Carmen**, of opera fame.

130

***Cleopatra and Mark Anthony (Antony):*** Florence delved into Egyptian history in order to depict the earliest subjects for her historical collection. Cleopatra (69-30 B.C.), queen of Egypt, stands boldly next to her larger than life companion, Mark Antony. Mark Antony was Marcus Antonious, a Roman general. In Rome, he met Cleopatra, who was then mistress of Julius Caesar. Together they are a formidable pair.

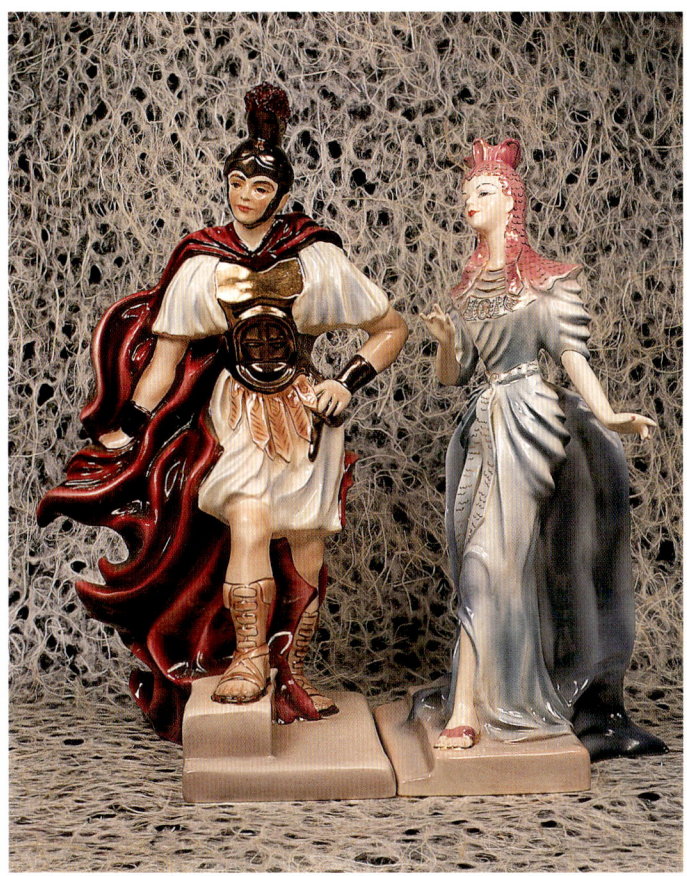

***Mark Anthony and Cleopatra***, Roman General and Queen of Egypt.

***Fair Lady:*** Fair Lady is almost certainly *My Fair Lady* of Broadway fame. One can imagine the Wards traveling to New York to see the play. We learned from Pamela Ward Perdue, granddaughter of the Wards, that her grandparents did indeed make several trips to New York. Seeing a Broadway show was always an integral part of their visits to New York.

*My Fair Lady* appeared on Broadway in the 1950s, and we know from the Florence catalogues that *Fair Lady* was created in 1957. Further, the original play – *Pygmalion*, by George Bernard Shaw – was written in 1905, the approximate setting for his story. Florence's *Fair Lady* wears a gown of this same time period, as does Eliza Doolittle in *My Fair Lady*. Finally, as one more piece of evidence, we note that perhaps due to copyright laws, Florence might have been reluctant to say specifically that *Fair Lady* was designed after the famous *My Fair Lady*.

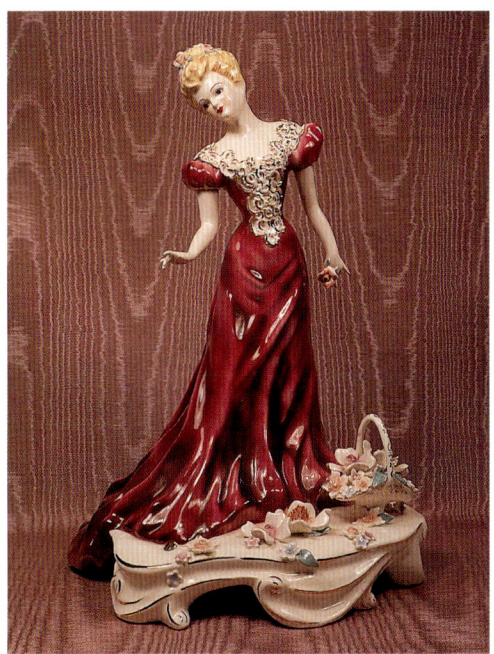

***Fair Lady***, from the Broadway play.

***Gibson Girl:*** The *Gibson Girl* was a figment of the imagination of Charles Dana Gibson, an American illustrator born in Roxbury, Massachusetts in 1867. Gibson studied at the Art Students League and in Paris, and his illustrations appeared in many magazines and books. He depicted women of the aristocracy at the turn of the twentieth century, which established him as the leading authority on fashion. His fashions were simply referred to as "Gibson Girls," and they were his own idea of the perfect woman. Florence, in turn, created the perfect *Gibson Girl(s)*.

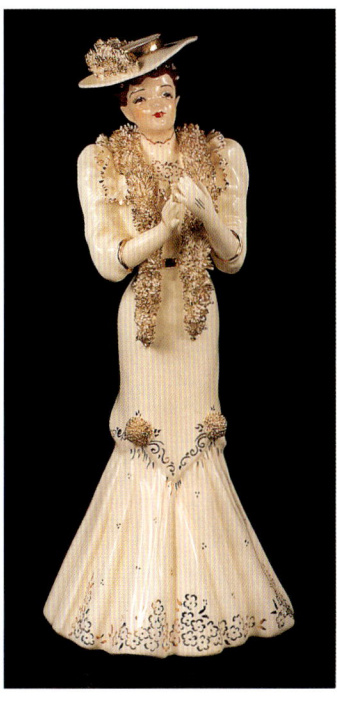

***Gibson Girl***, the perfect lady.

## 132  Historical, Literary, and Religious

**Godey Lady:** It has already been documented that Florence referenced publications of the *Godey Lady's Book of 1860. Godey's* originated as the *Lady's Magazine* begun by Louis A. Godey in 1830. In 1837, Godey merged with Sara Josepha Hale, owner and editor of the *American Ladies' Magazine.* Mrs. Hale moved from Boston to Philadelphia in 1837 to become Managing Editor of the new *Godey Lady's Book of Philadelphia.* She continued as the editor of this publication until 1877. During Sara Hale's tenure, *Godey's* became the most sought after publication for women's fashion. Most libraries have carried copies of *Godey's* throughout the years. In the example shown here, *Sarah* shows off the bow on the back of her *Godey* dress.

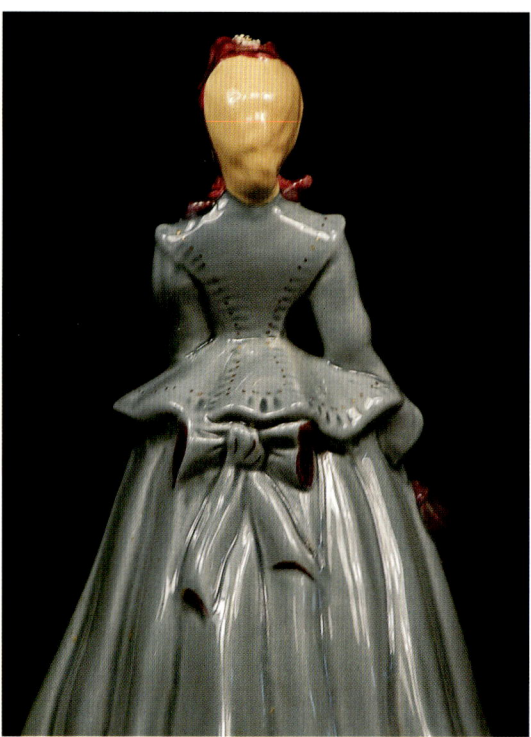

**Godey Lady,** *Sarah* with bow.

**Little Don:** If we can imagine, as mentioned earlier, the Wards journeying to New York to see *My Fair Lady,* then it is easy to believe that Florence would also visit the Metropolitan Museum in that same city. The painting of *Don Manuel Osorio De Zuñiga,* painted by Francisco de Goya in 1788, is part of the Jules Bache Collection of 1949 and has been on exhibit at the Metropolitan Museum since that time. Florence named her figurine *Little Don.* Shown here are Florence's *Little Don* and a picture of the Goya painting.

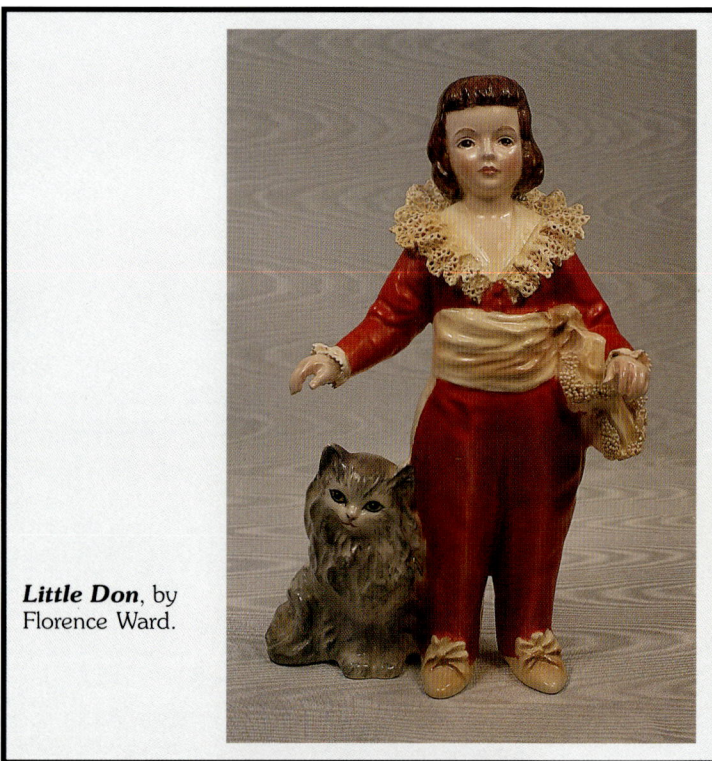

**Little Don,** by Florence Ward.

**Lillian Russell:** The legendary beauty of Lillian Russell also gained entrance to Florence's list of historic figurines. Lillian Russell was born in 1861 in Clinton, Iowa, but lived most of her life in Chicago. A trained singer and actress, she appeared in theatres in Chicago, Los Angeles, and New York, and at the Gaiety Theatre in London. Most of her roles were light opera; she sang only the occasional grand opera. Near the end of her stage career, she wrote articles on beauty for the women's pages of the *Chicago Herald* and the *Chicago Tribune.*

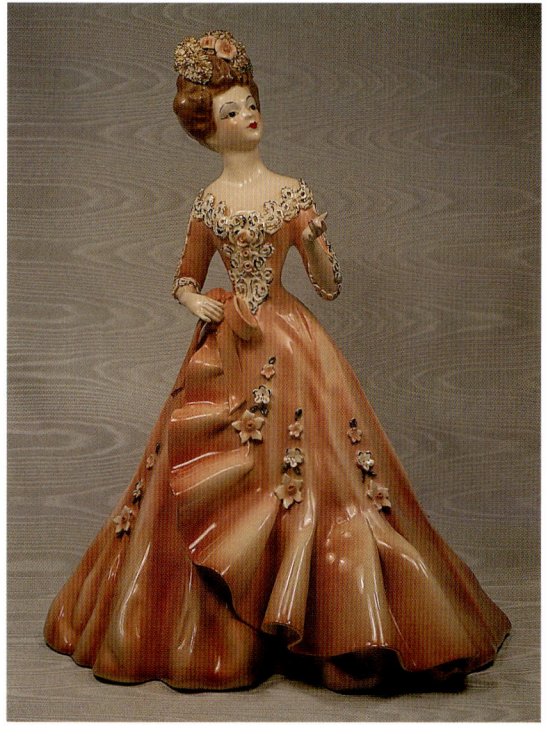

**Lillian Russell,** leading lady and fashion writer.

**Historical, Literary, and Religious** 133

**Little Princess:** While *Little Princess* can be a complement to *Little Don*, it is not believed they are a pair. In keeping with her presentations of sculpted figures from paintings by the Old Masters, Florence chose another young figure in *Portrait of the Infanta Margarita*, by Diego Velazquez (c.1660). The *Infanta Margarita* is the daughter of Philip IV of Spain. Philip ordered Velazquez to paint several variations of this picture, and in each one the dress was to be a different color. Florence's figural rendition of the variants is wonderfully true to the originals.

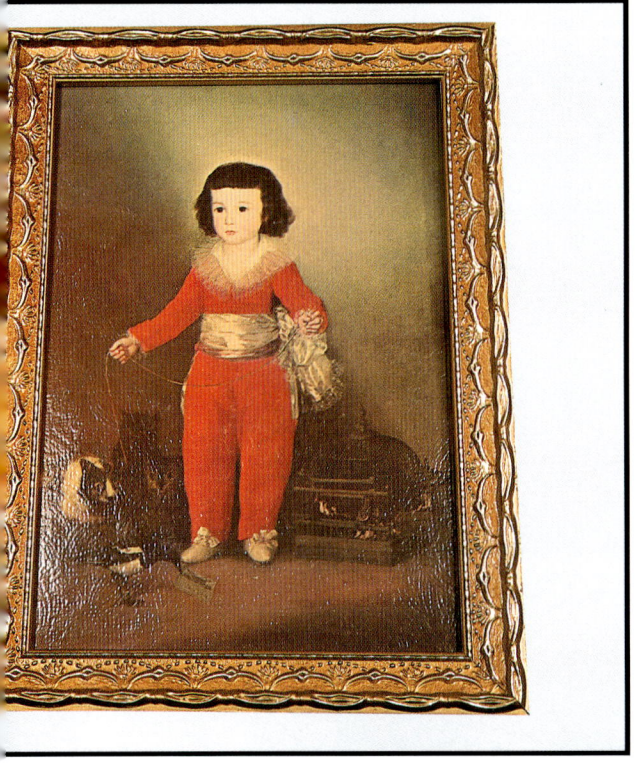

**Don Manuel Osorio**, painting by Francisco de Goya.

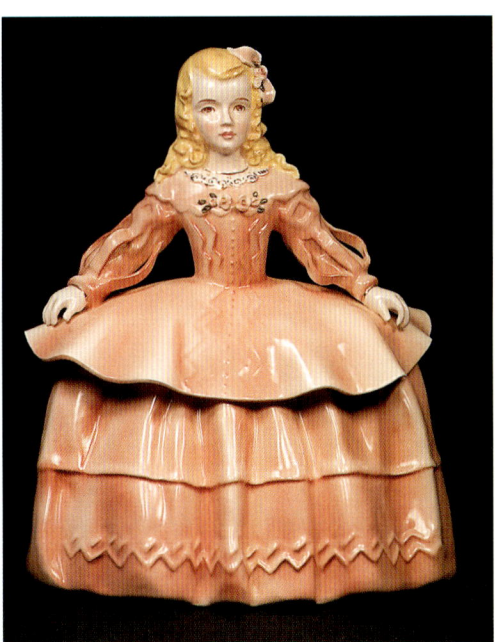

**Little Princess**, the Infanta Margarita.

**Madame DuBarry:** Madame DuBarry was born Comtesse Marie Jean Becu in France in 1743. Her notoriety came from her being the mistress of Louis XV. She was a favorite among Parisian society and was often seen accompanied by the king. Florence's artistic creativity is never more apparent than in this bust of the vainglorious Madame DuBarry.

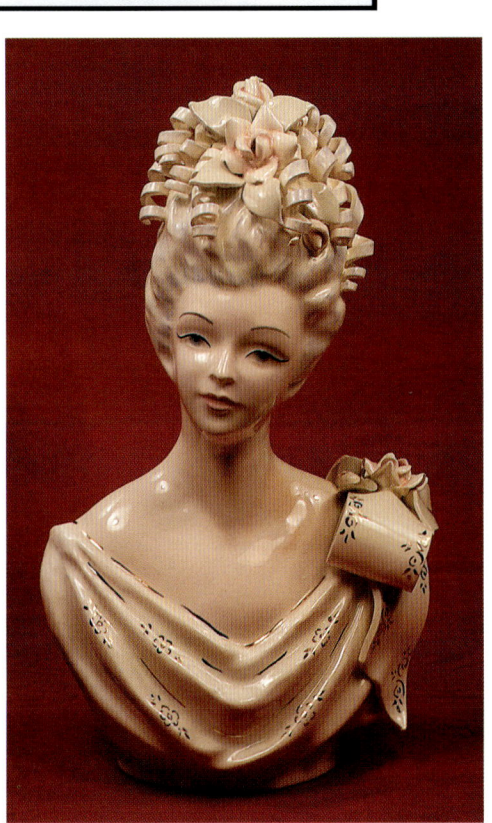

**Madame DuBarry**, eighteenth century French beauty.

## 134  Historical, Literary, and Religious

**Madame Pompadour and Louis XV:** Florence continued her representation of members of the French Court with Madame Pompadour and Louis XV. The opulence of the aristocracy is clearly recognized in these two figurines. Madame Pompadour was the mistress of Louis XV until 1764.

**Marie Antoinette and Louis XVI:** Austrian born Marie Antoinette married Louis XVI at Versailles in 1770. The queen immersed herself in the society and frivolity of the court, to the detriment of herself and the king. Her proclivity for annoying the populace was costly! Florence created two superb examples of the haughty grandeur of a time gone forever.

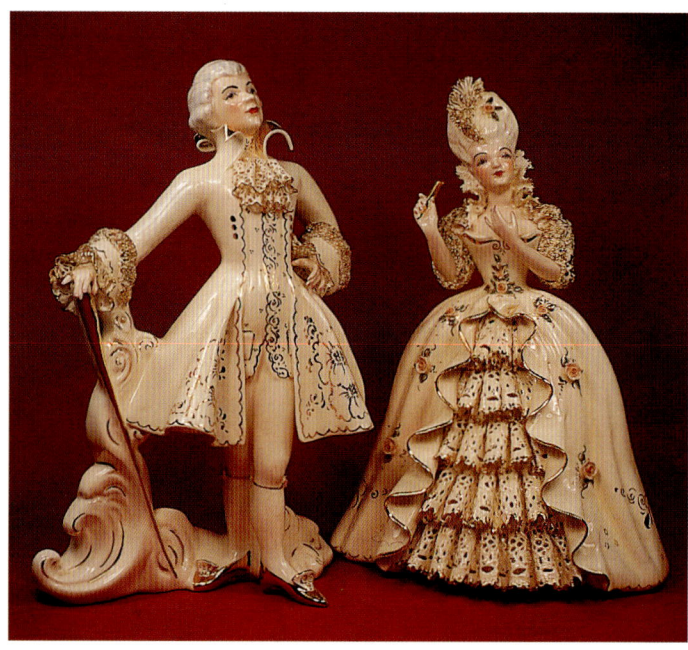

**Louis XVI and Marie Antoinette,** the grandeur of Versailles.

**Louis XV and Madame Pompadour,** famous French Court figures.

**Madonna and Child:** Florence painstakingly studied more than one thousand paintings of the Madonna by many different artists. She was looking for just the right painting that would best lend itself to the sculpted form. She chose Raphael. Florence said in an interview for *The Pasadena Star-News* of August 14, 1949, "In so far as I know, Florence Ceramics is presenting the first Madonna and Child in ceramics with each of the figures separate. The effect is pleasing, because it borrows much from the artistry of the immortal Raphael."

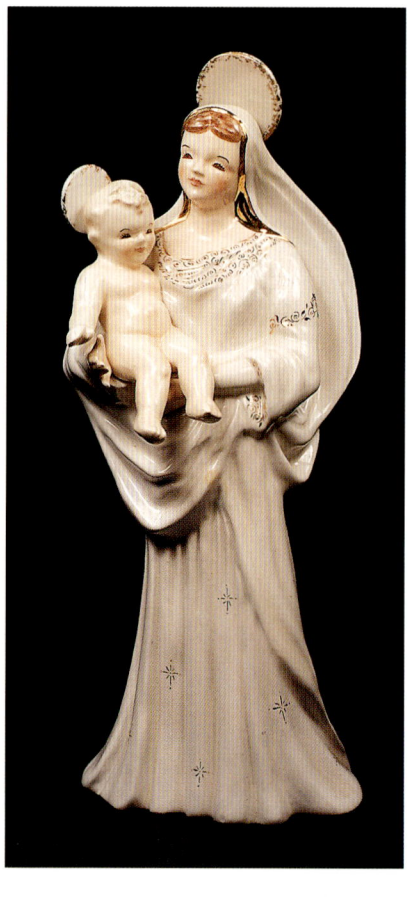

**Madonna and Child,** in the style of Raphael.

## Historical, Literary, and Religious   135

***Nell Gwynn (Gwyn):*** Nell Gwyn was born in London in 1651. She became an actress at the age of fifteen and was immediately successful. She was described variously as "piquant rather than pretty, reckless, generous, good tempered, witty, high-spirited, and finally, indiscreet." Her liaison with King Charles II may have had something to do with the latter. Florence created in *Nell Gwynn* a highly sought figurine.

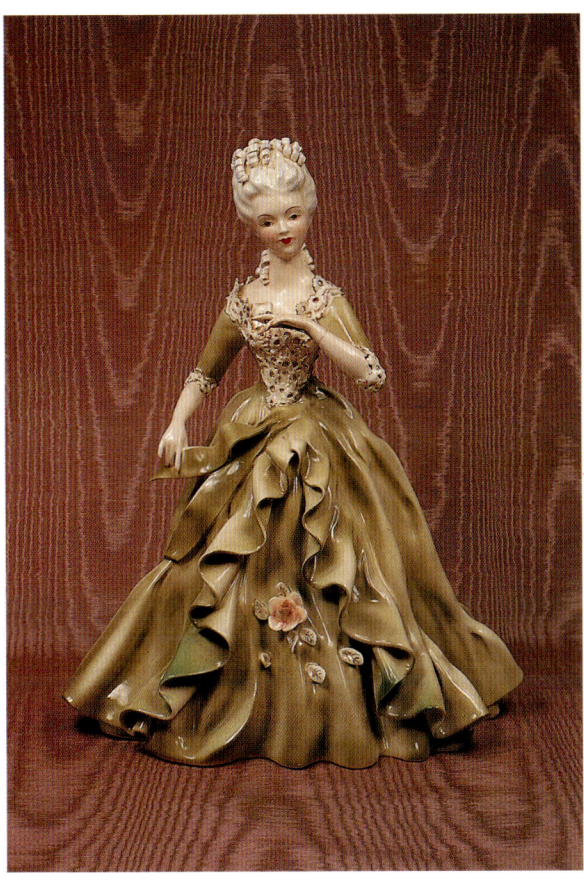

***Nell Gwynn***, seventeenth century London born actress.

***Pinkie and Blue Boy:*** Florence received permission from the Huntington Museum in Pasadena, California to sketch the portraits of *Blue Boy* and *Pinkie*. She spent countless hours doing so and thus was able to create two exemplary figures of the art world's portraiture. Thomas Gainsborough painted *Blue Boy* in 1770. Gainsborough was born in 1727 in Sudbury in the eastern part of England and became one of the foremost British portraitists of his day. Sir Thomas Lawrence, born in Bristol in 1769, painted *Pinkie* in 1794. It is generally believed that his painting of *Pinkie* was simply a commissioned portrait of Sarah Barrett Moulton, and was not intended to be anything other than that.

**Pinkie and Blue Boy**
Left: Created by Florence Ward from a painting by Sir Thomas Lawrence.
Right: Created by Florence Ward from a painting by Thomas Gainsborough.

***Priscilla and John Alden:*** Interestingly, Florence chose two austerely clad figures of early American history. These two Pilgrims are the antithesis of the elaborately gowned representatives of France and England. Neither do they have the flamboyance of the American theater. It is quite possible that Florence had nothing more in mind than to offer a more affordable pair for the average collector. (It may also be that she was merely making table decorations for Thanksgiving!) In any case, the simplicity of these two figurines makes them instantly identifiable and unique.

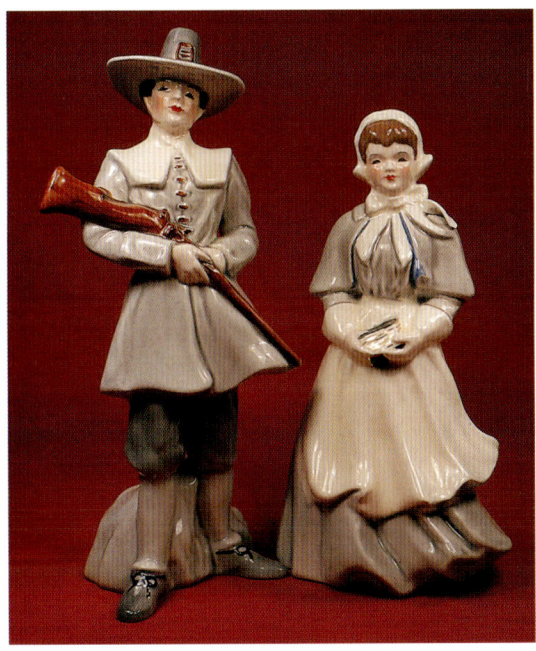

***John Alden and Priscilla***, Pilgrims.

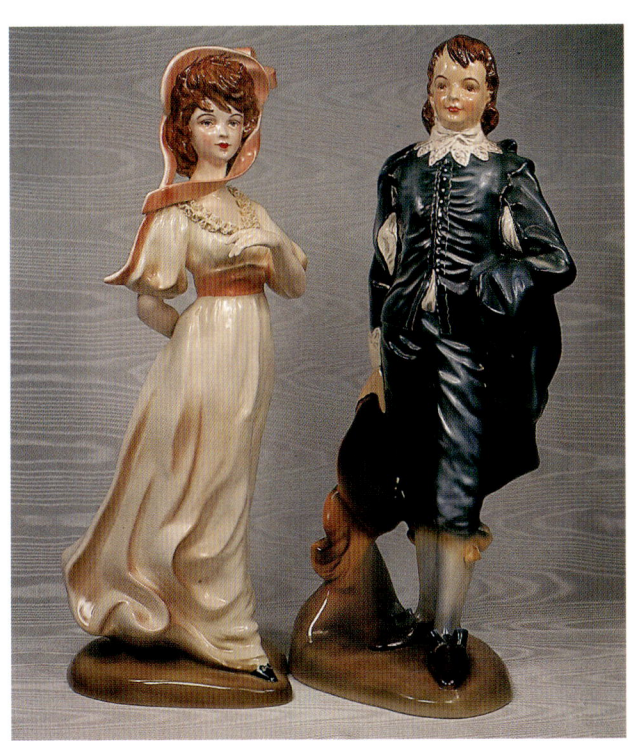

## 136  Historical, Literary, and Religious

**Sarah Bernhardt:** Sarah Bernhardt was born Rosine Bernard in Paris in 1845. She aspired to be an actress and made her acting debut at the *Comedie Francaise* in 1862. Over time she became known as the greatest actress of her day, and began a series of world tours. She visited several continents more than once and continued acting until 1922. Florence has made a very large imposing figure for Sarah Bernhardt, befitting someone of her stature and talent. This is the third and last figure of the triumvirate of theatre actresses.

**Wynkin and Blynkin:** The spelling on these two miniatures may at times appear as *Winken* and *Blinken*. As the last of the historic, religious, and literary lineup, we leave you with this verse:

*So shut your eyes while mother sings
Of wonderful sights that be,
And you shall see the beautiful things
As you rock in the misty sea,
Where the old shoe rocked the fisherman three:
Winken,
Blinken,
And Nod*

—Origin Unknown

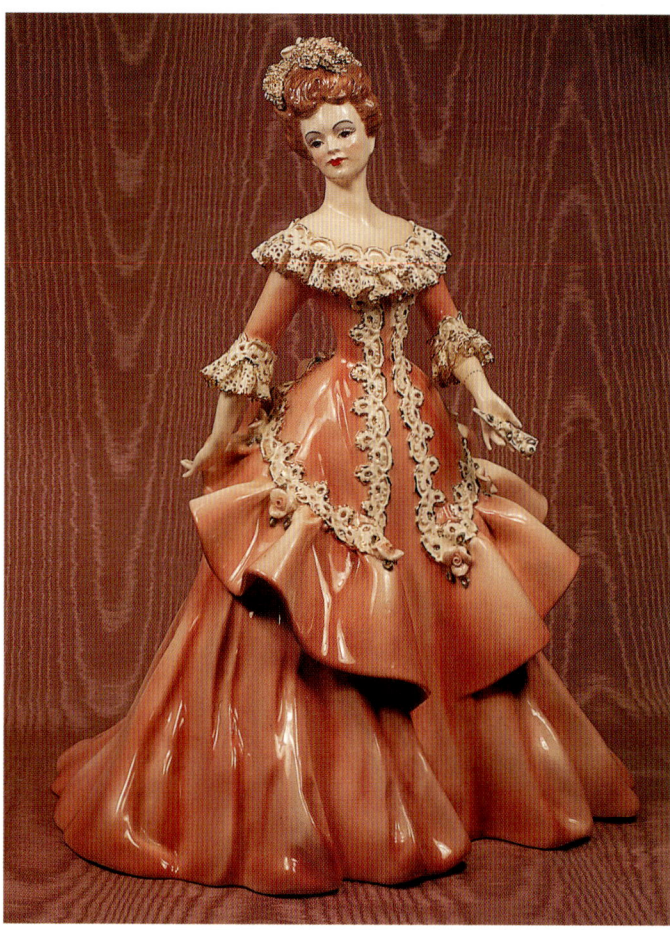

**Sarah Bernhardt**, Parisian born actress.

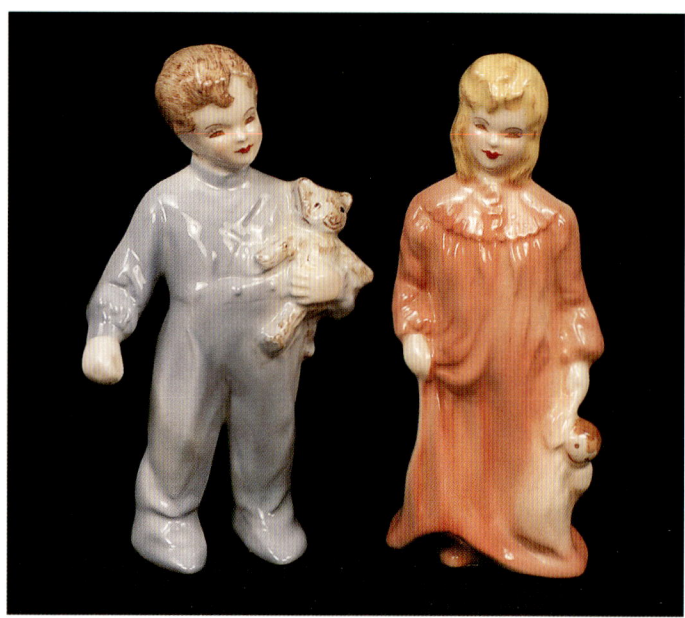

**Wynkin and Blynkin**, a lullaby.

**Sue Ellen, Scarlett, Rhett, Melanie:** The only criticism of this wonderful group is that one might have hoped all of the characters from *Gone With The Wind* had been included in Florence's literary lineup! These figurines are, of course, from the aforementioned book by Margaret Mitchell, written in 1936. They are highly collectible, not only by Florence Ceramics collectors, but by collectors of *Gone With The Wind* memorabilia as well. There is no allusion to *Gone With The Wind* in any of the Florence catalogs.

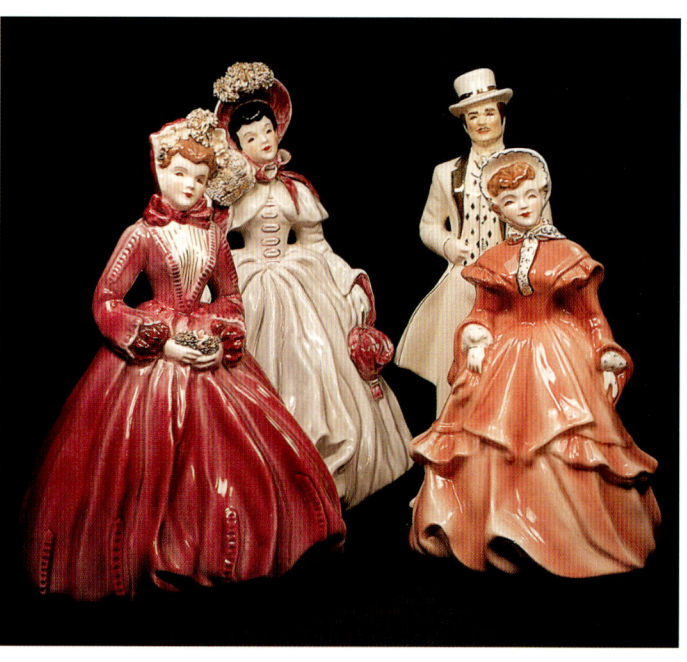

**Sue Ellen, Scarlett, Rhett, Melanie**, favorite book characters.

# Chapter VII
# *Birds and Animals*

*My sculpturing for Florence Ceramics came about in the 1950s. I worked with Cliff on his bird items as well as sculpting a shaggy dog coin bank...I definitely remember a pheasant and a swan...Cliff and I had a good relationship.*
—Don Winton, Winton Sculptures (Corona Del Mar, California, June 2001)

Stunning! That is the word that comes to mind for this group of birds and animals.

They are designed using lustrous colors and with perfect conformation and accuracy of detail.

Many of the birds were designed by Don A. Winton, a famous California sculptor who has sculpted for many different commercial enterprises during his career. The animals were designed by Betty Davenport Ford, another prominent and well known California artist. The first issue of these bisque fired figures was introduced in the mid 1950s. The designs were created exclusively for Florence Ceramics and the company produced this line for a brief two years, therefore they are rare.

The prices shown here reflect the average values across the continent. The animals designed by Betty Davenport Ford are indicated by "BDF" following the name of the figure, while the initials "DW" designate those sculpted by Don Winton.

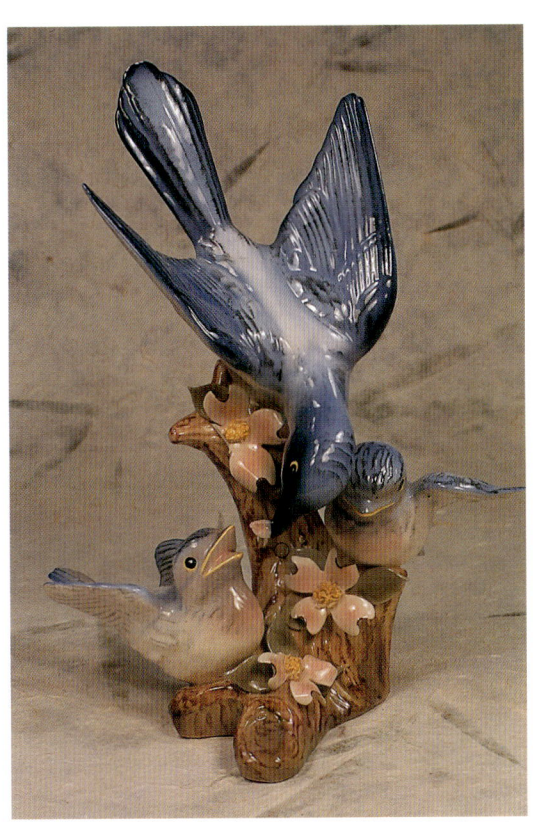

**Blue Bird Group**, 8.5"
$600-650

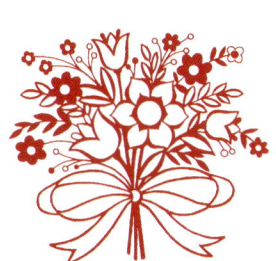

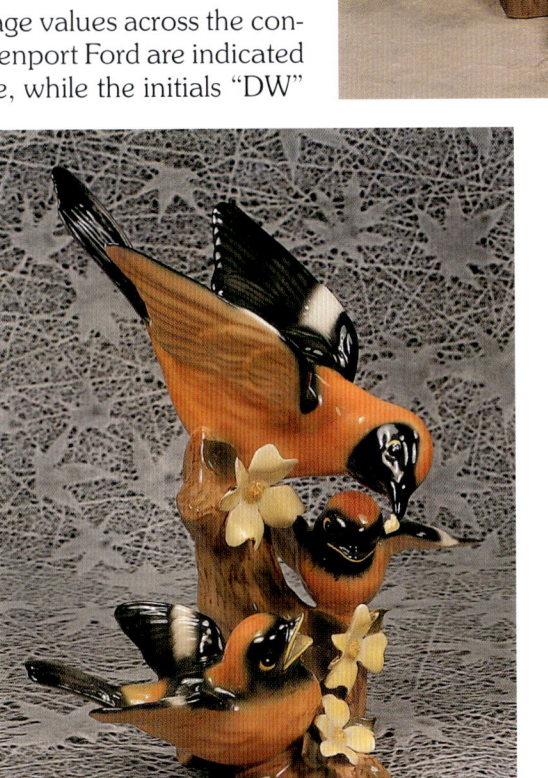

**Baltimore Oriole Group**, 8.5"
$600-650

## 138   Birds and Animals

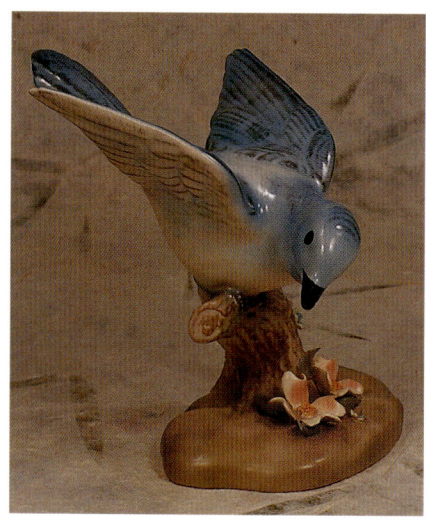

***Blue Bird Single***, 5.25"
$450-500

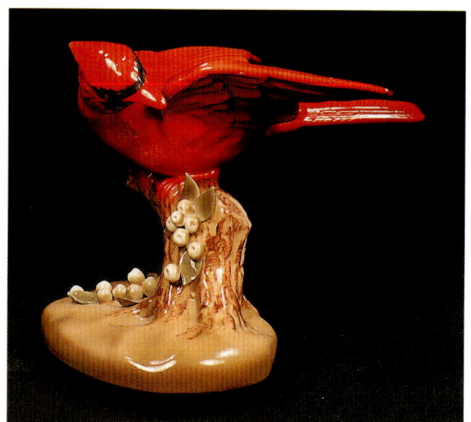

***Cardinal***, 4.75"
$450-500

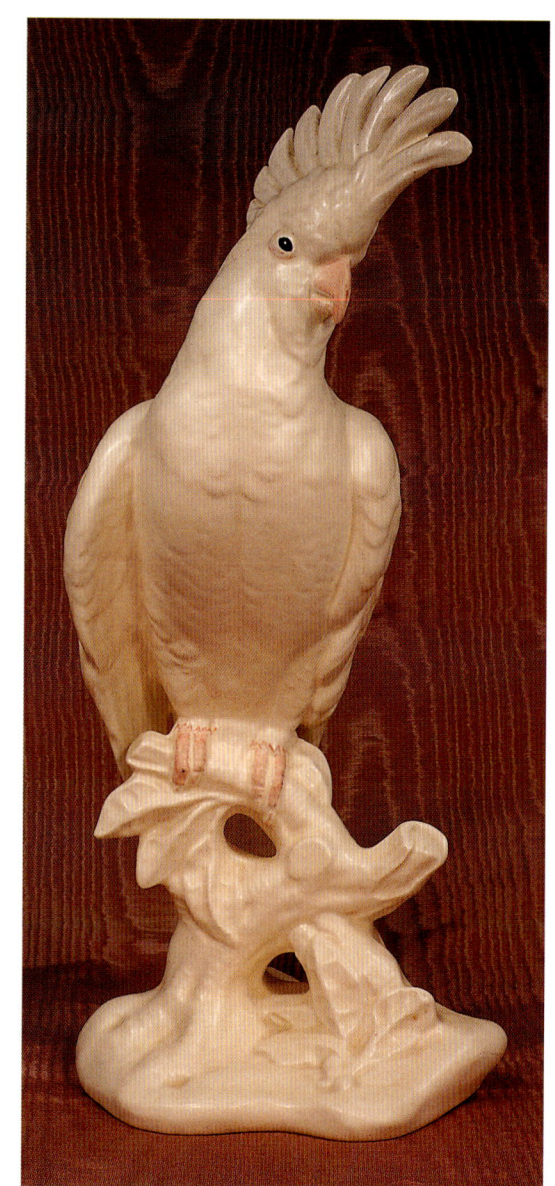

***Cockatoo***, 13.25" (DW)
$500-550

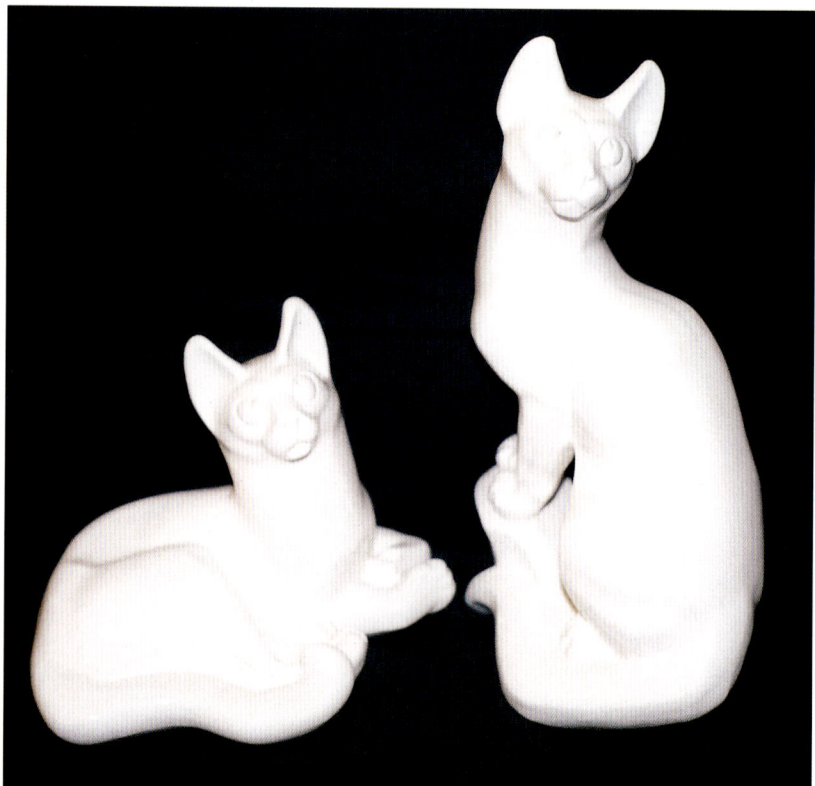

Left: ***Cat Reclining***, 7.75" (BDF); Right: ***Cat Sitting***, 11.5" (BDF)
$650-700 pair

**Birds and Animals** 139

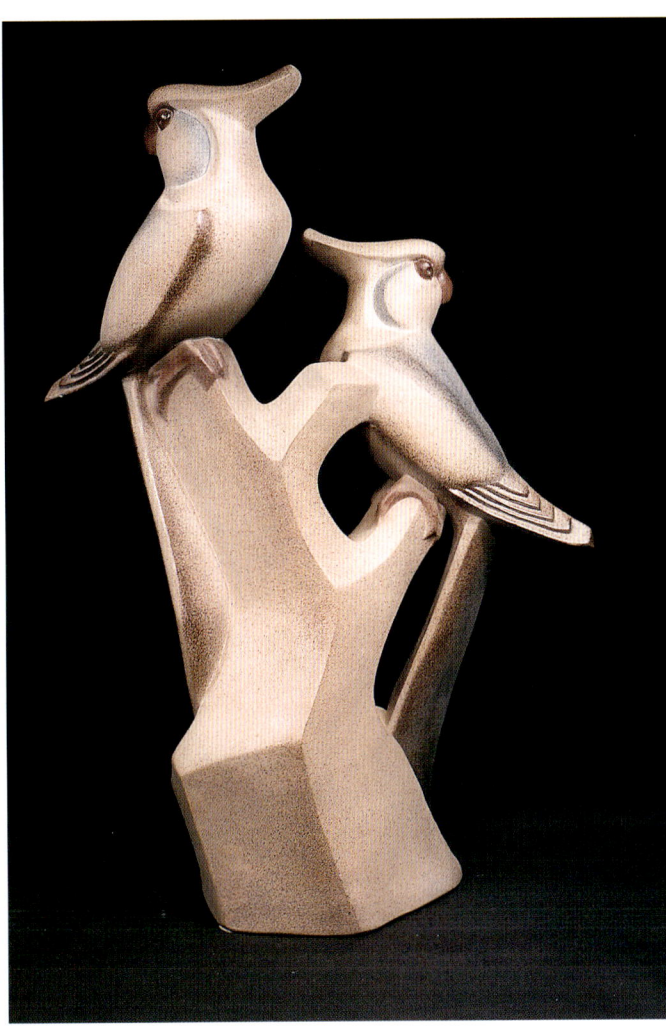

***Dove Flying***, 8" x 11" (BDF)
$375-400

***Cockatoos***, 15.5" (BDF)
$600-700

***Fox Running***, 9" x 16" (BDF)
$375-400

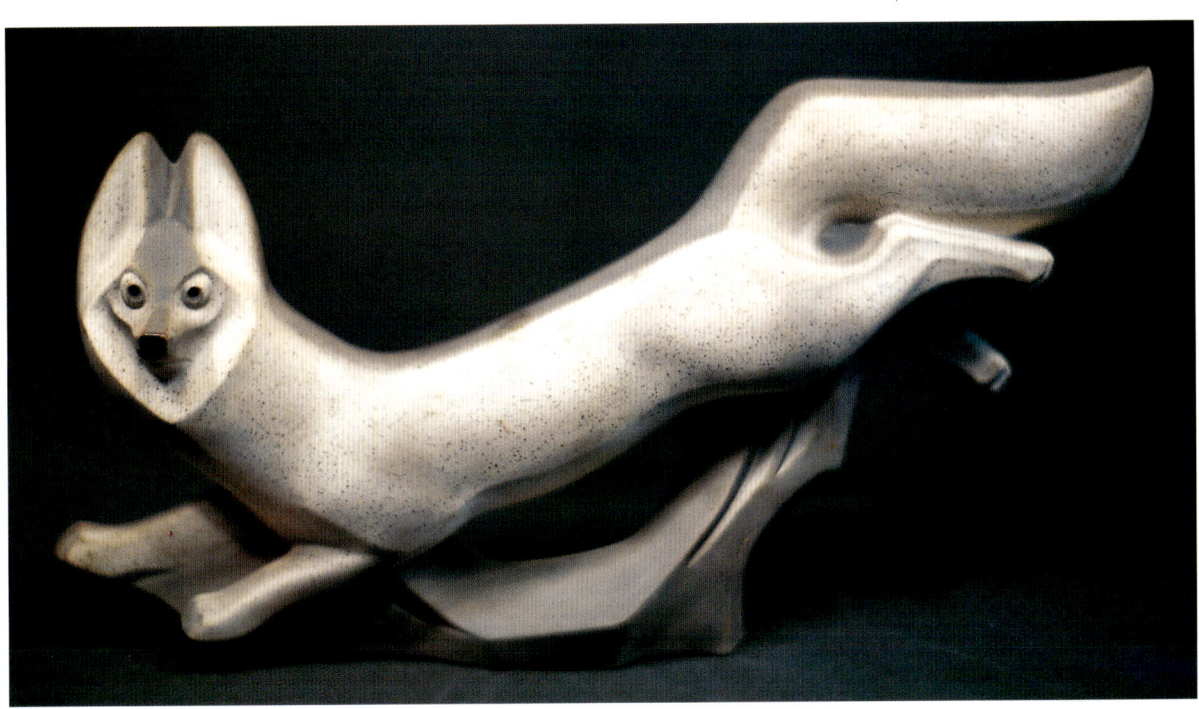

## 140    Birds and Animals

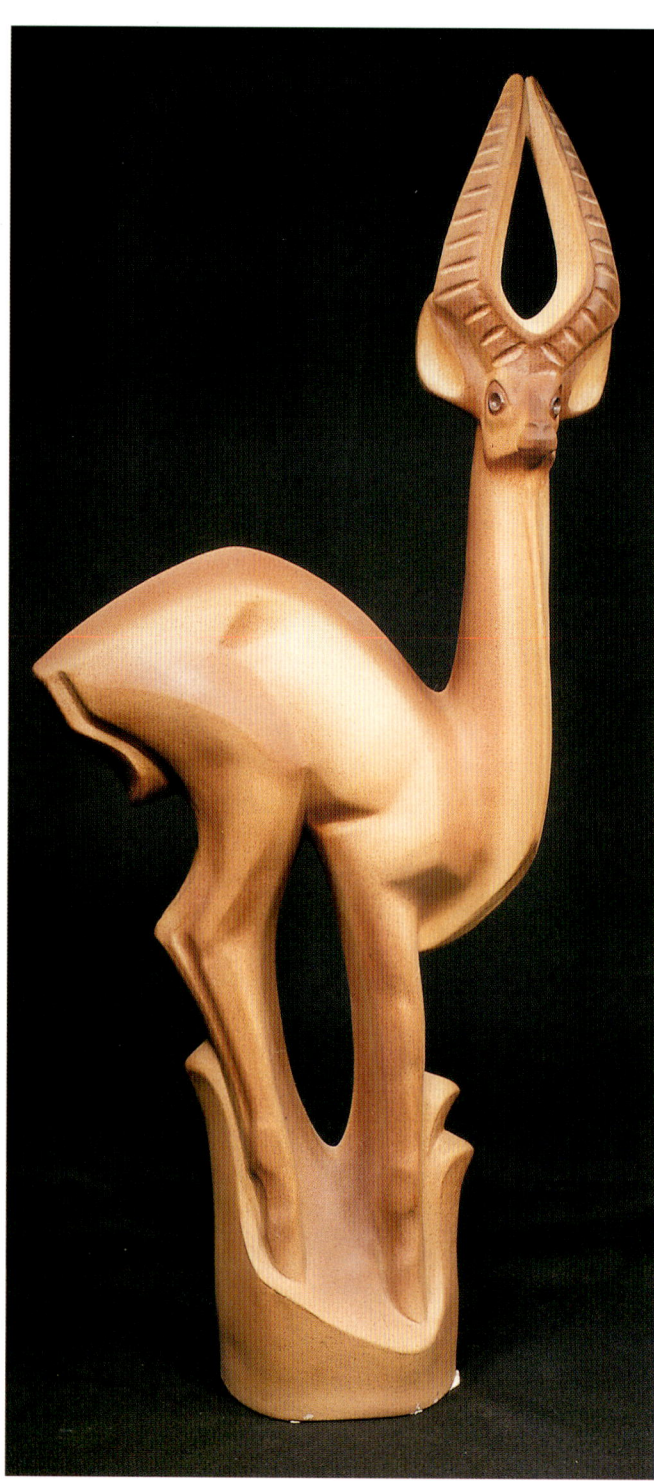

*Gazelle*, 19" (BDF)
$700-800

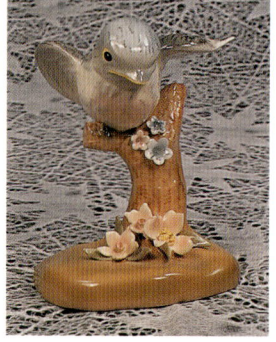

***Mocking Bird Baby***, 4.25"
$300-350

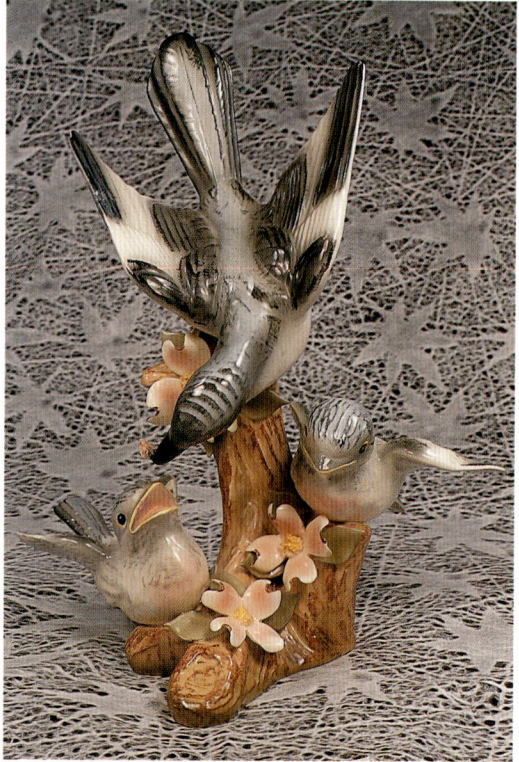

***Mocking Bird Group***, 8.5"
$600-650

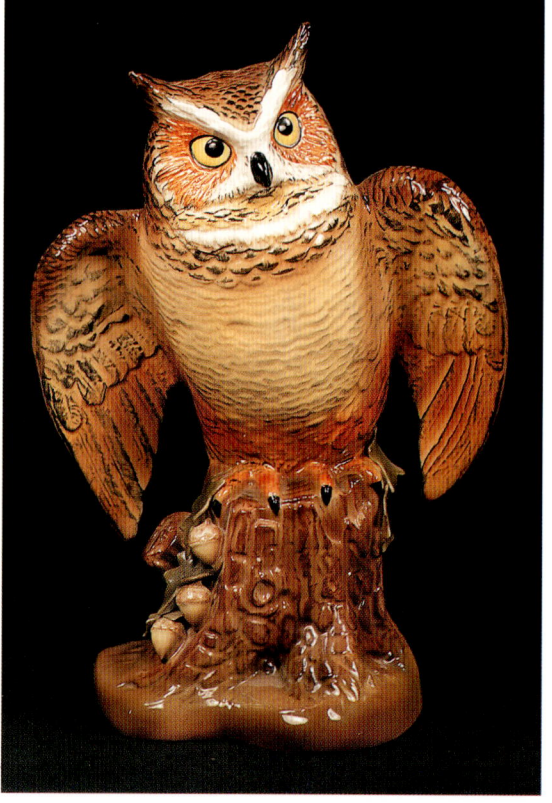

***Owl***, 9"
$500-550

**Birds and Animals**  141

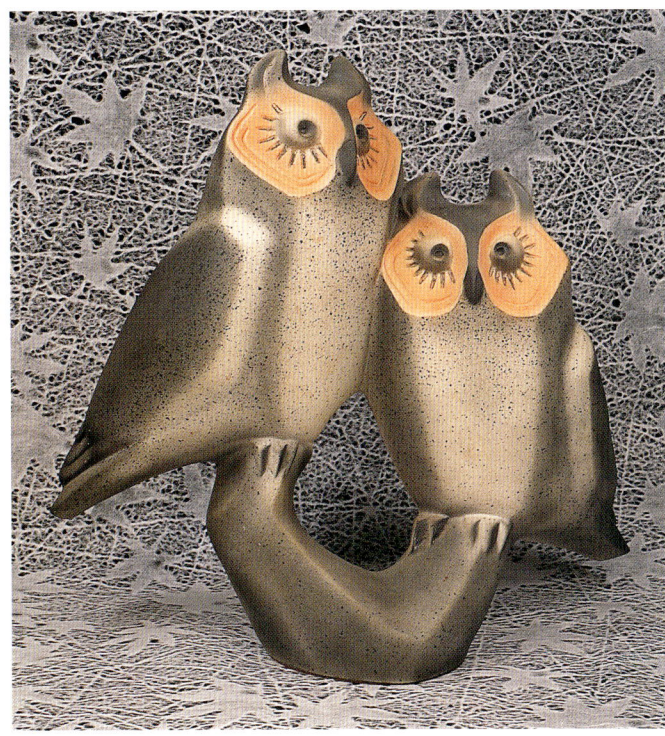

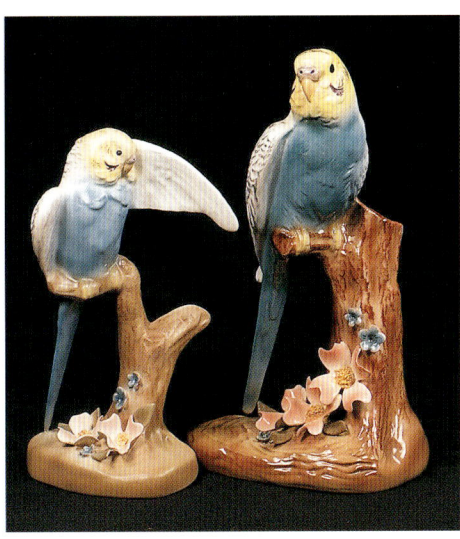

Left: ***Parakeet Wing Out***, 5.75";
Right: ***Parakeet Wing In***, 7.25" (both DW)
$750-850 pair

***Owls Double***, 12" (BDF)
$500-550

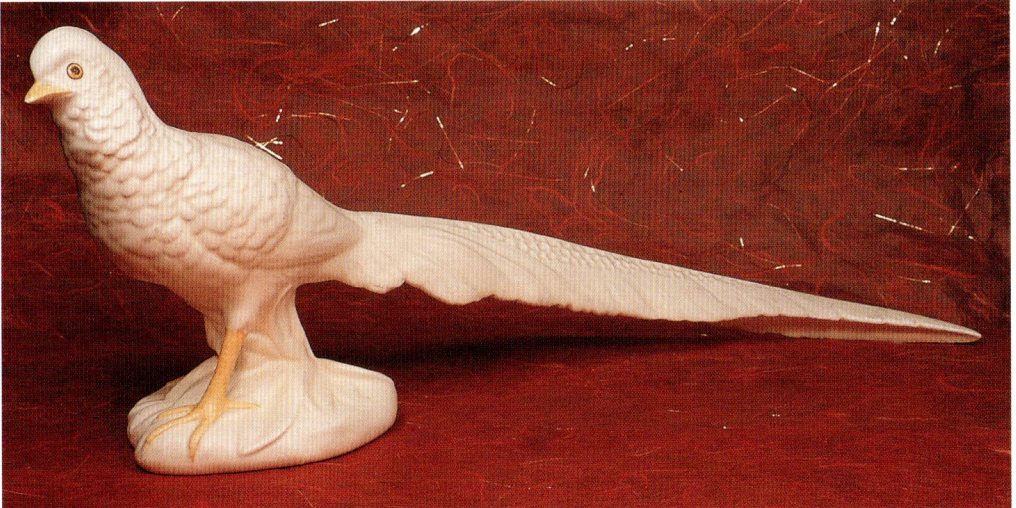

***Pheasant Tail Down***, 6.75" x 17" (DW)
$400-450

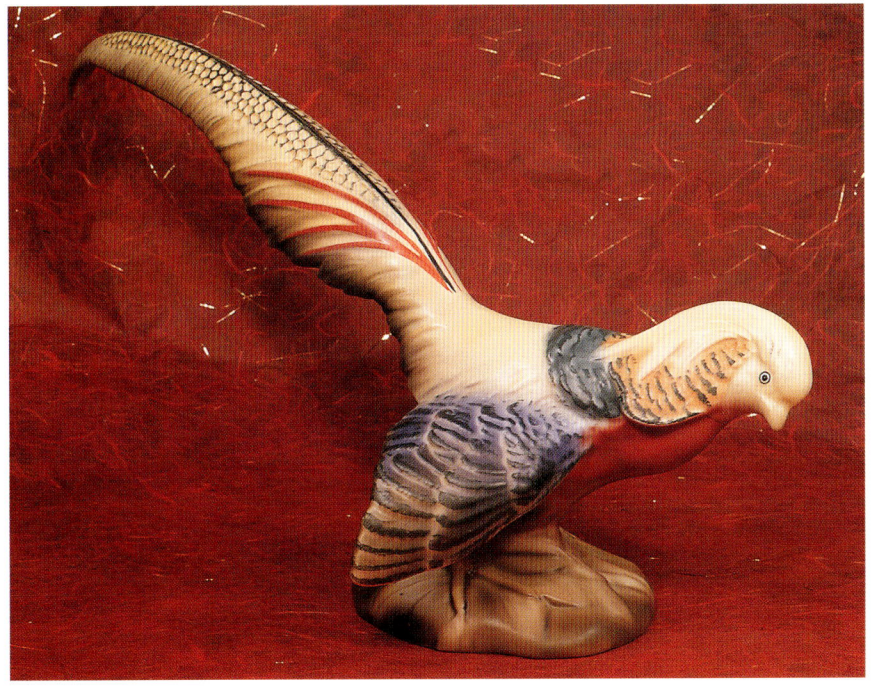

***Pheasant Tail Up***, 6.75" x 17" (DW)
$400-450

## 142   Birds and Animals

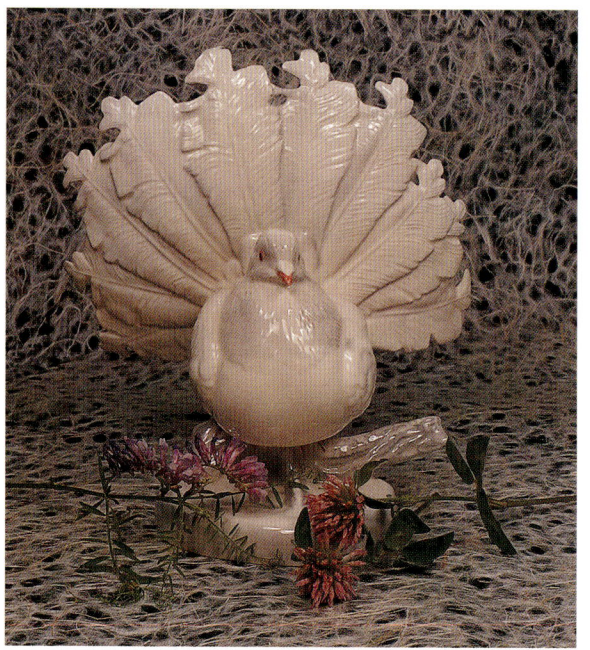

**Pigeon Fantail**, 8" (DW)
$450-500

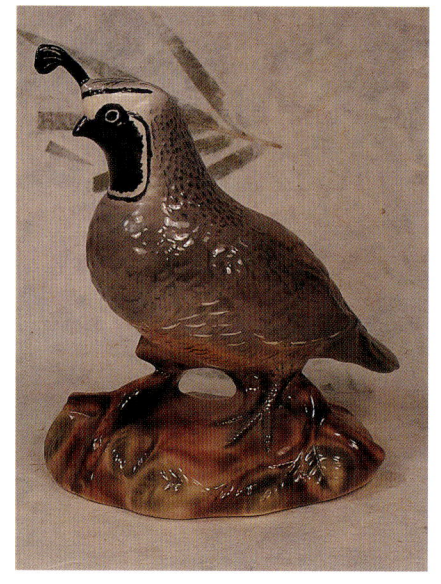

**Quail**, 7.5"
$500-550

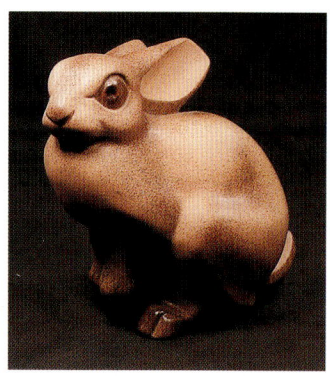

**Rabbit**, 5.5" (BDF)
$300-350

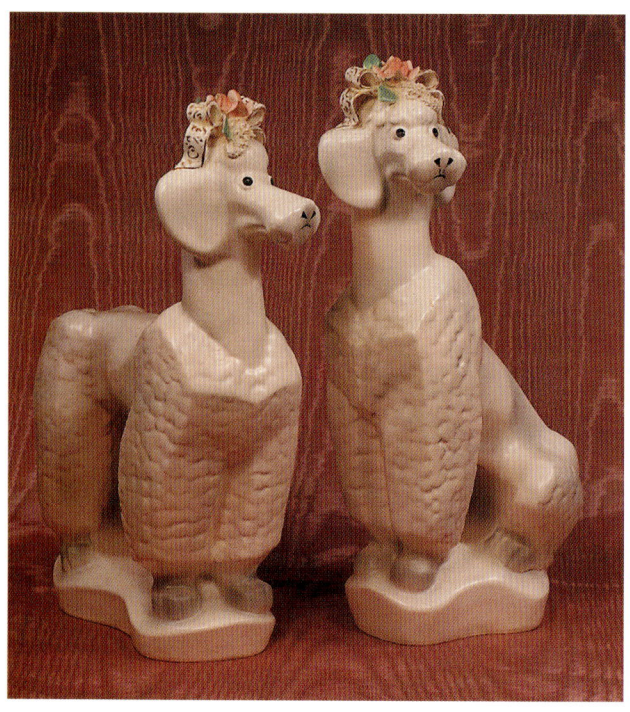

Left: **Poodle Sitting**, 9.5" (BDF);
Right: **Poodle Standing**, 8.75" (BDF)
$750-850 pair

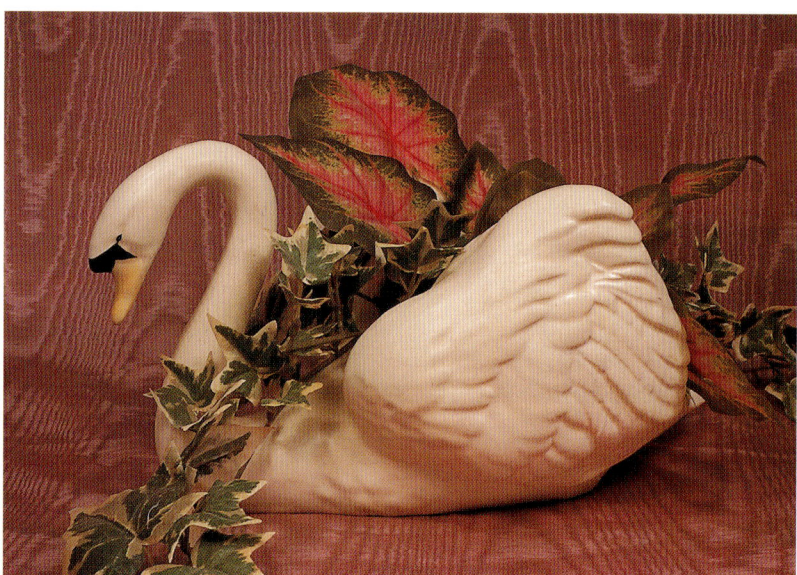

**Swan**, 11.75" x 6" (FH), (DW)
$400-450

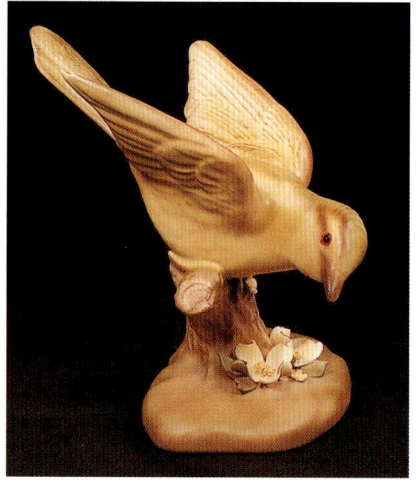

**Vireo**, 5.25"
$450-500

# Chapter VIII
# *Artware*

*...were such a close knit family...treated us all like we were family, too...we were always invited to their wonderful parties at the beach house...*
— Ann MacKellar (San Clemente, California, 2001)

In this chapter, we have provided a selection of Florence artware. The text briefly describes the various items and the pictures are numbered for ease of identification. Values shown are average prices realized across the continent.

The Florence Ceramics Company achieved a Meissen-like appearance with its artware pieces. Whether or not they intended to do so is unknown, but if such were the case they may have exceeded their own expectations. Florence designed and manufactured clocks, bonbon dishes, dresser or vanity sets, covered boxes, candleholders and picture frames (see Photos 1, 5, 6, 7, 10, 11, 12, 13, 19, 32). Other items are included in this chapter as well, and we identify them graphically and with a brief written description.

Two examples of shadow boxes are shown. They are part of the company's *Fashions in Brocade* line and were in production a very brief time. The backgrounds on the shadow boxes are velvet, while the hats are meticulously fashioned in genuine fabrics, feathers, and trimmings. Shown are *Bernice* with a poke bonnet and *Jacqueline* replete with pill box hat. These shadow boxes are apparently the only shadow boxes created by Florence Ceramics (see Photos 3, 4).

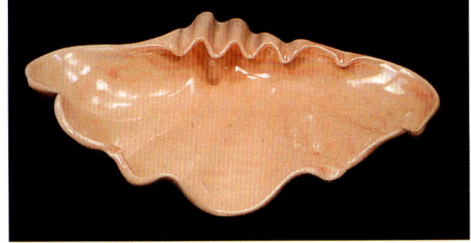

**#1: Florence Ashtray, Ming Tree Cigarette Box and Ashtrays, Bell, Sleigh, Bell**
$70-75, $275-300, $60-70, $200-250, $60-70

**#2: Shell Ashtray**, 11" x 7.25"
$80-100

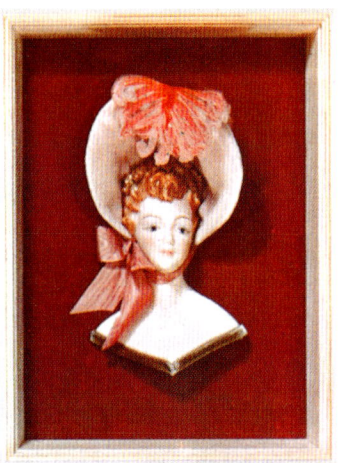

**#3: Bernice Shadow Box**,
9" x 12"
$400-500

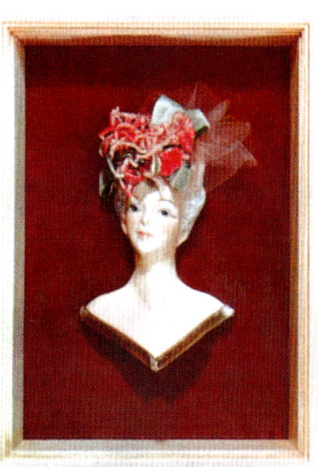

**#4: Jacqueline Shadow Box**, 9" x 12"
$400-500

143

Clocks are designed in the French style, and are electric with self-starting Sessions movements. Sessions movements are collectible in their own right. The clocks are designed for mantle, table, or boudoir; all are trimmed in 22-karat gold (see Photos 6, 9, 14, 23).

Bookends were produced using the various smaller sized children. These bookends also could be used as flowerholders (see Photo 8).

The company held a patent for their unique picture frames. This patent was filed in 1947 and approved in 1951. Edgar E. Kellems of Pasadena, California is the inventor and assigned the patent to Florence Ceramics. The basis of the patent is a picture holder comprising a flat single piece molded from ceramic material and defining a flat cavity, a viewing opening at the front, and an access opening at the base. Florence Ceramics produced picture frames in several sizes with a variety of applied decorations. Flower decorations are referred to by the company as "Dresden flowers" (see Photos 10, 12).

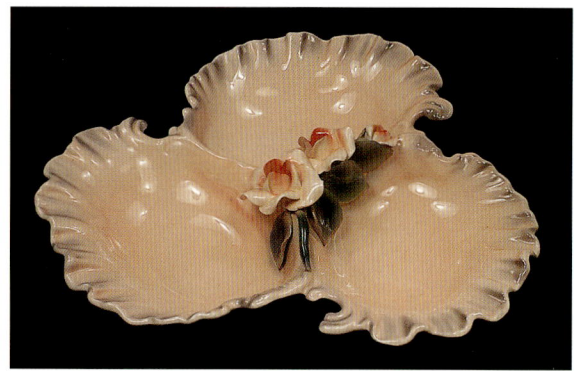

**#7: Triple Bon Bon Dish**
$160-180

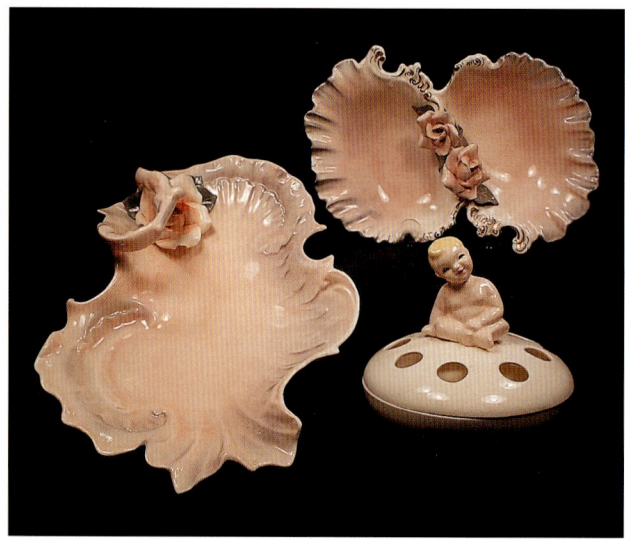

**#5: Console Bowl with Handle, Bon Bon Double, Lipstick Holder with Baby**
$120-140, $125-140, $450-500

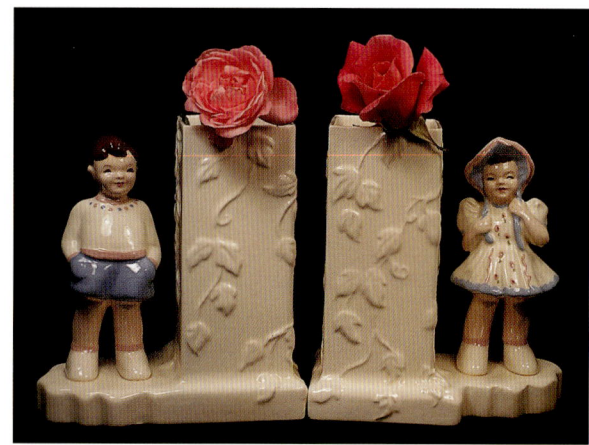

**#8: Bookends, Butch and Susie** (FH)
$450-500

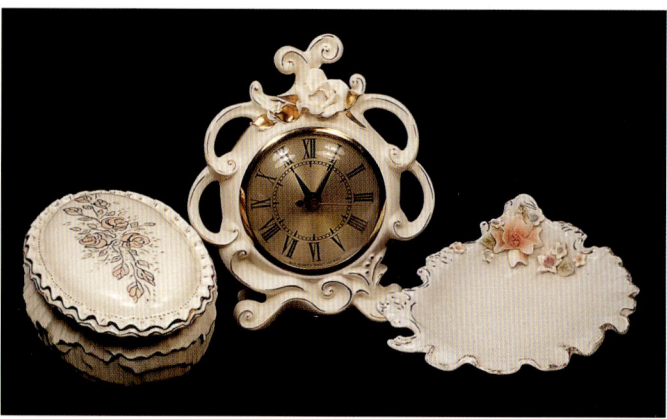

**#6: Powder Box 6", Boudoir Clock 7", Shell Bon Bon**
$135-150, $450-500, $110-125

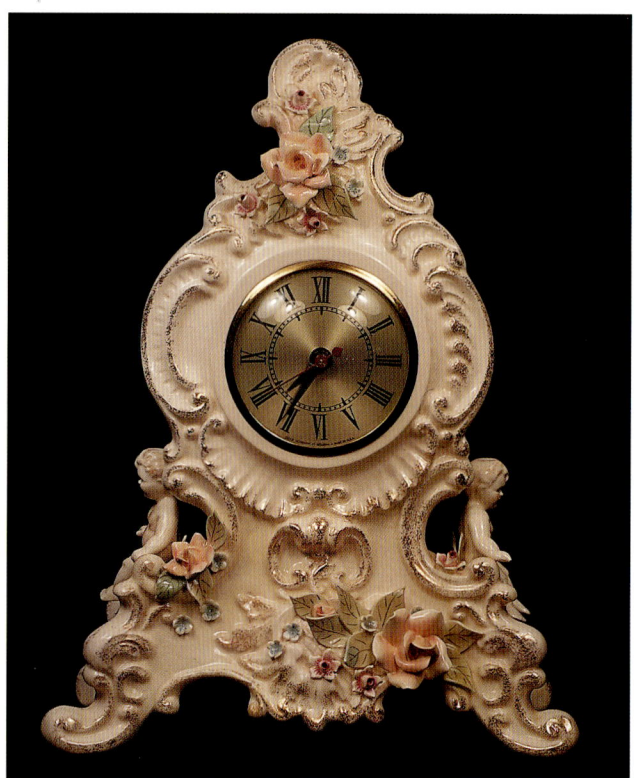

**#9: Mantle Clock**, 13"
$1,100-1,300

**Artware** 145

The company's covered boxes are almost always designed as cigarette boxes and often contain sets of individual ashtrays. Some of the lidded boxes are intended perhaps as playing card containers (see Photos 1, 13).

In 1951, the firm introduced their *Driftware* line. It is an original line in semi-porcelain of modern free-form bowls, accessories, and buffetware, unusual in shape as well as decoration. The *Driftware* bowls were designed in the manner of driftwood shapes. They can be used to hold floral arrangements or as planters, serving dishes, and even ovenware (they are oven-proof with normal precautions). Colors are Dark Pebble, Surf Green, and Fiji Coral (see Photos 41, 42, 43, 44, 45). For a short period of time, the company also made free form vases (see Photo 22).

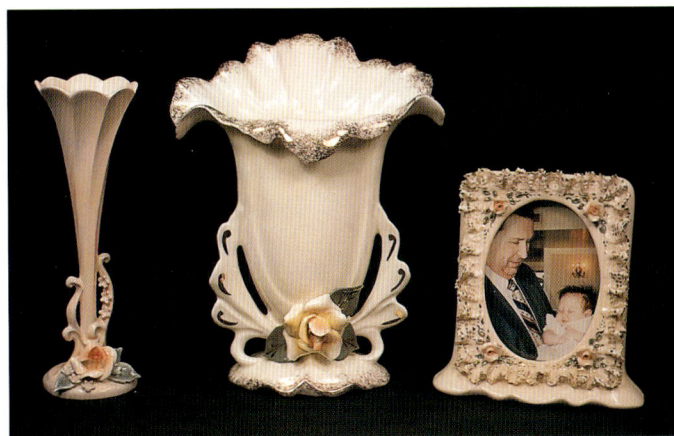

***#10: Bud Vase, Cottage Vase, Frame,*** 4" x 5"
$75-90, $115-130, $70-90

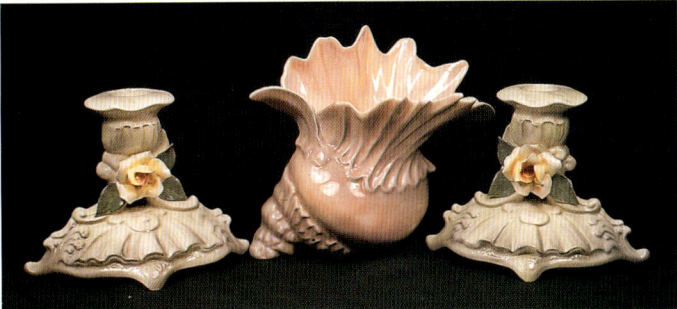

***#11: Candleholders, Shell Vase***
$110-125 pair, $75-90

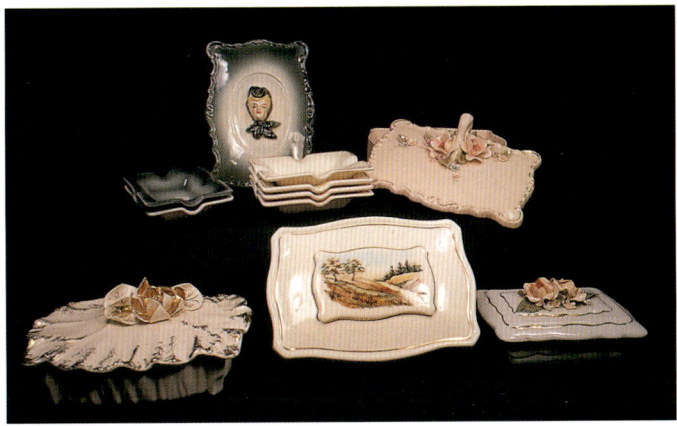

***#13: Cigarette Boxes with and without Ashtrays***
$180-225 box only, $275-300 box and four ashtrays

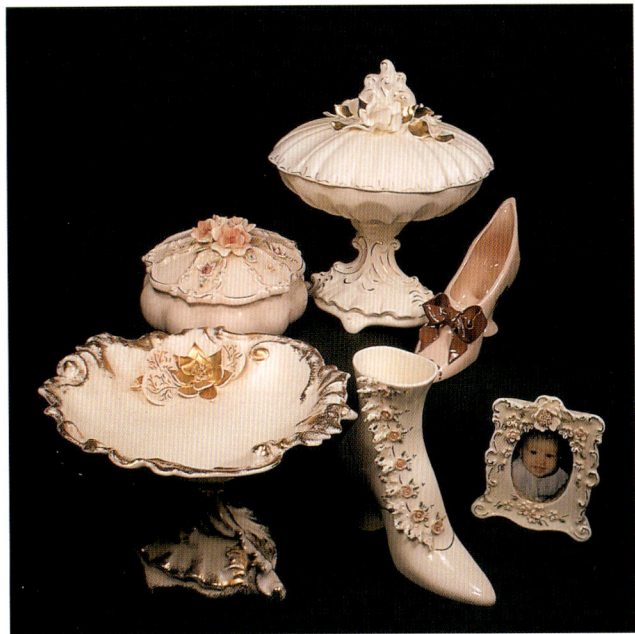

***#12: Tall Compote, Powder Box, Candy Dish, High Button Shoe, Slipper, Frame***
$150-175, $140-160, $135-150, $175-200, $115-130, $65-75

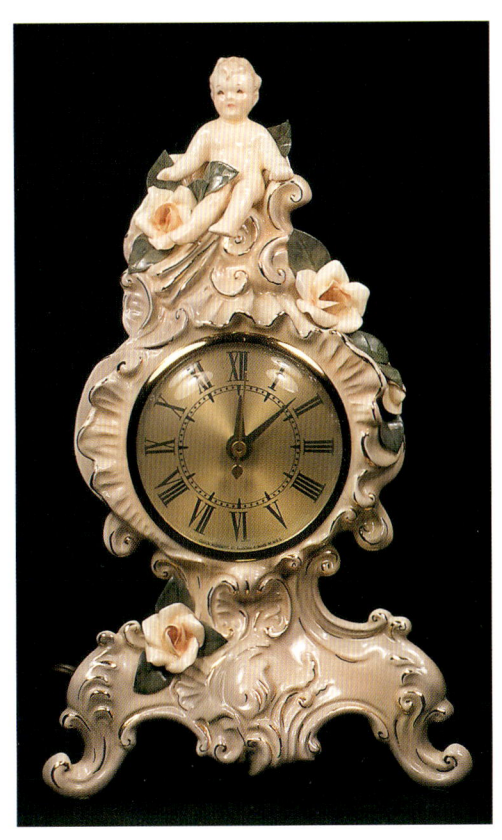

***#14: French Electric Clock***, 11.5"
$1,000-1,200

## 146 Artware

*Floraline,* the fascinating Rococo motif home accessory items, was introduced in 1950. Items consisted of console and Voltaire bowls, matching candleholders, Regency ashtrays, wall vases, and flower baskets. Colors are Grey Green, Maple Pink, and Ivory White, all with gold trim. Additionally, the *Floraline* group included two sizes of sleighs, a cornucopia, and a planter (see Photos 35, 36, 37, 38, 39, 40).

Florence Ceramics ventured into the tableware market with their *Florence Gourmet Pottery* line. *Scandia* is dramatically Nordic in design, produced for casual dining and entertaining. Its colors are Satin White, Persimmon, and Desert. *Sierra* is reminiscent of the splendor of the Sierra Mountains. This line of gourmet serving pieces was designed for patio or poolside serving, or any relaxed setting. *Sierra* colors are Satin White and Pastel Pink (see Photos 15, 16, 17, 18).

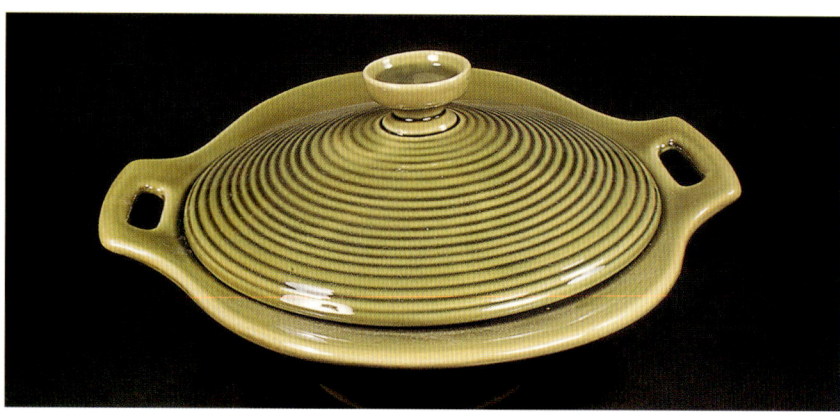

**#15: Casserole Bowl with Lid**
$100-120

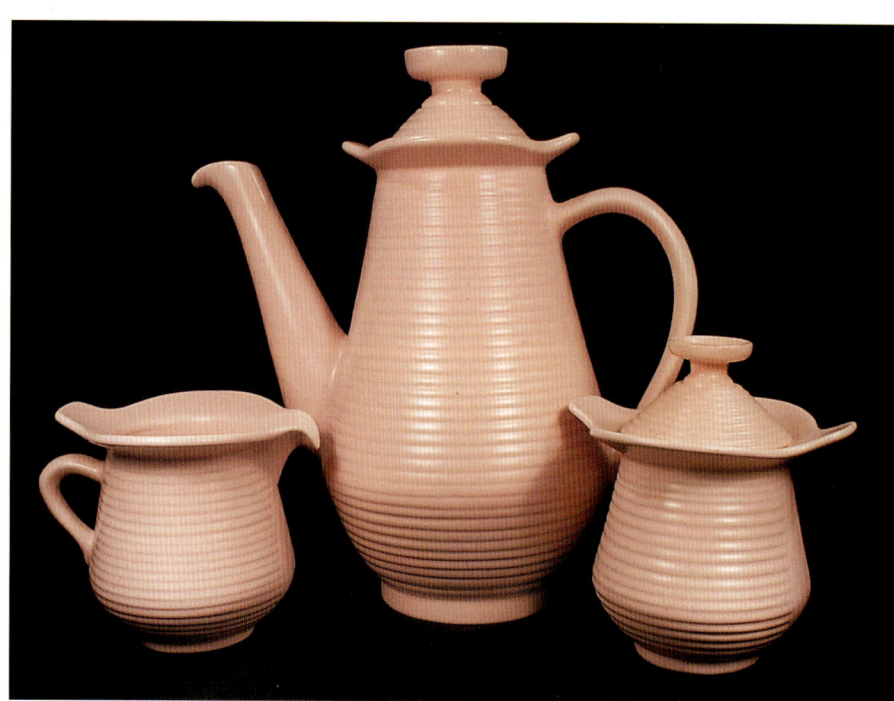

**#16: Coffee Pot, Cream, and Sugar,**
Pastel Pink
$600-700 set

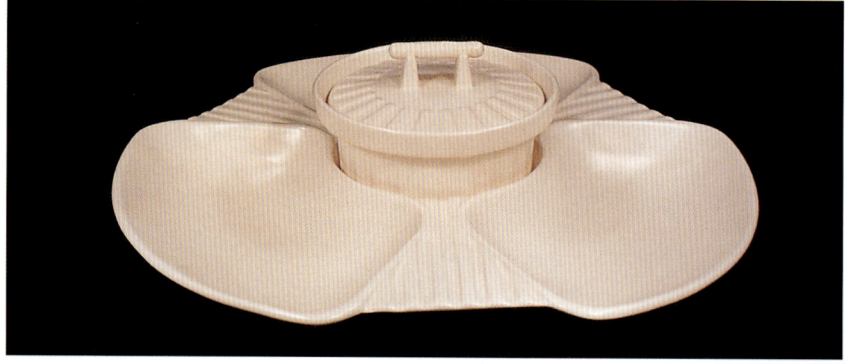

**#17: Divided Dish,** Satin White
$200-250

Artware 147

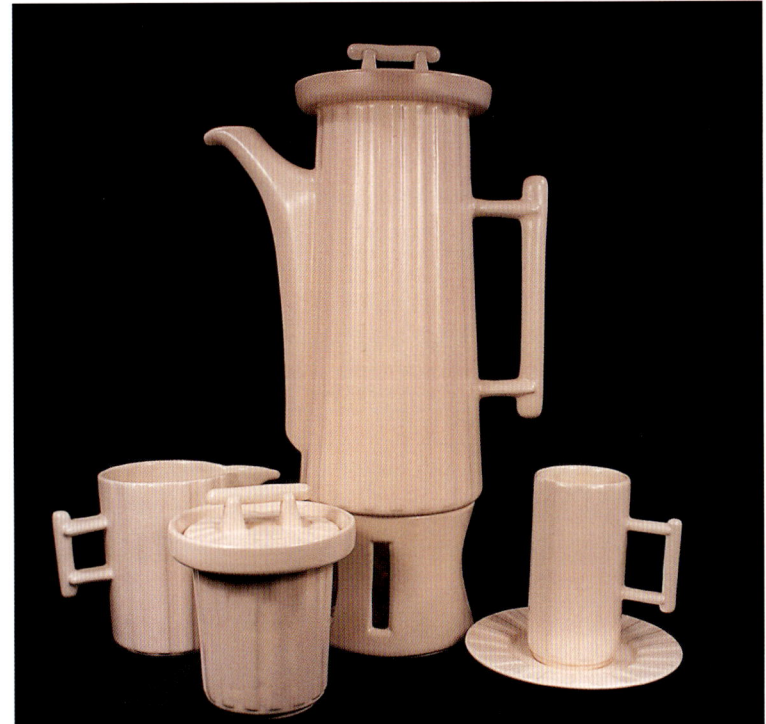

**#18: Coffee Set,** Satin White
$550-750

Offering a touch of whimsy, Don Winton's design of the Shaggy Dog is a must for the figural collector. The Shaggy Dog is adapted for a coin bank, originally contracted by the Southern California Ford Dealers Association (see Photos 20, 21).

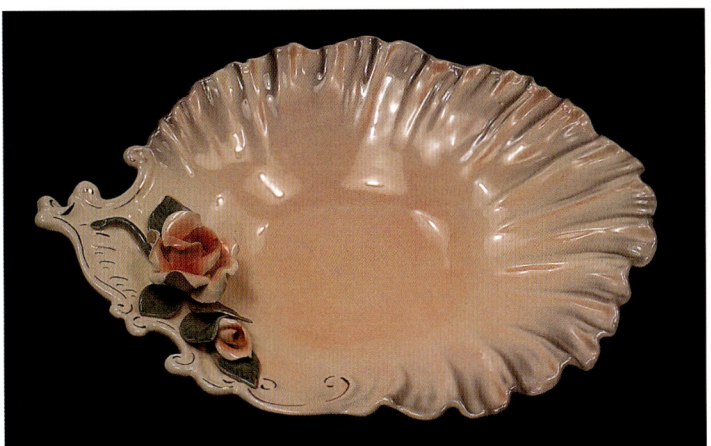

**#19: Console Bowl**
$150-170

**#20: Single Dog Ford Bank, Double Dog Ford Bank** (DW)
$100-115, $130-150

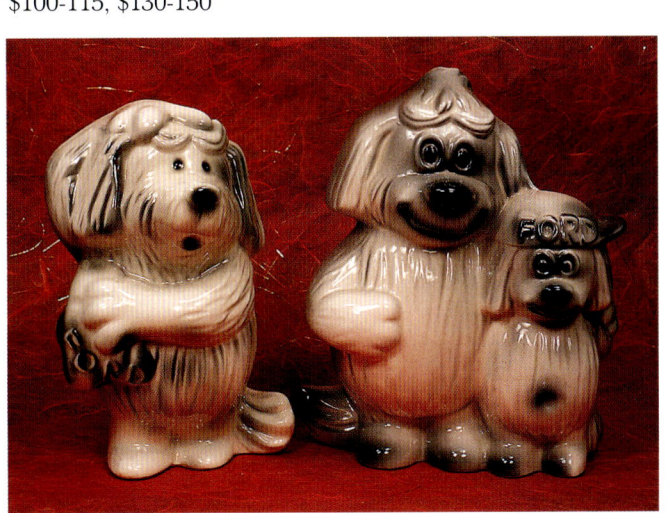

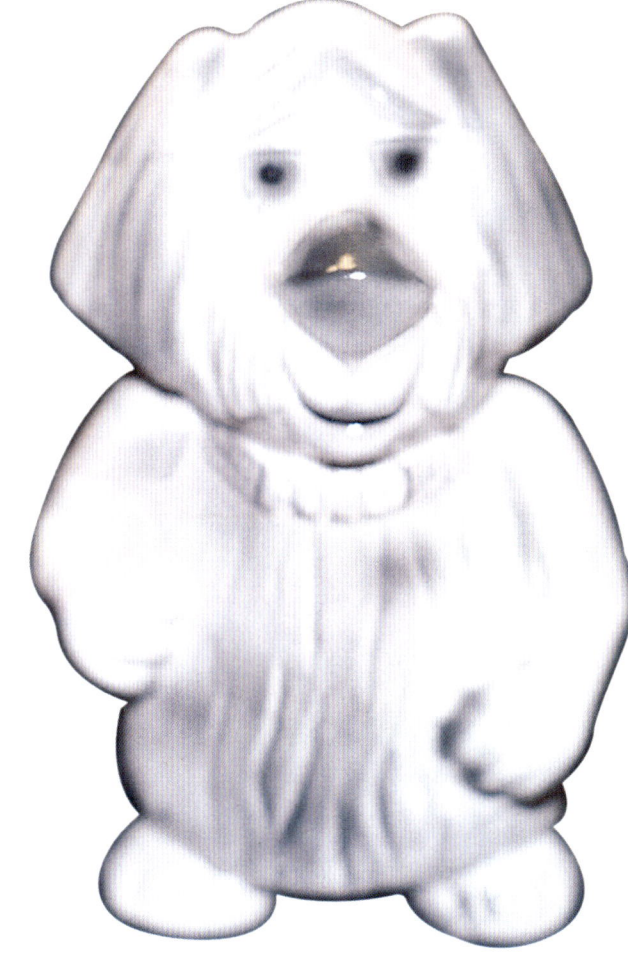

**#21: Large Ford Dog Bank** (DW)
$115-130

Another pretty and lighthearted design is the Shell Bowl. This lovely bowl with its luster color is perfect as a display unit for the Merrymaids. It is also a wonderful addition to the home or collection. There are other shell designs, including a Shell Ashtray and a Shell Wall Pocket, both of which are glazed in the same luster. Also shown is a unique Starfish Bowl (see Photos 2, 30, 31, 31A, 33).

While the wall plaques may be considered as figural display, they are also suitable for the artware line. Their rich overglazes highlight the color and beauty of design that make these plaques the perfect wall decor (see Photos 25, 26, 27).

Two lapel pins were produced as costume jewelry items. The lapel pins feature one lady with a bonneted head; the other has long tresses (see Photo 24).

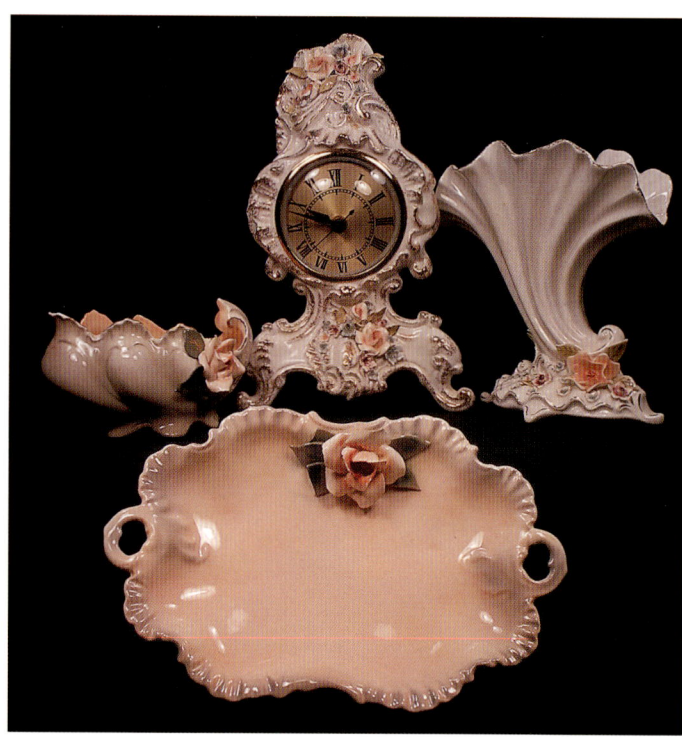

***#23: Deep Shell Bon Bon, Dresden Clock, Handled Tray, Cornucopia Vase***
$115-135, $900-1,000, $125-140, $140-160

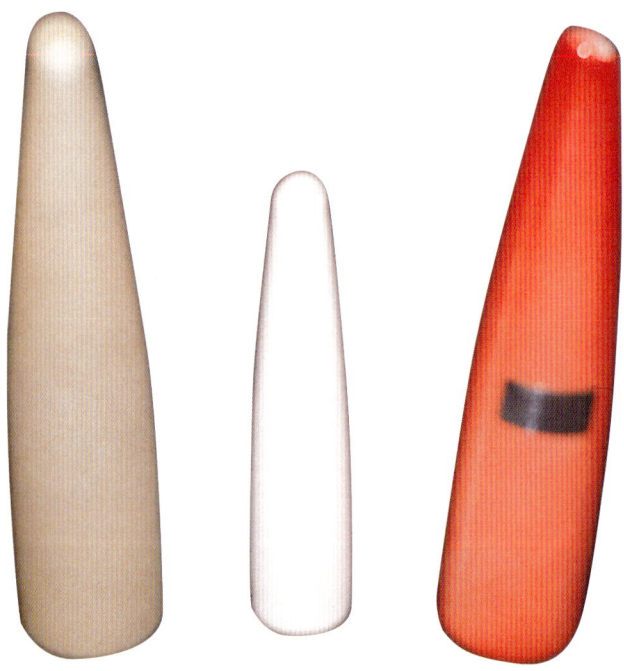

***#22: Free Form Vases*** in 7" and 10"
$50-75 each

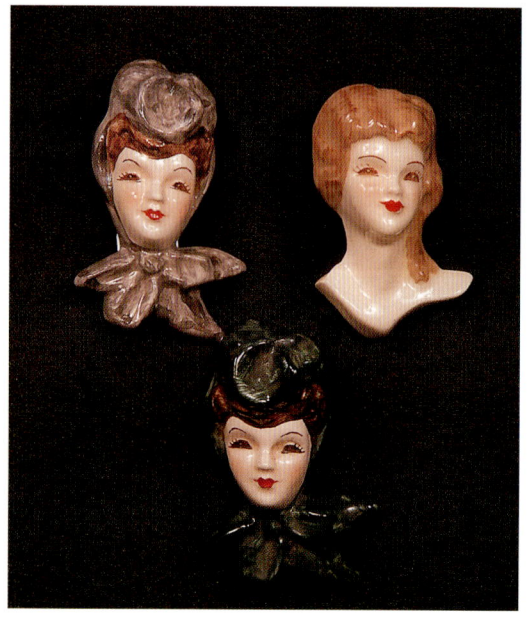

***#24: Lady Profile,*** small lapel pins
Left to Right: $225-250, $225-250, $300-350

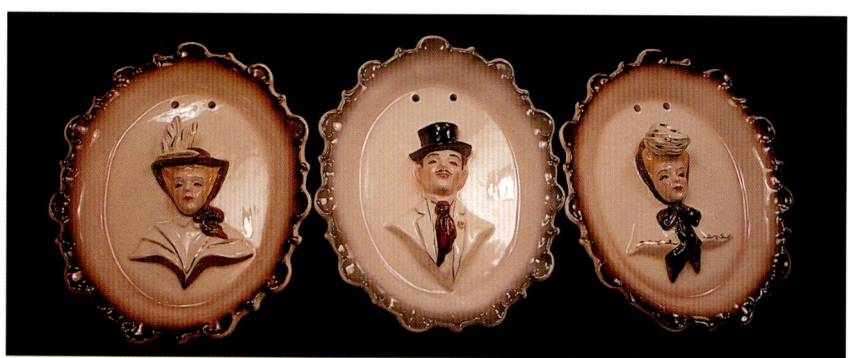

***#25: Cameo Plaques***: ***Lady, with Bow; Man, Top Hat; Lady, with Scarf***
$150-175, $200-225, $150-175

Collectors might want to include the few pieces from Scripto which are a postscript to Florence Ceramics production. We do not consider these items to be part of the Florence Ceramics Company's production, but we are including them so that they can be identified specifically as being produced by Scripto (see Photos 46, 47, 48).

The Crested Silver Mug was produced by the Florence Ceramics Company and not by Scripto, as mistakenly believed by some collectors (see Photo 34).

Lastly, we see the lovely, large and rare reindeer. This is one of the few pieces designed by Florence as a table or mantle decoration for Christmas. Combined with the large sleigh, it serves gloriously as a splendid holiday display (see Photos 28, 29).

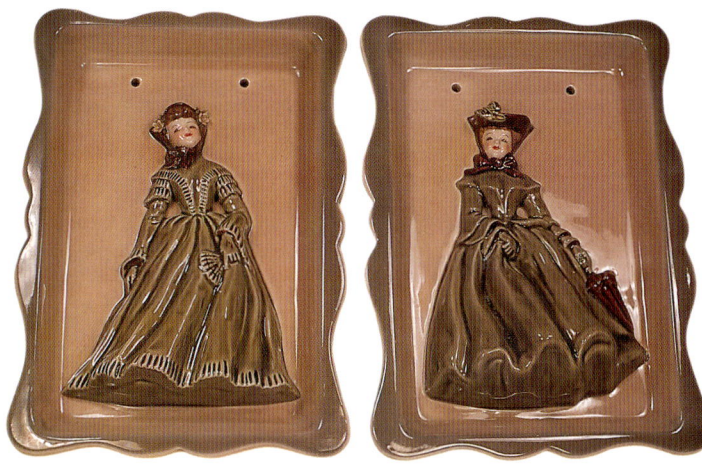

***#26: Figurine Plaques:** Lady, with Fan; Lady, with Parasol*
$130-150 each

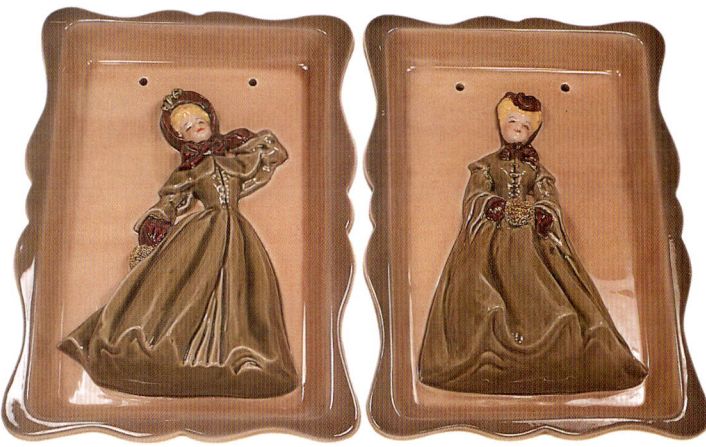

***#27: Figurine Plaques:** Lady, muff on side; Lady, muff in center*
$130-150 each

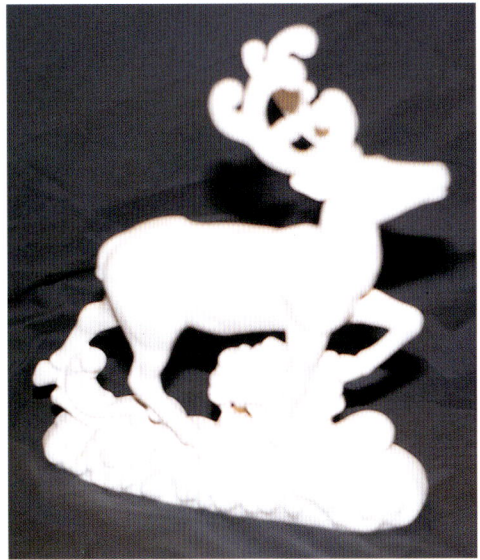

**#28: Reindeer**
$1,300-1,500

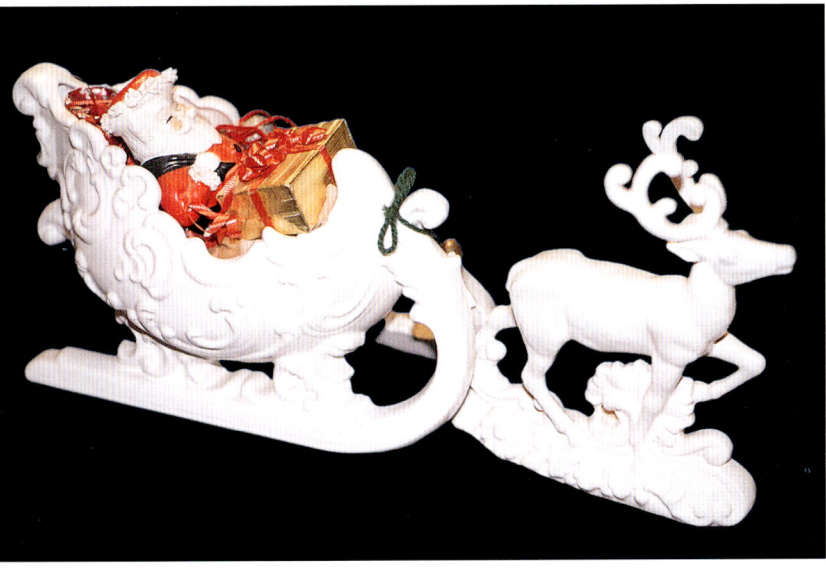

**#29: Reindeer and Sleigh**
$1,500-1,750

## 150  Artware

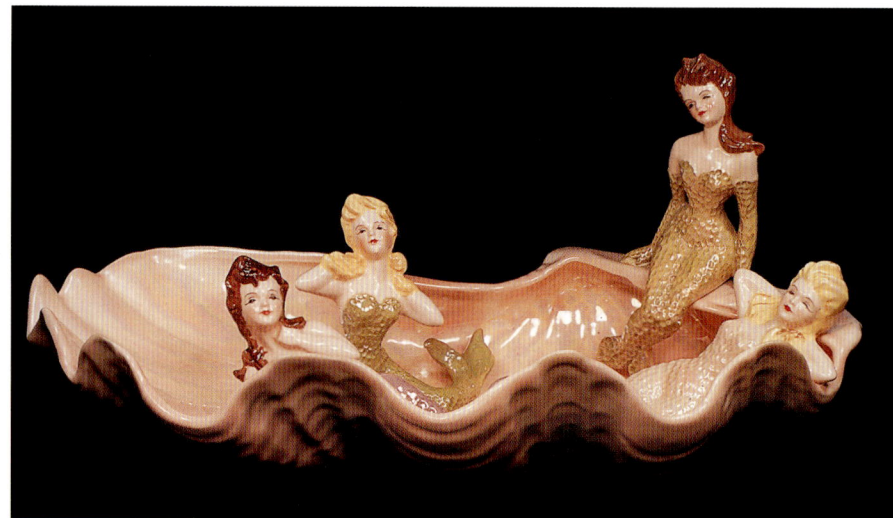

**#30: Shell Bowl for Merrymaids**, 15.5" x 9"
$275-325 bowl only

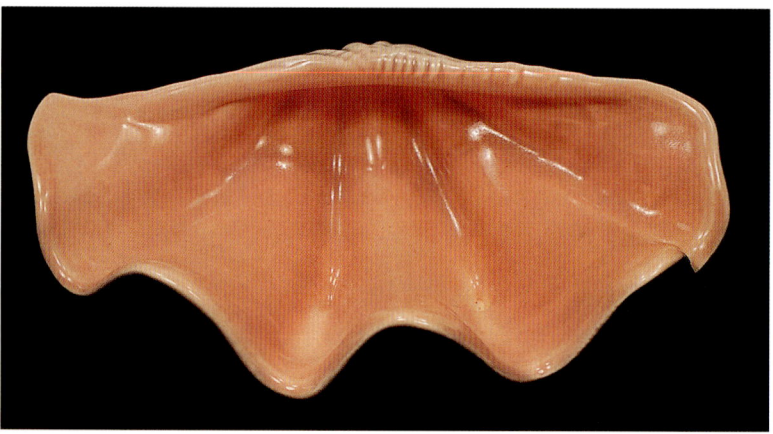

**#31: Shell Bowl for Merrymaids**, 11" x 7"
$200-250

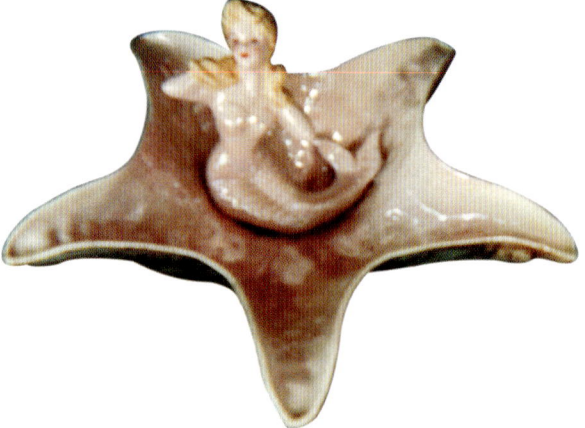

**#31A: Starfish Bowl for Merrymaids**
$300-350 bowl only

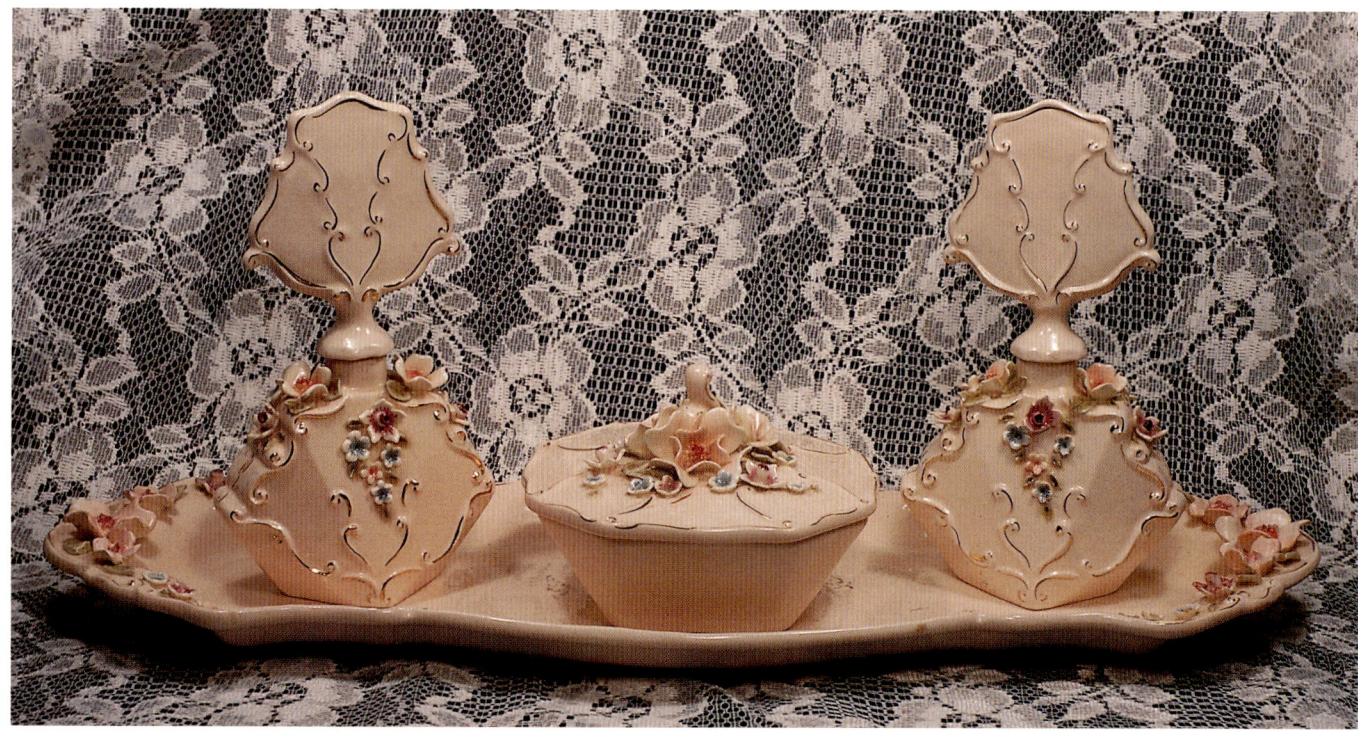

**#32: Vanity Tray with Cologne Bottles and Powder Box**
$650-700

Artware 151

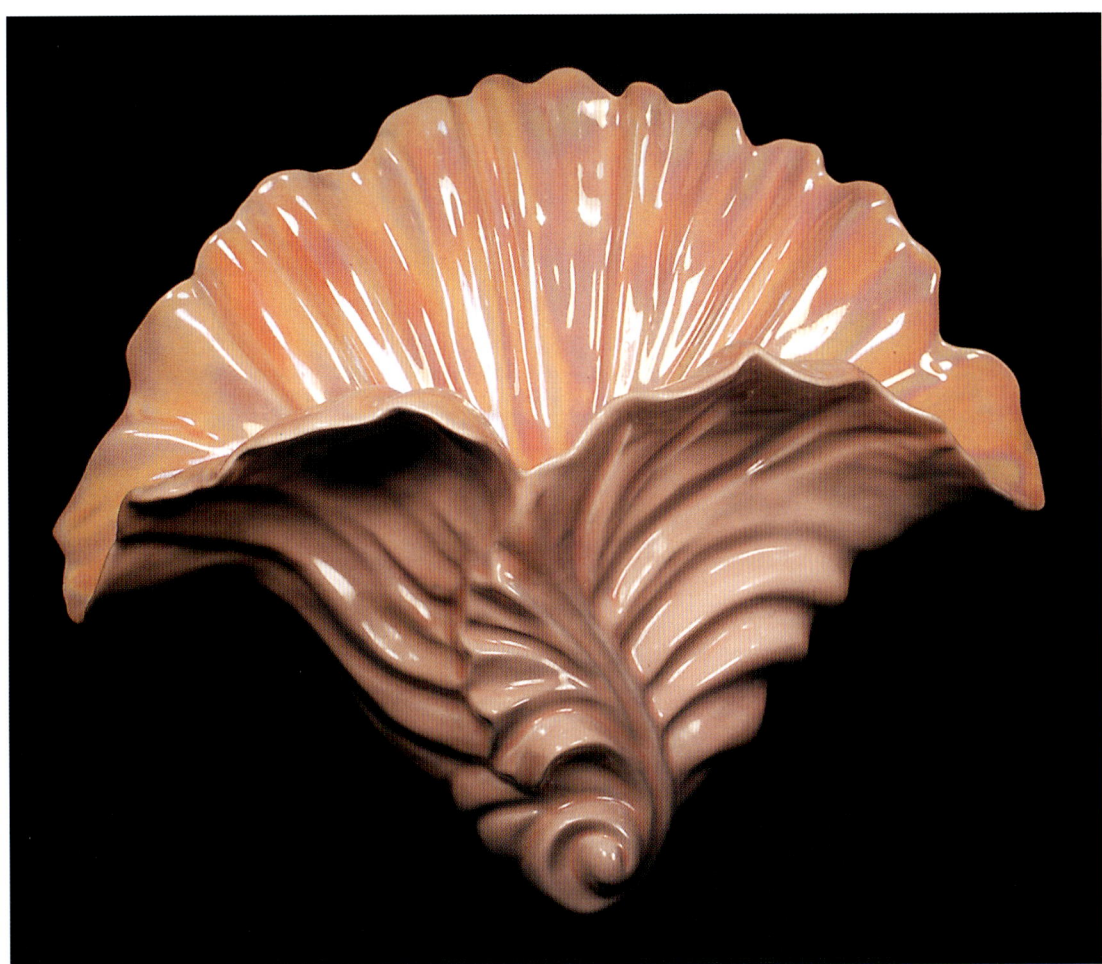

**#33: Wall Pocket**, Lustre Pink, 13" x 13"
$225-250

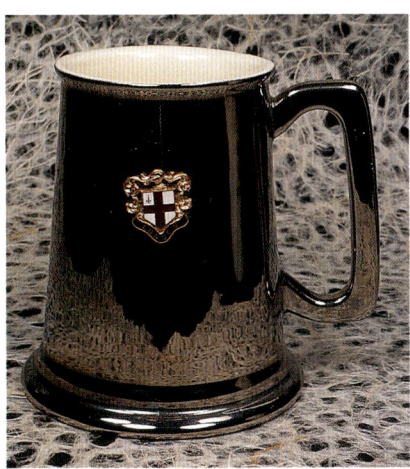

**#34: Crested Mug**, 5"
$140-160

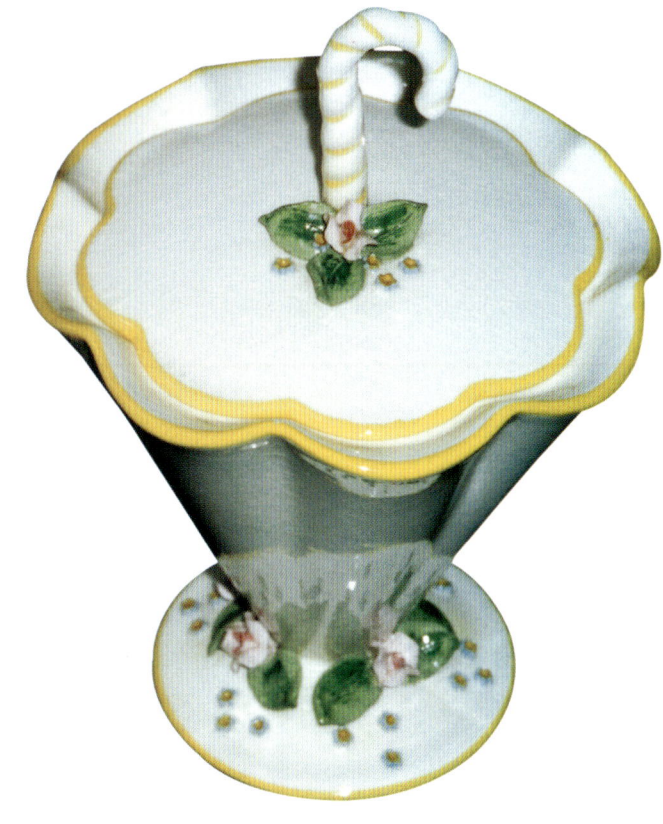

**#34A: Umbrella Vase**, 6"
$200-250

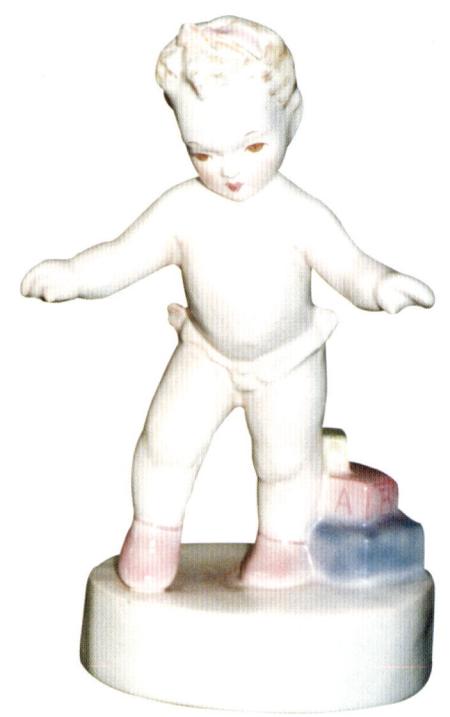

**#34B: Child with ABC blocks**, 10"
$350-400

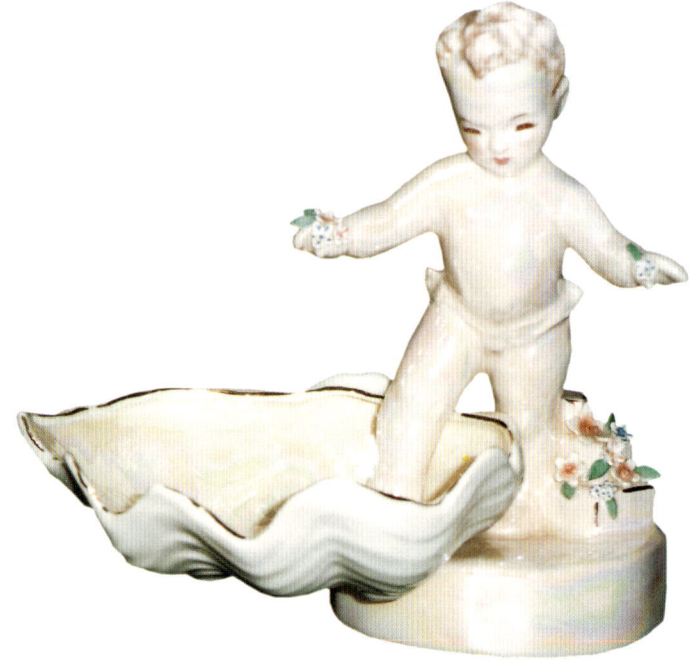

**#34C: Child and Shell Bowl**, 10"
$350-400

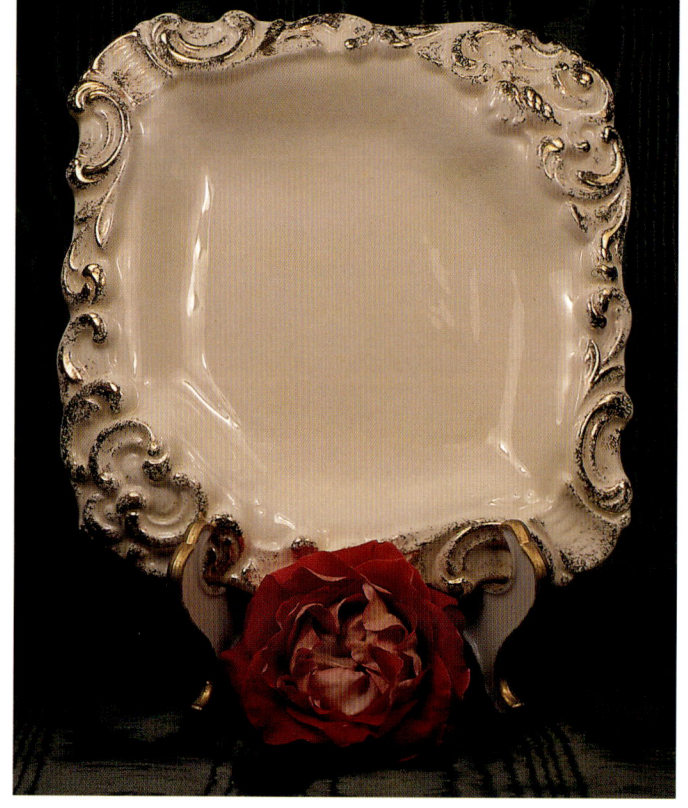

**#35: Floraline Regency Ashtray,** ivory and gold trim, 8.25" x 8.25"
$60-75

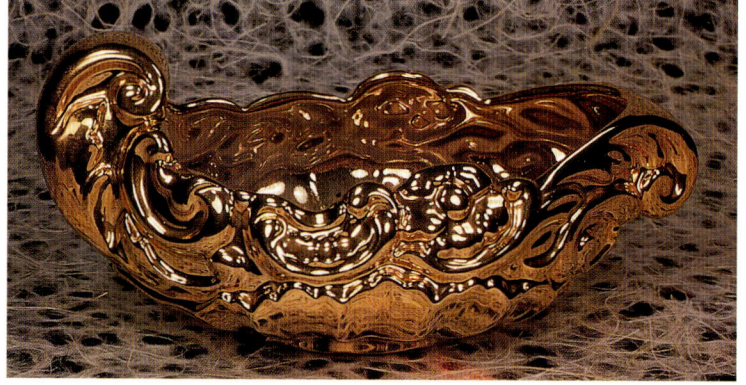

**#36: Voltaire Bowl**, in 22-karat gold , 4.25" x 7.75"
$85-100

Artware   153

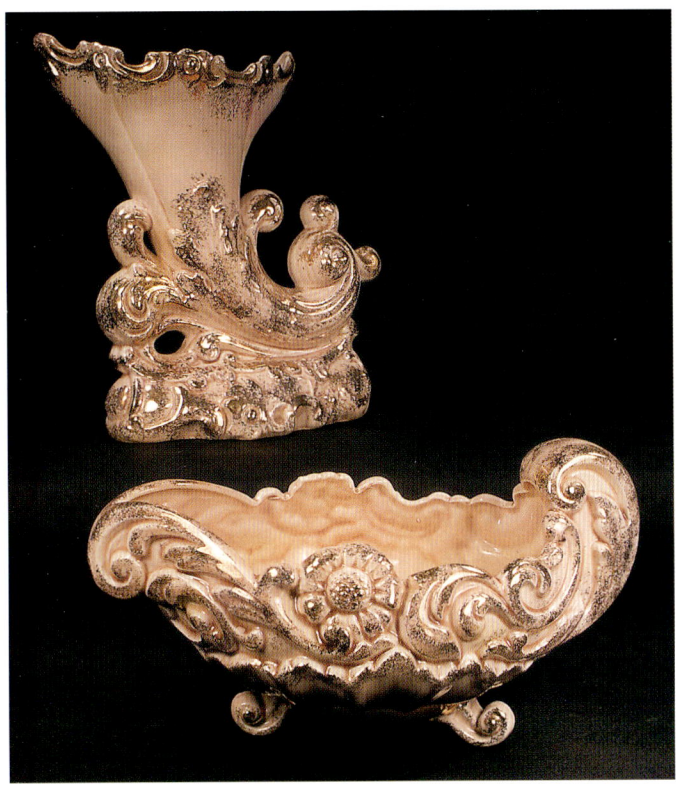

**#37: Floraline Cornucopia Vase**, 9.5", **Voltaire Bowl**, 5.75" x 9.5"
$175-200, $90-100

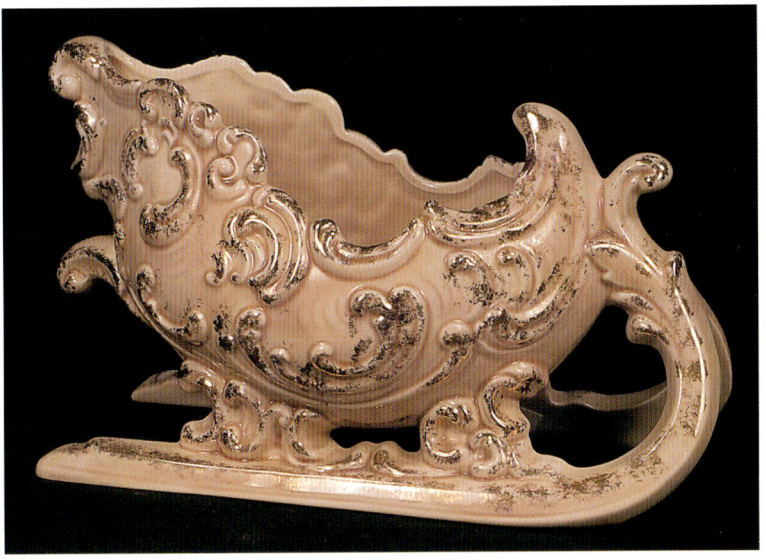

**#39: Floraline Sleigh**, 4.75" x 10.5" x 6.25"
$250-275

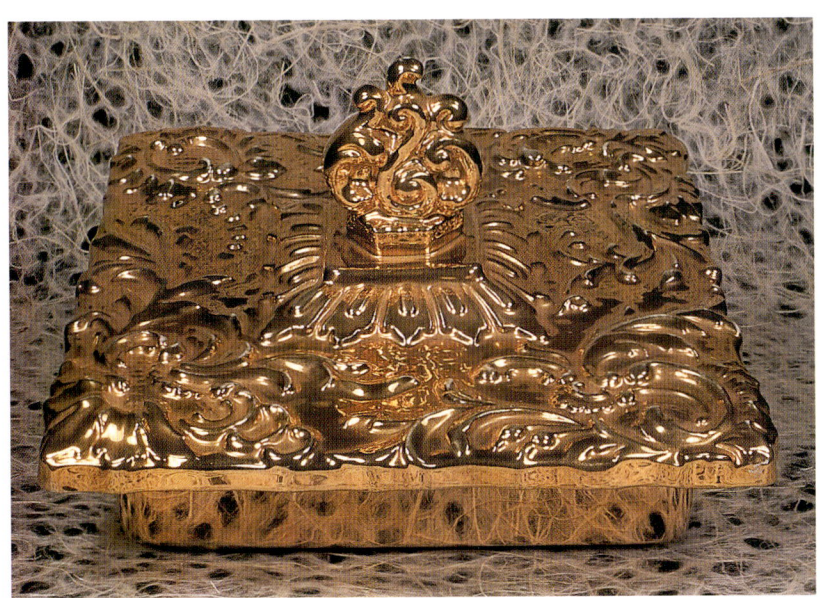

**#38: Regency Box**, in 22-karat gold, 8.25" x 8.25"
$150-175

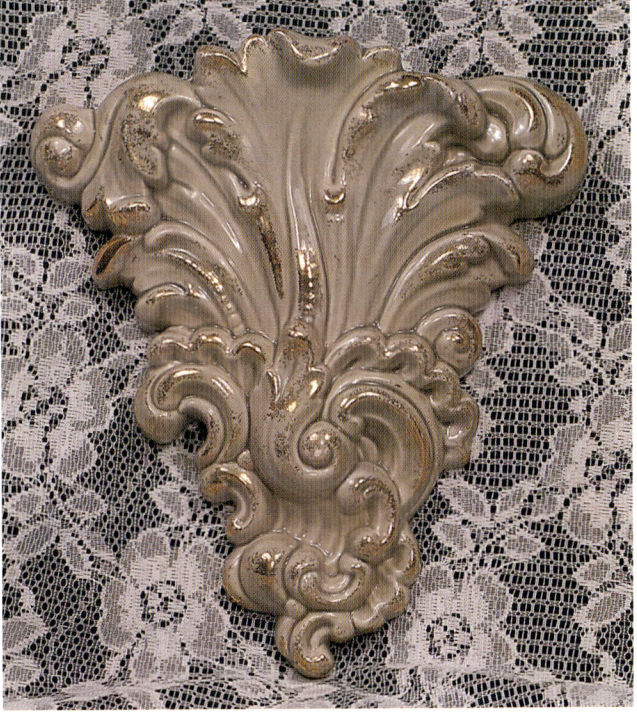

**#40: Floraline Wall Pocket**, in Gray/Green, 8.5" x 9.5"
$110-125

154   Artware

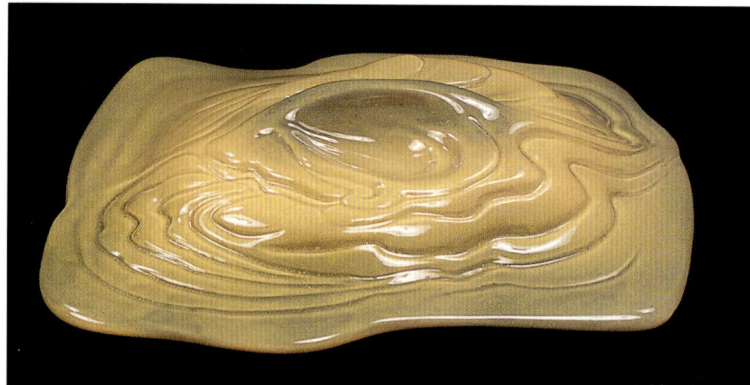

**#41: Driftware Candy Box**, 6" x 8"
$75-90

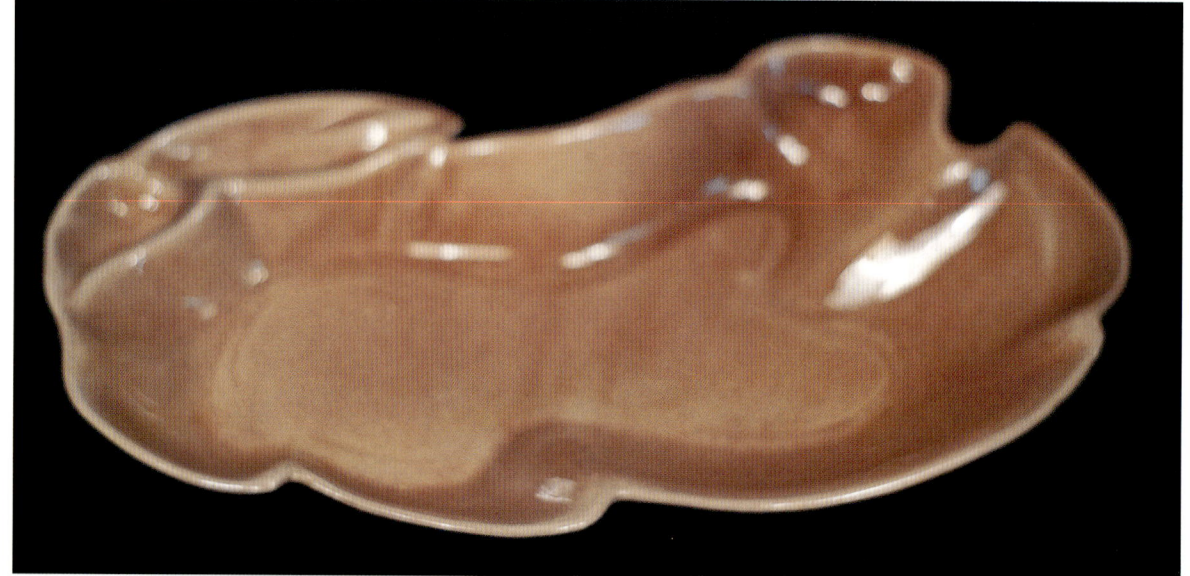

**#42: Driftware Flat Bowl**, 8.5" x 17"
$100-115

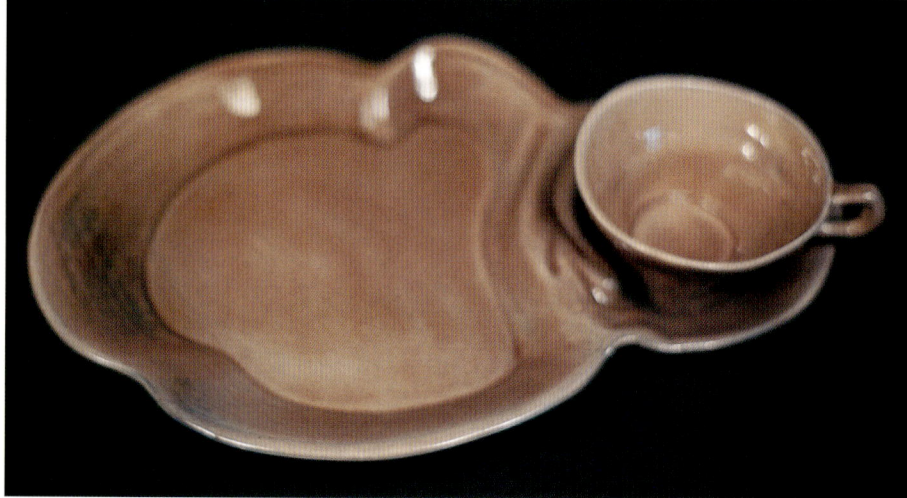

**#43: Driftware Buffet Plate and Cup**, 8.75" x 14"
$100-120

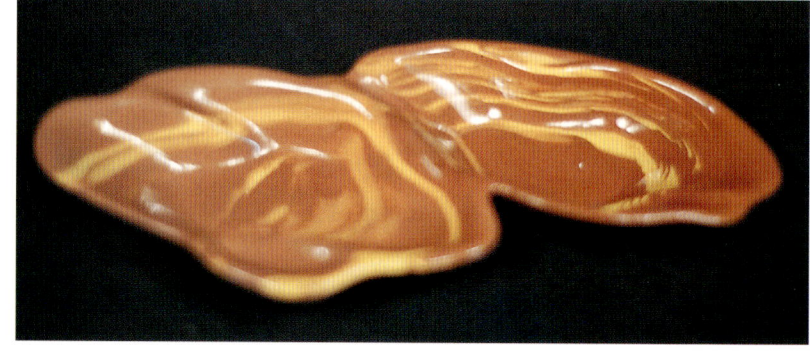

**#44: Driftware Relish Bowl**, 6.5" x 14.5"
$75-90

Artware 155

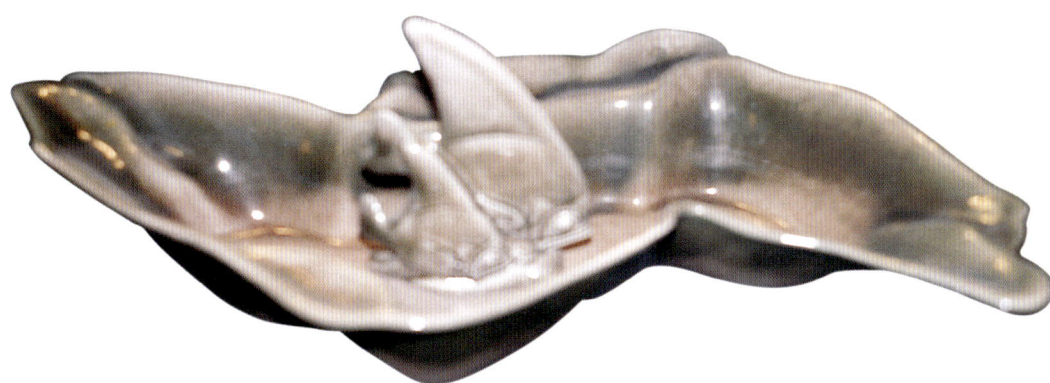

**#45: Driftware Bowl or Planter**, 9" x 21.5"
$85-100

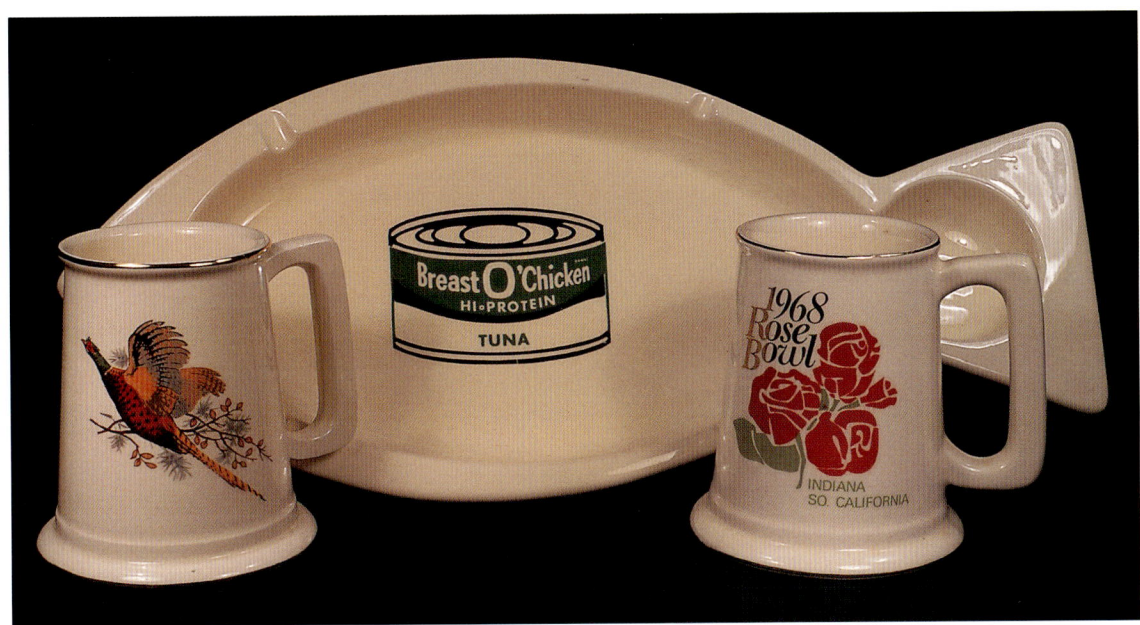

**#46: Scripto Mug, Fish Platter, 1968 Rose Bowl Mug**
$70-90, $80-100, $110-125

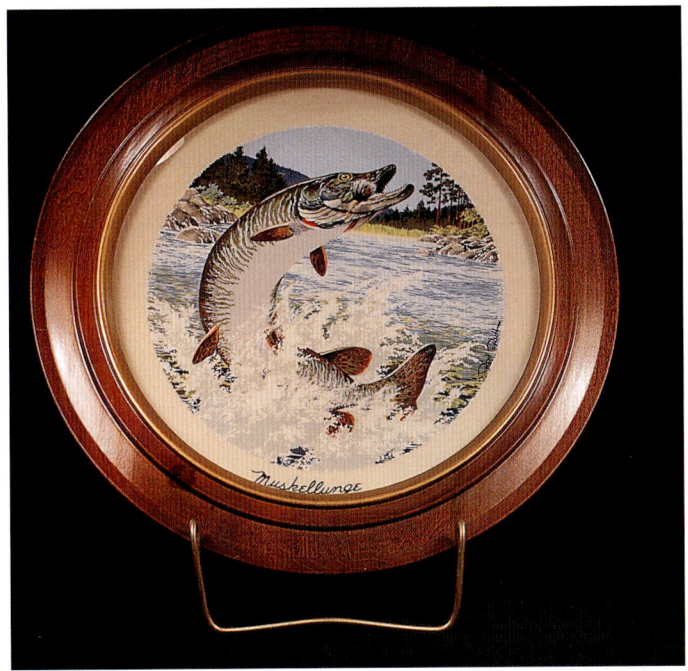

**#47: Scripto Framed Decal Fish Plate**, 13"
$100-120

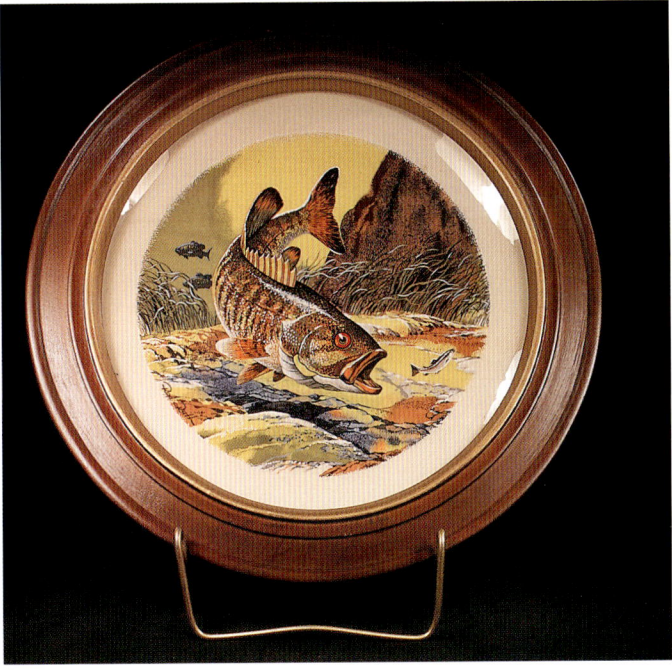

**#48: Scripto Framed Decal Fish Plate**, 13"
$100-120

# Chapter IX
## *Florence Particulars*

*The people in the clay room never got enough credit. They did such artistic work in there. They were all so talented.*
—Pearl Sylvester (San Clemente, California, 2001)

### *Backstamps*

During the twenty-four years that Florence Ceramics Company was in business it used twenty-six different backstamps to identify its products. As times changed, Florence protected its products with patents and copyrights. Many of the backstamps shown below reflect those changes. When Florence sold the company to Scripto, the name Florence Ceramics continued even though Scripto did not acquire the rights to any figurine production. The last two backstamps represent the Scripto era. All backstamps prior to those were used by the Florence Ceramics Company of 1940-1964.

Two of the items shown are applied stickers on figurines; all others are printed on the base of figures and artware. The printed backstamps are fired and cannot be removed. There is only one known incised backstamp, which appears on the picture frames. It is possible that other backstamps could be discovered, but as of this writing these represent all known backstamps.

Chronological order has never been definitely determined. To the best of our knowledge, we are listing the backstamps from the early 1940s to the 1960s.

From flowerholders in the 1940s.

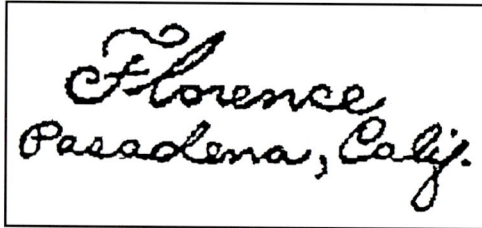

From tall flowerholders in the 1940s.

From various early figures.

From picture frames in the 1940s.

From early backstamp, Jo Ann flowerholder.

From figures with limited space.

From Nick and Nan.

FLORENCE CERAMICS COPYRIGHT

From figures with limited space.

From early garage figures.

156

# Florence Particulars 157

Florence Ceramics
Pat. No. 2540951

From a picture frame.

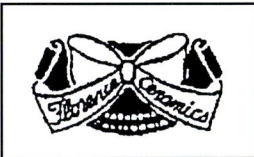

Sticker used on many figures.

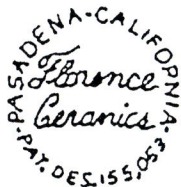

Chinese Girl (Design Patent 155053).

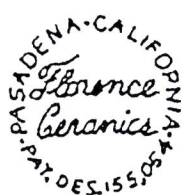

Chinese Boy (Design Patent 155054).

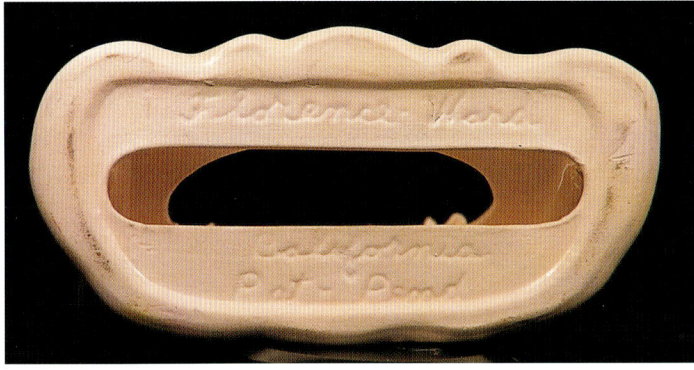

Florence Ward incised picture frame from 1940s.

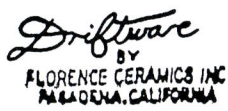

From Driftware line, early 1950s.

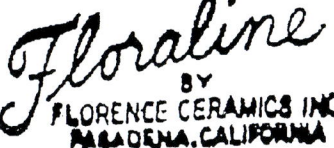

Floraline, from early 1950s.

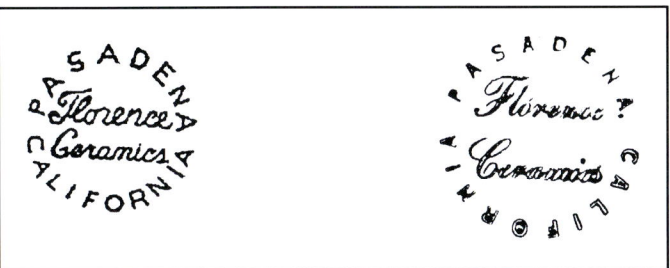

Both from 1940s pieces (note two versions of "California").

From bisque birds and animals by Betty Davenport Ford, 1956.

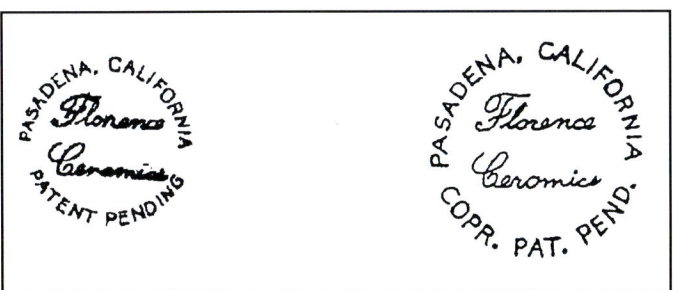

From many figures in the late 1940s to early 1950s, before patents.

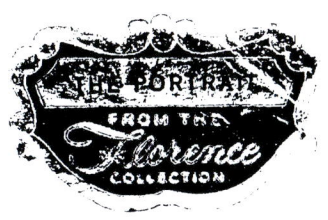

Sticker from fancy figures of the "Florence Collection".

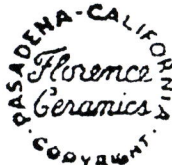

From 1950s figures.

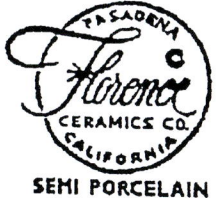

From fancier figures of 1950s to 1964.

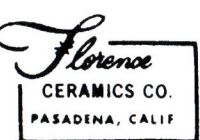

Scripto backstamp in 1964.

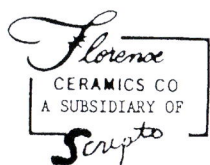

Final Scripto backstamp.

## Artist Initials

Many of the Florence figures bear the initials of the artists who worked in the "gold room." Most were signed in the 22-karat gold used to decorate the beautiful figures. Some signatures (initials) have also been found painted in black. The list below represents those initials that have been identified. More initials exist than those presented, but names to go with the others could not be determined at the present time so they are not included. Two different ways of signing the pieces can be found: one inside the backstamp, the other simply somewhere else on the bottom of the figure. The most commonly signed figurines are those that required gold decoration. Most of those not requiring gold were not signed.

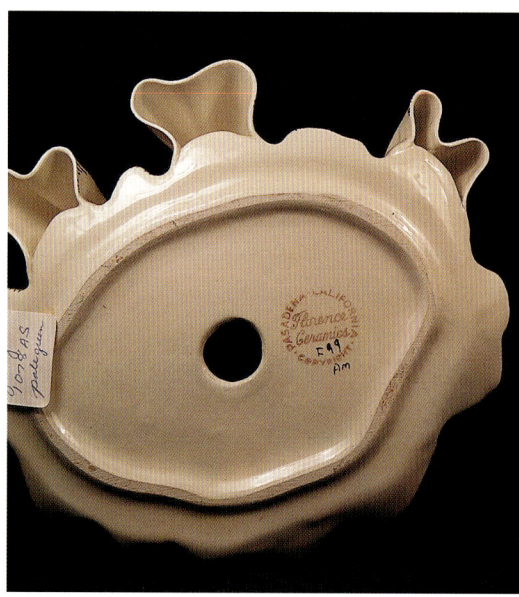

Artist initials, "AM" for Angie Maddox.

### Artist Initials on Figures

| | | | |
|---|---|---|---|
| AF | Anita Frye | LK | Lillian Kent |
| AM | Angie Maddox | LW | LaVerne Wilkison |
| BB | Bering'ere (Bea) Baluda | M | Madeleine Lormier |
| BG | Betty Gjerset | MB | Mildred Bartram |
| BJ | Billie Jeanne Hammer | MH | Marge Hill |
| CE | Cleo Eyre | MW | Margaret Wheeler |
| DB | Dorothy Blanch | MW | Myrtle Woodward |
| DS | Doris Soderquist | MW | Marie Wallace |
| G | Gerry Peterson | NL | Nancy Lee |
| H | Inga Hansen | NP | Norma Parkhurst |
| Hi | Hjardis Jensen | OS | Ollie Swinehart |
| HU | Helen Unfried | P | Pearl Sylvester |
| J | Josephine Silvio | T | Trudi Dahinden |
| LI | Louanne Irwin | V | Violet Kozar |

## Catalogs

Why are the Florence catalogs so hard to find? This is a frequently asked question by collectors. Florence did not sell directly to the public except at the salesroom of the factory located on South San Gabriel Boulevard in Pasadena, California. Florence sold its products through retail jewelry stores, gift shops, department stores, and florists. The catalogs that Florence did produce were directed towards these "wholesale" buyers rather than towards consumers.

The earliest catalogs were produced during the late 1940s. Others were produced throughout the 1950s and the latest ones relating to figurines were issued in 1965. In some cases the catalogs were only updated with a color change on the front cover and perhaps a few minor changes inside. Therefore, many catalogs appear to be the same, even though they were produced at different times. Some of the catalogs are dated and others are not.

Florence Ceramics also produced a single sheet insert to use in a California cooperative advertising booklet along with other pottery, porcelain, and giftware companies. These booklets were for buyers who attended shows in California and around the country. One of the cooperative efforts, entitled *Registered California Inc.*, was quite active in promotion of California companies. To date, eight different catalogs relating to the figurines have been found. Several others have been found for Driftware, Floraline and the contemporary bird and animal figures by Betty Davenport Ford, which were exclusive for Florence.

Interviews with Clifford Ward Jr., former president of the company, and with several other former employees confirmed that few catalogs were printed and distributed during the company's years of existence.

Florence did, however, market indirectly to the public with advertisements in a variety of specialty publications, such as *Home and Garden, Giftwares, The Gift and Art Buyer, Giftwares and Homewares, Giftwares and Home Fashions, Tradewinds, 225 Fifth Avenue Highlights*, and *House Beautiful*. In all cases, these advertisements listed a retail company one could contact. The catalogs were printed in color or black and white. The color catalogs were printed horizontally and the black and white ones vertically. The color catalogs were printed on heavy paper and some contained black and white glossy finished pages.

In most of the catalogs the first page or two feature the Florence Ceramics Company with a write-up about Florence Ward's attention to detail. The fancy large figures usually appear near the front of the catalog followed by more economically priced figures pictured in groups. The company would rotate various pages from one catalog to another depending on their marketing approach at a particular time.

**Florence Particulars** 159

These catalogs, which are difficult to find, are highly prized by collectors. The color catalogs give some insight into the variety of colors used by Florence. In the early days of collecting Florence, these catalogs were our only source of identification and information.

In general, a color catalog at retail value will sell for between $125 and $150, and a black and white one for $100 to $125. If a catalog contains an original order form with pricing, it would be worth 20-25% more.

Some selected examples of Florence catalogs and single sheet advertisements are shown below.

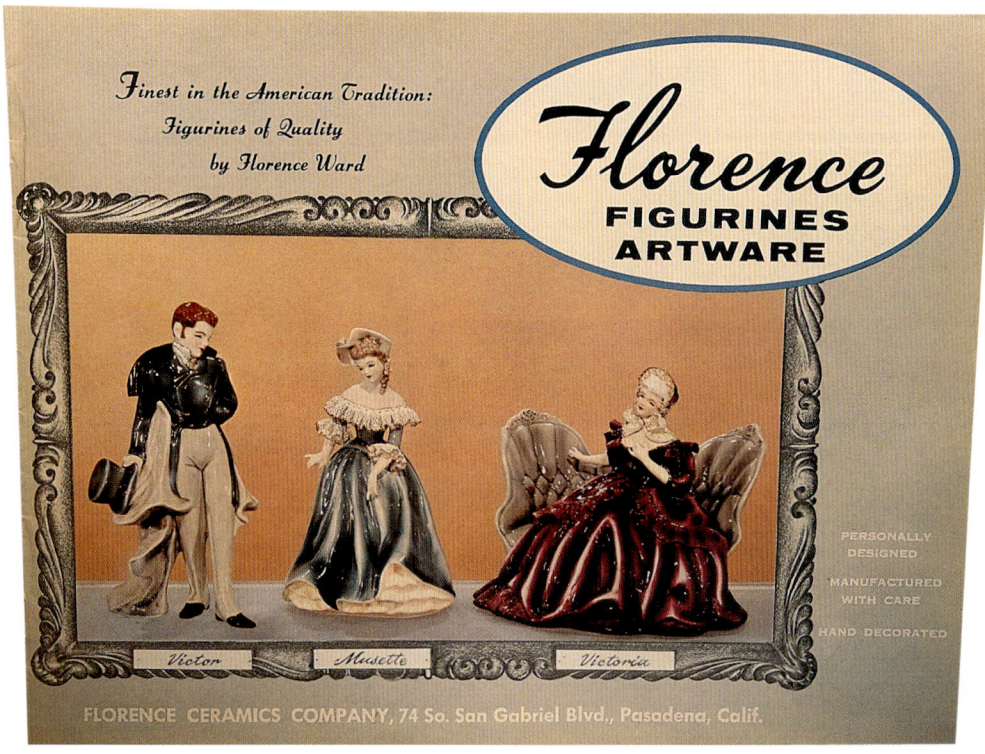

Front page of a Florence catalog from 1957 with Victor, Musette, and Victoria.

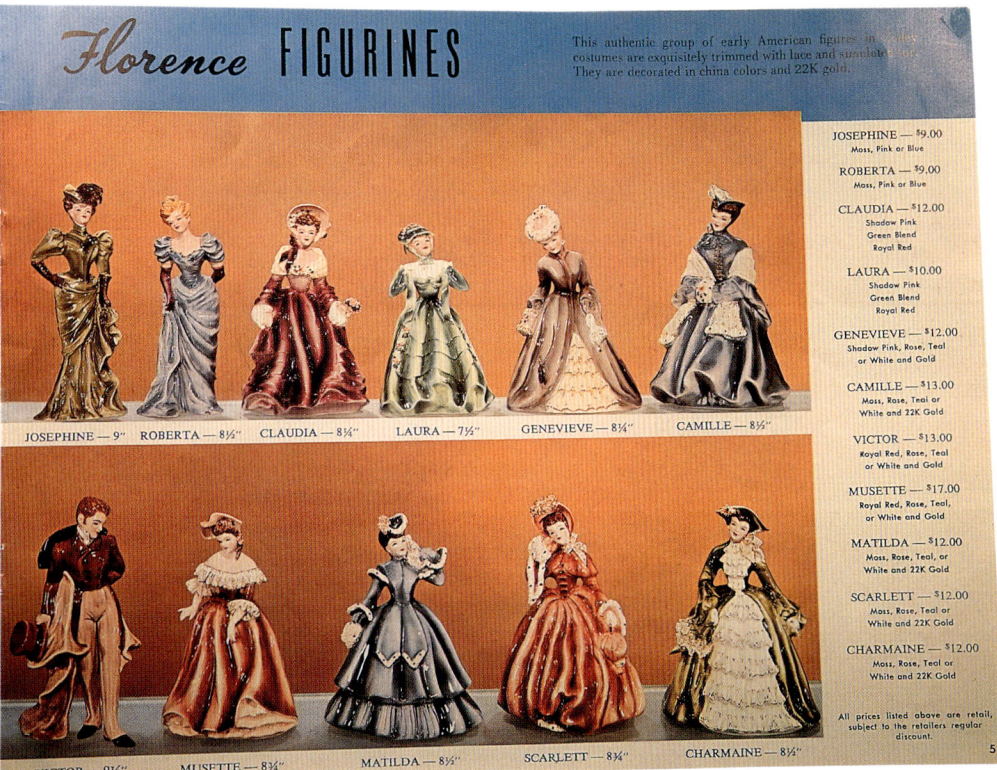

Page from Fall 1957 catalog featuring Godey costumes on ladies.

# 160 Florence Particulars

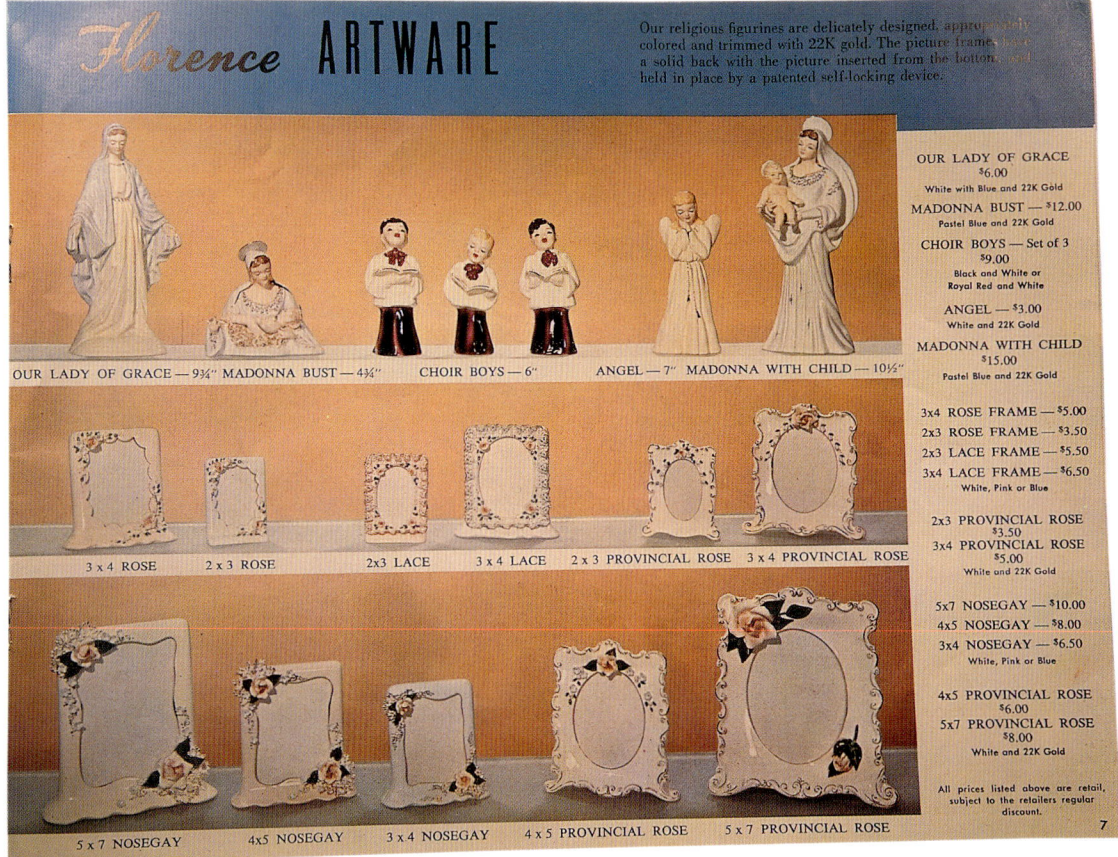

Page from July 1954 catalog with religious figures and picture frames.

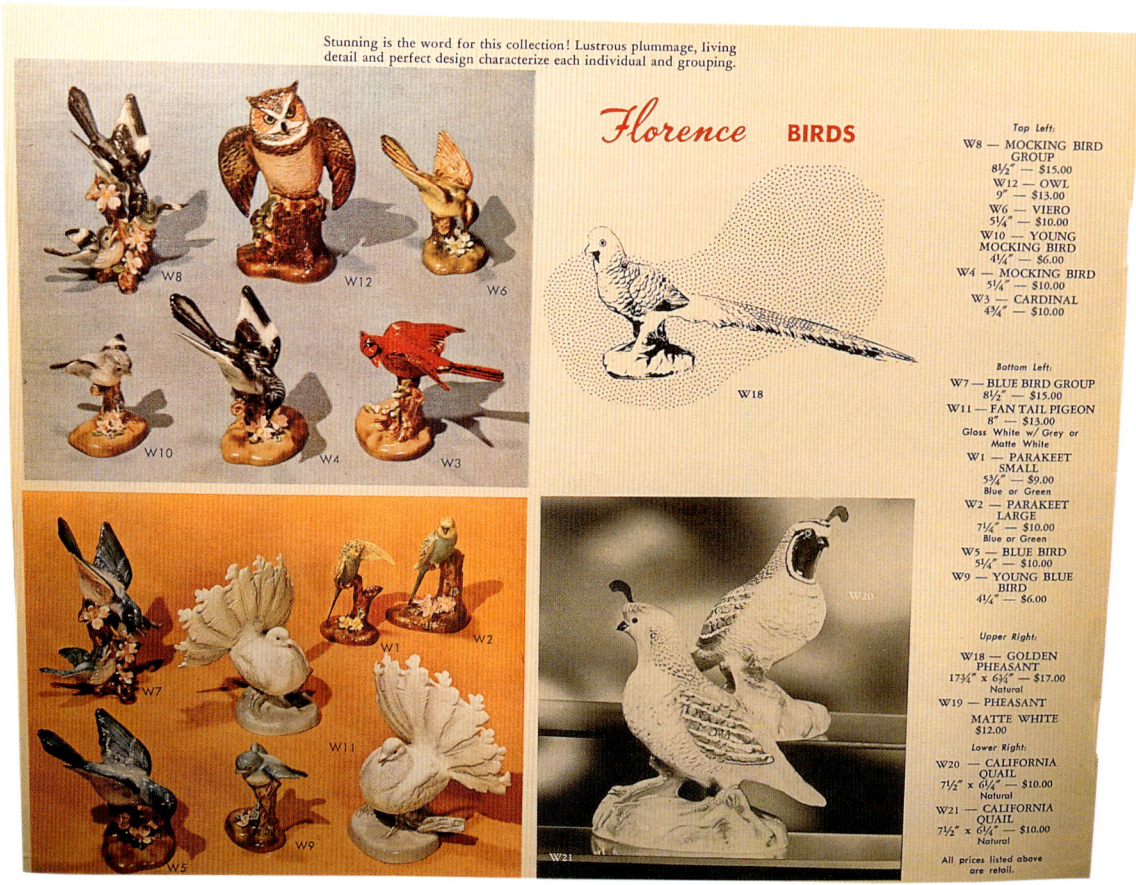

Page from Fall 1957 catalog showing the line of Florence birds.

**Florence Particulars** 161

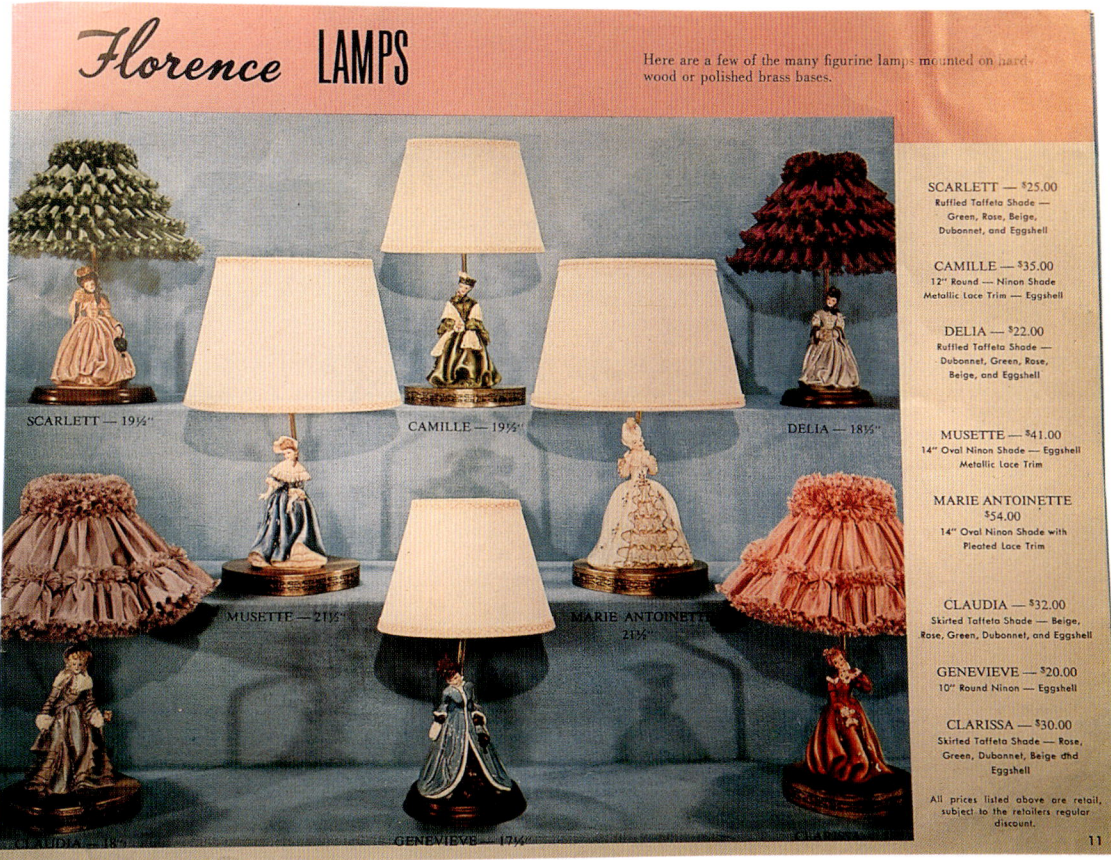

Page from July 1954 catalog showing lamps on either hardwood or polished brass bases.

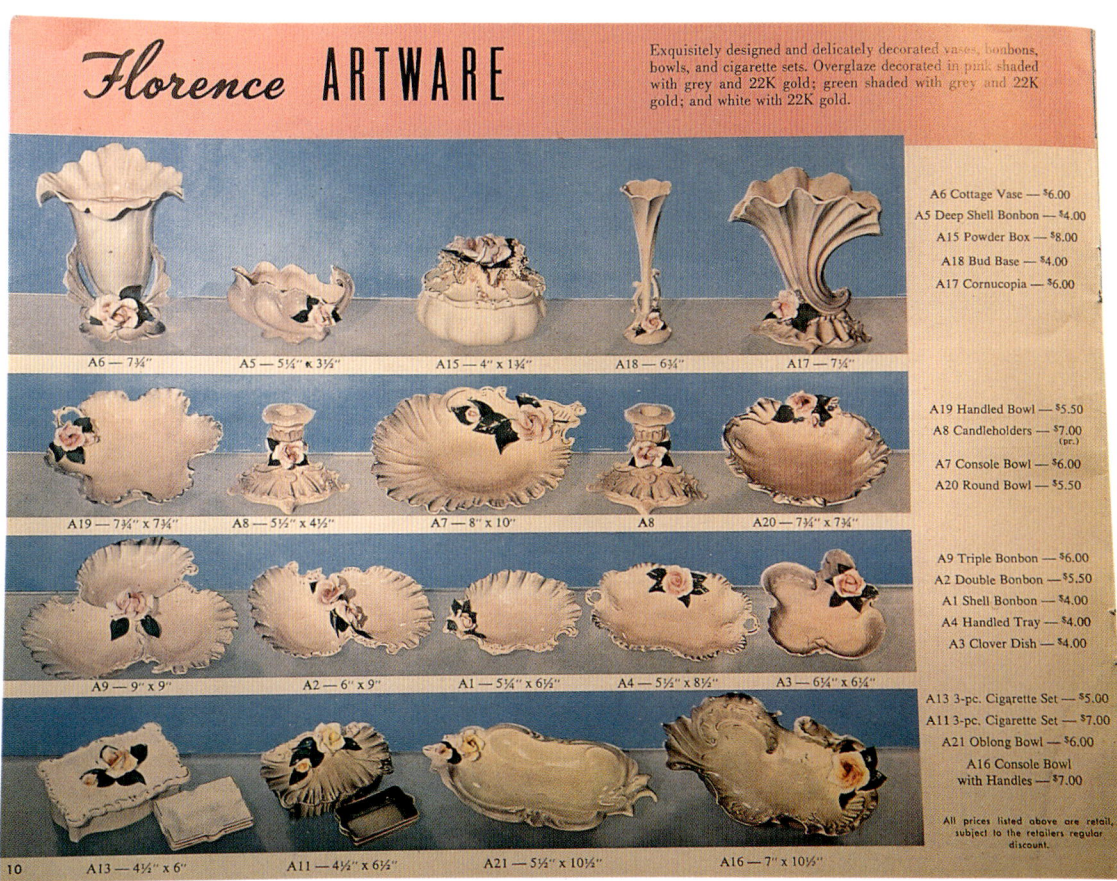

Page from July 1954 catalog featuring Florence artware items.

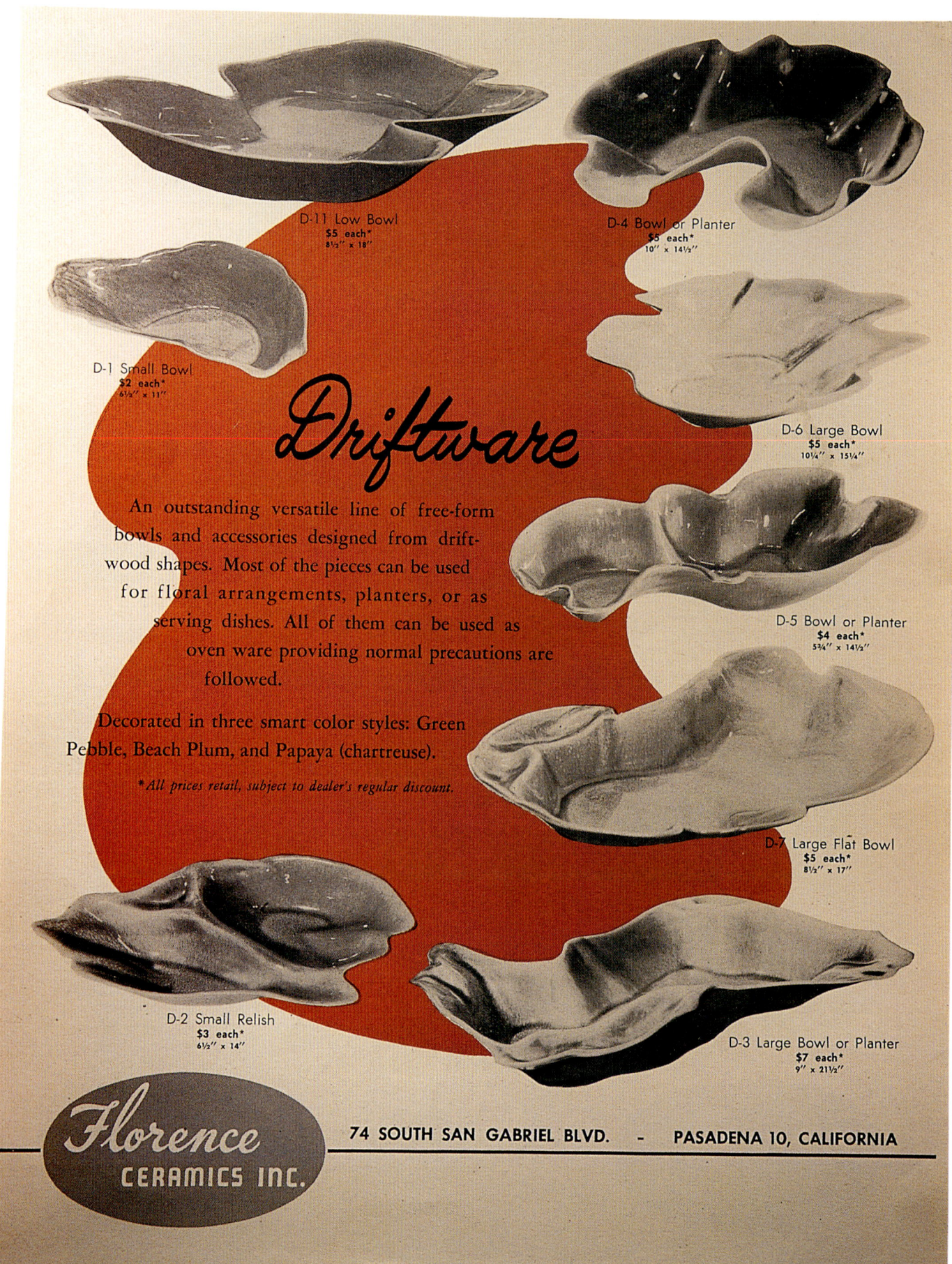

Page from 1951 catalog introducing the line of "Driftware" by Florence Ceramics.

# Florence Particulars 163

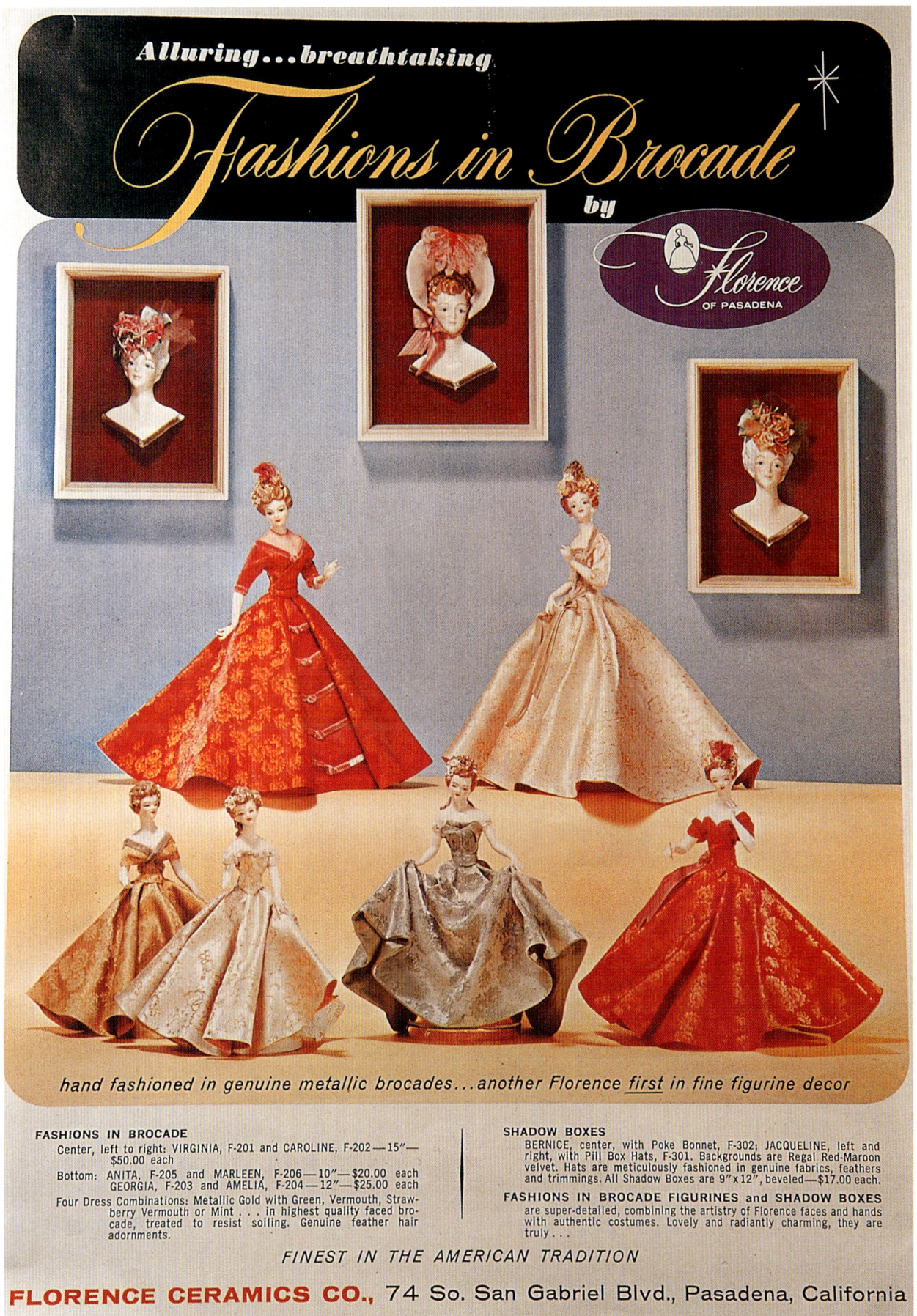

Single sheet brochure featuring brocades and shadow boxes from the mid 1950s, used to advertise at showrooms and gift shows.

**164** Florence Particulars

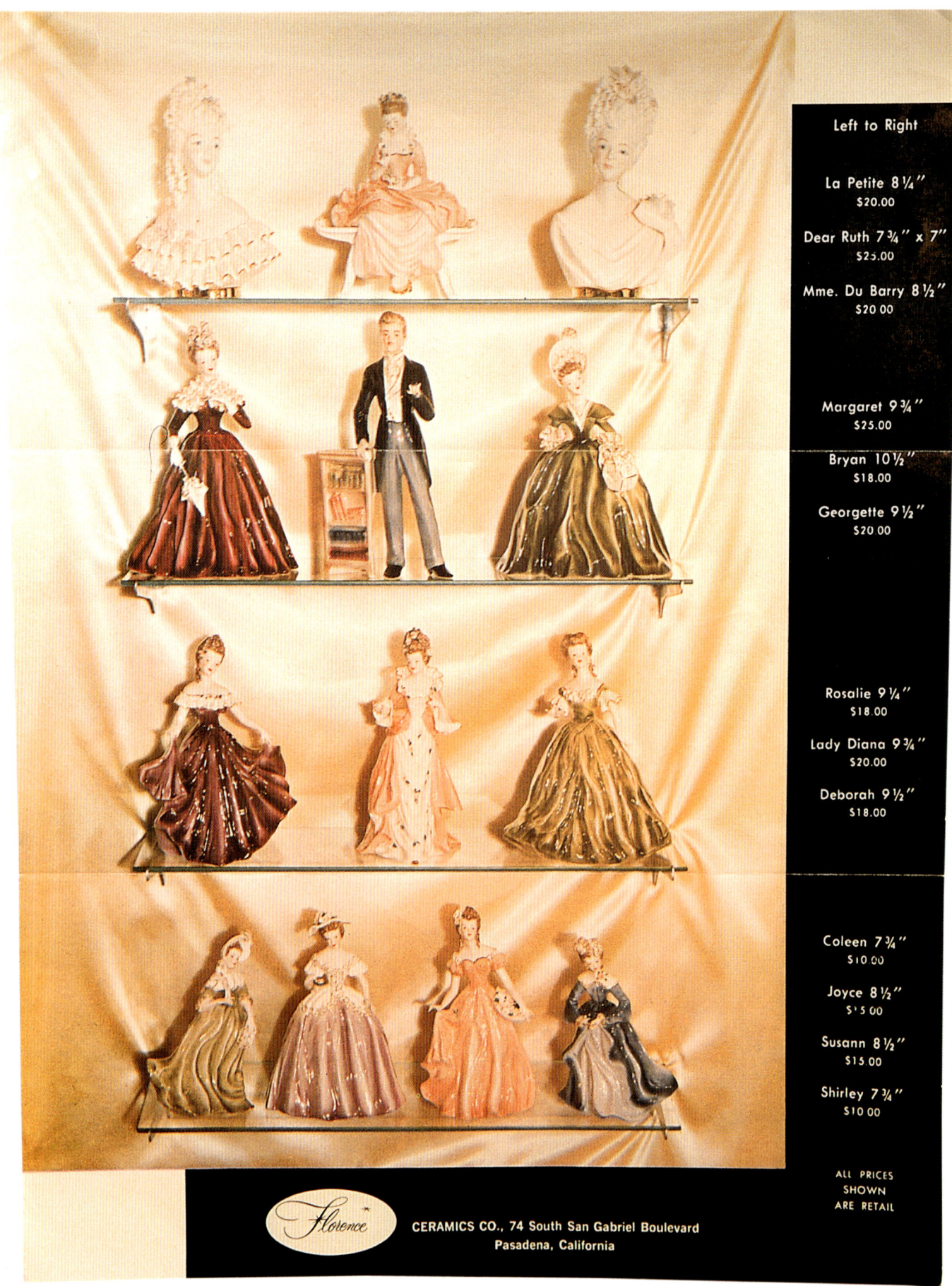

Single sheet brochure featuring Florence's better figures in 1962.

# Florence Particulars 165

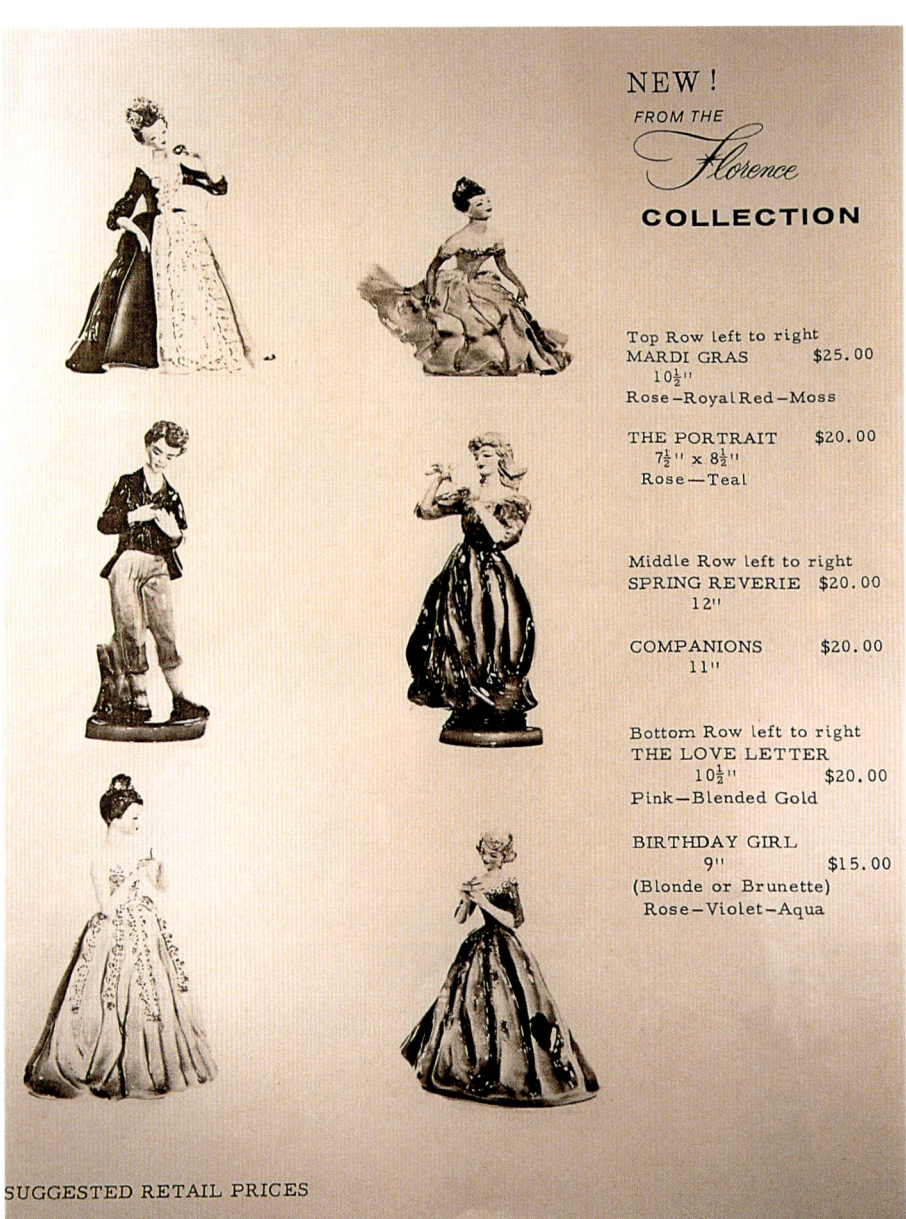

Brochure from the early 1960s showing "The Florence Collection" of top of the line figures.

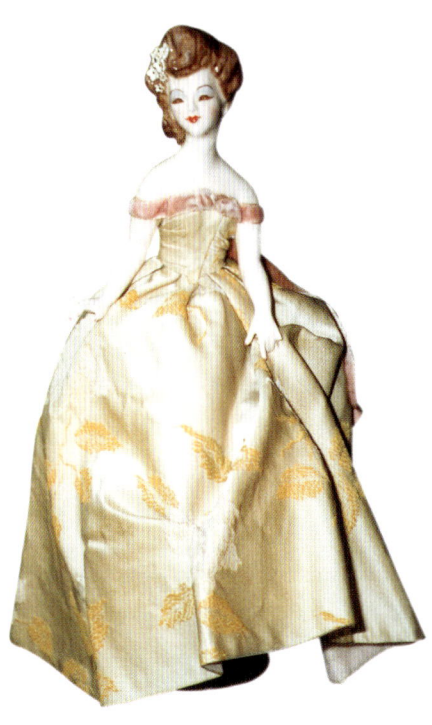
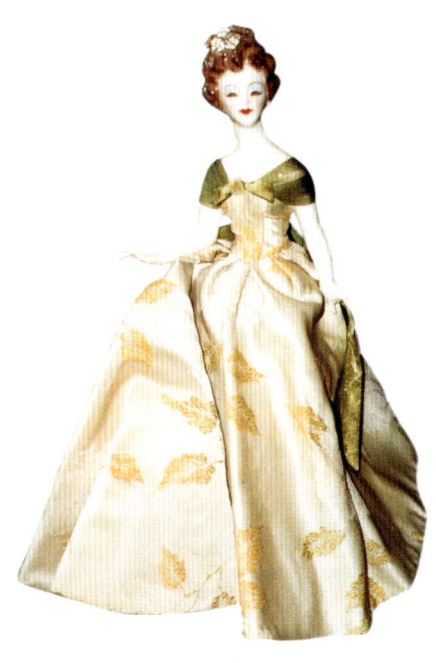

**Marleen Brocade** (left) and **Anita Brocade** (right), believed to be displays for dealers. May have been mounted in a frame or shadow box since the back of the porcelain is flat. They stand 12" high each.

## Colors Used by Florence Ceramics

Florence Ceramics Company used over forty different colors on their products.

Ideally, we would like to have presented a color chart and originally intended to do so. However, we found color to be defined by artistic interpretation. Shading, subtle nuances, and the artistic eye create endless variations of the same color.

Colors were applied to pieces in two different ways. Many of the plainer figures were dipped into a colored glaze and then fired. On glaze-dipped figures the color is universal over the entire piece. Most of the fancier figures were first dipped into a white underglaze, fired, and then china spray painted in the intended color. For that reason, the same color (on the white underglazed figures) can vary greatly in shade from one figure to another. It also explains why many of the fancier figures appear to have white highlights showing at the folds of a dress.

### Colors Used on Figurines

In the following table, the color listed on the left is most commonly used with the figurine(s) listed on the right. Of course, most of the colors could have been used on any figurine.

| Color | Figurine(s) |
|---|---|
| Aqua | Birthday Girl, Sherri, Josephine, Barbara |
| Aquamarine | Amber, Cynthia, Catherine, Sherri, Christening |
| Beige | Scarlett, Melanie, Delia |
| Black and White | Choir Boys |
| Blended Blue | Cleopatra |
| Blended Gold | Love Letter |
| Blue | Ann, Elaine, Sue, Ethel |
| Chartreuse | Chinese Boy & Girl, Lantern Boy & Blossom Girl |
| Emerald | Nancy, Victor, Yvonne, Jennifer |
| Gray | Priscilla and John Alden, Edward, Sarah |
| Gray-Green | Fern and Violet Head Vases |
| Green | Matilda, Sue Ellen, Deborah |
| Ivory | Most flowerholders, Don, Ruth, Eve, Stephen, children |
| Lustre Pink | Merrymaid Bowl and some Merrymaids |
| Lustre Blue | Merrymaids |
| Lustre Green | Merrymaids |
| Moss | Lillian, Irene, Douglas |
| Pastel Blue | Madonnas |
| Peacock | Jennifer, Richard, Catherine, Masquerade, Laura |
| Pink | Most figures were made in pink |
| Purple | Elizabeth |
| Rose | Victor, Gary, Yvonne, Claudia |
| Royal Purple | Elizabeth, Madame Pompadour, Louis XV |
| Royal Red | The most popular color used on many figures |
| Royal Red and Bronze | Mark Anthony |
| Royal Red and White | Choir Boys |
| Sage Green | Clarissa, Camille, and plaques |
| Satin White | Boy and Girl Busts |
| Teal | Genevieve, Charmaine, Grace |
| Turquoise | Gary, Grace, Rose Marie, Tess, Linda Lou, Master David |
| Velvet Green | Elizabeth, Madame Pompadour, Louis XV |
| Violet | Carol, Cindy, and many others |
| White | Many of the figures were white with gold trim |
| Yellow | Catherine, Tess, Sue Ellen, Susann, Claudia |

### Colors Used on Brocades

Metallic Gold
Mint
Strawberry Vermouth
Vermouth

### Colors Used on Birds and Animals

| Color | Item |
|---|---|
| Gloss White | Fantail Pigeon |
| Matte White | Pheasants |
| Natural | Quails |
| Woodland Brown | Contemporary Animals by Betty Davenport Ford |
| Dusk Gray | Contemporary Animals by Betty Davenport Ford |
| Tawny Rose | Contemporary Animals by Betty Davenport Ford |

### Colors Used on Artware

| Color | Artware Item |
|---|---|
| Brown | Cigarette Boxes and Ashtrays |
| Green and Yellow | Many of the artware pieces |
| Maple | Picture Frames |
| Matte White | Compotes, Sleighs, Vanity Tray, Bowls |
| Pink and Gray | Many of the artware pieces |
| Rose | Many of the artware pieces |

### Colors Used on Floraline, Driftware, Scandia, and Sierra

| Color | Item |
|---|---|
| Gray-Green | Floraline |
| Ivory White | Floraline |
| Maple Pink | Floraline |
| Dark Pebble | Driftware |
| Fiji Coral | Driftware |
| Surf Green | Driftware |
| Desert | Scandia Gourmet Pottery |
| Persimmon | Scandia Gourmet Pottery |
| Satin White | Scandia Gourmet Pottery |
| Pastel Pink | Sierra Gourmet Pottery |
| Satin White | Sierra Gourmet Pottery |

## "Cut From the Same Mold"

The following figurines are created by using the same mold. Different hands, arms, and heads are then applied. Where needed, different accessories are applied, and finally a change of color. Florence had created a whole new personality!

| Name of Figure | Name of Figure | Name of Figure |
|---|---|---|
| Adeline | Madeline | |
| Ann | Lea (FH) | |
| Annette | Juliet | Musette |
| Barbara | Cecile | Masquerade |
| Barbara Youth | Bee | |
| Blossom Girl | Blossom Girl (FH) | |
| Lantern Boy | Lantern Boy (FH) | |
| Bride | Darleen | Karen |
| Chinese Boy | Chinese Boy (FH) | |
| Chinese Girl | Chinese Girl (FH) | |
| Christening | Deborah | Giselle |
| Cinderella | Fair Lady | |
| Claudia | Margo | |
| Dora Lee | Rose Marie Adult | |
| Eugenia | Georgette | |
| Eve | Francis | Ruth |
| Fall | Wendy (FH) | |
| Ginger | Jeanie | Judy |
| Karlo | Taka | |
| Kathy | Kay (FH) | |
| Lee Ann | Virginia | |
| Lavon | Sherry | |
| Love Letter | Mardi Gras | Maybelle |
| Lyn (FH) | Sue | |
| Marianne | Marilyn | Martha |
| Marie Antoinette | Prima Donna | |
| Marsie | Nita | |
| Nell Gwynn | Princess | |
| Sarah Bernhardt | Virginia Brocade | Lillian Russell |
| Spring | Summer | |

## Florence Inventory Code System

The following charts indicate the inventory code letters and numbers for all product lines manufactured by Florence Ceramics.

Identifying the company's coding system is a very complex procedure, and not easily explained. Without benefit of computers, their records were kept by hand, and may not have been entirely perfect. We found some discrepancies and have listed them here. For instance, as older figurines were discontinued, those same inventory codes were used again for new production pieces, resulting in one inventory number belonging to two or more different figurines. Further, in the case of any figurine that was designed as both "plain" and "fancy," there are two inventory numbers – one for the "plain" and one for the "fancy." All figurines are designated with the letter "F" followed by a number, signifying figure number one, figure number two, and so on. However, there is a slight variation on that, too! A few non-figural items – picture frame, bell, and cigarette box – are also given the figurine code "F". Compounding the problem, not every figurine has an "F" number. Early on, no code numbers were used. After 1949, when Florence moved the company to the new plant, care was taken to insure that all figurines were assigned an inventory "F" code.

All other production pieces are categorized with their own code letters and numbers as listed in the remaining charts. We were able to determine the codes by examining original catalogs and company order forms. Original wholesale prices are also listed.

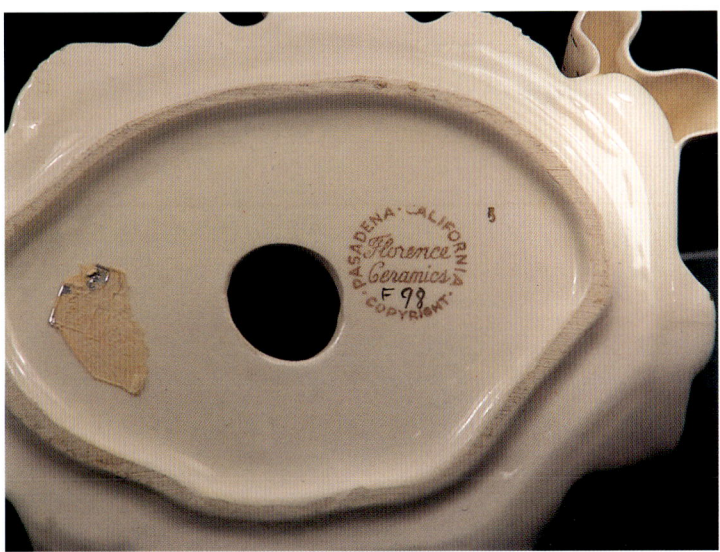

Figure number (F98) shown inside backstamp on some figures. This one is for Jeanie.

# Florence Particulars

| F-Code | Item | Size | Wholesale Price |
|---|---|---|---|
| 1 | Marie Antoinette | 10" | 14.00 |
| 2 | Eve | 8.5" | 9.00 |
| 2 | Catherine | 7.75" x 6.75" | 12.50 |
| 3 | Matilda | 8.25" | 8.00 |
| 4 | Ruth | 8.5" | 9.00 |
| 4 | Edward | 7" | 15.00 |
| 4 | Lillian Russell | 13.25" | 25.00 |
| 5 | Abigail | 8.25" | 8.00 |
| 5 | Georgette | 9.5" | 12.50 |
| 6 | Amelia | 8.25" | 8.00 |
| 6 | Dora Lee | 9.5" | 10.00 |
| 7 | Melanie | 7.5" | 6.00 |
| 7 | Rose Marie Adult | 9.5" | 10.00 |
| 8 | Ballet Powder Box | 6" x 6" | 10.00 |
| 8 | Madame Pompadour | 12" | 35.00 |
| 9 | Madonna and Child | 10" | 7.50 |
| 9 | Sherri | 8.5" | 5.00 |
| 10 | Madonna and Child Bust | 5.5" x 4.5" | 7.50 |
| 11 | Kay (FH) | 7" | 1.50 |
| 11 | Annabel | 8" | 7.50 |
| 12 | Kathy | 7" | 5.00 |
| 12 | Story Hour | 8" x 6.75" | 15.00 |
| 13 | Bee (FH) | 7" | 1.50 |
| 14 | Barbara Youth | 7" | 5.00 |
| 14 | Martin | 10.5" | 7.50 |
| 15 | Rose Picture Frame | 2" x 3" | 1.33 |
| 16 | Lace Picture Frame | 2" x 3" | 2.70 |
| 17 | Rose Picture Frame | 3" x 4" | 2.33 |
| 18 | Lace Picture Frame | 3" x 4" | 3.25 |
| 19 | Shen | 7.5" | 3.75 |
| 19 | Musette | 8.75" | 8.75 |
| 20 | Yulan | 7.5" | 3.75 |
| 20 | Victor | 9.25" | 6.25 |
| 21 | Nosegay Picture Frame | 4" x 5" | 4.00 |
| 22 | Nosegay Picture Frame | 4" x 6" | 4.50 |
| 23 | Nosegay Picture Frame | 5" x 7" | 5.00 |
| 24 | Master David | 8" | 4.00 |
| 24 | Marcella | 7" | 6.00 |
| 25 | David | 7.5" | 5.00 |
| 26 | Betsy | 7.5" | 10.00 |
| 27 | Acorn Picture Frame | 5" x 7" | 2.50 |
| 28 | Elizabeth | 8.25" x 7" | 25.00 |
| 29 | Choir Boys | 5.5" | 4.50 set |
| 30 | Angel Hands Clasped | 7" | 1.50 |
| 31 | Madonna | 10" | 3.00 |
| 32 | Louis XVI | 10" | 14.00 |
| 33 | Delia | 7.5" | 6.00 |
| 34 | Rita (FH) | 9.5" | 2.50 |
| 34 | Victoria | 8.25" x 7" | 25.00 |
| 35 | Yvonne (FH) | 9.5" | 2.50 |
| 35 | Ava (FH) | 10.5" | 8.00 |
| 36 | Sarah | 7.5" | 6.00 |
| 36 | Leading Man | 10.25" | 17.50 |
| 37 | Patsy (FH) | 6" | 1.50 |
| 37 | Jeanette | 7.75" | 5.00 |
| 38 | June (FH) | 6" | 1.50 |
| 39 | Polly (FH) | 6" | 1.50 |
| 40 | May (FH) | 5.5" | 1.50 |
| 40 | Prima Donna | 10" | 17.50 |
| 41 | Molly (FH) | 6.5" | 1.50 |
| 42 | Emily (FH) | 8" | 1.50 |
| 43 | Priscilla | 7.75" | 7.00 |
| 43 | Marsie | 8" | 3.00 |
| 44 | Butch Child | 5.5" | 1.50 |
| 44 | Susie Child | 5.5" | 1.50 |
| 44 | Jim Child | 5.5" | 1.50 |
| 44 | Peter Child | 5.5" | 1.50 |
| 44 | Becky Child | 5.5" | 1.50 |
| 44 | Joyce Child | 5.5" | 1.50 |
| 44 | Meg | 8" | 12.00 |
| 44 | Grace | 7.75" | 5.00 |
| 45 | John Alden | 9.25" | 7.00 |
| 45 | Jennifer | 8" | 5.00 |
| 46 | Fern (FH) | 7" | 5.00 |
| 47 | She-Ti | 10.25" | 15.00 |
| 48 | Kiu | 10.25" | 15.00 |
| 49 | Violet (FH) | 7" | 5.00 |
| 49 | Cinderella & Prince Charming | 11.75" | 25.00 |
| 50 | Apple Blossom Picture Frame | 5" x 7" | 6.00 |
| 50 | Fair Lady | 11.5" | 20.00 |
| 51 | Apple Blossom Picture Frame | 4" x 5" | 5.00 |
| 52 | Charmaine | 8.5" | 6.00 |
| 52 | American Lady Bust | 6.5" | .50 |
| 53 | Genevieve | 8" | 6.00 |
| 53 | Pompadour Bust | 6.5" | 7.50 |
| 53 | Amber | 9.25" | 12.50 |
| 53 | Margo | 8.5" | 5.00 |
| 54 | Peg (FH) | 7.5" | 5.00 |
| 54 | Barbara Youth | 7" | 7.50 |
| 55 | Belle (FH) | 8" | 5.00 |
| 56 | Acorn Picture Frame | 4" x 5" | 1.75 |
| 56 | Beth (FH) | 7.5" | 5.00 |
| 57 | Scarlett | 8.75" | 8.00 |
| 58 | Rhett (picket fence) | 9" | 7.00 |
| 58 | Modern Girl Bust | 9.5" | 3.00 |
| 59 | Pamela | 7.25" | 6.00 |
| 59 | Modern Boy Bust | 9.75" | 3.00 |
| 60 | Irene | 6" | 4.00 |
| 61 | Elaine | 6" | 4.00 |
| 62 | Charles | 8.5" | 9.00 |
| 62 | Dresden Picture Frame | 5" x 7" | 6.00 |
| 62 | Dresden Picture Frame | 4" x 5" | 4.50 |
| 63 | Chinese Girl (FH) | 7.75" | 5.00 |
| 64 | Chinese Boy (FH) | 7.75" | 5.00 |
| 64 | Dresden Picture Frame | 3" x 4" | 3.50 |
| 64 | Dresden Picture Frame | 2" x 3" | 2.50 |
| 65 | High Button Shoe | 5.5" | 3.00 |
| 66 | Slipper | 4.5" | 3.00 |
| 66 | Angel | 7" | 2.50 |
| 67 | Suzette (FH) | 7" | 1.50 |
| 68 | Rene (FH) | 8.5" | 2.50 |
| 68 | Tess | 7.25" | 12.00 |
| 69 | Chinese Girl | 7.75" | 3.75 |
| 70 | Chinese Boy | 7.75" | 3.75 |
| 70 | Ellen | 7" | 2.00 |
| 71 | Carol Child | 7.5" | 6.00 |
| 71 | Diana Powder Box | 6" x 6.25" | 10.00 |
| 72 | Francis | 8.5" | 9.00 |
| 72 | Ann | 6" | 3.00 |
| 73 | Louise | 7.25" | 6.00 |
| 74 | Lillian | 7.25" | 6.00 |
| 75 | Spring | 6.25" | 5.00 |
| 75 | Douglas | 8.25" | 6.00 |
| 76 | Summer | 6.25" | 5.00 |
| 76 | Jim | 6.25" | 4.00 |
| 77 | Fall | 6.25" | 5.00 |
| 78 | Mimi (FH) | 6" | 1.50 |
| 79 | Sally (FH) | 6" | 1.50 |
| 80 | Wendy (FH) | 6" | 1.50 |
| 80 | Rosalie | 9.5" | 8.75 |
| 81 | Cigarette Box with Ashtrays | 4" x 6" | 3.00 |
| 81 | Our Lady of Grace | 9.75" | 6.00 |
| 82 | Rose Marie Child | 7" | 12.00 |
| 83 | Blossom Girl (FH) | 8.25" | 2.50 |
| 84 | Lantern Boy (FH) | 8.25" | 2.50 |
| 85 | Reggie | 7.25" | 5.00 |
| 85 | Douglas | 8.25" | 6.00 |
| 86 | Chinese Twin Girl (FH) | 6.5" | 1.50 |
| 86 | Sue | 6" | 3.00 |
| 87 | Polly (FH) | 6" | 2.50 |
| 87 | Chinese Twin Boy (FH) | 6.5" | 1.50 |
| 87 | Provincial Rose Picture Frame | 3" x 4" | 3.50 |

| F-Code | Item | Size | Wholesale Price |
|---|---|---|---|
| 88 | Rebecca | 7" | 3.00 |
| 88 | Patsy (FH) | 6" | 2.50 |
| 88 | Joy (FH) | 7.5" | 2.50 |
| 88 | Provincial Rose Picture Frame | 4" x 5" | 6.00 |
| 89 | June (FH) | 6" | 2.50 |
| 89 | Genevieve | 8" | 3.00 |
| 89 | Jerry (FH) | 8" | 2.50 |
| 89 | Provincial Rose Picture Frame | 5" x 7" | 8.00 |
| 90 | Blossom Girl | 8.25" | 3.75 |
| 91 | Lantern Boy | 8.25" | 3.75 |
| 92 | Suzanna | 8.75" | 20.00 |
| 93 | Stephen | 8.75" | 9.00 |
| 94 | Karla Ballerina | 9.75" | 9.00 |
| 95 | Lisa Ballerina | 9.75" | 9.00 |
| 96 | Apple Blossom Picture Frame | 4" x 5" | 1.75 |
| 96 | Linda Lou | 7.75" | 12.00 |
| 97 | Apple Blossom Picture Frame | 5" x 7" | 2.50 |
| 97 | Sue Ellen | 8.25" | 8.00 |
| 98 | Ann | 6" | 2.00 |
| 98 | Jeanie | 8.75" | 10.00 |
| 99 | Sue | 6" | 2.00 |
| 99 | Judy | 8.75" | 10.00 |
| 100 | Ginger | 8.75" | 10.00 |
| 101 | Annabelle | 8.75" | 10.00 |
| 101 | Louis XV | 12" | 35.00 |
| 102 | Bud Cowboy | 7.5" | 2.50 |
| 102 | Scarlett | 8.75" | 7.50 |
| 103 | Rhett (stone wall) | 9" | 7.00 |
| 103 | Dot Cowgirl | 7.5" | 2.50 |
| 104 | Sandy Child | 7.5" | 2.50 |
| 104 | Louise | 8.25" | 2.50 |
| 105 | Blonde Child | 7.5" | 2.50 |
| 106 | John Child | 7.5" | 2.50 |
| 106 | Matilda | 9" | 6.00 |
| 107 | Mary Child | 7.5" | 2.50 |
| 108 | Don | 9.5" | 9.00 |
| 112 | Delia | 7.75" | 2.50 |
| 114 | Lea (FH) | 6" | 4.00 |
| 115 | Lyn (FH) | 6" | 4.00 |
| 115 | Lavon | 8.5" | 7.50 |
| 116 | Vivian | 9.75" | 10.00 |
| 117 | Eugenia | 9" | 10.00 |
| 119 | Lorry | 8" | 6.00 |
| 120 | Camille (fancy) | 8.5" | 13.00 |
| 121 | Clarissa (plain) | 7.5" | 5.00 |
| 122 | Camille (plain) | 8.5" | 8.00 |
| 123 | Clarissa (fancy) | 7.5" | 10.00 |
| 124 | Provincial Rose Picture Frame | 5" x 7" | 4.00 |
| 125 | Provincial Rose Picture Frame | 4" x 5" | 3.00 |
| 126 | Provincial Rose Picture Frame | 3" x 4" | 2.50 |
| 127 | Provincial Rose Picture Frame | 2" x 3" | 1.75 |
| 129 | Mary | 7.5" | 10.00 |
| 130 | Irene | 6" | 1.75 |
| 131 | Elaine | 6" | 3.00 |
| 132 | Jim | 6.25" | 3.00 |
| 133 | Pinkie | 12" | 12.50 |
| 134 | Blue Boy | 12" | 12.50 |
| 135 | Dear Ruth | 9" | 10.00 |
| 136 | Claudia | 8.25" | 6.00 |
| 137 | Josephine | 9" | 3.00 |
| 138 | Roberta | 8.5" | 3.00 |
| 139 | Sarah | 7.5" | 5.00 |
| 140 | Melanie | 7.5" | 5.00 |
| 141 | Laura | 7.5" | 5.00 |
| 142 | Richard | 7.5" | 4.00 |
| 142 | Rose Picture Frame | 2" x 3" | 2.00 |
| 143 | Joy | 6" | 2.00 |
| 143 | Rose Picture Frame | 3" x 4" | 2.50 |
| 144 | Rose Picture Frame | 4" x 5" | 3.00 |
| 144 | Pat | 6.25" | 2.00 |
| 145 | Mike | 6.25" | 2.00 |
| 145 | Anniversary Bell | 4.5" | 1.50 |
| 146 | Little Princess | 8" | 9.00 |
| 147 | Little Don | 7.75" | 8.50 |
| 148 | Story Hour with Boy | 8" x 6.75" | 18.00 |
| 149 | Annette | 8.25" | 8.50 |
| 150 | Madeline | 8.75" | 4.00 |
| 151 | Adeline | 8.75" | 4.00 |
| 152 | Wynkin | 5.5" | 2.00 |
| 152 | Grandmother and I | 9" x 7" | 20.00 |
| 153 | Blynkin | 5.5" | 2.00 |
| 153 | Princess | 10.25" | 12.50 |
| 155 | Deborah | 9.5" | 18.00 |
| 158 | Wynkin | 5.5" | 2.00 |
| 159 | Ethel | 7.25" | 2.00 |
| 159 | Blynkin | 5.5" | 2.00 |
| 160 | Memories | 5.75" x 6.5" | 12.50 |
| 164 | Carol (adult) | 10" | 10.00 |
| 165 | Denise | 10" | 10.00 |
| 166 | Cindy | 8" | 5.00 |
| 168 | Lady Diana | 9.75" | 20.00 |
| 169 | Cynthia | 9.25" | 8.75 |
| 172 | Susann | 8.5" | 15.00 |
| 173 | Joyce | 8.5" | 15.00 |
| 174 | Shirley | 7.75" | 10.00 |
| 175 | Coleen | 7.75" | 5.00 |
| 200 | Mardi Gras | 10.5" | 12.50 |
| 201 | Spring Reverie | 12.5" | 10.00 |
| 201 | Virginia (Brocade) | 15" | 50.00 |
| 202 | Companions | 11.5" | 10.00 |
| 202 | Caroline (Brocade) | 15" | 50.00 |
| 203 | The Portrait | 7.5" x 8.5" | 10.00 |
| 203 | Georgia (Brocade) | 12" | 25.00 |
| 204 | Love Letter | 10.5" | 10.00 |
| 204 | Amelia (Brocade) | 12" | 25.00 |
| 205 | Birthday Girl (Blonde) | 9" | 7.50 |
| 205 | Anita (Brocade) | 10" | 20.00 |
| 206 | Birthday Girl (Brunette) | 9" | 7.50 |
| 206 | Marleen, (Brocade) | 10" | 20.00 |
| 207 | Carmen | 12.5" | 20.00 |
| 208 | Madame DuBarry (Bust) | 8.5" | 20.00 |
| 209 | Summer Harvest | 12.5" | 15.00 |
| 210 | County Fair | 11.5" | 15.00 |
| 211 | Sweet Sixteen (probably never produced) | | |
| 212 | Maybelle | 10.5" | 10.00 |
| 301 | Jacqueline Shadow Box | 9" x 12" | 17.00 |
| 301 | Bernice Shadow Box | 9" x 12" | 17.00 |

## Artware Pieces

| A-Code | Item | Size | Wholesale Price |
|---|---|---|---|
| 1 | Shell Bon Bon | 5.25" x 6.5" | 4.00 |
| 2 | Double Bon Bon | 6" x 9" | 6.00 |
| 3 | Clover Dish | 6.25" x 6.25" | 4.00 |
| 4 | Bon Bon with Handles | 5.5" x 8.5" | 4.00 |
| 5 | Deep Shell Bon Bon | 5.25" x 3.5" | 4.00 |
| 6 | Cottage Vase | 7.75" | 6.00 |
| 7 | Console Bowl | 8" x 10" | 6.00 |
| 8 | Candleholders | 4.5" | 7.00 pr |
| 9 | Triple Bon Bon | 9" x 9" | 6.00 |
| 11 | Cigarette Set - 3 Piece | 4.5" x 6.5" | 7.00 |
| 13 | Cigarette Set - 3 Piece | 4.5" x 6" | 5.00 |
| 15 | Powder Box | 4" x 1.75" | 8.00 |
| 16 | Console Bowl with Handle | 7" x 10.5" | 7.00 |
| 17 | Cornucopia | 7.25" | 6.00 |
| 18 | Bud Vase | 6.75" | 4.00 |
| 19 | Handled Bowl | 7.75" x 7.75" | 5.50 |
| 20 | Round Bowl | 7.75" x 7.75" | 5.50 |
| 21 | Oblong Bowl | 5.5" x 10.5" | 6.00 |
| 22 | Flower Ring | 8.5" x 15" | 5.00 |

## Animals Designed by Betty Davenport Ford

| B-Code | Item | Size | Wholesale Price |
|---|---|---|---|
| 1 | Poodle Standing | 8.75" | 12.50 |
| 2 | Poodle Sitting | 9.5" | 12.50 |
| 3 | Squirrel on Stump | 8" | 9.00 |
| 4 | Running Squirrel | 5.5" x 7" | 9.00 |
| 5 | Standing Squirrel | 8" | 9.00 |
| 6 | Dove Sitting | 5.75" x 9.5" | 12.50 |
| 7 | Dove Flying | 8" x 11" | 13.50 |
| 8 | Doves Sitting | 9" x 11" | 22.50 |
| 9 | Doves Watching | 8.75" x 15" | 22.50 |
| 10 | Doves Flying | 12.75" x 11" | 27.00 |
| 11 | Sitting Cat | 14.50" | 25.00 |
| 12 | Resting Cat | 7.75" x 10.5" | 22.50 |
| 13 | Running Fox | 9" x 16 | 8.00 |
| 14 | Rabbit | 5.5" | 7.50 |
| 15 | Gazelle | 19" | 8.00 |
| 16 | Owls | 12" | 10.00 |
| 17 | Cockatoo | 11.5" | 13.50 |
| 18 | Cockatoos | 15.5" | 27.00 |

## Sierra Gourmet Pottery

| C-Code | Item | Size | Wholesale Price |
|---|---|---|---|
| 1W | Sierra Casserole with Frame | 11.75" | 7.00 |
| 2 | Sierra Cheese Tray with Board | 16" | 5.00 |
| 4 | Sierra Salad Bowl | 14" | 5.00 |
| 4S | Sierra Salad Bowl & Wood Servers | 14" | 6.00 |
| 5 | Sierra Pizza Platter | 15" | 4.00 |
| 6 | Sierra Chip and Dip | 8.5" x 14" | 2.50 |
| 12 | Sierra Deluxe Chip and Dip | 15" | 4.00 |

## Driftware

| D-Code | Item | Size | Wholesale Price |
|---|---|---|---|
| 1 | Driftware Small Bowl | 6.5" x 11" | 2.00 |
| 2 | Driftware Small Relish | 6.5" x 14" | 2.50 |
| 3 | Driftware Large Bowl | 9" x 21.5" | 3.25 |
| 4 | Driftware Bowl/Planter | 10" x 14" | 5.00 |
| 5 | Driftware Bowl/Planter | 5.75" x 14.5" | 4.00 |
| 6 | Driftware Large Bowl | 10.25" x 15.25" | 5.00 |
| 7 | Driftware Large Flat Bowl | 8.5" x 17" | 5.00 |
| 8 | Driftware Cigarette Box | 6" x 8" | 2.50 |
| 9 | Driftware Ashtray | 3.5" x 9" | .75 |
| 10 | Driftware Buffet Plate and Cup | 8.75" x 14" | 2.25 |
| 11 | Driftware Low Bowl | 8.5" x 18" | 5.00 |

## Clocks

| E-Code | Item | Size | Wholesale Price |
|---|---|---|---|
| 1D | French Electric - Dresden | 11.5" | 30.00 |
| 4 | Mantle Electric Clock | 13" | 35.00 |
| 4D | Mantle Electric - Dresden | 13" | 35.00 |
| 5 | Boudoir Clock | 7" | 20.00 |
| 5D | Boudoir Clock - Dresden | 7" | 25.00 |
| 8D | Boudoir Alarm - 30 Hour | 4.5" x 4.25" | 20.00 |

## Merrymaids

| M-Code | Item | Size | Wholesale Price |
|---|---|---|---|
| 1 | Merrymaid Betty | 4.5" | 1.50 |
| 2 | Merrymaid Jane | 7" | 1.50 |
| 3 | Merrymaid Rosie | 7" | 1.50 |

## Plaques

| P-Code | Item | Size | Wholesale Price |
|---|---|---|---|
| 1 | Plaque Lady w/Muff Center | 6.5" x 9" | 5.00 |
| 2 | Plaque Lady w/Muff Side | 6.5" x 9" | 5.00 |
| 3 | Plaque Lady w/Fan | 6.5" x 9" | 5.00 |
| 4 | Plaque Lady w/Parasol | 6.5" x 9" | 5.00 |
| 5 | Cameo Plaque Lady w/Scarf | 6" x 7.5" | 4.00 |
| 6 | Cameo Plaque Lady w/Bow | 6" x 7.5" | 4.00 |
| 7 | Cameo Plaque Man w/Top Hat | 6" x 7.5" | 4.00 |

## Floraline

| R-Code | Item | Size | Wholesale Price |
|---|---|---|---|
| 1 | Sleigh Large | 7" x 13" x 9" | 8.00 |
| 2 | Sleigh Small | 5" x 10" x 6" | 4.00 |
| 3 | Voltaire Bowl Large | 5.75" x 9.5" | 2.50 |
| 4 | Voltaire Bowl Small | 4.25" x 7.75" | 1.50 |
| 5 | Cornucopia | 9.25" | 3.00 |
| 6 | Candleholders | 7.75" | 3.50 pr |
| 7 | Wall Vase | 8.5" x 9.5" | 2.25 |
| 8 | Orleans Bowl Large | 10.5" x 16" | 4.00 |
| 9 | Orleans Bowl Small | 9" x 14" | 3.00 |
| 10 | Desk Frame | 4" x 5" | 3.00 |
| 11 | Wall Frame | 4" x 5" | 3.00 |
| 12 | Regency Ash Tray | 8.25" x 8.25" | 1.50 |
| 13 | Regency Box Covered | 8" x 8" | 3.50 |
| 14 | Planter | 6.25" x 12.25" | 3.50 |
| 15 | Flower Basket | 9.25" | 4.00 |

## Shell Bowls

| S-Code | Item | Size | Wholesale Price |
|---|---|---|---|
| 1 | Large Shell Bowl | 8" x 15.5" | 8.00 |
| 2 | Medium Shell Bowl | 11.5" x 8.5" | 6.00 |
| 3 | Shell Ashtray | 7.25" x 10.75" | 5.00 |
| 4 | Shell Vase | 6" x 6.5" | 5.00 |

## Television Lamp

| T-Code | Item | Size | Wholesale Price |
|---|---|---|---|
| 1 | Dear Ruth TV Lamp | 9" | 11.50 |

## Birds

| W-Code | Item | Size | Wholesale Price |
|---|---|---|---|
| 1 | Parakeet Small w/Wing Out | 5.75" | 4.00 |
| 2 | Parakeet Large w/Wing In | 7.25" | 5.00 |
| 3 | Cardinal | 4.75" | 5.00 |
| 4 | Mocking Bird | 5.25" | 5.00 |
| 5 | Blue Bird | 5.25" | 5.00 |
| 6 | Vireo | 5.25" | 5.00 |
| 7 | Blue Bird Group | 8.5" | 7.50 |
| 8 | Mocking Bird Group | 8.5" | 7.50 |

| W-Code | Item | Size | Wholesale Price |
|---|---|---|---|
| 9 | Young Blue Bird | 4.25" | 3.00 |
| 10 | Young Mocking Bird | 4.25" | 3.00 |
| 11 | Fantail Pigeon | 8" | 6.50 |
| 12 | Owl | 9" | 6.50 |
| 13 | Baltimore Oriole | 5.25" | 5.00 |
| 14 | Baltimore Oriole Group | 8.5" | 7.50 |
| 15 | Young Baltimore Oriole | 4.25" | 3.00 |
| 17 | Pheasant - Tail Up | 17.75" x 9.75" | 6.50 |
| 18 | Golden Pheasant | 17.75" x 6.75" | 8.50 |
| 19 | Pheasant - Tail Down | 17.75" x 6.75" | 6.00 |
| 20 | California Quail - Male | 7.5"x 6.25" | 5.00 |
| 21 | California Quail - Female | 7.5" x 6.25" | 5.00 |
| 22 | Swan | 11.75" x 6" | 5.00 |
| 23 | Swan - Flowerholder | 11.75" x 6" | 5.00 |
| 24 | Cockatoo | 13.24" | 6.50 |
| 26 | Quail in Antique Bronze, Male | 7.5" x 6.25" | 3.50 |
| 27 | Quail in Antique Bronze, Female | 7.5" x 6.25" | 3.50 |

## Florence Copyrights and Year

The Florence Ceramics Company held copyrights on most of the figures and artware they produced. In several of their catalogs they mention "Florence Figurines are fully protected by U.S. Copyrights." The following table lists the figures and the year they were copyrighted. In several cases, more than one year is shown – the latter date represents a second issue of that figure with changes having been made. The most common change is a different hand position. Florence Ward continually improved her creations and at the same time protected them with copyrights. Some figures are not copyrighted and the reason for this is not known. No figures were copyrighted from 1960 to 1964.

In the chart, the letters (BDF) or (DW) represent pieces designed for Florence by Betty Davenport Ford or Don Winton.

| Name of Figurine | Year | Year | Year |
|---|---|---|---|
| Abigail | 1951 | | |
| Adeline | 1955 | | |
| Amber | 1957 | | |
| Amelia | 1951 | | |
| Angel | 1956 | | |
| Annabel | 1956 | | |
| Annabelle, with bluebird | 1951 | | |
| Annette | 1955 | | |
| Ava | 1952 | | |
| Ballet | 1956 | | |
| Bea | 1956 | | |
| Belle | 1949 | 1952 | |
| Beth | 1952 | | |
| Betty, Merrymaid | 1955 | | |
| Blossom Girl | 1950 | | |
| Bluebird, single | 1957 | | |
| Blynkin | 1955 | | |
| Bride | 1957 | | |
| California Quail, female | 1957 | | |
| California Quail, male | 1957 | | |
| Camille | 1953 | 1958 | |
| Cardinal | 1957 | | |
| Carmen | 1959 | | |
| Carol with Pantaloons | 1949 | | |
| Cat Resting (BDF) | 1956 | | |
| Catherine | 1956 | | |
| Charmaine | 1954 | | |
| Chinese Twins | 1950 | | |
| Christening | 1960 | | |
| Cinderella & Prince Charming | 1957 | | |
| Clarissa | 1953 | 1955 | 1958 |
| Claudia | 1954 | 1958 | |
| Cleopatra | 1956 | | |
| Cockatoos (BDF) | 1956 | | |
| Cockatoos on branch (DW) | 1958 | | |
| Coleen | 1957 | 1958 | |
| Cynthia | 1958 | | |
| Dear Ruth | 1954 | | |
| Deborah | 1960 | | |
| Delia | 1951 | 1955 | 1958 |
| Diana | 1952 | | |
| Diane | 1956 | 1958 | |
| Delores | 1956 | | |
| Don | 1951 | | |
| Douglas | 1952 | | |
| Doves, double (BDF) | 1956 | | |
| Doves, flying (BDF) | 1956 | | |
| Doves, watching (BDF) | 1956 | | |
| Edith | 1955 | | |
| Edward | 1952 | | |
| Elaine | 1952 | | |
| Elizabeth | 1952 | | |
| Elizabeth, standing | 1949 | | |
| Ellen | 1958 | | |
| Ethel | 1955 | | |
| Eugenia | 1953 | | |
| Eve | 1949 | 1958 | |
| Fantail Pigeon (DW) | 1957 | | |
| Fair Lady | 1957 | | |
| Fall | 1950 | | |
| Fern | 1951 | | |
| Floraline 14" Sleigh | 1951 | | |
| Floraline Candleholder | 1950 | | |
| Floraline Orleans Low Bowl | 1950 | | |
| Floraline Picture Frame | 1950 | | |
| Floraline Regency Box | 1950 | | |
| Floraline Regency Tray | 1950 | | |
| Floraline Voltaire Bowl | 1950 | | |
| Floraline Wall Vase | 1950 | | |
| Ford Dog Bank (DW) | 1959 | | |
| Frances | 1949 | | |
| Gary | 1957 | | |
| Gazelle (BDF) | 1956 | | |
| Genevieve | 1954 | | |
| Georgette | 1958 | | |
| Ginger | 1951 | | |
| Giselle | 1959 | | |
| Grace | 1957 | 1958 | |
| Grandmother and I | 1960 | | |
| Haru | 1958 | | |
| Head Pins (Lapel Pins) | 1952 | | |
| Her Majesty | 1957 | | |
| Irene | 1952 | | |
| Jane, Merrymaid | 1955 | | |
| Jay, by wall | 1958 | | |
| Jean | 1951 | | |
| Jeanette | 1956 | 1958 | |
| Jennifer | 1958 | | |
| Jerry | 1950 | | |
| Jim | 1952 | | |
| John Alden | 1951 | | |
| Jose, with cart | 1953 | | |
| Josephine | 1954 | | |
| Joy | 1950 | 1954 | |

# 172 Florence Particulars

| Name of Figurine | Year | Year | Year |
|---|---|---|---|
| Joyce | 1958 | | |
| Judy | 1951 | | |
| Julie | 1958 | | |
| Juliet | 1956 | | |
| June | 1958 | | |
| Karla, Ballerina | 1950 | | |
| Karlo | 1959 | | |
| Kay | 1956 | | |
| Kiu | 1949 | | |
| Lady Diana | 1959 | | |
| Lantern Boy | 1950 | | |
| Laura | 1954 | | |
| Lavon | 1959 | | |
| Lea | 1952 | | |
| Leading Man | 1957 | | |
| Lila | 1959 | | |
| Lillian | 1949 | 1952 | |
| Linda Lou | 1952 | 1957 | |
| Lisa | 1958 | | |
| Lisa, Ballerina | 1950 | | |
| Little Don | 1955 | | |
| Little Princess | 1955 | | |
| Lorry | 1953 | | |
| Louis XV | 1953 | | |
| Louis XVI | 1949 | | |
| Louise | 1952 | | |
| Lyn | 1952 | | |
| Madame Pompadour | 1953 | | |
| Madeline | 1955 | | |
| Madonna with Child | 1949 | | |
| Madonna with Child Bust | 1949 | | |
| Marianne | 1957 | | |
| Marilyn | 1956 | | |
| Mark Anthony | 1955 | | |
| Marsie | 1957 | | |
| Martha | 1956 | | |
| Martin | 1954 | | |
| Mary | 1953 | | |
| Masquerade | 1955 | 1957 | |
| Master David | 1954 | | |
| Matilda | 1951 | | |
| Meg | 1952 | | |
| Memories | 1961 | | |
| Mikado | 1959 | | |
| Mike | 1954 | | |
| Ming | 1959 | | |
| Misha | 1958 | | |
| Mockingbird, single | 1957 | | |
| Musette | 1954 | | |
| Nancy | 1958 | | |
| Nita | 1956 | | |
| Oriole Group | 1957 | | |
| Owl, on stump | 1957 | | |
| Pamela, with basket of flowers | 1956 | 1957 | |
| Pamela, with tiered skirt | 1949 | | |
| Parakeet, head under wing (DW) | 1957 | | |
| Parakeet, with folded wing (DW) | 1957 | | |
| Pat | 1954 | | |
| Patrice | 1957 | | |
| Patsy | 1958 | | |
| Peg | 1952 | | |

| Name of Figurine | Year | Year | Year |
|---|---|---|---|
| Peter | 1956 | | |
| Pheasant, tail down, female (DW) | 1957 | | |
| Pheasant, tail up, male (DW) | 1957 | | |
| Pinkie | 1954 | | |
| Plaque with man | 1953 | | |
| Plaque, lady with fan | 1953 | | |
| Plaque, lady with muff in center | 1953 | | |
| Plaque, lady with muff on side | 1953 | | |
| Plaque, lady with umbrella | 1953 | | |
| Polly | 1958 | | |
| Poodle, sitting (BDF) | 1956 | | |
| Poodle, standing (BDF) | 1956 | | |
| Prima Donna | 1956 | | |
| Princess | 1960 | | |
| Priscilla | 1951 | | |
| Rabbit, (BDF) | 1956 | | |
| Rebecca | 1954 | | |
| Reggie | 1950 | | |
| Rene | 1949 | | |
| Rhett | 1952 | | |
| Richard | 1954 | | |
| Roberta | 1954 | | |
| Rosalie | 1959 | | |
| Rose Marie, 7" | 1952 | | |
| Rosie, Merrymaid | 1955 | | |
| Ruth | 1949 | | |
| Sally | 1950 | 1958 | |
| Sarah | 1951 | | |
| Scarlett | 1952 | 1958 | |
| Shen | 1949 | | |
| Sherry | 1958 | | |
| She-Ti | 1949 | | |
| Shirley | 1957 | 1958 | |
| Spring | 1950 | | |
| Squirrel, on stump (BDF) | 1956 | | |
| Squirrel, running (BDF) | 1956 | | |
| Squirrel, standing (BDF) | 1956 | | |
| Stephen | 1950 | | |
| Story Hour with Boy and Girl | 1955 | | |
| Story Hour with Girl | 1954 | | |
| Sue Ellen | 1952 | | |
| Summer | 1950 | | |
| Susann | 1959 | | |
| Suzanna | 1950 | | |
| Suzette | 1949 | | |
| Swan, (DW) | 1958 | | |
| Taka | 1958 | | |
| Tess | 1952 | 1957 | |
| Toy | 1959 | | |
| Victor | 1954 | | |
| Victoria | 1952 | | |
| Violet | 1951 | | |
| Vireo, on stump | 1957 | | |
| Virginia | 1960 | | |
| Vivian | 1953 | | |
| Wendy | 1950 | | |
| Wood Nymph | 1955 | | |
| Wynkin | 1955 | | |
| Yulan | 1949 | | |
| Yvonne | 1956 | 1958 | |

# Appendix: Collecting, Cleaning and Care of Figurines

As a collector of Florence Ceramics, you can build your collection in any number of ways. There's no right or wrong way, so choose for yourself. You might want to acquire one of every Florence figurine ever made! Perhaps you would like to collect all of the artware. Collecting the artware has gained popularity as people realize the beauty of these pieces. Some might collect by color. There are aficionados who collect by the various names inscribed on the figures. These names could be the same as one belonging to a loved one. Even flowerholders, with their innovative uses, would also make a great collection. Whatever your choice, it's safe to say that in all forms...Florence Ceramics is highly collectible!

Inasmuch as these ceramics have not been made since 1964, it is amazing that so many still exist. Considering the myriad ways these delicate pieces of art could have been destroyed over the years, it is exciting that many of the more elaborate figures are still found in good condition. Collectors find them in garages, attics, basements, and at yard sales, as well as at antique malls and antique shows. (Don't forget to look in Aunt Bertha's china cabinet!)

Collectors often ask "Do damaged pieces still have value?" We think so, but it depends upon the degree of damage. If it is a question of restoring an item for sentimental reasons, the answer is simply "Yes." If not restoring because of sentiment, or because you absolutely "have to have it" because it's the last one needed to complete your collection, then consider if the cost of the restoration exceeds the monetary value of the piece (see the Value Guide as shown in Chapter III, Showcasing Florence A-Z).

There are many fine professional restorers in the United States and Canada. Word of mouth among fellow collectors is an excellent way in which to find a good restorer of ceramics or porcelains. We suggest checking references before you proceed. As Florence Ceramics are now considered to be antiques, it is apparent that with each passing year proper restorations are of primary importance. Remember, a good restorer can work miracles! Do not discard any piece without professional advice.

Has anyone ever told you to water your china or porcelain? Well, it's a good idea to do so. Store or display figurines in areas of medium to high humidity, as moisture laden air keeps semi-porcelains from drying out and crazing. A simple method of doing this is to put a glass of water in an inconspicuous place in the curio cabinet or wherever you display your figurines. (Hint: All china and porcelains like to be kept in moist air. Humidifiers are helpful for whole room displays.)

Collectors ask, "How do I clean these delicate figurines?" Remember that the figurines have been fired at temperatures up to 1600 degrees. Using proper cleaning methods (unless a repair or "paint over" has been done), you cannot accidentally destroy decorations or gold trimming.

We suggest using cotton swabs for cleaning hard to reach places. A very soft toothbrush or camel hair brush can also be used. Dip the swab or brush into a mild solution of dishwashing liquid. Be aware that products containing trisodium phosphate, found in some automatic dishwashing detergents, can be harmful to restorations. (The trisodium phosphate can remove unfired paint.) Do not immerse the figurine in water, as you should never allow moisture to reach the unglazed inner surface. In addition, don't use toweling that can snag and break delicate lace or fingers. If a mild solution of liquid soap doesn't do the job, try a commercial product like Simple Green™. If you still aren't satisfied with the results, try paint thinner, lighter fluid, alcohol, or even acetone. (Remember, these stronger products will definitely have an adverse effect on restorations!) Avoid the use of abrasives, as they will scratch the high gloss finish.

**Florence Ceramics Collectors Society**

We are often asked: "Is there a collectors' club for this 'hot' collectible?" The answer now is yes! In the year 2000, the *Florence Ceramics Collectors Society* was formed. The Society's mission is to provide a forum for the exchange of information about the products and history of Florence Ceramics Company. As of this writing, the Society has over one hundred members and is growing daily. Annual conventions are held at different locations throughout the country. A quarterly newsletter (*The Floraline*) is published, which includes classified advertisements for buying, selling, or trading Florence. In addition, there are many interesting and informative articles in *The Floraline*. Everyone is invited to join the club, no matter how large or how small (and growing) his or her collection is. For more information and to join the club please send an e-mail to FlorenceCeramics@aol.com. You may also write or telephone to:

Florence Showcase/Sweet Pea Antiques
P.O. Box 937
Kodak, TN 37764
(865) 933-9060
**Please visit us at http://www.sweetpea.net**

Happy Hunting Everyone!
    —The Authors (Kodak, Tennessee, Spring 2002)

P.S. Like some former employees, we also wonder what happens after the lights go out...does Carmen dance with Jose? Does Delia date Douglas? Does Rhett really love Melanie more than Scarlett? We guess we'll never know!

# Bibliography

Allison, Grace C. "Florence – Choice of Discriminating Collectors." *Antique Week-Tri-State Trader*. Knightstown, Indiana (1985, February 25).

Austin, Ethel M. "Merchandising and Selling Figurines." *The Gift and Art Buyer*. Meriden, Connecticut (November 1954): 30, 31, 84.

Blum, Stella. *Eighteenth-Century French Fashions in Full Color*. Toronto, Ontario, Canada: Dover Publications, Inc., General Publishing Company Ltd., 1982.

Catalog, *Florence Ceramics Co.* 1949, Pasadena, California: Florence Advertising.

Catalog, *Florence Ceramics Co.* 1951, Pasadena, California, Florence Advertising.

Catalog, *Florence Ceramics Co.* 1954, Pasadena, California: Florence Advertising.

Catalog, *Florence Ceramics Co.* 1956, Pasadena, California: Florence Advertising.

Catalog, *Florence Ceramics Co.* 1957, Pasadena, California: Florence Advertising.

Catalog, *Florence Ceramics Co.* 1958, Pasadena, California: Florence Advertising.

Catalog, Order Form *Florence Ceramics Co.* 1962, Pasadena, California: Florence Advertising.

Catalog, Order Form *Florence Ceramics Co.* 1965, Pasadena, California: Florence Advertising.

"Ceramics Plant, Started in Garage Now Operating in New Building." *Pasadena Star-News*, August 14, 1949.

Cunnington, C. Willett. *English Women's Clothing in Nineteenth Century*. New York, New York: Dover Publications Inc., 1990.

Derwick, Jenny B. and Latos, Dr. Mary. *Dictionary Guide to United States Pottery and Porcelain (19th and 20th Century)*. Franklin, Michigan: Jenstan Research in United States Pottery and Porcelain, 1984.

*Encyclopedia Britannica*. London, England: William Benton, 1958.

"Fairy and Fairy Tale." Microsoft® Encarta® Online Encyclopedia, 2001. http://www.encarta.msn.com. ©1997-2001 Microsoft.

Florence Advertising, *The Gift and Art Buyer*, November 1948, 51.

Florence Advertising, *Tradewinds*, February 1952, 41.

Florence Advertising, *The Gift and Art Buyer*, June 1952, 115.

Florence Advertising, *Registered California*, February 1954, cover.

Florence Advertising, *The Gift and Art Buyer*, December 1954, 99.

Florence Advertising, *225 Fifth Avenue Highlights*, April 1955, 119.

Florence Advertising, *The Gift and Art Buyer*, March 1956, 149.

Florence Advertising, *House and Garden*, October 1957, 48.

Florence Advertising, *Giftwares*, July 1961, 71.

Florence Advertising, *Registered California*, July 1962.

Florence News Article. *Pasadena Star-News*. Pasadena, California, 1948.

Foland, Doug. *The Florence Collectibles, An Era of Elegance*. Atglen, Pennsylvania: Schiffer Publishing Ltd, 1995.

Janson, H. W. *History of Art*. Englewood Cliffs, New Jersey: Prentice Hall, Inc., 1963.

"Jonathan Buttall: The Blue Boy (c 1770)." The Huntington Library, Art Collections, and Botanical Gardens. http://www.huntington.org/ArtDiv/HuntingGall.html (November 19, 1996).

McLaughlin, E. B. "Modeling Hobby Starts Pasadena Family in Profitable New Business." *Pasadena Star-News*, January 18, 1948.

"Sarah Barrett Moulton: Pinkie (1794)." The Huntington Library, Art Collections, and Botanical Gardens. http://www.huntington.org/ArtDiv/HuntingGall.html (November 19, 1996).

United States Copyrights Office. *Copyrights 1948-1964*. Washington, D.C.: Copyright Office, 1964.

United States Patent Office. *Patents 1951-1963*. Washington, D.C.: Patent Office, 1963.

Van Doren, Charles. *Webster's American Biographies*. Springfield, Massachusetts: G.&C. Merriam Company, 1975.

# Index

## Figurines

Abigail, 17
Adeline, 17
Amber, 17, 97
Amelia, 18, 100
Amelia Brocade, 18
American Lady, bust, 18, 114
Angel, arms clasped, 18; wings spread, 19
Anita Brocade, 19
Ann, 19
Annabel, with flower basket, 19, 106; with card, 20
Annabelle, with blue bird, 20, 111
Annette, 20, 115
Ava, (FH), 20, 118
Baby, (FH), 21
Ballet, 21
Ballet Powder Box, 21
Barbara, adult, 21; youth, 22
Bea, 22
Becky, 22, 118
Bee, (FH), 22
Belle, (FH), 22
Beth, (FH), 22
Betsy, 23, 119
Betty, Merrymaid, 69, 126
Birthday Girl, 23
Blondie, 23, 119
Blossom Girl, (FH), 23, 119
Blue Boy, 24, 127, 135
Blynkin, 24, 119, 136
Bride, 24, 109
Bryan, 24
Bud, 5, 25, 122
Butch, 25, 118, 144
Camille, 25, 116
Carmen, 26, 110, 130
Carol, adult, 26; with pantaloons, 13, 26, 120
Caroline Brocade, 26, 111
Catherine, 27
Cecile, 27
Charles, 27, 123
Charmaine, 28
Chinese Boy, 28, 120; FH, 28, 120
Chinese Girl, 28, 120; FH, 29, 120
Chinese Twin, Boy (FH), 29, 120
Chinese Twin, Girl, (FH), 29, 120
Choir Boys, 29, 121
Christening, 30
Cinderella and Prince Charming, 30, 121, 130

Cindy, 30
Clarissa, 30, 116
Claudia, 31, 110
Cleopatra, 31, 121, 131
Clifford, (FH), * 32, 123
Coleen, 32
Cynthia, 32
Daisy, * 32
Darleen, 23
David, youth, 33, 119; bust, 33, 127
Dear Ruth, on bench, 34; TV lamp, 33, 112; oval base (no lamp) 34
Deborah, 34
Delia, 34
Delores, 35
Denise, 35
Diana Powder Box, 36
Diane, 36, 99
Dixie, * 36, 122
Don, 37, 124
Dora Lee, 37
Dot, 5, 37, 122
Douglas, 37
Edith, 38
Edward, 38
Elaine, 38, 122
Elizabeth, 38, 39; early figure, 39, 101, 123
Ellen, 39
Emily, (FH), 39
Emma, (FH), * 40
Ethel, 40
Eugenia, 40
Eve, 41, 123; from Lavon mold, 40
Fair Lady, Cover, 8, 41, 103, 109, 131
Fall, 41
Fall Companion (also called County Fair), 42, 122
Fall Reverie (also called Summer Harvest), 42, 122
Fern, head vase, (FH), 42, 123
Florence, (FH), * 42, 123
Florence Dealer Sign, Lady, 43; Rectangle, 43
Frances, 43
Gary, 43
Genevieve (also Jenevieve), 44, 98
Geoff, * 44, 97
Georgette, 44, 106
Georgia Brocade, 44
Gibson Girl, 45, 111, 116, 131
Gigi, bust, 46
Ginger, 46
Giselle, 46

Grace, 46, 100
Grandmother and I, 4, 47
Halloween Child, 7, 47
Haru, 47, 124
Hector, * 47, 122
Her Majesty, 48
Irene, 48
Jane, Merrymaid, 69, 126
Jay, 48
Jeanette, 48
Jeanie, 49, 117
Jenevieve (also Genevieve), 44, 98
Jennifer, 49
Jerry, (FH), 49, 124
Jim, 49, 122; child, 50, 118
Jo Ann, (FH), * 7, 50
Joe, (FH), * 50
John, 50, 119
John Alden, 51, 128, 135
Jose, (FH), 51, 118
Josephine, 51, 102, 124
Joy, 51; FH, 52, 124
Joyce, adult, 52; child, 52, 118
Judy, 52, 124
Julie, 53
Juliet, 53
June, (FH), 53
Karen, 53, 99
Karie, * 54
Karla Ballerina, 54, 125
Karlo, 54, 125
Kathy, 54
Kay, 55; FH, 55
Kiu, 55, 105, 128
Lady Diana, 55, 102, 113
Lantern Boy, (FH), 56, 119
La Petite, bust, 56
Larry, * 56
Laura, 56
Lavon, 57
Lea, (FH), 57
Leading Man, 57, 128
Lee Ann, 57
Lil, Merrymaid, 69, 126
Lila, 58
Lillian, 58
Lillian Russell, 58, 115, 132
Linda Lou, 58
Lisa, 59
Lisa Ballerina, 59, 108, 125
Little Don, 59, 132
Little Princess, 59, 133
Loraine, * 60; FH, 7, 60

Lorry, 60
Louis XV, 60, 125, 134
Louis XVI, 60, 125, 134
Louise, 61
Love Letter, 61
Lyn, (FH), 61
Madame DuBarry, bust, 62, 107, 133
Madame Pompadour, 62, 125, 134
Madeline, 62
Madonna, with arms outstretched, 62
Madonna and Child, 63, 134; bust, 63
Marcella, 63
Mardi Gras, 64
Margaret, 8, 64, 109
Margo, 64
Marianne, 64, 98, 101
Marie Antoinette, 65, 114, 125, 134
Marilyn, 65, 98
Mark Anthony, 63, 121, 131
Marleen Brocade, 65
Marsie, 65
Martha, 66
Martin, 66
Mary, 1, 66, 107; youth, 67, 119
Masquerade, 67, 114
Master David, 67, 127
Matilda, 67, 110
May, (FH), 68
Maybelle, 68, 115
Meg, 68
Melanie, 68, 128, 136
Memories, 69, 112
Merrymaids: Betty, Jane, Rosie, Lil, 69, 126
Mikado, 69
Mike, 70, 127
Mimi, 70; FH, 70
Ming, 70, 129
Misha, 70, 124
Modern Boy, 71, 126
Modern Girl, 71, 126
Molly, (FH), 71
Musette, 71, 126
Nan, (FH),* 72, 126
Nancy, 72
Nell Gwynn, 72, 135
Nick, (FH), * 72, 126
Nina, (FH), * 73
Nita, 73
Our Lady of Grace, 73
Pamela, Bust, 74; with basket, 74, 115, 127; youth, 73
Pat, 74, 127
Patrice, 74, 101
Patsy, (FH), 75
Peg, (FH), 75
Peter, 75; child, 7, 75
Pinkie, 76, 127, 135
Polly, (FH), 76
Pompadour Bust, 76
Portrait, 76
Prima Donna, 77, 113, 128
Princess, 77, 109
Priscilla, 77, 128, 135
Rebecca, 77
Reggie, 78, 120
Rene, (FH), 78
Rhett, 78, 128, 136
Richard, 79
Rita, 79; FH, 79
Roberta, 79, 102, 124
Rosalie, 79, 107
Rose Marie, adult, 80, 108; youth, 80
Rosie, Merrymaid, 69, 126
Ruth, 1, 80
Sabrina, (FH), * 81
Sadie, (FH), * 81
Sailor Boy, 7, 81
Sally, 81; FH, 81
Sandy, 82, 119
Sarah, 82, 132
Sarah Bernhardt, 82, 117, 136
Scarlett, 82, 128, 136
Shen, 83, 129; FH, 83, 129
Sherri, 83
Sherry, 84
She-Ti, 83, 128
Shirley, 84
Spring, 84
Spring Companion, 85, 121
Spring Reverie, 84, 103, 121
Stella, * 95
Stephen, 85, 129
Story Hour, 8, 85, 115, 117; with girl only, 85
Sue, 86
Sue Ellen, 86, 128, 136
Summer, 86
Susann, 86, 87
Susanna, 87, 129
Susie, 7, 87, 118, 144
Suzette, (FH), 87
Taka, 88, 125
Tess, 88
Toy, 88, 129
Victor, 89, 126
Victoria, 89, 100, 111
Violet, (FH), 89, 123
Virginia, 90, 107
Virginia Brocade, 90, 110
Vivian, 1, 90, 108
Wendy, (FH), 90
Wood Nymph Ballerina, 91
Wynkin, 91, 119, 136
Yulan, 91, 129; FH, 92
Yvonne, 92, 99, 112; early garage figure, 92; FH, 92

## *Lamps*

Camille, 93
Charles, 93,
David and Betsy, 93
Dear Ruth TV Lamp, 33
Delia, 93
Gibson Girl, 94
Louis XVI, 94, 95
Marie Antoinette, 94, 95
Stella, * 95
Story Hour, 95

## *Birds and Animals*

Baltimore Oriole Group, 137
Blue Bird, Group, 137; Single 138
Cardinal, 138
Cat, Reclining, 138; Sitting, 138
Cockatoo, 138
Cockatoos 139
Dove Flying, 139
Fox Running, 139
Gazelle, 140
Mocking Bird, Baby 140; Group 140
Owl, 140; Double 141
Parakeet, Wing Out, 141; Wing In, 141
Pheasant, Tail Down, 141; Tail Up, 141
Pigeon Fantail, 142
Poodle, Sitting, 142; Standing, 142
Quail, 142
Rabbit, 142
Swan, 142
Vireo, 142

## *Artware*

Ashtrays, 143, 145, 152
Bell, 143
Bon Bon, Deep Shell, 148; Triple, 144; Double, 144; Shell, 144
Bookends, Butch and Susie, 144
Bowl, Flat Driftware, 154; Relish, 154; Bowl/Planter, Driftware, 155
Bowl, Voltaire Floraline, 152, 153,
Box, Regency Floraline, 153; Cigarette, Ming Tree, 143; Powder, 145
Buffet Plate and Cup, Driftware, 154
Cameo Plaque, Lady with Scarf, 148; Man in Top Hat, 148; Lady with Bow, 148
Candleholders, 145
Candy Box, Driftware, 154
Candy Dish, 145
Casserole Bowl with Lid, 146
Child and Shell Bowl, 152
Child with ABC blocks, 152
Clock, 7" Boudoir, 144; Dresden, 148; French Electric, 145; Mantle, 144
Coffee Pot, Cream and Sugar, Pastel Pink, 146
Coffee Set for Six, Satin White, 147
Compote, Tall, 145
Console Bowl, 147; with Handle 144, 147
Cornucopia, Floraline, 153; Vase 148
Divided Dish, Satin White, 146
Dog Ford Bank, Single, 147; Double, 147; Large, 147
Lapel Pins, Lady Profile, 148
Lipstick Holder with Baby, 144
Mugs, 151, 155
Picture Frame, 145
Plaque, Lady, Muff in Center, 149; Muff on Side, 149; with Fan, 149; with Parasol 149
Plate, Framed Decal w/Fish, 155
Platter, Fish, 155
Powder Box, 144, 145
Reindeer, 149; with Sleigh, 149
Shadow Box, Bernice, 143; Jacqueline, 143
Shell Bowl for Merrymaids, Large, 150; Small, 150
Shoe, High Button, 145
Sleigh, Floraline, 153; White 143
Slipper, 145
Starfish Bowl for Merrymaids, 150
Tray, Handled, 148
Vanity Set, 150
Vase, Bud, 145; Cottage, 145; Free Form, 148; Shell, 145; Umbrella, 151
Wall Pocket, 151; Floraline, 153

*FH indicates Flower Holder*
* *indicates named by authors or FCCS*